DISCOVERING NATURAL SCIENCE

AN INTRODUCTORY DICTIONARY

Editorial Director PAUL E. KLINGE, A.B.

Executive Editor LEO CHARLES FAY, B.S., M.A., Ph.D.

ENCYCLOPÆDIA BRITANNICA
EDUCATIONAL CORPORATION
425 N. Michigan Avenue
Chicago, Illinois 60611

CONTENTS

These staff members of the David-Stewart Publishing Company of Indianapolis, Indiana, in cooperation with Encyclopædia Britannica Educational Corporation, are responsible for the editorial work in this book.

Editorial Staff

Director: David Rosenberg
Managing Editor and Art Director: James N. Rogers
Senior Editor: Charlotte Jeanes
Associate Editor: Jean M. White

Contributing Editors

Betty Holloway
Richard E. Kirk
Eth Clifford Rosenberg

Art Research

Betty Holloway
Jean M. White

Contributing Artists

Bonita Chandler
James Dixon
L. A. Gregory
Jean D. Kauper
David E. Kinney
Margaret Miller
Gale Reid
Edith Rozen
W. E. Shuman
Susan Yager

Research Staff

Laura R. Collins
Diana Sakmyster
Billie W. Stucky
Frances Weinberg

EDITOR'S PREFACE

The natural sciences are many. They include all the life sciences and all the earth sciences. This dictionary has been written in clear and simple language to help young readers in the early elementary grades expand their knowledge of the fascinating world of plants, animals and earth science. The dictionary provides definitions for over a thousand plants, animals and earth science subjects, as well as a glossary of more than a thousand words that are commonly used in writing and talking about natural science subjects.

As most readers know, a new subject usually requires a new vocabulary. The subject of natural science is somewhat of an exception, since most young readers already have a basic nature vocabulary. Learning the vocabulary of nature starts in early childhood. Most young readers already know that man, other animals, plants, oceans, deserts and mountains are all part of nature. They know what a rattlesnake is and what a volcano is, and they know the difference between a whale and a fish.

In writing about plants, animals and earth science subjects, the writers and editors have been able to avoid, for the most part, a scientific vocabulary. Even so, some common scientific terms such as *dorsal, bract* and *exoskeleton,* for which there are no easy synonyms, have been used. Such terms are both necessary and desirable, especially since a glossary is provided to define them—again, in clear, simple language. The glossary terms were drawn from the special vocabularies for each natural science.

The various plant, animal and earth science entries in the front section of the dictionary were selected by authorities in their corresponding sciences. Selection was based on frequency of use, particularly in early elementary curricula, textbooks, reference books, periodicals and nature study guides. Science authorities then wrote the text—not only a simple definition, but extended information about each entry. The artists who prepared the illustrations painted many of the pictures from actual specimens. Other illustrations were carefully researched and checked for accuracy. The text was carefully edited and checked for both accuracy and adequacy. Following this, the text was re-edited by reading experts to make sure it was in clear and simple language that a young reader could understand. The final step sent the re-edited text back to the science authorities, who checked to see that the readability revisions had not compromised scientific accuracy.

The names of the consultants, writers, artists and editors who produced this dictionary are listed earlier in this book. Both their knowledge of the subjects and their interest in helping others are reflected in the book, which will give pleasure as well as information to users of all ages.

HOW TO USE THIS BOOK

If you are a student in the early elementary grades, *Discovering Natural Science* was written especially for you. The dictionary is divided into three parts: the Main Text, the Glossary-Index and the Charts and Tables. Read on to understand how each part works.

The Main Text

The first part of the dictionary is the Main Text. It contains articles that tell about and illustrate many kinds of plants, animals, rocks, minerals, and other important subjects of natural science. All of the articles in the Main Text are in alphabetical order. Pronunciations are given for many of the natural science words you may not know.

Most articles in the Main Text tell about small groups of plants or animals. For example, the *blackberry* article tells about blackberries as a group. The article also tells about and illustrates the most common kind of blackberry, the *wild blackberry*.

Sometimes, an article in the Main Text tells about a plant or animal family, as in the *cat* article. In natural science, a family is usually a large, important group that contains many kinds of plants or animals. For example, the cat family contains lions and tigers as well as domestic (pet) cats. The article on *cat* tells what all cats look like, where they live on the earth, what their habits are and many other things about cats as a family. At the end of the *cat* article, you will find a list of the many different kinds of cats that have their own articles in the Main Text, as *lion* and *leopard*.

The Glossary-Index

The Glossary-Index is an important part of the dictionary. To save time, always look first in the Glossary-Index for the word you want. For example, suppose you are looking for the *African elephant*, which is one of the two kinds of elephants. First, look in the Glossary-Index. There you will find: **African elephant** p. 140. When you turn to p. 140, you will see that *African elephant* is described in the Main Text under the *elephant* article.

Many things in natural science have more than one name. For example, *crazyweed* is another name for *locoweed*. If you look up *crazyweed* in the Glossary-Index, you will find: **crazyweed** See *locoweed:* p. 260.

The Glossary-Index also defines many scientific words used in Main Text articles. For example, *flower* and *fang* are words used in some Main Text articles. They are words also used in your science textbooks and in many other places. In the Glossary-Index, several words are illustrated to make their meanings clearer.

The Charts and Tables

Between the Main Text and the Glossary-Index are eleven Charts and Tables. Each of these is listed in the Table of Contents. The Charts and Tables are useful because they bring together many related facts of natural science.

KEY TO PRONUNCIATION

ə	banana, bun, tickət, pert	j	job, edge
ə	sound preceding l, n and m, as in battle, eaten	ng	sing, ink
		ō	bone, snow
a	mat, map	ȯ	corn, saw, all
ā	age, vein	ȯi	coin, boy
ä	cot, cart, father	sh	shy, dish
au̇	sound, now	th	thin, ether
ch	chin, itch	th	then, either
e	bet, bed	ü	rule, fool, few\ 'fyü\
ē	even, beat, sleepy	u̇	pull, wood
i	tip, invent	y	yard, cue\ 'kyü\
ī	side, buy	zh	azure, vision

\ slant line used at beginning and end of all pronunciations.

' mark placed ahead of a syllable with strong stress or accent.

ˌ mark placed ahead of a syllable with some stress but not so much as '.

( ) parentheses showing a single sound or syllable which is pronounced by some speakers but not by others; also showing a stress—either (') or (ˌ)—which may or may not appear in a word, depending on the speaker.

a

aardvark\ˈärd-ˌvärk\(ant bear, Cape anteater)

This awkward-looking mammal moves about at night and sleeps in burrows during the day. During prehistoric times the aardvark probably roamed Europe and Asia, but now it is found only in Africa, south of the Sahara Desert.

The aardvark averages 4 feet in length and weighs about 100 pounds. Some aardvarks have a thin scattering of bristly hairs on their thick-skinned bodies. Others have soft-looking, black to reddish-brown fur. Aardvark legs are very strong, with 4 long, heavy claws on the front feet and 5 on the hind feet.

Fast diggers, aardvarks use their strong legs and claws to dig burrows and break open the tall earth nests of termites, their main food. They pick up the termites with their long, sticky tongues. The termites often attack the aardvark with their sharp cutting pincers, but the aardvark's thick skin protects it from injury.

Scientists believe that female aardvarks bear 1 young in July. When they are 6 months old, young aardvarks leave their families.

abalone\ˌab-ə-ˈlō-nē\(ear shell, rainbow shell, sea ear)

Abalones are large marine snails used both as food and for their shells. Because the shells are iridescent on the inside, buttons and other ornaments are often cut from them.

Abalone shells range from 4 to 12 inches across. The underside of the animal inside the shell forms a thick muscular organ called a foot. With this foot, the abalone grips rocks so tightly that a chisel may be needed to loosen it. The foot is a favorite food, especially in the Orient.

The tongue of the abalone is rough like a

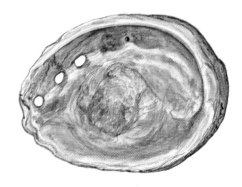

ABALONE

file and moves back and forth. It is used to scrape plant life, on which abalones feed, from underwater rocks.

Abalones are found in warm coastal waters of the Atlantic and Pacific oceans, but are most common in the Pacific Ocean. One kind, the red abalone (illustrated), lives in rocky areas of the California coast. So many abalones have been caught in California that they are protected by conservation laws.

acacia\ə-ˈkā-shə\

A group of shrubs and small trees, acacias belong to the legume family. The larger kinds of acacias are valued for their lumber, which is strong and long-lasting. Acacia bark is used for tanning leather. Acacias are sometimes planted as shade trees.

The tallest kinds of acacia grow to a height of 30 feet. The trunk may be as large as 12 inches across. Acacia bark is

ACACIA

fairly thin and smooth and is grayish or reddish-brown in color.

Acacias have graceful, fern-like leaves and seeds that grow in long, bean-like pods. The branches have sharp thorns, and the leaves are made up of many small, rounded leaflets.

Although acacias are found throughout the tropic and subtropic parts of the world, they are most common in Australia.

The cat claw acacia (illustrated) is found in the southwestern U.S. Its name came from the shape of its thorns. It grows as tall as 20 feet and has clusters of small yellow flowers.

African \ 'af-ri-kən \ violet

The African violet is a popular house plant that grows wild in central Africa. It was brought to the U.S. in 1894. The African violet is not related to the true violets that are so well known in temperate regions of the world.

African violets grow 4 to 6 inches tall. Their dark green leaves may be oval, broad or nearly round, and are clustered at the base of the plant. Both leaves and stems are thick and fleshy, and are covered with short, fuzzy hairs.

The flowers of the African violet are usually some shade of purple, but may be pink or white. They are about 1 inch across, and bloom all year.

AGATE

In order to grow well, African violets need moist air and a temperature of over 60° F. They can be grown from seed or leaf cuttings. If a leaf or a piece of stem is placed in moist sand, roots will develop and a new plant will begin.

agate \ 'ag-ət \

Agate is a beautifully marked and colored mineral. Its coloring and markings are due to layers of yellowish-white and dull green or brown chalcedony, a kind of quartz.

The markings of agate depend on where it is found in an igneous rock formation. If the agate fills a rounded hole in rock, its bands look like rings. If it fills a cut in the rock, the bands will be straight.

The chalcedony is carried to the holes and cuts in the rocks by water. When the water evaporates, a ring or wedge of agate is left.

Agate is found in many countries throughout the world. Most agate comes from Brazil. In the U.S., it is found in Wyoming and Oregon.

agave \ ə-'gäv-ē \

A group of flowering plants, agaves are both useful and decorative. They are native to Mexico and the warm parts of the U.S.

Agaves have stiff, gray-green leaves with spiny edges and sharp points. All leaves grow from the base of the plant. A

AFRICAN VIOLET

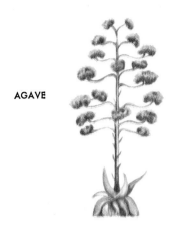

AGAVE

few kinds flower every year, but many bloom only after 10 or 20 years of growth.

Some kinds of agaves that grow in Mexico and Central America have many uses. Soap is made from the roots. The young leaves are used as food. Sap from the stem of one kind is made into a beverage. Fibers from the leaves of another kind of agave are made into rope.

The kind of agave best known in the U.S. and Europe is the century plant (illustrated). It grows wild in Mexico and has been brought into many areas of the U.S. as a decorative plant. Its leaves may grow as long as 6 feet. The plants may grow a long stalk 20 to 30 feet tall, bearing 100 or more large flowers.

agonic \ ə-'gän-ik \ **line**

An agonic line is a map line drawn to show places on the earth where a compass will point directly to the North Pole.

The earth turns around an imaginary axis. The north end of this axis is the North Pole, while the south end is the South Pole. Compasses point northward toward the earth's magnetic pole which is not in the same place as the North Pole. Therefore, a compass will not always point directly to the North Pole unless the compass is in a place on an agonic line.

In the U.S., an agonic line runs through Ohio, Kentucky and South Carolina. A compass anywhere on this line will point directly to the North Pole. In New York a compass points west of the North Pole. In California it points east of the North Pole.

Sometimes changes in the earth cause an agonic line to move. Two hundred years ago the agonic line now running through the U.S. was in the Atlantic Ocean.

agouti \ ə-'güt-ē \

There are many kinds of agoutis, but all are members of the rodent family. They live in wooded areas from southern Mexico to South America. Agoutis are great jumpers, and a 20-foot leap from a sitting start has been observed.

Agoutis look like rabbits but are tailless and have small ears. They are 18 to 20 inches long and have long, slim legs. Their forefeet have 5 toes but their hind feet have only 3. Their nails are long, flat and hoof-like. Agoutis can easily hold food in their paws.

During the day agoutis stay in burrows or holes in trees. At night they come out to eat grass, fruits, seeds and nuts.

Agoutis have 5 or 6 young at a time. Families stay together even after the young are fully grown. An agouti's normal life-span is 9 to 12 years.

The most common kind of agouti is the golden agouti (illustrated), native to Brazil, Venezuela and Guiana.

AGOUTI

ALBACORE

ALBATROSS

alabaster\ 'al-ə-ˌbas-tər\

A soft, fine-grained mineral, alabaster is a compact form of gypsum. It is easy to carve and polish, so it is often made into vases and small statues.

Alabaster is translucent and has a pearly luster. It is usually white, but may be lightly tinted or mottled.

Ordinarily found in beds, alabaster was formed in areas where. seawater evaporated. It is mined in Italy, in Great Britain and, in the U.S., in Colorado.

albacore\ 'al-bə-ˌkōr\

A kind of bluefin tuna, the albacore is famous for its extremely good eyesight and great speed. Because it is such a strong, determined fighter, the albacore is considered one of the finest saltwater game fish. Its white, tasty meat is canned and sold in stores as first-quality tuna.

The average weight of the albacore is 20 to 30 pounds, although much larger ones have been caught. Albacores are easy to recognize by their stout, streamlined bodies and their extremely long pectoral fins. The tail is large and widely forked.

Albacores are usually found in schools near the surface in both the Atlantic and Pacific oceans. They feed on small fish and microscopic plants and animals.

Scientists have found that albacores do not have regular migration patterns. Some swim great distances, while others remain in the same area.

albatross\ 'al-bə-ˌtròs\

Large sea birds that form a family, albatrosses are known for their long flights. They often stay at sea for months at a time, sleeping on the water and feeding at night on small marine animals.

There are about 15 kinds of albatrosses, and most have very large wingspans. The wandering albatross has a wingspan of 12 feet, larger than that of any other bird. Albatross bodies range from 2½ to 4 feet in length. Their legs and tails are short and their feet are webbed. Their heads are large and their large hooked bills have tube-like nostrils.

Albatrosses come to land only to breed. One egg is laid on the bare ground or in a simple grass nest. Both parents take turns sitting on the egg for 70 to 80 days. When the egg hatches, the parents feed the young bird fish which they have eaten and partly digested. Most albatrosses live in the South Pacific. Some kinds can be found in all parts of the oceans in the southern hemisphere.

The Laysan albatross (illustrated) breeds along the coast of Baja California and on Laysan and other islands in the South Pacific.

alder\ 'òl-dər\

Alders are a group of trees and shrubs closely related to birches and hazels. Some kinds of alders grow 100 feet tall and are used for lumber. Other kinds are

ALDER

low-growing bushes. Alder bark is sometimes used to tan leather.

Alder leaves are 2 to 5 inches long and have toothed edges and large veins. The leaves are usually oval in shape but taper to a short point at the tip. The flowers are clusters of purple and yellow tassels that appear in early spring.

Alders are common throughout the north temperate zone. They are most often found in moist areas.

The red alder (illustrated) is one of the largest kinds. It grows from 40 to 90 feet tall, and its trunk may be more than 2 feet across.

Red alder bark is smooth and light gray, sometimes marked with black patches. Its strong wood has a reddish color, and is used to make furniture. The red alder grows along the Pacific coast of North America.

alewife \ 'āl-,wīf \ (branch herring)

The alewife is a kind of fish belonging to the herring family. It is commercially important because it is netted in great numbers for food and fish meal and is also valued for its oil. Its scales are sometimes used to make imitation pearls.

The average length of an alewife is 13 inches. Average weight is about 1 pound. Alewives have a dark spot behind the gills, a narrow, silvery patch on the cheek and faint stripes along the side.

Alewives live in schools along the Atlantic coast from Canada to North Caro-

lina. They are also found landlocked in the deep waters of all the Great Lakes except Lake Superior, where they become a nuisance when large numbers die.

These fish feed mainly on plankton. Like other fish in the herring family, alewives swim into the mouths of rivers to lay their eggs. One female alewife normally lays more than 100,000 eggs each spring. The young swim out to sea when they are 3 to 4 inches long.

alfalfa \ al-'fal-fə \

A perennial plant grown from seed, alfalfa belongs to the legume family. It is important because of the nitrogen-fixing bacteria which live in nodules on its roots. The bacteria improve the soil by returning nitrogen to it.

Large fields of alfalfa are grown by farmers as pasture food for livestock. After it is cut and dried, alfalfa is called hay. Alfalfa does well in many different soils and climates.

Alfalfa grows in branching stalks 2 to 3 feet tall. Its leaves grow alternately along the stem, and each one is made of 3-inch-long leaflets. The roots sometimes grow as deep as 15 feet. Small, 5-petaled flowers grow in clusters at the tips of the branches. Spiral-shaped pods contain the seeds.

Alfalfa was first grown in Asia. The early pioneers brought it to America from Europe. It is now common throughout southern Canada and most of the U.S.

ALFALFA

algae \ 'al-ˌjē \

Algae are a large group of simple plants that include seaweeds 200 feet long, as well as plants visible only through a microscope. Some kinds of algae swim, other kinds just float and others anchor themselves to the ocean floor. A few kinds live on damp soil or tree trunks.

All algae are alike in that they have no roots, leaves or stems. Like green plants, algae contain chlorophyll. They use energy from sunlight to manufacture their own food from minerals in the water.

Some algae are single cells, and some are colonies of many cells. Some live in freshwater ponds and lakes. Many live in the ocean. A few live on land, in damp soil or on tree trunks.

Tiny, 1-celled algae reproduce by dividing. More complex kinds produce spores from which new plants grow.

Algae are important as food for fish and other animals that live in water. They are sometimes used to make fertilizer. Some seaweeds are eaten by humans, mostly in China and Japan. Scientists believe that certain kinds of algae which can be grown in tanks can provide fresh, nourishing food for men on long trips through space.

The simple cells of blue-green algae live together in colonies. The colonies are held together by a slimy jelly they produce. Blue-green algae are most common in fresh water.

Oscillatoria and Nostoc (both illustrated) are kinds of blue-green algae that form thread-like filaments. Each filament is a colony of cells clinging together end-to-end. When crowded together, the filaments form a slimy, tangled mass.

In Oscillatoria, one end of each colony clings to some underwater surface, while the other end moves about freely. In Nostoc, the filaments are rolled or tangled together in balls or sheets. Nostoc lives in stagnant ponds and on damp soil. Seen under a microscope, its colonies look like strings of small beads.

The cells of green algae are more highly developed than those of blue-green algae. In green algae, each cell contains a nucleus and 1 or more green-colored bodies called chloroplasts.

Chlorella, Oedogonium, Spirogyra and Volvox (all illustrated) are green algae that live in fresh water.

Chlorella lives in both fresh water and the ocean, singly or in colonies. Some chlorella live within the tissues of sponges. Oedogonium and Spirogyra look like green threads. A few cells in an Oedogonium act as anchors, and a few other cells act as reproductive organs. Volvox forms floating, ball-shaped colonies which are large enough to be seen without a microscope.

Fucus and kelp (both illustrated) belong to the brown algae group. They are tough, leathery seaweeds that grow in the shallower parts of the ocean where the water is cool or cold.

Fucus grows along rocky coasts, between high and low tide lines. Along its branching, ribbon-like strands are pairs of oval air pods that serve as floats.

Kelp is the largest of all the algae. Its strands grow as long as 200 feet. In Asia, kelp is used as human food. It is a source of iodine and of valuable mineral salts. Kelp is also used as food for cattle and as fertilizer.

Red algae have delicate, feathery shapes. They live deeper under water than the other algae, and their reddish or purple colors make them more sensitive to the dim sunlight that reaches them. Most kinds of red algae grow in warm, quiet parts of the sea.

Agar-agar, made from one kind of red algae, is used in scientific laboratories and in preparing some foods and medicines.

For other kinds of algae, see *diatom* and *euglena*.

Algae—Simple Plants

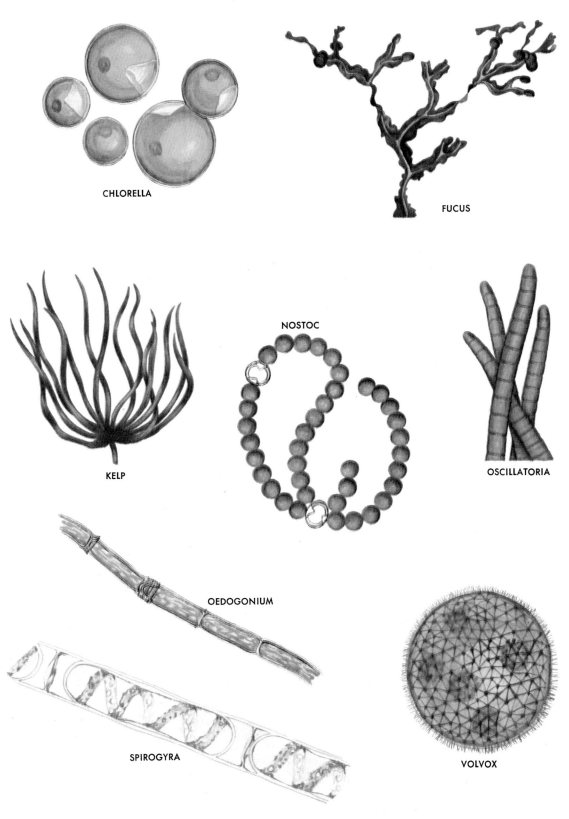

CHLORELLA

FUCUS

KELP

NOSTOC

OSCILLATORIA

OEDOGONIUM

SPIROGYRA

VOLVOX

ALLIGATOR

ALLUVIAL FAN

alligator

Alligators make up a small group of large carnivorous reptiles that live in and near fresh water in warm climates. Although alligators and crocodiles are related and look somewhat alike, crocodiles live in salt water as well as fresh water. The alligator has a broader snout, a more even arrangement of teeth and a more sluggish disposition than the crocodile.

Alligators have long heads with powerful jaws. Their long thick tails are used for swimming and as weapons. A single swish of a full-grown alligator's tail can break a man's leg.

While swimming, an alligator holds its short, stubby legs close to its scaly body. While its body is floating just under the surface of the water, an alligator can smell, see and hear because its nostrils, eyes and ears are above the water. On land an alligator can move very quickly for short distances.

One kind of alligator, the American alligator (illustrated), is large and slow-moving. About 9 feet long, it lives in rivers and swampy areas of the southeastern U.S. and Central America. In very hot or cold weather, it buries itself in mud. The female lays 30 to 40 eggs in a mound-like nest of mud and grass. In 9 to 10 weeks, the eggs hatch. The young are about 8 inches long.

alluvial \ ə-'lü-vē-əl \ fan

An alluvial fan is a large, fan-shaped deposit of pebbles, gravel, sand and mud.

Alluvial fans are formed in dry mountain areas when stream beds fill with fast-running water after a very heavy rain. Because the mountains are very steep and there are no plants to hold back the water, it flows downhill with great speed and force. As it moves downhill, the water picks up large amounts of mud and rocks.

When the water, mud and rocks reach the floor of a valley, the stream loses speed. Then, as the slow-moving water spreads out into a fan-shaped flow, it drops its rocks and mud. The largest rocks stop first, then the pebbles and sand and, finally, the mud. As the water sinks into the ground, the rocks, pebbles, sand and mud are left in a fan-shaped pattern.

almond \ 'äm-ənd \ tree

The almond tree, like the cherry, peach and plum trees, belongs to the rose family. It is grown for its sweet, nut-like seed and not for its fruit.

The almond tree usually grows from 10 to 20 feet high. The leaves are 3 to 4 inches long. They are thin, narrow and pointed. Along the edges of the leaves are tiny teeth.

The flowers bloom in early spring before the leaves appear. They are large and pink and have 5 petals. The flowers grow in bunches along the branches.

The oval fruit is about 1½ inches long. It has a thick skin and dry flesh. When ripe, the fruit cracks open and the seed can be seen.

Almond trees have been grown in southern Europe and Asia for hundreds of years. They were brought to California about 1900 and are now an important crop there.

alpaca \ al-'pak-ə \

Alpacas are domesticated animals that look like llamas but are smaller. They live only in the high parts of the Andes Mountains in South America. Alpacas are related to the prehistoric camels.

Alpacas are 3 to 4 feet high at the shoulder and are 4½ to 5 feet long. Hooked spurs on their hoofs help them climb steep mountain slopes. Although their main food is grass, they also eat lichens, mosses and leaves.

Long ago, alpacas were wild. Today they are raised by the natives of Bolivia and Peru for their soft, woolly hair. The hair may be red, white, dark brown or black. It is clipped from the animals and used to weave a soft, heavy cloth. This cloth is used to make very warm clothing.

Female alpacas have 1 young every 2 years. Alpacas live to be about 15 years old.

amber \ 'am-bər \

Amber is the fossilized resin of pine trees that grew at least a million years ago. It has been used to make jewelry since the time of the early Egyptians and is valued for its beauty. Its color ranges from pale yellow to red or dark brown.

Amber may be transparent or translucent. Usually occurring in small, rounded, irregular lumps, it sometimes contains perfectly preserved insects. These insects became trapped in the resin when it was still soft and sticky.

Like 3 other kinds of gems, amber was formed as a by-product of living organisms. The 3 other kinds of gems are pearl and coral, both parts of sea animals, and jet, a form of coal.

Amber washes ashore on beaches of the Baltic Sea, and on beaches in Sicily, France, England and China. It is mined commercially in East Germany and Burma.

American bison \ 'bīs-ᵊn \ (buffalo)

The American bison is a huge, hoofed mammal that is not a true buffalo. It once traveled in large herds across the Great Plains of North America. Indians hunted bison for food, clothing, shelter and bones to make tools. White settlers killed so many of these animals that by 1900 only 500 were left. The government then

ALPACA

AMBER

9

AMERICAN BISON

AMERICAN MOUNTAIN ASH

passed laws to protect bison, and by 1950 there were 23,000.

Bison weigh from 1,800 to 2,200 pounds. The males are 6 feet high at the shoulder and are about 11 feet long. The females are a little smaller. All bison have hollow, curved horns 15 to 16 inches long.

Bison cannot see very well, but they have very good hearing and a fine sense of smell. When frightened, they can run as fast as 40 miles per hour. Their coats are heaviest in December. In February they begin to shed. By the middle of the summer, they are nearly hairless.

During the month of May, 1 or 2 calves are born. They become adults in about 3 years.

American mountain ash

This tree is not a true ash, but a member of the rose family. The American mountain ash is also related to the apple and hawthorn trees. Although it is a good shade tree, its wood is not used commercially at all.

The American mountain ash may grow with more than one trunk, like a spreading shrub, or as a tree up to 25 feet tall. Its trunk may be as large as 12 inches across. The branches are slender, spreading and graceful.

The leaves are 6 to 8 inches long. There are 13 to 17 leaflets fastened to each thin stem. In the fall, the leaves turn bright yellow.

The flowers bloom after the leaves appear on the tree. White and very small, they grow in umbrella-shaped groups that are 3 to 4 inches across. In the fall, after the leaves have dropped, red-orange berries appear where the flowers were. The berries are about ¼ inch across.

The American mountain ash is common in southern Canada and around the Great Lakes. It is also found in the Appalachian Mountains.

American sable \ 'sā-bəl \ (marten)

This rare animal is a member of the weasel family. Its fine, soft fur is used to make expensive fur coats. So many of these animals have been trapped for their fur that they are almost extinct.

The American sable weighs about 4 pounds. It has a long, thin body, a long, bushy tail and short legs with curved claws. The fur is a rich brown. Sometimes the individual hairs are silver-tipped.

The American sable is now found only in Canada and southern Alaska. At one time it lived as far south as West Virginia and New Mexico.

AMERICAN SABLE

This animal is very active, hunting birds, eggs and squirrels both day and night. Sometimes it hunts for ground animals such as mice, snakes and frogs. It makes its den in treetops and does not hibernate. When frightened, the American sable gives off a very unpleasant odor. Its life-span is about 17 years.

American shad \ 'shad \

This saltwater fish, a member of the herring family, is a highly prized food fish. Its eggs, as well as its flesh, are eaten. It is also a popular game fish.

The American shad has a deep, slender body and a notch on its upper jaw. The male, which is smaller than the female, is usually 14 to 18 inches long and weighs 3 to 4 pounds. The female grows up to 30 inches long and may weigh as much as 12 pounds. American shad feed mainly on plankton.

Found from Newfoundland to Florida, American shad have been successfully introduced along the west coast of the U.S. They swim from the sea into freshwater rivers to lay eggs. One female may lay as many as 30,000 eggs at one time. Not all of these eggs hatch. The young remain in the river about 4 months. Then they move downstream and into the sea.

AMERICAN SHAD

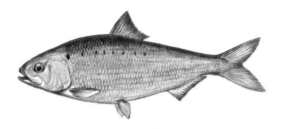

amethyst \ 'am-ə-thəst \

A crystal of quartz, the mineral amethyst is a gem when it is clear and flawless. It is one of the rarest kinds of quartz and one of the most valuable.

Amethyst is purple or violet-colored, and the darker crystals are popular as jewelry. Its color may be caused by the presence of a small amount of manganese. Some parts of an amethyst crystal may be darker than others. This is probably due to uneven spreading of the manganese in the crystal.

The best amethysts are found in Uruguay, but the biggest deposit is in Brazil. In the U.S., amethyst deposits are located in the states of South Dakota, Wyoming and Pennsylvania.

amoeba \ ə-'mē-bə \

Amoebas make up a group of 1-celled, microscopic animals with soft bodies that change shape as they move about. They live in water, moist soil and the bodies of animals. Even the largest amoebas are hard to see without a microscope.

Most amoebas are harmless, but 1 kind, sometimes found in the intestines of humans, causes the disease called amoebic dysentery.

An amoeba moves about by flowing. One side of the amoeba flows forward, forming a false foot called a pseudopodium. The rest of the animal then flows

AMOEBA

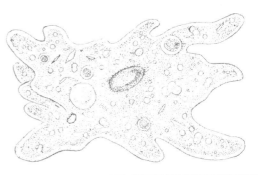

into the pseudopodium. In this way the animal moves from place to place.

Amoebas feed on other 1-celled plants and animals. Tiny bits of food are taken into the body, and wastes are pushed out at any place on the surface.

Amoebas have special organs for their needs. One type of organ controls the animal's response to light and temperature changes. Another organ controls the amount of water inside the animal. Still other organs contain and digest food.

A common kind of amoeba (illustrated) lives in clean, fresh water where there are green plants.

amphibian \ am-'fib-ē-ən \

Amphibians make up a large and important group of cold-blooded vertebrate animals. Their place in evolution is between the fishes and the reptiles.

Amphibians are divided into 3 types. One type is made up of legless, worm-like, tropical animals called caecilians. A second type is made up of salamanders, which are lizard-shaped animals with 4 short legs and a long tail. The third type is made up of toads and frogs.

All amphibians live in or near fresh water. They do not drink water, but soak it up through their thin skins. Amphibians breathe through lungs, gills or their skins. Certain kinds breathe in several of these ways. Many amphibians, such as toads and frogs, pass through metamorphosis (illustrated). From a gill-breathing stage, they develop lungs as they grow into adults. During winter, amphibians hibernate.

Most amphibians lay their eggs in water. Each egg is within a jelly-like substance. The eggs of most amphibians hatch into larvae. The best-known amphibian larvae are tadpoles.

amphibole \ 'am(p)-fə-,bōl \

A group of common minerals, amphiboles make up the biggest part of many rocks. They exist in many colors. They may be white to gray, green, or brown to black. All are fairly light in weight and most transmit light. Actinolite, hornblende and tremolite are common amphiboles.

All amphiboles are formed slowly, under medium amounts of heat and pressure. Water is always present. Amphiboles are usually found in metamorphic rocks.

Amphiboles are sometimes found as thin, rod-shaped crystals. The crystals may be in a tangled group. Broken pieces of amphiboles are often wedge-shaped, like a slice of cake.

There is no one chemical formula for amphiboles because their chemical content differs from piece to piece.

METAMORPHOSIS OF FROG

AMPHIBOLE

ANDALUSITE

anchovy \ 'an-ˌchō-vē \

Anchovies are a family of small marine fish related to the herrings. They are popular food fish and are also used as bait by fishermen.

The anchovy's body is long, thin and very flat. There are no scales on the head, which is long and pointed. The single dorsal fin is near the center of the back. The ventral fins are almost directly below the dorsal fin. The tail is deeply notched. A wide, silvery stripe runs along each side of the body, which ranges from 5 to 9 inches long.

Anchovies live off both the Atlantic and Pacific coasts, usually in warm waters close to shore. They travel in large schools, feeding on plankton, other marine organisms and small fish. Most kinds of anchovies spawn close to the shore, in spring and early summer. The eggs float out to sea and hatch in a few days.

One of the most common kinds of anchovies is the northern, or Pacific, anchovy. It is caught in large numbers as a food fish.

andalusite \ ˌan-də-'lü-ˌsīt \

Andalusite is a mineral that has several forms. One rare form, found only in Brazil and Ceylon, is a gem. When cut and polished, this gem looks green from one direction and reddish-brown from another.

Other forms of andalusite may be gray, brown or pink, and may be transparent or translucent. Andalusite crystals are sometimes cigar-shaped.

Andalusite is used commercially to make a kind of porcelain that will stand a great deal of heat. Such porcelain is used in the manufacture of spark plugs.

In the eastern U.S., andalusite is found from Maine to Pennsylvania. In California, it is mined commercially. Other sources are France, Austria, South Africa, Australia and Spain. In fact, andalusite takes its name from Andalusia, Spain, where it was first discovered.

angelfish

These tropical marine fish belong to the butterfly fish family. Although there are over 150 kinds of angelfish, none are valued as food or as game fish.

Angelfish have flat, oval-shaped bodies. Their heads are usually pointed, with a small mouth containing many small teeth. Many kinds of angelfish have long, thin dorsal and anal fins that sweep back as far as the tail fin. The cover over each gill has a large, sharp spine that can cause a painful wound.

Most angelfish are brightly and beauti-

ANGELFISH

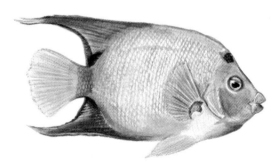

ANGULAR-WINGED KATYDID

fully colored. Often their mouths and lips are a different color from their heads. Some kinds of angelfish grow as long as 24 inches.

Angelfish are found alone or in pairs in shallow, warm, tropical waters. They often live in or around coral reefs or in brackish water. Their mouths are well shaped for picking up the small plants and invertebrates which they eat.

One of the most common kinds of angelfish is the queen angelfish (illustrated).

angular-winged katydid
\ 'ang-gyə-lər 'wingd 'kāt-ē-,did\

Angular-winged katydids are not true katydids, but are insects belonging to the long-horned grasshopper family. There are 2 kinds, the larger (illustrated) and the smaller. Except for their different sizes, they are almost alike.

The larger angular-winged katydid grows to a length of 2 inches. The thin wings of both kinds fold over their backs. On the head are 2 long antennae which look like threads.

In the fall, angular-winged katydids lay their eggs. The eggs lie on the edges of leaves and twigs and overlap like shingles. In spring, nymphs hatch from the eggs. The nymphs look like the adults but are wingless.

Angular-winged katydids are common in the eastern U.S. They eat tree leaves,

but not enough to be much of a pest. The color of angular-winged katydids protects them from being seen and eaten by birds.

annelid\ 'an-ºl-əd\

A large group of invertebrates, annelids are highly developed worms. This large group is divided into 3 smaller groups.

Annelids which live in salt water make up one of these smaller groups, called Polychaeta. Certain bristle annelids are not very often seen because they remain hidden in tube-like burrows most of their lives. Other bristle annelids swim about. Most of them are from 2 to 4 inches long and are very brightly colored.

Land annelids, such as the common earthworm and other kinds that live in fresh water, belong to the group called Oligochaeta. These worms usually breathe through their skins and are larger than Polychaetes. Most freshwater kinds of Oligochaeta do not swim. Some live their lives buried in the muddy bottoms of lakes and streams.

Over 300 kinds of leeches form the third group of annelids, which is called Hirudinea. Leeches live in seawater, in fresh water or on land. They grow from ¾ to 2 inches long.

For kinds of annelids, see *earthworm, leech, nereis* and *worm.*

ANNELIDS

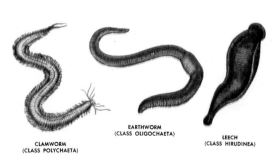

CLAMWORM
(CLASS POLYCHAETA)

EARTHWORM
(CLASS OLIGOCHAETA)

LEECH
(CLASS HIRUDINEA)

anole \ ə-'nō-lē \ (American chameleon)

These small reptiles make up a group of New World lizards. They change color just as the true chameleons of Europe, Africa and Asia do. However, the reptile often sold in pet shops as a "chameleon" is not a true chameleon, but the green anole (illustrated).

Anoles are 5 to 7 inches long, including the tail. True chameleons are up to 24 inches long. They differ from anoles in having stubby heads with bulging eyes and odd-shaped crests. Both anoles and true chameleons live in trees, but only true chameleons hold on to branches by wrapping their tails around them.

By expanding and contracting different-colored spots on their skin, anoles change color. The changes depend on the animal's emotions, or on light or temperature, rather than on the color of the animal's surroundings.

Anoles live in the warmer parts of North and South America, and in the West Indies. The green anole is found as far north as the Carolinas and as far west as Texas. It may appear light green or light brown, or a mixture of the 2 colors. The male has a throat fan he displays when courting. It is a flap of loose skin under the chin that appears pink when it is expanded and stiffened.

Young anoles hatch from eggs that the female lays among decaying leaves on the ground.

For a true chameleon, see *chameleon.*

ant

Ants make up a family of social insects related to bees and wasps. Over 6,000 kinds are known. Ants are found all over the world.

Most ants have large heads, slender thoraxes and large abdomens. The abdomen is joined to the thorax by a thin waist.

An ant's mouth has 2 sets of jaws. The outer jaws are used for carrying and digging, while the inner jaws are used for chewing.

Most ants live in large colonies. Like men, they adapt to many different living conditions. Their life cycle has 4 stages: egg, larva, pupa and adult. Like bees, ants have 3 castes: queens, workers and winged males. The workers are females who gather food and care for the young. They build, care for and defend the colony. Males do nothing but mate with the queen, who does nothing but lay eggs.

The carpenter ant (illustrated) is the largest ant in the U.S. and is common in the east and midwest. Carpenter ants

ANOLE

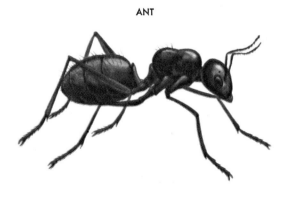

ANT

ANTEATER

ANTELOPE

sometimes damage wooden buildings by boring into them to build their nests. The nests are complicated chambers in buildings, logs or tree trunks.

Carpenter ants feed on plant juices, honey and insects. They sometimes enter houses in search of sweets.

anteater \ˈant-ˌēt-ər\

Anteaters make up a family of tropical mammals that live in Central and South America. They have long sticky tongues which they use to pick up the ants, termites and other small insects that they eat.

Anteaters range in size from 6 inches with 8-inch tails to 6 feet with 3-foot tails. Some kinds of anteaters have soft, silky hair while others have stiff bristles. Some have curved tails for climbing trees. Others have huge, bushy tails. Anteaters have long, thin snouts that are almost as long as their heads.

Some anteaters live on land or in trees while others like mud or shallow water and are good swimmers. Anteaters are quiet animals, but they will fight fiercely when angered.

One young anteater is born each year. It remains with the mother for a year, often riding on her back. The most familiar kind of anteater, the great or giant anteater (illustrated) lives in wet forests and shallow

water. It is about 6 feet long, including a 2½-foot tail. When sleeping, it curls up its tail for protection.

antelope

Antelopes make up a family of even-toed, hoofed mammals related to cattle, sheep and goats. Over 150 kinds of antelope are known. Most live in Africa, but a few live in Europe and Asia.

Antelopes live mainly in deserts, grasslands or mountains. Because they learn easily to live in captivity and are interesting to watch, antelopes are popular zoo animals.

All antelopes have unbranched horns that are bony growths. These growths are part of the skull and are covered with a hard, horny matter. Unlike deer, which shed their antlers every year, antelopes keep their horns. The horns grow as long as the antelope lives.

The Rocky Mountain goat (illustrated), which is not really a goat, is the only antelope found in North America. It lives on the high peaks of the northern Rockies, eating moss, grass and lichens. A surefooted climber, it has pads inside its hoofs. The pads act as suction cups to help the animal keep its footing on smooth rock or ice.

Instead of fighting or running away, the

Rocky Mountain goat tries to hide from its enemies, mostly bears and wolves.

Rocky Mountain goats are about 3½ feet tall and weigh up to 300 pounds. During the late fall mating season, the males fight fiercely over the females. One or 2 kids are born in the spring.

For other kinds of antelopes, see *chamois, gazelle, gnu, hartebeest, impala, klipspringer, kudu, oribi, oryx* and *waterbuck.*

anticline \ 'ant-i-ˌklīn \

An anticline is a group of sedimentary rock layers that have been folded up into the shape of an arch. The folding is caused by pressure deep in the earth's crust.

The sides of an anticline are called limbs. If the limbs slope at the same angle, a symmetric anticline is formed. But if the limbs slope, or "dip," at different angles, they form an asymmetric anticline.

An anticline tilted to one side is known as an overturned anticline. If it appears to lie on one limb, it is called a recumbent anticline.

Usually anticlines are found between synclines, or downfolds. Anticlines and synclines cannot always be seen on the surface of the earth. Sometimes, though, they can be seen in mountainous areas where all the soil has been washed away from the rock layers.

ANTICLINE

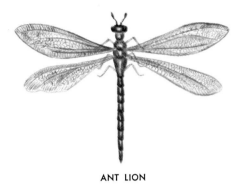

ANT LION

ant lion

Ant lions make up a family of insects that live throughout the U.S. and southern Canada. They are most common in the southwestern U.S.

There are several stages in the life of an ant lion. Adult ant lions lay their eggs on the ground. The eggs hatch into worm-like larvae with fat, hairy bodies.

Using their heads as shovels, most kinds of ant lion larvae dig holes in sandy ground. They hide at the bottom of these holes with only their heads and jaws sticking out. When an ant or other insect walks close enough to the hole, it slides down and into the larva's waiting jaws.

Most ant lion larvae build heavy cocoons in which they spend the winter. The adult ant lions are nocturnal, feeding on small flying insects which they stab and chew with their powerful mouthparts.

A common kind of ant lion (adult illustrated) is often mistaken for a damselfly because of its long narrow wings.

aphid \ 'ā-fəd \ (ant cow, plant louse)

Aphids are small, soft-bodied insects that make up a family of plant pests. They sometimes carry plant diseases and viruses that damage gardens, orchards and farm crops.

APHID

Aphids feed on plant sap, roots or bark. An aphid's mouth is a beak-like sucking tube which is sometimes longer than its body. Some aphids have wings, while others are wingless.

Most aphids produce a sweet fluid which they drop onto leaves. This fluid is a food for bees, wasps and ants. To have a good supply of this fluid, certain ants herd aphids from one plant to another. For this reason, aphids are sometimes called "ant cows."

Female aphids lay eggs near the buds on a host plant. The eggs live through the winter. The females hatch in the spring. Then the young female aphids produce many wingless young. Later in the summer, the winged males and females hatch. These mate, and the female lays eggs.

Aphids are eaten by spiders, ladybugs and lacewings.

The green peach aphid (illustrated) is found throughout most of the world. It carries diseases to garden crops and tobacco plants.

apple tree

Probably the best-known fruit tree, the apple tree belongs to the rose family. Apples of many different colors, sizes and flavors have been cultivated.

The apple tree grows 20 to 40 feet tall.

It has wide-spreading branches and scaly bark. The leaves are 3 to 5 inches long, oval and slightly hairy. The pinkish-white flowers are 1½ to 2 inches across and have 5 petals. The flowers and leaves both come out in May or June. The fruit ripens in the fall. With proper care, 1 apple tree can produce a crop each year for over 30 years.

The apple was probably native to Asia. Today it grows in nearly all parts of the world. It can be grown farther north than other fruit trees because it blossoms late. Frosts do not often kill the flowers or young fruit. Apple trees grow best in a cool, moist climate such as that of the Pacific Northwest in the U.S.

archaeopteryx \ ˌär-kē-ˈäp-tə-riks \

The archaeopteryx is thought to be one of the first kinds of bird that ever lived. Its name means "ancient wing" or "ancient one with wings." The archaeopteryx lived in Europe 135 to 140 million years ago and then died out. It was about the size of a crow, but it looked very different from the birds of today.

In the process of evolution, this animal was a step between the reptiles and the birds. Like a reptile, it had scales and a long tail, but like a bird, the archaeopteryx had feathers.

ARCHAEOPTERYX

Its beak was something like a bird's, but it had the sharp-pointed teeth of a reptile. Its feet were much like the feet of many birds living today.

The archaeopteryx was not a good flier; it had 3 sharp claws on the end of each wing to help it climb trees. It reproduced by laying eggs.

Only 3 fossil skeletons have ever been found. All 3 were found in southern Germany, the first 2 in 1861 and 1877, and the third in 1956.

archipelago \ ,ärk-ə-'pel-ə-,gō \

Many islands that are clustered together are called an archipelago. Archipelago is also used to describe that part of the sea or ocean that contains a number of islands grouped together.

The word "archipelago" was first used by the Greeks to describe their islands in the Aegean Sea.

One of the best-known archipelagos is the Malayan archipelago of southeast Asia. This includes the large islands of Borneo and Sumatra. The Alexander archipelago that is a part of Alaska includes over 1,000 islands.

arête \ ə-'rāt \

An arête is a sharp, jagged rocky ridge formed when glaciers on both sides of a mountain wear away the top of the mountain. Arête means "fish bone" in French.

Arêtes are found mainly in high mountainous regions where alpine glaciers form. Most arêtes are in the Swiss Alps, the Rocky Mountains of the U.S. and the Selkirk Mountains in Canada. Where there are continental ice sheets as in Greenland and Antarctica, arêtes are rare.

argentite \ 'är-jən-,tīt \

This mineral is an important silver ore. It is the ore that was mined at the famous Comstock Lode in Nevada, first discovered in 1856. Before the Comstock Lode was mined out, it produced over 200 million dollars' worth of argentite.

Argentite is blackish-gray in color. It shows a bright metallic shine on freshly broken surfaces. When exposed to air, the surfaces tarnish and become a dull blackish-gray. Like lead, argentite is so soft that it can be cut with a knife.

Argentite is found in veins running through other rock. It can be almost pure or mixed with other ores, such as gold or copper. When pure, it may contain over ¾ silver.

Large deposits of this mineral have been found in Mexico, Chile, Peru, Bolivia, Germany and Norway and, in the U.S., in Nevada, Colorado and Montana.

ARÊTE

ARGENTITE

ARMADILLO

ARTICHOKE

armadillo \ ˌär-mə-'dil-ō \

Small American animals, the armadillos make up a family of toothed mammals. They were named by early Spanish explorers. In Spanish, "armadillo" means "little armored thing." These words describe the bony, jointed plates which cover the upper parts of the animal.

If attacked, the armadillo rolls itself into a tight ball, with its head and tail tucked in. It is thus completely protected, as its enemies cannot bite or scratch through the bony plates.

Armadillos live in tunnels which they dig with their large claws. They sleep during the day and come out at night to eat worms, spiders, snakes and insects. Good climbers and swimmers, armadillos can stay under water as long as 6 minutes.

Several kinds of armadillos are found from the southwestern U.S. to Argentina. The only kind found in the U.S. is the 9-banded armadillo (illustrated). It is about 16 inches long. In spring, the female has 4, 8 or 12 young, always the same sex.

artichoke \ 'ärt-ə-ˌchōk \

The artichoke is a perennial plant grown as a vegetable. The large flower buds are the only part of the plant that is eaten.

The plant itself is large and heavy, growing from 3 to 5 feet tall. It looks very much like a thistle plant. Its leaves are long, heavy and unevenly notched. Some of the leaves have prickles or spines.

The flower buds grow at the tops of the larger branches, and are heavy and oval in shape. They are made up of fleshy, scale-like leaves called bracts. The center of the flower head, called the heart, and the thickened bases of the bracts are the only parts eaten. If not picked, the buds produce a thick cluster of small purple flowers.

Artichokes can be grown from seed or by rooting side stems of older plants. They are native to the Mediterranean region, but are grown in many warmer areas of the world. In California, they are an important crop.

ascaris \ 'as-kə-rəs \

Ascarides are a group of roundworms and are common intestinal parasites. They are found in man, in wild animals and in tame animals.

The male ascaris is 6 to 8 inches long. It has a hairy, down-curved tail. The female is straight and about 16 inches long. Both sexes have 3-lipped mouths.

The adult ascaris lives in the small intestine. The female lays millions of eggs. They leave the host animal in the intestinal waste matter. If eaten by a new host, the eggs hatch to larvae in the intestines of the new host. These larvae bore through the intestinal wall and enter the bloodstream.

Once in the bloodstream, the larvae travel to the liver, spleen and lungs. In the lungs, they grow and crawl or are coughed up the windpipe. Then they are swallowed and become adults in the small intestine. Humans become infected by eating infected, improperly cooked meat. Roundworms may infect an unborn animal if the mother is infected.

A widely known kind of ascaris is the common roundworm (illustrated).

ash

Trees that belong to the olive family, ashes are valued as shade trees and as a source of lumber. They are common through the northern hemisphere.

Some kinds of ash trees are shrub-like, but most grow 40 to 90 feet tall. Nearly all ashes have thick, rough bark marked with deep grooves. The compound leaves are opposite each other, with pointed or rounded leaflets. Ash flowers are green or purple and bloom before the leaves appear in spring. The seeds appear in autumn, dangling in clusters of samaras.

The red ash (illustrated), common in the eastern half of the U.S., is a small, slender tree. It is named for the reddish color of its winter buds and of the short hairs on the twigs and undersides of its leaves.

ASH

Growing from 30 to 50 feet tall, the red ash lives only in fairly damp soil along the edges of lakes and streams. The leaves are 10 to 12 inches long. Each leaf has 5 or 9 pointed leaflets about 2 inches long. The slender samaras are 1 to 2½ inches long.

asparagus \ ə-'spar-ə-gəs \

Asparagus is a perennial herb of the lily family. It is best known as a garden vegetable. The part that is eaten is the thick, fleshy stalk that sprouts from the ground in the spring. The young stalk is cut level with the ground when it is 4 to 8 inches tall. New sprouts then grow from the part still in the ground.

When fully grown, the asparagus plant is 5 to 6 feet tall. There are no true leaves. Thread-like divisions of asparagus branches make the plant look graceful and feathery. It is sometimes used in flower arrangements as a background for more colorful flowers.

Asparagus flowers are tiny, yellow-green bells. They dangle from the joints of the main and thread-like branches. The fruit is a bright red berry.

Asparagus is grown either from seed or root cuttings. It grows best in sandy soil. Native to Europe, asparagus is now grown in most parts of the world.

ASCARIS

aster \ 'as-tər \

Asters are a group of perennial flowering plants that grow both wild and in gardens. The name "aster" comes from the Greek word for "star" and describes the appearance of the flower head.

The flower head of the aster is made up of many narrow, petal-like flowers called rays. The rays surround a tight cluster of tiny, yellow, disk-shaped flowers.

The plant itself is bushy and branching, usually growing to a height of 3 to 5 feet. The leaves grow alternately along the stem, which may be hairy or smooth.

Asters grow from seed or from creeping rhizomes. They grow best in places having rich soil, plenty of sunlight and not too much summer heat.

The kind of aster best known in the U.S. is the wild New England aster (illustrated). It has narrow leaves and a rough, hairy stem. The flower heads are made up of 40 to 60 deep purple rays. The wild New England aster grows in roadside ditches and moist fields from the New England states and eastern Canada southward to North Carolina and westward to Colorado.

ASTER

ATLANTIC BONITO

Atlantic bonito \ ət-'lan-tik bə-'nēt-ō \

These fast-swimming fish are members of the mackerel family. Except in tropical areas, they are better known as game fish than as food fish. When feeding, they will often leap out of the water while chasing small fish and squid.

The Atlantic bonito is one of the most beautiful of saltwater fish. It has a silver underbelly and narrow, dark blue stripes on its upper back and sides. The bonito can weigh up to 12 pounds although most weigh about 6. Its streamlined body grows to a length of 3 feet.

The Mediterranean Sea and the warm waters of the Atlantic Ocean are living areas for the Atlantic bonito. It follows the warm Gulf stream as far north as Nova Scotia and Scandinavia.

Atlantic bonitos swim in schools and migrate irregularly. The females spawn in the spring.

Atlantic sailfish \ ət-'lan-tik 'sāl-,fish \

A large fish belonging to the same family as the spearfish and marlins, the Atlantic sailfish is prized as a game and food fish. It is named for its sail-like dorsal fin, which lies flat unless the fish is fighting or excited. Then the fin is always raised.

The Atlantic sailfish is a speedy swimmer and a strong fighter when hooked. It can leap clear of the water and has been known to travel 40 feet through the air.

ATLANTIC SAILFISH

ATOLL

The upper jaw of the Atlantic sailfish, like that of the spearfish, looks like a long, sharp spear. The long ventral fins fold back against the body when the fish swims.

Measuring from 6 to 8 feet long, Atlantic sailfish usually weigh about 50 pounds. They live in warm waters around the West Indies and Florida, and are rarely seen further north. They travel in schools or pairs and spawn during the summer in the shallower parts of the Gulf stream.

Atlantic tarpon \ ət-'lan-tik 'tär-pən \

A large, heavy-bodied fish, the Atlantic tarpon has become one of the most popular saltwater game fishes because of its strength and skill as a fighter. Its flesh is not good to eat.

Although it may grow to a length of 8 feet and a weight of over 300 pounds, the Atlantic tarpon is usually 4 to 5 feet long and weighs 50 to 60 pounds. Its dorsal fin is placed halfway back on the body and has a long, trailing spine. The underjaw is longer than the upper jaw and is protected by a bony plate on the underside. The mouth is large and is lined with small, sharp teeth.

The tough, silvery scales of the Atlantic tarpon measure from 1 to 3 inches across. These are used as sequins and for other ornamental purposes.

The Atlantic tarpon is most common in shallow waters of the Caribbean, the Gulf of Mexico and the Florida coast. The fish often enters rivers that empty into the ocean. Females are believed to spawn in the Caribbean during spring and summer. One female may lay up to 12,000,000 eggs at a time.

atoll \ 'a-ˌtäl \

An atoll is a ring of hard coral with a lagoon in the middle. Usually, a channel to the windward side connects the lagoon to the ocean which surrounds the atoll. Atolls are found only in tropical waters shallow and warm enough to support coral life. Most occur in the Pacific Ocean.

The naturalist Charles Darwin believed that atolls were formed by coral life growing on the crater of a volcano sinking beneath the sea. After World War II, scientists drilled deep into Eniwetok Atoll. The results showed volcanic rock under many layers of coral.

auk \ 'ȯk \

Chubby Arctic birds related to the puffin, auks have short necks, short heads and tails, webbed feet and large, thick beaks. Good swimmers and divers, they are poor fliers and are clumsy on land. Most kinds of auks are black and white.

Auks spend most of their time on the open sea. They feed mostly on small fishes, diving under the water for them and using their wings and webbed feet as paddles.

AUK

In spring, large colonies of auks gather on rocky ocean cliffs along the Arctic, north Atlantic and north Pacific coasts. Auks do not build nests; females lay 1 to 2 eggs on bare rock ledges. Because the eggs are almost pear-shaped, they do not roll away.

The great auk (illustrated) was the first bird in the western hemisphere to be killed off by men. A goose-sized bird that could fly, it was killed in great numbers for its meat and feathers. The last great auk was killed in Iceland in 1844. A few skins, skeletons and eggs are in museums.

aurora \ ə-'rōr-ə \

An aurora is a display of moving lights high in the atmosphere. The lights begin about 70 miles above the earth's magnetic poles, and look like bands, arcs, curtains or streamers. Their colors may include white, yellow-green, red, blue and violet.

Scientists believe that auroras are caused when electrically charged particles from the sun hit other particles in the earth's atmosphere. Then, the atmospheric particles give off light. Auroras appear most often when sunspots are most active, from March to April and from September to October.

In the northern hemisphere, an aurora is called an aurora borealis or the northern lights. In the southern hemisphere, an aurora is called an aurora australis or the southern lights.

azurite \ 'azh-ə-ˌrīt \

Azurite is a kind of copper ore formed by ground water seeping through it. Because it is produced by the action of ground water, azurite occurs near the surface of the ground or on the upper edges of a copper deposit.

Azurite was named after azure blue, the color of its most common form. Its color may vary, however, from light to dark blue.

It also varies from transparent, as in a large single crystal, to translucent, as in an irregular chunk of crystals.

Azurite is usually found along with the bright green mineral, malachite. These two minerals are both very much alike in chemical composition. In fact, azurite changes into malachite by losing carbon dioxide and picking up water.

In ancient times, azurite was ground for paint pigment. Today it is used chiefly as jewelry. Azurite is found in France, Greece, Romania and South Africa, but the best-quality crystals come from France. In the U.S., it is found only near Bisbee, Arizona.

AZURITE

b

baboon

Baboons are medium-sized apes that live in Africa, Arabia and Ethiopia. Some kinds of baboons have large, dog-like muzzles, highly colored faces and bright patches of color on their bottoms. Ancient Egyptian paintings show baboons on leashes. Young baboons can be tamed, but adults are usually too wild.

Although baboons use trees for sleep and protection, they are ground-dwelling mammals. The male is twice as large as the female and has much larger, sharper canine teeth. Both sexes have large cheek pouches and short body hair with shaggy manes on the neck and shoulders. Baboon tails curve downward.

Most baboons eat fruit and roots, as well as insects. They live in family groups ruled by large, strong males. Using the young males as scouts, baboons hunt in groups. They are fierce fighters and very quarrelsome even with each other. Their normal life-span is about 10 years.

The largest kind of baboon, the chacma (illustrated), weighs nearly 150 pounds. It is about 2 feet long and has an 18-inch tail. It eats reptiles, scorpions, insects and other small animals.

BABOON

BACHELOR'S BUTTON

bachelor's \ 'bach-(ə-)lərz \ button (cornflower)

The bachelor's button is an annual flowering plant that grows both as wild and garden varieties. Native to southern Europe, the wild bachelor's button has spread to this country.

The name of this plant comes from the shape of the flower head, which looks something like a small, round, almost flat button. The flower head is actually a tight cluster of many small, petal-like flowers. The individual flowers are tube-shaped, and the outer rows are notched so that the flower looks fringed. The flower heads are about 1½ inches across.

The plants are slender and branching, and are about 1 to 3 feet tall. The flowers grow singly at the tips of the branches. Most of the leaves look like narrow ribbons. Young leaves and branches are white and fuzzy. The flowers bloom all summer.

Two kinds of bachelor's buttons grow in the U.S. The blue cornflower grows wild, but the garden cornflowers (illustrated) are pink, white or bluish.

bacteria \ bak-'tir-ē-ə \

Bacteria are microscopic, 1-celled, plant-like organisms. Unlike most plants, they

BADGER

BALDPATE

cannot make their own food. They must take it from the bodies of other plants or animals, or from the soil or water in which they live.

Bacteria grow in 3 kinds of shapes: ball shape (coccus); rods with rounded ends (bacillus); or corkscrew shape (spirillum).

In many ways, bacteria help mankind. They turn milk products into cheese. They help decay dead plants and animals, so that basic chemicals are put back into the soil.

Bacteria can also be very harmful. They can cause diseases like typhoid fever, pneumonia and diphtheria. They can spoil food and milk and rot cloth.

High temperatures will kill bacteria. In the process called pasteurization, which was invented by Louis Pasteur to keep milk sweet and safe to drink, high temperatures are used to kill harmful bacteria.

Bacteria multiply by a splitting process called fission.

badger \ 'baj-ər \

Badgers are short-legged, nocturnal mammals that belong to the weasel family. The kind of badger that lives in Europe has black patches on its cheeks and forehead. From these patches, or "badges," the badger is supposed to have been named.

Badgers live in deep underground dens which they dig with their strong front legs and sharp claws. A badger den may be as long as 8 feet. At one end is a grass-lined nest. Badgers keep their burrows spotlessly clean. Unless winters are very cold, badgers do not hibernate.

Usually peaceful animals, badgers are fierce fighters when they are attacked. They eat mostly rodents, but roots, eggs, insects and young birds are also a part of their diet. One to 5 young badgers are born in May. A badger's life-span is 10 to 14 years.

The American badger (illustrated) is about 30 inches long with a 5- to 7-inch tail, and weighs from 13 to 25 pounds. It lives in open grasslands from southern Canada to central Mexico.

baldpate \ 'bȯl(d)-ˌpāt \ (American widgeon)

This shy, nervous bird is the most common kind of duck in California. It is named for the crown of white feathers on the head of the male, which gives it a somewhat bald appearance.

Baldpates range from 18 to 22 inches in length. They can be recognized in flight by the white patches on their fore wings. The females have more brown coloring than the males. The males whistle musically, while the females make rasping and squawking noises.

Although baldpates prefer inland swamps and ponds, they spend some time in saltwater bays. Because they are poor divers, they feed in shallow water, usually at night. They eat mostly water plants, but sometimes graze in fields of grain.

Baldpates winter from California to North Carolina and south to Panama. One of the last ducks to arrive north in spring, the baldpate breeds and spends the summer in Alaska, North and South Dakota and Montana. The female lays 6 to 12 creamy-white eggs, which hatch in about 3½ weeks. The life-span is about 17 years.

balsa \ 'bȯl-sə \

The balsa is a medium-to-large tree that grows in Central and South America. Balsa wood (illustrated) is very light. It is white or cream-colored and feels soft and smooth. The lightest balsa is only ⅓ the weight of cork.

Primitive South American tribes used balsa to build rafts and boats. Today it is used in place of cork for life rafts and life belts. It is also used as packing material and to build model airplanes and ships.

Balsa trees have smooth bark and alternate leaves. Each leaf is about 1 foot long and almost as wide, with irregular, saw-toothed edges. The white, cone-shaped flowers grow singly at the ends of the branches. Each flower has 5 large petals and is about 6 inches long. The fruit grows in a capsule or pod about 1 foot long.

Balsa grows in tropical jungles from southern Mexico as far south as Bolivia. Most of the wood cut for commercial use is grown in Ecuador.

balsam \ 'bȯl-səm \ (touch-me-not)

The balsam is an annual flowering plant belonging to the touch-me-not family. Native to India, it now grows in many parts of the world. Both wild and garden varieties of balsam grow in the U.S.

The name "touch-me-not" was given to the balsam because of its oval seedpods. When the seeds are ripe, the wind or a light touch will make the pods pop open and spray their seeds for several feet.

The balsam is about 1½ to 2½ feet tall. Its leaves grow alternately along the stem. They are tapering and have jagged edges. A cluster of leaves always grows at the top of the stalk above the flowers.

Balsam flowers may be red, white, pink, purple or yellow. Each flower has 5 petals. One sepal is large and grows in back of the flower like a spur. The flowers are short-stemmed. Both leaf and flower grow from the stalk at the same place.

BALSAM

BALSA

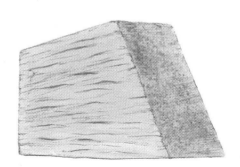

bamboo \ (')bam-'bü \

Bamboo plants are the tallest members of the grass family. They grow in clumps of slender, fast-growing stalks. Some kinds grow as much as 18 inches in 24 hours. One of the largest kinds of bamboo grows in India. It is a giant, growing as high as 120 feet.

Bamboo is among the most useful of all plants. Young sprouts can be eaten. Paper is made from the bamboo pulp or pith. Rafts, ropes, tools and even houses are made from whole or split stalks. Bamboo can be woven into furniture, baskets and mats. Because the stalks are hollow except at the node, a single section of stalk can be used to store food or water. In the U.S., bamboo is most often used for canes and fishing poles.

The leaf is short and blade-shaped. The fruit is a grain like wheat. Most kinds of bamboo have clusters of small flowers. Some flower every year, others only after many years.

Bamboo is found chiefly in China, Tibet and India, as well as in the U.S.

There are 2 kinds of bamboo in the U.S. One kind, the giant cane (illustrated), is found from Virginia to Louisiana. It grows to a height of 25 feet.

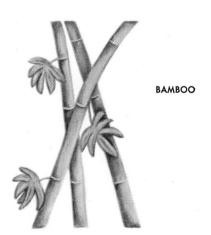

BAMBOO

BANANA

banana

Members of the banana family, banana plants grow in countries with hot, damp climates and rich soil. Although they may grow 10 to 30 feet tall, banana plants are considered herbs, not trees. In some countries, the fruit of the banana plant is one of the chief foods.

Banana leaves grow up to 2 feet wide and 12 feet long. The leaves overlap one another to form a strong stalk up to 16 inches thick. One stem grows from the center of the stalk. When yellowish flowers bloom in layers on the stem, the stem curves downward.

When the flower petals drop, tiny green bananas—the fruit—appear on the stem. The fruit is covered with a tough skin. As the bananas begin to ripen, they turn yellow.

Each banana plant bears only 1 crop and then dies, but 1 plant may produce more than 100 bananas. Young shoots sent up from the roots are replanted to start a new crop.

The banana plant is native to southern Asia. The largest banana plantations are in Brazil, Honduras, Ecuador and the Federation of Malaya.

There are many kinds of bananas. In the U.S., the most common kind eaten (illustrated) comes from South America, Jamaica and Central America.

banks

Banks are shallow areas of the ocean that occur where formations of hard rock resisted currents and other forces that wore away the softer surrounding areas. Not quite tall enough to rise above the surface of the sea, banks are made up of hills, valleys, ridges or plateaus. Most banks close to shore are important commercial fishing areas.

Some large banks are off the coasts of Miami and Nova Scotia. One of the largest banks in the world is the Grand Banks off the southeastern coast of Newfoundland. The Grand Banks curve 200 miles around the coast, reach out 300 miles into the ocean and are about 500 miles long. The shallow water over them is from 50 to 1,000 feet deep.

barberry \ 'bär-ˌber-ē \

Making up a group of prickly, low-to-medium growing shrubs, barberries belong to the barberry family. Some kinds are evergreens. All kinds have sharp spines and small oval leaves. The flowers have 6 petals and the berries, which are sometimes eaten, have from 1 to 3 seeds. A yellow dye can be made from barberry stems.

The most common kinds of barberry in the U.S. are the common barberry (illustrated) and the Japanese barberry. The common barberry is an alternate host for the wheat rust fungus, a serious crop disease, and is often destroyed where wheat is grown nearby.

The common barberry is native to Europe. In the U.S., it grows in gardens, wild along roadsides or in open woods, and is 6 to 8 feet tall. Its leaves are 1 to 2 inches long and have saw-toothed edges. The yellowish flowers and red berries grow in spike-shaped clusters about 2 inches long.

The Japanese barberry will not grow the wheat rust fungus. Its leaves are rounder and more smooth-edged than those of the common barberry. Its berries grow in pairs or singly along the stem.

barley

Barley is one of the oldest cereal grasses known. It is thought to have grown first in the Near East over 8,000 years ago. It was brought to the U.S. over 350 years ago by English colonists.

Barley grain is used in making malt drinks, barley flour and cereals, as well as for animal feed.

The barley plant looks like wheat but is not quite as tall. It is about 2½ to 3 feet in height, with a straight, smooth stem. Its flowers grow in spikes in vertical rows, which vary in number from 2 to 6. The

BARBERRY

BARLEY

spikes are about 4 inches long. The fruit is a hard, oval grain and is usually enclosed in pairs of bracts. The pointed leaves are about ¾ inch wide and 2 inches long. They surround the stem at its base.

Barley grows almost all over the world. It is an annual grown from seed, and can be grown in colder climates than wheat or rye.

barnacle \ 'bär-ni-kəl \

Barnacles make up a group of marine crustaceans. Large colonies of barnacles fasten themselves to the bottoms of ships, rocks and dock timbers, as well as to such animals as sea turtles.

The life cycle of a barnacle has several stages. Eggs develop inside the parent shell. They hatch into free-swimming larvae. As they grow and molt, they change form several times.

The rock barnacle (illustrated), a small kind of acorn barnacle, has an outer shell of 6 thick, limy plates joined together in a rough circle by thinner plates. A 4-plate door covers the top when the animal is alarmed.

The rock barnacle spends its adult life upside down. Six pairs of thin, feathery legs extend from the 4-plate door of the shell, waving above the opening. When the tide is in, the door opens and the legs kick food particles from the current into the shell.

Rock barnacles are found along the tide line of the North Atlantic coast of the U.S.

barrier \ 'bar-ē-ər \ beach (offshore bar)

A barrier beach is an off-shore, above-water sandbar. It may form along a seacoast where the land slopes gently under shallow water. Currents of water and waves moving toward the shore slowly deposit a ridge of sand. After a while, this ridge rises above the level of the sea. Then a narrow sandy island forms parallel to the shore line.

A barrier beach may move toward the shore if waves and currents are strong enough. Then it may form a lagoon which is protected from the ocean but still connected to it. Later, as waves carry more sand toward the land, and sediment washes from shore out toward the ocean, the lagoon may be gradually filled in.

Barrier beaches are common formations along the Atlantic coastline of the U.S.

basalt \ bə-'solt \ (trap, traprock)

Basalt is a hard, dark-colored, igneous rock. It is the most common of all igneous rocks. It is used most often as crushed rock in building highways.

BARNACLES
(ON SCALLOP SHELL)

BARRIER BEACH

BASALT

Basalt is formed when molten rock or lava cools very quickly on or near the surface of the earth. Because of this rapid cooling, basalt crystals are very small. The individual minerals in a piece of this rock cannot be seen without a very powerful microscope.

Large sheets or lava beds of basalt are found in India and Hawaii. In the U.S., it is found in the states of Oregon, Washington and Idaho. Veins of basalt, running through other rock formations, are found around Lake Superior and in the New York-New Jersey area.

basin \ 'bās-ᵊn \

A basin is a large or small area lower than the rock or ground surrounding it. A basin may be as small as a lake or as large as an ocean.

A dry basin is a dry, rocky area where all layers of rock dip toward the center.

Another kind of basin is made up of the whole drainage area of a stream system. For example, the Mississippi River Basin includes the land around all the rivers and streams that pour into the Mississippi River. This includes about ⅓ of the U.S., or over a million square miles.

Rivers and streams flowing into land areas having no outlet to the sea either form salty lakes, as Utah's Great Salt Lake, or they dry up completely. Such land areas are also basins. The Great Basin in the western United States is of this type. It covers 200,000 square miles and contains almost all of Nevada, as well as bits of California, Utah, Wyoming, Idaho and Oregon.

bass \ 'bas \

True bass make up a family of marine fish. Although true bass are called a marine, or saltwater, family, some are freshwater fish. Bass are both good to eat and popular game fish.

The black sea bass (illustrated) is the best-known kind of marine bass. It has a large head and a thick-lipped lower jaw that is longer than its upper jaw. Its average weight is about 3 pounds, but it may weigh as much as 8 pounds. Very large black sea bass may be 18 inches long.

Black sea bass are found along the Florida coast. They like dark places to hide and are sometimes caught in lobster traps. They eat small fish, crustaceans and squid that they find on the floor of the sea.

In the spring, black sea bass lay their eggs. The eggs float until they hatch. The young fish are mostly females, but some change sex before they are fully grown.

For other kinds of sea bass, see *grouper* and *white perch*.

Certain other fish are called bass, but

BASS

are really members of the freshwater sunfish family. For these kinds of bass, see *largemouth black bass* and *smallmouth black bass*.

bat

Bats are the only mammals that fly. Their wings are really arms with long fingers. A thin membrane connects these fingers with each other and with the sides of the body, legs and tail. The thumb is the only finger without a membrane, and it allows bats to climb and hold onto objects.

According to the food they eat, bats are divided into 3 types: insect-eating, fruit-eating and blood-sucking. Most U.S. bats are insect eaters.

Bats have very small, weak eyes and cannot stand bright light. During the day they hang upside down in caves or from trees. At sunset, they come out to eat.

The bat's ears are very sensitive. Their cry is a high-pitched squeak, too high for humans to hear. This squeak bounces back from objects, and the bat hears the echo. The time between the call and the echo is longer if the bat is far away from an object, and shorter if the bat is close. By judging the different echo times, bats avoid flying into objects. In the same way, insect-eating bats locate their food.

In the U.S., the most common bat is the little brown bat (illustrated), about 4½ inches long. Females produce 1 or 2 young in the spring.

bauxite \ 'bȯk-ˌsīt \

Bauxite is a rock that looks something like clay, but it is harder. It varies in color from white to brownish-red, and often has lumps or knobs that stick out from it, giving it an irregular shape.

Bauxite is the main source of the metal aluminum. In bauxite the aluminum is combined with oxygen. The aluminum is separated from the oxygen by a method called Hall's process. The bauxite is melted at a temperature of 1800° F. Then electricity is passed through the melted bauxite. The electricity separates the aluminum from the oxygen.

After aluminum is taken from bauxite, the aluminum is used in many ways. Foil, cooking pans, house siding and window frames are often made of aluminum. Airplanes and passenger train cars are also made of aluminum because it is so light in weight.

Bauxite is found in countries with warm climates. Some of these countries are Dutch Guiana, Guyana, France and Hungary. In the U.S., bauxite is found in Arkansas and Georgia.

BAT

BAUXITE

BEAN

BEAR

bean

Perhaps the best-known vegetable plants, beans are native to the warmer parts of America. Most are annuals, but a few are perennials. They are cultivated all over the world and are a very good source of protein. They belong to the pea family.

Bean plants are nearly always vines and are grown from seed. Each broad, pointed leaf is made up of 3 leaflets. Bean flowers are small and butterfly-shaped. The fruit is a long, curved pod containing a row of fat seeds. Both pod and seeds are usually eaten.

The common bean (illustrated) is an annual sometimes called the kidney bean. It was first cultivated by the Indians of Mexico, Central and South America.

There are many varieties of the common bean. Some, as the pole bean, are climbing vines. Others, as bush or dwarf beans, are erect plants. The flowers are ½ to ¾ inch long. They bloom singly or in small clusters where the leaves grow on the stalk. String or green beans are pods picked before they mature.

bear

Bears make up a family of the largest carnivorous mammals. They are found wild in parts of Europe, Asia and America. Whether walking upright or on all fours, bears walk flat-footed, just as men do.

Bears range in weight from 100 pounds to 1,500 pounds. All bears are intelligent and have a good sense of smell but have poor eyesight. Where they have enough food, bears do not really hibernate, but they do sleep soundly in the winter. They sometimes wake and walk around on mild winter days.

Most kinds of bears mate every other year. Usually, 2 blind and nearly hairless cubs are born.

The grizzly bear (illustrated) is the fiercest and most dangerous American mammal. Once common in the western U.S. and Canada, the grizzly was hunted so much that it has become rare. Today, most grizzlies live in parks, where they are protected from hunters.

Grizzlies eat almost anything, including ants, plants, birds, livestock, deer, snakes, small mammals and fish, which they scoop from rivers.

Male grizzlies may weigh as much as 1,500 pounds. Females are lighter.

One to 3 cubs are born every other year. They are only 8 inches long and weigh 1 to 2 pounds. In 3 years, they are mature adults. The life-span is about 30 years.

BEAVER

beaver

The largest member of the rodent family in North America, the beaver builds dams from trees and branches. The dams form ponds that help preserve wildlife, control floods and prevent land erosion.

Beavers average 30 pounds in weight and about 43 inches in length, including the tail. They have short ears and 5-toed feet. The hind feet are webbed. The long, paddle-shaped tail, which is about 16 inches long, is used on land for balance and as a propeller in the water.

Using their chisel-like teeth, beavers gnaw through trees near the water's edge. They strip the trees of twigs and branches and gnaw them into 4- to 5-foot lengths. Then they crisscross the sticks across a stream and cement them with mud to form a dam. Beavers store their food, usually bark, roots and twigs, against the base of this dam.

Beavers build a lodge in the middle of the pond formed by the dam. The lodge is built of sticks and mud. It has a nest chamber which is above the water but can be entered only under water.

In April or May, a female beaver gives birth to about 4 young, called kits. The kits mature in 2 to 3 years. The life-span is 16 to 18 years.

bee

Bees make up several families of insects that are most useful to man. There are about 20,000 different kinds of bees. As they move from flower to flower in search of nectar and pollen, bees pollinate plants. Without bees, there would be fewer fruit trees, garden vegetables and flowers. Farmers sometimes keep hives of bees to help pollinate their crops.

Bees range in size from less than ⅛ inch to over 1 inch. In the U.S., most kinds of familiar bees, such as the honeybee and the bumblebee, are social bees that live together in large colonies with their own kind. A colony may have over 50,000 bees.

The honeybee (illustrated) has 2 large compound eyes, 3 smaller, simple eyes and antennae that are very sensitive to flower smells. A honeybee colony has 3 castes: workers, drones and a queen. Each caste plays an important part in the life of a colony.

The drones are males who do nothing but mate with the queen, who does nothing but lay eggs. The eggs hatch into workers, drones and other queens. Workers are females who collect pollen and nectar from flowers. They make honey from the nectar and feed young bees with the pollen. They feed drones with honey. They change honey into beeswax to build

BEE

the many combs of the nest in which the colony lives. They keep the combs clean and protect the colony with their stings.

beech

Making up a group of tall, beautiful trees, beeches are valued for their strong wood. Beech wood is used for furniture and the manufacture of vinegar.

Beech trees grow 50 to 100 feet tall. The straight trunk, 2 to 3 feet in diameter, is covered with a smooth, blue-gray bark that is sometimes black and grooved at the base. Thickets of small young trees sometimes grow from a root system rather than from seeds.

The oval-shaped leaves are dark blue-green on top and lighter on the bottom. Three to 6 inches long, the leaves grow alternately on the slender, spreading branches. The leaves are heavily veined and have rough, jagged edges.

A beech tree bears both staminate and pistillate flowers, which bloom shortly after the leaves appear. The staminate flowers hang in ball-like clusters. The pistillate flowers form tiny spikes at the ends of the twigs. Three or 4 nuts form inside a hard, spiny capsule that bursts open when mature.

One kind of beech, the American beech (illustrated) is common in eastern North America from New Brunswick in Canada as far south as Kentucky and Missouri. It grows best in wooded areas containing rich, moist soil. Another kind, the European beech, is used widely as an ornamental tree.

beet

A popular vegetable that comes from the wild beet native to southern Europe, the beet is one of man's oldest-known foods. Swiss chard, garden beets, sugar beets and stock beets are very closely related to the wild beet.

Most kinds of beets are biennials. In the first year a small cluster of leaves appears, and food is stored in the root. If the plant is not picked the first year, it uses the stored food to produce a tall stem which bears many leaves and small flowers.

The familiar garden beet is a fleshy, red root. The young leaves are sometimes cooked. Swiss chard has large, fleshy leaves which are served as a green vegetable. Swiss chard stores its food in the leaves rather than the root.

Of all the kinds of beets, the sugar beet (illustrated) is most important commercially. It grows best where summers are late and cool.

More than half the world's sugar supply comes from sugar beets. In the U.S., Colorado, Utah and Montana are the biggest sugar beet producers.

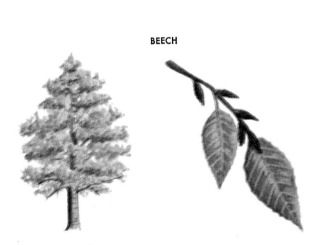

BEECH

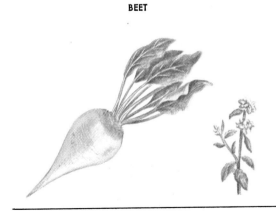

BEET

beetle

Beetles make up a very large group of more than 275,000 kinds of insects. Many of them destroy valuable crops, food and cloth, but others destroy harmful insects and weeds. Beetles live from the tropics to the arctic regions, in jungles, deserts, flatlands, forests and mountains, but not in the oceans. Fossils from Australia and Russia show that beetles have been on the earth at least 2 million years.

Although most beetles live on land, a few live in water. Some can fly. All have chewing mouthparts and jointed antennae. Each antenna usually has 11 segments. The legs of most beetles are well suited to running, digging, jumping or swimming.

All beetles have thickened, leathery fore wings that are not used for flying. If a second set of wings is present, they are thin and transparent. They are folded out of sight, under the fore wings, when the beetle is at rest.

Beetles, like other insects, have a 3-part body made up of head, thorax and abdomen. The abdomen usually has 10 segments. Each segment has a spiracle, or opening, into the breathing system of the beetle.

All beetles pass through the 4 stages of complete metamorphosis: egg, larva, pupa and adult. The eggs are usually laid on plants, where the worm-like larvae will find food to eat. The larvae of many kinds of beetles drop to the ground and burrow under the surface before passing into the pupa or resting stage. A few days or weeks later, or the following spring, adult beetles emerge from the burrows.

The adults of some beetles die soon after breeding. In other kinds, some adults live through the winter, hibernating in dead wood or plant stems.

All of the beetles illustrated are destructive pests except the 9-spotted ladybird beetle. Its larvae eat plants, but the adults eat aphids, plant lice, mealybugs and other harmful insects.

Both adults and larvae of the asparagus beetle feed on asparagus plants. The adults often hibernate in old asparagus stalks. In the spring they come out to feed on the tender shoots of new asparagus.

The adult carpet beetle eats mostly flower pollen, but the larvae damage some packaged foods and rugs. The adults have hairy or scaly bodies.

The click beetle and its larvae, called wireworms, are sometimes found on leaves or under the bark of trees. Click beetles eat seeds and roots of cultivated plants. If the adult falls and lands upside down, it may flip itself over with a clicking sound. The complete life cycle takes several years. Click beetles hibernate underground, usually in the pupal stage.

The Colorado potato beetle, once found only in the Rocky Mountains, damages potato plants throughout North America and in parts of Europe. The adult hibernates underground. In spring, the female lays eggs on potato plant leaves.

The green June beetle feeds on the leaves, stems and roots of garden vegetables and fruit trees.

The Japanese beetle, accidently introduced into the U.S. in 1916, damages the roots of grasses and farm crops.

The larvae of the long-horned beetle, called borers, burrow into tree trunks. The adults can fly, but they stay close to trees.

The rose beetle damages grape plants and fruit trees as well as roses. The adults eat rose and grape flowers and leaves, while the larvae feed on grass roots.

The adult striped blister beetle gives off a substance that causes blisters on the skin. The larvae feed on grasshopper eggs, while adults feed on cultivated plants.

For other kinds of beetles, see *borer*, *firefly* and *weevil*.

Beetles—Hard-bodied Insects

ASPARAGUS BEETLE

CARPET BEETLE

CLICK BEETLE

COLORADO POTATO BEETLE

GREEN JUNE BEETLE

JAPANESE BEETLE

9-SPOTTED LADYBIRD BEETLE

LONG-HORNED BEETLE

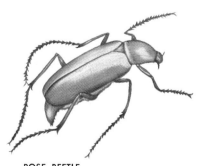

ROSE BEETLE

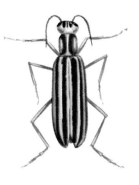

STRIPED BLISTER BEETLE

BEGONIA

begonia \ bi-'gōn-yə \

Begonias make up a group of tropical plants native to tropical Africa, Asia and Central America. They are prized for their beautiful flowers and leaves. In cool parts of the temperate zones, begonias are popular as garden and house plants. In frost-free tropical climates, they are grown outside throughout the year.

All begonias have thick stems, glossy leaves and flowers that grow in clusters. The staminate flowers of the single-flowering begonias have 2 sepals and 2 waxy petals. The flowers of pistillate-flowering begonias have 2 to 5 parts. The stamens and stigmas are yellow. Begonias with large, many-petaled flowers look something like camellias.

Begonias need warmth, partial shade and moist, rich soil. They are grown from bulb-like tubers, from rhizomes or from shoots or leaf cuttings.

The rex begonia (illustrated) is a cultivated kind grown for its flowers and its large, many-colored leaves.

bellflower \ 'bel-ˌflaủr \ (bluebell, harebell)

Making up a group of flowering plants, bellflowers include annuals, biennials and some perennials. Some kinds of bellflowers are wild, while others are cultivated.

Bellflowers vary in height from 6 inches to 4 feet. All kinds of bellflowers have alternate leaves and single bell-shaped flowers with 5 pointed lobes. The flowers bloom on thin stems or in clusters at the top of leafy stalks.

A common kind of bellflower grows wild in the cooler parts of Europe, Asia and North America. The leaves at the base of this delicate plant die before the flowers appear.

When new leaves appear, they are narrow and long, much like blades of grass. From 6 to 20 inches in height, this bellflower bears several blue blossoms at a time. The blossoms hang from short stems at the top of the stalk.

beryl \ 'ber-əl \

Beryl is a mineral that appears in many different forms. One of these forms is the emerald, a dark green gem which is very valuable. A good emerald is worth much more than a diamond of the same size. Emeralds are found in Russia and South America.

Other forms of beryl are aquamarine (illustrated) and golden beryl. These are not as valuable as emeralds. Aquamarines are blue-green, and golden beryls are yellow. Jewelry is often made from these stones. They are found in California, Brazil, Ceylon and Madagascar.

BERYL

One form of beryl is the source of a rare metallic element called beryllium. Each pound of beryllium is worth several thousand dollars. Like aluminum, beryllium is very light in weight, but it is also very hard. When it is mixed with copper, it makes the copper harder and lighter. Such mixtures of two metals are called alloys. Beryllium also forms a very strong alloy with aluminum.

betta \ 'bet-ə \

Bettas make up a group of small freshwater fish belonging to the labyrinth fish family. They are called labyrinth fish because they have a complicated breathing organ something like a lung. With this organ, labyrinth fish breathe oxygen directly from the air.

Before mating, the male betta builds a nest of sticky, floating bubbles. After mating, the female lays several hundred eggs just under the nest. Some eggs go into the nest while others sink. The male betta takes the sinking eggs into his mouth and spits them into the nest. From then on, he guards the nest by driving away the femmale and biting other bettas that come near the nest.

Native to Asia, bettas live in clear, weedy streams, irrigation ditches and rice paddies.

One kind of betta, the Siamese fighting fish (illustrated), is a popular aquarium fish. It is bred in a great many colors. Its dorsal fin is sail-shaped, while its anal fins are long and flowing. The male, which is larger than the female, is about 3 inches long. The life-span is about 1 year.

biotite \ 'bī-ə-ˌtīt \

An opaque mineral, biotite is a kind of mica and is sometimes called black mica. Usually black, biotite may be brown or dark green. It can be split into very thin sheets. These thin sheets are transparent but smoky, like the lenses of sunglasses.

Biotite contains iron, magnesium and a little water. It is found in all parts of the world, usually in igneous and volcanic rocks, less often in metamorphic rocks. In granite, biotite appears as small, dark specks.

birch \ 'bərch \

Graceful trees with smooth bark that peels off in thin sheets, the birches belong to the same family as the alders and hazels. Birches grow fast but they do not live very long or become very large.

Some kinds of birches are the source of hard, strong wood used for furniture and flooring. Some are ornamental trees planted for their beauty. The American

BETTA

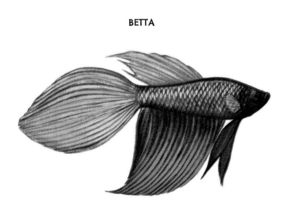

BIRCH

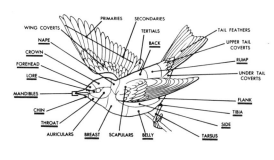

THE PARTS OF A BIRD

BIRD OF PARADISE

Indians used birchbark to cover their canoes and wigwams, and also to make baskets.

Birches grow in nearly all parts of North America and in Japan, China and southern Europe.

The branches are usually short and slender, and the twigs often droop down toward the ground. The leaves have ragged or saw-toothed edges. Tiny, yellow or green flowers appear in spring. The pistillate clusters are cone-like. The staminate clusters are tassels 1 to 4 inches long. In midsummer, seeds ripen in the cone-shaped clusters.

The white birch (illustrated) is an ornamental tree from Europe that seldom grows taller than 30 feet. It is one of several kinds that have white bark marked with scattered black spots. Other birches have gray or reddish-brown bark.

bird

Birds make up a large group of flying animals, although a few kinds are unable to fly. All birds have lightweight, hollow bones. Their forelimbs have developed into wings. Their bodies are covered with feathers which are quite different from the hairs or scales of other animals. Most birds have very keen eyesight.

Birds are thought to be descended from reptiles. They lay eggs as reptiles do, and their legs and feet are scaly. They differ from reptiles in being warm-blooded. The heart of a bird is 4-chambered, like the heart of a mammal.

There are about 8,500 different kinds of birds. They live in nearly all parts of the world, and they eat a wide variety of both plant and animal foods.

Many birds migrate to cooler climates in spring. They nest, lay their eggs and raise their young during the spring and summer months, when insects, fruit and berries are plentiful. In autumn, many birds migrate to warmer climates, where food is available during the winter. A very few kinds hibernate during the season when their food becomes scarce.

Some kinds of birds, such as chickens, ducks and geese, have been domesticated for centuries. They provide man with meat and eggs, and with feathers used for pillows and bedding.

bird of paradise \ 'par-ə-,dīs \

These unusual birds live only on New Guinea and a few nearby islands. The males are brightly colored and have long or odd-shaped plumes. They display their plumes in different ways to attract the females.

Some male birds of paradise have bibs

BITTERN

or neck ruffs that they spread wide around their heads. Other kinds have unusually long tails or skirts of feathers that extend out under their wings. Most kinds perch in trees when displaying their beauty before the females, while other kinds hang upside down. The females and the young birds are plain-looking and dull-colored.

Not much is known about the habits of birds of paradise, because it is difficult to study them in the wild jungles where they are found. Scientists believe that most males mate with several different females, and that males do not help incubate the eggs or feed the young.

The smallest birds of paradise are only about 6 inches in length. The great bird of paradise (illustrated) is about 40 inches long including its plumes, which are about 20 inches long. Highly valued for its plumes, the great bird of paradise is protected by law.

bittern \ 'bit-ərn \

Wading birds of the heron family, bitterns are hard to see among the reeds and cattails in the marshes where they live. When a bittern is frightened, it stands still, with its bill pointing straight up. Then, its stripes blend with the reeds and cattails around it.

Bitterns have a body length of about 28 inches. The head is carried close to the body, so that the neck looks shorter than it really is. Bitterns eat crayfish, frogs, eels, water insects and field mice, which they spear with their long, pointed bills.

Male bitterns make loud booming sounds during the mating season. The nest is a platform of plant stems, placed above water and well hidden among reeds. Three to 5 greenish-brown eggs are laid once a year.

Bitterns nest throughout central Canada and the northern part of the U.S. They spend the winter in the southern U.S., in Mexico and in the West Indies.

The American bittern (illustrated) is the most common bittern in the U.S.

blackberry

The blackberries are prickly shrubs of the rose family that bear edible fruit. They grow wild in many parts of the northern hemisphere, often forming dense, brambly tangles in woodlands or open fields.

The first year's growth is a long stem that stands erect or arches over. The second year flowers and fruit grow on short branches that grow out from the long stem.

Blackberry leaves are compound and are made up of 3 to 7 tooth-edged leaflets. The flowers have 5 white petals. The fruit is a cluster of tiny, juicy berries, each con-

BLACKBERRY

taining 1 small, hard seed. The fruit is attached tightly to its central core, and does not pull off easily as the fruit of the raspberry does.

Blackberries grow best in a cool, moist climate.

The kind of blackberry most common in North America is the wild blackberry (illustrated). It grows throughout southern Canada and in the northern part of the U.S., as far west as Minnesota. Several different cultivated blackberries have been developed from this wild plant.

blackbird

The birds called blackbirds in North America belong to the same family as the oriole, the meadowlark, the grackle, the cowbird and the bobolink. They are all 8 to 10 inches long, with pointed bills and rounded tails. The males are all or mostly black during the breeding season. The females are grayish or streaked brown.

Blackbirds are most often seen in open country, in farm fields and along fence-rows. They eat insects, along with some grain and seeds. Their neatly woven nests are made of grass and other plant materials. Two to 8 eggs are laid once or twice a year. The female usually incubates the eggs and feeds the young birds. The male may remain near to guard the nest.

Some kinds of blackbirds have musical songs. Others make only harsh squawking sounds.

Brewer's blackbird (illustrated) lives in the central part of the U.S. It often nests in orchard trees.

Red-winged, rusty and yellow-headed blackbirds all nest near ponds or marches, among reeds and cattails.

The European blackbird belongs to another bird family, the thrush family. It looks much like the American robin but has no red breast.

black-footed ferret \ 'fer-ət \

A mammal of the weasel family, the black-footed ferret lives only in western North America. It is the largest weasel and is closely related to the European polecat. When disturbed, the black-footed ferret gives off a strong, unpleasant smell.

Males are about 24 inches long, including the 6-inch tail. Females are a little smaller. Both male and female have a black mask on the face and black on the tail, back and feet.

Like other weasels, the black-footed ferret moves very quickly and fights fiercely when cornered. It eats mostly prairie dogs, gophers and ground squirrels, digging into their underground burrows to

BLACKBIRD

BLACK-FOOTED FERRET

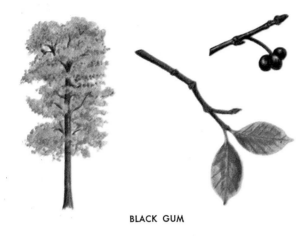

BLACK GUM

catch them. It sometimes takes over the burrow as its own home. Little is known about the mating habits of this animal.

The black-footed ferret was once common from Kansas and the Dakotas west to the Rocky Mountains, and north into Canada. It is now very rare in most of this area, probably because its main food, the prairie dog, is gradually disappearing.

black gum (sour gum, tupelo)

This fairly rare hardwood tree is sometimes called the sour gum or tupelo. It grows only in eastern North America, on mountainsides or in wooded areas where the soil is moist. The light-colored, very strong wood is sometimes used to make furniture.

The black gum grows 100 to 125 feet tall, with a straight trunk 3 to 5 feet in diameter. The bark is deeply furrowed. The smooth, glossy leaves are 2 to 5 inches long. Most of the leaves grow crowded together near the ends of the branches.

Small greenish flowers bloom in spring, soon after the new leaves appear. Staminate and pistillate flowers are usually on separate trees. The staminate flowers are in loose, umbrella-shaped clusters. The pistillate flowers appear 2 or 3 together, on a single stalk. The fruit is a small blue-black berry that is eaten by birds and small animals.

The black gum tree is often the first tree to change color in autumn. The leaves turn bright red, but only on the upper surface of each leaf.

black mollie \ 'mäl-ē \ (midnight mollie, mud pusser, permablack)

A small, tropical marine fish of the top-minnow family, the black mollie is popular with aquarium owners. It belongs to a group of mollies which are called sailfish mollies because of their very long, tall dorsal fins.

In its natural state, this fish is mottled green, with black markings. It lives in bays and estuaries along the Atlantic coast, from South Carolina to the Gulf of Mexico. The ones sold in pet shops are solid black, or have an orange border along the very large dorsal fin. These mollies were developed in captivity.

In the ocean black mollies are 2 to 3 inches long. In an aquarium they may become 4 inches long. Females are generally larger than the males, but males have larger dorsal fins.

Black mollies are related to the guppies, and the females give birth to living young just as female guppies do. The black mollie may bear as many as 20 young as often as once a month. The baby fish become adults in about 9 months.

BLACK MOLLIE

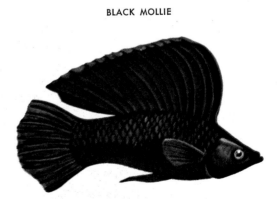

BLADDERWORT

BLEEDING HEART

bladderwort \ 'blad-ər-ˌwərt \

Bladderworts are unusual water plants that capture and feed on insect larvae and other small water animals.

Bladderworts grow in shallow ponds and quiet streams, with their leaves under the water. Attached to the leaves are hollow bladders. Each bladder has 1 opening surrounded by bristles or stiff hairs. When a small animal floats or swims inside a bladder, a kind of trapdoor closes the opening. The trapped animal soon dies, and its decaying body provides food that is absorbed by the plant.

Bladderwort leaves have many, very narrow sections. The bladders, which are very small, are on the undersides of the leaves. Flowers and seeds grow on a stalk that rises above the surface of the water. From 4 to 20 yellow or blue flowers appear on each stalk.

Bladderworts grow in nearly all parts of the world. One common kind (illustrated) grows as far north as Alaska. It has leaves 3 to 6 inches long, and its yellow flowers are shaped something like the flowers of snapdragons.

bleeding heart

Plants with odd-shaped, attractive flowers, bleeding hearts include both wild and cultivated kinds. The common wild flowers called Dutchman's-breeches and squirrel corn are bleeding hearts.

All bleeding hearts are perennials. They grow from small bulb-like rhizomes just under the ground. Their slender stems and leaves are divided into narrow sections.

The flowers appear in spring or early summer. Four to 20 flowers hang down from one stem. Each flower has 2 enlarged white or pink petals that enclose the other petals and form the 2 halves of the "heart." Small seeds develop inside a slender pod that splits into 2 parts when the seeds are ripe.

Wild bleeding hearts grow mostly in woodlands where the soil is moist and where the plants are shaded from the sun.

The garden bleeding heart (illustrated) is a cultivated kind from Japan. It is a bushy plant about 2 feet tall, with many rose-pink flowers that dangle from 1 side of a slender, arching stem. A hardy plant, it will grow almost anywhere.

blenny \ 'blen-ē \

The blennies are a large group of marine fish that live in both warm and cold seas. The smallest ones are only a few inches long. The largest ones are 2 feet long. In general, the smaller ones live in the tropics and the larger ones in colder, northern areas.

All blennies have long bodies and long dorsal and anal fins. Some blennies are so slender that they look something like eels. Many are colored like the rocks and seaweed on the ocean floor where they feed. Blennies eat some plant foods, along with small animals such as crustaceans.

Near their throats some blennies have slender pelvic fins that they use as legs. They can live out of water for some time if their skins are moist, and they are sometimes seen sunning themselves on rocks.

Male blennies make nests among rocks or underwater plants. After persuading a female to lay her eggs there, the male fans the eggs and guards them until they hatch.

The striped blenny is only 1 of some 500 different kinds. Others include the kelp blenny, the Molly Miller, the sarcastic blenny and the Carolina blenny.

bloodroot

A wild flower of the poppy family, the bloodroot is named for the color of its underground rhizome and its red juice. This juice was used by the Indians to make red dye. Some modern medicines are partly made from the bloodroot plant.

Each plant produces just 1 leaf and 1 flower. At first the leaf is rolled around the flowering stem. The flower often appears in early spring, before the leaf unrolls. The

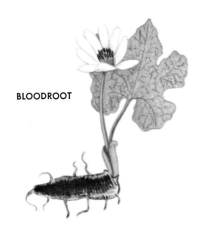

BLOODROOT

BLUEBERRY

leaf is about as wide as it is long, and it has irregular, wavy edges. The mature plant stands about 9 inches tall.

The flower is about 1½ inches across. It has 8 whitish petals that spread out around a yellow center. Sometimes 4 of the petals are larger than the other 4, so that the flower looks square. The seeds ripen inside a small, slender pod.

The bloodroot's rhizome is a thickened root that grows horizontally, just under the ground. It may be as thick as 1 inch and 2½ inches long, and it may divide or fork. The leaves and stems of the plants die after the seed ripens, but the roots live for many years.

The bloodroot is common in moist, wooded areas throughout southern Canada and most of the U.S.

blueberry

Blueberries are native North American shrubs related to the cranberry and the rhododendron. Blueberry fruit is often used in making pies, jams and jellies.

There are a number of kinds of blueberries. One of the best known is the high-bush blueberry (illustrated). It is a shrub that may grow as tall as 15 feet. Its green leaves are about 3 inches long and 1½ inches wide. Although the high-bush blueberry grows wild in swamps and woodlands, it is also cultivated and grown on farms.

The high-bush blueberry bears small white or pink flowers in May and June. The leaves are only half grown at flowering time. The deep blue berries are ripe in July and August. The berries of the wild plant are about ⅓ inch across. The cultivated berries are sometimes larger.

In the U.S., blueberries are widely grown as a commercial crop in Michigan, North Carolina and New Jersey. The plants are fairly easy to raise in sandy soil or peat moss. They can be started from cuttings. The berries are sold either fresh, frozen or canned. Wild blueberries are eaten by birds and animals.

bluebird

The bluebird is a small American songbird that belongs to the thrush family. In some areas, people think that the bluebird is a better sign of spring than the robin. Some people believe that the bluebird is a sign of happiness.

Bluebirds are blue with reddish-brown and white breasts. They live in cities, open country and orchards. They build nests of soft grass in holes in trees. They also build their nests in birdhouses built by men.

EASTERN BLUEBIRD

WESTERN BLUEBIRD

BLUEFISH

Bluebirds eat seeds, berries and insects. They are especially fond of the berries of poison ivy.

Bluebirds lay blue eggs. Four to 8 eggs are hatched twice a year. Both the father and the mother sit on the eggs, which take 12 days to hatch.

The eastern bluebird (illustrated) lives in the eastern half of the U.S. and Canada. It has a chestnut-colored breast. The young have brown and white spots and bright blue wings. The eastern bluebird is the state bird of Missouri and of New York.

The western bluebird (illustrated) lives in Mexico, the western U.S. and Canada. The male has a reddish breast. These bluebirds are poor singers. The female lays 4 or 5 dark blue eggs.

Another kind of bluebird, the mountain bluebird, is the state bird of Nevada and Idaho.

bluefish \ 'blü-ˌfish \

An ocean fish that fights fiercely when hooked and is good to eat, the bluefish is a favorite of sportsmen. Commercial fishermen catch and sell about 20 million pounds of bluefish every year.

The largest bluefish are 40 inches long and weigh up to 27 pounds. The average weight is about 4 pounds. Bluefish have stout, powerful bodies. The second dorsal fin is longer than the first, and the lower

BLUEGILL

jaw sticks out beyond the upper jaw. The large mouth contains strong, sharp teeth.

Bluefish live mostly in deep water, well away from shore. They swim rapidly in large schools, and they kill and eat large numbers of smaller fish.

In late spring or early summer, bluefish spawn. The newly hatched young fish swim toward shore and spend the summer in shallow, protected water near the coast. In autumn the young fish move out into the open sea. They grow fast, and are about 12 inches long when 1 year old.

Bluefish live in both warm and cool parts of the Atlantic Ocean. Along the east coast of North America, they are found as far north as Cape Cod and as far south as the Gulf of Mexico. Large ones are caught near the coast of Africa.

bluegill \ 'blü-,gil \

Fun to catch and good to eat, the bluegill is a favorite freshwater game fish in the eastern half of the U.S. It belongs to the sunfish family.

The bluegill gets its name from a dark blue spot on each gill cover. Below the gill covers are the long, pointed pectoral fins. The dorsal fins run together along the fish's back, and the tail is stout and slightly forked. The largest bluegills are 15 inches long and weigh up to 4 pounds. The average bluegill weighs much less.

Bluegills spawn in late spring or early summer. The male prepares a nest in shallow water near shore. He swims around and around, fanning his fins, until a shallow bowl appears in the sandy bottom.

Often a number of bluegills nest close together. The largest nests are about 2 feet across while the smallest ones are about 6 inches across. After females lay eggs in the nests, the males remain on guard to protect the eggs and the newly hatched young fish.

Bluegills live in fairly shallow, quiet water, where there are weeds and water plants. They eat insects, smaller fish and crustaceans.

blue gum (eucalyptus)

One of the largest trees in the world, the blue gum is an Australian evergreen of the myrtle family. Blue gum trees planted in California have grown 200 feet tall. In the forests of Australia, there are blue gum trees 300 feet tall.

The blue gum gives off a strong but not unpleasant smell which comes from an oil in the leaves, bark and flowers. Oil distilled from the leaves is used to make medicines to relieve cold symptoms.

As the tree grows, stringy brown bark peels off the trunk in long shreds, exposing a smooth layer of inner bark. Narrow

BLUE GUM

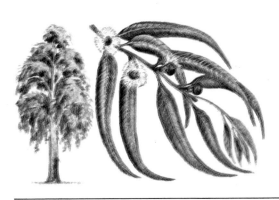

47

leaves, 6 to 12 inches long, hang down from the branches. The flowers and seeds of the blue gum tree are enclosed in hard, woody capsules that look like bells.

The blue gum tree gets its name from a bluish-white gum that covers the capsules. At first, the mouth of the capsule is closed by a hard cap formed of the flower's petals. The cap falls off as the other parts of the flower grow and expand. The seeds that ripen inside the bell in autumn are very small.

Blue gum trees have been planted in South America, Africa and southern Europe as well as in California.

bluet \ 'blü-ət \

An annual or perennial wild flower common in eastern North America, the bluet has dainty, pale blue flowers with yellow centers. The plant grows from a slender rhizome just under the ground.

The bluet grows 3 to 8 inches tall. Most of the leaves form a flat cluster on the ground. A few smaller leaves grow in opposite pairs along the slender stems. Most of the stems fork and bear a flower at the tip of each branch.

The flowers appear in May or June. Each one is about ½ inch long, and has a tube-shaped corolla that opens into 4 pointed lobes. Later in the summer, 4 to 20 round seeds ripen inside a small pod.

BLUET

BOBOLINK

Bluets grow in open fields where the soil is moist, or in soil among rocks. They often form a dense mat that covers the ground in wet meadows. They are found as far north as Nova Scotia and Wisconsin, and as far south as Georgia, Alabama and Missouri. In the southwest part of their range, bluets are fairly common in woods and thickets.

bobolink \ 'bäb-ə-ˌlingk \

The bobolink is an American songbird that belongs to the same family as the meadowlark, the cowbird, the grackle, the oriole and other birds called blackbirds. During spring and summer the male is black with white on the back and wings and yellow on the head. In autumn and winter the male is gray and brown, like the female.

The body of a bobolink is 7 to 8 inches long, with a 3-inch tail. The wingspread is about 12½ inches.

The bobolink lives in open country. It eats large numbers of harmful insects, along with some seeds and grain. Its nest of grass is placed on the ground, well hidden among weeds or tall grasses. To keep the nesting place a secret, the birds alight somewhere else and walk to the nest. Four to 8 eggs are laid in the spring, and are incubated for about 10 days.

In summer, bobolinks live throughout

southern Canada and in the northern half of the U.S., from New England west to the Rocky Mountains. The males arrive first in the spring and establish the territories where they will nest. Late in summer bobolinks gather in flocks and migrate to South America. Some spend the winter as far south as Argentina.

bobwhite (quail, partridge)

A group of medium-sized gamebirds related to pheasants, the bobwhites live throughout the eastern half of North America. They are easily identified by their call, a clear, whistling "bob-white!" heard most often in spring.

Bobwhites are about 10 inches long. They have small heads, plump bodies and small, narrow tails. They feed and nest on the ground, and fly only when frightened. Their flight is fast and usually straight.

These birds do not migrate. In summer they eat mostly insects. In winter they eat weed seeds and grain. They are usually seen in farm fields or along bushy fencerows.

The bobwhite's neat nest of grass is hidden under a bush or low tree. Six to 22 eggs are laid and are incubated for about 23 days. Although young birds are able to find their own food, a few usually stay together until the following spring. At night

BOOK LOUSE

a covey, or group, of bobwhites huddles together in a circle, each bird facing outward.

The eastern bobwhite (illustrated) is common from the Great Lakes south through Mexico.

book louse \ 'laůs \ (deathwatch)

The book louse is not really a louse at all, but belongs to a different family of wingless insects.

Book lice are very small, yellow or light-colored insects. They feed on the paste and paper in old books. In museums book lice may destroy dried plant and insect displays. They also creep into pantries and infest boxes of cereals.

The common book louse (illustrated) has biting mouthparts, long, thread-like antennae and a soft body. If they were laid end to end, it would take 1,000 book lice to equal an inch. Book lice do not undergo complete metamorphosis. The young look much like the adults.

Some book lice make a faint ticking sound by tapping their bodies on the surface they are resting on. Superstitious people once thought this tapping warned of coming death. They called the book louse "deathwatch."

Book lice are found in many parts of the world.

BOBWHITE

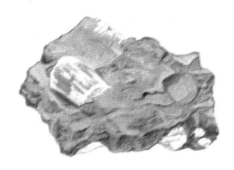

BORAX

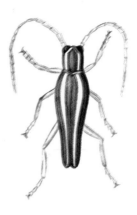

BORER

borax\ 'bōr-,aks\

Borax is a mineral salt which is white or colorless. Light will shine through it.

Crusts of borax are found around the edges of dry salt lakes. In the U.S., these dry lakes are in some desert areas of California and in Nevada. Scientists think that long ago the lakes were salty seas. The seas evaporated and left salts such as borax. About 90 percent of the world's borax comes from California. Borax is also found in Chile, Peru, northern Italy and Tibet.

Borax is used in many ways. Its greatest use is as a cleaner. It is used to make colored glazes on pottery. It is sometimes added to the family wash to soften the water by dissolving metallic impurities. Borax is also used in making glass, paint, paper and plywood, and it is put in motor oil, gasoline and fertilizers.

Forest fires are sometimes fought with borax. Chemists use borax in a special test for metals. The newest use of borax is in rocket fuel.

borer\ 'bōr-ər\

Borers are insects that as either adults or larvae bore into and damage wood. Borers feed on pine, locust, hickory, oak and many fruit trees.

The round-headed apple tree borer, a larva, attacks apple trees and related fruit trees, such as the quince and pear. The adult form (illustrated), which is a beetle, has well-developed mouthparts and very long antennae. The male beetle is usually ½ inch long. The female measures ¾ inch. Both sexes are light brown with 2 white stripes running the entire length of the body.

This beetle lays its eggs on the bark at the base of a fruit tree in early summer. The cream-colored larvae have small heads, round bodies and no legs. They bore into the sapwood of a fruit tree and burrow upward until they come out. Sometimes they burrow around the base of the tree. If they completely circle the tree, the tree dies.

A round-headed apple tree borer matures in 3 years. Pupation takes place inside the burrow in spring.

The round-headed apple tree borer is found throughout the U.S. and Canada east of the Rockies.

Boston\ 'bȯs-tən\ **ivy** (Japanese ivy)

Not a true ivy, Boston ivy is a hardy and attractive vine related to the grapes and to Virginia creeper. Boston ivy clings to stone, wooden and brick walls to form an attractive cover of dark green leaves.

BOSTON IVY

The woody stems of Boston ivy branch out in many directions. They grow to about 20 feet in length. The high-climbing vines have small sticky disks that hold them firmly to the wall.

The leaves are alternate and shiny. Most leaves on young plants are oval and have 3 lobes. Leaves on older plants are compound and are made up of 3 leaflets. The oval leaves are 2 to 5 inches long, while the compound leaves are 5 to 8 inches long. The tiny flowers and small, blue-black fruits are usually hidden by the leaves. In autumn, the leaves change to orange or red.

Boston ivy is a native of Japan and China and was brought to the U.S. many years ago. It is widely planted in America, especially in New England.

bougainvillea \ ˌbü-gən-'vil-yə \

Bougainvilleas make up a group of shrubs and vines that seem to have many large, colorful flowers. Actually, it is the 3 or more bracts, or leaves around the flowers, that are so colorful. In most other kinds of plants the bracts are green and small. In the bougainvillea they are large and brightly colored, ranging from red to rose to purple.

The bougainvillea was named for the French navigator, Louis Antoine de Bou-

gainville. It is native to South America but is now widely grown in southern California and in the southeastern states. Bougainvilleas need a warm climate and direct sunlight.

Bougainvillea plants have bright green alternate leaves. The leaves may be oval or wedge-shaped with pointed tips. The woody stems have many branches which are covered with hairs or sharp spines. Bougainvillea vines climb rapidly. Their trunk-like stems may be up to 1 foot in diameter and 10 feet tall.

One kind of bougainvillea (illustrated) has spiny stems that grow 30 to 40 feet long. The bracts are purple or red-purple. This plant was brought into the U.S. from Brazil.

box elder

The box elder is a hardy and fast-growing tree closely related to the maples. Unlike other trees of the maple group, it has compound leaves. Each leaf is made up of 3 to 5 pointed leaflets that are 2 to 4 inches long. They have irregular, saw-toothed edges.

The box elder usually has a short trunk 1 to 2 feet across. The trunk divides into several large branches near the base. The bark is gray or light brown, with deep ridges. The tree may grow to be 70 feet tall. Its wood is too soft to be valued as lumber.

BOUGAINVILLEA

BOX ELDER

Yellow-green, staminate and pistillate flowers grow on separate trees. The flowers hang down in long, graceful clusters. They appear in the spring at the same time as the leaves.

Samaras containing single seeds form in great numbers on the pistillate trees. Box elder samaras look very much like those of other maple trees. They hang from stems 1 to 2 inches long. The samaras mature early in the summer and hang in clusters.

The box elder is found throughout the eastern and southern U.S. It grows in both moist and fairly dry soil. Maple sugar is sometimes made from the sap of the box elder.

brine shrimp\ 'brīn 'shrimp\

These marine animals make up a group of crustaceans, but they are not true shrimps. They are members of the same family as the smaller fairy shrimps.

Brine shrimps are named for their shrimp-like appearance. Their eggs are sometimes dried and sold as fish food to breeders of tropical fish.

Unlike true shrimps, brine shrimps have no carapace. The body is about 4 inches long, with 11 to 19 pairs of abdominal appendages. The eyes are on stalks.

Brine shrimps are found in lakes and ponds that have a large amount of salt in them. The brine shrimp is one of the few animals that can live in the Great Salt Lake in Utah. It is also found in pools where seawater has evaporated, leaving a high salt content.

brontosaur\ 'bränt-ə-ˌsȯr\ (thunder lizard)

This huge dinosaur lived 160 million years ago. A giant reptile, the brontosaur was about 80 feet long and looked like a big lizard. It weighed 40 tons, more than some train locomotives.

The brontosaur had a long neck and a very small head. Its nostrils were at the top of its head. Its brain weighed less than 1 pound, and was smaller than man's brain. Both front and hind feet were short and wide like those of an elephant.

Although the brontosaur was a fearsome-looking beast, it ate only plants. Wading in streams and rivers, it fed on leaves from trees and plants along the banks.

The brontosaur lived in many places on earth, but the best fossils have been found in the Rocky Mountains and in Africa. Some scientists think that when cold weather killed many of the plants that the brontosaur ate, the brontosaur starved and became extinct.

Like most reptiles, the brontosaur laid eggs.

BRONTOSAUR

buckeye \ 'bək-ˌī \

Buckeyes are trees or shrubs of a group related to the horse chestnut tree. They get their name from the appearance of their seed. Each shiny brown seed has a light tan spot that looks like an eye.

Buckeyes grow to a height of 70 feet. The trunk diameter may reach 2 feet. The leaves are compound, and the 5 leaflets grow out from the end of the stem like fingers on a hand.

Buckeye flowers grow in loose clusters that are about 6 inches long. Each flower is yellow and about 1½ inches long. The fruit is a prickly pod which holds 2 or more large, smooth seeds. The seeds and leaves are poisonous to cattle. The bark is sometimes used in medicine.

Although the wood of the buckeye is used for paper pulp and lumber, the tree is more often cultivated for its beauty and shade than for its wood.

The Ohio buckeye (illustrated) is found in moist wooded areas from Pennsylvania west into Kansas and Nebraska. Ohio's nickname, the Buckeye State, comes from the Ohio buckeye, which is also the state tree of Ohio.

From 20 to 50 feet tall, the Ohio buckeye has rough, scaly bark. Its fruit is rough and prickly. The seeds are 1 to 1½ inches across.

BUCKEYE

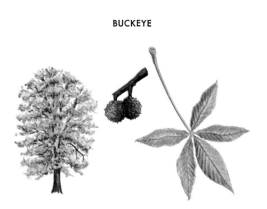

BUFFALO

buffalo

Buffalo make up a small group of mammals that belong to the bovine family. Buffalo are ruminants and are related to oxen. The North American mammal that is often called "buffalo" is a bison and not a true buffalo.

There are 3 kinds of buffalo. The Indian, or water, buffalo, is native to southeast Asia. It has been domesticated and is used as a beast of burden. The smaller forest buffalo is native to the islands of the western Pacific. The Cape buffalo (illustrated) of southern Africa is highly prized by big game hunters. It is strong, clever and nimble. Many consider the Cape buffalo to be the most dangerous of all wild game.

A Cape buffalo may stand 5 feet at the shoulder and weigh up to 3,000 pounds. The body of this animal may measure 7 feet with a 3- to 4-foot tail. A Cape buffalo's tongue is so rough that it can tear skin and flesh. The long, sharp horns have a total spread of 4 feet.

Cape buffalo usually travel in large herds. The animals forage at night and like wet swamp areas where there is plenty of grass. During the day they rest in shady areas and chew their cuds.

Bugs—Land and Water Insects

ASSASSIN BUG

BEDBUG

CHINCH BUG

GIANT WATER BUG

HARLEQUIN BUG

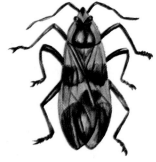

MILKWEED BUG

SQUASH BUG

STINKBUG

bug

Although the word "bug" is often used for any insect, true bugs are a certain group of insects that have piercing and sucking mouthparts. Some bugs feed on plant juices. Others feed on the blood and body juices of other insects, animals and man.

Like all insects, bugs have 3-part bodies and 3 pairs of legs that are attached to the thorax or middle section. The head is usually small, and the abdomen broad but not extremely long.

Bugs may be smooth, spiny or hairy. Some are bright-colored, while others are dull. The antennae may be short or long.

Some bugs have 4 wings, while others have none. If fore wings are present, they are thick and horny near the base, and are held crossed over the back when the insect is at rest. The hind wings and the back part of the fore wings are transparent.

All true bugs pass through the 3 stages of incomplete metamorphosis: egg, nymph and adult. The nymphs look much like the adults, but they are much smaller. They molt a number of times as they pass through the gradual changes that transform them into adults.

The female of many kinds of bugs deposits clusters of eggs on the undersides of green leaves. The newly hatched nymphs pierce veins in the leaf and suck out liquid sap.

In many kinds of bugs, including the chinch bugs, harlequin bug, milkweed bugs and squash bugs, the adult insect hibernates during the winter. The female lays eggs in early spring soon after she comes out of her hiding place.

Many but not all bugs produce a substance that has an unpleasant smell. Some bugs are pests that damage farm crops. Some bloodsucking bugs spread diseases. Others, such as the giant waterbug, are used as human food in some parts of the world.

The assassin bugs are fairly large and have very long antennae. Helpful to man, they kill many crop-destroying insects. The kind of assassin bug illustrated is called the wheelbug because of its crest which is shaped like a cogwheel. It is 1 to 1½ inches long.

The bedbugs feed on the blood of humans and other animals. They are active only at night, and can live for as long as a year without feeding at all. The bite of a bedbug is painless, but a chemical left behind by the insect may cause welts on the skin. The common bedbug (illustrated) is wingless and about ⅓ inch long.

The chinch bugs are a large group of insects that damage grain crops and lawns. They suck juices from the stems and roots of plants of the grass family, including corn and wheat. The small chinch bug (illustrated) is about ⅙ inch long.

The giant water bugs are a family of large insects 1 to 4 inches long. They live along the edges of streams and ponds, and they feed on the blood of other insects, snails, tadpoles and fish. At night, giant water bugs often leave their homes to cluster around lights. The kind illustrated is called the electric light bug.

The harlequin bug, less than ½ inch long, damages garden plants of the cabbage family. A crop pest from Mexico and Central America, this insect is now common throughout the southern U.S.

The milkweed bugs, related to the chinch bugs, eat mostly the juice of milkweed plants. The large milkweed bug (illustrated) is about ½ inch long.

The squash bugs are pests that damage gourd, pumpkin and squash vines. The common squash bug (illustrated) is a little more than ½ inch long.

The stinkbugs are green or brown insects that damage garden plants. The green stinkbug (illustrated) is about ½ inch long.

bullhead \ 'bu̇l-ˌhed \

Edible catfish closely related to the channel catfish, bullheads are common in most of the eastern U.S. Man has placed bullheads in some western streams. They can live in dirty water where few other fish can live.

The long, whisker-like barbels around the mouth are sense organs something like an insect's antennae. They help the fish feel its way along the bottom of a muddy stream or pond and find food that it cannot see. Bullheads eat plants and small animals such as snails and crayfish.

Like all catfish, bullheads have a smooth skin that is not covered with scales. At the front of the first dorsal fin is a sharp, poisonous spine.

Bullheads grow to be about 12 inches long and weigh 2 pounds. They spawn in the spring. A female bullhead may lay from 2,000 to 10,000 eggs. The male makes the nest and stays near it to guard the eggs and the school of young fish. If a young bullhead leaves the school, a parent takes the young fish in its mouth and spits it back into the school.

The most common kinds of bullheads are yellow (illustrated), brown or black. The yellow bullhead is found from the east coast west to Illinois, Missouri and Texas. It feeds at night.

BULLHEAD

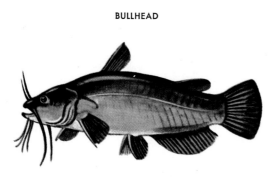

INDIGO BUNTING

PAINTED BUNTING

bunting \ 'bənt-ing \

Several kinds of birds that belong to the finch family are sometimes called buntings. Living and migrating in flocks, buntings spend much of their time on the ground eating crawling insects and seeds.

Different kinds of buntings vary in size. The length of the body ranges from 5½ to 7 inches, and the wingspan varies from 9 to 13 inches. Male buntings are usually brightly colored, while females are a duller color. Like most finches, buntings have short, strong bills and round heads.

Buntings live in Europe, Asia and North America. During the winter months they migrate to warmer climates, sometimes as far south as South America. During the summer they fly as far north as the Arctic.

The indigo bunting (illustrated) and the painted bunting (illustrated) are 2 common kinds of U.S. buntings. The indigo bunting is very helpful to farmers because it eats large numbers of caterpillars and weed seeds. The female indigo bunting is brown with faint streaks. The female painted bunting is greenish.

burbot \ 'bər-bət \

The burbot is the only fish of the cod family that lives in freshwater streams. All other codfish live in the ocean.

The flesh is edible but sometimes strong-flavored. The liver is a good source of

BURDOCK

vitamins, and it is sometimes used to make cod-liver oil.

A slender-bodied fish, the burbot may be 30 inches long and weigh 15 pounds. Some weigh up to 30 pounds.

The eyes are large and the mouth wide. There are 2 short, whisker-like barbels on the snout and 1 longer barbel on the chin. The second dorsal fin and the anal fin are long and extend almost to the rounded tail. The back and sides are spotted with brown or black, and there are small scales embedded in the tough skin.

Burbots live in the deeper lakes and larger streams of northern Europe and Asia and North America. They are most common in clear, cool water, where the bottom is covered with rocks or gravel. Active mostly at night, they feed on smaller fish and insects. They spawn in late winter or very early spring, often when the water is still covered with ice.

burdock \ 'bər-ˌdäk \

A group of coarse, weed-like plants, burdocks grow for 2 years before producing flowers and seeds. Burdocks look something like thistles. A few kinds reach a height of 9 feet in a fairly short time. Some burdocks are biennials that die after bearing seeds, while other kinds are perennials that live for many years.

The purple flowers grow in a loosely packed cluster which looks like a single flower. Around the flowers are sharp, hooked stickers which form burs. The oval or heart-shaped leaves grow alternately on the hairy stems. The stems branch out, making the plant bushy.

Burdocks are native to Europe but have been brought to the U.S. where they are common in many places.

The common burdock (illustrated) is also known as the cuckoo-button and cockle button. It grows to a height of 5 feet. Each flower cluster is about an inch across. Around each flower cluster is a green bur which often sticks to the clothing of anyone who brushes against it.

The common burdock is seen most often in rich soil. In pastures and open woodlands, it is sometimes a troublesome weed.

bush dog

A wild dog of Central and South America, the bush dog lives in thick forests and hunts at night in packs. It kills and eats small animals such as squirrels and rats. Because it is such a strong animal, the bush dog can kill other animals many times its size. It barks sharply, growls deeply and howls so loudly that it can sometimes be heard for miles.

The bush dog's legs are short in proportion to the length of its body. Its ears are small and rounded.

BUSH DOG

The strong, muscular body of the bush dog is about 25 inches long. It is covered with long, reddish-brown hair and has a short, bushy tail that is about 5½ inches long. Each foot has 5 large toenails that are used for fighting. Males and females are about the same size. Bush dogs live in burrows that they dig.

Once a year, the female bush dog has 2 to 12 puppies that stay with their mother for several months.

Bush dogs are most common in Panama, Brazil and Guyana. They have many natural enemies, including larger animals and man.

bushpig \ 'bush-,pig \ (river hog)

Closely related to the pigs on American farms, these mammals make up a group of wild pigs. They live in Africa and on the island of Madagascar.

Bushpigs, like farm pigs, have barrel-shaped bodies, short necks and long noses that are flat on the end. They have tough skin thinly covered with bristly hair that lies flat. The hair is thickest along the back and forms a short mane like that of a horse. Male bushpigs have small tusks.

The male bushpig is usually much bigger than the female. Males are about 30 inches high at the shoulder and weigh about 170 pounds.

Herds of 6 to 20 bushpigs live in forest areas near open fields. They feed at night on grass, roots, fruits, corn and other crops. Bushpigs have no dwelling, but hide in shrubs and brush. Most bushpigs are smart enough to keep away from the traps set by men who hunt them with dog packs.

A common kind of bushpig is the boschvark or South African bushpig (illustrated).

bushtit \ 'bush-,tit \

Six kinds of the small birds related to the titmice are called bushtits. They are about the size of a man's thumb. They are found in Europe, Asia, Java and western North America. Flocks of these noisy birds live in the woodlands of hilly or mountainous country.

Bushtits build hanging, sack-like nests 3 or 4 inches across and about 10 inches long. The nests are made of leaves and small plants, held together by spider webs. The inside of the nest is lined with soft animal hair.

Bushtits enter their nests through a spout-like opening on the side. Five to 8 white eggs are laid twice a year, and both parents care for the young birds. During nesting time, both parents sleep in the nest at night.

Very active birds, bushtits flutter their

BUSHPIG

BUSHTIT

wings as they move along tree trunks, digging for insects and worms through cracks in the bark. Their calls are high-pitched, buzzing sounds.

The common bushtit (illustrated) is the kind most often seen in the U.S. It is about 4½ inches long, including the tail.

butte \ 'byüt \

Steep-sided hills with flat tops, buttes are usually found in deserts. They are formed over a very long period of time by streams eroding away the soft land around them. They may look like large monuments rising from the desert floor.

The flat top of a butte is a cap of very hard, strong rock that was able to resist the usual forces of erosion.

Many buttes are found in western North America. Spanish explorers named the large, flat buttes *mesas,* meaning "tables." French explorers called those found in the Northwest *buttes,* their word for "mounds." The mesas of the Southwest are much larger than the buttes of the Northwest. The word "butte" is used for the smaller of these 2 formations.

The name "butte" is also used for certain steep-sided volcanic cones built of cinders or medium-sized volcanic rocks. These cones usually have tops that are more pointed or rounded than the tops of buttes formed by stream erosion.

BUTTE

BUTTERCUP

buttercup

Common wild flowers, buttercups are plants that bear bright yellow, cup-shaped flowers. There are many kinds of buttercups, and each kind looks somewhat different from the other kinds. They grow from a height of 6 inches to a height of 3 feet.

The flowers have 5 shiny petals. Each flower is about 1 inch across and is located at the tip of a long, branching stem. The leaves are attached near the bottom of the plant and are divided into sections. Some kinds of buttercups produce seeds in 1 year, while others take 2 years.

Buttercups grow throughout the cool, moist parts of the U.S. and far north in Canada. They are most often found along streams and swamps.

The tallest kind of buttercup (illustrated) is sometimes called the meadow buttercup. It was brought to the U.S. from Europe. From 2 to 3 feet high, its stems are stiff and straight. The broad leaves at the base of the plant are divided into 5 or 7 notched segments. The leaves at the top of the plant are smaller than those at the base.

The meadow buttercup grows from the Atlantic coast as far west as Kansas.

butterfly

Together with their close relatives the moths, butterflies make up a large group of harmless and colorful insects that have 2 pairs of broad wings. The worm-like larvae, called caterpillars, have chewing mouthparts and eat the leaves of plants. The adults have sucking mouthparts and eat only liquids such as flower nectar.

All butterflies pass through the 4 stages of complete metamorphosis: egg, larva (caterpillar), pupa and adult. The eggs are deposited in clusters on a plant that will provide food for the caterpillars.

A caterpillar has 3 pairs of legs plus 2 to 5 pairs of hooked, false legs on its abdomen. Some caterpillars are smooth-skinned while others are hairy. All have silk glands with which they spin the threads they use to make pupas around themselves. The pupa, which is called a chrysalis, is attached to a leaf or twig.

When the butterfly emerges from the chrysalis a few weeks later or the following spring, it is an adult with broad wings and a narrow body. The adult has 3 pairs of legs. The front pair of legs is usually too weak and small to be used.

The adults of some kinds of butterflies die soon after breeding. In other kinds, the adults hibernate through the winter or migrate to a warmer climate.

All of the butterflies illustrated are found in the U.S. They are seen most often over meadows or roadside weed patches, on sunny summer days.

The alfalfa butterfly is sometimes called the orange sulfur. It has a wingspread of 1 to 2 inches, and the female is usually more colorful than the male. The slender, green larva feeds on plants of the pea family and can be a crop pest. This butterfly is common in the central and southwestern U.S.

The blues are a group of butterflies with slender bodies and wingspreads of ¾ to 1½ inches. The females are usually darker and less colorful than the males. The larvae are chunky-bodied caterpillars that feed on flowers. The eastern tailed blue butterfly (illustrated) is found from the Atlantic coast west to Kansas.

The buckeye butterfly has large eyespots on its purplish-brown wings, which are about 2 inches across. This butterfly lives through the winter as an adult. It is found throughout the U.S. but is most common in the southern states. The larva is brownish-yellow and bristly.

The fritillaries are a group of butterflies with orange and brown wings 1 to 5 inches across. The larvae are black or brown caterpillars covered with bristles. They eat mostly flowers. The gulf fritillary is seen mostly in the southern states.

The monarch butterfly, 3 to 4 inches across, migrates in flocks to southern California, Florida and the West Indies, and flies back in spring to lay eggs. The larvae are plump yellow-and-black-striped caterpillars that feed on milkweed plants.

The painted lady butterfly, 1½ to 2 inches across, is sometimes called the thistle butterfly, since both adults and larvae feed on thistle plants.

The red-spotted purple butterfly common in the eastern U.S. has a wingspread of 3 inches or more. The larva is a spotted caterpillar that eats tree leaves.

The swallowtail butterflies are black and yellow, with wingspreads of 4 to 6½ inches. Their larvae are smooth-skinned, greenish caterpillars that feed on tree leaves and sometimes eat each other. The zebra swallowtail is found only in the central and southeastern states where papaw trees grow. The tiger swallowtail is found throughout the U.S. and into Alaska.

The violet-tip butterfly has odd-shaped, irregular wings about 2 inches across. Its larvae feed on elm or hackberry trees, hops and nettles.

Butterflies—Colorful Insects

ALFALFA

BLUE

GULF FRITILLARY

MONARCH

PAINTED LADY
(underside)

BUCKEYE

TIGER SWALLOWTAIL

RED-SPOTTED PURPLE

ZEBRA SWALLOWTAIL

VIOLET-TIP

C

cabbage

One of the most widely grown vegetables, cabbage belongs to the mustard family. Cabbage was first found in Europe growing along the seacoasts as a common weed. Today, there are many kinds of cabbage which are eaten. They include broccoli, Brussels sprouts and cauliflower.

Common cabbage (illustrated) is a low-growing plant with a short stem. At the end of the stem is a large head. The head, which is the part eaten, is made up of closely packed, alternate leaves. The outer leaves are green, shading to white within.

Broccoli was first grown in Italy and is sometimes called asparagus broccoli. The part of this plant which is eaten is the thick flower shoot.

Brussels sprouts are named for the capital of Belgium where they were first grown. The part of this plant that is eaten is the young shoot which looks like a tiny cabbage.

Cauliflower is a stemless form of cabbage with a thick white head. The parts which are eaten are the flower stalks and buds.

CABBAGE

CABBAGE PALMETTO

cabbage palmetto \ pal-'met-(ˌ)ō \ (palmetto palm)

A tall evergreen tree that grows in the southeastern part of the U.S. and in the Bahama Islands, the cabbage palmetto is a member of the palm family. At the top of the cabbage palmetto is a bud called the terminal bud which is very good to eat. If the bud is removed, however, the tree will soon die.

Its large, fan-shaped leaves are 3 to 6 feet long. They grow in a bunch at the top of a thin trunk. Each leaf is made up of 40 or more ribbon-like parts that are ragged and spiny along the edges.

The trunk is usually 1 to 2 feet in diameter. It may be smooth or covered with crisscrossed leaf stalks. Very small white flowers and round black berries grow in large groups that hang from the top of the tree.

Because the wood of the cabbage palmetto will last a long time in water, it is sometimes used for building piers. The cabbage palmetto is the state tree of South Carolina and Florida.

cacao \ kə-'kā-ō \ (cocoa tree)

Cacaos make up a group of tropical evergreen trees. They grow in Central and South America and Africa. They need rich, moist soil and a humid climate.

CACAO

One kind of cacao (illustrated) is sometimes called the cocoa tree because its seeds are the source of chocolate. Cocoa made from these seeds was once thought to have magic powers.

The cocoa tree grows to a height of 40 feet. It is a spreading tree with smooth bark. Its large, wide leaves are shiny and dark green.

The flowers and fruit of the cocoa tree grow in bunches attached to the trunk and the main branches of the tree. The small flowers have 5 petals which are pink and white. The fruit is a pod, 8 to 15 inches long and 3 to 4 inches thick, which looks like a melon. Inside are 5 rows of fat, white seeds ½ to 1 inch long. The pods are picked as they ripen, mostly between September and March.

Most chocolate made in the U.S. comes from the seeds of South American and African cocoa trees.

cactus \ 'kak-təs \

A large family of juicy, mostly tropical plants, cacti are native to North and South America. There are almost 2,000 different kinds of cacti. Some are 60-foot giants, while others are only a few inches high. Some are tree-like, while others are viny or shrubby. All are perennials.

Most cacti have bright flowers. The flowers of some kinds bloom at night. The petals of some kinds look like tubes or funnels, while the petals of others are widely spread out.

Most full-grown cacti do not have true leaves. If they do have leaves, they are small and flat. The green stems, which store water, are very large in some kinds of cacti.

The sharp spines and barbed bristles of many cacti make them hard to handle. The berry-like fruit of some kinds of cacti can be eaten.

Almost all cacti are found in desert or semidry areas where the yearly rainfall is less than 12 inches.

The giant or saguaro cactus (illustrated) is the largest kind of cactus. It is most common in Southern California and in Arizona, where it is the state flower.

calcite \ 'kal-ˌsīt \

Calcite is one of the most common of all minerals. Limestone, marble, travertine and chalk are some common forms of calcite. It is also found in some caves as stalactites and stalagmites. Water often has calcite dissolved in it. Calcite is one of the things which make water "hard."

Because there are hundreds of different forms of calcite, its appearance varies greatly. Most calcite, however, is white or colorless, and transparent or translucent.

CALCITE

CALDERA

Calcite is often found in the form of a crystal (illustrated). Certain other crystals of calcite are sometimes called Iceland spar. Such crystals are rare. They are unusual because objects seen through them appear double. Calcite crystals have more different forms than the crystals of any other mineral.

Calcite is the most important mineral in marble and limestone, which are widely used as building materials.

caldera \ kal-'der-ə \

A caldera is a large, steep-sided crater formed when the top of a volcano has blown off or has fallen into the volcano.

Referring to their shape, the Spanish described these special craters as caldera, which means "caldron" in Spanish. Because of the way they are formed, calderas are at least 3 times as wide as they are deep. Some are filled with water.

Crater Lake, in Oregon, is a famous, water-filled caldera. After the top fell into the volcano, the crater filled with water from rain and melting snow. New eruptions formed a cinder cone island in the middle of the caldera.

An even larger caldera is in the Jemez Mountains of northwestern New Mexico. It is about 16 miles across.

In 1883, the Krakatau volcano, in Indonesia, exploded and formed a caldera on the ocean floor.

California grunion \ 'grən-yən \

Sometimes called smelt, this small Pacific coast fish is found in warm water from San Francisco to Lower California. It is 5 to 8 inches long.

At the time of the nearly full moon during the spring and summer, large numbers of grunions follow the high tide and swim onto sandy beaches. The female digs a hole in the sand with her tail. She lays about 2,000 eggs in the hole. The male fertilizes the eggs as they are laid. Then the males and females are carried out to sea by the next tide. After the eggs have hatched 2 weeks later, the young fish are also carried out to sea by the tide.

Because California grunions come to the beach on a certain schedule, people often have large trapping parties to catch them. During such a time, grunions can be easily picked up by hand. To protect grunions, these trapping parties have been made illegal during part of the breeding season.

California laurel \ 'lȯr-əl \ (spice tree)

The California laurel is a handsome evergreen tree native to North America. The lumber from this tree is quite valuable. Because of its beautiful grain, the wood is used for wall paneling and furniture.

CALIFORNIA LAUREL

The California laurel grows to a height of 40 to 80 feet. The trunk often divides into branches near the ground. The bark is reddish-brown and scaly. The leaves are shiny and have a strong smell of camphor. They grow from 2 to 6 inches long and stay on the tree for 2 years or more. During the summer, the leaves change their color from green to yellow or orange.

The small flowers of the California laurel also have an odor. They appear in January and grow in bunches on the branches during the winter. The fruit is olive-shaped and is about an inch long. It ripens in the fall.

The California laurel is native to Oregon and California, where it grows along streams where the soil is moist.

calla \ 'kal-ə \ lily

The calla lily is a thick-stemmed, pleasant-smelling tropical plant. It is not a true lily, but a member of another plant family. It is often used for decoration and as a house plant. Calla lilies normally grow from 18 to 30 inches high.

The pretty white "flower" is really a leaf-like envelope, or spathe, wrapped around itself in a trumpet shape. This spathe is between 6 and 9 inches long. The real flowers grow on a stalk-like part in the middle of the white envelope. This stalk-like part has many tiny flowers that have no petals.

The large leaves of the calla lily are shaped like arrowheads. They grow on long stalks that branch out from the main stem near the ground.

The calla lily is native to South Africa. Although it will grow from seeds, florists usually cultivate it from a rhizome. Pink, red and yellow varieties have been developed. Calla lilies need rich, well-drained soil, quite a lot of water and some sunlight. Some calla lilies are grown as field crops in southern California.

camel

There are 2 kinds of these well-known mammals. One kind is the 1-humped Arabian camel (illustrated), sometimes called a dromedary. This kind of camel is found in the sandy regions of western Asia, India, Arabia and Africa. The other kind of camel has 2 humps and is called the Bactrian camel. It is found in the plains of central Asia, Chinese Turkestan and the Gobi Desert.

Camels have been tamed by man since prehistoric times. They are used as pack and saddle animals and are also raised for their milk, meat and hides. Camel skin is made into leather, while the hair is woven into light, strong cloth.

CALLA LILY

CAMEL

CANARY BIRD

Camels stand 6 to 8 feet tall at the shoulder and have long, thin legs. The humps on a camel's back store fat as a spare food supply.

A camel can go without water for 3 to 9 days. When there is plenty of water around, a camel drinks about 7 gallons a day. If a camel has gone without water for several days, it may drink as much as 16 gallons.

The normal life-span of a camel is 25 to 30 years.

canary bird

A member of the finch family, the canary bird is one of the best-known pet birds. It was brought into Europe from the Canary Islands, off the west coast of Africa. Canary birds are still found wild there, as well as in the Azores and the Madeira Islands.

Wild canaries live in small flocks. They perch in trees, hop on the ground and eat seeds. The birds live in pairs. The female builds a cup-shaped nest in a tree or bush. Three to 6 pale blue, brownish-spotted eggs are laid.

The upper parts of the wild canary bird are olive-colored, with streaks of brown and black. The lower parts are mostly shades of green. Body length, including the tail, is about 6 inches.

Hundreds of years ago man began to

catch these songbirds and keep them in cages. Through careful breeding, man has produced canary birds of many different colors and ways of singing. Because of their colors and songs, many people keep these birds as pets.

The canary bird is small and active. At times, it will sit and sing for hours. It eats seeds, which it crushes easily with its strong, cone-shaped bill.

cankerworm \ 'kang-kər-ˌwərm \

Cankerworms are not really worms. They are the larvae of moths. There are 2 kinds of cankerworms (illustrated), the spring cankerworm and the fall cankerworm. Both are very destructive, eating the leaves of fruit and shade trees, mostly apple and elm trees. Cankerworms are common in all parts of the U.S., except the southeast and along the Gulf of Mexico.

Both kinds of cankerworms are black with 1 yellow stripe and 3 white stripes. They are about 1 inch long. The spring cankerworm has spines on its abdomen.

Cankerworms change into moths with thin bodies. The male moths have wide, greenish-white wings. The females have no wings.

The female moth lays a mass of eggs in straight, even rows on the bark of deciduous trees. When the eggs hatch into cankerworms, they feed on the leaves of the trees.

SPRING CANKERWORM   FALL CANKERWORM

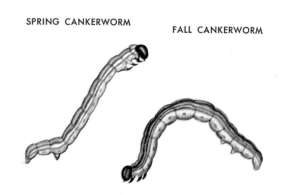

Cankerworms are sometimes called "measuring worms" or "inch worms," because of the way they move forward by throwing their bodies forward and then pulling them together.

capybara \ ˌkap-i-'bar-ə \
(cavy, water pig)

This clumsy-looking mammal is the largest of all rodents. It is 4 feet long and weighs from 80 to 100 pounds. It has a short neck, small ears and no tail, and is covered with coarse hair.

The hind legs are longer than the front legs. There are 3 toes on the hind feet, and 4 toes on the front feet. All the toes have stubby claws. They are webbed, much like a duck's foot.

The capybara lives in the eastern part of South America on the banks of lakes, marshes and rivers. It eats grass, water plants, tree bark, and melons and vegetables taken from gardens.

A quiet animal, the capybara rests near the water between feedings, always watching for danger. When it is frightened, it dives into the water and swims with great speed.

In zoos, the normal life-span of the capybara is 10 years. In the wild, its life-span is usually shorter because of its many natural enemies. Among these enemies is man, who hunts the capybara for its meat.

CAPYBARA

CARDINAL

cardinal \ 'kärd-nəl \

Although there are several kinds of songbirds called cardinals, the kind most common in the U.S. is often called cardinal or redbird (illustrated). It is the official state bird of Illinois, Indiana, Kentucky, North Carolina, Ohio, Virginia and West Virginia. The redbird belongs to the finch family.

The body of the male redbird is bright red. The female is brownish, with red-marked wings. Both male and female have a black patch around the bill, and are 8 to 9 inches long. Both male and female have tall, pointed crests on their heads. The stout, cone-shaped bill is reddish.

Redbirds make a variety of whistling calls. The call which is most often heard sounds like "what cheer?"

Redbirds are most common in the eastern half of the U.S. They are easily attracted to bird feeders. Many will return to the same bird feeder year after year. Redbirds eat mostly seeds, but some insects.

The redbird chooses a single mate and remains with that mate for its entire life. Nests are built in trees, bushes or vines. Three whitish eggs, marked with brown or purple, are laid each year. The life-span of the redbird ranges from 6 to 8 years.

caribou \ 'kar-ə-ˌbü \ (reindeer)

This useful mammal of the deer family has served Arctic peoples for hundreds of years. Caribou is the French-Canadian name for reindeer.

The caribou can carry a load of 150 pounds or pull a sled loaded with 450 pounds. Caribou meat is good to eat. Caribou skin can be tanned for leather. The fur makes warm clothes and robes. Caribou milk is good to drink and makes rich cheese.

The caribou stands 4 feet high at the shoulder and is about 6 feet long. It weighs between 300 and 400 pounds. Both male and female have broad antlers and 2-toed hoofs.

Although wild caribou travel in large herds in winter, they live alone or in families during the rest of the year. Caribou eat grass, lichens and moss. They live 13 to 15 years.

The woodland caribou (illustrated) is often pictured as the reindeer used by Santa Claus. Native to Canadian plains and lowlands, the woodland caribou is also found in the northeastern U.S. It lives mostly in birch and pine forests and is not found in mountain regions. It runs swiftly with a bounding motion.

CARIBOU

CARNATION

carnation \ kär-'nā-shən \

A perennial flowering plant, the carnation is popular for its attractive, long-lasting flowers. It is widely grown in both greenhouses and gardens.

Single flowers measure about 2 inches across. Each grows at the end of a long stalk, 1 to 3 feet in length. The flower may be red, white, yellow or pink. It has 5 wedge-shaped petals with fringed edges. Double carnations have many petals crowded together. Flower growers have succeeded in developing striped carnations, as well as carnations marked with 2 or 3 colors. Some carnation blossoms are very fragrant.

Carnation leaves are long, narrow and opposite each other. The stem is stiff, hard and jointed. The leaves grow from the joints. The fruit is an oblong capsule containing many seeds.

The carnation is a native of southeastern Europe. Although it is most often grown in America as a greenhouse plant, the carnation is also grown in gardens in mild climates. The scarlet carnation is the state flower of Ohio.

carp \ 'kärp \

Freshwater fish related to goldfish, carp are bottom-feeding fish that live in warm inland lakes and slow-moving

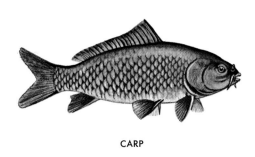

CARP

The garden carrot (illustrated) is an erect plant, 2 to 3 feet high. The small flowers are white or yellow and grow in flat, umbrella-shaped clusters. The fruit is a tiny, ribbed seed about ⅛ inch in length.

Carrot leaves, which have long stalks, are compound and pinnate. The leaves become fern-like at the ends.

The wild carrot is known as Queen Anne's lace. It has a pretty white flower, but is a troublesome weed that spreads rapidly. Dairy farmers try to keep it out of their pastures. When eaten by cows, Queen Anne's lace gives an unpleasant flavor to milk. The plant grows about 3 feet high and is found in most parts of the U.S.

Other garden vegetables related to the carrot are the parsnip, parsley and celery. About 2,000 herbs, including dill, anise and caraway, are also members of the parsley family.

cashew \ 'kash-,ü \

A tropical evergreen tree, the cashew is a source of edible nuts, lumber and oil. The cashew is related to American poison ivy and poison sumac.

The cashew grows as a shrub or low, spreading tree 20 to 40 feet tall. It has large green leaves that may be 6 inches long and 4 inches wide. The seed, or nut, looks

streams and rivers. They are both useful and harmful. Carp are edible fish, but they destroy the eggs and nests of other fish by disturbing the water in their search for food.

Full-grown carp may weigh 20 pounds or more and measure 3 feet in length, but are usually smaller. They have long, slightly flattened bodies. The mouth has no teeth, but the throat contains several rows of large teeth. The fins are soft. There are large spines in front of the dorsal and anal fin. The tail fin is forked. Most carp have scales.

Carp are native to eastern Asia, but were brought to America as a food fish in the 1870's. They have spread to many parts of the U.S. The female lays as many as 2 million eggs in the spring. The eggs are often laid on water plants, and hatch in 4 to 8 days. Young carp grow to about 6 inches the first year.

The goldfish belongs to the same family as the carp. Fishermen sometimes use small carp as bait.

carrot

This well-known vegetable is a member of the parsley family. Its orange root is a popular food around the world. Carrots need rich soil and are easily grown in most home gardens.

CARROT

CASHEW

like a curved bean ½ to 1 inch in length. It grows in a double-walled shell at the narrow end of a red or yellow fruit called the cashew apple.

Both apple and nut can be eaten. The nut must first be roasted to remove the poisonous oil between the double walls of the shell. The oil is very much like that found in poison ivy and blisters the skin.

The gum of the cashew tree is used in varnish. The poisonous oil is used as a lubricant, as an insecticide and in the production of plastic.

The cashew is native to Central and South America. It is now grown in other tropical countries such as India and parts of Africa. It needs rich soil and a warm climate.

Cassini's division \ kə'sē-nez də-'vizh-ən \

This name is given by astronomers to the gap between the 2 outer rings of the planet Saturn. The gap was named for Giovanni Domenico Cassini, an Italian-born astronomer who discovered it, as well as 4 of Saturn's moons.

Early astronomers thought that the band around Saturn was 1 wide, solid ring. In 1675, Cassini saw that a black line divided the band into 2 rings. He also suggested that the rings were made up of

small particles held in orbit by Saturns' gravity.

One hundred years later, William Herschel proved that the black line Cassini had seen was a gap between the 2 outer rings. In 1857, J. S. Maxwell proved that Cassini was correct in thinking that Saturn's rings were thousands of small particles in orbit.

Cassini's division is about 1,750 miles wide. The total width of Saturn's 3 rings is nearly 170,000 miles.

See *Saturn*.

castor-oil \ 'kas-tər-'öil \ plant

Although the seeds of this large, handsome plant are the source of castor oil, the plant is sometimes grown only for its handsome leaves and flowers.

The castor-oil plant grows from 3 to 40 feet tall. The leaves are shaped like big shields and may measure 3 feet across. They have deep lobes. Many small, dark red flowers grow in clusters up to 2 feet long at the ends of the stems.

The fruit is a capsule covered with soft, brown spines. Inside the capsule are silvery, oval seeds, ½ to 1 inch long. The leaves and seeds of the castor-oil plant are poisonous to eat.

Oil from castor seeds is clear and light-colored. It is used as a medicine and in

CASTOR OIL PLANT

CAT

making paints, varnishes, dyes, cosmetics, inks, greases and nylon plastics.

The castor-oil plant is native to tropical Africa. It is now grown in many parts of the world. It grows as an annual in cool climates and as a perennial in tropical climates. The tallest castor-oil plants grow in the tropics.

India and Brazil produce most of the world's castor beans and oil. The U.S. uses about half of the beans and oil produced.

cat

Cats make up a large family of mammals which includes both large wild beasts and small domestic pets. Cats live in many parts of the world and are many different colors and sizes. Through fossils, cats have been traced back over 40 million years.

All cats have strong, muscular bodies and rounded heads. Their legs are usually long in relation to the rest of their bodies. All cats have 5 toes on their forefeet and 4 toes on their hind feet. They walk softly and quietly on their padded toes. Their sharp claws can be drawn up into their footpads. The canine teeth of all cats are long and sharp.

In all cats, the tongue has a patch of sharp spines that point back from the tip. The spines help the cat lap up liquids and clean itself.

Most cats are good climbers. Cats like to hunt at night and often lie in wait for their prey. They are usually carnivorous, but the domestic cat (illustrated) has learned to eat the food furnished by man. Cats also like to catch and eat wild birds, chickens, mice and fish.

Domestic cats may have several litters of 1 to 8 kittens each year.

For other members of the cat family, see *cheetah, cougar, jaguar, leopard, lion, lynx, ocelot* and *tiger.*

catalpa \ kə'tal-pə \ (cigar tree)

This group of fast-growing, flowering trees is easy to identify. Catalpas have large, heart-shaped leaves 10 to 12 inches long.

Clusters of large, trumpet-shaped white, yellow or purplish flowers bloom in the spring. Long seedpods, 6 to 12 inches long, hang on the tree through the autumn and winter months. The pods, which are sometimes called Indian cigars, contain many winged seeds.

Catalpas usually grow to be 40 to 60 feet tall with a trunk 1 to 2 feet in diameter. The bark is reddish-brown and scaly. The wood of the trunk is used for fence posts and railroad ties.

Catalpas are found in the central and southern U.S. and in Asia. The hardy or

CATALPA

western catalpa (illustrated) is native to the upper Mississippi valley, from southern Illinois and Indiana to Arkansas and Texas. This catalpa has been widely planted as a shade tree in other parts of the U.S.

The caterpillar of the catalpa sphinx moth often feeds on the leaves of the hardy catalpa. These caterpillars sometimes strip a hardy catalpa tree of all its leaves.

cataract \ 'kat-ə-ˌrakt \

A cataract is a large waterfall that occurs where a stream drops steeply to a lower level. Waterfalls in which there is a small amount of water, or in which the water follows a less steep path, are called cascades or rapids.

Most cataracts are found in places where hard rock has worn away more slowly than the soil downstream. The difference in the speed of erosion leaves a steep cliff. The water falls over the cliff.

The most famous cataract in the U.S. is Niagara Falls in New York State. Its height is 167 feet. Niagara Falls is not the highest U.S. cataract. Many others are higher but have less water.

Cataracts are usually found in the mountains. They also occur where small streams flow into larger, lower bodies of water. The small streams do not cut away the earth to the level of the larger river valleys.

CATARACT

CATBIRD

catbird

This bird belongs to the same family as the mockingbird and thrasher. The catbird can usually be identified by its mewing, cat-like call. Like the mockingbird, the catbird also imitates the songs of other birds.

The male catbird measures up to 9½ inches in length, including the tail. The tail spreads out into a wide fan. Females are slightly smaller than males. Males, females and young birds are colored alike. They are slate gray with a black head cap and a rust-colored patch under the tail.

Catbirds usually live in thick shrubs and in vine areas near ponds or open swamps. They are also found in shrubs near houses. Their nests are made of twigs, bark and leaves, and are deep and cup-shaped. They are usually built from 3 to 10 feet above the ground. Catbirds feed mostly on worms and insects, but they also eat some fruit and berries. They sometimes damage the ripening fruit on grapevines and blackberry bushes.

Catbirds breed from Washington to Nova Scotia, south to Florida and west to Texas. The female lays 3 to 7 greenish-blue eggs 1 to 3 times a year. Both parents incubate the eggs for 12 to 14 days. Catbirds migrate to the gulf states, Cuba and Central America.

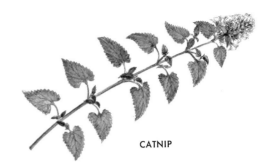

CATNIP

CATFISH

catfish

Catfish belong to a large group of about 2,000 kinds of freshwater and marine fish. All have barbels, which are whisker-like organs, on their snouts and jaws.

Catfish have smooth skins, broad heads and wide mouths. Sharp-pointed spines on the dorsal and pectoral fins can injure the hand of a person who handles a catfish.

Catfish are common in rivers and lakes throughout the U.S. Marine and freshwater catfish are found in almost all parts of the world. They vary in size from a few inches to more than 5 feet.

The channel catfish (illustrated) is perhaps the best-known kind of freshwater catfish. It is highly valued as both a food and game fish. Averaging 13 inches in length and 3½ pounds in weight, the channel catfish may grow to 4 feet and weigh 50 pounds.

Channel catfish are native to the Mississippi valley and have been widely introduced in other areas. They prefer moving water and feed on insects, worms, crustaceans and water plants.

Spawning takes place in summer. A female may lay as many as 20,000 eggs. The male guards the nest. After hatching, the young travel in schools for several weeks.

catnip \ 'kat-ˌnip \

The catnip plant is a perennial member of the mint family. Like many other plants in this family, it has its own scent by which it can be identified.

Catnip gets its name because cats seem to enjoy the odor of its crushed or bruised leaves. Cats eat the leaves and roll in them. The tops of mature catnip plants are sometimes harvested and used in medicines.

Catnip has white or lavender flowers that grow in a spike-like cluster on branches and the end of the square stem. The stem is straight and downy. It grows 2 to 3 feet high. The leaves are pointed and are covered with down on the underside. Large leaves may be 2 inches in length. The fruit of each flower produces 4 single-seeded nutlets.

Catnip is native to Europe but now grows in most parts of the northern hemisphere. It is becoming a common roadside weed in North America and Europe.

cattail \ 'kat-ˌtāl \

Cattails make up a group of wild plants that grow throughout the world in swamps and marshes.

The common cattail has leaves which may be as long as 9 feet and less than an

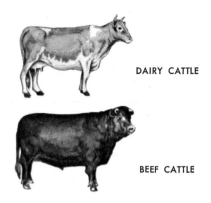

DAIRY CATTLE

BEEF CATTLE

inch wide. The stalk which bears the brown spike of flowers may be 6 to 8 feet long. The flower spike itself is about 1 inch in diameter and usually less than a foot long. The plant grows from a thick, starchy root.

The brown furry spike that gives the plant its name is formed by thousands of tiny, closely packed flowers. In early summer the spike has a tip made up of lighter-colored staminate flowers. After these shed their pollen they disappear, leaving the brown center. The center is made up of pistillate flowers without petals and sepals. Fluffy seeds are set free when the spike breaks.

Cattail reeds are used in basketmaking. The downy seeds are sometimes used for stuffing pillows and for insulation. Dried cattails are sometimes used as winter decorations.

Cattails grow from Newfoundland to Alaska and through most of the U.S. into Mexico.

cattle

Cattle make up a large group of hoofed mammals. In the U.S., the most familiar cattle are farm animals, but domestic and wild cattle live in many other parts of the world.

There are many differences in color and size, but all cattle are alike in a number of ways. They have heavy bodies and divided hoofs with an even number of toes. All cattle have long tails and they are ruminants.

Domestic cattle (illustrated) are believed to be descended from the wild Roman oxen. They are carefully bred to furnish milk and dairy products, or meat and leather. Domestic cattle have large heads, short legs and short necks. Some have horns while others are hornless. Each of the many breeds of cattle can be identified by its own shape, its own color or its own marking.

Female cattle are called cows, males are called bulls and young cows and bulls are called calves. A heifer is a young female that has not given birth to a calf. A steer is a male that has had the reproductive organs removed by an operation.

For other kinds of cattle, see *American bison, buffalo, musk-ox, yak* and *zebu.*

cattleya \ 'kat-lē-ə \

The cattleyas make up a group of American tropical plants belonging to the orchid family. They include the kinds of orchids most often sold in florists' shops. Cattleyas are named for William Cattley, an English flower grower.

All of the cattleyas have enlarged, club-shaped stems that store water and food.

CATTLEYA

One to 3 thick leaves and 1 to 3 large flowers are borne on each stem. The flowers are white, pink, lavender or purple. The 3 broader parts of the flower are the petals, while the 3 narrower parts are sepals. The largest of the petals, called the lip, curls around to form a tube or pouch.

The cattleyas are native to Brazil, where most kinds grow in trees. Hundreds of different kinds have been cultivated in greenhouses.

The most common of the cultivated cattleyas (illustrated) has 2 to 5 flowers about 6 inches across. The petals and sepals are usually pinkish or lavender, with some yellow and orange showing inside the lip. The edge of the lip is ruffled. The stem is flattened, and the leaves are about 6 inches long.

cedar \ 'sēd-ər \

The trees generally known as cedars in the U.S. are evergreens related to pines. They provide good-smelling wood and oil.

All cedars are similar in shape. Each is slender, with a broad base tapering to a pointed tip. The trunk is short and thick, with scaly, ridged bark. The leaves are small, dark, yellow-green scales that grow flat against the twigs. In late summer oval cones about ½ inch long grow in clusters near the ends of the branches.

CEDAR

CELERY

The western red cedar (illustrated), is often called giant arborvitae. It is the source of most of the fragrant cedar wood used for houses, fences and roof shingles. The wood is soft, long-lasting and easy to work with. The Pacific coast Indians used it for war canoes. They also used the inner bark, beaten thin, to make bark cloth.

Western red cedars grow from 150 to 200 feet tall. Some live to be 1,000 years old. They are found in cool, moist soil from the southern tip of Alaska south to northern California. Most western red cedars grow in Washington and Oregon.

For another kind of cedar, see *incense cedar.*

celery \ 'sel-(ə)rē \

Celery is an important crop plant related to parsley and parsnips. It produces leaves and roots the first year, and flowers, fruit and seed the second year. Celery to be eaten is gathered at the end of the first year of growth.

Native to Europe and Asia, celery is a biennial that needs a cool climate and moist, rich soil. It is hard to grow in most home gardens. Commercially it is grown in rich, drained soil in the Great Lakes area and in California in the winter.

The short, thick stem of the celery plant is called the "heart." It is completely surrounded by the leafstalks or petioles. These stalks have heavy, thread-like veins that carry food and water to the toothed leaves and leaflets growing at the petiole ends. Celery plants may be over 2 feet tall, and are eaten raw or cooked.

Celery is usually picked at the end of the first growing season. At the end of the second year, if allowed to grow, the plant produces small, white flowers in umbrella-shaped clusters. The fruit is oval. The seeds are used, either ground or whole, in cooking.

celestial \ sə'les(h)-chəl \ poles

The celestial poles are imaginary points on an imaginary line extending out into space from both ends of the earth's axis.

The north celestial pole is marked by the polestar Polaris, also called the North Star, which can be seen in the sky almost directly above the North Pole. The north celestial pole helped early explorers and navigators by giving them a fixed spot in the sky by which to find their positions on earth.

There is no visible nearby star to mark the position of the south celestial pole.

CELESTIAL POLES

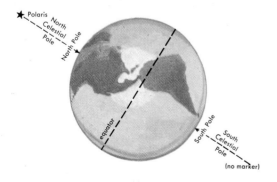

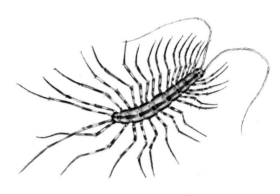

CENTIPEDE

centipede \ 'sent-ə-ˌpēd \

Centipedes are jointed-legged, invertebrate animals related to insects, spiders and crustaceans. Their closest relatives are millipedes, which look much like them but have shorter antennae and shorter legs.

Centipedes have long, jointed antennae, long, segmented bodies and up to 340 legs. The name centipede comes from the Latin words for "hundred" and "feet." There are over 1,000 kinds of centipedes.

According to the kind of centipede, there may be as few as 15 or as many as 170 segments in the body. Each of these segments has a pair of legs, except the last 2 and the segment behind the head. On this segment, the centipede has a pair of poison claws which it uses to kill the insects, worms, mollusks and other small animals that it eats. Except for certain kinds of centipedes found in tropical countries, its bite is not dangerous to man.

Centipedes are active only at night and can move very swiftly. Out of doors they live under stones or the bark of fallen trees.

The common house centipede (illustrated) lives in damp places. About 1 inch long, it has 15 pairs of very long legs. The last pair may be more than 2 inches long.

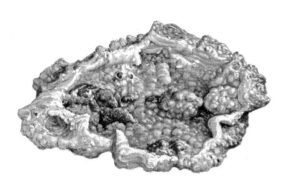

CHALCEDONY

chalcedony \ kal-'sed-ᵊn-ē \

Chalcedony is a kind of quartz mineral that does not form in crystals. It was named for Chalcedon, the town in Turkey near which it was first found. Chalcedony has been known for a long time and is mentioned in the last book of the New Testament. It is sometimes used to make necklaces, brooches and other ornaments.

Chalcedony forms when water containing silica fills holes or cracks in rocks or wood. In time, lumps or veins of chalcedony form. The petrified forests of Arizona were formed in somewhat the same way.

Usually brownish or gray, chalcedony may be white, dull green or blue-white. It is translucent, with a waxy luster. Various forms of chalcedony include the semiprecious stones agate, carnelian and onyx.

Deposits of chalcedony are found in Turkey, Scotland and Iceland. In the U.S., chalcedony is found in California and Colorado.

See *agate* and *onyx.*

chalcopyrite \ ˌkal-kə-'pīr-ˌīt \

Chalcopyrite is a valuable mineral because it is the most common copper ore. It may contain up to 35 percent copper. Chalcopyrite is found in veins or pockets, usually along with igneous rock, such as basalt or granite. Because it contains sulfur, chalcopyrite is sometimes called a sulfide ore.

When a chunk of chalcopyrite is freshly broken, its luster is a metallic, bright yellow. When left in open air, the surface often tarnishes first into iridescent colors and then into greenish-black. Some chalcopyrite contains small amounts of gold and silver.

Chalcopyrite is sometimes mistaken for iron pyrite, or "fool's gold." Iron pyrite, however, is a lighter color and much harder to scratch than chalcopyrite.

Chalcopyrite is widely distributed over the earth. In the U.S., large deposits are mined in Tennessee, Montana and Utah. The ore is also mined in England, Sweden, South Africa and Chile.

chalk

Chalk is the softest form of limestone. Very pure and fine-grained, it differs from other limestones only because it did not change into rock. Like all limestone, chalk is mostly made up of the mineral calcite.

Chalk was formed 130 million years ago during the Cretaceous Period. The Latin word for chalk, "creta," gave this period its name. Chalk formed when shells of tiny sea animals fell to the bottom of the sea,

CHALK

chameleon

CHAMELEON

CHAMOIS

forming beds of calcium carbonate or calcite.

All chalk beds were once at the bottom
of the sea, but some have since risen above
sea level. A large chalk bed in England
forms the famous White Cliffs of Dover.

Chalk is very brittle. It is easily broken
and ground into powder. Although chalk
is best known as a white stick used in
schools on chalkboards, it is also used in
paint, whitewash, fertilizer, putty and
tooth powder.

In the U.S., chalk is found in Texas,
Louisiana and Mississippi. In western
Kansas, fossils of flying reptiles and fishes
are preserved in chalk beds.

chameleon \ kə'mēl-yən \

True chameleons are reptiles belonging to
a large family of Old World lizards. There
are about 100 kinds of true chameleons,
found mostly in Madagascar or Africa. A
few live in Europe.

True chameleons range from 1½ to 24
inches long. All are tree lizards. Some have
prehensile tails that help them cling to
branches. Some have horns, and most
have a flaring crest at the back of the head.
All are covered with very small scales.

Chameleons can change their coloring
rapidly from dark to light to match their
surroundings, as can many other kinds of

lizards. The eyes of a true chameleon each
work separately. One eye can look up
while the other looks backward.

True chameleons are slow-moving animals with long, elastic, sticky tongues
which they shoot out to catch insects.
Most chameleons are born from eggs, but
some young are born alive.

The best-known kind of true chameleon is the common chameleon (illustrated). It lives in southern Spain, along
the coast of North Africa and as far east as
Palestine.

The chameleon most often sold in pet
stores is not a true chameleon but an
anole.

See *anole*.

chamois \ 'sham-ē \

A small goat-like antelope of the Pyrenees,
Alps and Carpathian mountain ranges of
Europe, the chamois is famous for its
surefootedness. It clambers easily over
sharp rocks and narrow ledges and jumps
nimbly across wide chasms. It is a favorite
of hunters, and its flesh and hide are
highly valued.

During the winter, chamois are most
often found in herds of 15 to 20 on forested
mountain slopes just below timberlines.
At dawn in the summer, they feed on
mountain herbs and flowers. In the win-

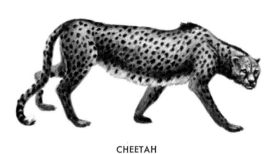

CHEETAH

ter, chamois feed on young pine shoots. During the day, they rest in the shade, chewing their cuds. During the summer or when frightened, chamois climb high into snowy, rocky areas.

About 2 feet high at the shoulder, the chamois is about 4 feet long and weighs 64 to 70 pounds. Both sexes have black horns that are never shed. Young chamois remain with their mothers for a year.

During the twentieth century, the chamois was successfully introduced into New Zealand.

cheetah \ 'chēt-ə \

The cheetah, a member of the cat family, is perhaps the fastest 4-footed animal alive. It can run up to 70 miles an hour for short distances. It climbs trees only when it cannot escape danger by running.

In India, cheetahs are tamed and kept for hunting. They are blindfolded and leashed until their owners see the animal being hunted. Then the cheetah is freed to chase and capture the hunted animal.

Weighing up to 100 pounds, the cheetah is about 7 feet long, including its long tail. Its height averages 2½ feet at the shoulder. Its legs are long and powerfully muscled. Unlike other members of the cat family, the cheetah cannot fully retract its claws.

At one time fairly common from south-

ern Africa to India, cheetahs were hunted for their skins until few were left. Today they are found only in the open hilly country and deserts of southern Africa and parts of India.

Cheetahs usually hunt in pairs during the day. Females have from 2 to 9 cubs. A cheetah's life-span is 15 to 20 years.

cherry tree

Cherry trees are members of the rose family and include both wild and culti-vated trees. They are valuable for both their lumber and their fruit. The wood of the cherry tree makes beautiful furniture.

Cherry trees were first cultivated in Europe and Asia but now grow in many countries. There are 3 types of crop cherry trees: the sweet, the sour (illustrated), and the "duke," a cross between the sweet and the sour.

All cherry trees have smooth, oval leaves with fine, saw-toothed edges. The pink or white flowers have 5 petals and bloom in clusters on the twig ends in early spring. The first is juicy and holds 1 large, hard, smooth seed.

The sour cherry tree is smaller than the sweet cherry tree. It can stand cold and heat better than the delicate sweet cherry. Sour or pie cherries are grown in Michi-gan, New York, Oregon, Wisconsin and

CHERRY TREE

Pennsylvania. One tree may yield from 15 to 40 quarts of cherries in 1 season. The U.S. is the world's leading producer of cherries.

chestnut

The chestnuts are tall, spreading trees, or shrubs, that are related to beech trees. They are native to Europe, Asia and North America.

Chestnuts have large oval leaves with coarse, saw-toothed edges. The flowers are tiny and cluster together on a long spike. The fruit is a nut covered with a prickly coat that splits open in autumn.

The American chestnut (illustrated) has been attacked by a fungus disease, and it is nearly extinct now. The Chinese chestnut, a kind much more resistant to diseases, has largely replaced it. Both are large and spreading shade trees.

The American chestnut may grow to 100 feet tall, with a trunk 8 to 10 feet around. Drooping flower spikes grow to a length of 3 to 8 inches. One, 2 or 3 glossy, reddish-brown nuts grow inside a spiny bur about 2 inches across.

The nut of the American chestnut contains crisp, white meat that is very good to eat, either raw or toasted. American chestnut wood is long-lasting and fairly soft. It is used for furniture, woodwork, fence posts and poles.

CHESTNUT

CHICKADEE

chickadee \ 'chik-ə-(,)dē \

The chickadees are small, active birds that are related to titmice. Their curiosity and acrobatic habits make them interesting birds to watch.

Chickadee bodies are round and chubby, ranging from 5 to 5½ inches in length. The tail is about 2 inches long, while wingspreads range to 8½ inches. The head is large and black-capped on adult birds, while the bill is small and sharp.

During the day, chickadees are active in woods, thickets and orchards. They eat insects and fruit, but seem to like soft acorns and poison ivy berries most of all. Chickadees do not migrate.

The most common kind of chickadee in America is the black-capped chickadee (illustrated). The black cap on its head extends from the bill to the upper part of the back.

The black-capped chickadee builds its nest in hollow trees, old woodpecker holes and bird boxes. The nests are made of mosses, feathers or fur. Six to 14 speckled eggs are laid once a year.

The black-capped chickadee is the state bird of Maine and Massachusetts.

The Carolina chickadee seen only in the southeastern states is similar to the black-capped chickadee but smaller.

CHICKWEED

chicken

The chicken is one of the most valuable birds in the pheasant family. It descended from jungle pheasants that lived in India more than 4,000 years ago. The chicken is raised for food, as a show bird and, in some countries, as a fighting bird. There are many breeds of chicken.

Chickens were first raised for fighting. In Rome they were used as temple sacrifices. Not until the Middle Ages were the meat and eggs widely used as food. Chickens were raised by South American Indians long before Columbus sailed. Early settlers brought the bird to North America.

Today, scientists use chicken eggs to study viruses. Drug companies also use eggs to make medicines. Ground eggshells make good fertilizer and are also used in making soap, paint and leather.

More chickens are raised in America than in any other country in the world. Over 2 billion chicks are hatched each year. Some chickens, grown for meat, are so heavy they cannot fly.

chickweed

Chickweeds are annual or perennial plants native to Europe and belonging to the family of flowers called pinks. There are about 100 kinds of chickweed, but only 1, the Easter bell, is a cultivated flower.

Chickweed has small, white, star-shaped flowers. Each flower has 5 deeply notched petals and 5 long sepals. The flowers grow in loose, branching clusters on the end of the thin stems. The stems are also branching and very weak.

The leaves of the chickweed are small, usually oval in shape, and opposite each other on the stem. The fruit is an oval, dry capsule growing on a short stalk from the place where the leaves join the stem. The fruit contains many seeds.

In mild climates, chickweed blooms throughout the year. In some cold regions, such as the northeastern U.S., chickweed can withstand heavy frosts.

The common chickweed (illustrated) is a garden pest and one of the worst lawn weeds. It grows all over the world, especially in damp ground, and is very hard to get rid of.

chicory \ 'chik-(ə)rē \

Chicory is a tall-stemmed perennial plant with ragged leaves that grow mostly low on the stalks, near the ground. It is both a weed and a crop. Chicory is native to Europe, where it is used as hay. Young, tender shoots are eaten in salads. The roots are sometimes ground and mixed with coffee or used instead of coffee. When mixed with coffee, ground chicory root

CHICORY

CHIMNEY ROCK

makes the coffee stronger and slightly bitter. In Belgium, the roots are boiled and eaten with butter.

The chicory plant grows 3 to 6 feet high. The bright blue flower heads are about 1½ inches across and bloom from June to October. They close in rainy or cloudy weather.

The thin leaves grow alternately along the stem, and have toothed or lobed edges. The stem is thick, hairy and filled with milky juice.

Chicory grows wild in Europe, Asia and North America. It is cultivated in the U.S. and southern Canada. It does best in limy soil and grows well either in fields or along roadsides.

chimney rock

A tall, thin shaft of rock that stands alone is called a chimney rock or stack. Chimney rocks are found along rugged seacoasts where waves beat constantly against tall cliffs. The weakest parts of the cliff break into pieces and are washed away. The strongest parts that remain become chimney rocks that are no longer connected with the mainland.

The tallest, straightest chimney rocks occur where a cliff had cracks or joints running up and down through it. Waves washed into the cracks, carrying along bits of sand. The grinding action of moving water and sand widened the cracks until some parts of the cliff broke away in square blocks. Chimney rocks are the parts that did not break away.

The Old Man of Hoy is a famous chimney rock 450 feet tall. It stands just off the coast of Hoy, one of the Orkney Islands near Scotland. Sailors have used it as a landmark for hundreds of years.

chimpanzee \ ˌchim-ˌpan-'zē \

The chimpanzee is the smallest and most intelligent of the anthropoid apes. Because chimps are affectionate, easily tamed and learn tricks quickly, they are favorite circus animals.

Chimpanzees have been known to make and use simple tools. Like man, they can make faces to show their feelings and can use reasoning to solve problems. Because their brains and bodies are something like man's, they are often used for scientific experiments.

Although chimpanzees can stand and walk on their hind legs, they usually walk on all fours. When standing, male chimps are from 4 to 5 feet tall. Females are usually smaller. Both sexes have long black hair on their bodies, but the skin on their faces, hands and feet is hairless. Skin colors range from pink to black.

CHIMPANZEE

Chimpanzees live in the forests of Africa, near the equator. Although they sleep in trees, they spend more time on the ground than any ape except the gorilla. Chimpanzees eat mainly fruit and plant shoots, but sometimes eat eggs, insects and birds.

In the wild, chimpanzees live about 35 years. In zoos, they may live as long as 40 years.

chinchilla \ chin-'chil-ə \

Making up a family of small rodents, chinchillas are native to the Andes Mountains in South America. The wild form is almost extinct, but chinchillas are raised commercially for their fur.

Chinchilla fur is probably the most expensive fur in the world. Over 135 chinchilla pelts are needed to make a fur coat. The soft, silky fur has been used for coats and trimmings for over 500 years, ever since the time of the Inca Indians.

Chinchillas are from 4 to 12 inches long, with tails almost as long as their bodies. In the wild state, they spend the day asleep in a burrow. At night they come out to feed on grain, seeds, fruit, moss and grass. In captivity, their diet includes yeast, molasses, carrots and orange juice.

The male chinchilla has only 1 mate. Females have 2 to 4 young at a time and have 2 or 3 litters a year. At 8 months chinchillas are fully grown and may live for 10 years.

Chinchillas are very excitable. If a mother is frightened, she may attack and kill her young.

The most valuable kind of chinchilla is the rare royal chinchilla (illustrated). It is 10 to 12 inches long.

chipmunk

Chipmunks are small, active members of the squirrel family. They are found in northern Asia, parts of Europe and all over North America. Although some kinds live in forests or mountains, most live in areas near people.

Chipmunks live in underground burrows with several entrances. When frightened, they dash quickly into one of these openings. When angry, they chatter loudly.

Adult chipmunks can often be coaxed to eat from a human hand. They feed on plants, grain, berries, seeds and nuts, which they carry or store in their large cheek pouches. Their chisel-like incisors, with which they open nuts, grow throughout their lives. Most chipmunks hibernate from early fall to March or April. Their life-span is 7 to 8 years.

In the eastern U.S., the eastern chip-

CHINCHILLA

CHIPMUNK

munk (illustrated) is the most familiar kind. It is 8 to 10 inches long, including its bushy 3-inch tail. Females often have 2 litters a year. Each litter contains 4 to 5 young, born furless and blind. If caught when young, an eastern chipmunk can be a good pet.

chiton \ 'kīt-°n \ (coat of mail shell)

A large group of sluggish marine mollusks, chitons live in the shallow waters of the Atlantic, the Pacific and other oceans. They have soft oval bodies covered by a hard shell. The hard upper surface of the shell is made up of 8 overlapping plates. There are over 600 kinds of chitons, and all but a few have a shell.

Chitons range in length from ½ inch to 6 inches. The underside of the chiton is made up of a flat, muscular foot. The head is very small.

The chiton burrows in soft mud or holds tightly to the undersides of rocks. If bothered, it rolls up in a ball so the soft underbody is protected. It moves about and feeds at night, scraping ocean plants off rocks with its rough, file-like tongue. A chiton may spend its entire life on 1 rock, or it may return to the same rock after feeding.

A fairly common kind of chiton is the hairy mopalia (illustrated). It is found from Alaska south to Lower California.

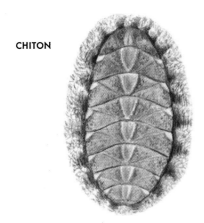

CHITON

CHLORITE

chlorite \ 'klōr-₁īt \

Chlorite is the name given to a group of minerals. All of them contain iron and aluminum mixed with silica and water, and many contain magnesium. Most chlorites are the products of the formation of other minerals. Chlorite may also form in cavities of igneous rocks.

Chlorites are almost always greenish, but rare forms may be brown, white, black, yellow or red. Light will shine through the edges of a piece of chlorite, but not through the center.

Like mica, chlorite can be split into thin sheets that will bend. A bent sheet of mica will snap back into shape when released, but a bent sheet of chlorite will remain bent.

Chlorite is common and widely distributed. Many schists and slates are green because of the flakes of chlorite they contain. Some forms of chlorite are old micas changed into chlorite by water.

chromite \ 'krō-₁mīt \

Chromite is a valuable mineral ore because it is the only source of the metal chromium. Chromium is added to steel to make it harder. Chromium is used to plate other metals because it does not rust and corrode easily. Furnaces used to melt other metals are lined with chromite

CHROMITE

bricks because they do not melt at temperatures hot enough to melt other metals.

Chromite is black or very dark brown. It is found in rock-like chunks or in grains. These grains are mixed with the sand on some beaches. The chromite makes the sand look black. Some chromite is slightly magnetic.

Chromite is also found near volcanoes or where great heat has melted old rocks and shaped new ones. Small amounts of chromite are found in Pennsylvania, Oregon and California. Larger amounts are mined in Russia, Cuba, Rhodesia, New Caledonia and the Philippines.

chromosphere \ˈkrō-mə-ˌsfir\

A chromosphere is a shell of hot gases that surrounds a star. However, chromosphere is most often used to mean the 8,000- to 10,000-mile-deep layer of reddish gases around the most important body in the solar system, the sun.

The chromosphere is the lowest layer of the sun's atmosphere, and is made up mostly of hydrogen. It surrounds the sun somewhat as the earth's atmosphere surrounds the earth. The chromosphere is seen most clearly during a total eclipse of the sun. As the chromosphere gives off radio signals, astronomers often study it with a radio telescope.

Because the gases of the chromosphere are so hot, they are very bright. The sun should never be looked at without special equipment to protect the eyes, even during a total eclipse.

The gases at the bottom of the chromosphere are hot enough to boil. Fast-moving currents of these gases rise to the top of the chromosphere and escape as fiery sprays. These sprays may be over 100,000 miles long before they fall back onto the sun's surface.

chrysanthemum
\kris-ˈan(t)-thə-məm\

Popular garden flowers, chrysanthemums were grown in Europe and Asia over 2,000 years ago. Today, there are over 150 kinds in gardens all over the world. The chrysanthemum is the national flower of Japan, where a holiday, the Feast of the Chrysanthemums, has been held for hundreds of years.

Most chrysanthemums are perennials. The stems are stiff and straight, with many branches. There are short kinds under a foot tall and others up to 3 feet tall. The plants may be grown from seed but are usually grown from cuttings.

The flower blooms in fall when days are short and evenings cool. The flower head has many rays or petals. These can be long

CHRYSANTHEMUM

CHUCKWALLA

CICADA

and thin, short and wide, or almost any shape in between. The flower can be tiny or almost flat, round as a ball or shaggy. Colors range from white through shades of pink, red, orange and copper.

In the U.S., the most common kind of chrysanthemum (illustrated) is often seen in flower shops. This chrysanthemum is believed to have originated in China.

chuckwalla \ 'chək-ˌwäl-ə \

One of the largest American lizards, the chuckwalla lives in the deserts in the southwestern U.S. It protects itself by running into a crack in a rock. There, it enlarges itself by taking a deep breath, wedging itself so tightly in the crack that it cannot easily be pulled out.

Chuckwallas are most common in the deserts of California, Utah, Arizona and Nevada. They are usually found in canyons, where there are rocks and caves for shelter. When unable to hide, a chuckwalla may defend itself by using its tail as a club.

The chuckwalla is usually about 16 to 18 inches long. Its skin is covered with very small scales, and hangs in a fold around its neck. Its head, legs and tail are stubby. As light and temperature change, a chuckwalla changes its color very slightly. Some adults are brownish, with striped tails. Young chuckwallas have dark bands crossing their bodies.

Once used as food by Indians, the chuckwalla feeds during the warmest part of the day. It eats plant materials, such as the leaves and flowers of the creosote bush.

cicada \ 'sə-'kād-ə \

Thick, heavy-bodied insects, cicadas make up a family of their own. They are best known for the loud, shrill noises made by the males in late summer. Widespread over most of the world, cicadas cause great damage to orchards.

Cicadas range in length from ½ to 1½ inches. The wings of adults are always longer than their bodies. The wide, blunt head has short antennae and bulging eyes. Males make their shrill noises by vibrating membranes over sound chambers on each side of their bodies.

Female cicadas damage trees by slitting twigs for a place to lay their eggs. After hatching, the nymphs fall to the ground where they burrow and remain from 4 to 20 years. During this time, the nymphs suck juices from plant roots. They also go through many molts while underground.

When fully grown, the nymph burrows to the surface of the ground. Then, the skin splits down the back and an adult comes out. Adult cicadas live about a week.

Many wild birds eat cicadas and help to control these pests.

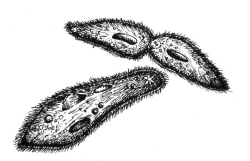

FISSION OF A CILIATE, PARAMECIUM

The periodical cicada (illustrated) is sometimes called the 17-year locust. It takes 13 to 17 years to come out of the ground. Periodical cicadas are common in the U.S. from Oklahoma eastward.

For another kind of cicada, see *harvest fly.*

ciliate \ 'sil-ē-ət \

The ciliates are a kind of protozoa, or 1-celled animal. They are among the largest and the most highly developed of all the protozoa.

Ciliates are named for their cilia, which are tiny, thread-like pieces of protoplasm. These may cover the entire cell surface or form only around the mouthparts of the animal. They are used like oars to push the animal through the water in which it lives.

The cilia are also used to brush food particles toward the mouthparts.

Most ciliates are oval in shape. Some live anchored down, but most swim free in fresh or ocean waters. A few ciliates are parasites.

Inside the ciliate are special parts. Each part does a certain thing. For example, one part takes in food while another part gets rid of body wastes.

Ciliates reproduce in either of 2 ways. One way is by fission (illustrated), a simple splitting into 2 parts.

Another way is by conjugation, a more complicated process. Here, 2 older cells come together and exchange material from their nuclei. Then, these cells separate and each of them splits into 2 younger, smaller cells.

The paramecium is a common kind of ciliate. *See* paramecium.

cinder \ 'sind-ər \ cone

A cinder cone is a steep, evenly sloped hill or mountain that surrounds the outlet of a volcano. The cone is made up of volcanic ash and other materials thrown out by the erupting volcano.

Included in a cinder cone are solid chunks of rock and cinders caught and held by the lava from the volcano.

The steep sides of a cinder cone slope up at an angle of 30 to 45 degrees.

cinnabar \ 'sin-ə-ˌbär \

Cinnabar is a valuable mineral ore because it is the chief source of the liquid metal, mercury.

Mercury is most familiar as the silver column in thermometers, but it is also used in medicines and paints. Mercury has an important place in the processes used to take gold and silver from their ores.

Cinnabar is a reddish ore that usually occurs in heavy, unevenly shaped lumps.

CINNABAR

Pure cinnabar is sometimes transparent, with a brilliant shine.

Like silver, cinnabar is found in veins. The veins occur in different kinds of rocks, but always near places where volcanoes or hot springs have been active.

Cinnabar is mined in Spain, Mexico, Russia, Yugoslavia and Italy. In Spain, it has been mined for over 2,000 years. In the U.S., cinnabar is mined in Alaska, Arizona, California, Idaho, Nevada, Oregon and Texas.

cirque \ 'sərk \

A cirque is a bowl-shaped hole near the top of a mountain at the head of a valley. Usually, a cirque is open on one side. The word "cirque" is a French word that means "stadium."

A cirque is formed by snow and ice wearing away rock. Every time water in the cirque freezes, the water expands and the cirque becomes larger. After many years, the ice breaks through a side of the cirque and moves down the mountain. This moving river of ice is a glacier.

In the past, climates have changed a great deal. Long ago glaciers covered most of the northern half of the U.S. When the glaciers finally melted, many empty cirques were left. When these cirques filled with water, they become lakes. Such lakes are called tarns.

CIRQUE

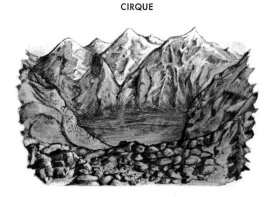

LEMON TREE   GRAPEFRUIT TREE

citrus \ 'si-trəs \ tree

Tropical evergreens, citrus trees have been grown for over 4,000 years. They are native to India and China. Oranges, tangerines, grapefruits, lemons and limes are well-known fruits from different citrus trees. In the 1890's, doctors found that the disease scurvy could be cured by drinking the juice of citrus fruits.

All citrus trees have shiny, dark green leaves that are leathery and pointed. Most of the branches have sharp spines. Citrus flowers are small and have 4 to 8 waxy white petals. The skins of the fruit are tough and oily. Each fruit is divided by membranes into 8 to 15 sections. Each section usually contains several large white seeds.

Orange and grapefruit trees grow 25 to 40 feet tall. Lemon and lime trees are generally smaller, 10 to 20 feet tall, and their branches are very thorny.

Citrus trees grow best in warm, moist places. They need warmth all year round and must be protected from frosts. A few kinds of orange trees have been developed that can stand cold weather.

Citrus fruits are valuable crops in Florida, Arizona, California and Texas. The fruits contain many minerals and vitamins, especially vitamin C.

CLAM

clam \ 'klam \

The clams make up a large group of bivalve mollusks. There are between 12,000 and 15,000 kinds. Most live in the ocean, but about 500 kinds live in fresh water. Several hundred kinds can be eaten. Certain kinds of clams, called oysters, grow pearls inside their shells.

Most clam shells are generally oval in shape and 1½ to 5½ inches long. The razor clam is longer and narrower, with squared-off ends.

Most shells are fairly smooth, but some kinds are rough and knobby. Clam shells from the temperate zone are cream-colored, gray or brown. Some kinds from the tropics are yellow, pink or purple.

A clam's 2 shells are held together by a strong muscular hinge. The animal inside has a wedge-shaped foot for moving or digging into sand. There are 2 sets of gills and 2 tubes for carrying water in and out of the shell. Clams feed on small pieces of plant matter which they take in with water through 1 of their 2 tubes.

Clam eggs are fertilized in the water and develop into free-swimming larvae.

The hardshell clam (illustrated) is a popular food. It lives in shallow waters, on sandy or muddy bottoms, from Cape Cod to the Gulf of Mexico. It is also called the cherrystone clam, the littleneck clam and the quahog. The Indians, who gave it the name quahog, used the 5- to 6-inch shells as wampum or money, and as decorations.

clay mineral \ 'min-(ə-)rəl \

A clay mineral is any of many mixtures of particles smaller than grains of sand. All clay minerals are made up of different amounts of silica, aluminum oxide and water. Iron, magnesium and other substances may be present. Common clay is a well-known clay mineral, while kaolin and kaolinite are others.

Widespread and very useful, clay minerals are a major product in many countries. They are used in making bricks, ceramic tiles, china and porcelain, and in paints, paper and rubber. When wet, clay minerals are slippery, have an earthy odor and can usually be molded.

Clay minerals usually occur mixed with other minerals. They are formed in soils by the effects that rocks and hot and cold water have on each other. Clay minerals are often washed into streams and deposited on stream beds. They also form on the bottoms of lakes and quiet rivers.

See *kaolin.*

CRYSTALS OF CLAY MINERAL (KAOLINITE)

Cloud Formations

ALTOCUMULUS

CUMULONIMBUS

ALTOSTRATUS

CUMULUS

CIRROCUMULUS

NIMBOSTRATUS

CIRROSTRATUS

NIMBUS

CIRRUS

STRATOCUMULUS

cloud

A cloud is a huge group of tiny water droplets in the air. Clouds form when warm, moist air rises above the earth and contacts cooler air. The warm air holds more moisture than the cool air can. When the warm air is cooled by the cool air, condensation takes place and water droplets appear. If the temperature is below freezing, the water droplets become particles of snow or ice.

When the droplets become too large and heavy to remain suspended in the air, they fall from the cloud as raindrops.

A cloud looks white if it is thin enough to reflect or diffuse sunlight. It looks gray or black if it is dense enough to absorb sunlight.

The names given to clouds are descriptive. Stratus means layered. Cumulus means rounded or curling. Cirrus means feather-like. Nimbus means rainy. Alto- means fairly high, usually 2 to 3 miles above the earth's surface.

Altocumulus clouds are the highest of the rounded "cotton ball" clouds. They look fairly small because they are 2 or more miles up, and they are scattered over a large part of the sky. They usually indicate fair weather.

Altostratus clouds are formless, light gray layers that cover a large part of the sky. They are usually about 3 miles up, and they often appear before a rain. The sun or moon may be visible through these clouds, but no halo surrounds them.

Cirrocumulus clouds are small, parallel clouds that lie close together over a large part of the sky. They are about 4 miles up, and they usually indicate fair weather. A sky full of these clouds may be called a mackerel sky because they look a little like a school of fish.

Cirrostratus clouds are thin, milky layers, about 5 miles up. The sun or moon may be visible through them, surrounded by a halo. They usually forecast cloudy weather but no rain.

Cirrus clouds are the highest clouds visible. They are the partly transparent wisps of white that form, sweeping, feathery lines across the sky. Five to 6 miles high, they contain slender ice crystals rather than water droplets. They appear during fair weather, but they often foretell the appearance of lower, heavier clouds that may bring rain.

Cumulonimbus clouds are very tall, rolling masses of cloud that shade from white to dark gray. The base may be only 1½ miles up, while the top is 5 miles high. The base is usually flat, while the top is either rounded or shaped like a flattened anvil. Cumulonimbus clouds are often called thunderheads, and they usually indicate storms.

Cumulus clouds are large, white cloud masses with flat bottoms and puffy, rounded tops. They are 2 to 4 miles up, and they usually indicate fair weather.

Cumulus clouds are the most common of all clouds, and also the most beautiful. They constantly change shape as they sweep across the sky. On fine days they grow smaller and farther apart toward evening. Larger masses that increase in number foretell possible storms.

Nimbostratus clouds are dark gray cloud layers less than 2 miles up. They indicate that rain or snow is likely.

Nimbus clouds are the very low cloud masses from which rain or snow is falling, or is likely to fall.

Stratocumulus clouds are very long, white or grayish clouds that stretch across a large part of the sky. They are fairly flat on the bottom and rounded on top but are not tall. They are usually 1 to 2 miles up, and they often appear before rain or snow.

Fog is a cloud so low that it rests on the surface of the earth.

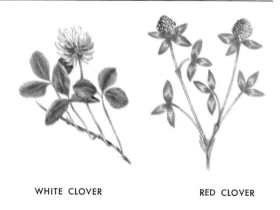

WHITE CLOVER   RED CLOVER

clover

Clovers are very useful plants that belong to the pea family. They grow all over the world in temperate zones. There are over 300 kinds of clover. Some are annuals and others are perennials. Some are weeds. Others are valuable crops that add nitrogen, a valuable fertilizer, to the soil.

Clovers have very small flowers crowded together in a rounded flower head. The compound leaves have finely toothed edges and are alternately placed. Usually, 3 leaflets are in a group, but there may be up to 6. Some people believe that finding a 4-leaf clover brings good luck.

Red clover (illustrated) is native to Europe and is the most common crop clover in the U.S. Its flower head is about 1 inch across, and its stem grows to 15 inches.

As it grows, red clover takes in nitrogen from the air and stores it. When a farmer plows the red clover under, it decays and gives up its nitrogen to the soil.

Red clover is also grown for cattle feed. Bees use its nectar to make honey. It is a biennial, living only 2 years.

Red clover is the state flower of Vermont.

White clover (illustrated) is a low, creeping perennial. It is a good ground cover and is often mixed with grass seed. The nectar makes very good honey. The flower head is smaller than that of red clover and has fewer florets. There are 3 leaflets on a stalk.

club moss

The club mosses make up a large group of primitive plants, sometimes called "ground pines." They are not true mosses. They are related to ferns, but are a more simple plant than ferns. Club mosses are low and creeping and may cover an entire forest floor.

Ancestors of today's club mosses included trees up to 100 feet tall. These plants, living hundreds of thousands of years ago, died out and decayed to help build up the beds of coal that developed over the centuries.

The main stem of club moss grows along the ground. From this stem, roots grow down and branches stand straight up. Both stems and branches are covered with tiny, narrow leaves and look like tiny pine twigs.

Some club moss branches may grow a club-shaped cone. This cone produces spores which grow into new plants without being fertilized. Other branches produce gametes, or eggs, that must be fertilized before a new plant can grow. True mosses and ferns also reproduce in both these ways.

HABITAT OF CLUB MOSS

COAL

coal

Coal is a sedimentary rock and one of man's most important fuels. It was formed from plant materials that decayed under water and were then pressed by the earth on top until they hardened.

Most coal in the eastern half of the U.S. was formed during the Pennsylvanian Period, about 300 million years ago. At that time the climate of the U.S. was much warmer than it is today. Many areas were swampy and overgrown with fern-like plants.

When the plants died, they sank to the bottom of the swamps, where they decayed. The carbon in the dead plants formed a black, mud-like material called peat. Peat is often burned as a low-grade fuel.

After many years, layers of clay and sand settled over the peat. The pressure of the layers hardened the peat into lignite, or soft brown coal, also used as a fuel. Then, as layers of sedimentary rock built up over the lignite, it hardened into bituminous coal (illustrated). Today, over 90 percent of the coal mined and used as fuel is bituminous coal.

Some deposits of bituminous coal were in areas that folded into mountains, as in Pennsylvania. The extra heat and pres-

sure that folded the land formed anthracite coal from the bituminous coal. Anthracite coal is the purest and hardest of all coals. It burns with less smoke and ash than any other coal.

coal sack

A coal sack is a dark cloud, or nebula, of gases or cosmic dust in deep space. Such a cloud absorbs, or covers up the light from stars behind it. A coal sack cannot be seen clearly without a powerful telescope.

One coal sack is in the constellation Cygnus near the blue star Deneb. Another coal sack is near the arms of the constellation called the Southern Cross. This coal sack is visible only from the southern hemisphere.

A group of coal sacks appears to divide the Milky Way. A coal sack called the Horse-head Nebula is in the constellation Orion. It can be seen through a small telescope as a black cloud against a background of hot, glowing gas.

coatimundi \ kə-ˌwät-ē-ˈmən-ˌdē \

The coatimundis are small mammals related to raccoons. They live in warm jungles from the southwestern U.S. through Mexico, Central and South America. They are very noisy, restless animals. The males live alone except at mating

COATIMUNDI

COCKATOO

time, but the females live in groups, with younger animals and other females.

Coatimundis are from 21 to 26 inches long and weigh from 24 to 28 pounds. The tail is unusual because it may be longer than the body. Coatimundi fur is brown with white on the chest and throat. The bushy tail is ringed with brown and yellow. The feet have long toes and sharp, strong claws.

Coatimundis feed on fruit, young birds, eggs, lizards and insects. They often climb trees in search of food. One of their favorite foods is the iguana lizard.

There are 2 kinds of coatimundi. One kind has red fur around its nose, and the other (illustrated) has white fur around its nose. In most other ways the 2 kinds are alike. If they are caught when young, coatimundis can be tamed. They are often kept as pets in South American Indian villages.

cockatoo \ 'käk-ə-ˌtü \

These birds, often seen in zoos, are members of the parrot family. Although a cockatoo looks something like a true parrot, it has a long crest of pointed head feathers which it can raise and lower. True parrots do not have such crests.

Cockatoos may be white, red, black, rose, gray and other colors.

Most kinds of cockatoos live in large, noisy flocks. Their call is a loud, shrill scream. Their food is seeds, nuts and fruit. All cockatoos have sharp, hooked beaks. They chip open their food, then they dig out pieces with their long, thick tongues.

Cockatoos nest in holes in high trees, lining the hole with wood chips. They feed their young with food that they first swallow and partially digest.

Although cockatoos are easily tamed, they cannot learn to talk and are noisy pets.

The largest cockatoo is the great black or palm cockatoo (illustrated), which lives in the forests of New Guinea. It is about 32 inches long, and it lives alone, rather than in flocks.

cockleshell \ 'käk-əl-ˌshel \

Cockleshells are saltwater clams and are near relatives of oysters. There are several hundred kinds of cockleshells. In some areas, especially in Europe, cockleshells are often used as food.

The shells of these clams vary from 2 to 6 inches in length, and may be very colorful. Shapes range from almost round to almost flat. The shells have a raised hump where the 2 halves join. Lines,

COCKLESHELL

called ribs, stretch from this hump to the outer edges, which may be toothed or scalloped.

Cockleshells are usually found in shallow waters along seashores. They burrow in the sand or mud, coming out as the tide comes in. Very active animals, cockleshells move rapidly over the wet sands, using a long, strong, pointed foot to push them along. They feed on plankton.

In the U.S., the common or yellow cockleshell (illustrated) is found from the Carolina coast on southward. The rounded heart-shaped shells are about 3 inches long and have several ribs. The outer edges of the shell are jagged and saw-toothed.

cockroach \ 'käk-ˌrōch \

Insects related to the grasshoppers, cockroaches are among the oldest creatures on earth, having existed for millions of years. They have flat bodies and small heads with chewing mouthparts and long antennae. Most are ½ to 1½ inches in length. Some can fly. Others lack wings but run swiftly on their long legs.

Although cockroaches are most common in the tropics, they live in nearly all parts of the world. In the cooler parts of the temperate zone, they live inside houses or barns, or burrow in the soil. During the day, they hide in dark, moist places. They move about at night, feeding on both plant and animal matter. Some kinds are pests that destroy stored food, clothing and books. Other kinds are known to spread diseases.

The female lays her eggs in a case or pod that she carries with her during at least part of the incubation period. The young are nymphs that look like adults but are smaller and lack wings.

The American cockroach (illustrated) is native to the New World tropics but it has become widespread in many other areas. It may be over 1½ inches long. This cockroach is most often seen in houses, where it feeds on food scraps and clothing. The American cockroach may transmit disease by carrying germs on its feet and body.

cockscomb \ 'käk-ˌskōm \

Garden flowers that make up a group of tropical plants, cockscombs have large, showy clusters of flowers. Originally tropical weeds, cockscombs have become popular garden plants grown from seed.

Cockscombs grow from 3 to 4 feet tall. Each flower is made up of many small, straw-like bracts crowded closely together in the shape of a plume or fan. The flowers may be yellow, purple, green or white. When picked, cockscombs last much longer than other flowers.

COCKROACH

COCKSCOMB

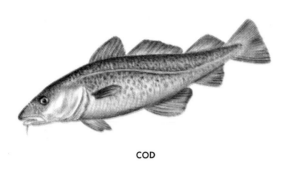

COD

The flowers of the most familiar kind of garden cockscomb (illustrated) are grouped in a ruffled crest that looks like the comb of a rooster. In most parts of the U.S., this cockscomb is planted outdoors in the late spring and blooms in late summer. It is usually placed at the back of a flower bed, with shorter plants in front.

cod

Making up a family of important food fish, cod live in the cooler, northern parts of the Atlantic and Pacific oceans. Some are sold as fresh fish, and some are dried or frozen. Their livers are the source of vitamin-rich cod-liver oil.

All cod have long bodies and small heads. Their scales are small and smooth, and a curving line shows up clearly along each side of the body. The 3 separate dorsal fins and the 2 anal fins are soft rather than spiny.

Cod swim in large, swift-moving schools, in fairly deep water. They eat smaller fish and other marine animal life. One female may lay as many as 8 million eggs.

The largest and perhaps most valuable kind of cod is the Atlantic cod (illustrated), which is common off the coast of New England and eastern Canada. It sometimes grows to 6 feet in length and can weigh as much as 200 pounds. Most Atlantic cod brought in by commercial fishermen are 2 to 3 feet long and weigh 10 to 25 pounds.

Atlantic cod, haddock, pollock, ling and tomcod are all well-known members of the cod family.

For other kinds of cod, see *burbot, haddock* and *hake.*

coelacanth \ 'sē-lə-ˌkan(t)th \

This odd-looking fish was known only from 60 million-year-old fossils until a few years ago. In 1938 fishermen caught a living coelacanth in the deep water of the Indian Ocean. It was 5 feet long and weighed 127 pounds. Since then, a few others have been caught and studied.

The coelacanth has strong, limb-like fins. It probably uses the pelvic and pectoral fins as legs when it moves along the bottom of the ocean. Scientists believe that other ancient fish used similar fins to pull themselves up on land. They also believe that such fins developed into the legs of land animals.

The coelacanth has bones in its skull and fins, but the rest of its skeleton is cartilage. Its lungs and heart are simpler than those of modern fish. The tail is broad and muscular, and the body is covered with large, overlapping scales.

Very few forms of life have survived for so many millions of years and changed so little as the coelacanth.

COELACANTH

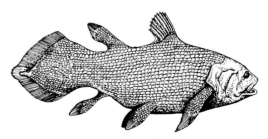

COFFEE TREE

coffee tree

Making up a group of tropical evergreen trees, coffee trees are cultivated for their berries, which contain coffee beans. The beans are dried, roasted and ground before they are made into the coffee people drink. One coffee tree produces 1 to 2 pounds of coffee beans each year. The beans contain caffeine, a nerve stimulant.

The first people to use coffee to make a beverage were the Arabians. The drink was introduced into Europe soon after 1600. Today the U.S. uses about half of all the coffee the world produces.

One kind of coffee tree (illustrated) produces most of the coffee used today. It grows to 40 feet high. To make it easier to pick the berries, most trees are trimmed to about 15 feet.

The glossy, dark green leaves grow in pairs along the twigs. Clusters of fragrant, white flowers appear along the twigs. The plump berries grow between the pairs of leaves. The berries turn bright red when they are ripe. Each berry contains 2 coffee beans.

Coffee trees first grew in Africa, but today most coffee comes from Brazil and Central America. The trees need rich, moist soil and a mild climate. They grow best on mountainsides about 1,500 feet above sea level.

col \ 'käl \

A col is a gap or pass high in rugged mountain country. In French, "col" means neck. Our word "collar" comes from the same word.

A col is very high, but it is not quite as high as the peaks near it. It occurs where 2 streams begin. One stream carries water down one side of a mountain range. The other stream carries water down the other side. Neither stream crosses the mountain range. Both carry away soil and stones so that the space between them is pulled down a little.

Cols are found in steep-sided, geologically young mountains like the Rockies, the Alps and the Himalayas.

St. Bernard's Col is a pass in the Alps that separates France from Italy. The South Col of Mt. Everest is one of the routes that mountain climbers take to the peak.

coleus \ 'kō-lē-əs \

Making up a group of annual and perennial plants widely grown for their colorful leaves, coleus belongs to the mint family. These plants are native to tropical and subtropical areas of the continents of Asia, Africa and Australia.

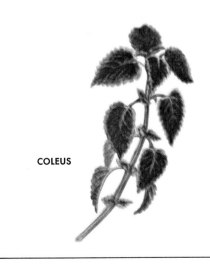

COLEUS

Coleus leaves combine different shades of purple, yellow and red with lines or borders of green or white. They have saw-toothed or scalloped edges. They are often ruffled and curled.

Coleus plants grow 2 to 3 feet tall if not cut back. They may be started from seeds. Cuttings take root quickly when planted in damp sand. Since even a light frost will kill them, they are usually grown indoors as house plants. They can be moved outside during the warm summer months and brought in again in autumn.

Most coleus plants grown in the U.S. have been developed from a kind found on the island of Java. The most commonly cultivated kind of coleus (illustrated) has blue or lilac flowers that are pinched off when they appear. The leaves are opposite, oval and richly colored.

columbine \ 'käl-əm-ˌbīn \

Perennial plants related to the buttercups, columbines are popular as garden border and rock garden flowers. The delicate flowers have 5 petals that form hollow tubes. The end of each tube contains a tiny drop of nectar. The tubes extend up, while the sepals hang down.

Columbine flowers are pink, red, yellow, white, blue or purple. The plants grow

COLUMBINE

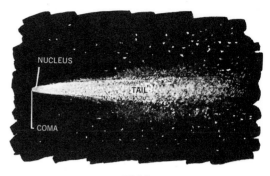

COMA

1 to 3 feet tall. Columbine leaves are divided into 3 parts and look something like a bird's footprint. Columbine seeds develop in small, dry pods.

In the U.S., the most common columbine (illustrated) is a wild flower that grows in wooded areas throughout the eastern half of North America. The flower is reddish on the outside and yellow inside.

Another kind of columbine, the Rocky Mountain columbine, is the state flower of Colorado.

coma \ 'kō-mə \

A coma is the circle of hazy brightness around the head or nucleus of a comet. The coma generally becomes larger as a comet approaches the sun.

A comet may have 1, 2 or 3 tails, or no tail at all, but it always has a coma. The coma makes it possible to tell a tailless comet from a planet or star.

Astronomers are not entirely sure what makes up a coma. They believe that it may be a cloud of small particles and vaporizing gases much like those in a comet's tail. They know the coma is not solid because they can see bright, faraway stars through it.

The meteorites that strike the earth may be fragments of the glowing comas or tails of old comets.

COMPOSITE CONE

comet \ 'käm-ət \

Comets are small heavenly bodies that move around the sun in an elliptical, or oval, orbit. At one end of its orbit, a comet is near the sun. At the other end of its orbit, a comet is far away from the sun. The time it takes a comet to make 1 orbit of the sun is called its period.

The solid, glowing head of a comet is called the nucleus. Scientists believe that the nucleus is made up of solid matter held together by frozen material, something like a dirty snowball. Around the nucleus is a circle of brightness called the coma. Streaming away from the nucleus may be 1 or more glowing tails hundreds of millions of miles long. The tail is made up of dust particles forced out from the coma by pressure of sunlight. The tail appears longest when the comet is nearest the sun. It always points away from the sun.

About 1,000 comets are known. They are usually named for the astronomers who discovered them. Only a few comets can be seen without a telescope.

Halley's comet takes about 76 years to make 1 orbit, or period. In 1910, it was near the center of the solar system and could be clearly seen from the earth. Halley's comet is expected to return again in 1986.

The shortest-known period is that of Encke's comet, which completes 1 orbit in 3.3 years.

composite \ käm-'päz-ət \ cone

A composite cone is a volcanic mountain built up of layers of lava and cinders.

The cinders in a composite cone are dry, odd-shaped fragments of rock thrown out of the crater of the volcano when it erupts. The lava is molten rock that flows out of the crater and down over its sides. The composite cone slopes gently near the base but rises to a steep peak at the top.

Mt. Rainier in Washington and Fujiyama in Japan are composite cones.

conch \ 'kängk \

The conchs make up a group of the largest gastropod mollusks found near American coasts. Their thick-walled shells are up to 12 inches long and weigh as much as 5 pounds.

Some conchs are good to eat. In the West Indies they are made into salads and chowders. The shells are sold as ornaments, or are shipped to factories where they are used in making porcelain.

Conchs live in warm, shallow parts of the sea, around coral reefs and where the ocean floor is sandy. They are snail-like animals with large eyes on stalks and 1

CONCH

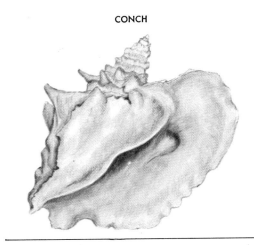

CONCRETION
(FLINT IN CHALK)

narrow but muscular foot. More active than most mollusks, conchs can move about quite rapidly.

Some kinds of conchs are fierce fighters that kill and eat clams and other mollusks as large as themselves. Other kinds are scavengers that eat only dead fish and small marine life.

Conch shells have cone-shaped spires and long, narrow openings. Mature shells have wide-spreading outer lips that are notched or ruffled along the edges.

The shell of the queen conch (illustrated) is 8 to 12 inches long. This conch is common in the West Indies and off the coast of southern Florida.

concretion \ kän-'krē-shən \

A concretion is an odd-shaped but usually rounded lump of hard rock found inside another rock. Concretions are made up of minerals that were once dissolved in water. The minerals were deposited, a layer at a time, around some object.

Concretions are found in sedimentary rocks such as sandstone, limestone and shale. These rocks were once beds of mud or sand at the bottom of a body of water. If a concretion is broken open, a fossil shell is sometimes found at its center.

Egg-shaped concretions found in Alberta, Canada, contain fossilized lobster claws. Longer, flattened concretions found in stream beds in the midwestern U.S. contain fossil prints of lacy ferns.

Concretions are nearly always harder than the rock that surrounds them. They often remain after the other rock has been broken up and carried away by wind or water erosion.

condor \ 'kän-dər \

Condors are the largest flying birds in the world and are native to America. They measure up to 5 feet from head to tail. They have wingspreads up to 12 feet and weigh 20 to 25 pounds.

Like other birds of the American vulture family, most condors eat dead animals. The huge birds soar in high, wide circles as their keen eyes search for food.

A condor's nest is usually built on a rocky mountain ledge 10,000 to 16,000 feet above sea level. One or 2 eggs are usually laid each year. Both parents care for the young birds at least 6 months.

The rarest of the 2 kinds of condors is the California condor. Once common from the state of Washington to Lower California, this bird is nearly extinct. Today, it lives only in a few counties of the state of California.

The Andean condor (illustrated) lives in the Andes mountains of South America, from Colombia south through Argentina.

CONDOR

Slightly larger than the California condor, this bird sometimes attacks living fawns and lambs. The Andean condor is pictured on the official seals of Colombia, Bolivia, Ecuador and Chile.

cone (cone shell)

Cones make up a group of tropical gastropod mollusks. Shell collectors value their beautifully patterned, glossy shells. The living cone is a snail-like animal that lives among coral reefs in warm seas.

Cones feed on marine worms, tiny fish and smaller cones. Some kinds of cones have a poisonous venom which they use to kill their prey. They inject this poison through sharp-pointed, hollow teeth similar to a snake's fangs. A large cone may produce enough venom to kill a human being. The venomous cones are found only in the Indian Ocean and in the Pacific Ocean near Asia.

The smooth, tapering shells are ¼ to 3 inches long, with a very narrow opening. Most are marked with attractive patterns of spots or stripes. One rare kind, called the glory-of-the-sea cone, is one of the most valuable of all seashells. Specimens have been sold for more than $1,000.

The alphabet cone shell (illustrated) is the largest of the cones found off Florida and in the West Indies. It is usually 2 to 3 inches long.

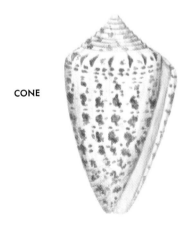

CONE

CONGLOMERATE

conglomerate \ kən-'gläm-(ə-)rət \

Conglomerate is a sedimentary rock made up of pebbles and small rocks. It is held together by a natural kind of cement made up of sand, clay minerals and calcite.

The materials in conglomerate were once carried by water. They dropped to the bottom of a stream, lake or ocean. The weight of other materials that dropped on top of them packed the materials together.

The pebbles in conglomerate are usually pieces of harder rocks such as quartz and granite. They have been worn smooth by running water in streams. The pebbles may be of the same or of different kinds of rocks.

Puddingstone is the name of a conglomerate found in New England. It contains colorful dark and light pebbles all about the same size.

continental \ ,känt-°n-'ent-°l \ shelf

A continental shelf is a gently sloping part of the ocean floor that lies next to a large land mass. The shelf extends out from shore to a depth of about 600 feet, where a steeper slope begins. In some places a continental shelf is only a few miles wide. In other places it is more than 800 miles wide.

Most of the plant and animal life of the ocean floor is crowded onto the shallower parts of a continental shelf. The richest fishing grounds lie over the shelf.

Scientists are not sure how continental shelves came to be. They may exist because the water level rose, or because land masses dropped down. They may be made up of sediments piled up by waves, or of sediments pushed off the land by glaciers.

continental \ˌkänt-ᵊn-'ent-ᵊl\ slope

A continental slope begins where a continental shelf ends. The slope drops 12,000 to 30,000 feet, and forms the walls of the deep basins that make up most of the ocean floor. In many places, deep, rugged canyons occur in the steep face of a continental slope. Underwater plant life ends where a slope begins, but some animal life is present.

coot \'küt\

Coots make up a group of medium-sized, dark-colored birds of the rail family. They have lobes on the sides of their toes to help them swim and to help them walk on soft mud without sinking in.

On dry land, coots can run very fast. They are excellent swimmers and usually nod their heads as they swim. Although coots are not strong fliers, some migrate long distances.

Coots are noisy, sociable birds that travel and feed in flocks. They eat fish and small aquatic animals. Coots nest near each other, among reeds and cattails at the edges of shallow lakes or streams.

The American coot (illustrated) has a white, pointed bill and a patch of bare brown skin between its eyes. It ranges from Canada to Ecuador, sometimes wintering in Hawaii. Other kinds of coots are found in Europe and Asia and throughout most of South America.

copepod \'kō-pə-ˌpäd\

Tiny relatives of shrimps and lobsters, copepods make up a group of crustaceans that live in both fresh and salt water. They help make up plankton, the food supply of many fish and other water animals.

Although copepods vary in size and shape, nearly all of them have 6 legs that they use as oars when swimming. The body is often pear-shaped. Like other crustaceans, copepods have exoskeletons.

A great many kinds of copepods are parasitic on larger aquatic animals. Other kinds of copepods feed on microscopic animals and plants smaller than they are.

The water flea (female, illustrated) is

COOT

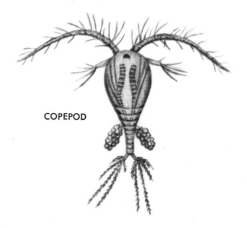

COPEPOD

a common freshwater copepod. The mature female carries bundles of eggs on each side. The water flea is greenish in color and about 1/10 inch long. It has just 1 eye in the middle of the front part of the body. Water fleas are most often found in ponds and lakes.

copper

Of all the metals used by man, copper is second only to iron in usefulness. It is soft and easy to work with. Copper is an excellent conductor of electricity. It is used in nearly all electrical wires and appliances. Copper is used to make 1-cent coins. It is combined with other metals to make alloys such as brass and bronze.

The primitive people of Asia learned to use copper before any other metal. It was the only metal that the North American Indians taught themselves to use.

Copper occurs naturally in a pure state more often than other metals do. Pure copper is found in rounded lumps, in flat plates or in branching forms that look like twisted wires or twigs. Freshly broken surfaces show the bright, reddish color of a new penny. Exposed to the air, copper turns black, sometimes with spots of blue or green.

Most of the copper used by modern industry is removed from ores such as chalcopyrite, cuprite and chalcocite.

COPPER

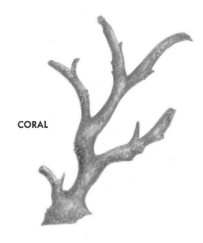

CORAL

coral \ˈkȯr-əl\

Corals are small ocean animals that take lime from seawater and use it to build cup-like skeletons around their soft bodies. When a coral animal dies, its skeleton remains and another coral animal builds on top. In this way large colonies may build up, and whole islands and long reefs of coral rock are formed.

Corals are closely related to the sea anemones, larger flower-like creatures that live on the ocean floor.

A living coral animal looks like a tiny flower. It has a fringe of waving tentacles around its mouth opening. Coral animals feed on copepods, tiny crustaceans that they paralyze with their tentacles.

Jewelry is made from pink or red precious coral (illustrated), which is found in the Mediterranean Sea and off the coast of Japan. Other kinds of coral, mostly gray or white, are called stony coral, brain coral, star coral and sea fan. All are found in warm, fairly shallow seas.

For a kind of coral, see *sea fan*.

cordillera \ˌkȯrd-ᵊl-ˈ(y)er-ə\

A cordillera is a series or chain of connected mountain ranges.

The word "cordillera" means "rope" in Spanish. The men who first explored

CORMORANT

South America called the long belt of mountains that runs from one end of the continent to the other "Los Cordilleras de los Andes." The word "cordillera" was later used to describe mountain ranges in other parts of the world.

Three cordilleras occur in the western part of the U.S. They are the Rocky Mountains, the Sierra Nevada and the Coast Range. Together they make up what is sometimes called the cordilleran region of North America.

cormorant \ 'kȯrm-(ə-)rənt \

Long-necked, dark-colored birds closely related to the pelicans, cormorants live along seacoasts and lakes. They dive and swim rapidly under water to catch the fish and eels on which they feed. Cormorants use both their legs and their wings when swimming.

In Japan and China fishermen still tame and train cormorants to dive from their boats and bring back fish. Thongs tied loosely around the birds' throats keep them from swallowing their catch.

Cormorants are 1½ to 3½ feet long. All 4 toes are webbed. When cormorants nest in cliffs, they build their nests of seaweed and guano. Tree nests are built of twigs. Two to 6 eggs are pale blue or green.

Guano is a valuable fertilizer made of cormorants' droppings. The guano is collected from rocky islands off the coast of Peru where great flocks of cormorants have nested for centuries.

The double-crested cormorant (illustrated) lives along the Atlantic coast of North America.

corn

A plant of the grass family, corn is one of the world's most important food crops. It is the only cereal grain native to the western hemisphere. Wheat, oats, rice and other cereal grains were brought to America by Europeans. Today, the U.S. produces over half the world's corn.

Like other grasses, corn has a jointed stem and ribbon-like leaves with parallel veins. The number of leaves on a corn plant varies according to the type of corn, and ranges from 8 to 48. The height of the stalk varies from 2 to over 20 feet.

One corn plant bears both staminate and pistillate flowers. The staminate flowers grow on the tassel at the top of the stalk. The pistillate flowers are the young ear and its silken tuft. The ear is covered with shucks, or husks, that are a kind of leaf. The wind carries pollen from the tassel to the silken tuft.

The main types of corn are dent corn, flint corn, flour corn (illustrated), sweet corn and popcorn. From each of these types, hundreds of hybrids have been developed.

CORN

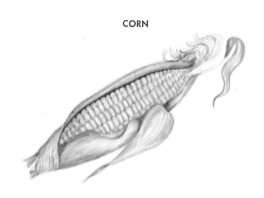

CORONA

corona \ kə-'rō-nə \

The corona is the outermost layer of the sun's atmosphere. It can be seen only during a total eclipse of the sun.

Astronomers believe that the corona is made up of electrically charged particles. They also believe that it reaches for millions of miles beyond the layer of luminous gases around the sun.

The corona appears pearly-gray or greenish-white. Its outer edge fades away. The shape depends on sunspot activity. During times of few sunspots, long rays or streams of light come from the equatorial region of the sun. Shorter, curved rays come from the polar regions. This makes the corona appear uneven.

When there are many sunspots, the equatorial rays are shorter and the polar rays are longer. This makes the corona appear circular.

The brightness of the corona as seen from the earth is about half the brightness of the full moon.

corundum \ kə-'rən-dəm \

Ordinary corundum (illustrated) is usually a hard, brown or gray mineral. It occurs in igneous, sedimentary and metamorphic rocks. Red rubies, blue sapphires and black, gritty emery are all different forms of corundum.

The different colors of corundum are due to small amounts of different elements present as impurities. Perfectly pure corundum would be colorless.

Rubies are corundum crystals tinted red by a little chromium. Sapphires contain a little iron or titanium. Emery, widely used in grinding and polishing other materials, is grainy corundum mixed with iron oxide.

Because it is very hard, corundum is used to make bearings for fine watches and some kinds of machines. It is the only fairly common mineral that is almost as hard as diamond.

Most rubies and sapphires have been found in Ceylon, Burma and Thailand. A few have been found in Montana and North Carolina. Emery comes from Turkey and Greece.

See *ruby* and *sapphire*.

cosmic \ 'käz-mik \ dust

Cosmic dust is made up of tiny particles of solid matter in space. Along with clouds of gas, cosmic dust occurs in the vast spaces between the stars. Astronomers know where it is because it hides the stars behind it, or causes starlight to appear red.

Although astronomers know that most of the gas is hydrogen, they are not so

CORUNDUM

sure what the cosmic dust is. Some think the particles are bits of ice. Others think they may be bits of the heavier elements such as iron.

Both cosmic dust and the gas with it seem to be the remains of old stars that exploded. A new star may be born when a cloud of gas and cosmic dust begins to whirl around. As it whirls, the cloud develops a center of gravity that pulls the scattered material together.

Astronomers know that cosmic dust is most plentiful at the outer edge of our galaxy, and that new stars are most likely to appear there.

cotton

Cottons make up a group of annual or perennial plants native to the tropics. Certain kinds of cotton are cultivated for their fluffy, white fibers which are used to make cotton cloth. The fibers are attached to the seeds inside egg-shaped capsules called bolls that burst open when ripe.

Cattle feed, fertilizer, salad oil, soap and many other useful products are made from cotton seeds after the fibers are removed from them.

The cottons are stiff, bushy plants with 3-lobed leaves. Cotton flowers have 5 yellow-white or pinkish petals. The bolls are the fruit.

COTTON

COTTONWOOD

Upland cotton (illustrated) is an important farm crop in the southern U.S. It grows 2 to 5 feet tall. The leaves are 3 to 6 inches wide. Many hybrid forms have been developed.

Cottons need a long growing season with a great deal of hot weather. The plants will bloom in the northern U.S., but the bolls ripen only in the southern states. Other areas where cotton is grown commercially are India, China, Egypt, Brazil and southern Russia.

cottonwood \ 'kät-ᵊn-ˌwu̇d \

Cottonwoods are fast-growing trees belonging to the willow family and closely related to poplars. Cottonwoods are found in nearly all parts of North America, from Alaska south to the middle of Mexico.

The wood of these trees is used as lumber and pulpwood. Cottonwoods are valued as shade trees and windbreaks on western prairies where few large trees are able to grow. The cottonwood is the state tree of Kansas and Wyoming.

The name "cottonwood" comes from the cottony tufts of fluffy fibers attached to the seeds. In early summer, the seeds and their fibers fall off the tree and drift with the wind. The flowers are tassels that hang down from the twigs in spring. Cottonwoods grow from 40 to 100 feet tall.

COUGAR

The leaves of the eastern cottonwood (illustrated) and of most other kinds are triangular and have toothed edges. A few kinds of cottonwoods have narrow leaves like the willows.

The eastern cottonwood is common in the U.S. from Pennsylvania to Texas. Its soft wood is used to make pulp products, excelsior and packing boxes.

cougar\ 'kü-gər\ (catamount, mountain lion, panther, puma)

The cougar is one of the largest animals of the cat family and is native to North America. Five to 6 feet long and weighing 150 to 200 pounds, a cougar is strong enough to kill a moose or a horse. Its loud scream can be hair-raising. It is very good at climbing and leaping.

Cougars once lived throughout most of the U.S. Today they are found only in wild, mountain areas of the western U.S. and Canada. They hide in caves or underbrush during the day and hunt at night. They may roam as far as 50 miles to kill deer, antelope or a rancher's sheep or calves. Cougars also feed on small animals such as rabbits and birds.

Young cougars, called kits, are born in late winter or early spring. There are 1 to 5 kits in a litter. They stay with their mother for about 2 years. Cougars live to be about 20 years old.

counterglow\ 'kaunt-ər-,glō\

Counterglow is an oval area of faint brightness that is sometimes visible in the night sky. It is a part of the zodiacal light, a band of faint light that follows the yearly path the sun seems to make in the sky.

Counterglow is exactly opposite the sun, so it is seen in the part of the sky where the sun appeared to be 6 months earlier.

Because counterglow is so faint, it can be seen only at certain times. In summer and winter it is usually lost in the brightness of the Milky Way. Sky watchers usually look for counterglow in spring and fall.

Astronomers believe that counterglow is probably sunlight reflected from meteoric particles opposite the sun and outside the earth's orbit.

See *zodiacal light*.

cowbird\ 'kau-,bərd\

This bird of the North American blackbird family never builds its own nest. Instead, the female cowbird lays eggs in the nests of other birds. The other birds care for the young cowbirds and feed them, along with their own young.

Cowbird eggs often hatch before the other eggs in the borrowed nest. As a result, a young cowbird sometimes pushes the other young birds out of the borrowed nest.

COWBIRD

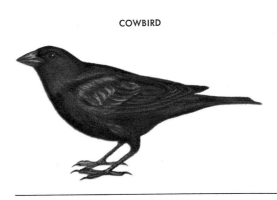

The male cowbird is black with a brownish head. The female is gray. Eight to 8½ inches long, cowbirds have a 3-inch tail and a wingspread of 13 inches.

Cowbirds often feed on the insects which collect on cattle. The Indians called cowbirds buffalo birds, since they followed the buffalo herds.

In spring and summer, cowbirds feed on insects in fields and meadows throughout central and southern Canada and most of the U.S. In the fall, large flocks of cowbirds migrate to the southern states and Mexico.

cowrie \ 'kau̇r-ē \

Cowries make up a group of tropical gastropod mollusks. Their attractive shells have been used as money by some primitive peoples. Other peoples, including the American Indians, used them as beads and ornaments.

The living cowrie is a snail-like animal that lives among coral reefs, in fairly deep, warm parts of the ocean. The young cowrie lives inside a spiral shell. As the animal grows older, the inner twists of the shell disappear so that only the outer lip remains. The mature cowrie has an unusually large mantle that spreads around and covers nearly all the outside of the shell.

COWSLIP

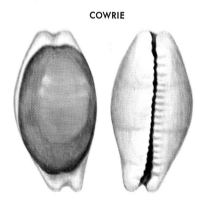

COWRIE

Cowrie shells are 1 to 4 inches long. All have a smooth, shiny surface like china. The colors and patterns of the shells vary greatly. Some kinds of cowrie shells are rare and valuable.

The chestnut cowrie shell (illustrated) is usually 1 to 2 inches long. It is sometimes found washed up on California beaches. Other cowries are found off Florida and in Asiatic waters.

cowslip \ 'kau̇-ˌslip \ (marsh marigold)

A perennial wild flower, the cowslip is related to the buttercup. The cowslip grows in marshy areas and along streams and blooms early in spring. It grows well in gardens if the soil is moist and soft.

Cowslips grow in bushy clumps 8 to 12 inches high. The thick stems are hollow. The bright green leaves are round or heart-shaped, with uneven edges. The bright yellow flowers are 1 to 2 inches across. They have no petals, but the 5 to 9 oval, yellow sepals are often mistaken for petals. Both leaves and flower parts are glossy. Cowslip seeds mature inside small dry pods.

The cowslip is found throughout eastern North America, as far south as the Carolinas and as far west as Nebraska. The cowslip also grows in Alaska.

COYOTE

CRAB

coyote \ 'kī-ˌōt \

The coyote is a fast-running, intelligent mammal related to the dog and wolf. It is known for its sad howl. It lives in open prairie country from Iowa to California and from Alaska to Central America. Its den is usually a burrow left by a prairie dog or badger.

In the evening, the coyote begins its "song." It starts with 3 short, rising barks, and ends with a drawn-out, sad howl. On moonlit nights 12 or more coyotes may "sing" together.

The coyote roams over a wide area. It hunts at night for rabbits and other small wild animals. It may also eat farmers' chickens.

A coyote can run as fast as 50 miles an hour. It is clever and usually avoids traps and hunters.

Coyotes mate for life. The female gives birth to 3 to 10 blind, helpless pups in early spring. When they are about 10 weeks old, the pups go with their parents on hunts. An adult weighs about 40 pounds and is 2 feet high at the shoulder.

crab

Crabs make up a large group of crustaceans that live in fresh water, in the ocean and on land. Most kinds burrow in sand or mud to escape their enemies. Some kinds can run rapidly, sideways, and some are fierce fighters. Some are very popular as food.

Crabs have 3-part bodies. The head and thorax are covered by a broad, flattened shell called a carapace. The eyes of most crabs are on stalks. The very small abdomen is folded back underneath the carapace.

Five pairs of legs are attached to a crab's thorax. The front legs end in pincers that the crabs use both in fighting and in feeding. They eat smaller crustaceans and other animals, along with some plant materials.

The female crab lays eggs which remain attached to her body for several weeks. The young, called zoeae, are swimming larvae with heads and slender tails.

The fiddler crab (illustrated) is found on sandy beaches along the Atlantic coast of North America. Only the male fiddler crab has the left pincer larger than the right. The female, like all other kinds of crabs, male or female, has 2 pincers the same size.

This crab's name is suggested by the way the male waves his large claw. He looks a little like a violinist drawing his bow back and forth across his instrument.

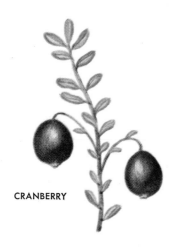

CRANBERRY

cranberry

Cranberries are low-growing, evergreen shrubs related to blueberries. The fruit of certain kinds of cranberries is valued for its sour taste. Such fruit is used to make cranberry sauce and a fresh fruit drink.

The American cranberry (illustrated) grows wild in the northeastern U.S. and in parts of Canada. Its thin, trailing stems form a thick tangle that covers the ground in bogs and moist lowlands.

The leaves of the American cranberry are round-tipped and about ½ inch long. Pink, bell-shaped flowers dangle along the stems in summer. Round, oblong or pear-shaped berries ½ to ¾ inch across ripen in the autumn. The color of the berries varies from pink to dark red.

In some cool areas, mainly New Jersey, Massachusetts, Wisconsin, Washington, and Oregon, American cranberries are an important crop. The plants are grown in a very acid soil and are heavily watered. In winter, cranberry growers flood their fields to keep the plants covered with water. Plants not under water would be killed by the first heavy frost.

In the U.S., about 3 million bushels of cranberries are grown each year. Over half the U.S. crop is made into canned cranberry sauce.

crane \ 'krān \

Cranes make up a family of long-legged, long-necked wading birds. They are found in marshy areas in many different parts of the world. Some kinds of cranes have become quite rare because they have been hunted, or because the marshes where they lived have been drained and turned into farm fields.

During the mating season, both male and female cranes take part in countship dances that include bowing, marching about and jumping up and down. At other times cranes seem stately and dignified. During flight, they stretch out their long necks and trail their long legs out behind them.

Cranes feed on insects, worms, snails, frogs and other small animals. The female lays 1 or 2 eggs in a large ground nest made from grasses and weed stalks.

The very rare whooping crane (illustrated) is 5 feet tall. It is the tallest bird in America. Its loud trumpeting call can be heard for several miles.

Whooping cranes spend the winter in Texas and the summer in northern Alberta, Canada, 2,500 miles away. There are probably less than 60 whooping cranes living today, including a dozen or so in zoos.

CRANE
(COURTSHIP DANCE)

CRAPE MYRTLE

crape myrtle \ 'krāp 'mərt-ᵊl \

Making up a group of flowering trees and shrubs, crape myrtles are native to warm parts of India and Australia. In the U.S., they are most often grown in the southern states as ornamental trees on lawns or in gardens. A few grow as far north as Kentucky and Maryland.

Crape myrtles are usually 10 to 50 feet tall. All during the summer months they bear large clusters of white, pink, red or purple flowers at the ends of the branches. The leaves are opposite.

Each flower is 1 to 1½ inches across and has 6 ruffled or fringed petals. The flowers are grouped in loose clusters 6 to 10 inches long. The seeds develop inside capsule-like fruits about ½ inch long.

The most common kind of crape myrtle in the southern U.S. is the queen's crape myrtle (illustrated). It grows to 50 feet tall. Its leaves are long, thick and leathery. The flowers are purplish.

crappie \ 'kräp-ē \

Making up a group of popular freshwater game fish, crappies are the largest members of the sunfish family. They are native to the U.S., where they are fairly common east of the Rocky Mountains. Twelve to 15 inches long, most crappies weigh 1 to 2 pounds.

Crappies have large mouths and foreheads that curve in. The 2 dorsal fins are together, with the second dorsal the longer. The ventral fins are directly under the pectoral fins.

Often traveling in schools, crappies feed on insects, crustaceans and smaller fish. They spawn in spring. The male stays near the nest and guards the eggs and young.

Crappies were once found only in the Mississippi River Valley and around the Great Lakes. In recent years they have been planted in many other areas.

All crappies are speckled with black. The white crappie has only a few dark speckles, while the black crappie has many more.

crater \ 'krāt-ər \

A crater is a bowl-shaped hole in the earth and is usually round and steep-sided. In the center of a crater, the floor may be nearly flat.

Some of the craters on the earth's surface are the vents or openings of old volcanoes. They may be at the tops of volcanic mountains.

Other craters show where meteorites struck with great force. A meteorite crater near Flagstaff, Arizona (illustrated), is 4,000 feet across and 500 feet deep.

CRATER

More than 30,000 craters have been seen in photographs of the part of the moon's surface visible from earth. Some are only ½ mile across, while others are as large as 150 miles across. Astronomers believe that many were made by meteors striking the moon, and that others may be parts of very old volcanoes.

crayfish \ 'krā-ˌfish \

Crayfish are small freshwater crustaceans which look something like lobsters. They are called crawdads or crawfish in some areas. Adult crayfish average about 3 inches in length.

A crayfish swims backward, with quick, downward flips of its tail. It can run either forward or backward. It is often found under a rock. Crayfish feed on smaller animals such as tadpoles, tiny snails and insect larvae. If a tidbit of food drifts by, the crayfish reaches out and grasps it with a claw.

In spring the female crayfish lays a number of eggs that look like small round berries. She attaches them to the underside of her tail, where they hatch 5 to 8 weeks later. The young crayfish cling to her body for several more weeks.

Crayfish are found in shallow ponds and streams in nearly all parts of the world. In some parts of the world they are considered good to eat.

CRAYFISH

CREOSOTE BUSH

creosote \ 'krē-ə-ˌsōt \ bush

The creosote bush is a desert shrub that gives off a strong but pleasant smell much like a balsam fir. Its leaves and twigs contain a sticky resin.

Creosote bushes grow 2 to 8 feet tall, with dense, tangled branches. The olive-green, compound leaves are made up of 2 tiny leaflets about $\frac{1}{3}$ inch long and joined at the base. They grow opposite each other on the twigs.

Small yellow flowers with 5 petals appear in spring. The white fruit looks like a dry, woolly berry.

The creosote bush grows in very dry, sandy places where most trees and shrubs cannot live. It is found in western Texas, Arizona, New Mexico and California.

cress \ 'kres \

The cresses are perennial plants that belong to the mustard family. Some are weeds and some are rock-garden plants. Some kinds of cress are eaten in salads.

All of the cresses have 4-petaled flowers and long, slender seedpods. They grow best in moist, shaded soil where the summer is not too hot.

Watercress (illustrated) is the best known of the edible cresses. It has very small white flowers and compound leaves of 3 to 11 leaflets.

CRESS

The leaves of watercress have a pleasant but sharp, slightly peppery taste. They are used in salads and sandwiches, and add flavor to vegetable soups. They may also be cooked and eaten like spinach.

Watercress is native to Europe, but it now grows wild in the cooler parts of North America. It is often found near springs or along cold, clear streams, with its leaves and stems floating in the water.

crevasse \ kri-'vas \

A crevasse is a deep, narrow crack in a glacier. When the different parts of a glacier move at different speeds, the parts may break away from each other, forming a crevasse. Several crevasses may appear where a glacier's bottom surface passes over uneven spots on the valley floor.

A crevasse usually becomes wider as time passes and as the ice melts a little at the top. Sometimes a crevasse becomes filled with loose snow and is invisible until a mountain climber steps on it and falls through.

A break in a levee along the Mississippi River is also called a crevasse.

cricket

The crickets are a family of insects closely related to grasshoppers and katydids. They often eat and destroy plants, but most people like to hear their cheerful chirping. Only the male cricket chirps. He makes the sound by rubbing one wing against the other.

In China and Japan, crickets are kept as pets, in tiny cages. In many parts of the world, a cricket living in the house is supposed to bring good luck.

Crickets are about 1 inch long and look something like grasshoppers. They have extra antennae that trail from the abdomen, and their wings fold flat on their backs. Crickets hear through slits in their forelegs.

In autumn the female lays eggs in the ground. Nearly all adult crickets die during the winter, but in spring the eggs hatch into nymphs.

One kind of field cricket (illustrated) is common in the U.S. It feeds on plants and damages some farm crops. Field crickets of other kinds are often found indoors. They may chew holes in clothing and bindings of books.

croaker \ 'krō-kər \

The croakers are a large family of marine fish important to both commercial fishermen and sportsmen. Croaker flesh is tender and has a delicate flavor.

Croakers are named for the odd noises they make by vibrating the muscles around their air bladders. The sound made in this way is like a low grunting or

CRICKET

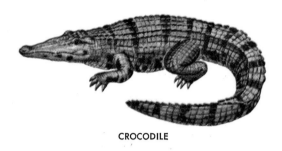

CROCODILE

croaking. It is thought that male croakers make these noises to attract females.

Six inches to 4 feet long, croakers are shaped like perch, and have rounded snouts. The dorsal fins may be together or be separated by a notch. Some kinds of croakers have a single barbel under the chin.

Most croakers live in the ocean, in fairly shallow, warm waters with sandy bottoms. A few live in brackish water at the mouths of streams. All feed near the bottom, on smaller fish, mollusks and crustaceans. Their floating eggs hatch soon after they are laid.

The Atlantic croaker grows to about 4 pounds. It is found off the east coast of America, from Massachusetts to as far south as Argentina.

crocodile

Crocodiles are large, 4-legged reptiles closely related to alligators and caimans.

The jaw of a crocodile is narrower than that of an alligator and contains 2 large teeth visible when the mouth is closed. The crocodile lives in a warmer climate than the alligator, and it is more vicious.

About 25 different kinds of crocodiles live in moist, tropical parts of North and South America, Africa and Asia. They are found in rivers and swamps, and in

salt water along the coasts. Crocodiles feed on fish, frogs, water birds and animals as large as wild pigs.

Female crocodiles lay up to 50 eggs at a time and bury them in sand, where the heat of the sun incubates them. The young make peeping sounds when they are ready to hatch. The mother then uncovers the eggs.

The American crocodile (illustrated) is found in Florida, Mexico and parts of Central and South America. It is usually 7 to 12 feet long, but specimens 25 feet long have been caught.

crocus \ 'krō-kəs \

Crocuses make up a group of small perennial flowering plants that belong to the iris family. Crocuses are usually the first garden flowers to appear in the early spring. There are also fall-blooming crocuses.

The crocus grows from a tough, fiber-covered corm to a height of 8 to 10 inches. The leaves look like blades of grass. They are dark green with a stripe down the middle. The leaves do not always appear until after the crocus has bloomed.

The 3- to 5-inch flowers of the spring crocus (illustrated) are shaped like small goblets. They have 3 sepals, 3 petals and 3 stamens. The flowers may be yellow,

CROCUS

white or shades of purple. Some are white, with narrow purple stripes.

The fruit of the crocus is an oblong capsule. The plants may be grown from the corms or from seeds.

The crocus is native to the Mediterranean regions of Europe and Asia Minor. In many parts of the world, it is a popular garden flower. It is also grown in pots as a houseplant.

crossbill

Birds of the finch family, crossbills are the only birds with upper and lower bills crossed near the tip. They usually live in pine forests. Their bills are adapted to picking the seeds from pine cones.

Crossbills are about the size of sparrows. The males are dark red or pink. The females are greenish-gray or speckled yellow.

Two to 5 speckled eggs are laid once or twice a year in a nest made of evergreen twigs and moss. The adults eat some fruit and berries in addition to pine seeds. They feed insects to their young nestlings.

The red crossbill (illustrated) lives mostly in Canada and Alaska. Some small flocks spend the winter as far south as Kansas, South Carolina and Mexico. In Mexico red crossbills are sometimes kept in cages as pets.

CROSSBILL

CROW

crow

Bold and clever birds, the crows belong to the same family as the jays, magpies and ravens. Their usual call sounds like "caw-caw," but they also make other sounds. Like parrots and parakeets, young crows raised as pets can be taught to imitate the sounds of a few words.

Crows are large, black birds with long, sharp-pointed bills. The common crow (illustrated) is found in most parts of North America and averages about 19 inches in length. It feeds on insects, bird eggs, weed seeds, nuts, fruit and small rodents such as mice. It damages some farm crops, particularly young corn.

Crows build bulky nests of sticks, high in tall trees. Three to 9 greenish-blue eggs with gray or brown markings are laid once or twice a year. The male and female birds take turns incubating the eggs.

Crows live as far north as the middle of Canada in summer. They spend the winter in the U.S., where they feed in woods, meadows and orchards.

crustacean \ krəs-'tā-shən \

Shrimps, lobsters, crabs, barnacles and crayfish all belong to a group of animals called crustaceans. All have an outside skeleton or shell.

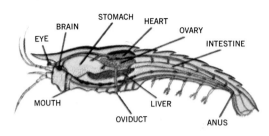

ORGAN OF CRUSTACEAN
(FEMALE CRAYFISH)

Nearly all crustaceans live in the sea, but a few live in streams and ponds or in damp earth. The smallest are microscopic. The largest are about 12 feet long.

Crustaceans have a 2-part body. The head and thorax together make 1 section; the abdomen is the other. Most have antennae and compound eyes on movable stalks. Most have 4 or more pairs of jointed legs. Crustaceans molt, shedding the old body covering and growing a new, larger one. All of them breathe through gills.

The crustaceans are valuable as food for fish and other animals. Some are also food for humans. A few crustaceans feed on dead plant and animal materials.

crystal \ 'krist-ᵊl \

Crystals are special shapes that substances take as they change from liquids or gases into solids. Crystals always have flat sides and angled corners.

Although crystals may be large or small, they keep their special shapes. For example, crystals of salt and galena are always cube-shaped, while crystals of quartz and calcite are always 6-sided. Other shapes are more complicated.

Perfect crystals form only under perfect conditions, when their atoms or molecules have time and space to arrange themselves in the proper pattern. Some substances form crystals more easily than others.

Many crystals are clear and beautifully colored. If they are also rare, they may be valuable gems. Amethysts, rubies and emeralds are crystals of different minerals.

cuckoo \ 'kü-ˌkü \

These slender-bodied, long-tailed birds make up a family. They are found in nearly all parts of the world.

Most cuckoos live in tropical forests. They feed on insects and caterpillars, and destroy many that are pests. In the U.S., cuckoos help control the tent caterpillars that damage many shade trees.

Cuckoos range from 6 to 27 inches in length. Both males and females are the same size and, in most kinds, the same color.

Cuckoos make many different clucking and chuckling sounds. Some kinds sing at night. Cuckoo clocks imitate the spring mating call of the male European cuckoo.

The black-billed cuckoo (illustrated) is found throughout the eastern half of North America in summer. It spends the winter in Central and South America.

The 2 to 6 bluish-green eggs are laid in a flimsy nest built of twigs and sticks. The nest is usually built in a shrub. Both male

CUCKOO

CUCUMBER

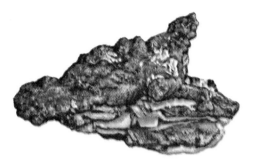

CUPRITE

and female incubate the eggs and feed the young birds.

The roadrunner, common in the southwestern U.S., also belongs to the cuckoo family.

See *roadrunner*.

cucumber \ 'kyü-ˌkəm-bər \

This garden plant belongs to the gourd family, along with pumpkins, melons and squash. Its fruit may be eaten as a salad vegetable, or it may be made into pickles. Cucumbers are grown in many countries as field or garden crops.

The cucumber is an annual vine that grows from seed planted in the spring. Its long stems sprawl on the ground. The leaves are oval or 3-cornered. Clusters of yellow, 5-petaled flowers about 1 inch across blossom all along the stems.

The fruit is 3 to 9 inches long. There are tiny bumps on its dark green skin, and its white flesh contains many flat, white seeds.

Cucumbers grow best in moist, rich soil, under warm sunshine.

cuprite \ 'k(y)ü-ˌprīt \

This reddish ore contains large amounts of copper, one of the most useful of all metals.

Cuprite is copper oxide, or copper that has combined with oxygen. It is usually found fairly near the surface of the earth, where pure copper or some other copper ore has been changed by weathering.

Although cuprite has a number of different forms, it is always some shade of red. The most common forms are solid masses (illustrated) or grains that are reddish-brown. A brick-red, powdery form is called tile ore. The most valuable form of cuprite looks like threads of red silk matted loosely together. Cuprite crystals are cube-shaped and a clear, bright ruby-red.

Large deposits of cuprite are found in Chile, Bolivia, Australia, Africa and in the southwestern U.S. The largest deposit in the U.S. is located near Bisbee, Arizona.

curlew \ 'kərl-(ˌ)(y)ü \

Slender, down-curving bills and long legs help identify these large wading birds. They belong to the same family as the sandpiper, snipe and woodcock.

Curlews live mostly in coastal marshes. They use their long bills to search in sand or mud for the worms, crayfish and other small crustaceans which they eat.

Most curlews spend the summer in the far north and migrate to winter homes south of the equator. One kind, the bris-

CURLEW

tle-thighed curlew, flies nonstop 5,000 miles between Alaska and a group of islands in the South Pacific.

The curlew's nest is a grass-lined hollow on the ground. Three or 4 spotted gray-brown eggs are laid once a year.

The largest of the North American curlews is the long-billed curlew (illustrated). It measures 20 to 26 inches from head to tail. Its bill is 6 to 7 inches long. Hunters once shot a great many of these large birds for sport. They are now protected by law and are increasing.

current \ 'kər-ənt \ marks

A pattern of small, side-by-side ridges or ripples, current marks are made by moving water which has disturbed sand or mud. Wind may cause current marks on dry sand, especially on sand dunes.

Current marks may be seen at the bottom of shallow streams, or at the edges of a lake where small waves lap at the shore. If the mud or sand hardens into rock, the current marks may last for thousands of years. They may prove that what is now dry land was once covered by water.

Sandstone and shale are the kinds of rocks that most often bear current marks. Both of these are sedimentary rocks.

The shape of each ridge indicates which way the water was moving. One side of each ridge is more gently sloping than the other. This gently sloping side marks the direction from which the water once flowed.

cutoff \ 'kət-ˌof \

A cutoff is a new, shorter path across the neck of a bend in a river.

Cutoffs are usually formed during a flood when a river overflows its banks. When the current is very fast, the river sometimes makes a new channel across the neck of a bend. Then, when the water level goes down, the river may continue to flow in the new channel. The old bend often becomes a crescent-shaped body of water, which is called an oxbow lake.

Cutoffs are found where a river flows through nearly level land on the floor of a broad valley. Such a river tends to enlarge its bends until it curves back and forth across the valley.

Map makers say that cutoffs shorten the lower Mississippi River about 50 miles each year. New cutoffs bypass some of the river's many loops and bends. In *Life on the Mississippi*, Mark Twain tells of the difficulties of piloting a steamboat on a river that forms new cutoffs between one trip and the next.

CUTOFF

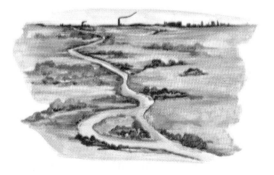

cuttlefish \ 'kət-ᵊl-ˌfish \ (sepia)

Closely related to the octopuses and squids, cuttlefish are found in fairly warm, deep parts of the oceans. They swim backward or forward by jet propulsion, filling a body cavity with water and then forcing it out rapidly.

The cuttlefish has a broad, oval body with 1 ruffled fin extending around it. It has a distinct head with 2 large eyes. The 10 arm-like tentacles can be drawn into pockets near the eyes. Inside the body is a flat, chalky shell called a cuttlebone. It is sold in pet shops and placed in bird cages as a source of the calcium that birds need.

When attacked, cuttlefish may release dye that turns the water around it dark. Sepia, a dark brown pigment used by artists in mixing paint, is made from this dye.

Cuttlefish feed on smaller mollusks and on crustaceans such as crabs. Rows of suckers on the tentacles help them grasp their prey.

Cuttlefish vary in size from a few inches to 6 feet long. The common cuttlefish (illustrated) is widespread in the Mediterranean and in European Atlantic waters. Up to 2 feet long, it can change color to match its surroundings. Its arms shoot out very rapidly when it nears a tidbit of food on the sea floor.

CUTTLEFISH

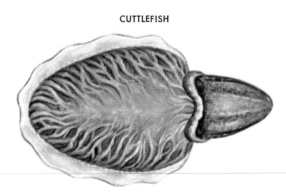

CYPRESS

cypress \ 'sīp-rəs \

Cypresses make up a group of evergreen trees belonging to the pine family. They are native to warm, fairly dry parts of Asia, Europe and North America. In the U.S., cypresses grow only in the mountains of Arizona and New Mexico and along the California coast.

Cypresses grow 15 to 70 feet tall. Those in windy areas are often gnarled and twisted by the wind.

The leaves are scale-like and overlap each other. Cypress cones are ½ to 1¼ inches across. When ripe, a cypress cone separates into 6 or more knob-like sections. Tiny winged seeds fall from the cracks between the sections.

The foliage of old cypresses is sometimes such a dark green that it looks black. This may be why the Greeks and Romans made the cypress a symbol of death.

The kind of cypress most common in the U.S. is the Arizona cypress (illustrated). It grows throughout the southwestern states. The Arizona cypress is valued for its reddish, long-lasting wood.

Also of the pine family and related to the true cypress is the bald cypress. It is a familiar sight in the swampy regions of the southeastern U.S. because of the strange-looking "knees" which grow from its roots. The bald cypress is the state tree of Louisiana.

d

dahlia \ 'dal-yə \

This widely grown garden plant exists in many different forms, with flowers of every color except blue. All of the many forms were developed by flower breeders from 1 plant that grows wild on mountain slopes in Mexico. The plant is named in honor of a Swedish botanist, Anders Dahl.

The largest dahlias are among the largest of all plants grown in flower gardens. They grow 7 to 8 feet tall, with giant flower heads 17 inches across. The stems are usually too weak to hold up such a heavy flower, so the plants have to be tied to wooden supports.

The flower head of the dahlia is a tight cluster of petal-sized blossoms. The cluster may be flat, like a daisy, or ball-shaped, like a chrysanthemum. The seeds are flat, with papery coverings.

Dahlias are most often grown from cuttings or from their tubers. Growing dahlias require rich, well-drained soil and plenty of water and sun.

The dahlia is a perennial but it cannot live through severe winter cold. In most parts of the U.S., gardeners dig up the plants each fall and store the tubers indoors till spring.

DAHLIA

DAMSELFLY

damselfly \ 'dam-zəl-ˌflī \ (darning needle)

Making up a group of large flying insects, damselflies are closely related to dragonflies. Damselflies have blue or green bodies and are a little smaller than dragonflies. When resting, damselflies hold their wings over their backs instead of out at the sides, as dragonflies do.

Damselflies feed on mosquitoes and other small insects. They capture their food while flying, in a basket-like trap they make by folding their legs together.

Damselflies are not strong fliers, and seldom travel far from the water where they were born.

The female damselfly drops her eggs onto water plants. The young are wingless nymphs that swim about. They breathe by pumping water through 3 leaf-like gills at the tips of their long abdomens. They may live in water for 5 years and molt as many as 12 times before becoming adults.

A common kind of damselfly is the blackwing damselfly (illustrated). As its name suggests, its wings are dark.

dandelion \ 'dan-dᵊl-ˌī-ən \

These plants make up a group of perennial weeds. They are troublesome, hard-to-

DANDELION

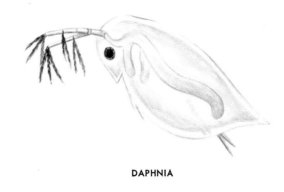

DAPHNIA

kill plants that grow in nearly all parts of the temperate zone.

A dandelion has a long, strong root that extends down into the earth for 10 inches or more. When the plant is cut off at ground level, its roots grow longer and stronger and they send up more leaves and flowers.

Dandelions do have some uses. In spring the young leaves can be cooked like spinach and eaten. In Russia, the milky juice of the leaves and hollow stems is used to make rubber. At one time the roots were made into medicine and the flowers were used to make wine.

The common dandelion (illustrated) is the kind most often seen on lawns and along roadsides. It bears flower heads that are clusters of tiny, petal-sized blossoms. Each yellow flower produces 1 dry, flat seed attached to an umbrella-shaped tuft of white hairs. The wind often carries the seeds long distances.

daphnia \ 'daf-nē-ə \

These tiny, flea-like animals make up a group of freshwater crustaceans. Often called water fleas, they are about 1/10 inch long. They are very common in most streams and ponds. Daphnia help to make up plankton, the major food supply of many fish and other water animals.

Dried daphnias are sold in pet shops as food for tropical fish. They are also used in certain scientific experiments. The oval, 2-part shell of a daphnia is nearly transparent. A biologist can place a living daphnia under a microscope and watch its heart and other organs in action.

A daphnia swims with 2 large, branching antennae that move like oars. Four to 6 pairs of smaller, weaker legs sweep bits of water plants and other food materials into the mouth.

The daphnia reproduces by laying eggs, several broods each week. Eggs laid in summer have thin shells and hatch quickly. Eggs laid in autumn have much thicker shells. Some of these autumn eggs live through the winter and hatch the following spring.

A common kind of daphnia (illustrated) occurs in large numbers in ponds, lakes and streams.

dayflower \ 'dā-ˌflaůr \

Dayflowers make up a group of low-growing, annual wild flowers. They bear many bright blue, heart-shaped flowers. Because the blossoms last only a day or less, the plants are called dayflowers. Most wither before noon, but the plants blossom from July to October.

Dayflowers are native to the tropics but they now grow throughout the eastern half of the U.S., as far north as New York and Kansas. They are usually found growing in moist soil along streams. The first frost usually kills them.

Each flower has 2 rounded petals about ½ inch long and a third, much smaller petal. The flowers appear 1 at a time or in clusters of 2 or 3. The seeds ripen inside small, 3-part capsules.

Some kinds of dayflowers grow to as much as 3 feet in height. The leaves wrap around the base of the stem. Both the flowers and the leaves grow from knobby joints in the stems.

The common or Asiatic dayflower grows to a length of 3 feet. It sprawls on the ground with only the flowering tips of the stems lifted up.

day lily

Day lilies make up a group of perennial plants which are related to true lilies. They are called day lilies because each flower lasts just a day. The plants themselves grow as tall as 8 feet.

Some kinds of day lilies are wild flowers that bloom along roadsides. Others are cultivated garden plants. All have fleshy, bulb-like roots and are native to central Europe and Asia.

The day lily's narrow, grass-like leaves and stalks grow in dense clumps. Six or more yellow or orange flowers grow on each bare, branching stalk. Day lilies produce flowers all during the summer months.

The common orange day lily (illustrated) grows wild in most of the U.S. It is 3 to 5 feet tall. The 6 to 10 flowers are orange-red and about 6 inches long. They have no fragrance. Large 3-part seedpods appear after the flowers are gone.

Cultivated day lilies usually do not produce seed. Gardeners start new plants by dividing the roots and replanting them. Some, like the kind called lemon lily, have very fragrant flowers.

deer

The deer family of hoofed mammals includes the moose, wapiti (elk) and caribou as well as the true deer. Members of the deer family are native to all parts of the world except Australia, southern Africa and Madagascar. Male deer are called bucks, while female deer are called does.

Deer leap gracefully and can run as fast as 35 miles an hour. They usually live at the edges of forests, where they feed mostly on the leaves and twigs of shrubs and young trees.

Male deer have branching antlers

DAY LILY

DEER

which are not true horns, but a form of tough skin. During the autumn mating season the males use their antlers to fight each other over females. They shed their antlers during the winter, before the young are born in early spring. During this time the males have only short, hair-covered antlers that are too tender to be used as weapons.

Three kinds of deer are found in North America. The black-tailed deer (illustrated) is a kind found along the Pacific coast of North America. Black-tailed males are about 3½ feet high at the shoulder and 7 feet long. They weigh about 300 pounds. The slightly larger mule deer is common in the Rocky Mountains, and the Virginia or white-tailed deer is found in the eastern states.

See *caribou, moose* and *wapiti.*

delphinium \ del-'fin-ē-əm \

Delphiniums make up a group of annual and perennial plants. Some delphiniums are native to the West Indies, while others are native to the eastern U.S.

Several kinds of delphiniums, including larkspurs, are popular garden plants. Most delphiniums have blue or violet flowers, but a few have red or white flowers. They grow from 12 inches to 8 feet tall. The perennial kinds are generally taller than the annual kinds.

DELPHINIUM

DELTA

Delphiniums grow best in cooler parts of the temperate zones. The flowers grow in tall, spire-shaped clusters. Each flower has a tail or spur extending back from it. The leaves are always divided into narrow, finger-like segments.

Both leaves and stems of all kinds of delphiniums contain poisonous juices. The kinds that grow wild on western ranches are called poisonweed and staggerweed because cattle that eat them become very ill and sometimes die.

The rocket larkspur (illustrated) is an annual delphinium that grows from seed planted in early spring. It is 12 to 24 inches tall, with flowers that are usually blue or violet.

delta \ 'del-tə \

A delta is an area of low, nearly level land at the mouth of a river. It is made up of sediment carried downstream by the river. From the air, a delta looks like a triangle, and is named for the Greek letter "delta," which is shaped like a triangle.

Deltas form when swift-moving water, which can carry more sediment than slow-moving water, slows down. When a river flows out into a larger body of water, its movement is slowed. Most of the sediment it carries drops to the bottom.

In time the sediment builds up to the level of the stream itself. The land built up in this way is valuable because it is so fertile. Of course, it is also very low, and much of it may be under water when the river floods.

One delta formed where the Mississippi River flows into the Gulf of Mexico is about 200 miles long. Another large delta is located where the Nile River flows into the Mediterranean Sea.

detritus \ di-'trīt-əs \

Detritus is loose material made of broken-up rock. Sand, clay and gravel are all different kinds of detritus. Soil is detritus that is mixed with rotted plant materials and water.

Freezing and thawing, and the action of moving water, are the main forces that break up rocks and turn them into detritus. Water expands as it freezes, and water that seeps into cracks in rocks may split them apart as it turns into ice. In stream beds, and at the edge of the sea, moving water grinds rocks together until they break.

The roots of moss and other green plants also help to break up rocks. The roots grow into tiny cracks in rocks and force the rocks to split into 2 or more pieces.

Another kind of detritus is talus. Talus is made up of pieces of rock that break loose from a mountain or cliff and pile up at the base.

See *talus.*

DETRITUS

CUT DIAMOND

diamond

This valuable mineral is both beautiful and useful. Its beauty as a gem is due to its brilliance when it is cut and polished. The diamond is useful as a cutting material itself because it is the hardest mineral known.

Only about 20 percent of the diamonds mined today go into jewelry. The other 80 percent are used by industry to edge saws and drills. These tools then cut into such hard materials as glass, metal and rock.

Diamonds are crystals of pure carbon. The finest ones are colorless or blue-white. Others are yellowish, brown or gray. Before they are cut and polished, most diamonds look like ordinary pebbles.

Some diamonds are found in stream beds. Others are dug from mines in rock formations that were once the necks of volcanoes. The world's largest diamond mines are in South Africa. Smaller mines are located in India and South America.

In the U.S., diamonds have been mined in Arkansas. A few diamonds have been found in gravel deposits or in stream beds in Wisconsin, California, Georgia, Indiana and other states. Artificial diamonds have been made by subjecting graphite to great heat and pressure.

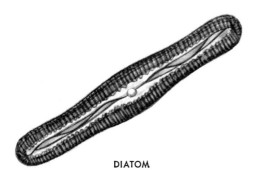

DIATOM

diatom \ 'dī-ə-ˌtäm \

Diatoms are unusual and very beautiful plants that make up a group of algae too small to be seen without a microscope. They are floating, 1-celled plants found in streams, ponds and the oceans. The great numbers of living diatoms help to make up about 9/10 of plankton, the food supply of many fish and other water animals. They are most common in the cooler parts of the ocean.

Unlike most plants, diatoms have hard coverings around them. Each diatom has a 2-part shell, like a box with a lid. Some diatoms are round, while others are triangular or star-shaped. Most have a pattern of dots on them. The shells are made of silica, and they are usually gold-colored or brown.

Like most 1-celled plants and animals, diatoms reproduce by dividing. Each of the new cells takes half of the old shell or box and builds a new half to go with it.

Diatom shells do not decay when the plants die. Some fall to the ocean floor where they build up deposits. This material is used in making polishes and filters, and in such products as soap, paint, plastics, brick and tile.

A common kind of diatom (illustrated) lives in fresh water.

dill \ 'dil \

An annual or biennial plant belonging to the parsley family, dill is grown for its seeds, flowers and leaves. All are used to add flavor and fragrance to foods.

Dill seeds and leaves are used in making dill pickles. The seeds and leaves are sometimes added to fish and seafood dishes, and to potato salad. The dill plant is also used to make some medicines and an oil that goes into perfume.

Dill grows 2 to 3 feet tall. It has slender, smooth stems and leaves that are divided into very narrow segments. Both leaves and stems are light green. Umbrella-shaped clusters of tiny, yellow flowers appear at the tops of the plants in July.

Dill grows wild in southern Europe. It was brought to North America by the early colonists. It now grows wild in the cooler parts of the U.S., where it is found in weedy fields and along roadsides. Dill is a popular annual plant in gardens, where it is picked in August, about 3 months after planting.

In some areas, dill is grown for market. In the U.S., Oregon and Idaho lead in dill production. In Europe it is grown mostly in Hungary.

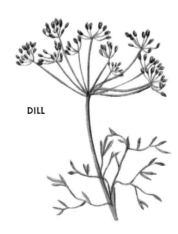

DILL

dimetrodon \ dī-'me-trə-ˌdän \ (fin-backed lizard, pelycosaur)

These prehistoric reptiles are known only through fossil remains. Dimetrodons lived about 260 million years ago, 100 million years or more before dinosaurs appeared on the earth.

Dimetrodons were 4-legged, heavy-bodied animals about 10 feet long. The bony fin on the back stood about 3 feet tall. It probably gave the animal some protection from its enemies. The fin may also have helped to control the reptile's body temperature.

The legs were short but sturdy, and these animals could probably run fast.

Aside from their fins, these reptiles looked much like some lizards and crocodiles of today. Dimetrodons had sharp claws on their toes and many sharp teeth in their large jaws. They were carnivores that fed on smaller animals and fish. They were probably fierce fighters. Like the dinosaurs, they were egg layers.

Dimetrodon fossils have been found in many different parts of Europe and North America. They are fairly common in Texas and New Mexico. Some dimetrodon fossils have been found in Russia and in South Africa.

DIMETRODON

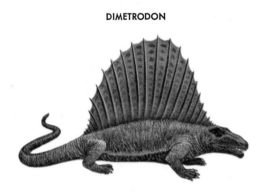

DINOFLAGELLATE

dinoflagellate \ ˌdī-nō-'flaj-ə-lət \

These very small, 1-celled organisms live in both the ocean and fresh water. One kind of dinoflagellate (illustrated) appears red in daylight and shines at night. During the day, when these dinoflagellates are together in large groups, they seem to turn the ocean red. This is known as the red tide. At night, they make the ocean sparkle with tiny dots of light.

Dinoflagellates, along with some other kinds of aquatic plant life, make up plankton, which is the main food for such marine animals as the whale.

Most dinoflagellates are covered with hard shells of varying shapes. Some shells are shaped like spheres. All dinoflagellates have 1 or more flagella. These are the long, whip-like parts that help the dinoflagellates move from place to place.

dobsonfly \ 'däb-sən-ˌflī \

Not true flies but relatives of lacewings and ant lions, dobsonflies are among the largest insects native to North America. Fierce-looking but harmless, they live near swift-running streams. They are sometimes seen clustered around lights at night. Dobsonfly larvae, called hellgrammites, provide food for many freshwater fish such as bass. They are often used as bait by fishermen.

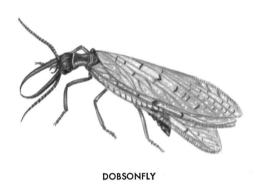

DOBSONFLY

Adult dobsonflies are 2 inches long, with a wingspread of 4 to 5 inches. Males have pincer-like jaws up to 1 inch long. Dobsonflies live only a short time as adults.

Female dobsonflies lay 2,000 to 3,000 eggs in white masses that cling to rocks or plants overhanging water. The newly hatched larvae drop into the water and live there for about 3 years. They shelter under rocks on the stream bottom, and feed on smaller insect larvae.

Fully grown larvae are 2 to 3 inches long. They have 3 pairs of short legs and many pairs of hair-like gills that extend out from their sides. When ready to pass into the pupal or resting stage, they creep out of the water at night and hide under a rock on the streambank. Less than a month later they appear as winged adults.

Dobsonflies live in nearly all parts of the world. One kind (illustrated) is rather common in the U.S. east of the Rocky Mountains.

dodo \ 'dōd-,ō \

This large bird of the dove family was killed off more than 250 years ago by Portuguese sailors. By 1681 there were no more dodo birds.

About the size of a turkey, the dodo lost the use of its wings after a while and no longer flew.

The dodo had a round body, small wings and a short neck. There were no feathers on its face, but its short tail was feathered like the tail of an ostrich. The dodo had strong, yellow feet and sharp claws. Its hooked bill was almost as long as its head.

The dodo lived on the island of Mauritius, in the Indian Ocean. Scientists do not know what it ate, but it is thought to have fed on plants, seeds and nuts. It laid 1 large white egg each year in a nest made of leaves.

dog

The written history of these carnivorous mammals goes back thousands of years. As early as 4000 B.C., men were using dogs as hunters and beasts of burden. In ancient Egypt, statues of gods were often given dog heads, and dogs were buried with great ceremony. Some American Indians believed eating dog meat would make them brave. They sacrificed dogs to their gods.

Today, man still uses dogs to hunt. They are also used to guide the blind, herd sheep or cattle and carry messages. But dogs are mostly valued now as pets rather than workers. The American Kennel Club recognizes more than 100 breeds of dogs.

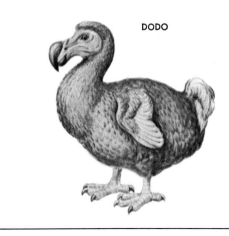

DODO

Dogs have a keen sense of smell and hearing, and are known for their intelligence. Coyotes, foxes, jackals and wolves are wild dogs. Most dogs have 5 toes on each paw, but some have 4.

Females bear 1 or 2 litters each year, at different seasons.

The number of pups in a litter varies. But all pups are born blind and helpless. They see in 9 days and hear in 10 to 12 days. Dogs mature in 1 year.

See *coyote, fox, jackal* and *wolf.*

dog fennel \ 'fen-ªl \ (Mayweed)

This bad-smelling weed is found along the sides of roads and in fields where flowers and weeds grow wild. Though its flowers look like small daisies, dog fennel should not be picked, for its crushed leaves may cause blisters.

The flowers of this annual plant appear from June through October. They have white petals and yellow, dome-shaped centers. Dog fennel has a small, dry, rough fruit.

Dog fennel grows to a height of 10 to 20 inches, with a number of branches that also grow upright. The alternate leaves are divided into many thin parts, which gives them a lacy appearance.

Dog fennel is native to Europe, but now grows wild in America, Australia, Asia and Africa.

DOG FENNEL

DOGWOOD

dogwood \ 'dȯg-ˌwu̇d \

Dogwoods make up a family of shrubs and trees that grow from 20 inches to 80 feet in height. Tool handles are sometimes made from the hard, close-grained wood of the larger kinds of dogwood trees.

Dogwoods bear flowers in early spring, before the leaves are fully grown. Some kinds bloom again, late in the summer.

The broad, oval leaves of the dogwood are marked by curving, parallel veins. In almost all kinds of dogwood, the leaves and twigs grow in opposite pairs. The flowers grow in clusters shaped like umbrellas. The fruit, a bright red, oval berry, is eaten by wild birds.

The best-known kind of dogwood is the flowering dogwood (illustrated). It grows throughout the eastern half of the U.S. These dogwoods grow to a height of 30 to 40 feet. They are broad-crowned trees with slender, horizontal branches and short trunks about 10 to 18 inches around.

The flower of this dogwood is yellow and very small. The 4 bracts, which are often mistaken for the flower, are whitish. Under each cluster of bracts are 4 shiny leaves, about 3 to 5 inches long. In autumn, the leaves turn a deep rich red.

The flowering dogwood is the state flower of North Carolina and Virginia, and the state tree of Missouri.

dolomite \ 'dō-lə-ˌmīt \

Dolomite is both a mineral and the principal part of a sedimentary rock. As a mineral, it is made up of calcium and magnesium carbonate. As a rock, dolomite contains other minerals as well. The rock is sometimes called dolomitic limestone.

Dolomite was named after the French geologist D. G. Dolomieu. Because of the large deposit of dolomite in the Italian Tyrol, these 10,000-foot-high mountains are called the Dolomites.

Lightweight and brittle, dolomite is colorless, white or pinkish, and usually translucent. Dolomite looks somewhat like calcite, but is harder.

In the U.S., there is a large deposit of dolomite in Joplin, Missouri.

Dolomitic limestone is fairly common throughout the world. It occurs most often in rocks containing marble and talc schists.

dolphin \ 'däl-fən \

Dolphins make up a family of small, toothed whales. Most kinds are highly intelligent, playful and friendly to humans. Because dolphins can communicate with each other by different sounds, they are being carefully studied by a number of scientists.

Dolphins live in all the earth's oceans. The most common kinds live along both coasts of North America. From 4 to 20 feet long, dolphins have slender, streamlined bodies and beak-like snouts. They have 2 paddle-like flippers longer than those of most whales. Halfway down their backs, dolphins have curved fins.

All dolphins are carnivorous. They eat fish and small marine animals.

The bottle-nosed dolphin (illustrated) is often mistakenly called a porpoise. It is the smallest of the toothed whales, which include the porpoises. The bottle-nosed dolphin is often seen in marine zoos. It is about 12 feet long.

An adult bottle-nosed dolphin can swim up to 35 miles per hour and leap high above the water. A single young is born 10 months after mating. In a month, the young dolphin begins to catch its own food. As an adult, a captive bottlenose eats about 12 pounds of fish a day.

For other dolphins, see *killer whale* and *pilot whale* under *whale*.

dome \ 'dōm \

A dome is a formation of rock layers shaped like an upside-down bowl. Domes form in different ways and vary in size and shape. They can be small with steep sides, or many miles across.

Some small domes are formed when molten rock forces its way up through layers of sedimentary rock. The molten rock forces the layers of sedimentary rock to

DOLPHIN

DOME

bulge upward. These small uplifts are called laccoliths.

Large rock domes are formed by the same forces that uplift whole mountain ranges. The Black Hills of South Dakota and Wyoming are large rock domes.

Some rock domes are underground. In certain oil fields petroleum has been trapped beneath underground domes, as in Oklahoma and Kansas.

Salt and sulfur are mined from underground domes in Texas and Louisiana.

See *laccolith*.

donkey (ass, burro)

Donkeys have been domestic animals since ancient times. Both donkeys and asses belong to the horse family and are the same animal, but donkeys are tame and asses are wild. Today, asses live in Asia and Africa. These wild asses are the ancestors of donkeys. Swift runners, wild asses are hunted for their flesh.

The largest donkeys are a little over 5 feet high. The smallest donkeys, which are called dwarf donkeys, are no more than 2 feet high. Donkeys have large ears, thin tails and wiry, upright manes. Their eyes are deep-set and their short legs have small hoofs. Donkeys do not whinny like horses, but have loud, noisy brays.

Donkeys are used all over the world as

DONKEY

DOUGLAS FIR

pack animals, especially in mountainous country. They can carry up to 200 pounds of cargo. Most of the time, donkeys are easily managed. Still, they can be very stubborn, kicking and biting when angry.

A group of donkeys is called a pace. Donkeys outlive horses by 25 to 50 years.

Douglas fir \ 'dəg-ləs 'fər \

The Douglas fir is a very large evergreen tree closely related to the pines. It is important as the main source of lumber and plywood in the U.S. Young Douglas firs are sold as Christmas trees.

This tree grows 100 to 200 feet tall. The straight trunk is from 2 to 12 feet in diameter. The thick bark is red-brown and has large scales. Twigs and branches form a dense but often patchy pattern. On trees that grow close together in the forest all but the top branches may die and fall.

The leaves of the Douglas fir are dark green needles ¾ to 1¼ inches long. In spring, the tips of the branches bear small orange or red cones. The mature seed cone is 1 to 4 inches long and has a shaggy look. This shaggy look is due to the leaf-like parts, called bracts, which extend past the broad, short scales of the cone.

The Douglas fir is native to western Canada and the U.S. The tallest Douglas firs grow in Washington and Oregon. Tree farms plant great numbers of Douglas firs. They are also planted as ornamental evergreens. The Douglas fir is the state tree of Oregon.

DOVE

dove (pigeon)

Doves, sometimes called pigeons, make up a family of nearly 300 kinds of birds. They live in both tropic and temperate regions.

Doves are from 7 to 13 inches long. All have scaled legs and strong claws. Their bills are short, thin and curved at the top. Doves are the only birds that keep their bills in water while swallowing. Their feathers are usually iridescent. Doves are strong, swift fliers.

Much of the day, doves scratch on the ground for food. They eat seeds, grains, fruits and even acorns and leaves. Doves build flimsy nests of twigs and sticks either on the ground, on cliffs or on buildings. Most kinds of doves lay 2 glossy, white eggs.

The European rock dove (illustrated), more often called domestic pigeon, is the dove most often seen in streets and parks. Several breeds of domestic pigeons have been developed by pigeon fanciers. Some are bred for show, others for racing or food. Domestic pigeons are most often seen in flocks.

The color of domestic pigeons varies, but most are marked with gray or blue. Many domestic pigeons have iridescent shades of green, pink or purple.

The passenger pigeon, once common in the U.S., is now extinct.

For members of the dove family, see *dodo* and *passenger pigeon*.

dragonfly \ 'drag-ən-ˌflī \ (darning needle)

Making up a large group of flying insects, dragonflies are closely related to damselflies. Dragonflies are larger than damselflies and are also stronger fliers.

Dragonflies have thin bodies about 2 inches long. The large compound eyes cover most of the head. Dragonflies have 2 pairs of long, thin, transparent wings. The hind pair is the larger. The wings remain spread when the insects are resting. Although color varies with the kind of dragonfly, many kinds are marked with green or yellow.

These insects are found at the edges of ponds or lakes where they feed on mosquitoes, small flies and other insects. Scientists believe that dragonflies have very keen eyesight.

Dragonflies lay their eggs on water plants or drop them in the water. The nymphs live in the water, molting many times before they become adults. The nymphs have thick bodies, big jaws, strong legs and 10 pairs of breathing tubes.

The large, brightly colored, green darner dragonfly (illustrated) has a bright green thorax and head and a blue abdomen. The body is about 2½ inches long. Green darners are fairly common and are most often seen near lakes, ponds and streams.

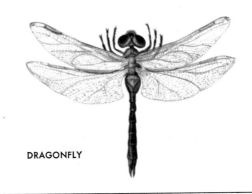

DRAGONFLY

duck

Together with their close relatives, the geese and swans, ducks make up a large family of aquatic birds. Ducks have heavy bodies, webbed feet and broad, flattened bills. They are good swimmers, with short legs placed far back on their bodies, but they waddle awkwardly on land. Most kinds are strong fliers. Ducks are active only during daylight hours.

Male ducks, called drakes, are nearly always much more colorful than females. They do not help build the nest or incubate the eggs.

The female duck lays 6 to 20 eggs, once a year. The nest is usually a pile of plant materials on the ground, near water. The wood duck, the goldeneye, and a few other kinds nest in hollow trees.

Duck nests are lined with soft down feathers that the female duck plucks from her breast. She uses these feathers to cover and hide the eggs when she leaves the nest to look for food. The young ducklings are covered with down. They can swim very soon after hatching.

Ducks feed and migrate in large flocks. Some are gamebirds and are highly valued by hunters.

The black, mallard, pintail, shoveler, and wood ducks and the teal (all illustrated) belong to the group called river or dipping ducks. They live in freshwater streams and lakes, and they feed in shallow water. They eat mostly plant materials, such as the seeds and roots of water plants, along with smaller amounts of animal foods such as snails, crayfish and insects. When feeding underwater they sometimes tip their bodies so that only the tails stick up, but they do not dive under the surface.

The black duck is closely related to the mallard and is rarely seen in the western half of North America.

The mallard is the most common and best-known kind of American river duck. Mallards are swift fliers and have been clocked at over 60 miles per hour.

The pintail is the only river duck with a long tail. It is a favorite gamebird and very good to eat.

The shoveler is named for its large, spoon-shaped bill, which it uses to strain insects, larvae and crustaceans from water.

The wood duck is often called a percher because it sometimes sits in trees. It has sharp claws that make perching possible.

Teal differ from all other ducks in that their hind toes have nearly disappeared.

Most of the river ducks migrate between their breeding grounds in the northern states and Canada and their winter homes in the southern U.S. and Central America. Some kinds of river ducks are year-round residents of the central states.

The goldeneye, the scaups and the scoter (all illustrated) are diving ducks. They eat more animal food than do river ducks, and may be found in salt water.

The goldeneye is a fish-eating duck that breeds throughout Canada and winters in most of the U.S. When goldeneyes fly, their wings make a loud, whistling sound. On the water, they are noisy quackers. Because of their fish diet, goldeneyes are not very good to eat.

Greater and lesser scaups eat some plant food, along with snails, crayfish and insects. They breed chiefly in Canada, and winter in the southern U.S. The lesser scaup is lighter in weight and breeds further south than the greater scaup. Both scaups are good gamebirds.

The surf scoter is seen only in the ocean and in the largest of the inland lakes. It feeds almost entirely on crustaceans. When diving underwater, it uses its wings as well as its feet. It may dive to 30 feet below the surface.

For other kinds of ducks, see *baldpate* and *eider*.

Ducks of North America

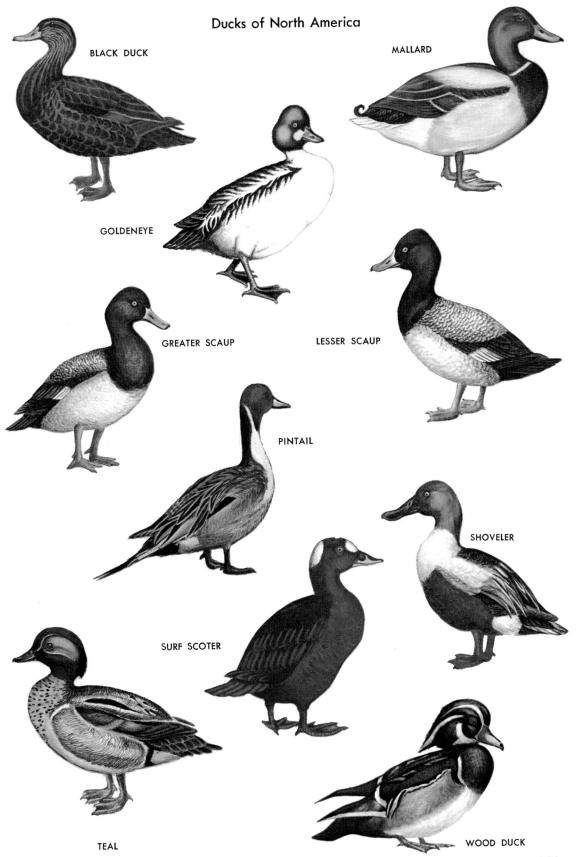

BLACK DUCK

MALLARD

GOLDENEYE

GREATER SCAUP

LESSER SCAUP

PINTAIL

SHOVELER

SURF SCOTER

TEAL

WOOD DUCK

133

duck-billed platypus\ 'dək-ˌbild
'plat-i-pəs\

This very unusual animal is a warm-blooded, fur-bearing mammal that lays eggs. Scientists once refused to believe that a mammal could have fur like a beaver and a bill like a duck, and lay eggs but nurse its young.

The platypus is about 2 feet long, with a black, leathery bill 2½ inches long. The feet are webbed and the tail is flattened. When in danger the male produces a strong poison that he forces out through sharp spurs on his hind legs.

Good swimmers, these animals live along streams and ponds in parts of Australia and Tasmania. They feed on worms, crayfish and insects. Long tunnels with openings both on land and under water lead to their dens. The dens are lined with leaves.

Once a year, the female platypus lays 1 to 5 round eggs about ¾ inch in diameter. She keeps them warm by curling her body around them until they hatch, about 10 days later.

The young are hairless, blind and helpless. For 4 to 5 months they remain in the den, feeding on milk from glands on the mother's abdomen.

Today, the platypus is so rare that it is protected by law.

DUCK-BILLED PLATYPUS

DUGONG

dugong\ 'dü-ˌgäng\

A harmless, warm-blooded mammal belonging to the sea cow family, this rare animal was once hunted for its hide, body oil and tasty flesh. Today, the dugong is almost extinct.

The dugong's only close relatives are the manatees, which live only in the Atlantic Ocean. Manatees are larger than the dugong, and their tails are squared-off rather than crescent-shaped.

The dugong has hairless skin. The forelimbs are flippers adapted to swimming, and the hind limbs have disappeared. This animal is almost never seen on land.

The male has tusks in the upper jaw.

Seen from a distance, with only its head and shoulders out of the water, a dugong looks almost human. A quick look from a ship may have started sailors' stories about mermaids.

Adult dugongs are about 10 feet long. Both males and females have wrinkled, whiskered faces. When feeding her single pup, the female dugong holds it in her flipper, much as a human mother holds her baby.

Dugongs live in the shallower parts of the Indian Ocean and the Red Sea, and along the coasts of Africa and Australia. They are usually found in quiet bays and near the mouths of rivers, feeding on seaweeds and other water plants.

e

eagle

Birds of prey that belong to the same family as hawks and kites, eagles are large and powerful. They have keen eyesight, hooked beaks and long, strong claws with which they catch their victims.

During the day, eagles hunt, capture and eat field mice, rabbits, fish, birds and animals as large as newborn deer and sheep.

Eagles live to be 30 to 80 years old. Most kinds mate for life. They build large, untidy nests of sticks in the tops of tall trees or on mountain ledges.

One to 3 eggs are laid, once a year. The newly hatched eaglets are blind, helpless and covered with down. The baby birds are fed and cared for in the nest for as long as 3 months.

Eagles were once common from the Arctic Circle south to Mexico, and throughout Europe and Asia. Although they are protected by law, they are now rare in most areas.

The bald eagle (illustrated) is also called the American eagle, and it is the national bird of the U.S. It is about 3 feet long, with a wingspread of 6 to 7 feet. Nearly extinct, the bald eagle now breeds only in limited areas of Alaska and Florida.

EAGLE

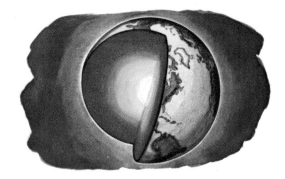

EARTH

earth

The earth is the fifth largest planet in the solar system. It is 7,927 miles in diameter at the equator, slightly pear-shaped and flattened at each pole. The earth is about 93 million miles from the sun. Only Mercury and Venus are closer to the sun.

In its orbit around the sun, the earth is moving at a speed of about 18½ miles per second. This orbit is 600 million miles long, and the earth completes 1 orbit in a year. At the same time, the earth is rotating on its axis once every 24 hours.

The earth's surface covering is a layer of rock and soil 2½ to 30 miles deep. About ¾ of this surface is covered with water. Beneath the surface is a layer of solid rock 30 to 50 miles deep. Together, these layers make up the earth's crust.

The earth's crust is thickest under the continents. It is thinnest under oceans. It is the only part of the earth that scientists know very much about.

Under the earth's crust there is thought to be a layer of hot rock about 600 miles thick. Below this layer is the core of the earth. Scientists believe that the earth's core contains molten rock, and probably such metals as iron and nickel, all under great pressure.

See *The Earth* on p. 498 and *The Sun, the Moon and the Planets* on p. 502.

EARTHWORM

earthworm

Making up a family of segmented worms (annelids) that live in the soil, earthworms are found in all parts of the temperate and tropic zones. The largest kind is 11 feet long. The smallest kind is microscopic.

The pointed, tapering end of the earthworm is its head, which has no eyes or ears. The thicker end is the tail. The 200 to 400 ring-like sections of the body are powerful bands of muscle that help the worm burrow through soil.

Earthworms swallow soil as they burrow. Their food is decaying plant and animal matter in the soil they swallow. Earthworms help man greatly by loosening and purifying the soil as they burrow through it.

Each earthworm has both male and female reproductive organs. After mating, each earthworm deposits in the soil a cocoon containing 2 to 20 fertilized eggs. Tiny but fully developed earthworms hatch from the eggs 60 to 90 days later.

The common earthworm (illustrated) is usually 5 to 8 inches long.

eastern goshawk \ 'gäs-ˌhȯk \

This keen-sighted bird of prey belongs to the same family as the hawks, eagles and kites. It hunts in daylight, swooping down to capture smaller birds in the air or animals on the ground.

The adult eastern goshawk is about 2 feet long, with a wingspread of 3½ to 4 feet. Like the eagle, it has a hooked beak and long, sharp claws. Its tail is marked with 5 broad, black bands.

The eastern goshawk lives in the woods, but it flies over prairies and farm fields when hunting food. Its nest is a rough pile of sticks and twigs in a large tree. Three to 5 eggs are laid once a year and are incubated for about 28 days. The blind and helpless young birds are fed and cared for in the nest for several months.

Their summer range is the northern half of the U.S., Canada and Alaska. In winter, the range includes all the U.S. and the southern part of Canada. Eastern goshawks are becoming very rare.

echidna \ i-'kid-nə \

Somewhat like porcupines in appearance, these small, odd mammals lay eggs, as the duck-billed platypus does. They are sometimes called spiny anteaters, though they are not closely related to the true anteaters of Central and South America.

Echidnas have narrow, tapering snouts. They do not have teeth or a tail. Echidnas use their long, sticky tongues to capture the insects and grubs they eat. Their short legs end in long, curved claws that they use for digging. During the day

ECHIDNA

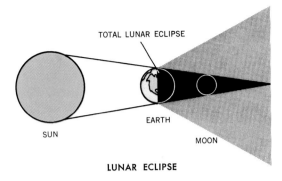

LUNAR ECLIPSE

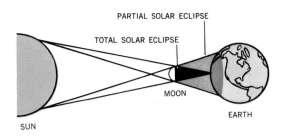

SOLAR ECLIPSE

they sleep in underground burrows. For protection from enemies, an echidna rolls itself into a spiny ball, just as a hedgehog does.

The female echidna lays 2 eggs with leathery shells and carries them in a pouch during the incubation period. The young remain in the pouch for about 2 weeks after they hatch.

Echidnas live in Australia, Tasmania and New Guinea.

The 4-toed echidna (illustrated) is usually 1 to 2 feet long. The 3-toed echidna is up to a foot longer.

eclipse \ i-'klips \

An eclipse of the moon takes place when the earth moves between the sun and the moon, so that the earth's shadow falls on the moon. Such an eclipse is often called a lunar eclipse.

A lunar eclipse can always be seen from a large part of the earth's surface. Although the moon is darkened, it does not entirely disappear. Some sunlight reflected to it from the earth gives it a dull, reddish glow. A total lunar eclipse may last 1½ hours.

An eclipse of the sun takes place when the moon passes between the sun and the earth, so that the moon's shadow falls on the earth. Such an eclipse is often called a solar eclipse.

A total solar eclipse is visible from only a small area, since only the tip of the moon's cone-shaped shadow touches the earth's surface. During a total solar eclipse, the sun's corona is visible as a ring of white light around the black disk of the moon. The sky becomes so dark that a few stars can be seen.

A partial solar or lunar eclipse is one in which only a part of the sun or moon is shadowed, or hidden from the earth.

eel \ 'ēl \

The eels are a large group of unusual fish with long, slender bodies. They look something like snakes. One narrow fin runs along the back and underside of the slippery body and around the tail.

Some eels have no scales. Others have very small scales hidden under the skin. All eels have sharp teeth. They feed on animal life such as smaller fish, worms and insects. In Europe and Japan, eels are highly valued as food.

All eels lay their eggs in deep parts of the ocean, far from shore. Newborn eels hatch from colorless eggs. They are flattened larvae that do not look like the

EEL

EELGRASS

adults. The larvae change into young eels, which are called elvers.

The common or American eel (illustrated) is the only kind that lives in freshwater lakes and rivers. The males are 1 to 2 feet long. The females are sometimes 4 to 5 feet long. Common eels are brown until they are ready to spawn. Then they turn silvery and begin the long trip down stream to the ocean. They lay their eggs in the Atlantic Ocean southwest of Bermuda, and then die.

The young live in the ocean for about a year, until they are 3 to 4 inches long. Then they swim up rivers and creeks to inland waters where they live until they are mature and ready to spawn. Some common eels swim as much as 1,000 miles to inland waters.

eelgrass \ 'ēl-ˌgras \ (grass wrack)

A grass-like marine plant, eelgrass grows underwater in tidal bays near ocean coastlines. It is a common plant in the cooler parts of the temperate zone. The seeds and plant parts of eelgrass are an important food for ducks and geese.

Eelgrass has long, ribbon-like leaves that resemble blades of grass. The branches grow upward and divide. The leaves sometimes grow to a length of 4 feet. At low tide, the tops of the leaves may be above the surface of the water.

An eelgrass plant bears both staminate and pistillate flowers. They grow alternately on the central rib of leaf-like spike and are hidden by leaf sheaths. Eelgrass seeds are barrel-shaped, with ribs running from one end of a seed to the other end.

Eelgrass spreads by means of creeping rhizomes that grow under mud or wet sand.

egret \ 'ē-grət \

Wading birds that belong to the heron family, egrets grow long and very beautiful plumes during the breeding season. Around 1900, the feathers of the American egret (illustrated) and the snowy egret were used to decorate women's hats. The birds were hunted until few were left alive. Laws were passed to protect them, and they are now becoming more common.

Egrets live throughout the temperate and tropical areas of the world. In the U.S., they live in swamps and marshes, mostly in southern states. They feed on fish, frogs, crustaceans and insects.

An egret's nest is a crude platform of sticks built in the top of a tree. Three to 6 eggs are laid once a year. The eggs are incubated by the female for about 28 days. Young egrets are very clumsy and pull themselves about the nest with their beaks.

EGRET

The American egret is sometimes called the common egret. It has a body length of about 24 inches, with plumes that may grow as long as 50 inches. It spends the winter south of South Carolina. In summer the American egret lives as far north as Ontario and Maine. Three to 5 pale blue eggs are laid once a year.

eider \ ˈīd-ər \

Ducks that live along seacoasts in the far north, eiders dive into the coldest parts of the ocean for the fish and mollusks they eat.

Thick layers of soft down feathers protect these ducks from the cold. The females pluck down from their breasts and use it to line their nests so that the eggs will not freeze. In Iceland and some other areas, men collect the down after the young birds leave the nest, and sell it. It is used to make fine pillows, quilts and sleeping bags.

Eiders breed along the coasts of Alaska, Greenland, northern China and in Siberia. During very cold winters, some eiders wander as far south as Japan, central Europe and the northern U.S.

The common eider (illustrated) nests in large colonies in Iceland, southern Alaska and the Aleutian Islands. The female, who is less colorful than the male, incubates the 4 to 10 eggs for about 26 days.

EIDER

ELECTRIC EEL

electric eel \ ˈēl \

This unusual freshwater fish generates electricity which it uses to shock and stun its enemies and the smaller fish on which it feeds. It is not a true eel, but a long, slender fish related to the catfish, the carp and the minnow.

The head and true body make up only about ⅕ of the total length. The rest is tail. Inside the tail are special kinds of muscle tissue that make and store electricity, much as a battery does.

The head end of the fish has a negative charge. The tail end has a positive charge. The greatest shock is given when the electric eel touches its head to one part of a victim and its tail to another part. A large electric eel gives off a shock powerful enough to knock a man unconscious. More than 500 volts have been measured from the shock of a large electric eel.

An electric eel may seek food by sending out radar-like electric signals that bounce back to it when they strike an object in the water.

The electric eel lives in the rivers of South America. It is 3 to 9 feet long and a sluggish swimmer. Little is known about its breeding habits, but the adults probably care for the young until they are about 6 inches long. The young eat insect larvae and worms.

ELEPHANT

elephant

Elephants make up a family of the largest of all land animals. They live in Africa and southern Asia, in tropical forests and on plains. Elephants have a keen sense of smell, but poor hearing and eyesight. When disturbed, they trumpet loudly.

Wild elephants usually feed and travel in herds of 10 to 20. Males are called bulls and females are called cows. Elephants eat only plant foods such as grass, tree leaves and bark. In captivity, they eat as much as 300 pounds of hay each day, and they drink about 50 gallons of water.

Elephant young are called calves. They grow up just about as fast as human babies do, since an elephant's life-span is equal to man's.

The Indian elephant (illustrated) is the kind most often seen in zoos and circuses. It is more easily captured and trained than the African elephant.

The Indian elephant is up to 10 feet tall, and can weigh as much as 5 tons. It has smaller ears than the African elephant, an arched back and just 1 "finger" at the tip of its trunk.

The African elephant is larger than the Indian elephant. There are 2 "fingers" at the tip of its trunk. The tusks are valuable sources of ivory and may weigh 100 pounds each.

elm

Elms make up a group of trees that grow in nearly all parts of the temperate zone except western North America. They are always mixed with other trees, and never grow in solid stands. In China and some other areas, food and medicines are made from the inner layer of elm bark. In the U.S., elm trees are valued more as shade trees than as timber trees.

Elm leaves have saw-toothed edges, and are a dark blue-green. Some feel rough. Some look lopsided because one half is longer than the other. Small, greenish-purple flowers dangle from the twigs in spring. The seeds are surrounded by a thin, papery wing.

The American elm (illustrated) is the largest and most beautiful of the elm trees. It may grow to 120 feet in height. It is now rare in many areas because of the Dutch elm disease and a bark disease caused by a virus.

Gracefully curved branches give the American elm tree its characteristic shape. The leaves and twigs droop down from the ends of the branches. The leaves are 3 to 6 inches long and feel slightly rough. They turn a bright yellow in autumn.

The American elm is the state tree of Massachusetts, of Nebraska and of North Dakota.

ELM

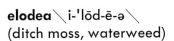

ELODEA

EMU

elodea \ i-'lōd-ē-ə \
(ditch moss, waterweed)

Elodea is a perennial plant which grows entirely underwater, with its roots in mud or wet sand. It is native to North America. It is often placed in indoor aquariums or outdoor goldfish ponds.

Like other underwater plants, elodea supports fish life by absorbing carbon dioxide from the water and giving off the oxygen that fish need.

Elodea is an attractive plant with graceful, feathery foliage. The many narrow leaves are slightly transparent and are crowded close together opposite each other on the stems. Very tiny flowers are hidden between the leaves. The seeds are small, hard nutlets that ripen underwater.

In most parts of North America, elodea grows in ponds and quiet streams. It often grows fast and in dense masses. When elodea grows too fast and chokes a pond, it becomes a nuisance.

emu \ 'ē-,myü \

This Australian bird stands 5 to 6 feet tall and weighs as much as 120 pounds. It is the second largest living bird. Only the ostrich is larger.

The emu cannot fly, but it swims well and can run as fast as 30 miles an hour. It has a broad, flat back, coarse feathers and very small wings. The male and female are the same color. The male is usually larger and makes a wider variety of sounds.

Emus live on the dry plains of Australia. They eat berries and fruits, as well as worms and insects. They are nuisances in some areas, where they break down fences and damage crops. Early settlers ate both the flesh and the eggs of emus.

The female emu lays 7 to 10 eggs once a year, in a flat nest placed on the ground. The nest is made of grasses, leaves and bark and is usually hidden under bushes or trees. Each egg is about 5½ inches long.

The male emu stays on the nest during the very long incubation period of about 2 months. He cares for the young birds after they hatch. Young emus are white, striped with yellow and black.

end moraine \ mə-'rān \
(terminal moraine)

An end moraine is made up of mounds or ridges of broken-up rocks, sand and soil that mark the place where a glacier stopped moving.

As a glacier moves, it pushes rocks, sand and soil ahead of it. When a glacier melts and stops moving, the rocks, sand and soil remain to form an end moraine.

Some end moraines look like curved banks across valleys. Other end moraines look like broad strips of broken and usually rounded hills. These end moraines are higher than the areas around them.

Geologists who dig into end moraines find gravel and rocks of different kinds and sizes, as well as sand and soil.

See *moraine*.

English sparrow

The English sparrow is not closely related to the other birds called sparrows in North America. It is a hardy little bird, native to Europe, that makes its home in crowded cities as well as in open country. The English sparrow eats almost anything, and it survives in all but the very coldest of climates.

A few English sparrows were released in Brooklyn, New York, in 1851, by men who hoped they would eat insects that were damaging shade trees. By 1900 English sparrows were common in nearly all parts of North America. The bird has also spread throughout South Africa, most of Asia, Australia and Hawaii.

The English sparrow is 5½ to 6½ inches

ENGLISH SPARROW

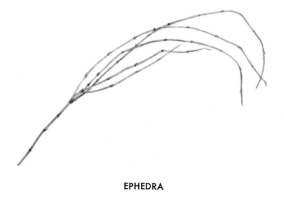

EPHEDRA

long. The male has a gray cap and a black throat patch. In winter, the feather tips of the male turn gray. The female is a streaked, brownish color with a pale brown stripe over each eye.

The bulky, untidy nest is built in bushes or vines, or under the eaves of buildings. The female lays 3 to 6 eggs several times a year, often raising a brood as early as February.

ephedra \ i-'fed-rə \

Ephedras make up a group of unusual desert shrubs that look something like horsetails. Botanists find ephedras interesting because their place in the plant kingdom is somewhere between angiosperms and gymnosperms.

Ephedras do not bear flowers. Their seeds, like those of conifers, mature inside cones. The stems are slender and jointed. The leaves are small scales that grow in pairs at the joints on the stem. The cones also grow at some of the stem joints.

One kind of ephedra, first cultivated in China, is the source of the medicine ephedrine. This medicine is used to relieve the discomfort of colds and hay fever by shrinking the mucous membranes in the nasal cavity. Today, most ephedrine is made in factories, from chemicals.

The kind of ephedra most common in North America is called Mormon tea (illustrated). It is a bushy shrub that grows 3 to 5 feet tall. Mormon tea grows in western Texas, New Mexico, Arizona and southern California.

escarpment \ es-'kärp-mənt \

An escarpment is a long cliff or steep slope that separates 2 fairly level areas, one higher than the other.

Some escarpments are due to faults or breaks in underlying rock layers. If the mass of rock on one side of the break is lifted higher than the mass of rock on the other side, an escarpment appears.

Other escarpments are due to erosion. Such an escarpment marks the end of a formation of hard rock. The hard rock remains after the softer rock, next to it, has been worn away by wind or moving water.

The end of a plateau may be an escarpment.

estuary \ 'es(h)-chə-,wer-ē \

An estuary is a long bay where the ocean enters the mouth of a river. The water in an estuary is a mixture of fresh water from the river and salt water from the sea.

Estuaries are sometimes called drowned valleys. They are found along submerged coastlines, where in fairly recent times the land has dropped down, or the level of the ocean has risen.

The upper end of most estuaries is above sea level. The streams that flow into the river at this upper end carry much sediment into the river. The sediment often forms many small deltas and mud flats at the mouth of the estuary.

The mouths of the St. Lawrence River, Chesapeake Bay, and the harbor at New York City are all estuaries. New York City harbor is the mouth of the Hudson River. Chesapeake Bay is the large drowned valley of the Shenandoah River.

euglena \ yu̇-'glē-nə \

Euglenas make up a group of 1-celled, swimming organisms. In some ways, euglenas are like plants, while in other ways they are like animals. Some scientists class them with animals because they are like certain protozoans. Other scientists class them with algae, or plants, because they contain chlorophyll.

Some kinds of euglenas live alone, while others live in colonies. Most kinds live in freshwater streams or ponds, but some live in brackish water or mud. Like plants, euglenas use energy from the sun along with chlorophyll to make their own food.

Seen under a microscope, different

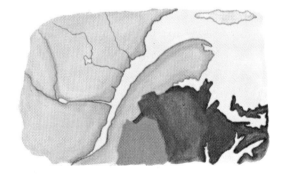

ESTUARY

EUGLENA

143

EUROPEAN CORN BORER

kinds of euglenas are rounded or oval. Like many protozoans, euglenas have the whip-like appendages, flagella, which they use to swim. Some kinds of euglenas have 1 flagellum, others have 2, and still others have 3.

Euglenas are brown, green or yellowish. They reproduce by dividing into 2 new cells, each like the parent but smaller.

A common kind of euglena (illustrated) is oval and has 1 flagellum.

European corn borer \,yủr-ə-'pē-ən 'kȯrn 'bōr-ər\

This insect pest is the larva of a moth. The larva (illustrated) attacks not only corn but other large-stemmed plants such as gladioli and dahlias. The larva was brought to the U.S. from Europe in 1910. Since then, it has spread from New England to all states east of the Rocky Mountains except Florida.

The adult moths have slender bodies, large heads and beak-like mouthparts. The wings are yellowish or white and measure over an inch from tip to tip.

In the summer, the female moth lays her eggs on the underside of the leaves of the host plant, usually corn. In about a week the eggs hatch and the tiny larvae feed on the outside of the plant. When they are half-grown, the larvae bore into the stalks and feed until winter. They hibernate and grow inside the stalks until spring. During the summer, they become adult moths.

The larvae are a pinkish color with hard, brown heads. Across each segment of the abdomen are 4 dark spots, each with a prickly, hair-like growth.

European wild boar \,yủr-ə-'pē-ən 'wīld 'bōr\

This wild mammal is one of the largest and most powerful of swine. It belongs to the same family as the domestic pig and is believed to be its direct ancestor.

Hunted for sport for centuries in Europe, Asia and Africa, the European wild boar was brought to U.S. by sportsmen. It is hunted in Tennessee, North Carolina, New England and California. Dogs track it easily from the strong odor it gives off from its scent glands.

The adult European wild boar is 5 feet long and stands 3 feet high at the shoulder. It may weigh as much as 375 pounds. Its solid, rounded body is covered with short, thick fur that is pale gray to black.

The long, sharp tusks may grow to over a foot in length. The boar sharpens them by rubbing them on trees or against its smaller, lower tusks. Its attack is fierce and its bite is very powerful, ripping flesh easily. The wild boar eats a wide variety of both plant and animal foods.

The piglets are born in litters of 3 to 12. They have dark spots and stripes that run lengthwise along the body.

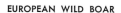

EUROPEAN WILD BOAR

EVENING PRIMROSE

evening primrose \ 'prim-ˌrōz \

Evening primroses make up a group of annual, biennial or perennial plants. They are not related to the true primrose. Evening primroses are widespread in North America. They are found in damp areas and along roadsides.

The flowers of the evening primrose are usually yellow but may be white or rose-colored. They have long tubes and 4 broad petals. One or 2 flowers appear at the point where the leaves join the stem. Some kinds bloom in the daytime, while others bloom in the evening. The flowers last only a short time.

The leaves grow alternately and may have smooth edges or rough, toothed edges. They may either have short stalks or be stalkless. The fruit is a 4-lobed seed-pod.

One evening primrose (illustrated) is called the sun drop. It is a perennial that blooms in the daytime. It grows 1 to 3 feet tall. The yellow flowers are about 2 inches across and have hairy stems, reddish in color. The leaves are 1 to 2 inches long and short-stalked. The sun drop grows throughout the eastern half of the U.S.

f

fairy shrimp \ 'shrimp \

Fairy shrimps belong to a group of fresh-water crustaceans that live mostly in fresh water. They are not true shrimps. They are called shrimps only because they look something like the true shrimps that live in the ocean.

Fairy shrimps have segmented bodies but no hard outer covering, or carapace, such as true shrimps have. The fairy shrimp has 11 pairs of appendages which it uses for swimming and for respiration, since the appendages contain gills.

The fairy shrimp swims on its back. As the gill feet wave back and forth, they push microscopic organisms, on which the fairy shrimp feeds, towards its mouth.

Fairy shrimps average 1 inch in length and are partly transparent. They may be red, bronze, green or blue. Females are more numerous than males and can be identified by the egg sac at the end of the thorax. The eggs are laid in summer and remain buried in mud until spring when the young hatch.

Although fairy shrimps live in fresh-water ponds all over the U.S., they are most common in the eastern U.S. They prefer cool to cold water. A common North American fairy shrimp (illustrated) is pale and translucent.

FAIRY SHRIMP

falcon \ 'fal-kən \

Falcons are swift-flying birds of prey that belong to the same family as hawks. Some kinds of falcons can fly as fast as 100 miles per hour and dive at speeds of 175 miles per hour. Falcons live in all parts of the world except Antarctica.

The body of the smallest kind of falcon is only 6½ inches long. Large kinds measure up to 24 inches. Most falcons have large heads with curved, notched beaks, long tails, broad shoulders and long, narrow wings. Their naked legs and feet have long, sharp talons.

Small falcons feed on insects. The larger kinds kill rats and mice, snakes and other birds. They do not build nests but lay eggs on the ground, on rocky ledges or in nests left by other birds. Small falcons lay 3 to 5 eggs, while large falcons lay 2 to 4.

Falcons can be trained to hunt. The sport of falconry dates back to ancient Egypt. The gyrfalcon (illustrated) is 1 kind of falcon used for falconry. It is the largest of the falcons and breeds in the Arctic. During winter months it ranges as far south as Russia, England and the northern U.S.

Some gyrfalcons are nearly pure white. The lighter-colored birds nest farthest north, on the snowy tundra.

FALCON

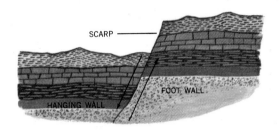

NORMAL FAULT

fault

A fault is a crack or break in part of the earth's crust. The earth or rocks on each side of a fault move past each other, upward, downward or sideways. The movement may be small and hard to see, or it may stretch for miles to form mountain ranges.

Most faults are caused by forces and pressures in part of the earth's crust. Some faults may be caused by forces and pressures far below the earth's crust.

Most earthquakes are due to movement along faults. An earthquake that shook New Zealand in 1929 was caused when ground on one side of a fault moved upward 15 feet and sideways 9 feet.

The side of a fault that slants underneath the other side is called the foot wall. The side that slants over the foot wall is called the hanging wall. The higher side of a fault is called a scarp.

A normal fault (illustrated) occurs when the foot wall moves upward and the hanging wall moves downward. The scarp slants and is often a smooth-faced cliff.

Normal faults are found throughout the world. In the Rocky Mountains in Utah and Nevada, normal faults mark the beginning of many mountain ranges. The

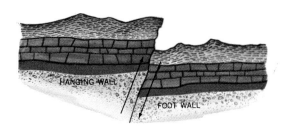

REVERSE FAULT

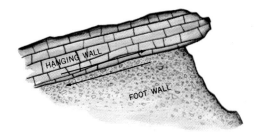

THRUST FAULT

mountains are several thousand feet higher on one side of the fault than is the valley on the other side. The Teton range of Wyoming is bounded on the east by a large normal fault.

A reverse fault (illustrated) occurs when the hanging wall moves upward and the foot wall moves downward. The scarp usually crumbles away in landslides or through erosion so that it has a rough surface.

A thrust fault (illustrated) is a kind of reverse fault in which the hanging wall forms only a small angle with the foot wall. It looks as if a hanging wall of older rocks had been pushed over a foot wall of younger rocks. The overhanging wall of a thrust fault is often folded over and deeply eroded.

One well-known thrust fault is in the Chief Mountains along the east side of the Rocky Mountains in Glacier National Park, Montana. Large thrust faults can be seen in the Appalachian region in Virginia and Tennessee.

The famous San Andreas Rift is a very long fault that extends about 600 miles along the West Coast, from northern California south into Mexico. The earthquake that destroyed San Francisco in 1906 was a horizontal or sideways slipping along the plane of this fault.

feldspar \ 'fel(d)-ˌspär \

Feldspars are a group of closely related minerals. About 60 percent of all the rocks in the world contain some kind of feldspar. Nearly all igneous rocks contain feldspars.

Feldspars may be white, pink, gray, yellowish-brown and occasionally green, bluish or black. They often can be seen as colorful crystals that shine on the face of cut stone.

Feldspars can be melted at high temperatures and are widely used in making pottery, glass and enamelware to give the objects a shiny surface.

It is hard to tell one kind of feldspar from another. Feldspars are classified by their chemical makeup and by cleavage. Although the color gives some clue to the content of a piece of feldspar, it can be accurately classified only by an expert.

Orthoclase is a potassium feldspar that is colorless in its pure state. Most orthoclase, however, is usually tinted pink or red by the iron oxide it contains. Orthoclase is a Greek word that means splitting at right angles, a characteristic of this form of feldspar.

Microcline is a kind of feldspar that is always some shade of green.

fern

The ferns are a group of primitive plants that do not produce flowers or seeds. Like the club mosses, ferns are the survivors of plants that grew thousands of years ago.

The smallest ferns are only a few inches tall. The largest, found only in the tropics, grow to 80 feet tall.

Fern leaves, called fronds, are nearly always made up of many small leaflets. The young fronds are often coiled at the tip. They uncurl as they grow larger.

Ferns are most common in the tropics, but some kinds grow in all parts of the temperate zone. All of those illustrated grow in North America. Most are found in shady places where the soil is moist.

Ferns reproduce by alternation of generations. The fronds are part of the sporophyte plant. In most ferns, the spores fall from small brown spots on the undersides of the leaflets. The gametophyte plant that grows from the spore is tiny and short-lived. It lies flat on moist soil, and it withers away as soon as the new sporophyte begins to grow from it.

The Boston fern is popular as a house plant. It is one of the very few ferns that will grow indoors, in a flowerpot. The fronds are light green and graceful. Each has a long center rib with narrow leaflets growing out from both sides.

The Christmas fern looks a good deal like the Boston fern but its leaves are thicker and glossier, more like holly. It stays green all winter. The shiny, dark green fronds are 8 to 20 inches long.

Bracken is a sturdy, weed-like fern that grows wild in almost all parts of the temperate zone. It is one of the few ferns that will grow in a dry, sunny field. The sturdy stalks of bracken grow from 2 to 9 feet tall. Each frond is a triangular group of coarse leaflets.

Maidenhair fern has a graceful, delicate appearance. It grows 10 to 18 inches tall. Its many small, scalloped leaflets grow from slender stems that branch repeatedly. It is found throughout the temperate zone, usually in woods where the soil is moist.

The walking fern is named for the unusual way that it sometimes produces new plants. One frond bends over until it touches the ground. Then it takes root at the tip. When the base dies, the fern has "walked" a step. Walking fern has blade-shaped leaves 2 to 8 inches long. Unlike most ferns, the leaf is not divided into leaflets. The walking fern grows among shaded, mossy rocks, from Quebec and Ontario to Georgia and Oklahoma.

In all the kinds of ferns mentioned so far, spores fall from the undersides of ordinary-looking, green leaflets. In certain other kinds, special leaflets that are a different shape or color produce spores.

Rattlesnake fern belongs to the group called grape ferns. Its spore-producing leaflets look like clusters of berries growing at the top of a slender stalk.

The interrupted fern, the royal fern and the cinnamon fern all belong to the group called the osmundas. They are large, coarse ferns that grow 2 to 9 feet tall, in swamps.

The cinnamon fern is named for the color of its spore-producing leaflets, which are clustered at the top of a separate stalk. This fern grows in large clumps 1 to 5 feet tall. It grows in most of the eastern U.S. and is also found in eastern Asia.

The royal fern is one of the largest ferns in temperate regions. The spore-producing leaflets are grouped at the ends of some of the long fronds. They are green at first but turn brown.

In the interrupted fern, the spore-producing leaflets are green but smaller than the others. They appear halfway along some stalks.

Ferns—Primitive Plants

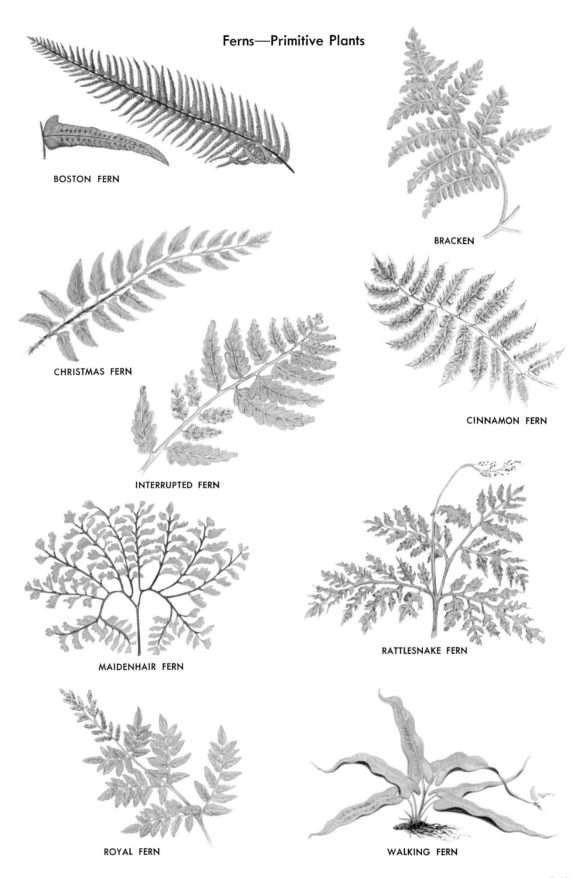

BOSTON FERN

BRACKEN

CHRISTMAS FERN

INTERRUPTED FERN

CINNAMON FERN

MAIDENHAIR FERN

RATTLESNAKE FERN

ROYAL FERN

WALKING FERN

ferret \ 'fer-ət \

Members of the weasel family, ferrets are carnivorous mammals native to Spain. European ferrets are dark brown and almost extinct. In the U.S., the ferret is called the domestic ferret (illustrated). It is a true albino and is yellowish-white.

Ferrets have short legs and long, thin bodies about 27 inches long, including the tail. Average weight is 4 pounds. The head is rat-like, with a pointed snout and short, round ears. The jaws are very strong, and the teeth sharp. Slender and quick-moving, the ferret darts into rabbit burrows and ratholes too small for most flesh-eating mammals to enter.

Wild ferrets are great hunters and some have been trained by man to catch rats and other unwelcome animals. Wild ferrets often raid chicken coops and pigeon lofts. Sometimes, they attack and kill animals larger than themselves. Domestic ferrets have become so dependent on man for food that they die in a few days if they are released.

Ferrets mate twice a year. The female ferret digs a den, often under a rock. The young ferrets are born blind and hairless, in litters of 6 to 9.

For another kind of ferret, see *black-footed ferret.*

FERRET

FRUIT AND LEAVES OF FIG TREE

fig tree

Fig trees include both trees and shrubs. All belong to the mulberry family. For thousands of years fig trees have been cultivated in warm countries. Cultivated fig trees are started from woody cuttings.

There are many kinds of fig trees and they produce figs of many sizes and colors. Some trees may be 35 feet tall. Others are shrubs 3 feet high. When ripe, the figs may be yellow, brown, purple or black. They are eaten fresh, dried or canned in many parts of the world. In the U.S., figs are widely used in fig bars and cookies.

The flowers of the fig tree are hard to see because they line the inside of the hollow, pear-shaped fig. The fig must be cut open to see the flowers and the true fruit, or seeds, which form inside. The female flowers are fertilized by the small fig wasp which crawls inside the fig.

In the U.S., figs are grown in California and Texas. In California almost all figs are grown under irrigation. In Europe, most of the figs are grown in Italy, Turkey, Greece, Portugal and Spain.

The common fig tree is native to the eastern Mediterranean area. Its leaves (illustrated) are alternate and irregular in shape, with 3 to 5 rounded leaflets.

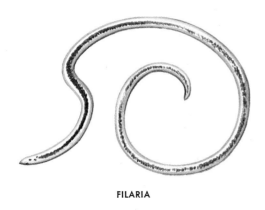

FILARIA

filaria \ fə-'lar-ē-ə \

Filarias make up a group of parasitic roundworms. They usually require 2 hosts to complete their life cycle. The first part of the life cycle takes place in the body of a biting insect. The second part takes place within the body of an animal bitten by the insect.

The larvae of a filaria live in the blood vessels of infected animals. The larvae are usually near the surface of the animal's skin. When an insect bites the animal, it picks up some of the larvae. The larvae then live within the insect and grow more mature there. Finally, when the insect bites another animal, the larvae pass from the insect to the second animal. There, the larvae develop into adult worms.

Many mature filarias are thread-like. Some grow to over 2 feet in length. A tropical kind of filaria (illustrated) is carried by a mosquito. This filaria matures and reproduces in human lymph glands. It may block lymph circulation and block the body's growth. A person severely infected with this filaria may develop elephantiasis, a condition where parts of the body swell. This disease is most common in Africa and in southern Asia. It is rare in the U.S.

finch \ 'finch \

Finches make up a large family of birds with members in every part of the world except Australia. They are perchers and seedeaters.

Most finches are from 5 to 10 inches long and have strong beaks well suited to cracking seeds. They also eat insects. The male is usually more brightly colored than the female. Finches that live in trees are usually more brightly colored than ground-dwelling finches. Most finches raise several broods each year.

The house finch (illustrated) is common in California and Mexico and looks something like a sparrow. The male has red on its head, breast and back. The female is gray-brown above and white below. The song is a long high warble.

A few house finches are found in the eastern U.S., near New York. They are descended from cage birds transported illegally and then released, in 1940.

In April, the female house finch builds a nest out of paper, grass and rags. She lays 4 to 5 pale blue, black-spotted eggs. While she sits on the eggs, the male stays nearby to protect the nest.

For other members of the finch family, see *bunting, canary bird, cardinal, crossbill, goldfinch, grosbeak, junco, linnet, sparrow* and *towhee.*

FINCH

FIR

fir \\ 'fər \\

Firs are cone-shaped evergreen trees with dense foliage and evenly spaced branches. They are closely related to the pines. Fir wood is weak and is used only for wood pulp and packing boxes.

The kind of fir most common in eastern North America is the balsam fir (illustrated). It is the source of a clear gum used to mount biological specimens on microscope slides. Young balsam firs are popular as Christmas trees because their needles stay on longer than most.

Mature balsam firs are 25 to 60 feet tall. Their lower branches often hang to the ground. The fragrant needles are a rich dark green on the top, and lighter underneath. The bark is gray on young trees and reddish-brown on older trees.

The cones of a balsam fir are oval, tapering and 2 to 4 inches long. They are dark purplish-green in color. The seed has a broad, purplish-brown wing.

Balsam firs grow best in cool, fairly moist climates. They are common in much of Canada. In the U.S., balsam firs are most common in New England, around the Great Lakes and south along the Appalachian Mountains to Virginia.

See *Douglas fir*.

firefly (lightning bug)

Lightning bugs make up a family of soft-bodied beetles that give off a flashing, almost heatless light. They produce this light by chemical reactions in the organs of the last segments of the abdomen. The number of flashes per minute depends on the kind of firefly and also the temperature. Scientists believe that the flashing lights bring male and female fireflies together.

Fireflies have wings with soft covers. The female of some kinds of fireflies has smaller wings or is wingless. The antennae are slender. The head is covered by the first segment of the thorax. Most fireflies are less than ½ inch long.

Female fireflies lay eggs in damp soil or near moisture-loving plants. The larvae, sometimes called glowworms, are flat with small, narrow heads and strong jaws. They live underground, and feed on snails, earthworms and slugs. The larvae may live 1 or 2 years before entering the pupal stage. The adult fireflies appear in early summer and usually eat nothing.

Fireflies are very widely distributed throughout the world. One kind of firefly (illustrated) is common east of the Rocky Mountains, near marshy areas and in woods.

See *glowworm*.

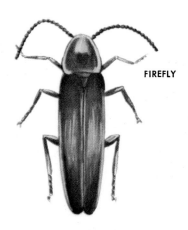

FIREFLY

firn\ 'fi(ə)rn\ (névé)

Firn is a mass of old snow that collects where glaciers begin. Firn is unlike newly fallen snow, which is light and fluffy because air is trapped between the crystals. Firn is made up of rounded particles that form when crystals of new snow melt and refreeze. The particles lie closer together and are heavier and denser than the crystals of new snow.

When new snow falls on top of firn, the particles are pressed even closer together. Repeated freezing and thawing turns firn into solid ice.

Firn collects in cirques on mountainsides and may build up to a depth of 100 feet or more. Each time it refreezes, firn expands slightly. This action, plus the weight of the ice, firn and snow, causes the mass to move slowly downhill. The result is the beginning of a glacier.

fish

Fish make up a very large group of cold-blooded chordate animals. They have a skin with many mucous glands and a backbone with vertebrae. The heart is formed of a folded tube with several chambers. Fish have no eyelids. Most fish have fins and scales. All have gills rather than lungs for breathing.

There are more than 30,000 kinds of fish. They differ greatly in size, shape and color. Some tropical fish are only ½ inch long. Some sharks are 70 feet long.

Because their bodies are streamlined, most fish can move easily through the water. An air bladder inside the bodies of most fish allows them to swim at different depths. Most fish are carnivorous. Nearly all fish hatch from eggs.

Almost every body of water has fish in it. Since early times, fish have been a large and important part of man's food. The economy of many countries depends greatly on fish. Fishing has long been enjoyed by sportsmen throughout the world. The by-products of fish include oils, meal, leather, fertilizer and glue.

In the sea, as on land, all animal life depends on plant life. Although most fish feed on fish smaller than themselves, the basic food of small fish is plankton.

fisher\ 'fish-ər\

This carnivorous mammal is a member of the weasel family. Its name suggests that it is fond of fish to eat. However, most fishers eat smaller mammals, frogs, nuts and fruits. Fishers are fierce hunters and are the only animals known that will attack porcupines.

The male fisher is fox-like in appearance and measures about 3 feet long with a 12-inch tail. It weighs 8 to 13 pounds.

PARTS OF FISH

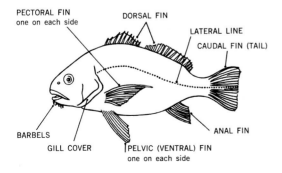

PECTORAL FIN
one on each side

DORSAL FIN

LATERAL LINE

CAUDAL FIN (TAIL)

BARBELS

GILL COVER

PELVIC (VENTRAL) FIN
one on each side

ANAL FIN

FISHER

The female is smaller and weighs 5 to 6 pounds. Both male and female have shaggy dark fur and bushy tails.

Fishers live in deep woods, where they build dens in hollow trees. They hunt at night. Like skunks, which belong to the same family, fishers give off an unpleasant odor if annoyed. They are good climbers and can leap easily from tree to tree.

Young fishers are born blind in litters of 2 to 6 in April. The mother cares for the young until fall.

The fisher was once common in New England, New York and the western states from Montana to California. Fishers were once widely hunted for their fur. They are now rare.

fissure \ 'fish-ər \

A fissure is a crack or break in a rock formation. It is usually long and narrow, but it can be very deep. Fissures are usually wider at the top than at the bottom.

Fissures are often found in layers of folded rock (illustrated). The top layer has pulled apart on the outside of a curve or anticline.

Some fissures were caused when there was a difference in pressure inside the rock. Other fissures were caused when hot melted rock cooled and shrank slightly. Such fissures are common in areas where volcanoes have been active.

FISSURE

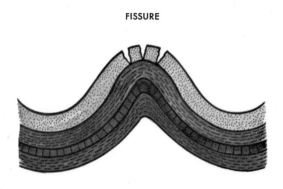

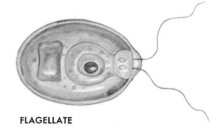

FLAGELLATE

A fissure can also be a crack or break in a glacier. Glacial fissures or crevasses are caused when the glacial ice moves along a rough, uneven surface. Instead of bending, the ice cracks. When a glacial fissure fills with soft snow it is hard to see. Such fissures, or crevasses, are a constant danger to mountain climbers.

flagellate \ 'flaj-ə-lət \

Flagellates are protozoans with 1, 2 or 3 whip-like appendages called flagella. They use these flagella to propel themselves through the water in which they live. The flagella are also used to draw food into the mouth opening. Flagellates are widespread in all tropical and warm temperate waters and in moist places.

Like all protozoans, flagellates are 1-celled. Some resemble plants and some resemble animals, while still others resemble both. Like animals, flagellates move about and digest solid food. Like plants and certain algae, some flagellates have chlorophyll and make their own food through photosynthesis.

Some flagellates are protected by shells, while others have no shells. Although most flagellates are parasitic, a few are free-living or symbiotic. Nearly all flagellates are solitary. They reproduce by binary fission. Many flagellates have small eyespots that are sensitive to light. Some have 2 flagella.

One kind of solitary flagellate (illustrated) has 2 flagella, 1 eyespot and a chloroplast.

For other kinds of flagellates, see *dinoflagellate* and *trypanosome*.

FLAMINGO

flamingo \ flə-'ming-ˌgō \

Flamingos make up a family of long-legged wading birds related to herons. The flamingo family contains the world's largest, bright-colored birds. Some stand more than 5 feet tall at the shoulder. Their length from bill to tail averages 6½ feet. Colors range from pink to crimson.

Flamingos feed by pumping mud and muck from the bottom of shallow bodies of water through their large hooked bills. Small mollusks, algae, protozoa and worms are strained out and swallowed.

At rest, the flamingo stands on one foot and rests its head on its back. In flight, the flamingo stretches its long neck and legs out and honks like a goose.

Flamingos gather in flocks of up to 2,000 and breed on islands or peninsulas surrounded by shallow water. The nest is built of muddy clay. It is 17 inches high and 12 to 15 inches across. The female lays 1 or 2 pinkish-white eggs. Male and female take turns sitting on the nest and feeding the young.

Flamingos are found in some areas of Europe, Africa, Asia, South America and the Caribbean. The greater flamingo (illustrated) is the best-known and most widely distributed kind of flamingo. It was once widely hunted for its plumage, but is now protected by law.

flatworm \ 'flat-ˌwərm \

The name "flatworm" has been given to 3 large groups of worms with flat bodies. There are about 7,000 kinds of flatworms. Some kinds are free-living, while others are parasites. Flatworms have many shapes, sizes and colors. Some are transparent. The smallest can be seen only through a microscope, while others may be hundreds of feet in length.

The flatworms are the simplest of all animals that have sense organs and nerves grouped in a kind of head.

The free-living flatworms live in ponds, streams and oceans. A few kinds live on land. The planaria (illustrated) is the most common free-living flatworm. It is a member of the Turbellaria group.

The parasitic flatworms usually depend on vertebrate hosts. Some of these flatworms complete their life cycle in 1 host. Others have 2 or 3 hosts. The fluke and the tapeworm (both illustrated) are parasites that cause disease and sometimes death in animals and humans. The fluke is a member of the Trematoda group, while the tapeworm belongs to the Cestoidea group.

Most flatworms have bilateral symmetry and are sensitive to light and vibration. Reproduction is either sexual or asexual, or in some kinds, it may be both.

See *fluke, planaria* and *tapeworm.*

THREE GROUPS OF FLATWORMS

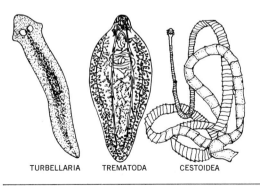

TURBELLARIA   TREMATODA   CESTOIDEA

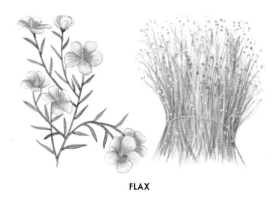

FLAX

flax \ 'flaks \

Flaxes make up a group of annual and perennial plants. They are among the oldest plants cultivated by man.

In Europe, Asia, Africa and America, flax is raised for its long-stemmed fibers, which are used to make linen cloth and rope. Linseed oil and cattle food is made from flax seeds. Some kinds of flax are grown as garden flowers and still others grow wild.

Flaxes grow best in a moist climate. They are 3 to 4 feet high. The flowers may be blue, white or pale pink. Each bloom has 5 petals, 5 sepals and 10 anthers that may be blue or yellow. The flowers open in early afternoon. The flowers are self-pollinating.

One kind of flax (illustrated) is grown for its fibers. It usually has blue flowers, although some plants may have white flowers. The crop is usually planted in early spring. It is picked for its fibers when about ½ of the seeds are ripe.

After the flax has been picked, it is tied in bundles and left in the field to dry. The seeds are removed by combing or beating the tops of the bundles.

Flaxseed (linseed) is ground, stemmed and pressed to remove its oil. Linseed oil is most often used in the manufacture of paints and varnishes.

flea

Fleas make up a group of very small insect parasites that annoy humans and animals. One kind of flea, the rat flea, carries the disease known as bubonic plague.

The body of a flea is smooth, flat, oval and reddish-brown in color. Some kinds are covered with bristles. Fleas have simple eyes or none, and piercing and sucking mouthparts. Two short antennae shaped like clubs lie close to the sides of the head. The well-developed legs have claws. Fleas are good jumpers and hard to catch.

Fleas live on the bodies of warm-blooded animals. The very small eggs are laid in the bed or nest of the animal. They go through a complete metamorphosis in 30 days.

Flea larvae look like slim worms and feed on decaying vegetable or animal matter. They have heads and biting mouthparts but no eyes and legs. They go through several stages of growth before they spin a cocoon and enter the pupal stage. Adult fleas feed on the blood of their hosts.

The dog flea (illustrated) lives on domestic animals and human beings. It looks like most other fleas except for the bristles on its head and thorax. The dog flea is about $\frac{1}{10}$ inch long.

FLEA

flicker \ 'flik-ər \

The flickers are woodpeckers that feed on the ground more often than most woodpeckers do. They eat ants and grasshoppers, along with other insects, seeds and berries.

Like other woodpeckers, flickers have strong, sharp bills and long tongues that are barbed and sticky at the tips. Their stiff tail feathers serve as props for their bodies when they cling to tree trunks. Their 2 center toes point forward, while the other 2 point backward. Flickers are about 11 inches long.

Flicker nests are holes up to 24 inches deep, hollowed out of trees or telephone poles. Both male and female incubate the glossy white eggs and feed the young birds.

Flickers live in both North and South America, in fairly open country rather than in deep woods. They help to control insects that damage shade trees and farm crops.

The yellow-shafted flicker (illustrated) is common in summer throughout the eastern half of the U.S. and southern Canada. It winters in the southern states.

The red-shafted flicker common in the western states is similar but has red under its wings rather than yellow. It also has a small red spot just above the bill.

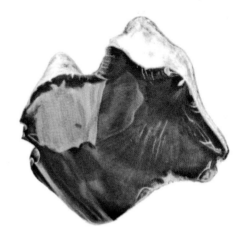

FLINT

flint \ 'flint \

Flint is a quartz mineral found in rocks in almost all parts of the world. It is made up of crystals so small that they can be seen only through a powerful microscope.

Because flint can be chipped to produce sharp edges, it was used by early peoples to make tools, arrowheads and other weapons. Later, man found that steel struck on flint produced sparks. He used this principle to start fires before the invention of matches. Flint and steel were struck together to produce the spark that set off gunpowder in old flintlock guns.

Today, flint is used in pottery. Several thousand tons of flint pebbles are used yearly to grind raw materials for ceramics and paints.

Flint is very dark gray, dark brown or black. When it is very thin, as around the edges of arrowheads, it is translucent.

Veins or nuggets of flint are sometimes found in limestone deposits. Flint is widely distributed in the United States and Canada and is even more common in the chalk deposits of western Europe.

Most often, flint is found in rounded lumps called nodules, 1 inch to 2 feet in diameter. The outside of the nodule is often white, like the chalk or limestone that once surrounded it.

FLICKER

FLOE

floe \ ˈflō \

A floe is a field of floating ice. Saltwater floes are formed in the summer when frozen areas of the sea around the North and South poles break up. These floes are loose collections of ice blocks 8 to 13 feet thick. Their tops are not far above the surface of the ocean.

An ice floe is less dense than pack ice, which is made up of floating blocks crowded together in a solid mass.

Freshwater floes are formed when icebergs break up as they drift into warmer water. Since icebergs are pieces that break off from glaciers, and glaciers are made of snow and ice, these floes are fresh water.

North Atlantic freshwater floes have been traced to glaciers in Greenland. Pieces of the glaciers break off and drift southward as icebergs. The rough waves, sun and warm water make them smaller and turn them into floes. The floes disappear south of Newfoundland.

Most of the floes that drift in the northern Atlantic and Pacific oceans are saltwater or sea ice floes. Because of the salt it contains, seawater does not freeze at 32° F. as fresh water does. Sea ice begins to form only when the temperature drops to about 28° F.

flounder \ ˈflaůn-dər \

Flounders belong to 2 families of flatfish. All flounders have flat bodies and nearly all live in salt water. Both eyes of the flounders belonging to 1 family are on the right side of the head. Both eyes of the flounders belonging to the other family are on the left side of the head.

Young flounders have 1 eye on each side of the head. They swim in an upright position. As the young flounders mature, the eye on one side moves to the other side, and the fish settles to the bottom on the eyeless side. The eyeless side turns whitish, while the eyed side becomes darker. Flounders feed on small crustaceans and other marine invertebrates.

One well-known member of the righteye flounder family is the halibut. It is the largest kind of flounder and may weigh as much as 700 pounds.

Most flounders are much smaller than the halibut and measure from 10 to 15 inches in length. All flounders are valued as food fish, especially the winter flounder (illustrated), which spawns in the winter. It is a righteye flounder, and is caught along the Atlantic coast from Labrador to Georgia. The winter flounder is often sold as sole.

For another member of the flounder families, see *halibut*.

FLOUNDER

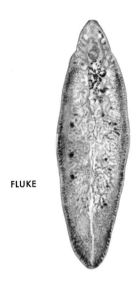

FLUKE

fluke \ 'flük \

Flukes make up a group of parasitic flat-worms. They are found mostly in fish, mollusks, turtles and frogs. Some are parasites of man and other mammals. Flukes are found all over the world. They are generally flat and leaf-like in appearance.

Some flukes live on the outside of animals, while others live within the organs, bloodstream or mouth. Some kinds of flukes require only 1 host. Many other kinds have 2 or 3 hosts and spend part of their life cycles in snails. Flukes reproduce either sexually or asexually.

One kind of liver fluke (illustrated) causes great losses each year in the U.S. to raisers of sheep, cattle and rabbits. The adults are about 1½ inches long. They live in an animal's liver, where they lay their eggs. The eggs pass from the animal in waste matter. The embryos bore into snails and develop into larvae.

The liver fluke larvae leave the snails and attach themselves to water plants that are eaten by sheep, cattle and rabbits. The larvae develop into adult flukes in the animal's intestine and move to the liver. They may live up to 11 years, if the host animal is not so heavily infected that it sickens and dies. Infected sheep and cattle are said to have "liver rot."

fluorite \ 'flur-ͺit \

Fluorite is a mineral valued for both its beauty and its usefulness. It is found on all continents of the world as transparent or translucent crystals of almost every color. Pure fluorite is colorless and is sometimes used for lenses. Pink or red fluorite is quite rare. The most common kinds are green, blue, yellow, purple, brown or nearly black.

Fluorite is often mixed with raw materials during the melting process to aid in the manufacture of steel. It is also used to aid in the removal of metals from their ores. Fluorite is used in the making of glass, enamel and fuels. It is also used in the production of hydrofluoric acid.

Cube-shaped fluorite crystals are highly prized by rock and mineral collectors. Some kinds of fluorite glow under ultraviolet light. The word "fluorescent" was coined to describe this characteristic. One kind of fluorite gives off a green light when it is heated.

Fluorite is usually found as veins or deposits in sedimentary rocks such as limestone and dolomite. Some fluorite is found in ores of silver, lead and copper. In the U.S., fluorite is mined in Illinois, Kentucky, Colorado, New Mexico and Utah. It is also mined in Europe. The British call fluorite fluorspar.

FLUORITE

Flies—Insect Pests

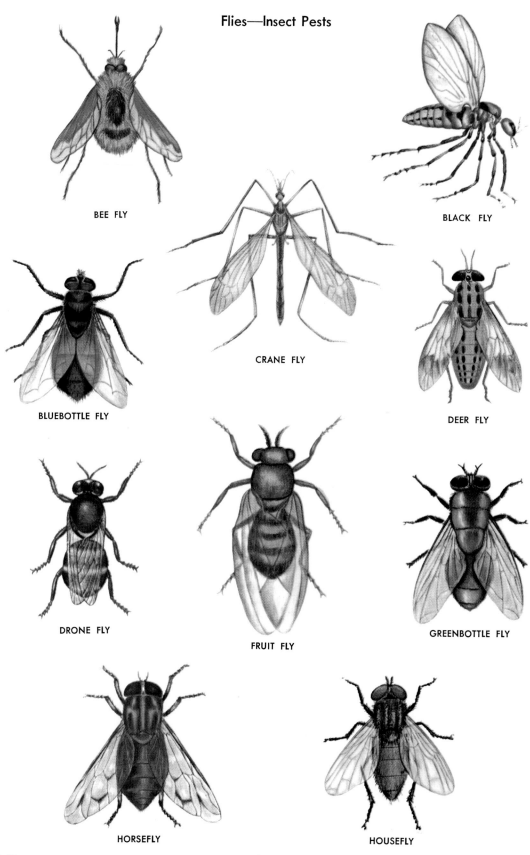

BEE FLY

BLACK FLY

CRANE FLY

BLUEBOTTLE FLY

DEER FLY

DRONE FLY

FRUIT FLY

GREENBOTTLE FLY

HORSEFLY

HOUSEFLY

fly

Flies are a large group of insects found in all but the very coldest parts of the world. As adults, all have soft bodies, short antennae and large eyes. Most have 1 pair of broad, transparent wings. Flies can fly faster than any other insect.

Some flies are pests, causing millions of dollars' worth of damage to crops each year. Some carry disease. Some benefit mankind by helping to pollinate flowers, and by providing food for songbirds, fish and other small animals.

Flies range in size from a fraction of an inch to over 2 inches. Most flies are black or brown, though some have bright blue or green abdomens. They have different kinds of mouths and eat many different kinds of food.

All flies pass through the 4 stages of complete metamorphosis: egg, larva, pupa and adult. In warm weather, some flies go through the cycle in 10 days.

Fly eggs are usually laid on decaying plant or animal matter. The legless, worm-like larvae are called maggots. A few kinds of flies make cocoons, but most pass through the pupa or resting stage inside a hardened skin.

The bee fly and the drone fly have plump, hairy bodies and look something like honey bees. The adults eat flower pollen and nectar. Bee fly larvae feed on caterpillars and the larvae of bees and wasps. Drone fly larvae float in stagnant water and eat algae.

The black fly is tiny, only $\frac{1}{25}$ to $\frac{1}{5}$ inch long, but it is a serious pest along northern streams in early spring. The adult female bites humans and animals and sucks blood. The larvae live underwater, feeding on algae and aquatic animals. When the larvae are fully grown, they spin a cocoon fastened to a rock. Later, the adult black flies rise to the surface and start laying eggs.

The bluebottle and greenbottle flies are loud-buzzing blowflies. They are about ½ inch long, with shiny blue or green abdomens. Their eggs and larvae are found in filth and garbage, and in open sores on the bodies of animals.

Crane flies look like mosquitoes, but are up to 2 inches long. The crane fly has a long, slender body with 2 pairs of narrow wings and 6 very long, thin legs. Because of its long legs, the crane fly is sometimes called daddy longlegs, a name also given to the harvestman. The adults are harmless, but the larvae burrow underground and damage the roots of farm crops. The gray, leathery-looking outer skin of the larvae has given them the nickname of "leather jacket." Craneflies are common along streams. They are used as a model for fishermen's artificial flies.

The deer fly and horsefly are pests that bother humans and livestock. They are known to spread diseases in animals. Both are thick-bodied with large eyes. The adult females suck blood. Deer flies and horseflies are widespread and prefer damp places. Adult males eat flower pollen. The larvae live in damp soil or mud.

The fruit fly is a very tiny insect widely used in laboratory studies of heredity because it breeds rapidly and has a life cycle of 10 to 12 days. The eggs and larvae are found on rotting fruit. The adult is yellowish with large red eyes and sucking mouthparts. Fruit flies are found all over the world.

The housefly is a serious pest that spreads diseases by carrying harmful bacteria to human food. Very widespread and probably the most familiar of all insects, the housefly is short and stout, has large eyes and is gray or black. Its eggs and larvae are usually found in filth and garbage. The larvae mature in 5 to 7 days. In warm weather, 1 female may lay as many as 200 eggs once a month.

flycatcher \ 'flī-ˌkach-ər \

In the New World, flycatchers make up a family of birds that are important and valuable insect eaters. Most kinds of New World flycatchers live in the tropics.

New World flycatchers vary in length from 4 to 15 inches. The broad, flat bill has a slight hook on the upper part and is usually surrounded with bristles at the base. The feet and short legs are covered with scales. Plumage is usually dull.

Flycatchers have strong wings and turn and dart rapidly as they chase insects in flight. A few kinds eat fruit and some eat reptiles. All kinds of flycatchers in North America migrate south in winter.

The great-crested flycatcher (illustrated) does not build nests of twigs and grasses as most flycatchers do. It uses a woodpecker's hole and often places the cast-off skin of a snake in the entrance. As the snakeskin dries and breaks, bits of it fall into the nest.

This flycatcher averages 9 inches in length. It lives in heavily wooded areas in eastern U.S. and Canada. Its 4 to 8 pale yellow eggs are marked with brownish-red blotches.

The scissor-tailed flycatcher is the state bird of Oklahoma.

For other kinds of flycatchers, see *kingbird* and *phoebe*.

FLYCATCHER

FLYING FISH

flying fish

Flying fish make up a family of marine fish that live in tropical waters. They have strong tails which they beat on the surface of the water to gain speed. Then, by stretching out their large wing-like fins, they are able to glide through the air for a few seconds at speeds up to 10 miles an hour. Some kinds of flying fish can make a single "flight" of almost 200 yards. The "flight" allows them to escape from such underwater enemies as dolphins.

Flying fish are from 6 to 18 inches long. Some kinds have 2 wing-like fins, while others have 4. All have blunt snouts and heavy, diamond-shaped scales.

The eggs of flying fish have silky hairs which stick to floating objects or seaweed. Some flying fish which live in the Atlantic Ocean build nests of seaweed.

The California flying fish (illustrated) is one of the best-known kinds. These flying fish travel in schools. A number of them may be in the air at the same time. Their chief food is invertebrates that live on the surface of the water.

foraminifer \ ˌfȯr-ə-'min-ə-fər \

These tiny animals make up a large group of protozoans, and are closely related to amoebas. Almost all kinds of foramini-

FORGET-ME-NOT

fers live in salt water. Most kinds are known from fossils (illustrated). The fossils prove that foraminifers have been on the earth for 420 million years. Over 20,000 different kinds of foraminifers are known.

Foraminifers have external shells. Some measure less than 4/100 of an inch but fossils measuring more than 2 inches have been found.

Foraminifers move, absorb food and reproduce with tiny net-like pseudopodia which reach out through holes in their shells. They reproduce both sexually and asexually.

When foraminifers die, the shells build up into limestone and chalk beds. Some of these beds have developed into thick deposits. About 30 percent of the ocean floor is covered with foraminifer shells.

Foraminifers are most common in warm, open seas. They soon die when blown into shallow waters. A few kinds live in brackish or fresh water.

Some kinds creep on the sea floor, or attach themselves to underwater plants.

FORAMINIFERS

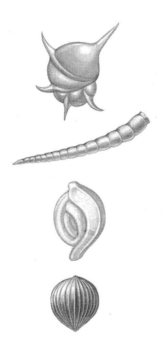

forget-me-not

Forget-me-nots make up a group of annual or perennial plants. Some kinds are popular, low-growing garden flowers. Other kinds grow wild in cool, damp places. Forget-me-nots are symbols of friendship and true love. They are the subject of many legends.

Throughout the northern and southern temperate zones, forget-me-nots are widespread. Most of the kinds grown in gardens are native to Europe. About a dozen kinds are native to the U.S. The forget-me-not is the state flower of Alaska.

Forget-me-not flowers are usually blue, but may be pink or white. They bloom in branching clusters. The leaves are long, smooth-edged and slightly hairy. They grow alternately on the stem. The fruit is made up of 4 small, smooth nuts.

The true forget-me-not (illustrated) is the kind most often grown in gardens. Although it is a perennial, it is often treated by gardeners as an annual or a biennial. It grows from 6 to 18 inches tall. Its stem is slightly hairy.

The flower buds of the true forget-me-nots are pink. As they bloom in small clusters, the flowers become bluish. The center of each flower is yellow.

FORSYTHIA

forsythia \ fər-'sith-ē-ə \

Forsythias make up a group of hardy plants that belong to the olive family. They bear bright yellow flowers early in the spring. Forsythias are widely planted in yards and gardens for their beauty. They are perhaps most colorful against a background of evergreen trees. Forsythia is named for the English botanist William Forsyth.

Forsythias grow to a height of 8 to 10 feet. The pointed leaves have toothed edges and are 3 to 5 inches long. They grow in opposite pairs on each side of the branch. In the fall, the leaves often become olive or purplish in color. The flower has 4 narrow lobes. It appears in March or April, before the leaves. The fruit is a woody pod that contains many small winged seeds.

One widely grown kind of forsythia (illustrated) is sometimes called weeping golden bell. It is native to China. It may grow up to 10 feet tall. The tips of its graceful, arching branches rest on the ground and sometimes take root there. Its flowers are a golden yellow and about 1 inch long.

According to folklore, 3 snows can be expected to fall after the forsythia first blooms.

fossil \ 'fäs-əl \

Fossils are the remains or traces of plants and animals that lived in prehistoric times.

Some fossils, such as large bones and shells, are hard objects that have lasted for a long time in their natural state.

Other fossils were preserved by a chemical change that took place after plants and animals were covered by water, sand or mud. Harder minerals replaced soft materials as the plants and animals decayed. On the sea floor, mollusk shells turned into limestone fossils (illustrated). In running streams that contained silica, fallen tree trunks turned into petrified wood.

Still other fossils are only prints or molds that show the shape of objects that decayed long ago. These include leafprints and the footprints of dinosaurs preserved when mud hardened and became rock.

Fossils of birds, fish and insects are rare, since they had delicate bodies that decayed rapidly. A few insects are preserved in lumps of amber from ancient pine trees.

The frozen bodies of mammoths are unusual fossils that have been discovered in the Arctic tundra.

See *amber, gastrolith* and *petrified wood.*

FOSSILS

FOX

fox

Foxes are carnivorous mammals related to the dogs and the wolves. Many kinds of foxes are found in the temperate zones of North America, Europe, Asia and northern Africa.

Foxes have large, bushy tails and long legs, with 5 toes on the front feet and 4 on the hind feet. The long, heavy fur may be yellowish to rusty, black or gray.

The fur of the Arctic fox is blue or white and is valued commercially. Most foxes hear, smell and see well. They are fast runners and are most active at night. During the winter they live in caves, dens or burrows, but they do not hibernate. Foxes are common in open country with stands of underbrush and woods.

Both parents care for the 4 to 9 kits, which are born blind, in the spring. They live to be about 12 years old. Foxes eat rabbits, rodents, snakes, birds and sometimes fruit and berries. Foxes stalk their prey with great skill.

The gray fox (illustrated) is the only fox that climbs trees. It has a gray coat touched with rusty red and is the only fox with a black streak down its bushy tail. The gray fox lives in swamps, forests and open country in most of the U.S. except for the western plains, and in northern South America. It is a shy animal and usually tries to hide when it is chased by hunters or dogs.

foxglove \ 'fäks-ˌgləv \

Foxgloves make up a group of biennial and perennial plants closely related to snapdragons. Foxgloves are native to Europe, western Asia and the Canary Islands. The name "foxglove" is believed to have come from the shape of the flowers, which look something like small fingers or bells.

Foxgloves grow to a height of 2 to 5 feet. The flowers grow in clusters at the top of a slender stem. They may be purple, rose, yellow or white. They usually bloom in June.

The dull green leaves of the foxglove grow alternately on the stem and are sometimes toothed. The lower leaves are larger than the upper leaves and grow closer together. The seeds are contained in oval capsules that ripen in August.

The common foxglove (illustrated) is a popular garden flower. Many varieties and colors have been developed from it. Some of the flowers may grow to 3 inches in length. The petal lobes have a fringe of very fine hairs.

Although the leaves of the common foxglove are poisonous, a valuable drug is made from them. The drug, digitalis, is used in the treatment of certain types of heart disease.

FOXGLOVE

frog

Together with their close relatives, the toads, frogs make up a group of amphibians that have long, strong hind legs and no tails. They are cold-blooded and mainly aquatic, and they hibernate underground where temperatures go below freezing.

Most frogs have smooth skins, streamlined bodies and webbed feet. They can jump long distances, and they can swim very fast. As tadpoles, they have gills for breathing underwater. As adults, they have lungs and breathe air, but most adults live in or near water. Some climb trees. Frogs are from 1 to 10 inches long.

Frogs have bulging eyes adapted to seeing small, moving objects in nearly all directions. When an insect comes near, a frog's wide mouth flies open and its long, sticky tongue snaps out to capture the insect. Frogs benefit mankind by helping to control many insect pests.

Both male and female frogs have vocal sacs opening off their mouths. They can make loud and varied sounds by rapidly contracting those sacs. Females seldom use their vocal sacs, but males make clicking, croaking or booming sounds, especially during the spring mating season.

All but a very few frogs lay their eggs in water, in the spring. The eggs are round and nearly transparent. They float in sheets and become attached to plants.

The young are tadpoles, with round bodies and slender tails. They have gills for breathing underwater, and they eat plant matter. As they become larger, tadpoles pass through a long series of gradual changes that transform them into adults, able to live on land and breathe air.

All of the frogs illustrated are native to North America. All except the barking frog are usually found near ponds or streams. The barking frog looks more like a toad than a frog. It hides in caves or under rocks in the hot, dry areas of southern Texas and Mexico. Its mating call is a loud yelp like the bark of a dog.

The bullfrog, with a body length of 4 to 7 inches, is the largest North American frog. Because its legs are highly valued as food, it is raised commercially. The tadpoles may grow to 6 inches before changing into frogs.

The leopard frog, 2 to 5 inches long, is perhaps the best-known, most widely distributed North American frog. It is more active during the day than most kinds of frogs. During the summer, the leopard frog ranges through woods and grassy meadows some distance away from water.

The barking frog, the pickerel frog and the wood frog are all medium-sized, with a body length of 2 to 3 inches. The pickerel frog and the wood frog are most common in cool, wooded areas.

The pickerel frog is one of the few frogs that has some protection against its enemies. Its skin secretes a substance poisonous or unpleasant to snakes and other animals that feed on frogs.

The wood frog lives as far north as Alaska, farther north than any other American amphibian. It has dark, masklike spots around the eyes and its head tapers to a pointed snout.

The cricket frog, the ornate chorus frog and the spring peeper are all small, with a body length of about 1 inch. All of them belong to the tree frog family. The cricket frog does not climb trees as the others do. Some kinds of tree frogs can jump farther than any other frogs.

Most tree frogs have sticky disks on their toes. Many tree frogs can change color by expanding or contracting differently colored areas of their skins. Tree frogs spend a good deal of time on land. The young tree frog is usually several months old before it develops lungs and is able to leave the water.

Frogs—Water Amphibians

BARKING FROG

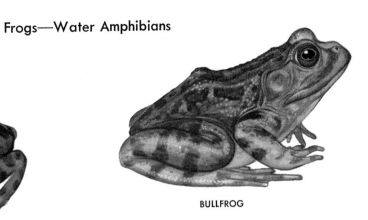

BULLFROG

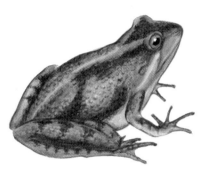

ORNATE CHORUS FROG

CRICKET FROG

LEOPARD FROG

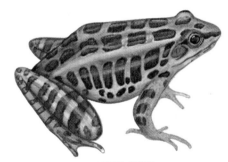

PICKEREL FROG

SPRING PEEPER

WOOD FROG

fuchsia \ 'fyü-shə \

Fuchsias make up a group of tropical shrubs and trees closely related to the evening primroses. Some kinds are cultivated in America and Europe for their brightly colored flowers. Fuchsias are named for the German botanist and physician Leonard Fuchs.

Most fuchsias are native to Central and South America and New Zealand. They cannot survive cold winters unless they are protected.

Fuchsias are usually between 1 and 4 feet tall, but a few kinds grow to 40 feet. Some have stems several inches around. Most kinds of fuchsias have alternate leaves. The flowers bloom from slender, twisted buds, and hang gracefully below the stems. The fruit is a berry containing several seeds. Cultivated fuchsias are grown from seeds.

In the southern U.S. and England, one well-known kind of fuchsia (illustrated) is a shrub that grows 2 feet tall. Its flowers are usually purplish-red, but may be blue or white. Each flower has a tube-shaped outside, or calyx, that opens into 3 petal-like lobes. The lobes surround 8 very long stamens. This plant is native to South America where it grows on mountain slopes, from Peru south to Argentina.

FUCHSIA

FUMAROLE

fumarole \ 'fyü-mə-ˌrōl \

A fumarole is a hole or crack in the ground from which smoke-like clouds of vapor arise. Somewhere beneath every fumarole is a formation of hot rock.

About 99 percent of the rising water vapor from a fumarole is steam formed when underground water comes in contact with the hot rock. Mixed with the steam may be such gases as carbon dioxide, hydrogen chloride, hydrogen, hydrogen sulfide and nitrogen. Since some of these gases kill plants, the area around some fumaroles is often bare.

Fumaroles are active in regions near volcanoes. They may give off vapor for many years after the volcano has erupted.

Many fumaroles could once be seen in the Valley of Ten Thousand Smokes in Alaska, around the crater of Katmai. Katmai erupted in 1912. Today, fumarole activity around it has almost stopped.

Fumaroles that fill with water may become hot springs or geysers such as those at Yellowstone National Park in the U.S.

fungus \ 'fəng-gəs \

Fungi make up a group of plants without chlorophyll. These plants have no roots, stems or leaves. They reproduce by forming spores or cells that develop directly into new organisms.

FUNGUS

Some fungi are very small, single-cell forms. Others are large organisms that measure 2 feet across, such as the puffball.

Fungi do not manufacture their own food. Some are parasites, taking their food from other living plants or animals. Others are saprophytes, plants that live on dead and decaying animals or vegetable matter.

The cells of most fungi are grouped in long, thread-like filaments. These in turn are grouped together to form a body called the mycelium. The mycelium usually has no special shape and is colorless. In most fungi, only the spore-producing part of the plant is visible.

Some fungi are useful. Yeast is important in making bread. Penicillin is a medicine. Mushrooms are a valued food. Other fungi cause diseases in animals and plants. Athlete's foot is a fungus disease of humans. Fungus-caused plant diseases destroy valuable crops and trees.

Bracket fungi make up a group of fungi that live on trees. Some kinds are saprophytes while others are parasites that infect living trees and cause them to rot from within. A common kind of bracket fungus (illustrated) has rings of different colors.

For other fungi, see *morel, mushroom, penicillium, puffball, rust and smut,* and *yeast.*

g

gabbro \ 'gab-ˌrō \

Gabbro is the name given to a number of kinds of igneous, coarse-to-medium-grained rocks having a dark color. Gabbro was formed deep underground at high temperatures. It looks something like granite. Like granite, gabbro is used for buildings and monuments.

Most gabbro is dark gray or greenish-black and quite heavy. It is made up of different-colored crystals all about the same size. The crystals are large enough to be seen easily and identified without the aid of a microscope.

The gabbros vary in appearance and makeup according to the minerals they contain. Most of these minerals, such as feldspar, hornblende and olivine, are fairly common. These minerals are present in rocks in many parts of the world.

Gabbro is found in large quantities in the Scandinavian countries and Canada. In the U.S., it is found in the Adirondack Mountains, Wyoming and around Lake Superior.

Valuable ores containing such metals as nickel, chromium, platinum and titanium are very often found near the gabbros, or even mixed with them.

GABBRO

galaxy \ 'gal-ək-sē \

A galaxy is a system of billions of stars, gases and dust in space. Each galaxy is held together by gravitation. Astronomers believe that there are millions of galaxies in space.

Galaxies are classified according to their shapes. Irregular galaxies have no regular shape. They contain mostly new stars and interstellar gas and dust. Astronomers believe that the new stars are formed from the gas and dust.

Elliptical galaxies have an oval shape and are made up of old stars. These galaxies have almost no gas and dust.

A spiral galaxy (illustrated) is shaped like a saucer and rotates around a nucleus of stars. The stars and gases outside the nucleus form arms which reach outward.

The galaxy of which the solar system is a very small part is called the Milky Way. It is a spiral galaxy. The solar system is about ⅔ of the way out from the nucleus to the rim.

The galaxy closest to the Milky Way is called Andromeda. It is a spiral galaxy a thousand times further away than the faintest star visible without a telescope.

Astronomers believe that the galaxies furthest from the Milky Way are moving outward at nearly ½ the speed of light. That is, the universe is expanding.

GALAXY

GALENA

galena \ gə-'lē-nə \

Galena is a valuable ore from which most lead is obtained. It is made up largely of lead and sulfur, but may also contain small amounts of silver, gold, zinc and copper. Because galena conducts electricity, tiny crystals of the ore were once widely used in crystal radio sets. Galena is used today in other electronic equipment.

Galena is dark gray or black, heavy and brittle. Broken surfaces usually have a brilliant metallic luster and show the cube pattern of the crystals.

Nearly every country of the world has deposits of galena. There are mines in Mexico, England, Germany, Spain, Australia and the U.S. Galena is found in veins and pockets of other rocks and sometimes occurs in veins of coal.

In the U.S., galena is mined for its lead in southeast Missouri. In Colorado, Idaho and Utah it is mined for its silver.

gallinule \ 'gal-ə-,n(y)ül \

Gallinules are marsh birds of the tropic and temperate zones. They belong to the rail family.

Gallinules are more slender than ducks, and their heads are smaller. Between the eyes and attached to the short, pointed bill is a broad plate that covers the forehead like a shield.

GALLINULE

Gallinules have strong legs and long-toed, unwebbed feet. They swim and run better than they fly. They fly only when threatened. In flight, their legs dangle awkwardly.

The well-built nests are hidden among reeds and rushes. Some nests float on the water while others are held up by the reeds. The 6 to 12 eggs are whitish, spotted with brown and purple.

The purple gallinule (illustrated) has deep-colored, glossy feathers that makes it one of America's most beautiful water birds. It is from 12 to 14 inches long. The plate on its head is pale blue. The bill is red tipped with yellow.

Most of the time the purple gallinule remains hidden in the tangled plants of swamplands. It feeds on seeds, young plants and small water animals.

In summer the purple gallinule ranges as far north as Missouri and Tennessee. Most purple gallinules breed along the Atlantic coast from South Carolina to Florida. They spend the winter in Texas and Louisiana south to Ecuador and the West Indies.

gannet \ 'gan-ət \

Gannets are large, white sea birds that make up a family. They dive from the air into the water to catch fish. Gannets sometimes dive as deep as 90 feet below the surface. Fishermen are often able to locate schools of fish by following gannets.

The average length of a gannet is 3 to 3½ feet, including a 4-inch bill and a wedge-shaped, black tail. Both legs and feet are scaled. The 3 webbed toes have sharp, black claws.

Gannets live in colonies. They build nests of seaweed and mud on narrow cliffs or steep sides of sea islands. The nests are used many times. In spring and fall, gannets migrate in small flocks.

Female gannets lay 1 pale blue egg in the spring. Both parents take turns sitting on it. The incubation period is about 42 days. In 10 to 12 weeks feathers develop on the young birds. They sometimes swim before they can fly. Gannets mature in 3 years.

The northern or North Atlantic gannet (illustrated) is white with a pale yellow head. Most northern gannets breed around the British Isles, but also on islands in the mouth of the St. Lawrence River, as well as Iceland and Labrador. In winter they migrate to northwest Africa and the Gulf of Mexico.

Young birds are brownish and speckled.

Two other kinds of gannets live south of the equator. They nest along the coasts of Australia and South Africa.

GANNET

GAR

gar \ 'gär \

These large freshwater fish make up a family that has not changed much since the Age of Dinosaurs. Gars often float like logs at the surface of quiet water. They have a lung-like swim bladder with which they sometimes breathe air.

Gars have little value to man. They are rarely used for food and are unpopular because they prey on game fish.

The bodies of gars are long and powerful. They measure from 2½ to 10 feet in length and weigh up to 300 pounds or more. Their jaws are narrow and their teeth are sharp and needle-like. Their diamond-shaped scales are thick and hard and are like those of many prehistoric fish. At one time, gar scales were used to cover shields. American Indians sometimes used them for arrowheads. Today, gar scales are painted and made into ornamental jewelry.

The small dorsal fin is located far back on the body near the rounded tail fin. The pectoral fins are low on the body.

In spring, female gars lay their eggs in shallow water. Newly hatched gars feed on minnows and grow very fast.

Gars are found in North and Central America in rivers and lakes. The long-nose gar (illustrated) is also called the common or bony gar. It grows to 6 feet and lives in streams along the Atlantic and Gulf coasts, the Great Lakes and the Mississippi River.

gardenia \ gär-'dē-nyə \

Gardenias make up a group of tropical evergreen shrubs and trees related to coffee trees. The gardenia was named for Alexander Garden, a Scottish naturalist.

In the U.S., gardenias are grown for their large, fragrant flowers. Because they cannot stand temperatures much below 65° F., gardenias are grown in greenhouses in the northern U.S. In the southern U.S., they are often grown outdoors.

Most gardenias grow from 3 to 6 feet tall. All have leathery, dark green leaves that grow opposite each other. They sometimes grow in groups of 3 at the stem joints. Each white, waxy flower grows at the end of a branch. The fruit has no stalk and is fleshy. Gardenias are grown from cuttings 6 to 8 inches long.

The Cape jasmine (illustrated) is the kind of gardenia most often grown in the U.S. It is a shrub, native to China, that grows 2 to 5 feet tall. Its very fragrant flowers are usually double, and are 2 to 3½ inches across. The smooth, dark green leaves are 3 to 5 inches long, and are broadest near the tip end.

The Cape jasmine gardenia is planted outdoors as far north as Virginia and Maryland, in protected locations, and in the states along the Gulf coast.

GARDENIA

garnet \ 'gär-nət \

Garnets make up a family of minerals usually found as hard, transparent crystals of many colors. They may be red, brown, yellow, green, black or colorless. The name garnet comes from the Latin word for pomegranate, a fruit containing bright red seeds. Some kinds of garnet look like pomegranate seeds.

Deep red and bright green garnets are classed as gems and are used in jewelry. Tiny garnet particles are used in industry to coat grinding wheels and sandpapers. They are also used as bearings in watches.

Garnets are fairly common and are found in many parts of the world. They occur in both metamorphic and igneous rocks. Garnet crystals an inch or more in length are fairly common. Within a garnet crystal may be many small grains of other minerals.

Garnets for industrial use are mined in New York State. At one place there, garnet crystals average 5 inches in length. The finest red garnets come from Brazil, Ceylon and Madagascar. Green garnets come from Russia.

Garnets were once used as bullets in ancient firearms. They were once worn by travelers because they were believed to protect the travelers from accidents.

GASTROLITHS

gastrolith \ 'gas-trə-,lith \

A gastrolith is a stone that was once in the body of a bird, reptile or fish. Like present-day birds, these animals swallowed grit, pebbles and sand to help digest the foods their teeth or beaks could not chew. Many gastroliths are believed to have been formed from the grit, pebbles and sand.

Groups of gastroliths have been found with the skeletons of dinosaurs. They are believed to have been in the reptiles' gizzards when they died. Such gastroliths are made up of different materials from other rocks nearby. These gastroliths are usually found only in rock layers of the Cretaceous and Turassic Periods, when dinosaurs were most common.

Gastroliths are smooth and highly polished. They usually measure from 1 to 4 inches in length and are made up of different kinds of rock, such as quartz, agate, granite and flint. The oldest gastroliths have the highest polish.

In the U.S., most gastroliths have been found in Colorado, Kansas, Wyoming, Montana and Utah. In Europe, they have been found in France, Germany and other countries.

Since they are evidence of prehistoric life, gastroliths are considered fossils.

GARNET

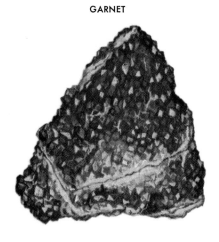

gastropod \ 'gas-trə-,päd \

Gastropods make up a large group of mollusks common in both salt and fresh water. Many kinds live on land, especially in the tropics. The snail is a well-known gastropod.

Most gastropods have shells with spiral or cone shapes. The body is soft and sticky. It has 1 large, fleshy foot which the gastropod uses to cling to and creep along a surface. The head usually has 2 eyes, 2 tentacles, gills, a mouth and a long, rough tongue. Land gastropods have pulmonary sacs and breathe air.

Most gastropods are nocturnal and carnivorous. They use their long tongues to bore holes in their prey, such as clams, and to eat the animal within. When gastropods with shells are attacked by other animals, they go into their shells for protection. If a tentacle is cut off, the gastropod grows another.

In most gastropods, the sexes are separate. Those that live in the water lay a great number of eggs in a jelly-like substance. The eggs hatch into free-swimming larvae. Some kinds of larvae pass through several stages before they become adults.

For kinds of gastropods, see *abalone, conch, cowrie, oyster drill, shell, snail* and *whelk.*

gazelle \ gə-'zel \

Gazelles are graceful animals that make up a group belonging to the antelope family. More than 30 kinds of gazelles are common in Africa and Asia. They live as far east as India.

Gazelles are about the size of deer, and grow to a height of about 3 feet at the shoulder. They have deer-like heads, with large pointed ears and big eyes. Their coats are sandy to yellowish-red above, with white underparts. Some kinds are lightly spotted. Most gazelles have white streaks on the sides of their faces, and some have tufts of hair on their knees. Both sexes have horns slightly curved like the letter S. The horns of the females are smaller than those of the males.

Herds of 50 to 100 gazelles graze open plains and deserts. They feed mainly on grass and leaves. Gazelles may group with other antelopes, giraffes and zebras.

Gazelles can run at speeds up to 40 miles per hour. Their ability to run is their best defense against larger animals.

The most common kind of gazelle is Grant's gazelle (illustrated) of east Africa. It stands 3 feet at the shoulder and is cinnamon brown in color. Beneath its tail is a white patch bordered with black. Grant's gazelle has 30-inch horns.

For another kind of gazelle, see *impala.*

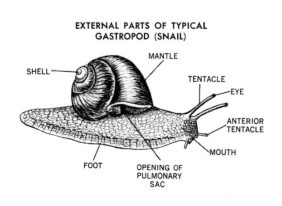

EXTERNAL PARTS OF TYPICAL
GASTROPOD (SNAIL)

SHELL
MANTLE
TENTACLE
EYE
ANTERIOR
TENTACLE
MOUTH
FOOT
OPENING OF
PULMONARY
SAC

GAZELLE

GECKO

gecko \ 'gek-ˌō \

Geckos belong to a family of lizards and are found throughout the tropics. They live on the ground, in trees or in houses. Most kinds of geckos have sharp claws and unusual toe pads covered with hair-like hooks that are hard to see without a microscope. The hooks allow geckos to run across ceilings and cling to window glass as easily as other lizards climb trees.

Usually brown or gray, geckos measure about 6 inches in length. A few kinds are bright-colored and have large, odd-shaped tails. Geckos are noisy reptiles and make chirping and peeping noises. Most are nocturnal and feed on insects.

The eyes are large and stick out from the animal's head. The pupils of the eyes look like those of a cat. Most geckos have eyelids that do not move.

Geckos lay white eggs with hard shells. The eggs are usually laid under tree bark or on the undersides of leaves.

The ground gecko or banded gecko (illustrated) lives in the U.S., in deserts and rocky areas from Utah south to Texas and southern California. It is a slender, long-legged lizard 3 to 5 inches long. The thin skin is light brown with darker bands. The ground gecko does not have the usual hair-like hooks on its toe pads.

For another kind of gecko, see *tokay*.

gentian \ 'jen-chən \

Gentians make up a large group of mostly perennial plants. Some of them are beautiful wild flowers that are often grown in gardens. Gentians are so popular as wild flowers that they are in danger of becoming extinct from being overpicked. They grow in the cool moist regions of all continents.

Gentian flowers are usually blue but may be purple, white or yellow. The plants grow from 1 to 3 feet tall and have straight stems. The leaves are opposite and often ribbed. They often grow in groups of 3, and they usually have no stalks. The fruit is a long, oval capsule that separates into 2 parts when it is ripe. Each part contains many small seeds.

The fringed gentian (illustrated) is a well-known gentian of North America. Its vase-shaped, pale blue flowers bloom on the end of each branch. They have 4 rounded lobes with fringed, or ragged, edges. The calyx is yellow-green. The leaves are oval and slender. The fringed gentian is a biennial, blooming in late summer and early fall.

The fringed gentian is most common in low moist ground, wet woods and meadows. It is a native of eastern North America. The plants are usually about 18 inches tall. The flowers, about 2 inches long, open only on sunny days.

GENTIAN

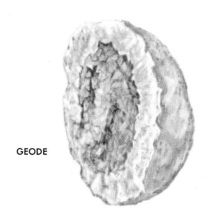

GEODE

geode \ 'jē-,ōd \

A geode is a round, partly hollow rock. Its inside is lined with calcite or quartz crystals that point inward, or with layers of minerals.

Geodes were formed when mineral-carrying water collected in a hollow place. The hollow may have been an underground hole or the shell left by a mollusk. When the water drained away or evaporated, the solid minerals were left. Layers of crystal and minerals built up inside the hollow. These layers can be plainly seen when geodes are broken open.

Geodes that are completely filled with crystals or minerals are called nodules. One geode of this kind is the bullseye agate.

Geodes are found in many parts of the world, usually in sedimentary rock such as limestone. Amethyst crystals are sometimes found in geodes.

Geodes containing quartz are fairly common throughout the limestone areas of the Ohio and Mississippi river valleys. Geodes may range in size from 1 to 10 inches across.

geologic \ ,jē-ə-'läj-ik \ **column**

A geologic column is made up of different rock layers that formed on top of one another. A geologic column may represent a small area of the earth, such as Texas, or an area the size of the earth's entire surface. A perfect geologic column would have 1 layer of rock for each period of the earth's history.

A geologic column must be "read" from the bottom. It was in this order that the layers were formed. The oldest rock formations are at the bottom. They usually contain granite, schist and gneiss. The youngest rocks are at the top. The layers of rock differ from each other in the minerals and fossils they contain.

In nature few geologic columns are complete. In drawing pictures of geologic columns, geologists usually piece together information from many different areas. One of the best places to see rock layers from many eras of history is at the Grand Canyon in Arizona.

geosyncline \ ,jē-ō-'sin-,klīn \

A geosyncline is a large, bowl-shaped trough that covers a large area of the earth's surface. After hundreds of centuries, geosynclines filled up with sediment. The sediment formed rock layers thousands of feet thick.

The sediment collected in the low area of a geosyncline when the sea flowed into it. The sea left traces of plants and animals. Ripple marks and fossils of shallow-

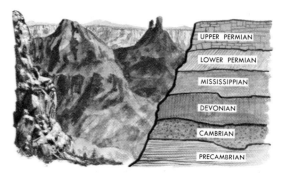

UPPER PERMIAN
LOWER PERMIAN
MISSISSIPPIAN
DEVONIAN
CAMBRIAN
PRECAMBRIAN

GEOLOGIC COLUMN
(of rock strata in Grand Canyon)

GERANIUM

water animals have been found in the sedimentary rock layers of geosynclines.

Sometimes the great weight of the layers of sediment caused the earth beneath to bend and crack. The geosynclines were lifted above sea level and folded into large mountain ranges. The Appalachian, the Sierra Nevada, the Andes and parts of the Himalayas are believed to have been formed in this way. Because the mountains were once under the ocean, remains of marine life are sometimes found on mountaintops.

Most geosynclines were located near the edges of continents. Some other geosynclines form the deepest parts of the oceans.

geranium \jə-'rā-nē-əm\

Geraniums make up 2 groups of annual, biennial and perennial flowering plants. One group contains both wild and cultivated kinds. The other contains only cultivated kinds.

Wild geraniums are most common in temperate regions. They have bright pink or light purple flowers 1 to 1½ inches across. The 5 petals are deeply toothed. The leaves are usually palmate and grow opposite each other. Many kinds of wild geraniums are cultivated in wild flower gardens.

The geraniums of the cultivated group are usually larger than wild geraniums. Cultivated geraniums differ greatly in the size and color of their flowers and in the shape and marking of their leaves. Two of the 5 petals of each flower are larger, smaller or differently marked than the other 3. The plants grow to a height of 1 to 6 feet. They require plenty of sunshine and enough water to keep their roots moist.

One kind of cultivated geranium (illustrated) is native to South Africa but is widely grown in the U.S. The red, pink or white flowers grow in umbrella-like clusters on the end of a strong stem. The leaves are 3 to 5 inches across. They are round or kidney-shaped with scalloped edges.

geyser \'gī-zər\

A geyser is a hot spring that throws water and steam high into the air through a hole in the ground. Geysers are located in regions where there have been active volcanoes. There, hot rocks lie near the surface of the ground. Water from nearby rivers and lakes seeps into cracks around the hot rocks.

When the water is heated by the rocks, steam forms. It cannot escape so the water around the rocks is heated to a still higher temperature, above its boiling

GEYSER

point. Slowly the pressure builds up. Finally, some of the heated water is pushed up out of the hole that leads to the surface. Then, because there is less pressure to hold the steam and hot water in the ground, it suddenly expands and erupts through the hole into the air.

After the geyser has erupted, water seeps back into the channel and the process is repeated.

Geysers are found only in Iceland, New Zealand and the U.S. The most famous geyser is Old Faithful at Yellowstone National Park. It spouts water on an average of once every 65 minutes the year round. Old Faithful spouts water and steam to as high as 150 feet.

giant panda \ 'pan-də \

This rare and unusual nocturnal mammal does not belong to any family of animals alive today. Only fossils remain of the other members of its family that lived long ago. Some scientists believe that the giant panda is related to the raccoon.

The giant panda is often called a bear because of its bear-like appearance. It has hyena-like back quarters.

About 6 feet long, the giant panda weighs around 300 pounds. Its body and head are mostly white. The legs are black and a black strip crosses the shoulders.

The large head has black ears and black patches around the eyes. The giant panda has a 5-inch tail and bear-like paws. Its fur is thick.

The giant panda is found only in the mountains of western China and Tibet. It lives in bamboo forests 6,000 to 8,000 feet high. It feeds on bamboo shoots and does not hibernate. The young are born in the winter. They are believed to be full grown at 4 to 5 years.

Giant pandas were first brought to American zoos in 1937.

For another kind of panda, see *lesser panda*.

giant tortoise \ 'tört-əs \

Giant tortoises make up a group of large land turtles. They are native to only a few islands in the Pacific and Indian oceans. Even in those regions there are few giant tortoises today, as they have been widely hunted for food.

Giant tortoises spend their entire lives on land. They go to water only to drink or bathe. They feed on plant matter such as grass, fruits and spineless cacti. During the mating season, the male makes a loud, bellowing sound.

The rough shell, or carapace, of the giant tortoise is 3 to 4 feet long. The weight of adults averages 300 pounds but may be as great as 600 pounds. The cara-

GIANT PANDA

GIANT TORTOISE

pace is divided into shield-shaped sections. The body within has a small head, long neck and a beaked jaw. Strong, thick legs lift the body well up off the ground.

The female lays her eggs in a shallow hole in soft ground. The round eggs are about 3 inches across and have hard shells. They are incubated by the heat of the sun. The young are 3 to 4 inches long.

Giant tortoises may live to be more than 150 years old. One kind (illustrated) is most common on the Aldabra Islands in the Indian Ocean.

gibbon \ 'gib-ən \

Gibbons make up 2 groups of apes with very long arms and no tail. They spend their entire lives in the forest. Moving easily from tree to tree, they often swing distances of 40 feet. On the ground they walk upright. While walking, they often lock their hands behind their heads.

Gibbons are very thin and have shaggy fur. They do not have cheek pouches like other members of the ape family. Gibbons are common in bamboo jungles of India, Burma, the Malay peninsula and the East Indies.

Gibbons are usually herbivorous but sometimes eat insects, spiders and birds, which they catch with their hands. They live in family groups. They make a sur-

GIBBON

GILA MONSTER

prising number of sounds from whoops to grunts.

The young gibbon stays with its parents for about a year. It often rides with its mother as she swings through the trees. Young gibbons become full grown in 6 years. These apes may live to be 20 to 25 years old.

The white-handed gibbon (illustrated) lives in Malaya and the East Indies. It stands 3 feet tall, has black or brown fur on its body, and whitish hands. A ring of whitish fur surrounds its face.

Gila monster \ 'hē-lə 'män(t)-stər \

The Gila monster is 1 of the only 2 lizards known to be poisonous. It kills small animals by biting and poisoning them with its venom. The venom comes from special poison glands beneath the skin of the lower jaw.

Adult Gila monsters grow to be 12 to 21 inches long. The color is dark brown or black with markings of pink or yellow. The skin is covered with small scales.

The Gila monster moves slowly. It searches out the nests of birds, small mammals and reptiles, and eats the eggs or young. It also eats insects and worms. The Gila monster has no known natural enemies.

These reptiles spend most of their time in their burrows. They come out only at night or in rainy weather. They can live

GINGER PLANT
AND ROOT

for months without food, since extra fat is stored in their tails and abdomens.

The female Gila monster lays 6 to 12 soft-shelled eggs in the sand, usually in July. The eggs are 2 to 2½ inches long. They are incubated by the heat of the sun and hatch 4 to 5 weeks after they are laid.

The Gila monster is native to desert areas in the southwestern U.S. and Mexico. In Arizona, it is protected by law.

ginger

Ginger is a perennial plant belonging to the ginger family and valued for its roots. It is native to the Pacific Islands and tropical forests of southeastern Asia.

The spice made from the ginger root gives gingerbread, gingersnaps and ginger ale their basic flavor. Oil of ginger is used in the food industry and in some perfumes. In the U.S., ginger is grown only in greenhouses in southern Florida.

The ginger plant grows to a height of 3 or 4 feet. It looks something like an iris plant. The flowers form in clusters on a spike. They are yellowish-white marked with purple. The narrow grass-like leaves are 8 to 12 inches in length. The stem is leafless but is surrounded by green bracts that are often yellow-tipped. The fruit is a capsule.

The root of the ginger plant is sold in

2 forms. Candied or preserved ginger is the whole root which has been boiled in honey or sugar syrup. The root is also ground into a powder and sold as a spice.

Ginger is an important crop in southeastern Asia, Nigeria, the West Indies, South and Central America. It is grown from root cuttings. The finest ginger is grown in Jamaica and Puerto Rico.

ginkgo \ 'ging-ˌkō \ (maidenhair tree)

Sometimes called a living fossil, the ginkgo tree is the only living member of what was once a widespread family of trees. All other members of the ginkgo family became extinct with the dinosaurs.

The ginkgo is thought to be native to Asia but probably no longer grows wild anywhere. Because the ginkgo is cultivated in Europe and the U.S. as an ornamental tree, man may have kept it from becoming extinct.

Growing 60 to 120 feet high, the ginkgo has a straight trunk with light gray bark. Its branches are slender and widely spaced. Its leaves are fan-shaped and 2 to 4 inches wide. They grow in clusters and look like the leaves of the maidenhair fern.

The fruit and pollen of the ginkgo appear in the spring on separate trees. The yellow-orange fruit, which grows on the female tree, has a bad odor. It ripens

GINKGO

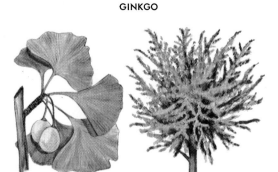

and falls in the autumn. The oily nut inside the fruit is pale yellow and about 1 inch long. It has a corn-like taste. In China, the nuts are a favorite food.

giraffe

Giraffes make up a family of ruminant mammals native to Africa. Their only relative is the okapi.

Giraffes are the tallest mammals in the world. Adults are 19 feet tall and weigh about 1,200 pounds. A young giraffe is 6 feet tall and weighs about 100 pounds at birth.

Giraffes were once common all over Africa. Today giraffe herds roam only the open plains in central and southern Africa.

Giraffes have slim bodies with very long legs and necks. Even though the neck is very long, it contains only 7 vertebrae, the same as man's. Male giraffes have manes of stiff hair down the backs of their necks. Both male and female have 2 to 5 short, skin-covered horns that end in tufts of hair. The coat is a pale, sand color, covered with dark markings.

A giraffe can go without water for a month. To drink, it must spread its forelegs widely. It usually feeds on leaves near treetops and can sleep standing up. The tongue may be 1½ feet long.

A giraffe can gallop at speeds up to 32 miles an hour. The giraffe's main enemy is the lion. Speed, keen hearing and keen eyesight are its best defenses, but it can kick hard and butt with its head.

The reticulated giraffe (illustrated) is often found in U.S. zoos. Its coat is marked in a net-like pattern. It usually has 3 well-developed horns.

glacial grooves \ 'glā-shəl 'grüvz \

Glacial grooves are the tracks left by a glacier. They are side-by-side grooves carved into bedrock by sharp-pointed, hard rocks that were carried by a glacier. Like the smaller marks called glacial striae, the grooves indicate the direction in which the glacier moved.

The best-known glacial grooves are those cut into the limestone of Kelleys Island on Lake Erie. Very deep glacial grooves a mile long occur in western Canada near the Arctic Circle.

See *glacial striae*.

glacial striae \ 'glā-shəl 'strī-ˌē \

Glacial striae are the marks and scratches left on bedrock by small pebbles and rocks in a moving glacier. Striae is a Latin word meaning small grooves or furrows. Glacial striae are smaller than glacial grooves.

GIRAFFE

GLACIAL STRIAE

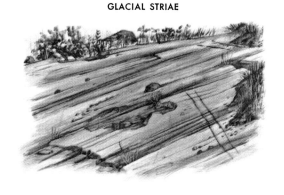

As the heavy ice of a glacier moves slowly downhill, it drags along rocks and other material in its path. The rocks in the glacier make small scratches, or striae, in the rocks over which they pass. The striae show the direction in which the glacier moved.

Sometimes the rocks under a glacier make marks on the rocks carried by the glacier. These marked rocks are dropped later by the glacier when it melts. They have flattened faces.

See *glacial grooves.*

glacier \ 'glā-shər \

A glacier is a mass of ice and snow that moves slowly across land. Glaciers begin in regions where the climate is too cold for snow to melt. As new snow falls, the old snow underneath becomes so tightly packed that ice forms.

When the ice and snow become thick and heavy enough, their weight causes them to flow downhill and form a glacier. The movement of a glacier cannot be seen. Glaciers move from a few inches to 150 feet a day. Like rivers, glaciers move slowest at the sides and fastest in the middle.

As a glacier moves, it picks up and drags sand, pebbles and rocks with it. The rocks may be huge boulders. The sand, pebbles and rocks scrape the land under a

GLACIER

GLADIOLUS

glacier as coarse sandpaper scrapes wood. In this way, a glacier smooths out the earth or rock over which it moves.

Glaciers which flow down mountain valleys are called valley glaciers. They are usually more than 50 feet thick. The Alps, the Rocky Mountains, the Himalayas and other mountains contain many valley glaciers. Some cover less than a square mile, while others are over 100 miles long.

Glaciers which cover large areas are called icecaps. Almost all of Antarctica is covered by an icecap 8,000 or more feet thick. The Greenland icecap covers about 650,000 square miles and is over 2 miles thick in one place.

If a glacier reaches the sea, chunks break off into the water. These become icebergs.

See *cirque, firn* and *glacial striae.*

gladiolus \ ,glad-ē-'ō-ləs \

Gladioli make up a group of perennial plants that belong to the iris family. They are native to South Africa and to Mediterranean regions of Europe and Asia. Gladioli are grown for their showy flowers by home gardeners and by florists in greenhouses.

Gladioli grow to a height of 4 feet. The flowers bloom in the summer and are shaped like small lilies. They grow in clusters along the tips of the straight stems. The flower petals are in 6 segments. The 3 upper segments are larger than the 3 segments below them. The lower part of each blossom is covered by a greenish bract.

The word gladiolus comes from "gladius," the Latin word for sword, and gladiolus leaves are sword-shaped. The fruit is a large, winged capsule. Gladioli are grown from seeds.

Florists have developed many varieties of gladioli, with many different colors of flowers. They may be white, red, purple, yellow or pink. The flowers of some varieties are as wide as 9 inches across.

One kind of gladiolus (illustrated) is a parent form of many varieties. It is native to moist parts of tropical Africa.

glowworm \ 'glō-ˌwərm \

Glowworms are the larvae of fireflies, or lightning bugs. The name glowworm is also used for the wingless female of the firefly. Both the larvae and the females give off a faint but steady greenish light.

Glowworms live underground. They have narrow heads which they can withdraw into their flat bodies. The organs that make light are in the eighth segment

GNATCATCHER

of the abdomen. Scientists do not know whether the light is of any use to glowworms.

Glowworms are useful to gardeners and farmers. They prey on slugs and snails that eat cultivated plants. The larvae first poison their victims with venom.

A year or more is needed for the larvae to develop into fireflies. The entire metamorphosis takes place underground.

In the U.S., fireflies and glowworms are most common east of the Rockies. They often gather near marshy or wet areas or at the edges of woods.

See *firefly*.

gnatcatcher \ 'nat-ˌcach-ər \

Gnatcatchers make up a small group of birds belonging to the New World warbler family. They are valuable because of the great number of harmful insects and insect eggs they eat and destroy. During the day gnatcatchers search constantly for food, their long tails flicking back and forth.

The blue-gray gnatcatcher (illustrated) is one of the smallest birds of North America. Its body is 4½ to 5 inches long, with a wingspread of 4½ to 5 inches. The tail is fan-shaped. Narrow white rings surround the eyes. The slender bill has a slight hook at the tip of the upper part. Both legs and feet are scaled.

GLOWWORM

The gnatcatcher builds a tidy nest of plant fibers. The nest is cup-shaped and lined with soft down. It is held together by lichens and spiderwebs. It is usually built in a tree 10 to 20 feet above the ground. Four to 5 spotted, pale blue eggs are laid in the spring.

The breeding range of the blue-gray gnatcatcher reaches from Canada to the Gulf of Mexico. In winter the bird migrates to the West Indies and Central America. The summer habitat includes open wooded areas.

gneiss \ 'nīs \

The word "gneiss" is used to describe a large and varied group of coarse-grained igneous and metamorphic rocks. They can be easily identified by the bands of minerals that run through them. The bands may be wide or narrow, short or long. The bands show where different light- and dark-colored minerals have been sorted into layers under great heat and pressure.

Gneiss was formed when rocks such as granite and shale were heated, twisted and squeezed. Because gneiss is made of different minerals, no 2 pieces look exactly alike. Gneiss may be white or gray, striped with black, red or green.

The minerals that form the light-colored bands in gneiss are most likely to be quartz and feldspar. The dark-colored layers often contain mica, amphibole, graphite, biotite, chlorite and hornblende. Many other minerals may be present in small amounts.

Gneiss is found in most mountain areas of the world. It is common in Scotland, Norway and Sweden, the Himalayas and eastern Canada. In the U.S., gneiss is found in New York and the New England states, the Piedmont plateau and the Far West.

gnu \ 'n(y)ü \ (wildebeest)

These strange-looking mammals are members of the antelope family. They are native to southern and eastern Africa. They were called "gnus" by the Hottentot peoples of Africa and "wildebeests" by the Dutch.

A gnu looks like a horse with the head of a buffalo and the back end of a cow. Standing about 4 feet high at the shoulder, gnus are about 7 feet long and weigh about 500 pounds. They have grayish-black bodies with dark stripes on the neck and shoulders. Both sexes have a heavy black mane and sharp horns that curve up and out at the tips. The tail is long and hairy.

GNEISS

GNU

GOAT

Gnus graze on grass in open plains. Bulls herd separately from cows. Both sexes often herd with antelopes, zebras and giraffes. Their horns and running speed are their best defenses against their enemies. Gnus are frisky animals and can be dangerous when cornered. Zookeepers handle them carefully.

The brindled gnu (illustrated) is fairly common in central and southeastern Africa. Because its grayish-black body has a bluish tinge, the brindled gnu is sometimes called the blue wildebeest.

goat

Goats make up a group of ruminant mammals of the same family as antelopes, cattle and sheep. Goats are found all over the world. They feed on grass and many other plants.

Goats are both wild and domesticated. Most kinds have short, straight hair, but some kinds have long, thick fur. Goats' horns arch backward from their long heads. They often have beards on their chins. Male goats are called bucks, while females are called does.

The domestic goat (illustrated) is one of the oldest kinds of animals raised by man. It originated from 3 kinds of wild goats. Domestic goats are generally divided into 2 groups. Milk goats are val-

ued for their rich milk and the dairy products made from it. Fleece goats are sheared twice a year for their hair, which is made into yarn. Domestic goats are usually kept in a herd made up of 1 buck and about 50 does.

As adults, domestic goats weigh from 100 to 120 pounds. Their hoofs are divided into 2 parts. One, 2 or 3 kids are born at a time. They are mature at 8 to 12 months. Goats may live 18 years.

The so-called Rocky Mountain goat is not a goat but an antelope.

For another kind of goat, see *ibex*.

goatsbeard \ 'gōts-,bird \

Goatsbeard is a perennial plant belonging to the rose family. It grows wild but is also cultivated by gardeners. Goatsbeard is native to eastern North America.

The goatsbeard plant grows to a height of about 7 feet. The large compound leaves are arranged like feathers on the erect stems. The leaves measure up to 20 inches long. The single leaflets are 3 to 6 inches long, with toothed edges. The olive-green fruit is slightly egg-shaped.

Goatsbeard flowers appear in late spring. Eight to 10 very small, stalkless, white flowers, each about ⅛ inch wide, grow along leafless branches. The spiky branches grow from 4 to 12 inches long.

GOATSBEARD

Staminate and pistillate flowers grow on separate plants that look much alike.

Goatsbeard grows best in shade and is usually found in mountainous areas, as far south as Georgia and Alabama.

goatsucker \ 'gōt-ˌsək-ər \ (nightjar)

Goatsuckers make up a family of nocturnal land birds. They have been called flying insect traps, as they swoop through the air with their mouths wide open, looking for swarms of insects to eat. Goatsuckers have long wings and large tails.

Because their small legs and feet are almost useless on the ground, goatsuckers fly rather than hop or walk, even for short distances. Their mouths are large and fringed with bristles. Their mixed gray and brown coloring makes them hard to see on the ground, where they often rest during the day. Some kinds have patches of white on the head, wings or tail.

Goatsuckers build no nest but lay their eggs on the ground. The 1 or 2 speckled eggs and the down-covered young are as well protected by their color as the adults.

Goatsuckers are found in all parts of the tropic and temperate zones where flying insects are plentiful. Most kinds live all year in the tropics. A few kinds, that live in temperate zones, migrate. Most goatsuckers have loud cries that they repeat over and over, usually at night.

The European nightjar (illustrated) is a goatsucker that has a very harsh cry. It was once believed to take milk from the udders of domestic goats. It winters in central Africa.

For other kinds of goatsuckers, see *nighthawk, poorwill* and *whippoorwill.*

goby \ 'gō-bē \

Gobies make up a family of fish in which there are more than 400 different kinds. They live in warm, shallow parts of the ocean and around coral reefs. The smallest vertebrate known is a tiny goby that lives in the Philippines. Fully grown, it is less than ½ inch long.

Some gobies are especially interesting because they form partnerships with animals and other fish. Some share burrows with shrimps, crabs or worms and act as guards at the burrow entrances.

Most gobies are brightly colored. The largest are about 4 inches long. None have the lateral line that most fish have on each side from head to tail.

One kind of goby, the neon goby, cleans tiny parasites from the skin of larger fish. In return, the larger fish protect the neon goby from its enemies.

The Catalina or blue-banded goby (illustrated) lives near Catalina Island, off the coast of southern California. It is just over 1 inch long. Like most other gobies, it feeds near the bottom, among rocks.

GOATSUCKER

GOBY

goldenrod \ 'gōl-dən-ˌräd \

Goldenrods make up a group of coarse, perennial weeds that belong to the largest plant family. Some kinds are admired for their beauty. Most goldenrods are native to North America and grow from 2 to 8 feet high.

The yellow flower heads of goldenrod are made up of many tiny ray flowers. The flower heads are crowded together at the end of a branch in long, arching clusters. In many kinds of goldenrod, the flower heads bloom on only 1 side of the branch.

Goldenrod leaves are alternate and usually toothed. They grow close to the erect, thin stems. The fruit is small and rounded. It contains 1 seed.

One kind of goldenrod common in eastern North America is the Canada goldenrod (illustrated). The flower heads grow in thick clusters on the upper sides of the spreading branches. Each of the narrow, toothed leaves is from 3 to 5 inches long. The stems may grow singly or in clusters. The upper part of each stem is covered with fine, downy hairs.

Canada goldenrod blooms from July through September. The plants are 3 to 5 feet tall. It is found as far north as Newfoundland and south to the Carolinas.

Goldenrod is the state flower of Kentucky and Nebraska.

GOLDENROD

GOLDFINCH

goldfinch \ 'gōl(d)-ˌfinch \

These small, American birds make up a group belonging to the finch family. They are related to the canary birds sold in pet shops, and are sometimes called wild canaries. Like all finches, goldfinches are seedeaters.

The kind of goldfinch common in the U.S. is the American goldfinch (illustrated). Its average length is 6 inches, including a 2-inch tail. The wingspan is about 9 inches. The American goldfinch is sometimes seen along country roads and at the edges of woodlands, where weed seeds are plentiful.

In summer, the male is bright yellow. The female is dull yellowish-green the year around. In winter, the color of the male changes to that of the female.

American goldfinches nest very late in the summer. The 3 to 6 eggs are laid in August or September, in a neat cup-shaped nest built in a bush or low tree. The nests are made of twigs and are lined with soft plant materials.

The American goldfinch breeds from southern Canada to the northern parts of the Gulf states and west to California.

The eastern goldfinch is the state bird of Iowa and New Jersey. The willow goldfinch is the state bird of Washington.

goldfish

Goldfish are attractively colored fresh-water fish closely related to carp. Goldfish are longer-lived than most fish. Some pet goldfish are known to have lived 25 years.

The ancestors of the modern goldfish were plain, dull-colored fish that lived in shallow streams in China. Centuries of careful breeding produced ornamental goldfish of many different shapes and sizes. Not all are gold. Some are black, white or spotted. Some have unusually long fins and tails.

If released in running streams to live outdoors, goldfish soon lose their decorative colors. Wild goldfish up to 16 inches long are common in streams and ponds in the U.S. east of the Rocky Mountains. They live mostly in shallow, weedy areas, and they feed on insects, small crustaceans and aquatic plants.

Goldfish spawn in early spring. All the young are dull-colored. The ornamental ones develop their bright colors as they mature.

Under natural conditions, 1 female goldfish may lay up to 500 eggs during the spawning season. The eggs are sticky and they cling to underwater plants until they hatch, 3 to 7 days later.

GOLDFISH

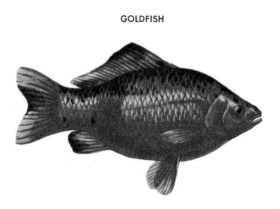

GOOSE

goose

Geese are water birds belonging to the duck family. Larger than ducks, geese also have longer necks and narrower bills. They spend more time on land than ducks do.

The geese raised on farms are descendants of wild geese native to northern Europe and China.

Geese feed on grasses, seeds and water plants. Males, called ganders, and females look alike, and they mate for life.

The wild goose seen most often in the U.S. is the Canada goose (illustrated). It nests throughout Canada and the northern U.S. in summer.

The largest ganders are 43 inches long and weigh more than 13 pounds. Birds from different parts of the country differ in size and in color, but all have black necks and heads with white on cheeks and chin.

The female lays 4 to 10 white eggs in a nest built on the ground, near water. She incubates them for about 28 days, while the gander stands guard.

In autumn, noisily honking family groups migrate to Mexico and the West Indies, where they spend the winter. They fly in long V-shaped formations. Each group is led by an old gander who knows ponds and fields along the way where the group can stop to rest.

GOOSEBERRY

gooseberry

The gooseberries and their close relatives, the currants, belong to a group of shrubs that bear edible fruit. The kinds of shrubs in this group that have prickly stems and bear white, yellow or green fruit are usually called gooseberries. The kinds that have smooth stems and red berries are usually called currants. All have small yellow or white, 5-petaled flowers and ragged-edged leaves about 1 inch across.

Gooseberries or currants are usually too sour to eat as they come from the bush. With much sugar added, the fruit is used to make pies, jellies and preserves. Gooseberries are more popular in Great Britain and northern Europe than in North America.

Gooseberries grow wild in cooler parts of the northern hemisphere and in the mountains of South America. The cultivated gooseberry (illustrated) was developed from a kind native to Europe.

The cultivated gooseberry has mild-flavored, greenish-yellow fruit about ½ inch across. The stems grow 3 to 4 feet tall, and have sharp thorns. Only leaves appear on the new stems. The flowers and fruit grow on stems a year old.

In America, gooseberries are attacked by powdery mildew, a fungus disease.

gopher \ 'gō-fər \ (pocket gopher)

Gophers make up a family of burrowing rodents related to beavers. They are fairly common in most parts of North America but they are seldom seen. They spend nearly all their time underground, and may leave their burrows only to seek mates.

Gophers are 6 to 13 inches long. They have sturdy forelegs, with long, curved claws for digging. On each side of the head is a fur-lined cheek pouch, or "pocket," used for carrying food.

These animals eat mostly roots. Large, yellowish teeth that extend outside the mouth are used to cut short lengths of root that will fit inside the cheek pouch.

Gophers damage some farm crops by destroying the roots, but they also help farmers by loosening and enriching soil.

During most of the year gophers live alone. Each gopher has its own network of tunnels and underground rooms. Female gophers give birth to 2 litters a year. There are 1 to 7 young in each litter.

The plains pocket gopher (illustrated) lives in open country, from Canada south to Texas and from Indiana west to Colorado. It is also found in some parts of Alabama, Georgia and Florida. The plains pocket gopher is about 12 inches long, including the hairless 4-inch tail.

GOPHER

GORGE

gorge \ 'gȯrj \

A gorge is a steep-sided valley, like a ravine but larger. The walls are likely to be of rock and nearly straight up and down. At the bottom of the gorge is the swift-flowing stream or river that formed the gorge by wearing away rock. A gorge may be hundreds of thousands or more years old.

Loose sand and bits of broken stones are the tools a river or stream uses to carve a gorge through solid rock. The movement of the water grinds these materials against the stream bed, and carries the loosened rock and sand away.

Very large gorges are usually called canyons. The Grand Canyon is a huge, deep gorge carved out of rock by the Colorado River. It is so deep because it is in an area that was being lifted up slowly at the same time the river was cutting its channel.

The gorge of the Niagara River, located just below Niagara Falls, is one of the most famous gorges in the world. Bryce Canyon, in Utah, is another well-known gorge. In Arkansas, the world's highest suspension bridge crosses Royal Gorge, a deep, narrow canyon.

The Olduvai Gorge in Tanganyika is famous for the wide variety of very old fossils found there in recent years.

gorilla \ gə-'ril-ə \

The gorilla is the largest of the apes. Although it has great strength, the gorilla is not as fierce as it looks. It seldom attacks smaller animals or men. It eats only vegetable matter such as the leaves, fruit and bark of trees. Gorillas have no natural enemies.

The male gorilla is usually larger than the female. Males stand 5 to 6 feet high and weigh 400 to 500 pounds. Gorillas usually walk on all fours.

Gorillas roam in small family groups through the forests north of the Congo of Africa. Each group is led by a strong, old male. The band stops each evening, wherever it happens to be, and the gorillas build crude nests in trees, where they sleep. They also stop during the middle of the day for a rest or nap period.

Newborn gorillas are as helpless as human babies and have to be carried by their mothers. They learn to walk when about 6 months old, but they usually stay with their mothers for about 3 years.

The gorilla is one of the few jungle animals that leads a peaceful life and usually dies of disease or old age. Gorillas live for about 30 years. Old ones have gray or silvery hair. Most are black, but some have tufts of reddish hair on their heads. Face, hands and feet are black and hairless.

GORILLA

gourd \ 'gōrd \

The gourd family includes many important food plants. All are native to the tropics. The ones called gourds have inedible but useful and ornamental fruit.

As early as 3000 B.C., men in both the Old and New Worlds used dried gourds for many different purposes. Small gourds were made into spoons, drinking cups and dippers. Large gourds were used as water bottles and as containers for storing grain. Gourds have been used to make musical instruments and tobacco pipes.

All gourd plants are climbing vines with hairy stems, large leaves and funnel-shaped flowers. Each plant bears 2 different kinds of flowers. The staminate flowers bloom first. The fruit forms at the base of the pistillate flowers that bloom a few days later.

The ornamental gourd (illustrated) was cultivated by the American Indians. Its fruit may be white, yellow, orange or green. The fruit is usually 4 to 10 inches long. The leaves end in 3 pointed lobes, and the flowers are yellow.

The bottle gourd or calabash is a plant from tropical Africa that bears much larger fruit. It has heart-shaped leaves and very fragrant white flowers.

For other plants of this family, see *cucumber, melon, pumpkin, squash* and *watermelon.*

GOURD

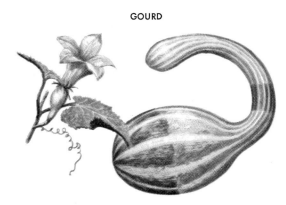

GRACKLE

grackle \ 'grak-əl \

These large birds of the New World blackbird family often gather together in large, noisy flocks during the fall and winter. At night, when they roost by the hundreds in city trees, they are a nuisance. In spring and summer, grackles are more often seen in open fields in pairs or small flocks.

All grackles have loud, unmusical voices. They make mostly squeaky, croaking noises.

Grackles are 12 to 14 inches long, with a wingspread of about 13 inches. Their tails are broad and long. The males have glossy feathers that are iridescent in sunlight. Females are smaller and usually dull black.

Grackles eat many insects, along with some grain and weed seeds. They usually nest in evergreen trees. The 4 to 7 spotted eggs are incubated by the female for about 2 weeks.

The purple grackle (illustrated) is common in the eastern U.S. It grows to a length of about 12 inches, including the tail. The eyes are yellow. The purple grackle ranges as far north as New England in summer. It spends the winter from New Jersey south to Florida.

The bronzed grackle is a larger, browner kind common in the Mississippi Valley.

granite \ 'gran-ət \

Granite is a colorful igneous rock that is both useful and beautiful. It is used as facing for many buildings and monuments, and tombstones are cut from it. Because granite is hard it resists bad weather for hundreds of years. It can be polished to a smooth, shiny finish.

Granite is usually gray, pink or yellowish-brown, speckled with black and white. Red granite also occurs, but it is not very common.

The colorless, glassy flecks in granite are quartz crystals. The black flecks are crystals of biotite mica or hornblende. The pink, gray or yellowish flecks are crystals of feldspar.

Granite was formed when molten rock, or magma, cooled slowly underground. The coarse makeup of granite is a result of this slow cooling. The mineral crystals in granite are about the same size. They are usually large enough to be identified without a microscope.

Granite is a common rock that is found in many parts of the world. It is often seen at the foot of a mountain range that has been uncovered by erosion. Red granite is most common in Scotland, and in the U.S., in Minnesota.

Much of the granite used in the U.S. comes from Massachusetts and Vermont.

GRANITE

GRAPE

grape

The grape plant is a vine with tough, woody stems and large leaves. It produces large clusters of edible fruit.

For 4,000 years or more, grape plants have been cultivated for their fruit, which is used to make wine. Much of the fruit also goes into grape juice, jam and jelly. Some is sold as fresh fruit, and some is dried in the sun to make raisins. The skins of the fruit are used to make a purple dye. An edible oil is squeezed from the tiny grape seeds.

Curling tendrils fasten the stems of the grape plant to treetrunks, fences or some other support. The stems are covered with stringy bark that peels off in loose shreds. The flowers are borne in a cluster. Each flower has 5 tiny petals joined in a sort of cap that falls off when the flowers open. The fruit is usually purplish-blue. It usually contains 2 to 4 small, hard seeds.

Wild grapes grow in nearly all parts of the temperate zone. The grapes cultivated in Europe, Asia and California are all varieties of a kind of grape (illustrated) that was probably native to the Mediterranean region. Hardier varieties, developed from wild grapes native to North America, are planted in cooler areas.

The Oregon grape is the state flower of Oregon.

GRAPE HYACINTH

Grapes are classed as wine grapes, raisin grapes, table grapes, sweet juice grapes and canning grapes. Some varieties are seedless.

grape hyacinth \ 'hi-ə-(,)sin(t)th \

Grape hyacinths make up a group of plants belonging to the lily family. They are among the first garden flowers to bloom in early spring. Grape hyacinths are among the smallest of the garden flowers. They may bloom when only 4 to 5 inches tall.

Most grape hyacinths have blue flowers that bloom in tight clusters. Each bell-shaped flower is about ⅛ inch long. A cluster looks a little like a tiny bunch of grapes. Some kinds of grape hyacinths have pink or white flowers. All have a faint fragrance.

The narrow leaves and the flowering stems all grow from an underground bulb like a small onion. The bulbs are usually planted in early fall, about 3 inches deep and 2 inches apart. The plants require little care and are not killed by cold winter weather. Some new plants grow each year from seeds that fall to the ground.

Grape hyacinths are native to the Mediterranean area. In some parts of the U.S. they have escaped from cultivation and grow as wild flowers.

graphite

A common kind of grape hyacinth (illustrated) is native to southern Europe and western Asia. In the U.S., it is a favorite for gardens and lawns. It grows from 4 to 12 inches high. The leaves are long and flat, and are about ¼ inch wide.

graphite \ 'graf-,īt \

A very soft, black mineral, pure graphite feels greasy to the touch and leaves a black mark on fingers or on paper. Graphite is most familiar as part of a pencil. The "lead" of a pencil is powdered graphite mixed with clay, then shaped into a thin rod and baked. Powered graphite is also used as a lubricant, and in some paints.

Graphite is a form of carbon. So is diamond, the hardest of all minerals. The two minerals are different because of the different patterns in which their molecules are arranged. In a diamond, carbon molecules fit tightly together in interlocking cube-like patterns. In graphite, the carbon molecules are in flat, 6-sided plates that easily slip apart.

Diamonds turn into graphite if they are heated to about 3,500° F., in a vacuum.

Although graphite is common and widely distributed, it usually occurs in small deposits. The black marks in marble are usually graphite. Graphite is mined only where it occurs as solid masses in veins. Today, most graphite is mined in Ceylon, Madegascar and Mexico.

GRAPHITE

193

Grasses—Mostly Useful Plants

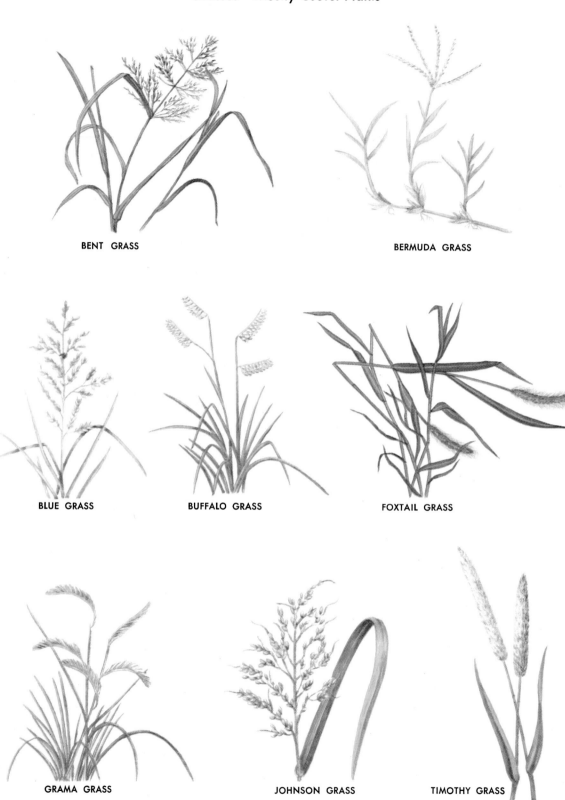

BENT GRASS

BERMUDA GRASS

BLUE GRASS

BUFFALO GRASS

FOXTAIL GRASS

GRAMA GRASS

JOHNSON GRASS

TIMOTHY GRASS

grass

Grasses make up a family that includes many of the world's most useful plants. Wheat, corn, bamboo, rice and sugarcane all belong to the grass family. Still other grasses provide food for livestock and wild animals. Grass roots help to hold soil in place and prevent erosion.

There are probably about 4,500 different kinds of grass. Most kinds are annual, biennial or perennial plants. Some kinds, like bamboo, have woody stems. Other kinds are climbing vines.

Grass grows in all parts of the world. Most kinds are of value to man in some way, but a few are troublesome weeds.

Grasses vary in size and appearance, but they have some things in common. All have jointed stems. Their narrow leaves are wrapped around the stem at the base end. All grass leaves have pointed tips.

Grasses have very small, green or yellowish flowers that are grouped in pointed clusters at the ends of the stems. Each flower is surrounded at the base by scaly structures which contain the reproductive organs and the hard, grain-like fruit.

The cultivated grasses used for lawns, pastures and golf courses are perennials. Their leaves and stems die in autumn, but the roots live through the winter.

Bent grasses are tall, delicate grasses. Some spread by creeping. Some are useful for lawns and pastures, while others are nuisance weeds. The leaves are somewhat rough and scaly. Redtop, the kind of bent grass illustrated, grows 3 feet tall. It is native to Europe and is used for lawns and pastures.

Bermuda grass spreads by means of creeping, horizontal stems. It is used for lawns where the climate is too hot and dry for other grasses. It is also used as pasture grass, but it sometimes spreads too quickly and becomes a nuisance weed. It will grow well in shade. Bermuda grass is sometimes planted to stop or prevent soil erosion. It grows 3 to 16 inches tall.

Blue grass, sometimes called Kentucky blue grass, is one of the finest grasses for lawns and pastures in the cooler parts of the temperate zone. It is a perennial grass that does not grow too well under great heat, shade or acid soil.

Buffalo grass is a low-growing, creeping grass native to the prairie states of the U.S. and Canada. It is a perennial that grows 4 to 12 inches tall. The leaves are very narrow and flat or folded.

Foxtail grass is an annual weed brought to the U.S. from Europe. It grows to 4 feet tall and is fairly common along road sides and in waste areas. The flowers are yellowish and are covered with stiff bristles, something like a fox tail. Foxtail grass has coarse leaves an inch or more wide.

Grama grass is a perennial that is native to the western prairies of the U.S. It grows 6 to 20 inches tall and has flat leaves that curl toward their tips.

Johnson grass is a perennial that was brought to the U.S. from the Mediterranean region. It is planted as hay and pasture grass in the southern U.S., and it has become a weed in some places. The leaves are coarse and wide, and droop toward the ground. They usually have red blotches caused by a bacterial disease. Leaves damaged by frost develop a poison that sometimes kills cattle. Johnson grass grows 3 to 6 feet tall.

Timothy grass is a cultivated perennial grass that is usually made into hay. It grows 2 to 5 feet tall. Its slender, spike-shaped flower clusters are up to 8 inches long. They are green when young, but become light brown when they are mature. The leaves are long and slender. Timothy grass is native to Europe.

For other kinds of grass, see *bamboo, barley, corn, oat, rice, rye, sorghum, sugarcane, wheat* and *wild rice*.

grasshopper

The grasshoppers make up 2 families of large, green or brown insects that feed on plants and damage farm crops. They use their long, strong hind legs to jump long distances. Most have wings when they are adults.

The grasshoppers that belong to the short-horned grasshopper family are sometimes called locusts. Most are brown. They have hearing organs on the sides of their bodies. The males make chirping noises by rubbing their hind legs against their wings. Short-horned grasshoppers lay their eggs in holes in the earth, or in dead wood.

The grasshoppers that belong to the long-horned grasshopper family have long antennae and are usually green. They have hearing organs in their knees. The males make chirping sounds by rubbing their wings together. Long-horned grasshoppers lay their eggs in the stems or leaves of green plants.

Grasshoppers lay as many as 100 eggs at a time, in a pod-like bundle. They hatch the following spring. The young, called nymphs, look like the adults but are smaller and paler, and lack wings. They molt 4 or 5 times while growing larger.

The American grasshopper (illustrated) belongs to the short-horned family and is about 3 inches long.

For other kinds of grasshoppers, see *angular-winged katydid* and *katydid*.

GRASSHOPPER

GREAT BARRACUDA

great barracuda \ˌbar-ə-ˈküd-ə\

This fierce and powerful marine fish probably attacks swimmers more often than sharks do. It has a great many teeth. Some are nearly an inch long and are almost as sharp as a razor. The great barracuda does not seem to be afraid of anything.

The great barracuda is popular with sports fishermen, as it will strike at anything bright-colored or moving. For short distances, the great barracuda is a fast swimmer and does not tire quickly when it is hooked. It is also popular as a food fish.

Great barracuda are usually about 5 feet long. Some become 8 to 10 feet long. They look a good deal like the pike and pickerel found in fresh water, as they have slender bodies, wedge-shaped heads and long jaws. The color is usually silvery, but changes according to the background.

Great barracuda live among coral reefs in warm, shallow parts of the Atlantic Ocean near Florida and the West Indies. They swim alone or in schools, chasing the smaller fish they feed on. Very large great barracuda usually swim alone. Great barracuda spawn once or twice a year, most often in early spring.

greater yellowlegs \ˈyel-ō-ˌlegz\

This slender, long-legged bird is related to the sandpipers. It is usually seen wading, less often than swimming, along sea-

GREATER YELLOWLEGS

GREBE

shores or in marshy places. It uses its long, slender bill to search in mud or wet sand for mollusks, small crustaceans, small fish and insects.

The greater yellowlegs is named for its bright yellow legs. The body is about 14 inches long. The back and head are gray to black. The underparts are white, with dark streaks on the breast. The bill is turned upward very slightly. Its call is a clear, loud whistle that is repeated 3 times.

Traveling in small groups, greater yellowlegs breed in a narrow area from Newfoundland west to British Columbia. They spend the winter along the Gulf coast as far south as Argentina.

The female lays 4 eggs once a year. They are gray, splotched with brown and lilac. The nest of reeds and other plants is built on the ground.

grebe \ 'grēb \

The grebes make up a family of water birds that swim and dive well but are nearly helpless on dry land. Their short legs are so far back on their bodies that they cannot walk easily.

Grebes live in lakes and reedy swamps in nearly all parts of the world. They feed on fish, crustaceans and other small animals they capture underwater.

Although grebes have trouble getting their heavy bodies up into the air, they are strong, swift fliers. Flaps of skin on the sides of the toes help them swim. The body is 12 to 29 inches long. The heads of some kinds of grebes have crests or tufts of feathers.

Grebes' nests are floating platforms of reeds and other plant materials. Two to 10 eggs are laid once a year and are incubated for 21 days. The young birds can swim as soon as they are hatched. They sometimes ride on their parents' backs, and may be carried along when the parents dive underwater.

The pied-billed grebe (illustrated) spends the summer in the U.S. and Canada. It is small for a grebe, with a length of 12 to 14 inches. It is the only grebe seen east of the Mississippi River during the summer. In winter, pied-billed grebes migrate to the southern U.S. and South America.

greenbrier \ 'grēn-ˌbrīr \

Greenbriers are climbing, prickly vines that belong to the lily family. They grow wild in nearly all temperate and tropical regions, and in many kinds of soil.

The leaves of the different kinds of greenbriers are narrow, broad or triangular. All of the leaves have ribs running from one end to the other, with a network of small veins between.

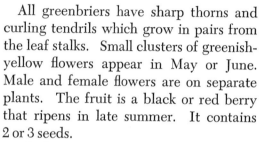

GREENBRIER

GROSBEAK

All greenbriers have sharp thorns and curling tendrils which grow in pairs from the leaf stalks. Small clusters of greenish-yellow flowers appear in May or June. Male and female flowers are on separate plants. The fruit is a black or red berry that ripens in late summer. It contains 2 or 3 seeds.

The kind of greenbrier most often seen in the northeastern U.S., and the Alleghany Mountains is the common greenbrier (illustrated), often called catbrier. It has broad, rounded leaves 3 to 4 inches across, and bluish-black berries. It is hard to kill, since it has many long roots.

Common greenbriers are a nuisance where they turn fence rows into dense tangles, or crowd out more valuable plants.

grosbeak \ 'grōs-ˌbēk \

These colorful, rather shy birds of the finch family are all tree dwellers. They live in nearly all parts of the world where there are forests, orchards or pine groves. They feed mostly on seeds, but also eat berries, buds and insects.

Most grosbeaks are 7 to 9 inches long. They have stout bodies, short tails and short, strong bills that are quite thick at the base. The males are usually bright-colored. The females are streaked yellow-gray or dull brown.

Some grosbeaks migrate, but they return early in the spring. Some build their

nests while there is still snow on the ground.

The female does most of the nest building. The nest is saucer-shaped and is built of twigs and grass. It is usually placed from 5 to 25 feet above the ground. Three to 5 spotted eggs are laid.

The black-headed grosbeak (illustrated) has a body length of about 7 inches. The female is streaked brown and black, with white stripes on the head and white wing-bars. A light yellowish color shows under the wings when the birds fly.

Black-headed grosbeaks breed in the far western parts of the U.S. and Canada in summer. However, they spend the winter in Mexico.

groundsel \ 'graȯn(d)-səl \

Groundsels make up a large group of annual, biennial or perennial plants belonging to the largest plant family. There are about 1,200 different kinds of groundsels. They are widespread throughout the world. A few are shrubs and small trees. A few are cultivated garden plants cultivated for their leaves and flowers. Many are common weeds.

Like the other plants in its family, the groundsels bear flower heads that are clusters of petal-sized blossoms. Rings of bracts surround the flower heads. Most groundsels have yellow flowers but some have red, purple, blue or white flowers.

The leaves grow either alternately or at the base of the stem. The fruit is small and has slender bristles around it.

The golden ragwort (illustrated) is a kind of groundsel common in the eastern half of North America. It is a perennial that grows 1 to 2 feet tall. The deeply lobed leaves have ragged edges and are about 6 inches long. At the tops of the branching stems are clusters of yellow flower heads about ¾ inches across. The golden ragwort is sometimes slightly hairy.

grouper \ 'grü-pər \

These large fish belong to the marine bass family. Some kinds are called rockfish because they live along rocky coasts or around coral reefs.

The groupers are important to commercial fishermen and, as game fish, to sportsmen and skin divers. They live in the warmer parts of both the Atlantic and Pacific oceans. Groupers feed on mollusks, crustaceans and smaller fish. They spawn in shallow water, in spring or early summer.

Groupers have large mouths with thick lips and many sharp teeth. Their bodies are short and stout, with squared-off tails. Their dorsal fins are spiny. Weight varies from less than a pound to nearly 1,000 pounds. Many groupers change color to match their surroundings.

GROUNDSEL

GROUPER

The Warsaw grouper or black jewfish (illustrated) may grow to 7 feet long and weigh as much as 500 pounds. It is dark brown, dark gray or bluish-black. It lives along the east coast of North and South America, from the Carolinas south to Brazil. The Warsaw grouper is valued by both commercial fishermen and sports fishermen.

grouse \ 'graús \

Grouse make up a family of game birds of the northern hemisphere. They are year-round residents of the cooler parts of the northern hemisphere. Grouse are the only gamebirds with feathers on their legs. The feathers help to keep their legs and feet from freezing in winter.

Grouse are dull-colored birds, but the males have unusual displays to attract the females. Some spread their tails and strut or leap. Some puff up air sacs on their throats. Most make loud drumming noises by beating their wings rapidly.

Some grouse have special "dancing grounds" where they gather in bands and show off before the females. The tribal dances of the Plains Indians may have been copied from these bird dances.

Most grouse are the size of chickens. They feed on berries and insects in summer. In winter they eat seeds and tree buds. The female lays 5 to 15 eggs in a ground nest well hidden under shrubs.

GROUSE

The eggs are incubated by the female for 21 to 29 days.

The male ruffed grouse (illustrated) is sometimes mistakenly called a partridge. Both sexes have feathers that stick out on each side of the neck. The young can walk and run as soon as they are hatched. A fast flier, the ruffed grouse is sometimes raised in captivity and then released for hunters. Many believe that it is the finest game bird in the U.S. The ruffed grouse is the state bird of Pennsylvania.

guava \ 'gwäv-ə \

The guava is a small tree native to Central and South America. Its fruit is used to flavor soft drinks and to make guava jelly. Guava fruit is eaten fresh and is also cooked or canned. The guava belongs to the myrtle family.

Guava trees grow 15 to 25 feet tall. The bark is scaly. Oval leaves grow in opposite pairs along the branches. The leaves are 3 to 6 inches long and have large veins. White flowers about 1 inch across bloom singly or in small clusters along the branches.

The fruit is round or pear-shaped and about the size of a small apple. Its smooth skin is usually yellow. Inside is a sweet, juicy pulp that is white, yellow or pink.

The guava tree has been planted in Florida, California and Hawaii. The trees are most often grown from seed, although they will also take root from root cuttings.

Guava trees grow well in many types of soil, but the soil must be moist and well-drained. The trees bear fruit when only 2 or 3 years old. The fruit appears in early summer, and continues to appear for many weeks.

The larva of 1 kind of small moth sometimes damages guava fruit.

guinea \ 'gin-ē \ pig (cavy)

Guinea pigs are small, furry animals that make up a group belonging to the rodent family. They make good pets and are widely used in scientific experiments. They are neat and clean, and can live in small cages.

Guinea pigs are native to South America where their wild relatives are called cavies. They live in underground burrows and feed on roots and grasses. Guinea pigs cannot live in cold climates.

Most guinea pigs are about 11 inches long and weigh about 1 pound. Some have long, shaggy hair, while others have short hair. They are reddish-brown, black, white or spotted.

Guina pigs have 4 toes on their front feet and 3 toes on their hind feet. Their tails are very small and are usually hidden by fur. The hind legs are shorter than the front legs.

Wild guinea pigs give birth to 3 or 4 young at a time. Tame ones have larger

GUINEA PIG

GULL

litters of 5 to 12 young. They grow to full size in about 15 months, but they often mate and bear young before that.

One kind of guinea pig (illustrated) is tamed and sold as a pet. It is sometimes used for testing new medicines or different kinds of diets. Scientists also use this guinea pig to study how characteristics such as color and length of hair are passed from one generation to another.

gull\ 'gəl\

Gulls make up a group of noisy, long-winged birds found along seacoasts in all parts of the world. Some are seen around inland lakes, and a few kinds spend part of the year in prairie country.

Gulls eat fish, crustaceans and floating garbage. Some carry clams high in the air and then drop them on rocks to break open the shells. Some follow ships for the food scraps thrown overboard. They can sleep floating on the water, even in high waves.

Gulls are 11 to 29 inches long. They have heavy bodies and strong beaks that hook down at the tip. The feathers are usually white and gray. Some adults have black on their heads in summer. Young birds are streaked with brown, and take several years to grow adult feathers.

Most gulls nest in flocks on coastal islands. The 2 to 4 eggs are laid in a nest of sticks and seaweed on the ground.

The herring gull (illustrated) is common along seacoasts throughout the northern hemisphere. It has a red spot on the beak. In the U.S., some herring gulls nest as far inland as South Dakota, where they feed on insects and worms.

The California gull, which is smaller than the herring gull but much like it, is the state bird of Utah.

gully\ 'gəl-ē\

A gully is a steep-sided valley where the soil has been eroded or washed away. The water runs downhill during and after heavy rains. The faster the water runs, the more soil it carries away.

The first soil to be washed away is the fertile topsoil. Few plants are able to grow in the subsoil that is left.

Where trees and grass grow, a network of roots often holds the soil in place. Gullies form after the trees are cut down and the grass has been plowed under.

Farmers prevent gullying and other forms of harmful erosion by leaving the natural cover of grass and trees on hillsides. When sloping land is to be used for growing a crop, they plow furrows around the slope rather than furrows that run up and down the slope. This process, called contour plowing, makes small steps or terraces that hold back water after a hard rain. Grass, shrubs and trees are often planted to heal gullies.

GULLY

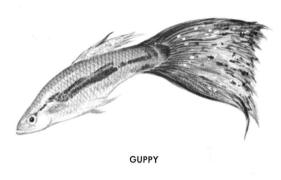

GUPPY

guppy \ 'gəp-ē \

This small freshwater fish is popular with aquarium owners because it is active and easy to care for. The guppies sold in pet shops are descended from wild guppies that live in streams and ponds in northern South America and on islands in the Caribbean.

Young guppies form inside eggs, as all fish do, but the female carries the eggs inside her body until they hatch. Female guppies may give birth to 100 live young as often as once a month. The young fish are almost too small to see, but most are able to swim and to find food for themselves. In home aquariums, newborn guppies must be separated from other kinds of fish, or they may be eaten.

The largest guppies are about 2 inches long. The females, larger than the males, are gray-green and move slowly. The slender, bright-colored males swim rapidly and gracefully all around the females. Guppies have long, flowing tail fins.

Because they multiply rapidly and require little care, guppies are sometimes used for scientific experiments. In the West Indies, guppies help control mosquitoes by eating the mosquito larvae.

Many different kinds of guppies have been developed by fish breeders.

gypsum \ 'jip-səm \

A white or gray mineral that has many uses, gypsum is found in many parts of the world. The chalky material doctors use to make casts around broken bones is gypsum that has been heated, ground to a powder and mixed with water to form a plaster. It is called plaster of Paris because it was first made near Paris, France.

Gypsum is used to make the plaster and plasterboard used in the walls of houses. It is also used in paints and cement. Farmers sometimes scatter gypsum on land to improve the soil. A small amount of gypsum goes into Portland cement.

Gypsum is usually a rather soft, lightweight substance. It occurs in different forms. Light can be seen through thin pieces of it. Alabaster is a rock-like kind of gypsum used to make vases and small statues. Clear crystals of gypsum are called selenite. Satinspar is a kind of gypsum that looks like silky threads.

Most gypsum is found in North America. It often occurs in flat beds where seawater evaporated. At White Sands, New Mexico, grains of gypsum cover the ground like sand. Most of the gypsum used by industries is mined in Michigan, California, Texas and New York.

For forms of gypsum, see *alabaster* and *selenite*.

GYPSUM

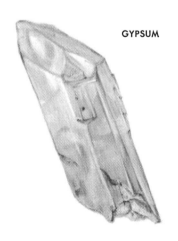

h

haddock \ 'had-ək \

This member of the cod family is an important food fish. Much of the frozen fish sold in the U.S. is haddock. Finnan haddie is haddock that has been salted and smoked.

The haddock has a dark line running along each side from head to tail. The first dorsal fin is tall and nearly triangular. A single barbel rangs from the lower jaw.

Most haddock brought in by commercial fishermen weigh 3 to 4 pounds. A few grow much larger, and weigh as much as 30 pounds.

Haddock swim in large schools and usually feed near the ocean floor. They eat bottom-living marine animals, squid and small fish. Haddock are common in cool, deep parts of the Atlantic Ocean and in the North Sea. Commercial fishermen catch haddock from the coast of New Jersey to the Grand Banks area off Newfoundland.

Haddock spawn in the spring. One female may lay several million eggs at a time. The eggs float in plankton and hatch in about 2 weeks. The young haddock drift about with the plankton until they have grown large enough to swim deep.

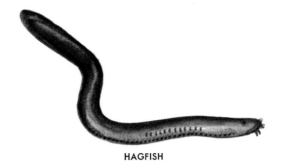

HAGFISH

hagfish \ 'hag-,fish \

These parasitic marine animals make up a primitive, eel-like family of fish. Blind and jawless, hagfish find food by smell. Around their mouths are 4 pairs of barbels that also help them find food.

Like sharks, hagfish have skeletons made of cartilage. They have round mouths, and are sometimes called borers because they use their sharp teeth to bore through the skins of fish and other marine animals. Hagfish often prey on other fish caught in nets and traps. They eat all of their prey except for skin and bones.

Hagfish live at the bottom of the sea, where the water is cool and deep. They bury themselves in mud so that only their noses and barbels show.

The female hagfish lays 25 to 30 eggs. Each egg is about 1 inch long and has a hook that fastens it to some object on the sea floor so it cannot float away.

Hagfish do not pass through a larval stage. The newly hatched fish look like the adults, but are much smaller.

When captured, hagfish secrete a slimy substance from glands in the skin.

The length of hagfish varies, but most are from 20 to 30 inches long.

The Atlantic hagfish (illustrated), is 2½ feet long when fully grown.

HADDOCK

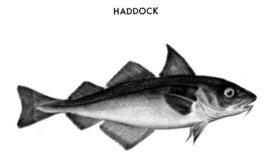

HAKE

hake \ 'hāk \

These ocean fish belong to the cod family. They are an important food fish in Europe, but they do not keep well because their flesh is so soft. Much of the hake caught by commercial fishermen is used to make cat food.

Sport fishermen consider the hake a good game fish. Because hake live near the ocean floor, commercial fishermen usually catch them in nets which are dragged along the bottom.

Hake are 1 to 4 feet long. Long-bodied, slender fish, they have sharp teeth, large mouths, long noses and small, weak tails. The second and third dorsal fins are joined to form a single long fin. A few hake weigh as much as 40 pounds. Hake live in the Atlantic Ocean, the Mediterranean Sea and in some northern parts of the Pacific Ocean.

Hake feed on smaller fish and crustaceans. Most spawn in early spring. The eggs are buoyant and float near the surface of the water.

The Atlantic silver hake (illustrated) is usually 1 to 2 feet long and weighs less than 5 pounds. It is found along the Atlantic coast of North America, from Newfoundland south to the Bahamas. The silver hake spawns during the summer. The transparent eggs hatch in about 2 days.

halibut \ 'hal-ə-bət \

Important food fish of the northern Atlantic and Pacific oceans, halibut are flatfish. They are members of the 2 flounder families. Like flounders, adult halibut have both eyes on the same side of the body.

Halibut are the largest of all flatfish. Some become 8 to 9 feet long and weigh up to 700 pounds. The females are usually larger than the males. The upper side of both sexes is dark brown, marked with pale blotches. The underside is whitish.

Halibut feed on smaller fish, mollusks and crustaceans. Scientists believe that they spawn in deep water as early as December. One female halibut may lay up to 1 million fairly large, buoyant eggs that drift with ocean currents. Newly hatched halibut swim upright, and have 1 eye on each side of the body. As they mature, 1 eye moves to the opposite side of the body.

The Atlantic halibut (illustrated) and the Pacific halibut are members of the righteye flounder family. The California halibut is a member of the lefteye flounder family.

Commercial fishermen bring in as many as 90 million pounds of halibut a year. About 70 percent of these are caught in the north Pacific. Although Atlantic halibut are caught as far south as New Jersey, they are most common in cold waters, farther north.

HALIBUT

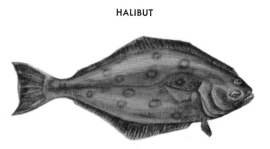

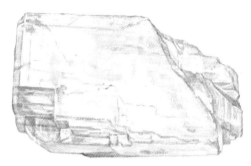

HALITE

halite \ 'hal-ˌīt \ (salt)

A common mineral, halite is better known as salt, or table salt. Thick beds of dry salt are found where the sea once covered the land. When the water evaporated, the salt remained.

Halite usually forms white or colorless, cube-shaped crystals. It dissolves easily in water.

Salt is used to season foods, and to preserve meat and fish. Both human beings and animals need salt to live. Animals such as deer travel long distances to reach natural salt deposits. Farmers place blocks of salt in their pastures for cows and sheep to lick.

Many chemical compounds are produced from halite. These are used mainly by the chemical companies and the food industry.

Halite is found in many different parts of the world. In Russia, in Rumania, along the Gulf of Mexico and the Mediterranean Sea, it is found in great domes. In the U.S., halite is mined in 15 different states. Most of this halite comes from New York, Michigan, Louisiana and Kansas.

halo \ 'hā-ˌlō \

A halo is the circle of light that sometimes appears around the sun or the moon.

A halo appears only when the sun or moon is shining through a high, thin layer of cloud. The tiny ice crystals in the cloud bend and spread the rays of light, somewhat as a glass prism does.

Sometimes the halo is white. Sometimes it is rainbow-colored. When it is colored, red is always at the inside of the circle, since the red rays are bent least. Blue shows at the outside of the circle.

There is some truth in an old saying that a halo appears before rain, and that the fewer stars there are inside the halo the sooner the rain will come. This is because the kind of cloud that causes a halo, called a cirrostratus cloud, usually moves ahead of a warm front bringing rain. As the warm front comes nearer, the cloud becomes thicker and the halo smaller, so that fewer stars can be seen inside it.

Halos are brighter and are seen much more often from the polar regions of the earth than from other regions.

hamster \ 'ham(p)-stər \

Hamsters are rodents with thick fur, large cheek pouches and short tails. They are well known as pets and are widely used in scientific experiments.

Native to Europe and Asia, hamsters were introduced in the U.S. about 1938, when they were first sold as pets and for use in laboratories. They are more active at night than during the day.

Hamsters are about 6 inches long. They have 4 toes on their front feet and 5 on their hind feet. Colors range from black and gray to golden brown and white.

HAMSTER

Wild hamsters dig burrows from 3 to 6 feet deep with several rooms and tunnels. They nest in one room and store grain and seeds in others. They feed on lizards, birds and other rodents as well as large amounts of grain and garden vegetables.

Pet hamsters will eat lettuce, dog biscuits and corn. They are clean and almost odorless. They are gentle and easy to care for.

Female hamsters bear 7 to 15 young at a time, as often as once a month. A hamster's life-span is seldom more than 2 years.

One of the most common kinds of hamster is the golden hamster (illustrated).

hare

Hares are furry mammals very closely related to rabbits. They are usually larger than rabbits, and their legs are longer and stronger than rabbit legs. Also, their ears are longer than rabbit ears.

Some hares are wrongly called rabbits and some rabbits are wrongly called hares. For example, the American jackrabbit is really a hare, and the Belgian hare is really a rabbit.

Hares bear their young in the open rather than in burrows, as rabbits do. Newborn hares are covered with fur. Their eyes are open, and they can hop when only a few hours old. Rabbits, on the other hand, are born naked, blind and helpless.

Hares eat mostly tender shoots, twigs, buds and leaves. They can do great damage to crops and orchards. Hares can run very fast and are able to leap as far as 12 feet. The color of their fur is so nearly the color of the fields in which they live that they are sometimes hard to see.

Female hares bear 2 to 8 young, as often as 4 times a year.

The arctic hare (illustrated) lives in Canada and Alaska, mostly north of the forest belt. Arctic hares are mostly white but turn grayish-brown for a short time in summer. They dig down through the snow to reach the moss and other plants they eat.

For another kind of hare, see *jackrabbit*.

hartebeest \ 'härt-(ə-)ˌbēst \

Probably the fastest of all antelopes, hartebeests are pony-sized African mammals. They are awkward-looking, with cow-like faces and long, unbranched horns that curve back in V or U shapes.

Hartebeests are native to sandy, grassy plains of Africa, where they once grazed in huge herds. Today, they are rarely found except in parks set aside to preserve wildlife.

HARE

HARTEBEEST

HARVEST FLY

Hartebeests are reddish-brown above and whitish below. Their markings differ with different kinds. The females give birth to single young 6 to 9 months after mating.

Perhaps the best-known kind of hartebeest is the South African or Cape hartebeest (illustrated), which is about 4 feet tall at the shoulder. Although once the Cape hartebeest lived from the Cape of Good Hope to Angola, it is now rare in southern Africa.

harvest fly (annual cicada)

Harvest flies are large insects of the cicada family. Their name comes from the fact that they are seen, and heard, in late summer and early autumn at harvest time. They are also called annual cicadas, since they appear once a year.

Harvest flies are about 2 inches long and have large, almost transparent wings. They have sucking mouthparts and feed on plant juices.

One of the loudest sounds made by any insect is the shrill buzzing the male harvest fly makes by vibrating plates on the sides of its thorax.

Female harvest flies lay eggs in slits they cut in the young twigs of trees. Wingless larvae hatch out and drop to the ground. There, they burrow under the surface and feed on juices they suck from roots.

When fully grown, the larvae climb to the surface of the ground and onto a tree trunk. The old skin splits down the back to free the winged adult.

Harvest flies are found throughout the U.S. and Mexico, and in eastern Canada.

The most common harvest fly is popularly called the lyreman (illustrated). It is about 2 inches long and is black and green.

harvestman \ 'här-vəs(t)-mən \ (daddy longlegs)

Related to spiders but not a true spider, the harvestman has a small oval body, with the head and thorax joined. The body seems to be hung in the center of 4 pairs of very long, slender, jointed legs. A pair of short antennae and 2 large eyes are on the head. On the body are glands that give off an unpleasant odor.

Male and female look alike, but the female is usually larger.

Harvestmen are common in most parts of the U.S., and there are at least 75 different kinds. In the late summer, they can be seen at dusk in fields, feeding on insects and on the juices of fruits and vegetables.

In autumn, harvestmen lay eggs under stones or in the ground. The eggs hatch in the spring. In colder climates the adults die after the eggs are laid, but in warmer areas they hibernate through the winter in rubbish or brush.

HARVESTMAN

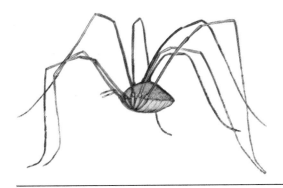

Hawks—Daytime Hunters

COOPER'S HAWK

DUCK HAWK

FISH HAWK

MARSH HAWK

PIGEON HAWK

RED-SHOULDERED HAWK

RED-TAILED HAWK

ROUGH-LEGGED HAWK

SHARP-SHINNED HAWK

SPARROW HAWK

hawk

Hawks are large, strong-winged birds of prey. All have long, sharp talons, which they use to grasp and kill the smaller birds and animals on which they feed. All hawks have strong, hooked beaks and unusually keen eyesight, but no sense of smell.

Hawks are found all over the world. Some hawks soar in wide circles as they watch for moving creatures below them. Others perch quietly in tall, dead trees waiting to pounce onto an unlucky bird or rodent. Although many hawks kill chickens and birds, others benefit man by killing large numbers of rats, mice and grasshoppers.

The larger hawks usually build untidy nests of sticks and twigs in large trees. Others nest on the ground or on rocky ledges. A few use nests left by other birds.

Two to 5 eggs are laid, once a year. The incubation period is unusually long, 4 to 5 weeks. The young birds are covered with down and are helpless. They must be fed in the nest from 4 to 10 weeks. Some hawks do not grow their full adult feathers until they are 2 years old.

All of the hawks illustrated are found in North America. The marsh hawk and the fish hawk live near lakes or streams. The others are most common in wooded or brushy areas.

Cooper's hawk, commonly called chicken hawk, and the sharp-shinned hawk belong to the accipiter family of hawks. Both of them are swift and fierce. Cooper's hawks are 18 to 20 inches long, with a wingspread of 2½ to 3 feet. Their tails are long and squared-off. Sharp-shinned hawks are slightly smaller.

Chicken hawks swoop down and dash off with chickens, smaller birds and small mammals. They live near chicken farms and in open woods from southern Canada to the Gulf of Mexico.

The duck hawk, or peregrine falcon, the pigeon hawk and the sparrow hawk all belong to the falcon family. Their wings are long and taper to a point. They can fly even faster than the other hawks, and sometimes dive through the air at speeds up to 175 miles an hour.

The duck hawk is 16 to 19 inches long. Its beak and talons are black. The pigeon and sparrow hawks are 9 to 13 inches long. All eat birds, small mammals and insects.

The red-shouldered, red-tailed and rough-legged hawks all belong to the buteo, or buzzard hawk, family. They are 20 to 24 inches long, with wingspreads up to 4½ feet. Their wings are broad, and their tails are fan-shaped. Buzzard hawks seem to float in the air as they soar high over the ground. They eat mostly rodents.

Their names show some of the differences among these buzzard hawks. The tail of the red-tailed hawk is red, or reddish-brown. The feathers on the back near the head of the red-shouldered hawk are copper-red.

The marsh hawk is also called harrier. It is about 24 inches long, has more rounded wings than other hawks and longer legs. Because its face is rounder than that of other hawks, it looks a little like an owl.

Marsh hawks are found in open fields, marshes and prairies in the eastern U.S. They feed on frogs and small reptiles, as well as birds and rodents.

The fish hawk, or osprey, looks something like an eagle. The fish hawk is the only hawk in North America that dives into the water. It is 21 to 24 inches long, with a wingspread of 4½ to 6 feet. Fish hawks are dark brown with white underneath. Active only during the day, fish hawks eat fish, which they catch in their talons by diving into the water feet-first.

For other kinds of hawks, see *eastern goshawk, falcon* and *kite.*

hawthorn \ 'hȯ-ˌthȯrn \

The hawthorns are prickly shrubs and trees belonging to the rose family. They are closely related to the apple tree. The larger kinds have hard, tough wood used in making small articles such as tool handles. In England, hawthorns are planted as hedges around farm fields, to serve as fences. In the U.S., some kinds of hawthorns are planted as ornamental trees.

Hawthorns grow 8 to 25 feet tall. They bear 5-petaled flowers in clusters near the ends of wide-spreading branches. The fruit looks like a small apple and contains large, hard seeds. Some kinds of hawthorn have leaves with jagged edges. Other kinds have smooth-edged leaves, while still others have deeply lobed leaves.

Hawthorns grow in most cool, moist parts of the temperate zone. They are most common in rich soil at the edges of woods or in open fields.

In North America, the largest kind of hawthorn (illustrated) grows 20 to 25 feet tall. It has flower clusters with red fruit and dark, scaly bark. The branches have long thorns and slender leaves that are smooth-edged at the base and jagged at the tip. This hawthorn is common in the eastern part of the U.S. as far south as North Carolina.

HAWTHORN

HAZEL
(LEAVES, FLOWERS AND FRUIT)

hazel \ 'hā-zəl \

Hardy shrubs or small spreading trees related to birches, hazels are valued for their sweet, tasty nuts. Hazels grow in many different soils and climates in most of Europe, Asia and North America. They are usually found in densely wooded areas.

Hazels have oval or heart-shaped leaves with jagged edges. The twigs are hairy. The flowers are dangling tassels about 1½ inches long. They appear before the leaves in early spring. The oval nut develops inside a thin, smooth shell. The nut ripens between July and September.

In southern Canada and the eastern U.S., the most common kind of hazel (illustrated) grows 8 to 10 feet tall.

heal-all \ 'hēl-ˌȯl \ (self-heal)

A hardy perennial plant belonging to the mint family, heal-all is usually thought of as a wild flower. It is a low-growing, spreading plant that can be a troublesome weed in a poorly drained lawn. In earlier times, heal-all was believed to have healing qualities and was used as a medicine.

The flowers are lavender, purple or white, and grow in clusters on a spike at the tip of a thick, squarish stalk. Pointed, bristly, leaf-like parts are mixed with the flowers, which are 2-lipped. The upper lip is broad and the lower lip is 3-lobed or

2-lobed. The outer lobes are rounded and the center is 1-toothed.

The long, lance-shaped leaves are opposite each other on the main stalk. The leaves have short stalks, or none, and smooth edges.

Heal-all is native to Europe and North American but now grows throughout the world, usually in woods and fields.

heather \ 'he<u>th</u>-ər \ (ling)

A low-growing evergreen shrub, true heather has delicate fern-like foliage, with clusters of white or purplish-pink flowers. Heather and Scotland are often thought of together, because heather is so often mentioned in songs and stories of Scotland. The plant is common in other parts of the British Isles and in much of Europe.

Thick growths of heather often cover hillsides. The plant itself grows from 6 to 36 inches tall. Its leaves are very small, sharp-pointed needles that grow in 4 rows. Flowers about ¼ inch long appear in erect, slender spikes in late summer.

Heather grows only in sandy or acid soils, in areas which have mild winters and cool summers. Large areas of heather are often called heaths. It has been planted in the eastern U.S. as an ornamental shrub. Heather grows wild in a few areas near the Atlantic coast north of New Jersey.

HEATHER

HEDGEHOG

hedgehog \ 'hej-ˌhȯg \

Small insect-eating mammals, hedgehogs are valued because they destroy many harmful pests. Although hedgehogs feed mostly on insects, they will also eat mice, snakes, voles and lizards. They are almost completely immune to the bites of poisonous snakes.

A typical hedgehog is about 10 inches in length, including the tail, and weighs about 1½ pounds. The face, legs and lower part of the body are covered with hair. The upper part of the body is covered with coarse, yellow-tipped spines. Normally these lie flat, but if the animal is alarmed, it raises its spines and rolls into a ball. Hedgehogs swim and climb well, and most are nocturnal.

Hedgehogs are found mostly in Europe, Africa and parts of Asia, in varied habitats. They build nests lined with leaves and plants, and they hibernate during the winter months.

Five to 6 weeks after mating, a litter of young is born. There are 2 litters a year. Life expectancy is 9 to 11 years.

A well-known kind of hedgehog is the European hedgehog (illustrated).

The European hedgehog has small, rounded ears and a very short tail. Its spines are stiff and sharp, but they are not barbed at the tip like porcupine bristles.

HELIOTROPE

HEMATITE

heliotrope\ 'hēl-yǝ-,trōp\

Heliotropes make up a group of over 200 kinds of tropical and subtropical plants. Some kinds are woody, some are classed as weeds, and some are garden and greenhouse flowers prized for their fragrance and beauty.

The small blue, purple or white flowers are borne in forking or coiled clusters. The flowers are often on alternate sides of the stalks. The hairy leaves grow almost opposite each other. The fruit separates into 4 nutlets.

The common heliotrope (illustrated) is a perennial but is usually treated as a tender annual in the garden. It grows 2 to 4 feet tall. The flowers are purple and about ¼ inch long. The leaves are oval or oblong. This kind of heliotrope is native to Peru, South America.

hematite\ 'hem-ǝ-,tīt\

The mineral hematite is a valuable ore, as it is 70 percent iron. Hematite is sometimes called red ocher. American Indians used it for red war paint, and it is still used as a pigment in mixing red paint.

Hematite is usually a brownish-red color. It occurs as earthy, fibrous masses, as rounded lumps or as shiny, black crystals that look like plates.

Hematite is worn away from old, iron-bearing rocks by weather. It is common in small quantities and gives a red color to many soils and rocks. Most of the large deposits of hematite have been heavily mined.

The world's greatest supply of hematite has been mined in North America, in the states surrounding Lake Superior and in Ontario. In this region, nearly 100 million tons of hematite were mined in 1 year. Other large deposits of hematite have been found in Brazil, Venezuela, Labrador, England, France, Russia, India, Newfoundland and Cuba.

hemlock\ 'hem-,läk\ **tree**

Hemlock trees are evergreens related to the pines. They are native to the Pacific coast, the eastern U.S., Japan and China. Their coarse, knotty wood is used to make paper pulp and rough crates.

Hemlocks grow 50 to 150 feet tall and sometimes live to be 600 years old. The thick, ridged bark is reddish-brown. Hemlocks have dense foliage made up of flat needles that appear to grow in 2 rows. Each short-stalked needle is dark green on its upper surface and has white bands on its green lower surface. The seed is attached to 1 end of a narrow wing of the light brown cone.

HEMLOCK TREE

Hemlocks grow in cool, moist areas. The trees cannot live without water.

The kind of hemlock found in New England is the eastern hemlock (illustrated). It is most common in the Appalachian Mountains and around the Great Lakes. The eastern hemlock grows 50 to 70 feet tall. It is Pennsylvania's state tree.

The western hemlock is the state tree of Washington.

hemp \ 'hemp \ (marihuana)

Hemp is an erect, strong-smelling, annual plant that is native to Asia. It is the source of hemp fiber, which is made from the rough, woody stem of the plant. Hemp fiber is used to make rope. The female flowers of hemp produce a sticky gum which is the source of the narcotic drugs, hashish and marihuana. Growing hemp is against the law in many countries.

Hemp flowers are greenish and very small. Staminate and pistillate flowers grow on different plants. Staminate flowers grow on hollow stalks in long, branching clusters. Pistillate flowers are almost too small to see. They grow in short, leafy clusters or spikes inside bristly, leaf-like parts.

Hemp leaves grow alternately on the stalks. Each leaf is large and thin, with 3 to 7 tapering leaflets having jagged edges.

hepatica \ hi-'pat-i-kə \ (liverwort)

A small group of low-growing, perennial plants, hepaticas are attractive, early-spring wild flowers.

The lavender-blue, rosy-pink or white flowers appear before the leaves. The flowers have no petals, but have 6 or more petal-like sepals, with 3 bristly, leaf-like parts below. The 3-lobed, rounded leaves rise on fuzzy stalks from the base of the plant. The leaves stay green through the winter but droop and turn brown when the flowers appear. New leaves follow later. The fruit is a dry, hard, 1-seeded pod.

Hepatica grows throughout the north temperate zone, chiefly in wooded areas.

The Mayflower or blue anemone is a common kind of hepatica in eastern North America from the east coast west to the state of Minnesota.

heron \ 'her-ən \

Herons make up a family of wading birds with long bills, long legs and long necks. The vertebrae in a heron's neck are of different lengths so that the neck usually has an S shape.

All herons have powder downs, which are patches of small feathers that are never shed. The ends of these feathers crumble

HERON

into a fine powder. Herons use this powder to clean their other feathers.

Herons live on animal food such as crustaceans, amphibians, reptiles, aquatic insects and fish. They capture much of their food by spearing it with their sharp bills.

Herons live throughout most of the ice-free lands of the world. Most kinds of herons migrate.

The only large heron in the northern U.S. and Canada is the great blue heron (illustrated). It lives in marshy wilderness areas from Alaska south to Florida and the West Indies. Four feet tall and 42 to 52 inches long, the great blue heron eats field mice and gophers as well as fish and frogs. These birds migrate to the southern U.S. and Central America.

For another kind of heron, see *egret*.

herring \ 'her-ing \

Making up a family of marine fish, herrings are considered the most important of all commercial food fish. Herrings are also important as food for other fish and some are valued as game fish and for bait.

Most kinds of herring have a sharp, scaly ridge on the underside. All have deeply forked tails. The herring grows to about 2 feet and 2 pounds. The mouth is large and nearly toothless.

HERRING

HIBISCUS

Herring live both in open seas and close to shore. A few enter brackish or fresh water. They travel in large schools, usually near the surface, and feed on plankton. Spawning habits vary with different species, but all produce many young.

There are probably more Atlantic herring (illustrated) than any other kind of fish in the Atlantic Ocean. Young Atlantic herring are sold as New England sardines. They are also an important source of food for other fish. A single female produces up to 40,000 eggs.

For other kinds of herring, see *alewife, American shad* and *sardine*.

hibiscus \ hī-'bis-kəs \

Hibiscuses make up a group of flowering shrubs or trees. They grow over large areas in the temperate and tropic zones, though the tree-sized kinds grow only in the tropics.

Most kinds of hibiscus have large, 2-petaled flowers that are white, pink, blue or purple. The seeds develop inside a 5-sectioned capsule.

The kinds of hibiscus that grow wild in most of the U.S. are commonly called mallows. Most are found in swamps. They grow 3 to 6 feet tall and have pink or white flowers, 4 to 7 inches across.

The kind of hibiscus most often cultivated in the northern U.S. is the rose of

HIPPOPOTAMUS

Sharon (illustrated). It is a hardy shrub that grows 4 to 12 feet tall. It has triangular-shaped leaves and produces flowers from midsummer to the time of frost. The rose of Sharon is native to eastern Asia.

The red hibiscus is the state flower of Hawaii.

hickory tree

The slow-growing, long-living hickory trees are members of the walnut family. They are native to North America and China.

Some kinds of hickory are valued for their nuts, while others are valued for their hard, tough wood. The wood is used to make tool handles and it is often used as fuel for smoking meat.

Hickories grow 50 to 150 feet tall. The gray bark is smooth on young trees, but rough on old trees. Each leaf is made up of 5 to 13 pointed leaflets.

The pecan (illustrated) is the largest kind of hickory tree. It grows 90 to 150 feet tall, and has a trunk 5 to 6 feet around. The pecan is a source of valuable lumber. Its flowers are dangling tassels which become clusters of sweet, thin-shelled nuts called pecans. They are among the most popular of edible nuts.

The pecan is native to the Mississippi Valley where it grows in rich, moist soil from southern Iowa to Louisiana.

HICKORY TREE

hippopotamus

A family of hoofed mammals native to Africa, hippopotamuses are among the largest land animals. Although they are called land animals, hippos spend much of their time on river banks or in the water. They can float or swim or stay under water up to half an hour, and can walk on a river bottom with amazing speed.

Hippos usually feed at night, on water plants and grasses. In certain parts of Africa, hippo meat is eaten, and the huge teeth are valued as ivory. The female hippo bears a single young that often rides on its mother's back while she is swimming.

The common hippopotamus (illustrated) once lived all over Africa. Today, it wanders in large herds south of the Sahara Desert.

A full-grown male hippo is barrel-shaped, is 12 to 17 feet long and weighs up to 4 tons. Its mouth is about 2 feet wide, and its jaws are 3 to 4 feet long. Common hippos have almost hairless skin that is 2 inches thick in certain places. The color is grayish-black, with some pink in the lighter areas.

The pygmy hippopotamus is similar in appearance but much smaller. It is about the size of a barnyard pig. Pygmy hippos live only along a few lakes and streams in West Africa, mostly in Liberia.

hoarfrost \ 'hōr-ˌfròst \

Hoarfrost is a white, feathery kind of ice that looks like light snow. Hoarfrost is found on the ground, on grass blades and on the tops of automobiles after a clear cold night. It forms when air touches surfaces colder than 32° F. When this happens, the water vapor in the air changes directly into ice crystals.

holly \ 'häl-ē \

Many different-looking kinds of trees and shrubs make up the holly family. Holly grows widely through the tropic and temperate zones. American holly and English holly have prickly evergreen leaves and are used in Christmas decorations. Other kinds have round-tipped, smooth-edged leaves. Not all hollies are evergreen.

Most hollies grow 5 to 20 feet tall. Small, white or green flowers bloom along the smaller branches in spring. Holly fruit is a round, red or black berry.

In the U.S., hollies grow all along the Atlantic coast and throughout the southern states from Kentucky to Virginia south to Texas and Florida.

The hard, white wood of American holly (illustrated) looks like ivory and is used for decorative objects and inlays. The leathery, dark green leaves and bright red berries remain on the branches all winter. The American holly is the state tree of Delaware.

hollyhock \ 'häl-ē-ˌhäk \

The hollyhock is a tall, straight garden plant belonging to the mallow family. It was once a perennial plant but is now raised in gardens as a biennial. A hollyhock plant does not produce flowers and seeds until the second year.

Hollyhocks grow from 5 to 9 feet tall. Many large, showy flowers appear on a tall central stalk late in the summer. The flowers have 5 wide, notched petals. They are usually red and white, but hollyhocks have been developed in many colors.

The alternate leaves are large and rounded or heart-shaped, and have long stalks. They are rough or wrinkled, and hairy, and often have jagged edges. The fruit is a circle of pods, each of which contains 1 seed.

Native to China, hollyhocks are now grown widely in North America and Great Britain. They grow best in sandy loam.

honeysuckle \ 'hən-ē-ˌsək-əl \

The honeysuckles are a large group of shrubs and climbing plants best known for their very sweet-smelling flowers. Honeysuckles are native to the temperate zones of North America and Asia.

HOLLY

HONEYSUCKLE

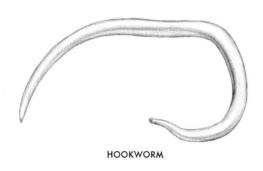

HOOKWORM

The honeysuckle has oval leaves which grow in opposite pairs. The flowers are white, yellow or red. They are shaped like slender tubes, and they open out in 5 rounded lobes. In some kinds 4 lobes combine to form the upper lip. The fruit is a red, blue or orange berry.

One kind of climbing wild honeysuckle (illustrated) has blue-green leaves and small, yellow or red flowers. The inside of the flower is hairy. The stems and the edges of the leaves are smooth. This kind of honeysuckle grows in fairly dry, rocky or sandy soil in southern Canada, and in the U.S., as far south as Tennessee.

hookworm \ 'hùk-,wərm \

One of the roundworms, the hookworm is a white, thread-like parasite less than ½ inch long. Hookworms live in the small intestines of human beings. There they drain enough blood to weaken an adult or to slow the development of a child.

Hookworms are most often picked up in warm, moist climates by people walking barefoot in unsanitary places. The larvae bore through the soles of the feet and enter the bloodstream. They travel to the lungs and enter the air passages. Finally they reach the throat where they are swallowed.

Once inside the small intestine, the hookworms cling with the hooks or teeth inside their mouths. In the intestine, they grow for a year or more. There they mate and produce thousands of eggs which are passed out with the host's body wastes.

Some kinds of hookworm infect domestic animals, such as dogs, sheep and cattle. Other kinds infect wild animals, such as foxes.

Hookworm can be prevented in humans by proper sanitation and by the wearing of shoes.

One kind of hookworm (illustrated) was discovered in America in 1901. It was probably brought by slaves from Africa to America.

hop

Hops are a small group of vines of the hemp family and are native to the north temperate zone. One type, native to Eurasia and North America, is widely used as a source of lupulin. Lupulin is a fine, yellow powder which contains 2 bitter chemical substances. These substances are used commercially to give beer its bitter flavor. They are also used in medicines to kill certain fungi and bacteria.

Hop flowers are green. The staminate flowers grow in clusters on one plant. The pistillate flowers grow in pairs on another plant. Each pair forms under a large bract, producing the cone-like "hops" which contain the lupulin.

The rough leaves grow opposite each

HOP

other on coarse stems. The small, dry fruit has 1 seed. Hop vines often become so tall that they must be held up by a fence or trellis.

The common cultivated hop vine (illustrated) can grow so swiftly that it may overrun a garden and become a nuisance.

hornblende \ 'hȯrn-ˌblend \

Hornblende is a mineral that makes up the largest part of many common rocks. It occurs most often in metamorphic rocks, but is sometimes present in igneous rocks. Granite, gneiss and schist are all likely to contain hornblende. As a rule, the darker these rocks are, the more hornblende they contain.

Hornblende is dark green, very dark brown or black. When pure, it looks like very dark glass. It is translucent through thin, broken edges. Crystals of pure hornblende are long and slender. Broken pieces are usually wedge-shaped.

Hornblende contains aluminum as well as calcium, magnesium, iron and smaller amounts of other elements. It belongs to a family of minerals called the amphiboles. Actinolite and tremolite are other minerals of this family. All amphiboles contain magnesium and iron. The lighter-colored ones contain more magnesium and less iron. Hornblende is one of

HORNBLENDE

HORNET

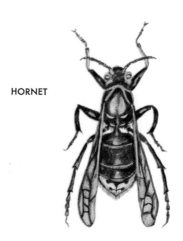

the darker-colored amphiboles that contain more iron than magnesium.

A very common mineral, hornblende is found in many different parts of the world. It is more common in mountains than in lowland areas.

hornet \ 'hȯr-nət \

Hornets are a group of large, social wasps that make paper nests. They harm trees and shrubs because they use the living bark and wood for their nests. They chew up wood to form the nests which are made up of many little, room-like cells with a strong paper-like covering.

Hornets average about 1 inch in length. They have rounded heads and short, thick abdomens attached to the middle part of the body by a short "waist." Hornets are black or reddish-brown with yellow or white markings. The sting of the female can be painful.

Most hornets live only 1 season. After mating in the fall, the female hibernates until spring, builds a new nest and deposits an egg in each cell. The first larvae are fed with freshly killed insects by the queen for about 10 days or until they enter a pupal stage. In about 2 weeks the larvae develop into adult workers. These workers take over nest building and feeding the young, while the queen lays eggs, as many as 25,000 in a season. Most of these become workers. Only about 100 become queens and males.

Hornets' nests are large and round. They are found around buildings, in hollow trees or under rocks.

The bald-faced hornet (illustrated) is a common kind of hornet found all over the U.S. and Canada. The bald-faced hornet is black with white stripes on the abdomen and a white face.

horntail \ 'hȯrn-ˌtāl \

Horntails are a group of wasps. They are called horntails because the female has a long, horn-shaped organ used to drill into dead or dying wood to lay eggs.

Horntails have large heads but do not have the narrow "waists" of many wasps. They have 2 pairs of transparent wings, 1 pair smaller than the other. Horntails are usually black with yellow stripes and they grow to be about 2 inches long.

Horntail larvae have stout, cylinder-shaped bodies about 1½ inches long. The larvae have large heads with sharp, pointed horns, and very small legs. They bore deep tunnels in trees and make thin, paper-like cocoons when ready for the pupal stage.

The pigeon horntail (illustrated) is one of the largest and best-known horntails. It is common everywhere in the U.S., except the southwest, and damages many kinds of trees.

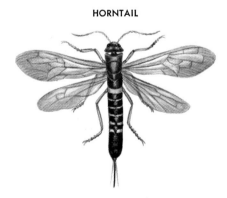

HORNTAIL

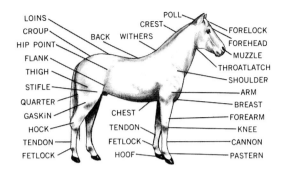

THE PARTS OF A HORSE

horse

Horses make up a family of hoofed mammals. They are the only hoofed mammals with 1 well-developed toe on each foot. Modern horses probably have the best foot for running of any mammal.

Modern horses are descendants of much smaller, prehistoric, horse-like mammals with 4 and 5 toes. Zebras are a family of wild horses. The donkey, the mule and the pony are all types of horses.

Male horses are called stallions. Females are called mares and newborn horses are foals. Young male horses are colts and females are fillies.

Horses differ widely in size and shape. They are usually large, from 56 to 80 inches tall at the withers, or highest point of the back, and can weigh up to 2,000 pounds. They have long legs, hairy tails and manes, and smooth, shiny coats.

About 1 year after mating, 1 foal is born. Wild horses live about 25 years, but domestic horses sometimes live 50 years.

Horses are found all over the world today, but they first lived in the steppes and deserts of Asia and Africa. They feed on grasses and grains.

Domestic horses have been widely used as beasts of burden and for transportation. Many are especially bred and raised for sports like racing.

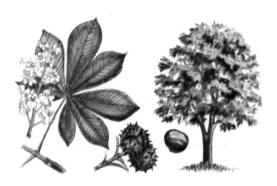

HORSE CHESTNUT

Horse meat is used as pet food and is sometimes eaten by human beings. Horses are also used to produce serums for medical uses.

For members of the horse family, see *donkey, Merychippus, Mesohippus, mule, pony, zebra* and illustration for *mammal.*

horse chestnut \ 'ches-(,)nət \

The horse chestnuts make up a group of strong, beautiful trees with large flowers and seeds. They are native to Asia but are much like American buckeyes. Horse chestnut flower clusters are larger than those of buckeyes and their leaves are wider at the tip end.

A common kind of horse chestnut (illustrated) is often planted in European cities and the eastern U.S. It grows 75 to 100 feet tall, and has a trunk 2 to 3 feet across. The leaves, made up of leaflets, grow opposite each other and are from 10 to 15 inches long. The rough, dark-brown bark is used in making medicines.

Flower clusters about 12 inches long appear at the ends of branches in May. The flowers are white with purple markings. Each flower is about 2 inches long. Smooth, chestnut-brown seeds about 1½ inches wide develop inside a spiny husk. The husk breaks open in 3 sections when the seed ripens, in October.

horseshoe crab

Horseshoe crabs are not true crabs, but make up a group of marine arthropods. Horseshoe crabs have existed since the Silurian Period of the Paleozoic Age and are often called "living fossils." The horseshoe crab's nearest relatives are spiders and scorpions.

The average length of the horseshoe crab is 2 feet. Females are larger than males. The shiny, brown shell has 2 sections. The front, horseshoe-shaped part protects the head and the middle part of the body. The smaller section is edged with spines. There are 2 pairs of eyes. One pair of eyes is simple. The other pair is compound.

The front part of the body has 5 pairs of clawed spines and 1 pair of movable spines called pushers. There are 2 gills for breathing. Each gill is made up of several thin plates. The pointed tail is as long as the body.

Horseshoe crabs are found only along the Atlantic coast of the U.S. and the east coasts of Asia. They live in shallow waters, and move about only at night. They feed on worms and soft mollusks.

Eggs are laid in early summer on sandy beaches, above the high-tide mark. The female deposits the eggs in hollows which

HORSESHOE CRAB

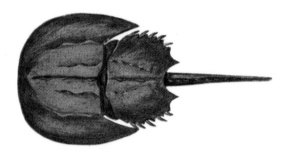

she digs in the sand. The larvae go through a long series of molts and do not mature for several years.

horsetail \ 'hȯrs-ˌtāl \

Horsetails make up a group of plants that have existed from ancient times. They are related to ferns and club mosses. Horsetails belong to the horsetail family, which once included tree-sized plants.

Most kinds of horsetails grow 6 to 24 inches tall, but 1 kind reaches 12 feet. Tiny, scale-like leaves and sometimes slender branches grow in circles or whorls at some joints of the stem. All kinds of horsetails bear a cone-like organ that produces spores. Horsetails are most common in shaded, moist or sandy soil.

The common horsetail (illustrated) produces 2 separate, aerial stems. One is green and branching and carries on photosynthesis. The other stem is colorless, has no branches and produces the cone. The colorless stem appears in early spring before the green stem. Horsetails reproduce by alternation of generations.

The slender branching parts are stems. The true leaves are tiny and wrap around the stems at the joints.

The common horsetail grows 18 to 24 inches tall. It is found in Eurasia and North America.

HORSETAIL

HUCKLEBERRY

huckleberry

Huckleberries make up a group of thick, bushy shrubs that bear many small, black or blue berries. They are native to North and South America. Huckleberry fruit has some use as human food, but most of it is eaten by birds and wild animals. The fruit is seedier than the blueberry and is not as sweet.

Huckleberries are usually found in dense thickets. They sprout from underground stems and grow best in dry, sandy or rocky soil.

Most kinds of huckleberries grow 1½ to 6 feet tall. They have small, oval leaves. On 1 or both sides of each leaf are many small dots of resin. The dots are too small to be seen easily without a microscope. The small, white flowers appear in clusters at the ends of the branches in May and June. The berries ripen between July and September. Each berry contains 10 large seeds.

Black huckleberry (illustrated) is the kind of huckleberry most common in eastern Canada and the U.S. It grows 2 to 3 feet high and has leaves 1 to 3 inches long. The black berries hang in long, drooping sprays. This plant grows only in acid soil, under taller shrubs and trees.

HUMMINGBIRD

hummingbird

Hummingbirds make up a family of swift-flying, bright-colored birds. They live throughout the American continent from Alaska to South America. There are about 300 kinds of hummingbirds, varying in size from 2½ to 8½ inches long.

The hummingbird's flight is unlike that of any other bird. On tiny wings beating 50 to 200 times per second, hummingbirds zoom forward or backward or hover in one place. At times, they swing rapidly back and forth like a pendulum. When the male is trying to win a mate, he stages a show of fancy aerial acrobatics for her.

Hummingbirds are most often seen hovering above flowers. They thrust their long, slender bills deep inside the flower and feed on the nectar and insects they find there. They also pick insects from the leaves and bark of trees.

The females build tiny, cup-shaped nests in trees. They incubate the 2 white eggs and feed the young without help from the males. Most kinds of hummingbirds raise 2 or 3 broods a year.

The ruby-throated hummingbird (illustrated) breeds from Canada to Texas. The female has no red on the throat. A few of these birds winter in southern Florida, but most fly 500 miles across the Gulf of Mexico to South America.

hyacinth \ 'hī-ə-(ˌ)sin(t)th \

The hyacinths are popular garden plants related to the lilies. There are about 30 different kinds of hyacinths. They are native to the lands around the Mediterranean Sea and to South Africa.

All hyacinths have waxy, fragrant flowers grouped in spike-shaped clusters. The flowers are bell-shaped and may be pink, red, blue, white, yellow or purple. The flowering stem and all of the narrow leaves grow from the base of the plant. The fruit is a 3-angled capsule. The plant grows from a large, round bulb which gardeners plant 5 to 6 inches deep in rich soil.

All hyacinths bloom in early spring. For even earlier flowers, the bulbs are planted indoors, in pots of soil or in water. Bulbs grown in glass containers are kept in a dark place until the roots are well developed. Then the plants are placed in sunlight.

The common garden hyacinth (illustrated) exists in many different colors and sometimes has double flowers. Its stem is up to 15 inches tall. The leaves are up to 12 inches long and about 1 inch wide. This kind of hyacinth is native to Greece and Asia Minor.

In the common garden hyacinth, each plant bears just 1 flower cluster.

HYACINTH

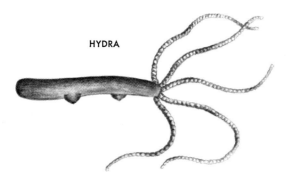

HYDRA

hydra \ 'hī-drə \

Small, freshwater animals that look a little like plants, hydras make up a group of simple, multicellular creatures. They are common throughout the world in streams, lakes and ponds. They die when the water temperature rises above 70° F.

Hydras have slender, tube-like bodies 1/10 to 1 inch long. Their color is pink, brown, green or nearly transparent.

The mouth opening at one end of the body is surrounded by stinging tentacles. As a hydra grows, both the number and size of its tentacles increase. The animal fastens a sticky disk at the other end of its body to an underwater rock or plant.

Hydras feed on small crustaceans and insect larvae. They sometimes eat animals larger than themselves. Their waving tentacles sting and capture their food and sweep it inside the mouth opening.

When parts of its body are destroyed, a hydra is able to grow new parts to replace them. Hydras reproduce either sexually or by budding.

A common kind of hydra is the brown hydra (illustrated).

hydrangea \ hī-'drān-jə \

Hydrangeas are a group of flowering shrubs native to North and South America and to Asia. They are upright and bushy.

The small flowers have 4 or 5 white, pink or blue petals. They are grouped in very large clusters at the ends of the branches. Some kinds have flat-topped or pointed flower clusters, while others have round, ball-shaped clusters. The large, coarse leaves grow in pairs opposite each other.

Hydrangeas grow well in direct sunlight, in well-drained, rich soil. They bloom as far north as the Great Lakes and southern Canada.

hyrax \ 'hīr-ˌaks \ (coney)

Hyraxes are small mammals that look like marmots or small-eared rabbits. Many zoologists place hyraxes in a group of their own. Others believe that they are related to rabbits. In the structure of their teeth, feet and blood, hyraxes resemble elephants. They are native to Africa and the Middle East.

Usually, hyraxes are about 1 foot long. They are dark gray or brown above, with lighter fur below. Some long hairs scattered over their bodies may act as feelers. Hyraxes have very short tails or no tails at all. Their small feet are hoof-like.

Hyraxes are found at sea level as well as at high altitudes. Some kinds live in trees. Others prefer grassy plains or deserts or are rock dwellers.

Little is known about the reproduction of hyraxes except that there are usually 2 to 3 young in a litter.

The most common kind of hyrax, the Syrian hyrax (illustrated), lives in Ethiopia, and near the Red Sea in Syria and Arabia. Zoologists believe the Syrian hyrax is the coney mentioned in the Bible.

HYRAX

i

ibex \ 'ī-ˌbeks \

Ibexes are wild goats with large, curved horns. They live in the Alps, Pyrenees, Himalayas, and mountains of Africa, south Arabia and southern Siberia. A male ibex's horns may be from 2 to 4½ feet long and weigh about 30 pounds. Females' horns are about $\frac{1}{3}$ this size.

Ibexes are about 3½ feet tall at the shoulder and are often 5 feet long. Fully grown males weigh as much as 200 pounds and have shaggy beards and manes. They have rough, gray or brown fur that changes color with the seasons.

Ibexes live on mountain crags or meadows just below snow lines. During most of the year males and females travel in separate herds, feeding on mountain vegetation. Mating takes place in fall, and 1 or 2 kids are born in summer.

Because ibexes are hunted by man and are the prey of flesh-eating animals, they have become rare in most areas.

The Alpine ibex (illustrated), perhaps the best-known kind, is now found only in the Italian Alps. It has knobby ridges on the upper surface of its horns.

In summer, the Alpine ibex is gray. In winter it turns yellowish-brown. It lives near the snow line all year.

IBEX

IBIS

ibis \ 'ī-bəs \

Ibises make up a family of medium-sized wading birds related to herons. Ibises live in marshy areas and along seacoasts in many parts of the world. Some kinds have slender, pointed bills that curve downward at the tip. Other kinds have broad, flat bills.

Ibises are 20 to 40 inches long, from tip of bill to tail. They are white, red or brownish-green. Many kinds are voiceless, but some make croaking or cackling sounds.

Feeding during the daylight hours, ibises eat crayfish, frogs, small fish and insects that they find in shallow water. Ibises travel and nest in large flocks. When they fly, they hold their necks straight out ahead of them and their long legs trail behind. Their nests are crude platforms of sticks placed in trees, often over water.

The kind of ibis most common in North America is the white ibis (illustrated), sometimes called the white curlew. It is 24 to 30 inches long, with a 9-inch bill and legs about 12 inches long.

The white ibis nests in wooded areas of the southern U.S. and in Mexico. Three to 5 spotted eggs are laid in June or July and are incubated by both parents for 21 days.

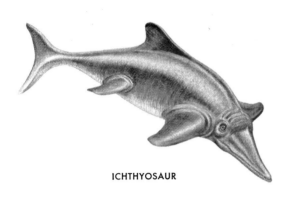

ICHTHYOSAUR

The young birds are gray-brown marked with white, and look quite different from the adults.

ichthyosaur \ 'ik-thē-ə-ˌsȯr \

A group of prehistoric, swimming reptiles, the ichthyosaurs lived about 200 million years ago, during the Mesozoic Era. They are known only from fossil remains that have been found in many different parts of the world. Some fossils have been found with pieces of skin and with eggs in the abdominal cavity.

Shark-like in appearance, the ichthyosaurs had streamlined, neckless bodies covered with smooth skin. Their heads were large, and their long, pointed jaws contained many sharp, cone-shaped teeth. They probably swam as sharks do, by moving their powerful tails rapidly from side to side. The large fin on the back may have acted somewhat as a ship's keel. Ichthyosaurs probably used their limbs only for steering.

Ichthyosaurs ate fish and squid. The females carried the fertilized eggs inside their bodies during the incubation period and gave birth to living young.

Different kinds of ichthyosaurs lived at different times. The largest ones were about 40 feet long. The earliest ones had legs, like their ancestors that lived on land.

A later kind of ichthyosaur (illustrated) had 4 limbs that looked like flippers.

Most ichthyosaurs lived during the Jurassic Period, shortly before the largest of the dinosaurs appeared on land.

iguana \ i-'gwän-ə \

Fierce-looking but harmless reptiles, the iguanas are large lizards with pointed spines on their backs or under their chins. They belong to the same family to which most American lizards belong.

Most iguanas live in the tropical jungles of the warmer parts of North and South America, in the West Indies, and on the Fiji Islands and Madagascar. The kinds that live in trees are mostly green, while the kinds that live on the ground are brownish. One kind of iguana lives in the deserts of the southwestern U.S., while another lives in the ocean off the Galápagos Islands.

Like other lizards, the iguanas have dry skin covered with small scales. Most iguanas eat only plant materials. Like most reptiles, iguanas lay eggs.

The common iguana (illustrated) is sometimes called the tree iguana. It is 3 to 7 feet long and weighs as much as 30 pounds. The common iguana lives in the dense forests of Mexico, Central and South America and the West Indies. Long toes with strong claws help this iguana cling to branches. Its color blends with the leaves

IGUANA

225

around it. Common iguanas are sometimes caught and tamed as pets.

When angry, the common iguana makes a loud hissing sound. It can run fast on the ground, and may plunge into water to escape its enemies. It is a good swimmer.

In the areas where it lives, both the flesh and eggs of the common iguana are valued as food.

impala \ im-'pal-ə \

This swift and graceful African gazelle belongs to the antelope family. It can run very fast and jump very high, covering up to 30 feet at one bound.

Taller than most antelopes, the impala stands over 3 feet high at the shoulder. The body length is 6 to 7 feet. The underparts are white, and there are some white markings around the eyes and inside the ears. The tail is black. Only the males have horns, which are slender and curving, with ring-like ridges near the base.

The impala lives south of the Sahara, as far north as Kenya and Angola. Traveling in herds of 10 to 50, the animals roam brushy plains and grasslands, always near water. They eat grass and leaves. The only sounds they make are short, sharp barks.

The impala's best defense against its

INCENSE CEDAR

enemies is its running speed. Lions and leopards stalk impala herds, killing and eating any animals they can capture. Even when grazing quietly, impalas are alert for signs of danger. Any sudden noise sends them bounding away at top speed.

A male impala usually mates with several different females. The females bear 1 to 3 young, about 8 months after mating.

incense cedar \ 'in-sen(t)s 'sēd-ər \

Incense cedars are tall, straight-trunked trees related to the pines. They are named for their pleasant smell. Incense cedars are the source of soft but strong wood which is used for poles, fence posts, shingles and lead pencils.

Once incense cedars grew only along the Pacific coast of North and South America, on mountain slopes 2,000 to 9,000 feet above sea level. They now grow in other parts of North America and in Europe, where they have been planted as ornamental trees.

The leaves of the incense cedars are small scales. The twigs with their leaves form flattened sprays of foliage. The bark on the trunk of the tree is reddish-brown and scaly.

The incense cedar common in Oregon

IMPALA

and California (illustrated) grows 80 to 150 feet tall. The large trunk is 3 to 5 feet across. Some of these trees live to be 300 years old.

The new leaves near the ends of the branches are yellow-green. The small cones are yellow when they appear in spring. When the seeds ripen in autumn, the cones are reddish-brown and about 1 inch long.

Indian paintbrush \ 'pānt-ˌbrəsh \

Indian paintbrushes make up a group of colorful plants belonging to the figwort family. They grow wild along seashores and in low, moist places. Indian paintbrushes are found in northeastern Asia and in many parts of North America.

The flowers of the Indian paintbrushes are small and greenish. They appear in clusters at the tops of the stalks, where they are nearly hidden by bracts that turn red or yellow. The fruit is a pod containing many small seeds. The stems are hairy, and the plants grow 10 to 20 inches tall.

Indian paintbrushes are nearly always parasitic, taking at least part of their food from the roots of other plants. For this reason it is very difficult to transplant them or grow them from seed. They are almost never seen in flower gardens.

The kind of Indian paintbrush most common in the eastern U.S. (illustrated) is sometimes called painted cup. Its flowers are surrounded by red-tipped bracts. Some of the light green leaves are oval, while some are ragged at the tip end.

The Indian paintbrush is the state flower of Wyoming.

insect

The insects make up the largest group of animals on the earth. All have 3 pairs of jointed legs. About 850,000 different kinds of insects are known. They live nearly everywhere except in the ocean.

Although insects differ in size and appearance, all are alike in many ways. All have 3-part bodies divided into head, thorax and abdomen. All have a hard body covering rather than an inside skeleton. As adults, all breathe air. They reproduce by laying eggs. Most live only a short time, but they produce many young.

Insects have different kinds of mouths adapted to biting, sucking or chewing. Some kinds eat green leaves or suck juices from plant stems, while others feed on dead plant and animal matter. Some kinds feed on the tissues and body fluids of living animals.

Many kinds of insects pass through the 4 stages of complete metamorphosis (egg,

INDIAN PAINTBRUSH

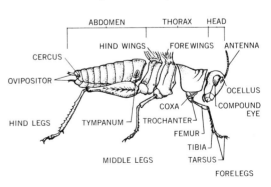

PARTS OF A TYPICAL INSECT
(GRASSHOPPER)

IRIS

larva, pupa and adult). Other kinds look like tiny adults when they hatch from the eggs.

Some insects are pests that carry diseases or destroy food crops. Others are useful because they help pollinate flowering plants and because they provide food for birds, fish and many other animals.

iris \ 'ī-rəs \

Irises make up a large group of flowering plants related to the crocus and gladiolus. Wild irises grow in nearly all parts of the temperate zone. Hundreds of different varieties have been developed by flower growers.

All irises are perennials. Most grow from a thickened, underground stem called a rhizome. The long, narrow leaves of all irises are folded along the center rib.

The most common kinds of iris have flowers that are some shade of blue or purple. Some kinds have white or yellow flowers. Three of the 6 petals stand upright, while the other 3 spread apart and bend down. The fruit is a 3-part pod containing smooth, flattened seeds.

About 30 kinds of wild irises are native to North America. All are swamp plants that grow in moist soil. Most have narrow blue or purple petals, with some yellow and white showing at the center of the flower.

The cultivated iris (illustrated) was developed from irises native to Europe and Japan. It has large, showy flowers that may be many different colors. The plants are up to 24 inches tall. The cultivated iris grows equally well in full sunlight or in mixed shade and sun. The iris is the state flower of Tennessee.

isthmus \ 'is-məs \

An isthmus is a narrow strip or neck of land that connects 2 large land masses. It may lie between 2 continents, or between a continent and a large peninsula. The name "isthmus" was first used for the Isthmus of Corinth, in Greece.

The very narrow neck of land that connects North and South America is called the Isthmus of Panama. At one point it is only 28 miles wide.

The Isthmus of Suez connects the large land masses of Africa and Arabia and separates the Mediterranean Sea from the Red Sea.

Both the Isthmus of Panama and the Isthmus of Suez have been cut by canals that greatly shorten shipping routes.

Isthmuses are important to plant and animal geography because they provide a way for plants and animals to migrate between 2 land masses. Early man also crossed these land bridges.

ISTHMUS (OF PANAMA)

IVY

ivy (English ivy)

Ivy is an attractive and hardy vine that keeps its green leaves all winter. It can climb up to 90 feet above the ground, covering brick walls or tree trunks with a dense curtain of leaves. Along the stems are tiny rootlets that cling tight to any rough surface.

Ivy will also grow flat on the ground, as a creeping vine. It makes a good ground cover for shady places where grass will not grow.

Native to Europe, ivy now grows in many other parts of the world. It has been widely planted as an ornamental vine, and a number of different varieties have been developed.

Ivy leaves are dark green and smooth. The upper surface is sometimes marked with lighter green veins, and the underside may be reddish. Most of the leaves are divided into 3 pointed lobes. Leaves on very old plants may be broad and rounded.

Only very old ivy plants bear flowers and fruit. The small, green flowers have 5 petals. They are grouped in umbrella-shaped clusters. The fruit is a small, round berry containing 3 to 5 seeds.

As a house plant, ivy will grow either in water or in soil.

j

jackal \ ˈjak-əl \

Jackals are wild dogs that live only in the Old World. Although they look like foxes, they are more closely related to wolves. In many ways, jackals are like the New World coyotes. Like coyotes, they make many different sounds, including barks, yelps and long howls.

Jackals are 2½ to 3 feet long. They are gray or brownish, sometimes marked with faint stripes on their sides. Their bushy tails hang loosely behind them.

Jackals live in Africa, southeastern Europe and southern Asia. They are probably most common in Africa. During the daylight hours jackals hide in caves or burrows, or under bushes.

When hungry, jackals will eat almost anything. They roam at night, in large noisy packs. They eat dead animals they find in the forest, or visit farms and villages to feed on garbage. Jackals kill and eat small mammals and poultry. Large packs of jackals will sometimes attack animals as large as sheep and goats.

The females bear litters of 7 to 9 young called pups. Jackals live 10 to 12 years.

The Oriental jackal (illustrated) ranges from the Balkans through India and Iran to Burma and Thailand.

JACKAL

jack-in-the-pulpit \ 'pŭl-ˌpit \
(Indian turnip)

Jack-in-the-pulpit is an unusual wild flower that grows in moist, shaded places throughout eastern North America. It is a perennial plant that usually blooms in April or May.

The true flowers of the jack-in-the-pulpit are very small. They are crowded together on the lower part of the upright column that is usually called the "jack." Botanists call this part of the plant the spadix.

The spadix is surrounded and covered by a bract that forms the "pulpit." The bract is funnel-shaped, with a pointed end that arches over and forms a kind of roof. The bract is green, marked with purple.

A jack-in-the-pulpit usually produces just 1 flowering stalk and 2 leaves. Each leaf is made up of 3 pointed, dull green leaflets about 2 inches long. Under the ground is an enlarged stem, or tuber, that stores food for the plant. When cooked, the tuber can be eaten. It was a favorite food of the American Indians and is sometimes called Indian turnip.

Jack-in-the-pulpit grows as far north as Nova Scotia and as far west as Minnesota.

JACK-IN-THE-PULPIT

JACKRABBIT

jackrabbit \ 'jak-ˌrab-ət \

Jackrabbits are hares, not rabbits. The 2 groups of mammals are closely related, but hares are more muscular than rabbits and they have longer ears and legs. Hares do not live in burrows as rabbits do, and their young are not blind and helpless as young rabbits are.

Jackrabbits live in the western half of North America, on deserts and prairies and in the mountains. They need little water. They eat any soft plants available, and are nuisances in some areas where they damage farm crops.

Famous for their speed, jackrabbits run as fast as 40 miles an hour. They can jump as far as 25 feet.

Although they do not dig burrows of their own, jackrabbits may hide in the dens of other animals. At other times they take shelter under bushes or rocks. Hawks and coyotes are among the natural enemies of jackrabbits.

In summer, female jackrabbits bear litters of 1 to 5 young. The young jackrabbits are covered with fur, and able to hop about and hide from danger when only a few days old.

The white-tailed jackrabbit (illustrated) is about 2 feet long and weighs up to 10 pounds.

JACOB'S LADDER

Jacob's\ˈjā-kəbz\ **ladder** (Greek valerian, polemonium)

The flowering plants called Jacob's ladder are closely related to phlox. Their compound leaves have narrow leaflets in opposite pairs, and the longer leaves that grow near the base of the plant look a little like ladders.

Most kinds of Jacob's ladder have blue or purplish flowers, but a few kinds have white, yellow or pinkish flowers. The bell-shaped flower opens out into 5 broad lobes. A dry, 3-sectioned seedpod is the fruit of the plant.

The Jacob's ladder most common in North America (illustrated) is a slender-stemmed wild flower that blooms in May. It is about 12 inches tall, and its longest leaves have 17 leaflets. Its blue flowers are borne in loose, branching clusters. It grows in moist, shaded soil, from New York west to Minnesota and south to Arkansas and Alabama.

Other kinds of Jacob's ladder grow in the western U.S., and in swamps near the Atlantic coast. A cultivated kind from Europe and Asia has been planted in many U.S. flower gardens. It grows wild in a few places. It is 36 inches tall, with blue flowers grouped in large, fairly tight clusters. Its longest leaves have 31 leaflets.

jaguar\ˈjag-ˌwär\

A swift and powerful member of the cat family, the jaguar is a good climber. Unlike most cats, it is also a good swimmer. The jaguar is native to America.

Although the jaguar looks much like the leopard of Africa and Asia, it has a larger head, a shorter tail and sturdier legs. Most jaguars are yellowish with white underparts. The yellowish coat is marked all over with irregular black circles called rosettes. Black jaguars, so dark that their spots are hard to see, are very rare.

Jaguars live in forests, deserts and on mountains, from the southwestern U.S. south to Paraguay. North American jaguars are generally smaller than the South American ones.

Male jaguars are 6 to 8 feet long and weight up to 300 pounds. Females are smaller than males. In some areas jaguars live almost entirely in trees.

Jaguars kill and eat a wide variety of wild animals including monkeys, birds, fish, turtles and alligators. In some areas they visit ranches and kill livestock. They are hunted for sport, and for their valuable skins.

Female jaguars bear litters of 1 to 4 young, called kits, at different times during the year. The kits stay with their mother for about 2 years.

JAGUAR

JAY

jay

Jays are noisy, active birds that belong to the same family as crows. Jays are found in nearly all parts of the world, but they are most common in America and southern Asia. They are usually year-round residents of their areas.

Most jays are blue or gray, and about 12 inches long. Some but not all have pointed crests of feathers on their heads. The females look like the males but are somewhat smaller.

These birds eat a wide variety of foods, including insects, berries and seeds. They sometimes eat the flesh of dead animals, as well as eggs and young birds from other birds' nests.

The nests are often placed in pine trees. They are built of sticks and twigs, and are lined with grasses and lichens. The 3 to 5 eggs are incubated by both male and female.

The blue jay (illustrated) is a loud-voiced bird that makes whistling and shrieking sounds. It is most common in coniferous forests of southern Canada and the U.S., from the Rocky Mountains east to the Atlantic coast. Its 3 to 5 eggs are laid in early spring. They are greenish, spotted with brown. Both parents incubate the eggs and feed the young birds.

jellyfish

Jellyfish are not fish, but hollow-bodied animals that make up a group of marine invertebrates. They are related to the corals and sea anemones. Jellyfish are soft and partly transparent. When washed up on the beach, they look something like mounds of jelly.

The umbrella-shaped body is 1/16 inch to over 6 feet across. Around the edge are 8 sense organs that include eyespots sensitive to light. A mouth is located in the center of the underside. A fringe of long, stinging tentacles trails from the body.

Jellyfish live in shallow water near coasts, in all oceans. They float with the waves and currents, but can swim a little by expanding and contracting their bodies. Jellyfish feed on small invertebrate animals that float in the sea. They reproduce both sexually and by budding, and pass through several different stages of development as they grow to maturity.

The sun jellyfish (illustrated) is also called the pink jellyfish or sea blubber. Its body is 1 to 8 feet across, edged with 32 rounded lobes. As many as 800 tentacles trail behind it. Some of the tentacles are 75 to 200 feet long.

This jellyfish lives in cooler parts of the sea, as far north as the Arctic.

JELLYFISH

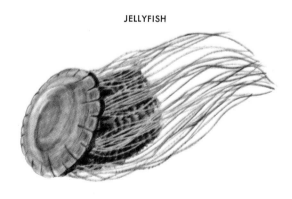

JERBOA

JIMSONWEED

jerboa \ jər-'bō-ə \ (jumping mouse)

The jerboas are small, nocturnal rodents with silky fur and long, tufted tails. Jerboas live in desert areas of Africa, Arabia and central Asia.

Most jerboas have a body length of about 7 inches, not including the tail, which is about 8 inches long. The tail helps them balance as they sit erect or walk backward or forward on their hind legs.

When they become frightened, jerboas can move very fast, covering 2 to 3 feet with each jump, and holding their tails stiffly out behind them.

All jerboas are sand-colored, with white underparts. Some kinds have very big ears.

Social animals, jerboas live in large colonies. Their homes are deep underground burrows. They sleep in their burrows during the day and move about looking for food at night. They eat a few insects, along with grass, plant roots, seeds and fruit. Like mice, they make shrill squeaking sounds.

Little is known about the breeding habits of jerboas.

The African jerboa (illustrated) is common in North Africa, Syria and Arabia. It lives in dry, sandy places.

jimsonweed \ 'jim(p)-sən-ˌwēd \

Jimsonweed is a poisonous, annual plant related to nightshade. When the plant is wilted, its juice is deadly. Jimsonweed is also one of the sources of a useful drug, atropine.

Jimsonweed blooms in late summer and early autumn. The large, trumpet-shaped flowers appear where the branches fork from the stems. The flowers are about 4 inches long, and may be white or pale violet. The envelope surrounding the base of the flower is pale green, with 5 pointed lobes. The plant grows to about 4 feet high.

The thin leaves of jimsonweed grow alternately along the stems. The leaves are broadly toothed and have slender stalks. The stout, smooth stems are branched, and may be tinged with purple. The fruit is a large, rounded capsule about 2 inches long. It is usually covered with stout spines, and it contains several dark, flattened seeds.

Jimsonweed grows in waste areas, barnyards and fields wherever the soil is rich. Although it is widespread in the U.S., jimsonweed is most common in the southern states. It was probably brought to the New World from tropical Asia or Africa.

JUNCO

JUNIPER

junco \ 'jəng-,kō \

Juncos make up a group of dark, medium-sized birds found throughout North America. They belong to the same family as the sparrows and the buntings. Like the sparrows, they have strong bills for cracking seeds. The chirping call of the junco is also like the sparrow's call.

Juncos are often seen on lawns, in gardens and on farmland during the winter months. In spring, they move to thick wooded areas where it is cool and damp. During the summer months, they feed on insects.

Junco nests are built on the ground and are well hidden in rocks or between tree roots. Juncos lay from 4 to 6 grayish-white eggs spotted with brown or purple.

The most colorful kind of junco is the Oregon junco (illustrated). Body length averages about 6 inches.

The Oregon junco breeds in Alberta and Saskatchewan and as far south as the middle of California. During the winter months, it ranges from the Canadian border south to New Mexico. It is sometimes seen as far east as Nebraska and Texas.

juniper \ 'jü-nə-pər \

Junipers make up a group of evergreen trees closely related to the pines. All juni-pers bear large cones which look like berries. The wood from the juniper is used to make pencils and to line cedar chests.

Juniper trees are native to North America, Asia and Africa. Some are more like bushes than trees. Others have slender trunks that grow as tall as 100 feet. The bark of juniper trees is made up of reddish-brown scales. The prickly leaves are sharp-pointed scales that cling tightly to the slender twigs.

When ripe, juniper cones are blue or blue-black. They are about ¼ inch across. Each contains 1 to 12 tiny seeds.

One kind of juniper (illustrated) is sometimes called red cedar, although it is not a true cedar. This juniper is most common in southern Canada and the eastern U.S. It grows 60 to 100 feet tall and is fairly important as a source of lumber. The so-called red cedar grows in dry, rocky soil, usually on hillsides.

Jupiter \ 'jü-pət-ər \

Jupiter is the largest of the 9 planets in the solar system. It is the fifth planet away from the sun and is about 483 million miles away from the sun. Jupiter makes 1 complete orbit of the sun in about 12 years. Its day is 9 hours and 50 minutes long.

Astronomers believe that Jupiter's core is made up of very dense rock or hydrogen,

JUPITER

and that the core is surrounded by a shell of ice at least 20,000 miles thick. The atmosphere of Jupiter is probably made up of hydrogen, ammonia and methane gas. Because so much of Jupiter is made up of gas, it is fairly light for its size. If there were an ocean big enough, Jupiter would probably float in it.

Seen without a telescope, Jupiter is usually the second brightest planet in the sky. Through a powerful telescope, Jupiter is a bright disk with flattened poles and a bulge at the equator. It has brown, tan and yellow bands and a large spot. The spot changes color from brick-red to gray, and sometimes changes position. It seems to be floating in Jupiter's atmosphere. At times, this floating spot almost disappears.

Jupiter has 12 moons. At least 4 of these can be seen with good binoculars or a small telescope. Three of these 4 moons were the first bodies in the solar system discovered with a telescope, in 1610.

The smallest of Jupiter's moons is only 14 miles in diameter. It was not discovered until 1951.

Because Jupiter is far away from the sun, it is very cold. The surface temperature is probably about —200° F.

See *The Sun, the Moon and the Planets* on p. 502.

k

kame \ 'kām \

A kame is a rounded hill or short ridge made up of layers of materials deposited by water from a glacier.

Kames are formed at the sides or ends of large glaciers. As the glacier melts, flowing water picks up sand, soil and gravel. The flowing water dumps these materials as it flows away from the glacier.

Kames are not like terminal moraines because kames contain only small pieces of sand, soil and gravel. Terminal moraines often have pieces of all sizes.

Kames are sometimes found behind terminal moraines. Such kames occur mostly in the glacier valleys of Scotland and the north central U.S.

kangaroo

Kangaroos make up a family of marsupials native to Australia and Tasmania. They vary in size and color, but most kinds have short front legs, long, muscular hind legs and long, muscular tails. Most have small heads with long noses and large ears.

The largest kangaroos roam open country in bands of 40 to 100. Smaller kinds live in trees, alone or in small groups. In Australia, kangaroos are hunted as pests because they eat the same plants needed by cattle and sheep.

KANGAROO

Kangaroos are well-known for their speed and leaping ability. They are easily stampeded, and may run into trees or other objects. Their major enemies are wild dogs. Kangaroos usually defend themselves by kicking with their hind feet.

Kangaroos give birth to single young. After it is born, the young kangaroo crawls into its mother's pouch where it nurses for several months. Even when it is old enough to take care of itself, a young kangaroo re-enters the pouch when tired or frightened.

The great gray kangaroo (illustrated) weighs up to 200 pounds and is about 10 feet long, including the tail. In 1 bound, it can leap 10 feet into the air and cover more than 30 feet on the ground.

For another member of the kangaroo family, see *wallaby*.

kaolin \ 'kā-ə-lən \

Kaolin is a rock made up of crystals and pieces of the clay mineral kaolinite, which is silvery-white powder in its purest form. As found in the earth, kaolin is white, gray, reddish-brown or black. It usually contains some quartz, feldspar and other minerals, which give it a scaly look. These other minerals are removed before the kaolin is used commercially.

Some kaolin is formed when water

KAOLIN

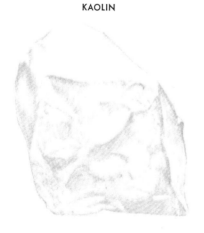

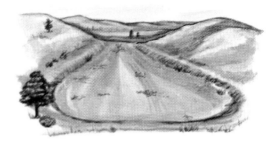

KARST TOPOGRAPHY

changes the form of a granite-like igneous rock. Kaolins in France, Germany and North Carolina were formed in this way. Kaolin also occurs in sedimentary form, in large beds. These beds of kaolin were formed when kaolinite was carried by rivers or streams. The minerals in the water changed the kaolinite to kaolin, which settled out of the water to form beds. Florida, Georgia and South Carolina have kaolin deposits of this kind.

Kaolin is used in making china, porcelain, rubber, paper, paint, ink, plastics and many other products. About ½ the kaolin produced is added to wood pulp from which paper products are made. Kaolin is widespread and occurs in most parts of the world.

karst topography \ 'kärst tə-'päg-rə-fē \

Geologists use this phrase to describe land that has been shaped by water sinking down into the earth. The phrase originally stood for the Karst region of Yugoslavia, east of the Adriatic Sea.

Karst topography occurs where there are large beds of limestone under the soil. Much of the water that falls as rain seeps slowly down through this rock, instead of forming streams on the surface.

Part of the rock is dissolved by the seeping water and carried away, leaving caves and tunnel-like passages. The soil sinks

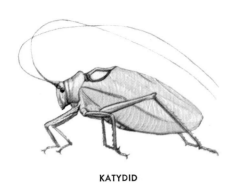

KATYDID

down over these hollowed-out places, and the land surface is no longer flat. The hollowed-out places are called "sinkholes."

Springs and underground rivers are common in karst topography regions. Streams flowing on the surface are rare.

In the U.S., there are regions of karst topography in southern Indiana, Kentucky and Tennessee. In Europe, karst topography occurs in southern France as well as in Yugoslavia.

katydid \ 'kāt-ē-,did \

The katydids make up a group of insects with very long antennae. They are best known for the loud, shrill sounds the males make by rubbing their wings together. The mating call of the northern katydid (illustrated) sounds like "katy did, katy did" repeated rapidly, over and over again.

Nearly all katydids are green, and they are sometimes hard to see when they are clinging to green leaves. A few kinds of katydids are brown or pinkish. Most kinds are a little more than 1 inch long. Their antennae are often longer than their bodies. They have long, strong hind legs for jumping, and they seldom fly.

Katydids are common in the U.S., from the Atlantic coast west to the Rocky Mountains. They feed on leaves, and damage some shade and fruit trees and shrubs.

All female katydids have a slender, pointed, egg-laying organ at the tip of the abdomen. In autumn the female lays flat, oval eggs in overlapping rows on the edges of leaves. The young insects hatch in spring. They look something like the adults but are smaller and paler, and have no wings.

The so-called angular-winged katydid is not a katydid but a grasshopper.

kettle

Kettles are bowl-shaped basins formed by the continental glacier that covered North America during the Ice Age. Some are dry, but many are filled with water and form lakes.

Kettles were made when heavy blocks of ice broke off from the main body of the glacier. Loose gravel and soil that had been carried by the glacier were left piled up around each ice block. When the climate became warmer, the ice melted, and a basin or hollow marked place where each block had been.

Kettle lakes are generally fairly shallow and more or less round in shape. They are common in eastern Canada and in Minnesota, Michigan and northern Indiana.

Many of the shallower kettles have filled up with plant materials and turned into peat bogs. Some are only visible as low places in pastures and farm fields.

KETTLE

KINGBIRD

kingbird \ 'king-ˌbərd \

Kingbirds are a group of medium-sized, dark-colored birds belonging to the fly-catcher family. Fierce fighters, they pick quarrels with larger birds such as crows and hawks. They are nearly always able to drive the larger birds away.

Kingbirds eat mostly insects that they catch in the air. They also eat some fruit. They live in open country, and are almost never seen in cities. Kingbirds often perch in the very top of a tall tree to watch for insects and for the other birds they con-sider their enemies.

The nests of kingbirds are bulky but neat. They are built of grasses and twigs, and are placed high in large trees. Both male and female birds incubate the 3 or 4 pinkish or cream-colored eggs.

Kingbirds live in nearly all parts of North America. The eastern kingbird (il-lustrated) spends the summer in southern Canada and the eastern half of the U.S. It winters in Mexico and Central America. The eastern kingbird has a wide whitish band at the end of its tail. The male has a crown spot of red feathers that shows only when he is angry or courting.

The western kingbird is brownish-gray, with yellow underparts. It spends the summer in the western half of the U.S., and in Manitoba and British Columbia.

kingfisher \ 'king-ˌfish-ər \

The kingfishers are a family of land birds that dive into water for their food. They live near streams and lakes, in nearly all parts of the world.

The smallest kinds of kingfishers are about 5 inches long, while the largest kinds are about 17 inches long. Most kinds are bright-colored. All have large heads and long, strong bills. The feet are small and weak.

Kingfishers capture and eat fish, frogs, water insects and small crustaceans. Skillful fliers, they hover over the water and then drop on their prey in a swift dive. Their nests are deep burrows dug into stream banks. Both male and female birds incubate the 5 to 8 white eggs and carry food to the young birds. Newly hatched kingfishers are blind and helpless. They remain in the nest 3 to 4 weeks. Most kingfishers raise 2 or more broods of young each year.

The only kind of kingfisher found in North America is the belted kingfisher (il-lustrated). It is about 13 inches long. The male has 1 reddish chestband, while the female has 2.

The belted kingfisher spends the sum-mer in nearly all parts of southern Canada and the U.S. It migrates to Central and South America in autumn.

KINGFISHER

KINGLET

kinglet \ 'king-lət \

Kinglets make up a group of tiny, quick-moving birds belonging to the Old World warbler family. They live in nearly all parts of the northern hemisphere. Only the males have bright-colored crests that stand up when the birds are excited.

Kinglets are 3 to 4 inches long, with tiny bills and short tails. Their fluffy feathers are greenish-gray above and white below. On the wings are 2 white bars.

Except when nesting, kingbirds fly and feed in flocks. In winter they are often seen in mixed flocks, with chickadees, nuthatches and other seed-eating birds.

These birds eat insects, insect eggs and larvae and some seeds. Their neat nests of moss, lichens and soft bark are hung from the branches of evergreen trees. The female incubates the 7 to 12 small eggs. The eggs are cream-colored, speckled with lavender and brown. Both parents bring food to the young birds.

The golden-crowned kinglet (illustrated) breeds in the spruce forests of the northern U.S. and southern Canada. It winters in most parts of the U.S. Both male and female have white around the eye. The female has a yellow crown spot on her head, while the male has a bright, orange-red crown spot.

kinkajou \ 'king-kə-ˌjü \ (honey bear)

The kinkajou is an odd, bear-like mammal related to the raccoons. It lives in the tropical forests of Mexico and of Central and South America.

The kinkajou is about the size of a domestic cat. Its body is slender, and its hind legs are longer than its forelegs. The head is round, with small ears and very large, bright eyes. The soft, woolly fur is dark gold, brown or gray.

Good climbers, kinkajous spend much of their time in trees. They can swing by their long tails, as some New World monkeys do. They sleep during the day and move about at night, looking for food.

Kinkajous eat a wide variety of both plant and animal foods. They are very fond of honey, and use their 6-inch-long tongues to take it from trees where bees live. Kinkajous eat many kinds of fruit, and kill and eat small animals, birds and large insects.

Intelligent and easily tamed, kinkajous are sometimes kept as pets. They are usually friendly but should be handled with care as they have sharp teeth and may bite.

KINKAJOU

KITE

Young kinkajous are black. They are born in litters of 1 to 2, and grow very quickly. They are able to climb about and hang by their tails when only 7 weeks old.

kite

Long-winged birds of prey, the kites are closely related to the hawks and eagles. Graceful in flight, kites soar easily in wide circles and dive at great speeds. They live in all of the warmer parts of the world.

The many different kinds of kites vary widely in size and appearance. They are 12 inches to 4 feet long. Most are fairly slender birds, with long tails and strong, hooked beaks. All are skillful fliers.

Most kites eat insects and also kill and eat small animals such as field mice, snakes and frogs. Some kinds eat the flesh of dead animals. One kind feeds on bats, while another kind feeds on snails.

All kites nest in trees. The 2 to 5 eggs are incubated for as long as 4 weeks.

The swallow-tailed kite (illustrated) is about 24 inches long, including the long, V-shaped tail. The wingspread averages about 4 feet. The back, wings and tail of adults are blue-black. Young kites are speckled with white.

Once common in most parts of the U.S., the swallow-tailed kite now nests only near the Gulf coast, from Florida west to Texas. It winters in Central and South America.

kiwi \ 'kē-(ˌ)wē \

Kiwis are unusual birds that cannot fly. They are not closely related to any other living birds. The kiwi is the national emblem of its native land, New Zealand. Once hunted for food and for its feathers, the kiwi is now protected by strict laws.

Kiwis are about the size of plump chickens. They are usually brown or gray, but albinos are not uncommon. Their legs are stout, and their heads are small. Their nostrils are located at the tips of their long bills.

Shy birds, kiwis live only in the dense swamps and forests of New Zealand. They sleep in nests during the day and move about looking for food at night. They eat worms and insects that they scratch from the ground. A keen sense of smell and sensitive bristles around the bill help them locate food that they cannot see in the dark.

KIWI

Kiwi nests are underground burrows. For its size, the kiwi lays the largest egg of any bird. Each year, the female lays just 1 egg, about ⅓ the size of her body. The male incubates the egg for a long time, 75 to 80 days, without help from the female.

The common kiwi (illustrated) is the largest of the 3 different kinds. It is up to 2 feet long, and weighs as much as 4 pounds.

klipspringer \ 'klip-ˌspring-ər \

The klipspringer is a small, very nimble member of the antelope family living in the mountains of Africa. More sure-footed than other antelopes, it stands on the very tips of its tiny, round hoofs. It runs fast in rough country and easily jumps from rock to rock.

The klipspringer stands only about 2 feet high at the shoulder. Its yellow-brown coat is made up of very stiff, bristly hairs. When the klipspringer is gripped by an enemy, this coat may pull away in patches, but it grows back later.

The large ears are rounded, and are marked inside with dark, ray-like lines. The males' horns are straight spikes about 4 inches long.

Klipspringers are usually seen in pairs rather than in herds. They range through most mountainous parts of Africa, from the Cape of Good Hope north to Ethiopia. Within their range, they are least common in southern Africa. There, they have been widely hunted both by natives and by sportsmen on safari.

koala \ kō-'äl-ə \

The koala is an odd Australian mammal that looks something like a plump, gray Teddy Bear. It belongs to a family of marsupials, and the female carries her young in a pouch that opens from the back.

Koalas are 2 to 3 feet long and weigh up to 30 pounds. They have thick, woolly fur. A fringe of hair surrounds the large ears. The eyes are small, and the large nose looks as if it were made of black rubber. The forepaws look much like hands, but they have very strong, sharp claws. Koalas have no tails.

This animal spends nearly all its time in trees. During most of the year it eats only the leaves of certain eucalyptus trees.

The koala was once common in many parts of Australia. It has now disappeared from many areas because the trees bearing the leaves it eats have been

KLIPSPRINGER

KOALA

destroyed. Many koalas have been killed for their fur. Today, koalas are protected by law.

Female koalas bear 1 or 2 young every other year. The newborn koala is only about 1 inch long. It creeps into the mother's pouch and remains there for about 6 months. For a year longer it travels with the mother, clinging to the fur on her back.

kudu \ 'kü-,dü (koodoo) \

Kudus are African antelopes that travel in small family groups. There are 2 kinds of kudus, the greater kudu (illustrated) and the lesser kudu. Female kudus have no horns.

The lesser kudu is about 3 feet tall and weighs up to 200 pounds. It lives on the grassy plains and in thorn forests from Abyssinia to southern Tanganyika.

The greater kudu, which is more common than the lesser kudu, stands about 5 feet tall and weighs about 600 pounds. The male greater kudu is hunted for its long, twisting horns, which are widespread and up to 4 feet long. Greater kudus are mountain dwellers that sometimes live above timberlines.

All kudus are brownish or red-brown, with a line of white fur along the center

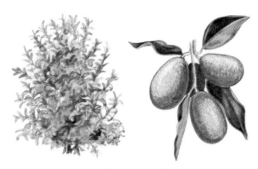

KUMQUAT TREE

of the back. Thin stripes of white run up each side of the kudu. The greater kudu has a throat mane and a crest on its shoulders.

Each year, the female kudu gives birth to 1 or 2 young. The life-span of a kudu is about 10 years.

kumquat \ 'kəm-,kwät \ tree

A group of small, oriental trees or shrubs, kumquat trees are closely related to citrus trees. Kumquat trees are grown for their fruit, which can be eaten raw or made into jellies and preserves. The fruit is the size of a large nut and looks like a tiny, flattened orange. The taste of the kumquat fruit is sharper than the taste of the orange.

Kumquat trees are native to China but are now grown in Japan and the U.S. California and Florida both grow large numbers of this tree.

Kumquat trees usually grow 8 to 12 feet tall. The leaves grow alternately along the branches. They are about 3 inches long and 1½ inches wide, with smooth edges and pointed tips. The flower is sweet-smelling, small and white.

The most common kind of kumquat tree is the oval kumquat tree (illustrated), which bears oval fruit about 1 inch in diameter.

KUDU

I

laccolith \ 'lak-ə-ˌlith \

A laccolith is a dome-shaped rock formation. It is formed when molten rock has pushed between layers of older sedimentary rocks such as shale. This causes the top layers of rock to be pushed upward, just as a blanket would be pushed upward by a balloon blown up underneath it.

A laccolith looks like an oval or circle-shaped mound or a small mountain. If the molten rock had pushed all the way through to the surface of the earth by melting or blowing through the topmost layer of rock, a volcano would have resulted. Instead, the molten rock spread out sideways, 7,000 to 10,000 feet below the surface.

In most cases, the top layers of a laccolith have been eroded away by weathering. When this has happened, the core, which is usually an igneous volcanic rock such as granite, can be seen. Ridges of sedimentary rock surround the dome-shaped core. The ridges are all that is left of the eroded cover layers.

The Henry Mountains of Utah, Little Sundance Hill in Wyoming and Bear Butte in South Dakota are all laccoliths. Other formations of this kind are found in western South America and in England.

LACCOLITH

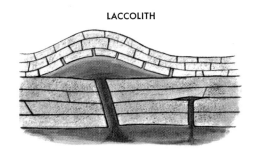

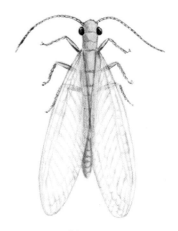

LACEWING

lacewing \ 'lā-ˌswing \

Making up 2 families, the brown lacewing family and the green lacewing family, these insects are related to dobsonflies. The families are named after the color of the adult. Lacewings are nocturnal and feed entirely on smaller insects.

Lacewings have slender bodies, 2 pairs of large, thin-veined wings and long, thin antennae. The larvae of lacewings are called aphis lions or aphis wolves. They have piercing and sucking mouthparts, and are valued because they feed on aphids and scale insects. All lacewings undergo complete metamorphosis.

Adult green lacewings are about an inch long. They are found in almost all parts of the world on shrubs, trees, grasses and weeds. When handled, they give off a bad smell and are sometimes called "stinkflies."

Adult green lacewings live 4 to 6 weeks. The female lays several hundred eggs, which hatch into larvae. The larvae spin cocoons in which they stay 1 or 2 weeks before coming out as nearly adult insects.

A common kind of green lacewing in the U.S. is the goldeneye lacewing (illustrated).

lady's slipper

A group of perennial plants, lady's slippers belong to the orchid family. They include wild flowers and plants grown commercially. The commercial kinds are the orchids sold by florists. The wild kinds are sometimes called moccasin flowers.

There are several hundred kinds of lady's slipper, from 4 inches to 3 feet tall. There are 1, 2 or 3 flowers to a stem. The flowers grow in many colors, and are called lady's slippers because some of the petals curve into a sort of moccasin or slipper shape.

Lady's slipper leaves are broad, shiny and large-veined. They cover the base of the stem. The root system is large, tangled and easily broken. The fruit is a pod divided into 3 parts by a Y-shaped membrane.

The showy lady's slipper (illustrated) is often called the pink and white lady's slipper. It is the state flower of Minnesota. Once found wild throughout the eastern U.S., it has been picked so much that it has almost disappeared. It grows in shady, damp places, to about 2 feet tall. One or 2 flowers about 3 inches wide bloom from May to July.

LADY'S SLIPPER

LAGOON

lagoon \ lə-'gün \

A lagoon is a shallow, quiet body of salt water or fresh water that is formed in different ways. One of the most common types of saltwater lagoons is formed by a barrier beach. Ocean waves deposit sand in a long sandbar or island which is off-shore but parallel to shore. Miami Beach is this sort of island, while Biscayne Bay is the lagoon between the island and the mainland.

Another kind of saltwater lagoon forms when sandbars build up across a bay. An atoll made of coral animals can also form its own lagoon.

Freshwater lagoons are made either by nature or man. When a river flows into the sea, the channel may be so small that the sea does not disturb the quiet water at the mouth of the river. Such quiet water is called a lagoon.

A protected bay opening off a freshwater lake is also called a lagoon.

See *barrier beach*.

lake

A lake is a body of still water surrounded by land. It may be large or small, deep or shallow. A very large lake is often called a sea. The Dead Sea in Asia and the Caspian Sea in Europe and Asia are really lakes.

PLAYA LAKE

If a lake has a way for water to flow out of it as well as in, it remains a freshwater lake. If there is no outlet, water can only leave the lake by evaporation. The remaining water becomes more and more salty, as the mineral salts in the water remain. The Great Salt Lake in Utah is 4 to 7 times as salty as the ocean.

Lakes are formed in many ways. Most of the lakes in the northern parts of Europe and North America are in mountain regions and other areas where glaciers have been. The lakes were dug out by the action of the moving glaciers, which scooped out hollows that filled with water. In other places, rocks and boulders dropped by melting glaciers dammed up rivers to form lakes.

Another kind of lake, the oxbow lake, forms when a stream or river changes its course and flows across one of its bends. The water left in the old bend may then become a lake.

Rainwater can collect to form lakes in craters of extinct volcanoes, as at Oregon's Crater Lake.

A lake that is full of water only part of the time is a playa lake (illustrated). It may be a dusty plain, or a broad, shallow body of water, depending on the rainfall. Playa lakes are fairly common in California, Nevada, Utah and Arizona.

See *kettle* and *tarn*.

lake herring \ 'her-ing \ (cisco)

The lake herring is a small North American freshwater fish and an excellent food and game fish. Although it is called a herring, the lake herring does not belong to the herring family.

The lake herring looks something like a salmon or trout. It has a silvery, narrow body that is thickest through the middle. The lower jaw is longer than the upper jaw and the snout is pointed. The base of the tail is thick and the tail forked. The average lake herring is 12 inches in length and weighs about 1 pound. A few grow to twice this size.

A fast swimmer, the lake herring prefers shallow water. It will go into deeper water in midsummer and midwinter. Lake herring travel in large schools and feed on plankton, insects, small fish and some crustaceans.

The lake herring spawns in late fall or winter. The eggs are laid in shallow water on the bottom of the lake, usually on gravel or sand.

Lake herring range from northwest Canada through the Great Lakes region and east to Labrador.

lamprey \ 'lam-prē \

Lampreys make up a family of primitive fish with slender bodies like eels. Although the eel is a true fish, the lamprey is not. The spine of a lamprey is not

LAMPREY

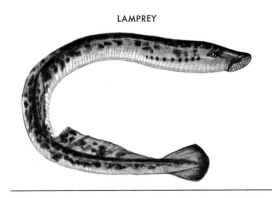

bone, as are fish spines, but is soft cartilage. The lamprey does not have paired fins or jaws. Lampreys are scaleless, smooth and slimy. Many are parasites, feeding on true fish.

Lampreys once lived only in the Atlantic and Pacific oceans. In 1930, the sea lamprey (illustrated) entered the Great Lakes, where it adapted to fresh water. Sea lampreys have killed so many lake trout and whitefish that they have almost ruined the Great Lakes fishing industries.

The mouth of the sea lamprey is a round, flat disk. This disk acts as a suction cup and allows the lamprey to fasten itself to the side of a victim. The tongue of the lamprey is covered with over 100 horny teeth. Using these as a file, the lamprey cuts a hole in the side of a fish. Then, by sucking the fish's blood, the sea lamprey often kills it.

All lampreys spawn between March and May in freshwater rivers and streams along seacoasts. A shallow nest is scooped out and several hundred thousand eggs are laid. Adults die after spawning. The young grow slowly. As adults, they may reach 3 feet in length.

landslide \ 'lan(d)-,slīd \

A landslide is a downhill movement of loose rock and soil. It may be a slow movement, called "creep," or a fast slide.

One cause of landslides is earthquakes. A more common cause is erosion by action of wind or water. When soil near the base of a slope is worn away, some of the support for the rock masses higher up is gone, and a landslide may result. The action of glaciers, waves or rivers against cliffs often causes landslides.

Landslides are most likely to occur in early spring, when heavy rain and melting snow wet the soil and rocks. These become heavier and more likely to slip. Because the mud formed is slippery, the rocks and soil are more likely to slide once they start to shift positions.

lantern fish

Odd-looking deep-sea fish, lantern fish make up a family. They are named for the rows of light organs along their sides.

Lantern fish are small, ranging from 3 to 6 inches in length. They have rounded heads and large eyes. Most kinds have an adipose fin in front of the forked tail. The first dorsal fin and the anal fin are long. The ventral fins are on the abdomen. Most lantern fish have large, silvery scales.

Spawning takes place in late winter or early spring. The larvae are transparent and float on the water's surface. As they mature, the larvae swim deeper.

One kind of lantern fish (illustrated) lives in the Atlantic Ocean. This fish

LANDSLIDE

LANTERN FISH

feeds on plankton. It spends the day deep under the surface, as the plankton also sinks deep under the surface during the day to avoid the warmth of the sun. At night, as the surface of the water cools and the plankton rise, the lantern fish follows the plankton to the surface.

Some kinds of lantern fish stay deep under the ocean surface all their lives.

lapis lazuli \ˌlap-ə-'slaz(h)-ə-lē\

This semiprecious mineral is used to make jewelry and small ornaments. It is deep blue or blue-green, and opaque. Flecks of gold and other colors show within it.

Lapis lazuli has a grainy structure. Within it are bits and pieces of other minerals such as pyrite, amphibole, feldspar, mica, zircon and calcite. Lapis lazuli is found only in small, round masses, usually in beds of limestone near granite deposits.

The use of lapis lazuli as an ornament is very old. Egyptians and Romans used it as jewelry. It was also used as medicine. It was believed that ground lapis lazuli, mixed with milk and made into a paste, would heal ulcers or boils.

Today, the main sources of lapis lazuli are Afghanistan, Siberia and Chile. The best, most highly colored stones come from Afghanistan.

LAPIS LAZULI

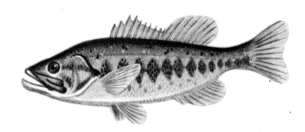

LARGEMOUTH BLACK BASS

largemouth black bass
\'lärj-ˌmaủth 'blak 'bas\

One of the most popular native freshwater game and food fishes of the U.S., the largemouth black bass is the largest member of the freshwater sunfish family. It is named for its large mouth, which extends further back than the eye. The mouth of its close relative, the smallmouth black bass, extends only as far back as the eye.

Once found only in the eastern half of the U.S., the largemouth black bass was taken by man to other waters and now lives from the Great Lakes south to Florida.

In northern waters this fish averages 3 pounds. In the south it may grow nearly 3 feet long and weigh over 20 pounds.

Largemouth black bass prefer warmer waters and weedy or muddy-bottomed places in lakes, rivers and ponds. They eat small fish, large aquatic insects and crustaceans such as crayfish.

Spawning occurs in late spring and early summer. The male makes a nest on gravelly bottoms and attracts as many as 5 females to deposit eggs in the nest. Over 2,000 eggs may be laid in 1 nest. When the young fish hatch, they are guarded by the male.

For another kind of black bass, see *smallmouth black bass*.

lark \ 'lärk \

Larks make up a family of grayish or brownish birds best known for their flute-like song, sung while flying. The meadowlark common in the U.S. is not a lark but a member of the New World family of blackbirds and orioles.

Larks range in length from 5 to 9 inches. They have pointed, slightly down-curved bills. Most kinds have a feathered crest on their heads. The back toe ends in a long, sharp claw.

Most larks live in grassy, open country. They spend much of their time on the ground, hunting for insects, worms, seeds and berries. The cup-shaped nests are built on the ground, of grass, feathers and plant fibers. Two to 6 eggs are laid twice a year.

Most kinds of larks are native to Africa, but a few are native to Europe and Asia. Only one kind of lark, the horned lark (illustrated), is native to the New World.

The horned lark is named for the small black feathers that stick up above its eyes like 2 small horns. Its face has a black eye marking and its throat is marked with black. The 3 to 5 eggs are whitish, marked with purple or brown.

Horned larks live from the edge of the Arctic Circle southward to Central America. They do not migrate.

LARK

LAUREL

laurel \ 'lȯr-əl \

Laurels are a group of evergreen shrubs and small trees native to lands near the Mediterranean Sea, the Canary Islands and Madeira. They are now grown in many other countries as well. The family includes cinnamon and camphor trees as well as avocado and sassafras.

Many kinds of laurel are important sources of spices. Others are valuable timber trees.

The ancient Greeks used one kind of laurel, the sweet bay (illustrated), to make wreaths for honoring winning athletes.

The sweet bay is a kind of laurel that grows from 20 to 40 feet tall. Its oval leaves are leathery and dull green. Small yellow flowers bloom early each spring. The fruit is a dull purple berry containing 1 large seed. The sweet bay grows in southern Europe and in western Asia, near the Mediterranean Sea.

lava \ 'läv-ə \

Lava is hot liquid rock or rock that was once liquid. Lava breaks out of an opening in the surface of the earth. It may flow slowly like thick syrup or squirt high in the air. As it cools it becomes hard rock again.

LAVA

All lava is fine-grained, because it cools too fast for large crystals to form. Dark-colored lava is basalt. Light-colored lava is felsite.

Lava takes different shapes as it hardens. Sheet lava is a smooth flow that covers a wide area. Pillow lava, which is rounded and puffy, flows into the sea and hardens under water. Pumice and scoria are rough and full of holes. Pahoehoe (illustrated) is smooth and shiny. It is lava hardened in a flowing, rope-like form.

Lava caves and tunnels form where lava hardens on the outside while the inside remains liquid and pours out.

Unusual lava formations may be seen in Hawaii and Alaska, at the Craters of the Moon National Monument in Idaho and at the Lava Beds National Monument in California.

See *pumice* and *scoria*.

lavender \ 'lav-ən-dər \

Lavender is a plant that belongs to the mint family. It has been grown for hundreds of years for its fragrant, pale purple flowers. The color lavender is named after this flower.

In ancient Rome, lavender leaves and flowers were floated in bath water. For years, oil from the flower buds has been used to make perfume. When dried, the flowers keep their fragrance for months. Dried lavender is still put with stored linens and clothing to perfume them.

Lavender is native to the Mediterranean countries but is planted in gardens around the world. It is often used as a low hedge. It is an evergreen and therefore pleasing in appearance all year long. The rounded, bushy plant is from 12 to 18 inches tall. The narrow, gray-green leaves are velvety to the touch. They grow in opposite pairs along the stalks and are each about 1½ inches long. The flowers are borne in crowded, spiky clusters, rising from the leaf axils in midsummer. The fruit is a collection of dry nutlets.

leafhopper \ 'lēf-ˌhäp-ər \

Leafhoppers make up a large family of small insects that are very harmful to plants. They suck plant juices and also carry virus, fungus or bacterial diseases from plant to plant. Leafhoppers live all over the world. There are over 700 kinds in this country.

Most leafhoppers are ⅛ to ½ inch long. They are usually yellow or green. Some, living on the west coast, are striped or of more than 1 color.

All leafhoppers have slender, tapering

LEAFHOPPER

bodies. On their heads, between the large eyes, are short, slender antennae. There are 2 rows of sharp spines on the undersides of the hind legs.

The female lays rod-shaped eggs in slits which she makes in stems or leaves. The eggs hatch either in late summer or early the next spring. Both nymphs and adults hibernate under dead leaves.

The potato leafhopper (illustrated), one of the most destructive kinds of leafhopper, spreads a leaf disease called hopperburn. It damages apple trees, berry bushes and such garden flowers as hollyhocks, roses and zinnias.

The adult potato leafhopper is about ⅛ inch long. It is pale yellow-green with white splotches on the head. It is common as far west as Kansas.

leatherwood \ 'le<u>th</u>-ər-ˌwu̇d \

Leatherwood is a common North American shrub named for its tough, springy bark. The Indians used strips of the bark to make bowstrings and fishlines.

Leatherwood is usually bushy, with many slender, spreading branches. The twigs are jointed and bend without breaking. Tiny, pale yellow flowers appear at the ends of the twigs in early spring, before the leaves.

The smooth-edged leaves are 2 to 3

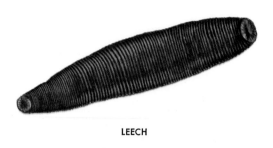

LEECH

LEATHERWOOD

inches long and 1 to 2 inches wide. They are rounded at the base and taper slightly toward the tip. The fruit is an egg-shaped, red berry a little less than ½ inch long.

Leatherwood grows in rich, moist soil, usually in wooded areas, where it is shaded by taller shrubs and trees. It grows in the eastern half of North America, north to Quebec and Minnesota, and south to Arkansas, Alabama and Florida.

leech \ 'lēch \

The leeches are a group of unusual segmented worms.

Some leeches live on land and some live in water. Water leeches swim by curling and uncurling. Land dwellers hump along like inchworms. Some leeches kill and eat smaller living creatures. Others eat dead animal and plant materials. Others are parasites that suck blood from larger animals.

Until about 100 years ago doctors used blood-sucking leeches to draw blood from sick people. They thought that this practice reduced fever.

The leech's body is flattened and oval. At one end is a mouth surrounded by a small sucking disk. At the other end is a larger round sucker used for holding itself in place. The leech breathes through its skin. Unlike most worms, it has a pouch for storing food and can live for as long as 3 months after a large feeding.

All leeches have both male and female reproductive organs. After 2 leeches mate, each lays eggs. The eggs are laid in a protective cocoon, either on land or in the water.

Leeches common in the U.S. are 1 to 2 inches long. The European medicinal leech (illustrated) is about 4 inches long, but when sucking blood it may swell up until it is 12 inches long.

lemming \ 'lem-ing \

Lemmings are small mammals, the most common rodents of the arctic regions. They are also found in the Scandinavian mountains and the forests and tundra of northern Canada.

Lemmings live in shallow burrows. While some kinds are constantly active, some sleep all day and still others sleep only at night. They eat roots, grasses, moss and lichens.

Every 3 or 4 years, hundreds of millions of certain types of lemmings leave their homes to travel straight across the northlands. Many of them die of starvation or exhaustion along the way. Those that reach the ocean jump in and swim till they drown. It is thought that overcrowding or lack of food triggers these suicide marches.

Female lemmings bear 3 to 9 young at a time. When food is scarce, they have only 1 litter a year. When food is plentiful, they bear litters as often as once a month.

Lemmings are 3 to 7 inches long. While they are usually gray, brown or black, the collared lemming (illustrated) is white in winter and brown or gray in summer. It is the only rodent that changes color. Its name comes from a stiff ruff of hair that covers the animal's ears. In autumn it grows an extra claw on each foot to help it burrow under the snow as well as walk on top of it.

lemur \ 'lē-mər \

Although they resemble foxes, the lemurs are a group of primates related to the monkeys and apes. Most kinds live in trees. They are found only on Madagascar and a few nearby islands.

The largest lemurs are the size of large dogs, while the smallest ones are the size of mice. Their woolly fur is gray, brown, reddish or white. Their hind legs are longer than their forelegs, and their paws look a little like hands. Nearly all have long tails.

The smaller kinds of lemurs sleep during the day and search for food at night. Larger lemurs sometimes feed during the day, and they are seen on the ground

LEMMING

LEMUR

lentil

LENTIL

more often than the smaller ones. All eat leaves and fruit, along with some insects, snakes, birds and eggs.

Female lemurs bear 1 to 3 young, once a year. While they are small, young lemurs cling to the mother's chest, where they are hidden by her long hair.

The best-known kind is the ring-tailed lemur (illustrated). In southwestern Madagascar it is often seen on the ground, in rocky places. It runs rapidly on all fours, holding its tail straight up.

lentil \ 'lent-ᵊl \

One of the oldest food plants known, the lentil is a heavily branched annual legume, a member of the pea family. The lentil has been cultivated for almost 4,000 years and is mentioned in the Old Testament. It grows in southern Europe, Egypt, western Asia and America.

The plant grows about 18 inches tall. The tiny, blue-white flower grows on a thin stalk which sprouts where the leaf joins the stem. The leaves are compound, with 4 to 14 narrow leaflets, each about ½ inch long. The fruit is a pod which looks like a pea or bean pod. It is less than an inch long and holds 2 seeds.

Lentil seeds are dark red-brown, gray or black. They are flattened and less than ½ inch across. They contain a large amount of protein and carbohydrate. They make a very good soup and also can be used as a table food like peas or beans.

The plant grows best in a light, dry soil. After the seeds are harvested, the leaves and stems can be dried and used as cattle fodder.

leopard \ 'lep-ərd \

A large and beautiful member of the cat family, the leopard lives in Africa and Asia. Males are 4 to 5 feet long and weigh 150 to 200 pounds. Females are somewhat smaller.

Most leopards are brownish-yellow marked all over with irregular black spots called rosettes. Those that live in forests are generally darker than those that live on dry plains. A few are black.

Like other cats, the leopard has sharp, strong claws that help it climb trees. It often waits on a tree limb, then jumps down on its victim's back. It may drag its kill up into a tree and eat it there.

Leopards hunt singly or in pairs. They kill monkeys, goats, sheep, deer and wild hogs. They have little fear of man, and sometimes enter native villages in search of food. They sleep during the day and prowl at night.

Leopard cubs are born in the spring. There are 2 to 4 in the litter. The cubs remain with the parents until they are fully grown.

LEOPARD

LESSER PANDA

LETTUCE (HEAD AND LEAF)

lesser panda \ 'les-ər 'pan-də \

The lesser panda is a small mammal that looks much like its distant relative, the raccoon. Its closest relative is the black and white giant panda.

This animal lives on forested slopes of the Himalayan Mountains in Asia, from 6,000 to 12,000 feet above sea level.

The lesser panda has a body length of about 2 feet. It is reddish-brown, with white on the face and ears, and black rings around the very long, bushy tail. Like the giant panda, it walks bear-like on rather short, stout legs, but it can run rapidly on all fours.

Strong, sharp claws make the lesser panda a good climber, and it spends most of its time in trees. It sleeps in a hollow tree, but it often seeks food on the ground. It eats bamboo shoots and other plant foods such as fruit and nuts, along with some small animals and birds' eggs.

The lesser panda is often seen in zoos. It does not make a good pet, since it is likely to scratch or bite anyone who tries to pet it.

In the forest, lesser pandas usually live in pairs or family groups. One or 2 young pandas are born to the female in early winter, and they stay with the parents for a year or more.

lettuce

Lettuce is a well-known garden vegetable. Its leaves are eaten raw in salads.

This plant once grew wild in Europe and Asia, near the Mediterranean Sea. It was known to the ancient Greeks and Romans, who used it to make medicines. Today wild lettuce has disappeared, but many different cultivated kinds are grown all over the world.

The lettuce plant is an annual with thin, ruffled leaves that wrap around the stalk. If the whole plant is not harvested when the leaves are ready to eat, the stalk becomes 3 to 4 feet tall and bears flowers in late summer, and seeds in autumn. The flowers are yellow and open only in the morning. The small oblong seeds are yellow or black.

Plant breeders have produced 3 main types of lettuce. Leaf lettuce (illustrated) is the easiest kind to grow, and it is probably most like wild lettuce. Head lettuce (illustrated) leaves form a round, solid ball. Cos or romaine lettuce has long leaves that overlap each other and form a tall roll.

Lettuce grows best in cool weather, in moist, rich soil, protected from heat and sunshine. In the U.S., California and Arizona lead in growing lettuce for market.

libration \ li-'brā-shən \ of the moon

As the moon moves around the earth, the same face is always turned toward the earth. The visible area, however, does change slightly. These changes are due to slight movements, as if the moon were rocking a little from side to side and up and down as it moves around the earth. The slight changes collectively are called the libration of the moon.

Libration in latitude changes what is visible at the top and bottom of the moon, near the moon's poles. It is due to the tilt of the moon's axis in relation to the plane of its orbit. At one time during the month an observer on earth sees a little more at the top of the moon and a little less at the bottom. At another time of the month he sees more at the bottom and less at the top.

Libration in longitude changes what is visible at the sides of the moon. It is due to changes in the speed at which the moon orbits the earth. When the moon is near the earth, it moves faster. When farther away, it moves more slowly. At the same time, the moon is rotating on its axis, always at the same speed. When the 2 speeds are "out of step," an observer on earth sees more of the moon's surface at one side and less at the other side.

See *moon.*

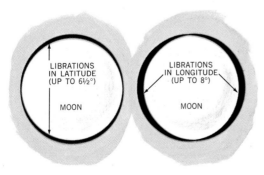

LIBRATION OF THE MOON

LIBRATIONS IN LATITUDE (UP TO 6½°)

MOON

LIBRATIONS IN LONGITUDE (UP TO 8°)

MOON

LICHEN

lichen \ 'lī-kən \

An unusual form of plant life, lichens are made up of an alga and a fungus living together and depending on each other. The alga manufactures food for the fungus. The fungus stores water for the alga and shelters it from the sun and wind. Together, the two can live in places where neither could live alone, and where no other plants can live.

About 15,000 different kinds of lichens are known. Most are gray, gray-green or black, but some kinds are yellow, brown, pink or red. Some kinds form a thin, crust-like growth on a rock or tree trunk. Some kinds have wrinkled, branching parts that look like leaves. Others look like tangled, leafless shrubs.

Lichens are used to make litmus, a dye for chemical testing. They are also food for some animals. Reindeer moss (illustrated) is the chief food of the arctic reindeer, musk oxen and caribou. It is bushy and grows 12 inches tall, taller than any other lichen.

Lichens grow higher on mountains and nearer the poles than any other plants. About 400 different kinds grow in Antarctica, where there are almost no other plants. Still other kinds of lichens grow on deserts and in the tropics.

LICORICE

licorice \ 'lik(-ə)-rish \

A plant belonging to the pea family, licorice is valued for flavoring material extracted from its roots. The flavoring is used in such products as chewing gum, candies, tobacco, soft drinks and cough medicines. After the flavoring has been taken from the root, the root fibers themselves are used in such products as fire-fighting foam and insulation board.

The plant is a perennial that grows from 2 to 3 feet tall. Pale lavender flowers bloom in short, spiky clusters in late summer or early fall. The compound leaves have 4 to 8 pairs of oval leaflets. These are slightly notched on the end and sticky underneath. The fruit is a pea-like pod 3 to 4 inches long.

Widely grown in the Mediterranean areas of Europe and Asia, licorice is not an important crop in the U.S.

lignite \ 'lig-ˌnīt \

A kind of coal, lignite contains less carbon and more water and other impurities than other grades of coal. It is soft and burns well but it gives off a great deal of smoke and a strong smell. When it is dry, it crumbles easily and is rather hard to handle.

Lignite is found where beds of sedimentary rock have formed on top of peat. It is yellowish-brown, dark brown or black. It is more solid than peat but crumbles more easily than soft coal.

Like other forms of coal, lignite was formed from plants that grew millions of years ago.

See *coal*.

lilac \ 'lī-lək \

The lilacs are a group of hardy shrubs belonging to the olive family. They are native to eastern Europe and Asia.

The small, fragrant flowers are tube-shaped and open out in 4 rounded lobes. They bloom in late spring, crowded in pointed clusters at the ends of the branches. The common lilac has lavender flowers, but kinds bearing white, pink and purple flowers have been developed.

The purple lilac is the state flower of New Hampshire.

lily

One of the largest plant families, the lily family includes over 2,000 kinds of plants and over 100 kinds of garden flowers.

Most lilies have showy, funnel-shaped flowers that open out in 6 equal sections. They blossom in late spring or early summer, singly or in clusters at the tops of the stalks. They are usually red, orange,

LILY

LILY OF THE VALLEY

yellow or white. They may also be spotted, striped or plain.

Leaves of lilies are narrow and smooth-edged and grow all along the stem or in a thick cluster from the ground. The fruit develops in a capsule, with flat seeds in each section. Lilies grow from bulbs or rhizomes. They are found all over the north temperate zone.

The leopard lily (illustrated) grows wild in the mountains of California, Oregon and Washington. It grows best in moist but well-drained soil. The spotted orange flowers that give the plant its name blossom in summer.

The sego lily is native to the western U.S. and is the state flower of Utah.

For other members of the lily family, see *asparagus, day lily, grape hyacinth, green-brier, hyacinth, lily of the valley, onion, star-of-Bethlehem, trillium* and *yucca.*

lily of the valley

A plant of the lily family, lily of the valley has been grown in flower gardens for many hundreds of years. Its tiny flowers have a sweet, very delicate scent. Oil from the flowers is used in perfumes.

The broad, dark green leaves and the slender, flowering stems grow about 9 inches tall. The white flowers are bell-shaped and about ¼ inch long. They dangle from short stalks, all along the flowering stems. The flowers bloom in late spring. The fruit that appears on the plant in late summer is a red berry about ¼ inch across.

Lily of the valley is native to Europe and Asia, but it has been planted in many other parts of the world. It is a hardy perennial that will grow in almost any part of the temperate zone. It grows best in shaded places where the soil is rich and moist. The plants spread by means of creeping, horizontal roots.

Lily of the valley is planted by burying sections of the root that have bud-like sprouts on them. These sprouts, called pips, are sometimes planted in flowerpots indoors so that they will bloom early in the spring.

limestone \ 'līm-,stōn \

One of the most useful rocks, limestone can be crushed for roadbeds, carved or cut for building stone, or treated chemically to make rock-wool insulation. When limestone is heated to 900° F., lime is produced. Lime is used in cement, fertilizer, paper, glass and soap.

Limestone is white, pale gray or light brown. There are many different forms. Oolitic limestone is fine-grained and even-textured. Coquina is loosely

LIMESTONE

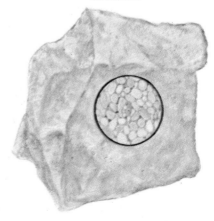

packed and contains many sea shells. Tufa is a porous, lightweight kind. Chalk is very soft, white limestone.

Limestone is made up of calcium carbonate (calcite) that was once dissolved in seawater. When the water became warmer, or when plants used up carbon dioxide in the water, some of this mineral material settled out and dropped to the sea floor. Tiny living animals, such as protozoa and corals, took calcite from the water and used it to build shells around their soft bodies. When they died, these shells fell to the bottom and helped to build up the thick beds of limestone.

Large beds of limestone are found in many different parts of the world, often in the middle portions of the continents. These beds show that the continents were once at the bottom of the sea.

linnet \ 'lin-ət \

A member of the finch family, the linnet is a favorite songbird in Europe. Linnets were once trapped and kept as pets, in cages, but laws now protect them.

In size and habits, the linnet is much like the American goldfinch. Both birds are about 5 inches long. They have short but strong, cone-shaped bills for cracking seeds. They live in open country rather than in forests, and they usually nest in low, bushy shrubs.

Linnets are not all colored alike. Most males are reddish-brown and most females are gray-brown, but some birds are spotted and some are pale gray or nearly white. Some of the reddish-brown males have bright red around the head during the mating season.

The linnet's song is a sweet, twittering melody, but it does not have much variety. The same short phrase is repeated over and over.

The nest is a neat, cup-shaped structure placed fairly near the ground. Four to 7 eggs are laid twice a year. They are pale blue, spotted with brown.

The linnet nests in most parts of Europe and Asia. Some birds winter in the northern part of Africa.

lion

A large and powerful cat, the lion was once common throughout Europe, Asia and Africa. Today it is extinct in Europe and nearly so in Asia. In Africa, it lives mostly in game preserves.

Male lions are up to 11 feet long and weigh up to 600 pounds. Females are much smaller, often only half the size of the males. Only the males have heavy manes of longer hair around the neck and shoulders. The mane is usually light on young animals and darker on older ones. The shorter hair on the body

LINNET

LION

LIONFISH

LIVERWORT

is reddish-brown or yellowish-brown. The tail is long and slender, with a brushy tuft of longer hair on the tip.

In the wild, lions live in groups called prides. They sleep hidden in thickets during the day. They hunt at night, prowling over deserts, plains and mountains. Often, the male chases an animal toward the female who kills it. Lions kill and eat many different kinds of animals. As a rule, only old and weak lions kill humans.

The female lion gives birth to 1 litter of 2 to 6 cubs, once a year. The newborn cubs are blind, and are covered with spotted, grayish wool.

lionfish \ 'lī-ən-ˌfish \
(scorpion fish, tigerfish, turkeyfish)

An odd-looking, poisonous fish belonging to the scorpion fish or rockfish family, the lionfish has striped spines and tentacles that help it hide among rocks and seaweed.

About 10 inches long, this fish eats smaller fish, crustaceans and other forms of sea life. It is a slow and lazy swimmer, but it will attack very quickly, jabbing its victim with the stiff, sharp spines along its back. Each spine is connected to a gland that secretes poison.

The lionfish's poison is much like snake venom. There is usually not enough of it to kill a human being, but it can cause great pain. Tropical fishermen are careful not to touch this fish.

Like other members of the scorpion fish family, the lionfish has a bony plate on each cheek.

The lionfish lives in the warmer parts of the sea, in the Indian Ocean and in the Pacific, from the East Indies to the islands of Polynesia. It is usually found near rocky coasts or coral reefs.

liverwort \ 'liv-ər-ˌwərt \

Liverworts are small green plants closely related to mosses. They have no stems or true roots, and they do not bear flowers or seeds. The main part of the plant, called the "thallus," is an irregular, rather leaf-like body which grows flat on the ground. The plant got its name because early observers thought the thallus was shaped like the human liver.

On the underside of the thallus are tiny rootlets that absorb food. Reproductive parts appear on the upper surface.

The male reproductive cell swims through a film of water along the top of the plant to fertilize the egg cell. This type of reproduction alternates with a spore-producing generation of plants, as in ferns and mosses.

Common in moist areas all over the world, liverworts are most often seen in woods in early spring. The largest kind is 6 inches across, but most kinds are

LIZARD

much smaller. They are often hidden among mosses and ferns that grow in the same moist, shaded places.

In a common kind of liverwort called Marchantia (illustrated), the thallus is like a branching ribbon. The reproductive parts are like tiny palm trees.

lizard

Lizards make up a large group of quick-moving reptiles with scaly skins. They are closely related to snakes. Most lizards are harmless. There are many kinds of lizards found in much of the world, although most live in tropical and mild temperate regions.

The bodies of all lizards are covered with scales. They have long tails. Most kinds are able to grow a new tail if the old one is broken off. Almost all kinds of lizards have 4 short legs.

Some lizards are only 2 to 3 inches long, while the largest kinds are 8 to 10 feet in length. All lizards eat insects.

Most North American lizards feed during the day and lie in the sun. Many tropical kinds come out only at night. Because lizards are cold-blooded animals, those that live in cold regions hibernate in winter.

Most lizards mate in the spring. The females lay oval, leathery-shelled eggs in sand or under rocks.

The collared lizard (illustrated) lives

in Kansas, Missouri and the southwestern states. From 7 to 10 inches long, it may be green, gray or brown, but usually has red or yellow markings on the head. The 2 black lines around its neck give the collared lizard its name.

For other kinds of lizards, see *anole, chameleon, chuckwalla, gecko, Gila monster, iguana, skink* and *tokay*.

llama \ 'läm-ə \

Llamas are ruminant mammals that make up a group of animals native to South America. Llamas look something like camels without a hump. The domestic llama (illustrated) is descended from the wild llama still common in the Andes Mountains. Domestic llamas are used as beasts of burden. Their wool is used for cloth.

Llamas average about 4 feet high at the shoulder. Their long, woolly fur is brown, black, yellowish or white, with white underparts. Their necks are long and slender, while their sheep-like heads have long, pointed ears.

Llamas live all along the Andes range, at altitudes of 13,000 to 16,000 feet. In the northern part of their range, they sometimes stray down to 7,000 feet. In colder southern parts of the Andes, they often graze on grassy plains lower than 7,000 feet. Llamas eat any plant materials they can find.

LLAMA

259

lobster

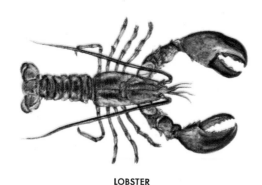

LOBSTER

The domestic llama is most common in Bolivia and Peru, where 1 herd may include up to 1,000 animals.

Smaller than the wild llama, the domestic llama is about 4 feet long, with a 6-inch tail and a 22-inch neck. The coat is often speckled or spotted. Domestic llamas breed every 2 years, and live 12 to 18 years.

lobster

Lobsters make up a family of crustaceans that live in the ocean. They look much like freshwater crayfish, but are usually larger. Lobsters are a popular seafood.

Lobsters have skeletons on the outside of their bodies. The eyes are on the ends of movable stalks, and the antennae are very long. Most kinds of lobsters have large pincers at the ends of the first pair of legs, and smaller pincers on the second and third pairs of legs. Small limb-like parts called swimmerets are attached to the jointed sections of the abdomen. At the end of the abdomen is a fan-shaped tail used for swimming.

The largest lobsters are about 2 feet long and weigh up to 30 pounds. Most lobsters caught in traps and sold as seafood weigh 1 to 3 pounds.

Lobsters live in shallow water near shore during the summer. They move out to deeper water in winter. They feed mostly at night, walking on the sea floor and searching in the sand for snails, starfish and crustaceans. They also eat fish and some underwater plants.

The female lobster lays thousands of tiny round eggs that cling to the underside of her abdomen until they hatch.

The American lobster (illustrated) is found off the east coast of the U.S., from Maine south to the Carolinas.

locoweed \ 'lō-(ˌ)kō-ˌwēd \ (crazyweed)

This group of plants belongs to the pea family. Locoweeds are poisonous to animals that eat them. The name "locoweed" is suggested by the convulsions, or wild behavior, of cattle or sheep that have eaten the leaves. In a short time these animals fall to the ground, unable to move. They often die.

Several different kinds of locoweed grow wild in the western U.S. All have compound leaves made up of many small leaflets.

Woolly locoweed (illustrated) is a very poisonous kind. It is covered with silky white hairs. The leaves, 5 to 8 inches long, are made up of as many as 29 leaflets attached to a slender midrib. Each leaflet is rounded at the tip and about ½ inch long.

The small flowers are purplish and about ½ inch long. They are borne in spike-shaped clusters at the tops of the

LOCOWEED

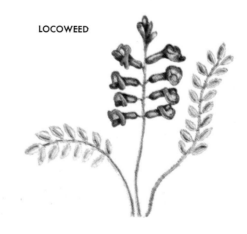

LOCUST

branching stalks. The clusters look a little like sweet pea flowers. The seeds look like small garden peas. They ripen inside a dry, leathery seedpod about 3 inches long.

Woolly locoweed has a very long, tough root that grows down into the soil as far as 6 feet.

locust \ 'lō-kəst \

Trees with beautiful, lacy leaves, the locusts belong to the pea family. Because their wood is very hard and strong, some kinds are valued as timber trees. Other kinds are planted to control erosion, or for shade.

All locusts have compound leaves made up of many small leaflets. Most kinds bear clusters of fragrant flowers in spring. The fruit is a long seedpod that remains on the tree all winter.

Locusts are often divided into 2 main groups. The black locust and its relatives have leaves with an uneven number of leaflets, so that 1 leaflet stands alone at the end of the leaf. These locusts are native to the U.S. and Mexico.

The honey locust and its relatives usually have an even number of leaflets so that there is a pair at the end of each leaf. These locusts are native to North and South America, Africa and Asia.

The honey locust (illustrated) has sharp thorns about 2 inches long on the trunk and larger branches. The leaves vary in size. The largest leaves are branching sprays of 100 or more small leaflets. The small flowers are greenish white. This tree is named for the sweet, sticky pulp found inside the long, twisted seedpods. The honey locust is native to the southeastern U.S.

loess \ 'les \

Loess is a kind of soil made up of tiny bits of rock carried and then dropped by the wind. Large parts of continents are covered with layers of loess 5 to 100 feet deep. Loess is very rich soil, and it forms some of the finest farming areas.

Loess is usually a yellowish color. It is a loose material, but it clings together because it is made up of odd-shaped particles with points and corners. It does not slide and pour like sand, which is made up of larger, rounded bits of rock. Loess may be seen in straight-up-and-down cliffs, along streams or highway cuts.

Thick beds of loess cover parts of Iowa, Nebraska and most of the Mississippi valley. Most of this loess was ground as fine as flour by glaciers that once covered the land farther west. Since the winds of the U.S. blow mostly from the west, this loess was carried toward the east.

Loess is also found in central Europe and in parts of Australia. Loess that forms thick beds in China was blown as dust from deserts farther west.

LOESS

loon \ 'lün \

The loons are a group of large water birds not closely related to any other birds. They are best known for their strange calls, which sound like crazy laughter or wails.

Twenty-four to 36 inches long, loons have streamlined bodies, short necks and pointed bills. They have small wings and short legs.

In summer, all loons are handsome black-and-white birds marked with neat patterns of dots and stripes. In winter, they are dull gray with whitish underparts. Males and females look alike.

Expert swimmers and divers, loons eat fish that they catch underwater. They are seen on land only during the nesting season. The nest is on the ground, always within a few feet of water. The 2 large eggs are brown, spotted with black.

Loons spend the summer on lakes and streams in the far northern parts of North America, Europe and Asia. They winter along seacoasts as far south as Florida and Japan.

The common loon (illustrated) nests in Alaska, northern Canada, Greenland and Iceland. It winters along both coasts of North America, off Great Britain and in the Mediterranean Sea. The common loon is the state bird of Minnesota.

LOON

LORIS

loris \ 'lōr-əs \ (slow lemur)

Lorises make up a group of nocturnal, tree-dwelling mammals related to the monkey. They are native to India, Indochina and Malaysia.

Lorises grow up to 16 inches long, and have no tails. Their long, woolly hair is usually dark cream or grayish-brown. They have reddish-brown markings on their faces. Some have black stripes which continue over the head and circle the eyes.

Lorises very seldom come to the ground. They sleep during the day in hollow tree trunks. At night they eat almost anything that they can find in the tree branches. Often lorises catch large insects with their hands while hanging by their hind legs.

The best-known kind of loris is the slender loris (illustrated). It is the size of a squirrel and lives in southern India and Ceylon. It has long, thin legs, a pointed nose and very large, close-set eyes. The slender loris does not have the dark back stripe of some other kinds of lorises.

louse \ 'laùs \

Lice are small, wingless insects that prey on warm-blooded animals. All lice are pests, and some carry serious diseases.

There are 2 general kinds of lice. One kind is the sucking louse. It sucks the blood of many kinds of mammals. The sucking louse lives on dogs, cats, cattle, hogs, sheep, goats, horses, rats, mice and many other mammals, including man.

The other kind of louse is the biting or bird louse that has chewing mouthparts. Biting lice feed on the hair, feathers and the outer skin of the animal on which they are found. They are found on birds, domesticated animals and rodents.

The body louse is a very small kind of sucking louse. It became known as the "cootie" during World War I. The body louse lives on humans, mostly on the chest and back. It is closely related to the head louse, which also attacks humans. Both the head louse and the body louse carry diseases such as typhoid fever, trench mouth and relapsing fever.

lumpfish \ 'ləmp-ˌfish \ (lumpsucker)

A deep-water, ocean fish, the lumpfish is also known as the lumpsucker because the bottom fins join together to make a sucking disk. With this disk, the fish can attach itself to the ocean floor. There it waits for currents to bring it the crustaceans, small fish and jellyfish on which it feeds. The lumpfish is found mostly in the Atlantic Ocean.

The body of the lumpfish is short and thick. The underside is wide and flattened. The back of the fish is narrow, and the top fin looks like a hump.

A lumpfish's skin does not have scales but is covered with wart-like bumps. Colors vary from greenish to slate blue to olive-brown, with a lighter underside.

A female lumpfish may be 24 inches long and weigh up to 20 pounds. The male is about half as large.

During the breeding season, the male lumpfish turns purple-blue above and bright red beneath. After mating, many small, sticky, pink eggs are laid by the female. These eggs sink to the bottom and are guarded by the male until they hatch.

lungfish \ 'ləng-ˌfish \

Lungfish make up a large group of primitive fish which have changed very little over millions of years. They are sometimes called "living fossils."

Lungfish have long, slim, eel-like bodies and long tails. Besides gills, they have a lung-like air bladder. They range in length from 2 to 7 feet.

Lungfish feed on many ocean plants and small animals. They can live out of water for several years. During this time they make a damp cocoon in the mud and breathe with their air bladders.

The female lays her eggs in a nest that is about a foot deep. The male guards the eggs until they hatch.

LUMPFISH

LUNGFISH

LUPINE

Lungfish are found in African and South American Atlantic coastal waters, and 1 kind is found near Australia. They often move into swampy areas.

The South American lungfish (illustrated) is more gentle than other kinds of lungfish. It has pairs of lacy-looking fins and scales half buried in the skin.

lupine \ 'lü-pən \

Lupines make up a group of annual and perennial plants and shrubby trees belonging to the pea family. Many kinds of lupines are found in North America, especially in the West, in South America and around the Mediterranean.

The Texas bluebonnet is one of the best-known wild lupines. It is the state flower of Texas. The bluebonnet has bright blue flowers with a white or yellow spot. Thousands of Texas bluebonnet blooms are seen in open fields in the late spring.

Some lupines are grown as border flowers in gardens.

The smaller lupines also have blue flowers, almost like those of the garden pea. They grow from 1 to 4 feet tall. Their leaves have as many as 18 leaflets, each from 1 to 1½ inches long.

The tree form of lupine is shrubby, growing from 4 to 8 feet high. Showy, blue flowers grow at the ends of the branches. Both sides of the leaves are hairy.

The common wild lupine (illustrated) is called the Quaker bonnet. It grows in eastern North America.

lynx \ 'ling(k)s \

Lynxes are a large group of wild cats found in all parts of the world except Malaysia, Australia and South America.

Male lynxes are about 3½ to 4 feet long and weigh 30 to 40 pounds. The female is usually slightly smaller. Lynxes have long legs and short tails. They have grayish fur which is spotted with either lighter or darker shades. Their eyes are bright yellow. The pupils of the eyes are shaped like those of the ordinary house cat.

Lynxes are vicious animals. They attack larger animals, such as sheep and calves, as well as smaller mammals, especially rabbits.

Lynxes can climb well and are excellent swimmers. They can walk for many miles but are poor runners. Lynxes sleep during the day and hunt during the night.

Lynxes become adults at 1 year. Their life-span is about 12 years.

The lynx most common in the U.S. is the bay lynx (illustrated), often called bobcat or wildcat. It ranges from the Canadian border south through central Mexico.

LYNX

m

macaw \ mə-'kȯ \

Macaws are a group of long-tailed parrots native to Central and South America. They include the largest kinds of parrots. All have strong, curved beaks which they use to crack nuts.

The smaller macaws, which are about the size of a pigeon, are mostly green. The larger kinds are bright shades of red, gold and blue. Their call is a loud, high scream.

In their native jungles, macaws are usually seen in pairs. They nest in hollow trees. The female lays 2 or more round, white eggs. Both parents feed the young birds after they hatch.

Macaws can be captured and are often kept as pets. Unlike some other kinds of parrots, they seldom learn to say more than a few words.

The largest kind of macaw is the 30- to 36-inch gold-and-blue macaw (illustrated). It can be found in jungles from Panama south to Peru.

mackerel \ 'mak-(ə-)rəl \

Mackerel make up a family of fish valued by both commercial fishermen and sportsmen. Most kinds of mackerel are very good to eat.

Mackerel are streamlined fish. They

MACAW

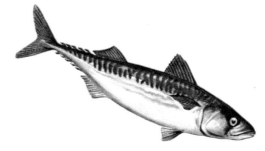

MACKEREL

have pointed heads, large mouths and narrow tails. Their tail fins are deeply forked. On the top and bottom of the fish, along the tail, are tiny finlets. Mackerel vary greatly in size, with small kinds weighing less than 2 pounds and larger kinds more than 60 pounds.

Mackerel are found in temperate parts of both the Atlantic and Pacific oceans, in open seas or near the shore. They are fast swimmers and travel in schools. Most mackerel feed on other fish.

The Atlantic mackerel (illustrated), sometimes called common mackerel, is an important food fish. Unlike most mackerel, the Atlantic mackerel grows to about 2 feet and weighs about 4 pounds. Atlantic mackerel also feed on plant material as well as small fish.

In May or June, a female lays up to 500,000 floating eggs. The young fish hatch in 5 days.

For members of the mackerel family, see *albacore, Atlantic bonita, tuna* and *wahoo*.

Magellanic \ ˌmaj-ə-'lan-ik \ clouds

Magellanic clouds are 2 oddly shaped galaxies that can be seen only from the southern half of the earth. They were discovered by and named for the famous explorer, Magellan, in 1516.

Without a telescope, the Magellanic

clouds look like hazy patches. Each is made up of thousands of stars, star clusters and nebulae. More than 500,000 giant stars have been counted in the larger of these 2 galaxies.

The smaller galaxy is 84,000 light-years away. The larger galaxy is 75,000 light-years away from the earth. The 2 galaxies are 30,000 light-years apart.

The Magellanic clouds are thought to be satellites of our own Milky Way galaxy. The larger galaxy, called Nubecula Major, is found in the constellation Dorado. The smaller one is called Nubecula Minor and may be seen in the constellation Tucana.

magnetic \ mag-'net-ik \ poles

The magnetic poles are the 2 places on earth toward which a compass points. The north magnetic pole and the south magnetic pole are the positive and negative poles of the earth's magnetic field.

The earth's magnetic field is probably caused by electrical currents in the earth's core. The needle of a magnetic compass is attracted to the north magnetic pole and pushed away from the south magnetic pole.

The magnetic poles are always moving slowly from place to place on the surface of the earth. They are not located at the same place as the true, or geo-

MAGNETITE

graphic, North and South poles. These poles are always in the same place.

The north magnetic pole is now located in the Arctic Ocean about 1,000 miles from the true North Pole. The south magnetic pole is located between Antarctica and Australia, about 1,500 miles away from the true South Pole.

magnetite \ 'mag-nə-ˌtīt \

Magnetite is a form of iron oxide. The lodestones or natural magnets known to the ancient Greeks were pieces of the mineral magnetite. In Scandinavia, where magnetite is found in large quantities, it is mined as iron ore.

All magnetite is attracted by magnetic force. Some magnetite has been naturally polarized so that it is itself magnetic.

Always black or dark gray, magnetite is hard and fairly heavy. It is usually found in irregular, grainy lumps. Crystals of magnetite have a metallic shine.

This mineral is always found among igneous rocks, where there were very high temperatures at some time in the past. In the U.S., magnetite is found in New York, New Jersey, Pennsylvania, Utah and near Lake Superior.

In some parts of the world tiny particles of magnetite washed up by ocean waves form black sand beaches.

MAGNETIC POLES

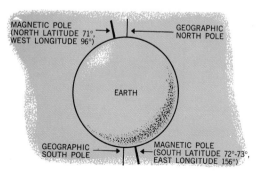

MAGNETIC POLE (NORTH LATITUDE 71°, WEST LONGITUDE 96°)

GEOGRAPHIC NORTH POLE

EARTH

GEOGRAPHIC SOUTH POLE

MAGNETIC POLE (SOUTH LATITUDE 72°-73°, EAST LONGITUDE 156°)

MAGNOLIA

magnolia \ mag-'nōl-yə \

The magnolias are a family of handsome trees and shrubs that bear large flowers in early spring. They grow in eastern Asia and in the warmer parts of North and South America.

The largest magnolias are trees up to 120 feet tall. They are the source of strong, very durable wood. All require moist soil and a mild climate.

The magnolias native to the U.S. have white, yellow or greenish flowers that appear after the new leaves. Cultivated magnolias from Asia have pink or purple flowers that appear before the leaves.

All magnolias have large leaves that are thick and leathery. Some kinds keep their leaves during the winter.

The flowers, usually very fragrant, are borne near the ends of the branches. The cone-shaped fruit is reddish. The ripe seeds dangle from the fruit on threads.

The southern magnolia is the state tree of Mississippi and the state flower of both Louisiana and Mississippi.

The umbrella magnolia (illustrated) grows 20 to 50 feet tall. Its bright green leaves are 12 to 20 inches long, and its flowers are about 10 inches across. This tree grows in the eastern U.S.

For another member of the magnolia family, see *tulip tree.*

magpie \ 'mag-ˌpī \

Noisy but attractive birds, magpies belong to the same family as the crows and jays. Like crows, they can sometimes be taught to imitate human speech.

Magpies live in southern Europe, northern Africa, China, Japan and the western part of North America. They are mostly black and white but some are marked with green, blue, brown or red. All have long tails. They eat seeds, acorns, insects and some animals, such as field mice and young birds, which they kill with their sharp, strong beaks.

Magpies build unusually large nests. The males collect material and bring it to the females, who do the actual building. Nests 2 to 3 feet across are common. Some kinds of magpies build a dome-like roof of thorny twigs over the top of the nest. There is only a small entrance, at the side.

Six to 10 eggs are laid once a year and incubated for 16 to 20 days.

The yellow-billed magpie (illustrated) lives only in the San Joaquin Valley of California, and ranges from San Jose to Santa Barbara. It is about 17 inches long. The similar but larger black-billed magpie, about 20 inches long, is found throughout western North America, and in Europe and Asia. In the U.S., magpies are never seen east of Nebraska.

MAGPIE

MAHOGANY TREE

mahogany \ mə-'häg-ə-nē \ **tree**

A tropical evergreen, the mahogany tree is probably the most valuable of all timber trees. Its beautifully grained wood is used for paneling, fine furniture and musical instruments.

Mahogany wood is pinkish or light brown when freshly cut. Surfaces exposed to the air turn a deep reddish-brown.

The wood is hard but easily worked, and it takes a high polish.

The mahogany tree grows 150 feet tall, with a trunk up to 6 feet in diameter. The leaves are compound. Each is made up of 4 to 12 pointed leaflets that are dark green and glossy.

Small, white or yellow flowers with 5 petals are borne in clusters near the ends of the branches. The seeds ripen inside pear-shaped pods that split into 5 sections, from the base end. The tiny seeds are attached to wings.

A few mahogany trees grow in southern Florida. Most grow in the forests of Central America and the West Indies. Some have been planted as ornamental trees in other areas, and in some places they are grown on timber plantations. The trees need a warm climate and much rainfall.

malachite \ 'mal-ə-ˌkīt \

A beautiful green mineral, malachite is sometimes used in making jewelry. Where it is abundant, it is mined as an ore of copper. Rock and mineral collectors value it for its beauty.

Rounded lumps of malachite are most common. They may be light, bright green or a deep, very dark green. Stripes or bands may run through them. Malachite is translucent so that light passes through a thin piece of it.

Malachite is made up of copper combined with oxygen, hydrogen and carbon. It is found where copper minerals have been exposed to water and air, so it is always near the surface rather than deep underground.

When copper is exposed to the weather, some of it is likely to combine with oxygen, hydrogen and carbon from the air to form malachite. The green tarnish that appears on copper roofs and weathervanes is a thin layer of malachite that has been formed in this way.

Malachite is found where other copper minerals are common. Large deposits are in Russia, Africa and Australia. In the U.S., it is found mostly in Arizona and New Mexico. Azurite, another copper mineral, is often found with it.

MALACHITE

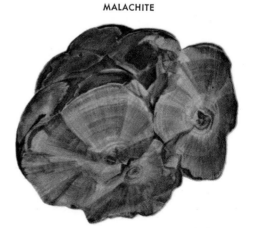

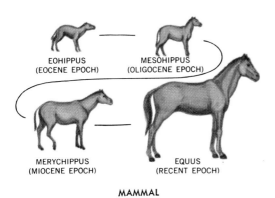

MAMMAL

mammal \ 'mam-əl \

The mammals are a group of animals that vary a great deal from each other, though they have important characteristics in common.

All mammals are warm-blooded, and all have hair on at least part of their bodies. Their young are fed on milk produced by special glands in the females' bodies.

All mammals bear living young except the echidna and duck-billed platypus, which lay eggs. Most live on land, but a few, like the whales, live in water. Most have tails, but a few, like bears, apes and man, do not. Most have 4 limbs, but a few, like the whales and manatees, have only 2, and even these limbs have changed into flippers. Bats have forelimbs that have changed into wings, and they are the only mammals that can fly.

The mammals vary in size from whales 100 feet long to tiny shrews a few inches long. Some live in trees and some burrow underground. Some hibernate as cold-blooded animals do.

The many different kinds of mammals eat a wide variety of both plant and animal foods, and they are able to live in a wide variety of climates.

mammoth \ 'mam-əth \

The mammoths are extinct kinds of elephants that lived in cold climates rather than in the tropics as modern elephants do. Mammoths disappeared about 1 million years ago, probably because of a change in the earth's weather or plant life.

Fossil tusks and bones of mammoths have been found in many different parts of the northern hemisphere. Some of the tusks are 10 feet long. Bodies complete with skin and hair have been found preserved, in frozen mud and snow, in Siberia and Alaska.

Primitive men who lived in Europe during the Ice Age hunted and ate mammoths, and painted pictures of them on the walls of caves.

Mammoths looked much like the modern Indian elephant, but they had coarse, shaggy hair all over their bodies and longer, more curving, tusks. Their ears were rather small.

The curved tusks may have been used to push snow off the grass they ate. They also ate the leaves of trees and shrubs.

The woolly mammoth (illustrated) stood about 10 feet tall. It lived in northern Europe, Siberia and North America during the Pleistocene Epoch.

MAMMOTH

man

Modern man, called *Homo sapiens* by scientists, is the only living form belonging to the family of man. Fossil bones and stone tools are the only evidence of other, older kinds of men. These ancestors and relatives of modern man disappeared long ago.

There is no clear-cut timetable of man's development. Recent fossil finds seem to show that man-like creatures lived in Africa about 1 million years ago. They stood erect and used tools.

Early man ate meat, as well as plants. Man's first tools were stones that he used as clubs to kill the animals he ate.

As he developed, man became less hairy. His skull bones became thinner, and his forehead was taller and more straight up-and-down. The brain within his skull became larger.

Man is the most adaptable of all mammals. He can live in different climates and eat many different kinds of food. Using his brain and his hands, he can change surroundings to meet his needs.

Zinjanthropus is usually called a pre-human or near-man. He lived in Africa, perhaps as early as 175,000 years ago. He was ape-like, but his teeth were smaller, more like human teeth, and he stood erect. His only tools were very simple ones, mostly broken pebbles that happened to fit into his hand.

Zinjanthropus ate meat, but he could probably kill only the smaller, weaker animals. He ate frogs, birds, snakes and young wild pigs.

Java man and Peking man lived in Asia about 360,000 years ago. Java man is known only from parts of skulls and legbones. The shape of the legbone shows that he stood erect.

Peking man is known from many teeth and bone fragments, as well as other remains found in ancient caves in China. He knew how to light fires to cook his food, and he made crude stone tools. He killed and ate deer. Some scientists believe that Peking man was the earliest man to develop speech.

Heidelberg man lived in Europe about 150,000 years ago. No tools or other remains have been found, so little is known about his intelligence or how he lived.

Neanderthal man lived in Europe 50,000 to 150,000 years ago. Like the "cave man" of comic strips, he had a low sloping forehead and heavy eyebrow ridges. He stood about 5½ feet tall. He wore skins for clothing, but he did not know how to sew. Using stone weapons, he killed animals as large as mammoths.

Cro-Magnon man lived in Europe about 50,000 years ago. He may be the direct ancestor of modern man. He was about 6 feet tall, and looked very much like modern man.

Using a variety of stone weapons, Cro-Magnon man hunted and killed reindeer, rhinoceroses, wild oxen and horses. He learned to make needles, and he sewed skins together for his clothing. On the walls of his caves he painted pictures of animals. Some of his caves may have been used as places of worship.

Australian man is a form of modern man but he is more primitive, both physically and culturally, than other living humans.

Scientists believe that Australian man is descended from Stone Age men who wandered south from Europe or Asia 30,000 or more years ago. Once isolated on the Australian continent, they did not mix with the other, changing races of the world. They went on using crude stone tools and weapons. They did not learn to use metal, or to cultivate crops. When Europeans arrived in Australia 200 years ago, they found these men living much as their Stone Age ancestors had.

The Forms of Man

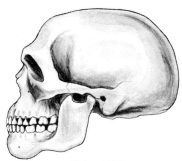

AUSTRALIAN MAN

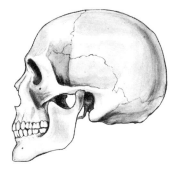

MODERN MAN

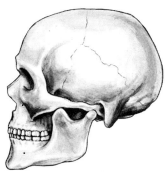

CRO-MAGNON MAN

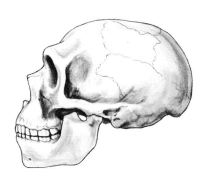

NEANDERTHAL MAN

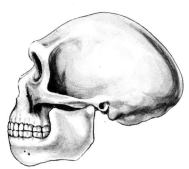

HEIDELBERG MAN

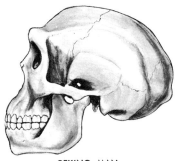

PEKING MAN

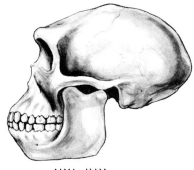

JAVA MAN

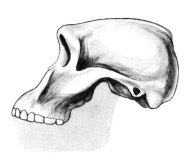

ZINJANTHROPUS MAN

manatee \ 'man-ə-ˌtē \ (sea cow)

The manatees are mammals that live in the warmer parts of the sea. They have been hunted for their skins, flesh and oil until they are now quite rare.

Manatees have dark gray, hairless skin and broad, bristly muzzles. Males are 10 to 15 feet long and weigh up to 2,000 pounds. Females are about 7 feet long.

About a year after mating, the female gives birth to 1 or 2 young. The newborn manatees have to be pushed above water every few minutes to breathe, and the females often help each other care for the young. Young manatees drink their mothers' milk for about 1½ years.

Adult manatees eat plants that grow in water. They usually rise to the surface every 10 or 15 minutes to breathe, but when frightened they may remain under water for as long as 30 minutes. They live in shallow parts of the sea and in the mouths of rivers. They are almost never seen on land.

The lamantin manatee lives in the Atlantic, from the West Indies south to Brazil. Other manatees live in the Pacific and Indian oceans.

mandrill \ 'man-drəl \

The mandrill is the oddest-looking and the most colorful animal of the Old World monkey family. It lives in the forests of western Africa.

Adult mandrills are 2 to 3 feet long. They have stocky bodies and very short tails. Their small eyes are set close together under a heavy brow ridge.

Adult males have red noses and bare, blue-purple cheeks. Whitish or yellow fur forms a beard and ruff around the face. Bare skin on the buttocks is bright red or purple. The females and young males are less brightly colored.

Though mandrills live in trees, they usually feed and travel on the ground. They eat a wide variety of foods, including fruit, leaves, insects, lizards, snakes and other small animals.

Mandrills have sharp teeth and they can be ferocious fighters, though they do not often attack men or animals larger than themselves. A tribe of mandrills will fight fiercely any other monkeys that invade the part of the forest they consider their own.

mango \ 'mang-ˌgō \ tree

A handsome evergreen tree, the mango is cultivated in the tropics for its delicious fruit. It grows larger and lives longer than most fruit trees.

Mango trees are usually 50 to 90 feet tall. The glossy, dark green leaves are 10 to 12 inches long and 3 to 4 inches wide.

MANDRILL

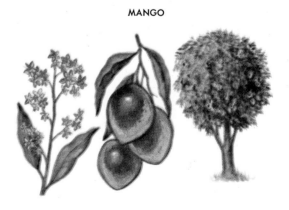

MANGO

MAN-O'-WAR BIRD

Loose clusters of small pink flowers are borne at the ends of the branches. The fruit is generally oval and 3 to 4 inches long. The leathery skin and the sweet, spicy pulp are yellow, orange or red when the fruit is ripe. In the center is 1 large, flat seed.

The mango probably came from India or Burma. It has been cultivated for about 3,000 years, and it now grows in many parts of southern Europe, Africa and Central America. In the U.S., mango trees have been planted in Florida and California.

The mango tree grows best where there is a dry season during part of the year. It will bear fruit only where there is no frost.

man-o'-war bird (frigate bird)

Large, swift-flying seabirds with very long wings, the man-o'-wars are a family related to the pelicans.

These birds are named for their pirate-like habits. While flying, they attack and rob other seabirds carrying fish. Man-o'-wars cannot easily catch fish for themselves, since they cannot swim or dive. They do manage to scoop up some jellyfish and baby turtles that float on the surface of the sea. If forced to land on water, however, they drown.

Man-o'-wars have a body length of about 4 feet and a wingspread of about 8 feet. Both males and females are blackish with white underparts. During the mating season, the male's throat turns bright red. He can expand it like a balloon.

Though they can fly very well, man-o'-wars are seldom seen very far from the tropical islands where they nest. The male builds the nest in a tree or shrub, using twigs collected by the female. Both parents incubate the 1 white egg and bring food to the young bird.

The magnificent frigate bird (illustrated) is a man-o'-war found near the Atlantic and Pacific coasts of America.

manta \ 'mant-ə \ (devil ray)

The mantas are a family of large, odd-shaped fish related to the sharks. They are the largest of the rays. Some are 22 feet wide and weigh as much as 3,500 pounds.

Like the sharks, rays are primitive fish that have skeletons of cartilage and that bear living young. They all have long tails and huge, wing-like fins that extend out on either side of the body. In addition, the mantas have smaller fins that extend out from the head.

Mantas have large mouths with small teeth in the lower jaw. They are usually peaceful, but if molested they may attack and capsize a small boat.

MANTA

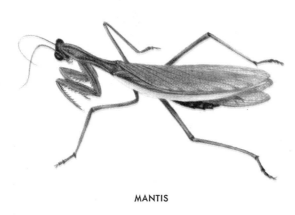

MANTIS

Most rays swim and feed near the sea floor but mantas are often seen at the top of the water. Alone or in pairs, they loll on the surface, sometimes jumping into the air and falling back with a slap. They eat mostly crustaceans and fish.

Mantas live in the warmer parts of the sea, usually near shore. The Atlantic manta (illustrated) lives along the east coast of America, from Virginia south to Brazil.

mantis \ 'mant-əs \

The mantises are a family of very large insects related to the crickets and grasshoppers. Although they are 2 to 4 inches long, their green and brown coloring makes it easy for them to hide among the leaves of plants.

These insects are often called praying mantises because of the way they sit with their forelegs raised in front of them. The forelegs are equipped with sharp hooks and are used to grasp and hold the insects' prey. The other 4 very slender legs are used for walking.

All mantises are harmless and very helpful to man. They eat many insects that damage farm crops.

The female mantis often eats the male immediately after they mate in autumn. The eggs are laid in sticky egg cases that are fastened to the branches of trees or shrubs. One female may deposit 3 to 6 egg cases, each containing 50 to 400 eggs. The young insects hatch the following spring. They resemble the adults but are yellowish-brown.

The Chinese mantis (illustrated) was brought to North America from Asia in 1895. It is now common in the eastern U.S. Females are 4 inches long and the males a little smaller.

maple

Making up a family of valuable shade and timber trees, the maples grow in nearly all parts of the northern hemisphere. Most maple trees have a straight trunk and wide-spreading branches that form a broad, rounded crown. The largest kinds grow 120 feet tall.

Nearly all maples have broad leaves that are divided into 3, 5 or 7 pointed sections. The leaves turn red or yellow in autumn.

Small green or reddish flowers appear on the twigs in early spring, before or with the new leaves. The seeds are joined together in pairs. Each seed is attached to a flat, papery wing.

The sugar maple (illustrated) is the source of hard, strong wood that is used to make furniture and flooring. Sweet

MAPLE

sap drained from the trunk of the tree in early spring is boiled down to make maple sugar and maple syrup.

The leaves of the sugar maple are 3 to 5 inches long. They turn brilliant colors in autumn. The sugar maple grows in southern Canada and the northeastern U.S. It is the state tree of New York, Vermont, West Virginia and Wisconsin. The red maple is the state tree of Rhode Island.

marble

A kind of rock that is both beautiful and useful, marble is pure white or streaked and mottled with different colors. Marble is durable, but it cuts easily and takes a high polish.

Statues and monuments are often made of marble. It is also used to finish the walls of public buildings, and for tabletops and floor tiles.

Marble is a metamorphic rock. It is limestone changed by heat and great pressure. Marble containing only calcite is snow white. Colored marbles contain small amounts of other minerals along with calcite. Black marble contains graphite. Red or yellow marble contains iron. Green marble contains chlorite.

Like other metamorphic rocks, marble is usually found where the earth's crust has been squeezed and folded into mountains. The finest of pure white marbles are quarried in Greece, Italy and Colorado. Colored marbles are quarried in Vermont, Tennessee and Georgia, and in Africa, France, Greenland and Australia.

marigold \ 'mar-ə-ˌgōld \

Marigolds are plants that have showy, strong-smelling, yellow or orange flowers. They are annuals that grow from seed and bear flowers in 1 season.

Most marigolds are bushy plants. Their leaves are divided into narrow, ragged-edged sections. The many flowers are borne singly or in clusters at the ends of the branching stems, from midsummer until frost kills the plants. The seeds are dry, flat achenes with parallel lines running from end to end.

The African marigold (illustrated) grows 30 to 48 inches tall. The French marigold grows 9 to 30 inches tall. Dwarf marigolds grow 6 to 12 inches tall. The names "African" and "French" are misleading however, since all marigolds were developed from plants native to Central and South America.

The African marigold is sometimes called the Aztec marigold, a better name for it since it came from Mexico. Its flowers are 2 to 4 inches across.

MARBLE

MARIGOLD

Marigolds grow well where the summer is hot and dry. For a long season of blooming, gardeners plant the seed indoors in early spring. They set the young plants outdoors when all danger of frost is past.

marlin \ ˈmär-lən \

The marlins are large, fierce-fighting game fish that live in the warmer parts of the oceans. They belong to a family which includes sailfish and spearfish. All of these fish have upper jaws that extend out into slender, rounded spears. They use these weapons to stun or kill the smaller fish they eat.

The largest marlins are 14 feet long and weigh more than 1,000 pounds. Fish weighing 350 pounds are common. Because of their fighting ability, these fish are among the favorite targets of deep-sea fishermen. Marlins are also a popular food fish.

Marlins usually swim alone or in small groups rather than in large schools. They are found far from shore, in deep water. They often jump out of the water, and sometimes they appear to stand on their tails on the surface.

The blue marlin (illustrated) is found in the Atlantic, as far north as New York, in the warm waters of the Gulf Stream.

The white marlin is a smaller kind that lives in the Atlantic. Black and striped marlins are found in the Pacific.

marmoset \ ˈmär-mə-ˌset \

The marmosets are a group of New World monkeys that includes the smallest of all primates. Most marmosets are the size of squirrels, but the smallest ones can curl up comfortably in a teacup.

Marmosets live in Central and South America. They are most common in the rain forests of Brazil.

Swift-moving and curious, marmosets make a variety of bird-like, chirping sounds as they scramble through treetops. They have very long tails, but they do not swing by them as some New World monkeys do. Like most monkeys, marmosets feed and travel in tribes, usually 16 or more together. They eat insects, spiders and fruit.

Females give birth to 2 or 3 young at a time. The smallest marmosets are only about an inch long when they are born. The young are usually carried by the fathers, except at feeding time. They grow to full size in about 9 months.

The golden lion marmoset (illustrated) has bright orange fur that forms a long, silky mane around the face and neck. It is about 16 inches long, including an 8-inch tail.

MARMOSET

MARLIN

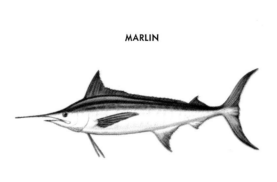

MARMOT

marmot\ˈmär-mət\(woodchuck, groundhog)

Marmots are gnawing rodents with plump bodies and thick fur. They belong to the squirrel family, and are related to chipmunks and prairie dogs. They live in nearly all parts of the northern hemisphere. In Russia they are trapped for their fur.

The smallest marmots are about 19 inches long, including the bushy tail, and weigh 4 pounds. The largest are 30 inches long and weigh 15 pounds.

Marmots live in burrows they dig in the ground, or in holes among rocks. They hibernate 7 to 8 months of the year. During the summer, they eat mostly grass, along with some other plants and a few insects.

Litters of 2 to 5 young are born to the females in midsummer. The young remain with the mother for about a year, sharing her burrow during the winter. The family groups break up the following summer, when new litters are born to the mothers.

The hoary marmot (illustrated) grows up to 30 inches long, including the 10-inch tail. It lives in the mountains of western North America from Alaska south to New Mexico.

Mars\ˈmärz\

Mars is a planet that circles the sun in an orbit just outside the earth's orbit. It is the fourth planet from the sun. At one point, it comes within 30 million miles of the earth. At another point, it is 200 million miles away from the earth.

Mars is about half the size of the earth. It rotates on its axis once in 24½ hours. One complete orbit around the sun takes 687½ days. Mars has 2 small satellites named Deimos and Phobos.

Seen with the naked eye, Mars has a reddish color. Viewed through a telescope, it is mottled with gray-green and orange and has white icecaps at the poles. These colors change somewhat with the seasons. In summer, the icecaps become smaller and the greenish patches larger and darker. Scientists believe that the greenish color may be due to some kind of plant life similar to lichens and moss, and that the brown or orange areas may be desert.

The atmosphere of Mars has traces of water vapor, along with much carbon dioxide. Winds blow on Mars, and clouds sometimes hide parts of the surface. The temperatures vary from 85° F. to −150° F.

See *The Sun, the Moon and the Planets* on p. 502.

MARS

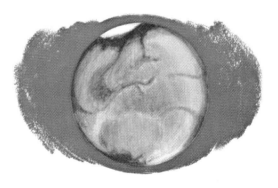

marsh

A marsh is a level place where the land is mostly covered with shallow, quiet water. Marshes are always located in places where the land does not slope enough for water to drain away quickly. Part of the water may disappear during a dry season, but the soil remains wet and muddy.

Freshwater marshes are common in many parts of the world. They contain water that falls to earth as rain or snow. Many marshes are found where land was scraped flat by glaciers. Some are found where slow-flowing streams dropped mud and sand until the stream's channel was blocked.

Salt marshes are found along the seacoasts, in places where the land slopes very gently down to the shore. Some salt marshes are located at the mouths of rivers that flow into the sea. All salt marshes contain water from the ocean mixed with water that has fallen to earth as rain or snow.

Marshes are inhabited by many water birds, such as wild ducks, bitterns and cranes. Snakes, turtles, frogs and salamanders also live in marshes.

A swamp is much like a marsh except that it has some solid land in it. Trees and bushes grow in swamps, but only grasses and low plants grow in marshes.

MARSH

MARTIN

martin \ˈmärt-ᵊn\

The martins are birds belonging to the swallow family. They live in nearly all parts of the world. All are dark-colored, but some have light gray or brown on the breast. The American martins, about 9 inches long, are the largest of the martins and also the largest of all swallows.

Martins have long, pointed wings and streamlined bodies. Their short, triangular bills are held open as they fly. They eat insects that they catch in the air.

Like the other swallows, the martins are skillful fliers that can swoop and dart gracefully. Most kinds live in colonies. In wild places, they nest in hollow trees or in nests made by other kinds of birds.

The purple martin (illustrated) nests in apartment-style birdhouses in nearly all parts of the U.S. It winters as far south as Brazil. The female has a gray breast. The 4 or 5 eggs she lays are white.

The purple martin is not an outstanding singer, but it makes pleasant twittering sounds as it flies. It is valued and protected by man because it eats many mosquitoes, as well as some other insects.

mastodon \ˈmas-tə-ˌdän\

Huge mammals that lived about 22 million years ago, mastodons are known from skeletons that have been found in many different parts of the world.

MASTODON

The mastodon looked something like an elephant. It was not a true elephant, however, as was the mammoth that lived at the same time. The mastodon was a little larger than the mammoth, and it had a lower forehead. Teeth, jaws and tusks of the animals were quite different.

A little larger than the Indian elephant of today, the mastodon stood 9½ feet tall at the shoulder. Its body was covered with thick, shaggy hair. The eyes and ears were small, but the tusks were up to 12 feet long. The legs were very sturdy.

Scientists believe that mastodons lived mostly in forests. They ate evergreen twigs, along with leaves and grasses and other plant foods. They could live in very cold climates.

Mastodons once roamed throughout Europe, Asia and North America. They must have been very common in the U.S., since a great many mastodon bones, teeth and tusks have been found in this country.

mayflower\ˈmā-ˌflaûr\(trailing arbutus)

An evergreen plant, the mayflower bears fragrant flowers early in the spring. There is often snow on the ground when they appear in early April.

The tough, hairy stems of this plant lie flat on the ground. The leaves are rounded at the tip end and are about 2½ inches long. They feel rough to the touch. They remain on the stems all winter but are dull green or brownish by spring. New leaves replace them in June.

The tube-shaped flowers are white or pale pink. They are borne in clusters along the creeping stems or at the ends of branches that stand 6 to 12 feet tall. The fruit is a 5-part seedpod containing many small seeds.

Mayflower grows from Canada south to Florida and as far west as Minnesota. It is most often seen on rocky hillsides, or in dry, sandy soil. It oftens grows among evergreen trees.

Once common throughout the eastern U.S., the mayflower is now rare in most places. The mayflower is the state flower of Massachusetts.

mayfly\ˈmā-ˌflī\

The mayflies make up a large family of insects that live only a very short time as winged adults. As nymphs, they live in water. Though these insects are very small, they hatch in great numbers and are eaten by birds, frogs, bats and fish. Many of the artificial flies used by trout fishermen are patterned after mayflies.

Adult mayflies have slender bodies and tails that look like 2 or 3 threads. Their antennae are short, and their mouths are not well developed. They do

MAYFLY

not eat as adults. The wings are transparent, and many kinds have just 1 pair.

Mayflies are seldom seen far from lakes or streams. They are active at night, and sometimes cluster around lights. After mating, the female lays tiny eggs on or in the water.

The nymphs that hatch from the eggs live in water for as long as 3 years. Some kinds swim, while others crawl on the bottom. They eat water plants. When fully grown, the nymph rises to the surface. The skin splits along the back, freeing an adult with small wings. A short time later it molts once more and appears with full-sized wings.

A mayfly with very short antennae and 2 long tails (illustrated) is common in the U.S. as far west as the Rockies.

meadowlark \ 'med-ō-ˌlärk \

Not true larks, meadowlarks belong to the American family of birds that includes the blackbirds, orioles and grackles. Their sweet, whistling song is heard in open country, in the early spring.

Plump birds 10 to 11 inches long, the meadowlarks have yellow breasts marked with a black V. There are 2 kinds, the eastern meadowlark (illustrated) and the western meadowlark. They look much alike, but their songs are different.

MEADOWLARK

MEANDER

The western meadowlark is the state bird of Kansas, Montana, Nebraska, North Dakota, Oregon and Wyoming.

Meadowlarks eat many insects, along with weed seeds and grain. They nest on the ground, in hayfields and pastures. The cleverly hidden nest has a dome-shaped roof of grass over it, and the birds enter from the side. The 4 to 7 eggs are spotted. The female incubates the eggs and does most of the nest building, but the male helps feed the young.

Meadowlarks are found only in the New World. Some birds spend the summer as far north as Canada and some winter as far south as Brazil. They nest in all parts of the U.S., and are year-round residents in the southern states.

meander \ mē-'an-dər \

A meander is a wide, loop-like bend in a river's course. Such bends are found only where the land is nearly level. They are common in flat-bottomed valleys like the lower Mississippi valley.

Slight bends develop into meanders because the swifter-flowing water swings to the outside of each curve. This current cuts away the bank on that side of the stream, and carries away soil and sand. At the same time, slower-flowing water at the inside of the curve drops the soil and

MELON

sand it carries. In time, the river's channel becomes a series of S-curves.

When the meanders become very wide, the river is likely to make new channels that are shortcuts between 1 curve and another. This often happens when the river floods. The cut-off loops then become U-shaped bodies of water called oxbow lakes.

Meanders make a river much longer than it would be if it ran straight from one place to another. Because of its meanders, the lower Mississippi River flows 1,050 miles between two points that are only 600 miles apart.

melon \ 'mel-ən \

The melons are vine-like plants that belong to the gourd family and are closely related to squashes, pumpkins and cucumbers. Native to eastern Asia, these plants have been cultivated for their fruit for hundreds of years, and many different kinds have been developed.

Melon plants are annuals that grow from seed and produce fruit in 1 season. The long stems sprawl on the ground. The leaves are mostly 3 to 5 inches long. Some leaves are broad and rounded, while others have 3 or more pointed lobes. Both leaves and stems are covered with prickly hairs, and there are curling tendrils along the stems.

The funnel-shaped flowers, about an inch in diameter, are made up of 5 petals. There are both staminate and pistillate flowers, but they grow on the same plant. The fruit develops at the base of the pistillate flowers. The sweet pulp of the fruit is green or orange.

The kinds of melons grown most in the U.S. are the muskmelons, cantaloupes and winter melons such as the casabas and honeydews. Most of these plants need a warm climate, rich soil and much moisture.

The American muskmelon or cantaloupe (illustrated) has a net-like pattern of white lines on the outside of the fruit.

For another kind of melon, see *watermelon*.

Mercury \ 'mər-kyə-rē \

Mercury is the smallest of the planets and the one closest to the sun. Mercury's diameter is about 3,100 miles, less than half that of the earth. Its average distance from the sun is 36 million miles.

Because it is so near the sun, Mercury is hard to see. It is usually in the sky at the same time as the sun. At certain times of the year it can be seen just before sunrise or just after sunset, always very low in the sky. Sometimes Mercury passes between the earth and the sun. Then astronomers see it as a dark dot crossing the sun's face.

MERCURY

Mercury moves faster than the other planets as it swings about its short orbit. It completes 1 trip around the sun in 88 days, while rotating once on its axis. It always has the same side turned toward the sun. This side of Mercury is very hot, perhaps 650° to 800° F. The other side is always dark and very cold.

Astronomers know that Mercury has a solid surface. They think it is probably rough, with jagged mountains and deep craters. There is a very thin atmosphere or none at all. It is unlikely that there is life of any kind on this planet.

See *The Sun, the Moon and the Planets* on p. 502.

Merychippus \,mer-ē-'kip-əs\

Merychippus is an extinct animal known only from fossils. It is an ancestor of the modern horse and is usually considered the third stage in the horse's evolution. It lived about 25 million years ago.

The earlier kinds of horses called Hyracotherium and Mesohippus were the size of dogs. Merychippus was the size of a small pony. It had a stocky body and sturdy, fairly long legs.

There were 3 toes on each foot, but only the large, center toe touched the ground. The center toe had a small hoof.

Merychippus held its head higher than

MERYCHIPPUS

MESA

earlier horses. Its ears and teeth were much like those of modern horses. Scientists believe that Merychippus had a short mane and a plume of long hair at the end of its slender tail.

This animal lived on prairies, where it ate grasses and other low-growing plants. Fossil bones of Merychippus have been found mostly in Europe and Asia.

mesa \'mā-sə\

A mesa is a broad hill with a flat top and steep sides. The word "mesa" means table in Spanish, and hills of this kind are often called tablelands.

A mesa was once part of a larger highland. The rest was worn away by running streams. The mesa remains because it is topped with a layer of hard rock that resisted erosion.

A butte is much like a mesa but smaller. Both mesas and buttes are found where there is little rainfall. In the U.S., they are common in the southwestern states.

Mesohippus \,me-zə-'hip-əs\

Mesohippus is an extinct animal known from fossils found in Europe, Asia and North America. It is usually thought of as the second stage in the evolution of the modern horse. It lived about 36 million years ago.

MESOHIPPUS

MESQUITE

Larger than the "dawn horse" called Hyracotherium or Eohippus, Mesohippus was 2 to 4 feet tall. The forelegs were shorter than the rather dog-like hind legs. The head slanted downward, on a line with the down-slanting back. There was a ridge of loosely folded fat on the animal's back.

Mesohippus had just 3 toes on each foot. All 3 touched the ground, but the animal's weight was carried by the center, larger toe. This toe had a heavy nail that was beginning to develop into a hoof.

The teeth of Mesohippus were quite different from the teeth of modern horses. They were adapted to chewing the broad, soft leaves of bushes and trees rather than grass. This animal lived mostly at the edges of forests, but it may have visited the open prairies at times.

Many fossil bones of Mesohippus have been found in the Big Bad Lands of South Dakota.

mesquite \ mə-'skēt \

The mesquites are thorny shrubs and small trees that belong to the pea family. Because of their deep root systems, they can live where there is very little rainfall.

Some kinds of mesquite grow 50 to 60 feet tall. Most kinds are bushy shrubs. All kinds have compound leaves made up of very small leaflets. Small greenish-white flowers appear on the twigs in spring. The fruit is a long pod containing a row of seeds that look like peas.

The hard, strong wood is used for fence posts and fuel. In places where no other kinds of trees grow, mesquite wood is sometimes used to build houses. The seeds provide food for horses and some wild animals. In some places mesquite is a nuisance because it crowds out the grasses needed by cattle.

Common, or honey, mesquite (illustrated) grows in the southwestern U.S., from Texas west to California. Other kinds of mesquite grow in Mexico, Central America and western South America.

metal

Metals are elements that are good conductors of heat and electricity, and that are generally hard and shiny. They can be pounded into different shapes, or melted and poured into molds. Most kinds can be made into wires. They are generally heavier than the other elements.

Most metals are found in ores, which are mixtures of different elements. A few kinds, such as copper and gold, are sometimes found in a naturally pure state. Man first learned to use these pure metals

METEOR

to make such objects as jewelry and weapons. Later he learned to take metals from ores, and still later to combine different metals to make alloys.

Mercury is the only metal that is a liquid at normal temperatures. Other metals become liquid when they are heated.

Some common and useful metals are aluminum, copper, gold, iron, lead, magnesium, nickel, silver, tin and zinc.

meteor \ 'mēt-ē-ər \

A meteor is sometimes called a shooting or falling star. It is not really a star at all, but a small mass of solid material that passes into the earth's atmosphere where friction heats it till it glows. Most meteors burn up before they reach the earth's surface.

Meteors may be bits of old, dead stars. Scientists think that millions of them strike the earth's atmosphere every day. Many of them are as small as grains of sand.

The few meteors that do reach the earth's surface are called meteorites. They look like dark-colored rocks or lumps of metal. They contain iron and nickel, along with other elements.

Most meteors are traveling 15 to 40 miles per second when they enter the earth's atmosphere. They become visible when they are less than 100 miles high, and they usually disappear when they are about 40 miles high. An observer on the earth's surface sees only a light streak in the dark night sky.

There seem to be more meteors in summer than in winter, and they are usually seen more often after midnight than before midnight. On any clear night, an observer watching the sky very closely can see about 10 meteors an hour.

mica \ 'mī-kə \

The micas are a group of minerals that can be split and peeled into flat sheets. The sheets can be split again and again, until they become so thin they are nearly invisible.

Thin sheets of mica will bend and stretch. Light will pass through them, but electricity will not. Mica is often used as an insulator in electrical switches.

Muscovite is a clear, colorless kind of mica that is also called isinglass. Long ago, pieces of muscovite were used to make windows in Russia. This material was also used for windows in stoves and ovens before heatproof glass was invented.

Biotite mica is black or dark brown. Phlogopite mica (illustrated) is yellowish-brown.

All mica is made up of silica and aluminum, combined with smaller amounts of

MICA

other elements. The micas are found in granite and other kinds of rocks in many different parts of the world. The finest large crystals of pure mica come from India and Canada. In the U.S., mica is mined in South Dakota, New Hampshire and North Carolina.

For a kind of mica, see *muscovite*.

mid-ocean ridge \ ˌmid-'ō-shən 'ridj \

The mid-ocean ridge is a giant mountain range under the sea. About 40,000 miles long, it passes through all the oceans. Scientists are still not certain how the ridge was formed.

The mid-ocean ridge is 300 to 1,200 miles wide. Along its slopes are many live volcanoes. A crack or gash as much as 1 mile deep and 30 miles wide runs along the center of the ridge. Most underwater earthquakes seem to begin along this crack.

Iceland and other islands are bits of the mid-ocean ridge that stick up above the water, and some of the mountain ranges of Africa seem to be branches of it.

The mid-Atlantic section (illustrated) of the mid-ocean ridge curves south from Iceland through the Atlantic Ocean. It lies about halfway between North America and Europe and between South America and Africa. In some places it takes up a third of the ocean floor.

In the southern hemisphere, the undersea mountain chain curves around Africa and Australia. It ends in the Pacific Ocean near South America.

milkweed \ 'milk-ˌwēd \

The milkweeds are a group of flowering plants that grow mostly in North and South America. Some kinds are troublesome weeds, while others are handsome wild flowers.

Nearly all of these plants contain a sticky white juice that looks like milk. Some scientists have made rubber from the juice. The tufts of silky hair attached to milkweed seeds were once used to stuff life preservers and pillows.

Most milkweeds are tall perennials with large leaves that grow opposite each other on the stems. They bear large clusters of fragrant flowers. Each flower is made up of 5 scoop-shaped hoods surrounded by 5 down-curved petals. The fruit is a pointed pod that splits open when the seeds are ripe. Winds carry the tufted seeds long distances.

Common milkweed grows 4 to 6 feet tall. The stems, pods and the undersides of the leaves are hairy. The pale, purplish flowers are borne in large, rounded clusters near the tops of the stalks. Common milkweed grows from the Atlantic coast west to Nebraska.

MID-OCEAN RIDGE

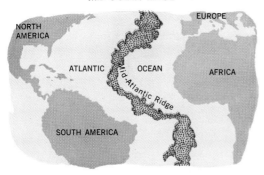

MILKWEED POD AND SEED

millipede \ˈmil-ə-ˌpēd\ (thousand-legged worm)

Millipedes belong to the group of joint-legged animals called arthropods. Their closest relatives are the centipedes, which have longer antennae and fewer legs. Although they are worm-like, they are not true worms.

Millipedes have 4 short legs on each section of the body. Some have 100 sections and 400 legs. When they walk, the many legs seem to move in waves.

Like insects and spiders, millipedes have hard skeletons on the outsides of their bodies. On their heads are 2 short antennae and 2 clusters of tiny eyes.

Millipedes live only in dark, damp places. They are most often found under rocks or logs. They eat decaying plant material, such as dead leaves and roots.

Some kinds of millipedes curl up in a spiral when disturbed. Other kinds give off a bad-smelling and poisonous liquid.

Like other arthropods, millipedes reproduce by laying eggs. Newly hatched millipedes have short bodies and only 3 pairs of legs. They molt a number of times as they grow larger, each time gaining more body sections and more legs.

One kind of millipede common in the U.S. (illustrated) has 30 to 35 body sections, and 120 to 140 short legs. It is usually about ½ inch long.

MILLIPEDE

MIMOSA TREE

mimosa \mə-ˈmō-sə\ **tree** (silk tree)

The mimosa tree is a member of the pea family admired for its showy flowers.

This tree is native to the warmer parts of Asia, from Persia to southern China. It has been planted in many other parts of the world because of its beauty. It needs a warm, moist climate.

The mimosa tree grows 20 to 30 feet tall, with slender, wide-spreading branches. The doubly compound leaves are 8 to 20 inches long. Each is a spray of 100 or more, pointed leaflets about ½ inch long.

Clusters of pink flowers are borne near the ends of the branches in June and July. In late summer, seedpods 2 to 4 inches long dangle from the branches.

In the U.S., the mimosa tree has been planted mostly in the southeastern states. A few trees grow as far north as Maryland.

mineral \ˈmin-(ə-)rəl\

Minerals are the nonliving materials that make up the earth and the planets. About 2,000 different minerals are known today. All of them are found somewhere in or on the earth's crust.

Nearly all minerals are solid substances, but a few liquids are usually classed as minerals. One of these is mercury and another is water. Coal is not a true mineral, since it is made of plant material that was once alive.

Some minerals, such as gold and copper, are single chemical elements sometimes found in a pure state. Most minerals are chemical compounds or combinations of several different elements.

A mineral can be identified by how it looks, how heavy it is and how it reacts to certain tests. Some minerals, like salt, can be identified by taste.

Rocks are made up of different minerals that have been bound together by heat, pressure or some chemical change.

mink \ 'mingk \

Minks are slender-bodied mammals of the weasel family. They are best known for their valuable fur. Very thick and glossy, mink fur is durable as well as beautiful.

Minks were once common in most of the northern hemisphere, as far south as Mexico. Today they live only in wilderness areas and on mink farms, where thousands of them are raised in cages for their furs. Wild minks are dark brown. Other colors have been developed by breeding from lighter animals born in captivity.

The American mink (illustrated) is usually 12 to 20 inches long, including the bushy, 8-inch tail. Old World minks are similar but usually have some white spots on the face or underparts.

Expert swimmers and divers, minks spend much of their time in water. They eat fish and frogs, along with birds, snakes and such animals as water rats. They

MINNOW

have sharp teeth and will fight fiercely to defend themselves or their young. They have an unpleasant odor.

Minks sleep in underground burrows or in hollow logs. They usually live alone, except during the mating season. The female bears a litter of 3 to 8 young in March or April. During the summer, the young minks follow the mother when she hunts for food. They are full-grown when about 1 year old.

minnow \ 'min-ō \

Several different kinds of small fish are called minnows in different parts of the world. Most of them are related to the carp, and all live in freshwater lakes and streams. The largest are 18 inches long.

Minnows are most important as food for larger fish. They are used as bait by both sportsmen and commercial fishermen.

All minnows have slender, streamlined bodies covered with round scales. Their heads are usually scale-less. They have teeth in the throat but none in the jaws.

Most kinds of minnows have notched tail fins and a single dorsal fin that begins about the middle of the back. In some kinds, the male develops knobs all over the body during the breeding season.

Most minnows are active, quick-moving fish. Some kinds live in muddy water, while others live only in clear water. They are found in a variety of climates and at different altitudes.

MINK

The cutlip minnow (illustrated) is found in clean, gravel-bottomed creeks in the northeastern U.S. and eastern Canada. It is up to 6 inches long and has a blunt snout that extends forward.

For another kind of minnow, see *shiner*.

mint

The mints make up a large family of perennial plants native to northern Europe and Asia. Some are garden flowers, some are kitchen herbs and some are weeds. Many kinds have fragrant leaves that are used to flavor foods and medicines.

Peppermint, spearmint, marjoram, thyme, rosemary, sage and horehound all belong to the mint family. Their leaves have tiny glands containing fragrant oils.

Most mints grow 1 to 3 feet tall. They spread by means of creeping roots (illustrated) that grow out in all directions, just under the surface of the soil.

Most kinds have small, smooth-edged leaves that grow in opposite pairs along the square stems. Small white, pinkish or purple flowers are borne along the stems, or in pointed clusters at the tops of the plants. The flowers are irregular in shape, usually 2-lipped with the upper part cut into 2 lobes and the lower part cut into 3. The fruit is a collection of small nutlets.

Plants of the mint family were brought to North America by early settlers, and

ROOT STRUCTURE OF SPEARMINT

MISTLETOE

a number of kinds now grow wild in many places.

For members of the mint family, see *catnip, coleus, lavender, peppermint, rosemary, sage, spearmint, sweet basil* and *thyme*.

mistletoe \ 'mis-əl-ˌtō \

The mistletoes are shrubby evergreen plants that grow on the branches of trees. Partly parasitic, they take some of their food from the tree they cling to. A heavy growth of mistletoe can kill a tree.

The mistletoes grow in Europe and in North America. They are found mostly on oak, alder or cottonwood trees, near water. In winter the drooping, bushy clusters of mistletoe show up clearly on the bare branches.

All mistletoes have oval, yellowish-green leaves that grow in opposite pairs along the woody stems. Clusters of tiny, yellowish flowers appear in late winter or very early spring. The fruit is a round, white or cream-colored berry.

Birds spread mistletoe from tree to tree when they eat the berries. Inside each berry is a sticky seed that often clings to the bird's bill until the bird wipes it off on a tree branch.

American mistletoe (illustrated) grows mostly in the south. It is sometimes found as far north as New Jersey and Kansas. It is the state flower of Oklahoma.

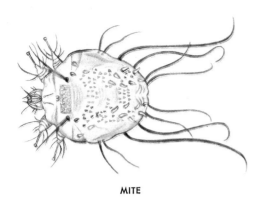

MITE

mite \ 'mīt \

The mites are a group of small, joint-legged animals related to spiders. The mite group includes the ticks and chiggers. Mites live on larger animals, in water, in soil or on plants. Many kinds spread diseases. Other harmful mites destroy farm crops, fruit trees and stored food, such as cheese and grain. A few kinds of mites feed on dead plant and animal materials and are generally helpful to man.

Most mites are less than ¼ inch long, and many kinds can be seen only through a microscope.

All mites have flattened, oval bodies. The head is joined with the body, or is very small. As adults, nearly all kinds have 4 pairs of legs. All kinds reproduce by laying eggs. The young look much like the adults but are smaller and usually have just 3 pairs of legs. The young molt many times as they grow larger.

Many kinds of mites are parasites that feed on the blood or flesh of larger animals. Some kinds, like the human itch mite (illustrated), burrow into the skin and cause painful itching. Other kinds of mites live in the lungs or stomachs of larger animals. Some kinds carry diseases of poultry and farm animals. In the tropics, some kinds carry human diseases.

For another kind of mite, see *tick*.

mockingbird \ 'mäk-ing-ˌbərd \

Mockingbirds are American birds known for their skill at imitating the songs of other birds. They belong to the same family as the catbird and the thrasher.

Mockingbirds are 8 to 12 inches long, with large, long tails and slender bills. All eat mostly insects, along with some fruit and berries. All build open, cup-shaped nests fairly near the ground.

The mockingbirds live mostly in the tropics. One kind, the eastern mockingbird (illustrated), is common as far north as Maryland and Iowa.

The eastern mockingbird is dark gray, with gray-white underparts and white markings on the wings and tail that show up clearly when the bird flies.

The loud, cheerful song of the eastern mockingbird is heard at night and during the day, at all times of the year. This bird imitates human and animal sounds, as well as the songs of other birds.

Active and fearless, the eastern mockingbird will fight fiercely to defend its territory from other birds, or from dogs and cats. It usually nests in a bushy shrub. The female incubates the 3 to 6 spotted eggs. Both parents feed the young birds.

The mockingbird is the state bird of Arkansas, Florida, Mississippi, Tennessee and Texas.

MOCKINGBIRD

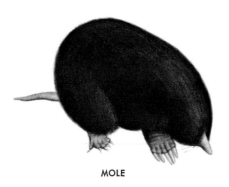

MOLE

MOLYBDENITE

mole \ 'mōl \

The moles are a group of small, insect-eating mammals related to the shrews. They live in Europe, northern Asia and North America. Some kinds crawl on the surface of the earth, swim in streams or even climb low trees. Most kinds live entirely underground. Some have weak eyesight, while others are blind.

Most moles are 6 to 9 inches long. Their plump bodies are covered with velvety fur that is dark brown, dark gray or black. Short legs, broad feet and strong claws make these animals expert diggers. As the mole tunnels along, its rubbery snout feels in the soil for earthworms, grubs and beetles. Moles are generally helpful to man because they control harmful insects and loosen the soil.

Most moles dig 2 sets of tunnels. Feeding tunnels are only a few inches under the surface, and often make raised ridges. The animal's home is another set of tunnels, deeper underground.

Males and females generally live apart, except during the mating season. Females bear 1 or 2 litters of 1 to 6 young each year. Newborn moles are blind and hairless. They grow to full size in about a month.

The eastern mole (illustrated) is common in the U.S. from the Atlantic coast to the Great Plains. It is 8½ inches long.

mollusk \ 'mäl-əsk \

Mollusks make up a large group of invertebrate animals that includes the snails, clams and octopuses. All but a few of them live in water. Nearly all use lime to build hard shells around their soft bodies.

The snails and their relatives, such as the whelks, have just 1 shell usually twisted into a spiral. The clams and their relatives, such as the scallops, have a pair of matching shells hinged along 1 side.

The slugs, squids, octopuses and some others have small shells hidden inside their bodies, or no shells at all.

A layer of flesh called the mantle covers most of the mollusk's body. The mantle secretes the shell, building it from the inside out. A strong, muscular foot attached to one end of the body is used for creeping, digging or swimming.

Mollusks breathe through gills. They feed on both plants and animals. Some kinds have both male and female reproductive organs. Most lay eggs but some bear living young.

Many kinds of mollusks are eaten by man. Others are valued for their shells or for the pearls they produce.

For kinds of mollusks, see *abalone, chiton, clam, cockleshell, conch, cone, cowrie, cuttlefish, murex, mussel, nautilus, octopus, oyster, oyster drill, scallop, shell, snail, squid* and *whelk*.

molybdenite \ mə-'lib-də-,nīt \

The mineral molybdenite is a valuable ore of molybdenum, a rare silver-white metal that is added to steel to make it very strong. Steel made with molybdenum is used to make metal-cutting tools, guns and armor plate.

Molybdenite is found in small plates or scales attached to igneous rocks such as granite. The bits of molybdenite are black or dark gray and fairly soft. They feel greasy to the touch.

Most of the molybdenite mined as an ore comes from Colorado. Smaller quantities have been found in the New England states, Utah and New Mexico, and in China, Australia, Norway and Sweden.

monadnock \ mə-'nad-,näk \

A monadnock is a hill or small mountain of solid rock that stands in a fairly level area.

Monadnocks are found where the general level of the land has been lowered by stream erosion. Monadnocks are formed slowly over millions of years. Running water first carries loose stones and soil away, and then the softer rocks are worn away. Finally, an isolated mass of very hard rock that resists erosion remains as a monadnock.

Formations of this kind are named for Mt. Monadnock, the highest point in southern New Hampshire. It is a rock peak that stands 3,166 feet above sea level. Stone Mountain near Atlanta, Georgia, is another famous monadnock. It is a rounded outcropping of pale gray granite.

mongoose \ 'män-,güs \

Mongooses are a group of swift-moving, furry animals native to the Old World. They are best known for their skill at killing snakes. The ancient Egyptians kept mongooses in their homes to rid them of both snakes and rats. They are still used for this purpose in some countries.

Mongooses raised in captivity make interesting pets, but strict laws keep them out of the U.S. They have become serious pests in some areas. Like all mammals, they can carry rabies.

Most mongooses are about 20 inches long, including the fairly long, bushy tail. All have pointed snouts, small ears and coarse gray or brown fur.

Mongooses are native to Africa, Asia and the countries around the Mediterranean Sea. They kill and eat lizards, insects and birds, as well as snakes and rats. They live in underground burrows. Females give birth to 2 or more litters each year. There are usually 2 or 3 young in each litter.

The common Indian mongoose (illustrated) is silvery-gray and about 33 inches long.

MONADNOCK

MONGOOSE

monkey

The monkeys are primates closely related to the apes. They are generally smaller than apes and have longer tails. Monkeys live in forests in nearly all of the warmer parts of the world.

In the Old World, monkeys live in Africa, southern Asia and on the Rock of Gibraltar. Old World monkeys include the largest as well as the oddest-looking kinds, which have patches of bare, bright-colored skin.

New World monkeys live in Central and South America. They have broader noses and more teeth than Old World monkeys. Many kinds of New World monkeys have prehensile tails. Some, but not all New World monkeys, can swing by their tails. Old World monkeys do not have prehensile tails.

All monkeys are good climbers, and all spend at least part of their time in trees. They eat plant materials such as leaves, fruit and nuts. Some kinds also eat insects, small animals and bird eggs.

Nearly all monkeys live in groups called tribes. Most tribes are made up of 10 to 25 monkeys of different sizes and ages, led by 1 old male. The tribe travels and feeds together, and will often fight another tribe that invades its territory.

Unlike most animals, monkeys can breed at any time during the year. The young are usually born singly, but twins are not uncommon.

The capuchin, howler, spider and woolly monkeys are all native to the New World. The howler monkey seldom lives long in captivity, but the other kinds are easy to care for, and they make good pets.

Capuchin monkeys are intelligent and easily trained. They are often seen doing tricks in circuses and zoos. Fourteen to 19 inches long, they are brown or black, with lighter hair on the face and chest.

Most kinds of capuchins have a cap of dark fur on top of the head.

Spider monkeys are small and very quick-moving. Their bodies are slender, and their arms and legs are unusually long. Some spider monkeys easily jump 30 feet from one tree to another.

Woolly monkeys are larger and move more slowly than spider monkeys. They make good pets, since they are more gentle than most monkeys and are very neat and clean. Their thick, soft fur is white, brown or dark gray.

The howler monkeys have dog-like faces. They are the ugliest and the noisiest of all the New World monkeys. Old males make loud roaring sounds that can be heard from 2 miles away.

The green, proboscis and rhesus monkeys all live in the Old World. The green monkey is native to South Africa. Equally at home in trees or on the ground, it climbs nimbly and can also run fast on all fours.

The large, odd-looking proboscis monkey lives in the lowland forests and swamps of Borneo. Old males are 30 inches tall, with tails 30 inches long. Some weigh as much as 50 pounds. Females are smaller. Only males have the long, grooved noses. Both males and females have hairless, pinkish faces that turn red when angry. The proboscis monkey seldom lives long in captivity.

The hardy and intelligent rhesus monkey is widely used in scientific research, as it lives well in captivity. Because it reacts to many drugs in the same way humans do, the rhesus monkey is used for developing and testing vaccines and medicines. In the early phases of the space program, rhesus monkeys were sent on rocket flights beyond the atmosphere.

Adult rhesus monkeys are about 24 inches long. Their tails are fairly short, and their hands look much like human hands. They are native to India, southern China, Burma and Thailand.

Monkeys of the World

CAPUCHIN MONKEY

GREEN MONKEY

HOWLER MONKEY

PROBOSCIS MONKEY

RHESUS MONKEY

SPIDER MONKEY

WOOLLY MONKEY

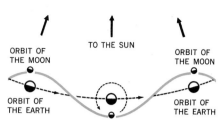

MOON'S ORBIT IN RELATION TO THE SUN

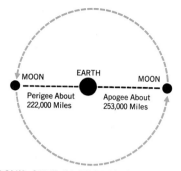

MOON'S ORBIT IN RELATION TO THE EARTH

moon

The moon is the earth's only natural satellite. Its diameter is ¼ that of the earth. Its average distance from the earth is 238,857 miles. It rotates once on its axis as it completes 1 fairly circular orbit of the earth every 29½ days, so the same face is always turned toward the earth.

The moon has rugged mountains, circular craters, softly rolling surfaces and broad, flat plains that were once thought to be seas. The surface of the plains appears to be covered with a dry, dust-like material. Temperatures on the surface range from 215° F. to −240° F.

As it orbits the earth, the moon's position in relation to the sun's light is constantly changing. This change causes the phases of the moon (illustrated). The phase called full moon takes place when the moon and sun are on opposite sides of the earth, so that all the visible face of the moon is lighted. The phase called new moon takes place when the sun and moon

are on the same side of the earth. At this time almost none of the visible face of the moon is lighted by the sun.

A gibbous moon occurs when more than half but less than the full face is lighted. It is a crescent moon when less than half the face is lighted. The first quarter moon has the right half illuminated. The third quarter moon has the left half illuminated.

A waning moon is passing from full to new, so that each night less of the face is lighted. A waxing moon is passing from new to full, so that each night more of the face is lighted.

In the northern hemisphere, the full moon nearest September 23 is called the harvest moon. The next full moon after the harvest moon is called the hunter's moon.

See *The Sun, the Moon and the Planets* on p. 502.

moonstone \ 'mün-ˌstōn \

A semiprecious mineral used in jewelry, moonstone is white with a pale blue sheen. It has a pearly luster, and faint rainbow colors may be visible in it.

Moonstone is a rare kind of albite, a mineral of the alkali feldspar group. Crystals of moonstone usually show a pattern of fine parallel grooves or lines along broken surfaces.

Most of the valuable moonstones come from Ceylon. Some have been found in Switzerland and, in the U.S., in the New England states and Virginia.

PHASES OF THE MOON

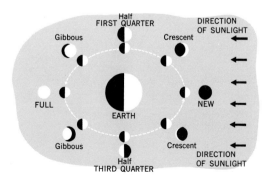

MOOSE

moose

Moose are grazing animals of the deer family. They are the largest hoofed mammals native to North America. Moose are 6½ to 7 feet tall at the shoulders, with long legs, large heads and very short tails.

Both male and female moose have growths of skin and hair that hang down under the neck. The males have large, branching antlers with broad, scoop-like parts. Some antlers weigh as much as 100 pounds.

Males shed their antlers in January and grow new ones by August, before the autumn mating season. Young moose, called calves, are born in early spring and stay with the parents for about a year.

Moose live in forested areas near shallow lakes. They are expert swimmers, and they eat plants that grow in water. They also eat the leaves and twigs of trees, grass, moss and lichens.

The Alaskan moose (illustrated) weighs up to 1,800 pounds, and is powerful enough to fight off a large bear. The slightly smaller common moose lives as far south as Ontario, Maine and the Dakotas.

moraine \ mə-'rān \

Moraines are hills, ridges or plains made up of different sizes and kinds of rocks and smaller particles deposited by a melting glacier. These different materials never occur in layers, as do sediments dropped by running water.

End or terminal moraines are ridges that mark the farthest point reached by a glacier. They contain the loose material that was pushed ahead of the glacier. These moraines are at right angles to the direction the glacier was moving.

Lateral moraines are long, low ridges. They were formed at the sides of the glacier and are parallel to the movement of the glacier.

Ground moraines are level deposits that lay beneath the glacier.

Moraines are common in northern Europe and Asia, and in Canada. In the U.S., they are found as far south as New York City, Cincinnati, St. Louis and Omaha.

See *end moraine.*

moray \ mə-'rā \

Morays make up a family of eels with sharp teeth and strong jaws. Vicious hunters, these fish hide in cracks between rocks until their prey moves near. Then they dart out to attack. Skin divers have been painfully bitten by them. There are 80 or more different kinds of morays.

Like other eels, morays have very long, snake-like bodies, ranging from 2 to 10 feet in length. Their tough skin is scaleless. They have ribbon-like dorsal and anal fins that run to the tip of the tail.

Morays have no pelvic and pectoral fins. Their gill openings are round and very small, like pores in the skin. Little is known about their reproduction, but sci-

MORAY

entists think that young morays do not pass through a larval stage.

Morays live in all the warmer parts of the oceans, but they are most common along rocky coasts and near coral reefs. Some kinds are good to eat. Other kinds are believed to be poisonous.

The spotted moray (illustrated) is common in waters around the West Indies.

morel \ mə-'rel \

The morels are a group of fungi that look like sponges set on short, smooth stems. Some kinds are very good to eat.

Like their relatives the mushrooms and toadstools, morels are plants that lack chlorophyll and cannot manufacture their own food from minerals in the soil. Instead, they exist on dead plant materials such as fallen leaves and rotting wood.

The largest part of the morel lives underground and is nearly invisible. It is like a tangle of slender, colorless threads. The part of the morel plant that appears aboveground in spring is a kind of fruit. When it ripens, tiny spores fall from the hollows near the top. Spores that fall on moist, rich soil grow into new plants.

The common edible morel (illustrated) is yellow-white or light brown. It grows 4 to 8 inches tall. It is found in most parts of the U.S., in wooded, moist places.

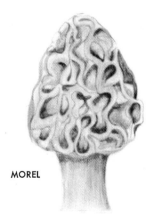

MOREL

MORNING GLORY

morning glory

Morning glories make up a family of about 400 kinds of climbing vines. Some kinds are annuals, while other kinds are perennials. Some kinds are weeds, others are garden flowers and still others useful food plants. The sweet potato belongs to the morning glory family.

Morning glories are native to tropical South America, but they have been planted in many other parts of the world. In some places they have escaped from cultivation and become weeds.

These plants are named for their flowers, which open early in the morning but usually close soon after noon. Shaped like bells or funnels, the flowers are blue, purple, red or white. In most kinds, the flower untwists as it opens from the bud. The fruit is an egg-shaped seedpod.

The leaves are oval or heart-shaped. Most kinds have simple leaves, but some kinds have compound leaves.

Common morning glory (illustrated) is an easy-to-grow garden vine. An annual, it grows 10 to 20 feet tall from seed planted in the spring. Many large flowers appear along the stems from early summer through autumn.

For another member of the morning glory family, see *sweet potato*.

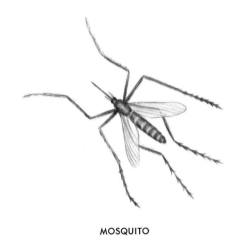

MOSQUITO

mosquito \ mə-'skēt-o \

Mosquitoes make up a family of almost 2,000 kinds of small flies. They are pests and can be carriers of diseases such as yellow fever, malaria and elephantiasis. Mosquitoes are found as far north as the Arctic Circle. Much money is spent to control these insects.

Mosquitoes have long, slender abdomens and narrow, transparent wings. They are yellowish or greenish, red-brown, dark brown or black. Males feed on flower nectar and other plant juices. Some kinds of females are bloodsuckers.

Eggs are laid on water and hatch the next year. The larvae, called wrigglers, live in water and breathe through an air tube near the end of the body. They feed on water plants and go through 4 molts before becoming pupae and adults. Their entire life cycle takes 2 to 3 weeks. The male adult lives about 1 week. The female adult lives about 1 month.

The house mosquito common in the U.S. (illustrated) is a pest but not a carrier of human disease.

The anopheles mosquitoes that carry malaria look much like the house mosquito but have spotted wings. The females hold their bodies tilted down when they bite.

moss

The mosses are a group of primitive plants that do not have true roots, stems or leaves. The mosses and their close relatives, the liverworts, may be much like the first plants that lived on land billions of years ago. Mosses are found in all but the driest and coldest parts of the world.

Moss plants grow crowded together. The largest kinds become 8 inches tall. Most kinds cling to moist, shaded soil, rocks or tree trunks. Some kinds grow in shallow water.

Alternation of generations takes place in mosses. Green moss plants produce 2 kinds of gametes that join when rain or dew covers the plants with a film of water. From the joined gametes, a second kind of plant grows on top of the first. Usually brown, it looks like a slender stem with a tiny pod at the tip. Spores fall from this pod onto moist soil and grow into new green moss plants.

Common haircap moss (illustrated) grows 2 to 8 inches tall and is found in most parts of North America. The green gamete-producing plants look like tiny pine trees growing close together. The slender spore-producing plants form a "hairy cap" over the green moss at some times during the year.

MOSS

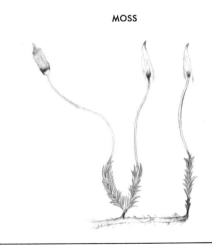

Moths
Insects of the Night

BROWNTAIL MOTH

CECROPIA MOTH

WHITE-LINED
SPHINX MOTH

HUMMINGBIRD MOTH

IO MOTH

LUNA MOTH

POLYPHEMUS MOTH

PROMETHEA MOTH

298   CYNTHIA MOTH

UNDERWING MOTH

moth

Moths make up a group of insects closely related to butterflies. Both moths and butterflies have 2 pairs of wings. There are a number of differences, however. Moths have plumper bodies than butterflies, and they are not so colorful. They fly at night, while butterflies are active during the day. At rest, a moth holds its wings straight out, while a butterfly holds its wings up. Moths live in all but the coldest parts of the world.

The largest moths have a wingspread of about 6 inches. Both body and wings are hairy. The antennae are slender or feathery, and they seldom have a knob at the end. A few kinds are bright-colored, but most are soft shades of gray or brown.

Adult moths eat only nectar which they suck from flowers. By feeding on nectar, adult moths help to pollinate flowers. Moths have tube-like mouths that coil up like springs. Some kinds of moths do not eat at all. All moths have short life-spans.

All moths pass through the 4 stages of complete metamorphosis: egg, larva, pupa and adult. The small eggs are usually laid in groups on green plants. The larvae that hatch from the eggs are caterpillars. Most kinds of moth caterpillars eat leaves, and some are pests that damage fruit trees, shade trees and farm crops.

Moth larvae molt a number of times as they grow larger. When they are ready to pass into the pupa or resting stage, they spin a silk thread and use it to build a cocoon. Some kinds fasten their cocoons to twigs, or place them inside rolled-up leaves. Other kinds hide their cocoons in the soil, or in wood.

Most kinds of moths pass the winter in the pupa state, inside cocoons. They are adults when they come out in spring. Some kinds lay eggs in autumn which do not hatch until spring.

The browntail moth is a pest that was accidently brought to North America from Europe. It is now common in the New England states and in southern Canada. The adults are up to 1½ inches across. The browntail has a dark body and pale, creamy-white wings. The larvae live together in groups on trees. They spin silk threads and construct a large, tent-like nest around their colony.

The cecropia, io, luna, polyphemus, promethea and cynthia moths all belong to 1 family called the saturnids. As adults, most are quite large, with broad, strongly patterned wings. On the wings of some are spots that look like eyes. All adult saturnids have poorly developed mouths and do not eat.

Saturnid moth larvae are large caterpillars that are usually spiny rather than hairy. Some are bright-colored. They feed on the leaves of trees and shrubs. Io and luna moth larvae drop to the ground and spin their cocoons under grass or dead leaves. The others attach their cocoons to leaves or twigs on a tree.

The white-lined sphinx and the hummingbird moths belong to a family called the hawk or sphinx moths. As adults, they have broad bodies and slender, pointed wings. They have tube-like mouths up to 6 inches long.

Hawk moth larvae are large caterpillars. They are sometimes called hornworms because of the horn-like growths at the ends of their bodies. They damage some farm crops. The caterpillars called tomato worms and tobacco worms are both hawk moth larvae.

The underwing moth is hard to see when it clings to a tree trunk, because it folds its colorful rear wings under the dull brown forewings. Its eggs remain unhatched during the winter. The larvae are dull, hairless caterpillars that taper at both ends. They feed on forest trees and form their cocoons on the ground.

COMPLEX MOUNTAIN

MOUNTAIN LAUREL

mountain

Mountains are large masses of rock and earth much higher than the land around them. They become narrower as they rise, and the top is usually a single peak or a narrow ridge. The sides generally slope at an angle of from 20 to 40 degrees.

Mountains cover almost ⅕ of the land area of the world. Almost always grouped in long ranges or belts, they are often near an ocean, running parallel to shore.

Young mountains are sharp and rugged, with surfaces of bare rock. Old mountains have gentle slopes rising to rounded summits. They are usually covered with soil, trees and other plants. Many mountains are the result of movements of the earth's crust.

A block mountain, such as the 400-mile-long Sierra Nevada range, is a single mass of rock that was tilted upward.

A complex mountain (illustrated) is an irregular formation caused by a combination of forces. Horizontal pressures, volcanic eruption and folding and slipping of rock layers may all be involved. Most large mountain ranges, including the Alps, Rockies and Appalachians, are complex mountains. The Alps and Rockies are young mountains, while the Appalachians are very old.

mountain laurel \ 'lȯr-əl \

Mountain laurel is an evergreen shrub or small tree which bears clusters of white, purple or pink blossoms in late spring.

Mountain laurel usually grows from 5 to 25 feet tall. The short, often crooked, trunk is covered with smooth brown bark. The thick, leathery leaves are 3 to 5 inches long. They are dark green on the upper surface and paler green underneath. Most of the leaves grow crowded together near the ends of the branches.

The flowers are about 1 inch across, and open out into 5 broad lobes. They are grouped in rounded clusters 4 to 5 inches across. The fruit of the plant is a ball-shaped seedpod that splits apart into 5 sections to release tiny, winged seeds.

Mountain laurel grows wild in eastern North America from New Brunswick to Florida and as far west as Kentucky and Louisiana. It is the state flower of Connecticut and Pennsylvania.

mouse

Mice make up a large group of small rodents. They live in all parts of the world except for a few Pacific islands. There are 4 families of mice: Old World mice, New World mice, jumping mice and pocket or kangaroo mice.

MOUSE

The Old World mouse family includes kinds that carry diseases and destroy great amounts of stored foods. The common house mouse (illustrated) is typical of this family. Native to Asia, it is now found wherever man lives, even on ships at sea. It lives in houses and barns, as well as in fields and wooded areas. It is about 4 inches long, with a 3-inch tail.

The house mouse usually sleeps during the day and moves about looking for food at night. It will eat almost anything, and it damages clothing and books.

The white mouse used in scientific experiments and sometimes kept as a pet is an albino house mouse.

Mice mate frequently and produce large litters. The young are often full-grown and ready to breed when 2 or 3 months old. One male and female house mouse may produce 1,000 descendants within a year.

mudcrack \ 'məd-ˌkrak \

Mudcracks are shallow splits in mud. They form when clay-rich soil deposited by water is dried by the sun and wind. The clay in the soil expands as it absorbs water. It shrinks as it dries, causing the surface to pull apart into odd-shaped sections. The breaks in the surface are mudcracks. Mudcracks often form on the beds of dry lakes, and along the edges of streams. They often form a network.

Mudcracks generally disappear when water flows over them. If there is no rain for a very long time, however, the clay may harden and become rock.

Geologists sometimes find mudcrack patterns in desert rocks. This tells them that there were once heavy rains there, or large rivers that flooded the land.

mudminnow \ 'məd-ˌmin-ō \

The mudminnows make up a family of small, freshwater fish something like topminnows but more closely related to the pike. Mudminnows are valuable as bait fish and as food for larger fish.

Mudminnows have a chunky body about 2 inches long, a stubby snout and a rounded tail. Both head and body are covered with large scales. The dorsal fin is near the rear of the fish's body, opposite the anal fin. All fins are transparent.

These fish are found in the northern U.S. and southern Canada, throughout the upper Mississippi valley and the Great Lakes regions. Their chief foods are insects, crustaceans and water plants.

Mudminnows are most often found in slow-running waters with mud bottoms. When startled, they bury themselves, tail first, in the mud.

The largest kind, sometimes reaching 6 inches, is the central mudminnow (illustrated). It is found from the Great Lakes to the Mississippi basin.

MUDMINNOW

MUD PUPPY

mud puppy

The mud puppy is a large salamander. Unlike other salamanders, the mud puppy has feathery gills outside its body even when it is an adult.

Larger than most salamanders, the mud puppy grows 12 to 18 inches long. It has a flat body, short legs and a long tail. The smooth skin is greenish-brown or gray, spotted with yellow or black. The gills that extend out from both sides of the body, just behind the head, are dark red.

Mud puppies live at the bottom of muddy streams and ponds. They usually sleep during the day and move about looking for food at night. Mud puppies eat insect larvae, crayfish, fish eggs and tiny crustaceans.

Although mud puppies mate in autumn, the female does not lay eggs until spring. She fastens the 100 or more tiny jelly-covered eggs to rocks or plants under water. She usually remains near the eggs until they hatch 5 to 8 weeks later. Newly hatched mud puppies are striped and less than 1 inch long. They grow to full size in about 5 years.

Mud puppies are fairly common near the Great Lakes, throughout the central U.S. and southern Canada.

mulberry \ 'məl-ˌber-ē \

The mulberries make up a family of fruit-bearing trees and shrubs native to eastern North America, Asia, and parts of Mexico and South America. The long-lasting wood is often used for fence posts and boats. Indians made cloth from mulberry bark.

The leaves may be heart-shaped, mitten-shaped or deeply cut into 3 to 7 irregular lobes. All have fine, saw-toothed edges. The flowers are green tassels that dangle from the twigs in spring. Staminate and pistillate flowers grow on separate branches or on different trees. The female flower develops into the fruit, which is a cluster of small juicy berries.

The red mulberry (illustrated) grows throughout the eastern half of the U.S. It is valued for its fruit. The berry cluster is bright red when it first appears. When ripe, in midsummer, it is dark purple and about 1 inch long. The tree grows 50 to 75 feet tall, with a short trunk and heavy spreading branches. The blue-green leaves have a rough surface and are 3 to 9 inches long.

The white mulberry is native to China, where its leaves are used to feed silkworms.

For other members of the mulberry family, see *fig tree, osage orange* and *paper mulberry.*

MULBERRY

MULE

mule

The mule is a hybrid animal, the offspring of a male donkey and a female horse, or mare. When a male horse, or stallion, is mated with a female donkey, the resulting foal is a hinny, an animal not nearly so valuable as the mule.

Mules were first bred and used as work animals in Asia, 3,000 years ago.

The mule stands 4 to 5½ feet at the shoulders and weighs from 600 to 1,400 pounds. It has the large body and strong muscles of its mother and the long ears, short mane, tufted tail and loud bray of its father. The mule also inherits the donkey's patience, sure-footedness and endurance.

Because mules are less likely to be affected by fatigue or illness than horses, they were once widely used for rough work in mines, in construction camps, on military bases and on farms. Today, most mules in the U.S. are found in the southern states. In other parts of the country they have been largely replaced by tractors and trucks.

The mule's life-span is about the same as that of the horse. All male mules and most female mules are sterile and cannot reproduce.

mullet \ 'məl-ət \

The mullets make up a family of about 100 different ocean fish. Most kinds are good to eat. The flesh is sometimes smoked. Mullets are not important commercially because they cannot be caught in large numbers.

Most mullets are 2 to 3 feet long. They have rounded bodies, blunt snouts and small mouths. The first dorsal fin contains 4 stiff spines. The tail fin is long and V-shaped. The scales are medium-sized, and the color is greenish-gray or silvery.

Mullets are schooling fish that live in the warmer parts of the sea, in shallow water near shore. In the tropics, some kinds enter streams and live in freshwater.

Mullets that have teeth eat smaller fish. Kinds that lack teeth eat aquatic plants along with tiny worms and crustaceans they find in mud or sand.

All mullets move to deeper water, farther from shore, to spawn. The different kinds spawn at different times of the year.

The striped mullet (illustrated) is found along both Atlantic and Pacific coasts of the U.S. In Florida it is called the black mullet. One of the largest kinds, it grows up to 3 feet long and weighs as much as 15 pounds.

The red mullet, popular as a food fish in Europe, is a different kind of ocean fish belonging to another family.

MULLET

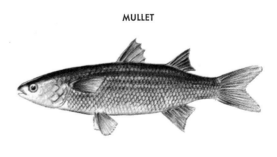

murex \ 'myŭr-,eks \

The murexes make up a group of gastropod mollusks. They live on the sea floor in warm, shallow parts of the oceans. Murexes are most common in the tropics.

Some kinds of murexes feed entirely on other mollusks. Such murexes are considered pests in areas where they destroy valuable oysters.

The murex has eyes set on stalks and a long, narrow tongue that is edged with sharp teeth. The animal travels by means of a muscular foot. The murex has a horny plate which can be used to close the opening when it withdraws into its 1-piece, spiral shell.

Murex shells are thick and heavily ridged. Most kinds have pointed spines and rows of knobs. They are 1 to 6 inches long. The outer surface is yellowish-white, light brown or gray, and is marked with darker spots or stripes. The opening is broad and rounded, and the inner surface is pink or rose-colored. Murex shells from the tropics are usually more colorful and spinier than shells from the temperate zone.

The apple murex shell (illustrated) is usually 1 to 3 inches long. It is pale yellow, marked with reddish brown. Common on Florida beaches, it is sometimes found as far north as the Carolinas.

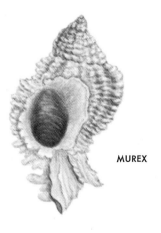

MUREX

MUSCOVITE

muscovite \ 'məs-kə-,vīt \

The mineral muscovite, sometimes called isinglass, is the most nearly colorless kind of mica. It is widely used in electronic equipment and as an insulating material in electrical appliances.

Like other kinds of mica, muscovite is found in crystals which can be split into very thin sheets. These are both flexible and elastic. Thin sheets of muscovite are colorless and perfectly transparent. Thick sheets are yellowish or greenish.

Muscovite is found in granite and other coarse igneous rocks such as gneiss. It is seldom found in fine-textured volcanic rocks such as basalt.

Most muscovite is mined in India. It is also mined in Brazil, in Canada and, in the U.S., in North Carolina, South Dakota and Connecticut.

This mineral's name comes from Muscovy, an old name for Moscow, where muscovite was once used as window glass.

mushroom

Many different kinds of fungi are commonly called mushrooms. Some are very good to eat, while others that look almost exactly like them are highly poisonous.

Like other fungi, the mushrooms are plants that have no chlorophyll and cannot manufacture their own food from minerals in the soil. Mushrooms are

MUSHROOM

saprophytes, plants that feed on decaying plant material. The true plant body of the mushroom lives underground. The growth that appears aboveground is a reproductive part something like a fruit. Tiny spores that fall from slits under the cap grow into new mushroom plants.

Some kinds of mushrooms grow in wooded places, while other kinds grow in open fields. They are found around the world, in nearly all parts of the temperate zone. Most kinds are white or light brown, but some are bright-colored.

The meadow mushroom (illustrated) is 2 to 5 inches tall. When it first appears above the ground, the cap is ball-shaped. The gill slits under the cap are pinkish, but turn purplish-brown as the spores ripen. This kind of mushroom is grown commercially and sold, fresh or canned, in food markets.

muskellunge \ 'məs-kə-ˌlənj \

The muskellunge is a large freshwater fish that belongs to the pike family. Because of its vicious nature, strength and energy, it is considered one of the finest freshwater game fish. It is an excellent food fish.

There are several ways to spell muskellunge, among them "muskalonge" and "musquilongue." Fishermen often call the fish a "muskie" or "musky."

The muskellunge has a long, rounded body which may grow more than 5 feet long. It has a long, pointed head and a protruding underjaw. Both jaws have long, sharp teeth. The tail is forked. The dorsal fin is far back on the body, opposite the anal fin. While the average weight is 15 pounds, the fish may reach 70 pounds.

The muskellunge lives in lakes and rivers that have cool, clear water and weedy bottoms. It is found in southern Canada, the upper Mississippi Valley, the Great Lakes and the St. Lawrence and Ohio rivers. It lives in deep water in summer, and in shallower water in spring and fall.

This fish eats frogs, fish, snakes and any other small animals that come its way. Spawning occurs in spring, usually in shallow water or flooded marshes.

musk-ox \ 'məsk-ˌäks \

The musk-ox is a shaggy mammal belonging to the family that includes oxen, sheep, antelopes and goats. It looks something like a buffalo. It was named for a musky smell once thought to be produced by glands in front of its eyes. Actually, unless greatly excited, the musk-ox has no odor at all. It is an ancient animal, and fossil remains dating back thousands of centuries have been found.

The bull musk-ox is about 8 feet long and 6 feet tall at the humped shoulder. The cow is smaller than the bull. The coarse, shaggy, dark-brown or black fur

MUSK-OX

MUSKRAT

hangs almost to the ground. The fur is curly or matted over the shoulders but straight on the rest of the body. Both sexes have horns and whitish feet.

Musk-oxen live in large herds, staying in higher areas in winter but returning to the valleys in summer. They graze on grasses, twigs and leaves.

Mating is in August, every other year. The single calf weighs about 25 pounds at birth and is able to join the herd about 2 hours after it is born.

Hunted widely for their meat and fur, musk-oxen are now found only in small areas of northern Canada and Greenland. Centuries ago, they also roamed the barren Arctic regions of Europe and Asia.

muskrat \ 'məsk-ˌrat \

The muskrat is a large water rodent. It is named for its musky odor. More muskrats are trapped each year for their fur than all other fur-bearing animals put together.

The muskrat is dark brown to grayish yellow above and gray underneath. It is about 18 to 22 inches long, including a 10-inch tail. The tail is black, scaly and hairless, and is flattened vertically. The hind feet are partly webbed.

Muskrats are native to the U.S., from Alaska to the Gulf of Mexico, but they are not found on the west coast south of Oregon. They live in large groups in fresh or saltwater marshes, ponds, rivers and lakes. Active both day and night, they eat cattails and other plants and, sometimes, crayfish and mollusks.

In summer, muskrats dig a burrow in a stream bank, with an entrance above water or underwater. In fall, a cone-shaped house is built in the center of a swamp or pond, which may be many miles from the burrow. The house may extend 3 or 4 feet above the water.

Two litters of 5 to 9 pups are born each year. One litter is born in spring and the other in late summer.

mussel \ 'məs-əl \

Mussels make up several families of bivalve mollusks. There are several hundred kinds of mussels, both saltwater and freshwater forms. They are all important as food for water animals. Some of both kinds are used by man for food. Pearl-like buttons are made from the shells.

The mussel shell has 2 halves joined by a ligament and hinged teeth. It is held shut by strong muscles. The animal lacks eyes and tentacles and sometimes has no head. Two siphon tubes take in and pass out water. In this manner, plankton and other organic food are taken in and wastes are passed out. Some mussels move with a heavy muscular foot.

Saltwater mussels are usually found in the cooler seas, often in dense beds or

HABITAT OF MARINE MUSSEL

MYNAH BIRD

clusters (illustrated). Their shells vary in size from 2 to 6 inches and range in color from dark blue to greenish-brown. Between April and September females cast out millions of eggs. The young pass through several changes of shape before becoming anchored and taking adult form.

Freshwater mussels live in all parts of the world, but mostly in North America. From ½ to 4 inches long, the shells are rounded and clam-like, with circular growth lines. They may range in color from white to greenish-brown.

mustard \ 'məs-tərd \

The mustard family contains over 200 kinds of annual and perennial plants. It includes many important, cabbage-like food plants as well as many weeds.

On mustard plants, yellow or white flowers bloom in summer or early fall, clustering at the end of the stem. The small, blue-green leaves may be lobed, toothed or cut. If picked while young, the leaves of some plants may be eaten in salads. They are very rich in vitamins A, B and C.

The stalked seedpod is long and narrow and contains several seeds. The seeds of some plants are ground and used as a powder to season foods. They are also made into the familiar yellow paste used to season hot dogs and sandwiches.

MUSTARD

Most prepared commercial mustard is made from the seeds of the black mustard plant (illustrated). Black mustard has clusters of small, yellow flowers and hairy, lobed leaves. Fruit pods 1 inch long stand along the sides of the main stem.

Mustard was once used as a home medical remedy. It is still used to cause vomiting in certain cases of poisoning.

For other members of the mustard family, see *cabbage, cress, radish* and *turnip.*

mynah \ 'mī-nə \ bird (myna)

Mynah birds are large, dark-colored birds of the starling family. Pet mynah birds are often taught to imitate human speech and other sounds. Mynah birds are native to forests of India, Ceylon and some other parts of southern Asia.

Mynahs are 12 to 15 inches long. They are brown or black, with some white on the wings. The stout bill is orange, and there are usually patches of bare orange or yellow skin on the head. The short legs are yellow. Male and female birds look alike.

Wild mynah birds make many different chuckling and whistling sounds. They eat mostly fruit.

As cage birds, mynahs are hardy and easy to care for. They often live to be 25 years old. They do not breed in captivity. Young mynahs in pet shops all

MYRTLE

come from Asia, where they are taken from the nests of wild mynahs.

The greater Indian hill mynah (illustrated) sometimes learns to imitate human speech and other sounds very clearly. It is the kind most often seen in pet shops. Usually about 13 inches long, it is glossy black with flaps of yellow skin under the eyes and at the back of the neck.

myrtle \ 'mərt-ᵊl \

The myrtles make up a family of evergreen shrubs and trees that grow in the warmer parts of the world. Common myrtle (illustrated) was considered sacred by the ancient Greeks. Today, it is planted as an ornamental shrub. Its bark can be used for tanning leather.

The myrtle shrub is 3 to 9 feet tall and has many branches. It has glossy, dark green leaves which grow in opposite pairs.

Pink or whitish flowers about ½ inch in diameter blossom in spring and are clustered along the branches. The fruit is a fragrant, purple-black berry. Both berry and leaf are used in making perfumes.

Myrtle is easily transplanted through cuttings but needs a warm climate to grow well. In the U.S., it can be planted outdoors only in South Carolina, Florida, California and along the Gulf of Mexico.

For members of the myrtle family, see *guava* and *pimento.*

n

narcissus \ när-'sis-əs \ (daffodil, jonquil)

Narcissuses are a group of fragrant, hardy plants belonging to a family that also includes the amaryllis and the spider lily. Narcissuses are grown chiefly from bulbs, and are among the most popular of all garden flowers. They are native to Europe.

The flowers are yellow or white, or both. The central part of the flower is either a shallow ring or a long tube, and is surrounded by 6 spreading petals. The flower blooms at the end of a long stalk. Leaves are tall and thin, growing from the base of the plant. The bulb looks something like an onion and the fruit is a 3-lobed, many-seeded capsule.

Narcissuses are grown widely. The paper-white narcissus bears clusters of sweet-smelling, white flowers and is often grown indoors in winter.

Plants of the narcissus group which are called jonquils have small, orange-yellow flowers which also bloom in clusters, on a stalk about 18 inches long. Those called daffodils (illustrated) have single blossoms on an 18- to 24-inch stalk. The center part of the flower is tube-like and is about 2 inches long.

NARCISSUS

nasturtium \ nə-'stər-shəm \

Nasturtiums make up a family containing both annual and perennial plants. Most of them are climbers, some reaching as high as 10 feet. Native to South America, the nasturtium is now a widely grown, summer-blooming garden flower.

Brightly colored, red, orange or yellow flowers grow singly on a stalk from the leaf axil. Each flower has 5, long-clawed petals ending in a spur. The flower is about 2½ inches across. As the flower stalks grow, they curl around anything available to support the climbing plant.

The light green leaves are rounded or shield-shaped. Thick veins branch out from the center of the leaf where it is attached to the stem. The fruit has 3 parts, each containing 1 seed.

The common annual nasturtium is sometimes called Indian cress. The leaves are spicy and somewhat tart and have been used to season salads.

Several double-flowered kinds of nasturtium have been developed. They grow easily in sunshine but must be protected from aphids by spraying.

nautilus \ 'not-ᵊl-əs \

Nautiluses make up a group of mollusks that are closely related to the squids, cuttlefish and octopuses. Only a few kinds of nautilus are now alive, but scientists estimate that 500 million years ago, there were about 2,500 different kinds.

The nautilus has a smooth, coiled shell made up of a series of chambers lined with mother-of-pearl. The shell and the compartments are made of a substance produced within the animal. New chambers form as the animal grows, and it lives in the newest one. The smaller, older compartments are then filled by the animal with a gas used as ballast for floating or swimming.

The chambered or pearly nautilus (illustrated) is found along shores and coral reefs in the South Pacific and Indian oceans. Its shell is usually 4 to 6 inches in diameter. The animal has a large head and a powerful, horny-jawed mouth surrounded by 60 to 90 tentacles. The tentacles feed the animal, help anchor it down and act as organs of smell. By squirting water through a funnel-like opening under the head, the animal moves backward through the water.

nebula \ 'neb-yə-lə \

A nebula is a cloud-like mass of dust and gasses in space. It is thought to be the remains of a star that has exploded. Made up chiefly of helium and hydrogen, it has no light of its own but reflects light from nearby stars.

NAUTILUS

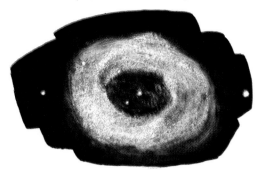

BRIGHT NEBULA
(RING NEBULA OF LYRA)

There are different types of nebulae, varying in brightness and shape. Some are in our galaxy and some are outside it. Only 4 can be seen with the naked eye.

When a nebula is near enough to a star to be brightly lit by it, it is termed a bright nebula (illustrated). A dark nebula (illustrated) is too far away to reflect light. A planetary nebula is round and surrounds a star. The nearest planetary nebula is 1,000 light-years distant, and none is visible to the naked eye.

A diffuse nebula (illustrated) sometimes looks like a small, hazy area or a large, formless cloud. Diffuse nebulae can be seen through binoculars or a telescope.

A nebula may be a combination of types. The Crab nebula is a diffuse planetary nebula, resulting from the explosion of a very large star in 1054. The Crab nebula is still expanding.

NEEDLEFISH

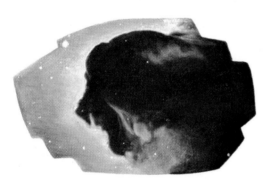

DARK NEBULA
(HORSEHEAD NEBULA OF ORION)

DIFFUSE NEBULA
(GREAT NEBULA OF ORION)

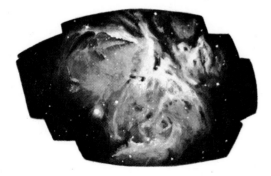

needlefish \ 'nēd-°l-ˌfish \

Needlefish make up a family of warm-water marine fish closely related to gars and flying fish. Needlefish are active, rapid swimmers. Like flying fish, they often jump clear out of the water. Needlefish are not important fish commercially, although the flesh is edible.

These fierce-looking fish are long and cigar-shaped. They have long jaws containing many sharp teeth. The long dorsal and anal fins are placed far back on the body, near the tail. The lobes of the tail are widely separated and V-shaped. Although the average length is 2 feet, needlefish have been known to reach 5 feet.

Needlefish are surface swimmers. They live close to shore in tropical or warm seas. They feed on smaller fish but are themselves eaten by larger fish.

The most common of the 60 kinds of needlefish known is the Atlantic needlefish (illustrated), also called the billfish.

Neptune

Neptune is the fourth largest of the 9 planets in the solar system. It is the eighth planet away from the sun and is about 2.8 billion miles away from the sun. Neptune makes a complete orbit of the sun in about 165 years. Its day is about 15 hours and 48 minutes long.

Neptune was not discovered until 1846. Astronomers had noticed that the orbit of the planet Uranus was not regular. They decided that some large mass was pulling

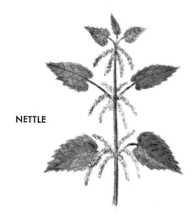

NETTLE

Uranus out of its expected orbit. Through exact calculations, the position of the large mass was fixed. The new planet was then discovered and named Neptune, after the Roman god of the sea.

Over 17 times as large as the earth, Neptune has a diameter of about 28,000 miles. Its equator is tilted 29 degrees to the plane of its orbit. The planet has 2 moons. One travels around the planet from east to west. The other travels from west to east.

Like Uranus, Neptune is thought to have a small rock core wrapped in ice and solid hydrogen. The surface temperature is extremely low. Through a telescope, Neptune is greenish.

See *The Sun, the Moon and the Planets* on p. 502.

nereis \ 'nir-ē-əs \ (clamworm, mussel worm)

Nereis is the name for a group of saltwater annelids, or segmented worms. Only a few rare kinds can live in fresh water.

While most nereides range from 2 to 12 inches in length, some reach 24 inches. They have many paired appendages along their bodies and many tentacles, each with several eyes. The head has sharp, horny, retractable jaws. They breathe with gills.

Living in burrows along seashores, nereides swim freely at night. They are meat eaters, feeding on other worms and small sea animals.

NEREIS

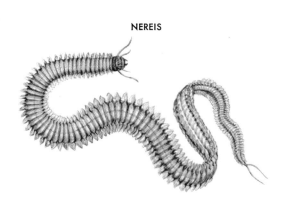

Different kinds of nereides reproduce in different ways. One tropical kind breeds in timed cycles, probably connected with the phases of the moon. In another kind, the male eats the female and incubates the eggs himself.

The commonest member of the nereis group in this country (illustrated) is found along Atlantic and Pacific shores, especially near San Francisco.

nettle \ 'net-ᵊl \

Nettles make up a family of about 500 kinds of flowering plants. They are mostly native to the tropics, but are widely distributed in moderate climates. Nettles are usually small plants, but some kinds are bushy, and a few kinds look like trees.

The nettles found in America are annual or perennial weedy plants. Most of them have a bristly or hairy leaf. The bristles contain a juice that produces a brief but severe irritation when it touches the skin.

The greenish flowers have no petals and are borne in spiky clusters. Staminate and pistillate flowers are separate on the same plant. The leaves are saw-toothed and grow in opposite pairs along the stem. The leaves are stalked and have small, leaf-like bracts at the base of the stalk. The fruit is small and dry and contains 1 seed.

The stinging nettle (illustrated) is a common weed in eastern North America as far south as Virginia. It grows in neglected areas, reaching 30 inches in height. The flower clusters are forked and the leaves are large and heart-shaped, with large teeth. Leaf surfaces and stems are heavily bristled.

newt \ 'n(y)üt \

The newts make up a family of salamanders. Many newts live on land for over a year before maturing. While on land, they are called efts.

Most common in the eastern half of the U.S. is the red-spotted newt (illustrated), called the red eft while living on land. Newly hatched red-spotted newts are yellow-green and have external gills. When 2 to 4 months old, they turn bright red-orange and develop lungs. For 1 to 3 years they live as efts in wooded areas away from streams. They grow to 2 to 3½ inches long, developing rough skins and a slender tail and legs. Red spots on the back are bordered in black.

Adults go back to streams and ponds to mate and lay eggs. At this stage they are 3 to 4½ inches long and have smooth olive-green skin marked with 2 rows of red dots along the back. The tail is large and has a vertical fin or keel to help in swimming.

Red-spotted newts eat insects and insect larvae, frog eggs and worms.

NEWT

NIGHTHAWK

nighthawk \ 'nīt-ˌhȯk \

Nighthawks are not true hawks, but are members of the goatsucker family of birds. They are most often seen feeding at dusk. They fly in swoops and darts, with their large mouths open. They feed entirely on insects caught in flight.

Nighthawks have long, curved wings and fairly large tails. Their feet are small and so weak that the birds are nearly helpless on the ground.

The common nighthawk (illustrated) is 8½ to 10 inches long. Its coloring is a mixed black, white and brown. It has white bars on each wing.

This bird, once living only in the country, is now fairly common in cities. Nests are built on the ground in gravel, or on flat, gravel-covered roofs of buildings. The texture of the gravel helps to conceal the 2 gray-white eggs marbled with brown. Young birds are fed by both parents.

The common nighthawk inhabits most of the U.S. and Canada, and winters in South America.

nightingale \ 'nīt-ᵊn-ˌgāl \

Nightingales are members of a group of birds belonging to the thrush family. They are found only in western and central Europe. The clear, bell-like notes of the nightingale form a song that has been

NIGHTINGALE

admired for centuries. The young nightingales learn the song from their parents, but if hatched and raised apart from other nightingales, the fledglings will imitate any song they hear.

The nightingale lives deep in woods or hedges. Ground-living insects, which it catches as it hops along, are its main food.

The male nightingale helps to build the nest and to incubate the eggs. Made of moss, twigs and grass, the nest is built on or near the ground. The 4 to 6 eggs are olive-brown or whitish. There is 1 brood a season. Nightingales winter in Africa.

Plain in appearance and shy in habit, the European nightingale (illustrated) looks something like the North American hermit thrush. The European nightingale is small, only about 6½ inches long. Its body is brown, with a brighter reddish-brown tail and rump. The underparts are pale brown or beige.

nightshade \ 'nīt-ˌshād \

The nightshades make up a family of several thousand plants that includes trees, shrubs and nonwoody plants. Many of them are important food plants. Some of these are the tomato, the potato and the eggplant. Tobacco and petunias also belong to the nightshade family. Some nightshade plants contain a deadly poison.

Flower petal colors range from blue-white to purplish blue, with pointed, yellow centers. The flower clusters are borne at the leaf axil. The leaves are alternate. The fruit is a berry, edible in some kinds but poisonous in others. Although native to the tropics, nightshades are now found all over the world.

The black nightshade is a spreading annual weed that grows 12 to 24 inches tall. It is common in the eastern part of North America. Small white flowers bloom from May to early autumn. The dark green, oval leaves are somewhat sticky, and may have either even or toothed edges. The juice of the wilted leaf is a dangerous poison. When ripe, the fruit is a dull black berry.

For other members of the nightshade family, see *jimsonweed, pepper, petunia, potato, tobacco* and *tomato*.

northern sea robin (Carolina sea robin)

The northern sea robin is a marine fish fairly common off the east coast of North America. Its flesh is edible, but it is used mostly for making canned cat food.

Most northern sea robins are about 1 foot long. They are reddish-brown or gray, with lighter underparts and some black spots on the chin and back.

The large head is covered with hard, bony plates and is armed with stiff spines. There is 1 spine on each cheek and there are longer spines on the sides of the neck.

NORTHERN SEA ROBIN

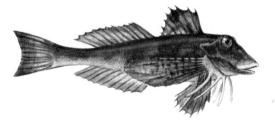

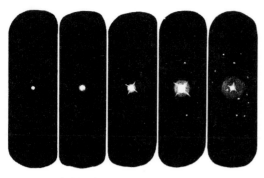

NOVA (STAGES OF EXPLOSION)

The tapering body is covered with small scales, and the tail fin is concave. The broad, rounded pectoral fins are used like legs as the fish creeps along the sea floor seeking food. It eats smaller fish, crustaceans, marine worms and squid.

The northern sea robin spawns in late spring or summer. The eggs float on or near the surface of the water, and they hatch in 2 or 3 days.

In summer, the northern sea robin is found near shore, where the bottom is sandy. In winter it moves into deeper water farther from shore. It is most common south of Cape Cod, but it is sometimes caught as far north as Maine.

nova \ 'nō-və \

A nova is a star that becomes much brighter for a time and then fades. Some novae flare up just once, while others repeat the cycle again and again.

At their brightest, some novae are 10,000 to 80,000 times brighter than their normal state. The period of greatest brightness usually lasts only a few days. The fading may take several years.

Novae are quite rare. They are usually dim or faraway stars that are visible without a telescope only during their brightest periods. They are most common in the densest part of the Milky Way. The rarest and brightest novae are called supernovae.

Astronomers are not certain what causes a nova. They think that the sudden brightening may be due to something like an explosion. They know that during its brightest period a nova throws off clouds of gas and dust.

It is probable that novae are old stars, though the name means "new." As stars become very old, their makeup may become unbalanced. A kind of nuclear explosion may burn away part of the star's matter and restore the balance for a time. A star may also flare up when matter thrown off by another star strikes it.

See *supernova*.

nuthatch \ 'nət-,hach \

Nuthatches make up a family of small, quick-moving birds. They are often seen perching head-down and tail-up on tree trunks. Nuthatches live in nearly all parts of the northern hemisphere and in Australia.

Four to 6 inches long, nuthatches have short necks, slender bills and short tails. The head is black, and the back and wings are gray or brownish. The call is a repeated whistle.

Nuthatches eat mostly insects and worms that they find on the bark of trees, as well as some seeds and berries. Sometimes the bird will wedge a nut into a crack in the bark and then tap with its bill until the nutshell breaks open.

NUTHATCH

The nest is usually built in a hollow tree. The female nuthatch incubates the 4 to 10 eggs, which are white or pinkish, speckled with brown. The male helps feed the young birds.

The red-breasted nuthatch (illustrated) spends the summer in Alaska and Canada, and the higher mountains of the U.S. It winters as far south as Arizona and the Gulf coast. A shy bird, it lives mostly in evergreen forests.

The white-breasted nuthatch is a year-round resident of the eastern U.S.

nutmeg \ 'nət-,meg \ tree

The nutmeg tree is a tall evergreen that grows in the tropics. Its fruit contains 2 kinds of spices, mace and nutmeg.

Golden, pear-shaped fruit and shiny gray-green leaves make the nutmeg an attractive tree. The leaves are about 5 inches long and 2 to 3 inches wide. The pale yellow flowers look something like lilies of the valley. They hang in clusters.

A nutmeg tree may be 40 to 70 feet high. It does not bear fruit until it is about 9 years old. The fruit is grooved on 1 side and, when ripe, splits open along the groove. The kernel is the nutmeg. Around the kernel is a bright scarlet membrane known as mace. Removed from the kernel and dried, mace turns a soft orange-brown color. The tree bears 2 or 3 crops of fruit each year.

The nutmeg tree is native to the Spice Islands. It is now grown widely in both the East and West Indies. It grows best in areas where rainfall is plentiful.

nutria \ 'nü-trē-ə \ (coypu, coypu rat)

The nutria is a plump rodent native to the Andes mountains of South America. It is sometimes confused with the beaver. The nutria is smaller than the beaver, and it has a more slender tail, but both are fur-bearing, gnawing mammals that swim well and spend much of their time in water.

The nutria's soft, yellowish-brown underfur is used to make women's coats. The coarse brown hairs on the back are used to make felt for hats.

Most nutrias are about 3 feet long, including the tail. Good swimmers but poor divers, they live along the edges of quiet ponds and streams. Their homes are burrows in the streambank, or platforms of plant materials hidden among reeds. They eat mostly green plants, along with some shellfish.

Female nutrias bear litters of 4 to 12 young, as often as 3 times a year. Newborn nutrias look like rats, and they can swim well when only a few days old.

Many nutrias have been brought to the U.S., where they are raised for their fur on nutria farms and ranches. Some have escaped and now live wild.

LEAVES AND FRUIT OF NUTMEG TREE

NUTRIA

O

oak tree

Oaks are sturdy, long-lived trees that grow throughout the northern hemisphere. There are 2 large groups of oak trees, the black oaks and the white oaks. Trees in the black oak group have dark brown bark. Their leaves are sharp-pointed. Trees in the white oak group have light brown or gray bark and leaves with smooth edges.

The black oak tree (illustrated) belongs to the black oak group. It usually grows from 60 to 90 feet tall, with a trunk diameter of 2 to 3 feet.

The leaves of the black oak are 5 to 6 inches long and are divided into 7 bristle-tipped lobes. They are reddish in early spring, dark green in summer and dull red in autumn. The leaves cling late, falling gradually during the winter. The plump, reddish-brown acorns measure ½ to ¾ inch long. They take 2 years to mature.

The inner bark of the black oak is bright orange. The bark is used in dyes and medicines, and the wood is used in furniture.

The black oak is found throughout the eastern half of the U.S.

Iowa has adopted the oak as its state tree. The bur oak is the state tree of Illinois, the red oak of New Jersey and the white oak of Maryland. The live oak is the state tree of Georgia.

OAK TREE

OAT

oat

Oats make up a group of plants that belong to the grass family. They are widely cultivated as a cereal crop. The grain makes fine food for man and farm animals. The straw left after the grain is removed makes good fertilizer and animal feed.

Oats may be either perennial or annual. Annual oats are planted in the spring and usually harvested in July. Winter oats are planted in the autumn.

The small, greenish flowers are borne in loose, branching clusters at the tops of the stalks. Each seed is surrounded by a protective husk.

The common oat (illustrated) is a spreading annual. It grows 2 to 4 feet high. The flower clusters spread on each side of the stem in flat, drooping spikes. The grass-like leaves measure up to 9 inches long and are slightly rough. The plant is bright green when young and turns pale gold when the grain is ripe.

Oats are believed to be native to Europe and western Asia. They are widely cultivated in all parts of the temperate zones. Some kinds of oats have been grown near the Arctic Circle.

obsidian \ əb-'sid-ē-ən \

Obsidian is a smooth, glassy, dark-colored rock. It is usually black or gray but may be striped with red, green or violet. A thin section of obsidian is translucent.

316

Obsidian is actually natural glass. It was formed when molten lava flowed out onto the surface of the earth. The lava cooled so quickly that crystals had no time to form. The same lava, cooling underground, might have become granite.

Obsidian is quite brittle and breaks easily. It was used by the Indians in making arrowheads.

Over a period of centuries, obsidian turns into a dull, fine-grained rock. It may then break up and be washed away. Thus, obsidian is found only where volcanoes have been active in recent times. It is fairly common in some parts of the western U.S. and Mexico, but it is never found in the eastern part of the U.S.

ocean sunfish \ 'sən-,fish \ (headfish)

The ocean sunfish is a large, strange-looking, warm-water fish. In spite of its name, this fish is not related to the freshwater sunfish found in U.S. lakes.

The Japanese consider sunfish liver good to eat. The rest of the body is poisonous.

This fish is often called headfish because it looks like a fish head with fins. It ranges in length from 6 to 11 feet and may weigh up to 2,000 pounds. It has a small mouth with a bony beak. The eyes are directly in line with the mouth. The fish has tough, leathery skin about 1½ inches thick. The bones are soft and weak.

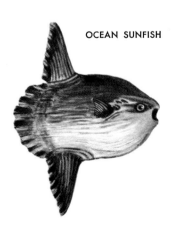

OCEAN SUNFISH

OCELOT

Often seen floating near the surface, the ocean sunfish seems lazy. It drifts along, flapping its fins above the water. It captures small marine animals, such as jellyfish, by sucking in whatever floats by.

The ocean sunfish usually lives in open seas. It has been found as far north as Newfoundland.

ocelot \ 'äs-ə-,lät \ (leopard cat, tiger cat)

The ocelot is a member of the cat family. It is a slender, medium-sized wild cat with smooth, buff-colored fur, marked with brown and black spots, circles, bars and stripes. Each ocelot is marked differently. Even the 2 sides of the same animal may have different patterns or markings.

The body measures about 2 feet long, and the tail about 15 inches. An adult weighs 30 to 35 pounds. The ocelot's eyes are brown. There is no white surrounding the pupil.

The ocelot hides in thickets of wild woods. Its home is a den well hidden among rocks. Ocelots mate in June or July, and the young, usually twins, are born 3 months later. The young are marked like the adults. An ocelot, if caught when it is young, can be tamed and kept as a pet.

This cat is native to western America from Paraguay to Texas. It once roamed as far east as Ohio.

octopus (devilfish)

Octopuses make up a group of 8-armed, marine mollusks. Unlike most mollusks, they have no protective shell. Most live in shallow tropical waters of both the Atlantic and Pacific. In Europe and the Far East, they are used for food.

Octopuses are usually small, timid and harmless. The smallest is less than 2 inches long. One kind can spread its arms to 32 feet.

The large head is fastened to the soft body by a short neck. The animal has 2 well-developed eyes and beak-like jaws.

The arms, or tentacles, are fastened to the head by a web. Each of the 8 tentacles has 2 rows of sucker disks on its underside with which the octopus captures and holds its prey. The tentacles also enable the animal to crawl about on the ocean bottom. If a tentacle is destroyed, the octopus grows a new one.

A funnel-shaped siphon projects from the body beneath the head. The octopus swims by forcing water out of the siphon. It is also able to squirt an ink fluid from the siphon when in danger.

The female octopus lays a large number of very small eggs in holes or under rocks. In 4 to 8 weeks, the eggs hatch. The tiny octopuses closely resemble adults.

The common octopus (illustrated) has a tentacle spread of 1 to 3 feet.

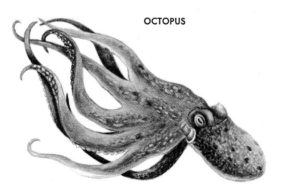

OCTOPUS

OKAPI

okapi \ō-'käp-ē\

The okapi is a ruminant mammal that was discovered in 1900 in the dense forests of the Congo valley in Africa. It is related to the giraffe and resembles it in some ways. The neck and legs are shorter, however.

The okapi is about 4 feet tall at the shoulder. The chest is deep, and the legs are long. The head is cone-shaped, and the tongue is very long.

The thighs, haunches and upper forelegs are marked with zebra-like black and white stripes. The face, throat and upper legs are grayish-white. The body is chestnut red. The male okapi has 2 short, skin-covered horns tipped with white.

Okapis live singly or in pairs. The animals are so shy that they are hard to observe. Very little is known about their habits. They stay in dense, damp forests and feed only at night. They usually eat leaves that may be as high as 8 to 10 feet above the ground.

The young are born 1 at a time, after a gestation period of 425 days. They nurse for 3 or 4 months.

oleander \'ō-lē-ˌan-dər\

The oleanders make up a group of evergreen shrubs that bear clusters of pink, yellow or white flowers. Oleanders are often grown in pots or tubs as house plants and are popular garden plants in warm climates.

Oleanders are native to the Mediterranean region but have been widely planted in other areas of the world where the climate is mild.

There are many kinds of oleanders. The stems of all of them contain a white juice that is poisonous. All have narrow leaves that grow in opposite pairs or in 3's along the stems.

One common oleander grows 8 to 25 feet tall. Its leathery, dark-green leaves are 4 to 8 inches long. Its flowers shade from pale pink to a deep rose-purple.

The flower clusters appear at the end of the branches. The fruit is a double pod containing many seeds. Each seed bears a tuft of silky hairs.

olive tree

The olive tree is a sturdy member of the olive family, which includes lilacs, forsythia and ash trees. The long-lived olive tree is an evergreen that has been cultivated for its fruit since 3000 B.C.

The olive tree is native to the eastern Mediterranean region. It was brought to the U.S. by Spaniards in 1769. It is now grown in southern California and Arizona.

Olive trees live to be more than 1,000 years old. The narrow, silver-green leaves are 1 to 3 inches long and grow in pairs. Small, white flowers appear on the twigs and smaller branches in May. The oval fruit contains 1 large seed. The fruit is green during the summer months, yellow or red in autumn and black when fully ripe in midwinter.

In the U.S., much of the fruit is harvested green and preserved by pickling. In Europe, the fruit is allowed to ripen on the tree and is used to make olive oil. Both the seed and the flesh contain oil.

The valleys of Spain, Italy, Greece and Portugal lead in the production of olives.

For other members of the olive family, see *ash, forsythia* and *lilac*.

olivine \ 'äl-i-ˌvēn \

Olivine is a mineral which is found in many dark-colored rocks. It has also been found in meteorites.

Olivine is olive-green to brownish-green in color. It is translucent, hard and fairly heavy. It is made up of silica, magnesium and iron combined with oxygen. Pieces of olivine are usually found scattered through gabbro and basalt. The pieces may be large masses or small grains.

One rare kind of olivine is called peridot. It is a gem stone used in jewelry. It is transparent and deep green.

In the U.S., olivine is fairly common in New Hampshire, Pennsylvania, Virginia and in the Rocky Mountains. Olivine is also found in the Mediterranean area.

onion

The onions make up a group of plants belonging to the lily family. Although onions have a strong smell of their own,

OLIVE TREE

ONION

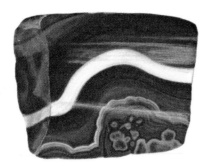

ONYX

they are closely related to such sweet-smelling flowers as the hyacinth and lily of the valley.

Included in the onion group are the common garden onion (illustrated), chives, leeks, garlic, shallots and some attractive wild flowers and ornamental plants. Most of the edible onions are perennial plants from Asia. Wild onions grow in all parts of the U.S.

All of the onions have long, narrow leaves and smooth stems that grow from bulbs. The leaves are usually rounded and hollow, but some are flat. The white or greenish flowers are borne in umbrella-shaped clusters at the tops of the stalks. The fruit is a lobed pod containing small seeds.

The common onion has hollow leaves that are usually a dark blue-green color. The edible bulb is made up of many layers. The outer layer is papery. The flowering stem grows about 18 inches tall and bears clusters of many small flowers.

The common onion is believed to be native to Mongolia, but it is now grown in all parts of the northern hemisphere.

onyx \ 'än-iks \

The mineral onyx is a kind of chalcedony that can easily be identified by its light and dark stripes. The light stripes are white. The dark layers are usually black. When layered in brown or red, the mineral is called sardonyx.

Onyx is very much like agate. Both are fine-grained quartz. The stripes in onyx are fairly straight. The markings in agate follow curves or circles.

This beautiful mineral is strong and hard. It can be polished until it is as smooth as glass. It is widely used in making such items as jewelry, lamp bases and pen stands. Sheets of onyx are sometimes used to cover the fronts of buildings.

The chief sources of onyx are South America, Mexico and India. It is found in the U.S. in Utah, Arizona, Kentucky and California.

opal \ 'ō-pəl \

Opal is a mineral. Some kinds are gem stones used in fine jewelry. An opal gives off flashes of many colors when it is turned in different directions. Ancient people thought that the opal had magic powers and brought bad luck.

Strangely enough, opal is made up of the same materials found in common sand, or silica. The milky or colorless opal is best known. It shows changing rainbow colors in the light. The fire opal is a clear orange-red. The rare black opal is dark blue or gray. It, too, shows rainbow colors. The common opal is translucent with a white or light tint. It does not have changing colors.

Opal is formed by the acid waters from hot springs. Silicate materials dissolve in the acid water. As the water evaporates,

OPAL

a layer of solids is left behind. The layers build up slowly. The rainbow effect comes from the bending of light rays as they pass through the different layers.

Gem opals come from Australia, India, Honduras and Mexico. They have also been found in the western U.S.

opossum \ō-'päs-əm\

The opossums make up a family of marsupial mammals. They are the only marsupials native to the western hemisphere. There are several different kinds of opossums, but the most well known is the common opossum (illustrated).

The common opossum has a body length of 12 to 20 inches. It can hang from branches by its hairless tail, which is 10 to 18 inches long. The soft fur is light or dark gray. The face is white with dark markings around the small eyes. The ears are large, black and hairless.

The opossum has sharp teeth but usually does not use them. Instead, it tries to trick its enemies by rolling up into a ball and pretending to be dead.

The female gives birth to 6 to 18 young at once. They are about the size of bees. They crawl at once into the pouch on the mother's stomach, where they stay for the next 4 to 8 weeks.

The opossum has adapted itself to city living and is often found in city parks and near houses. It feeds at night on roots, garbage, insects, birds and reptiles.

The common opossum lives in southern Canada, throughout the eastern half of the U.S. and in Central and South America.

orangutan \ə-'rang-ə-,tang\

The orangutan is a mammal that belongs to the ape group of primates. The orangutan is native to Borneo and Sumatra. Its name comes from a Malayan word that means "man of the woods." The orangutan somewhat resembles the chimpanzee and gorilla. It is a popular animal in zoos. Young orangutans can be trained to eat, dress and behave almost like humans.

The heavy body is 4 to 5 feet tall and weighs 160 to 200 pounds. The legs are short and thick. The arms are long and powerful. When the animal is standing upright, the fingers nearly reach the ground. The span from hand to hand with arms outstretched may be as much as 7 feet.

The head of the orangutan is pear-shaped with a high forehead. The nose is flat and the ears are small. The mouth has narrow lips and projects outward. The face is flesh-colored but turns black with old age. On a young animal the fur is reddish, but it turns gray with age.

In the wild, the orangutan lives alone or in family groups high in the trees. It builds its nest on platforms made of branches. It lives largely on vegetation, although a captive orangutan will eat the same foods that man does.

OPOSSUM

ORANGUTAN

ORCHID HABITAT
(RATTLESNAKE PLANTAIN)

orchid \ 'or-kəd \

The orchids make up a large family of flowering plants. There are thousands of kinds of orchids, most of which have beautiful, colorful flowers.

These plants grow all over the world, except in the coldest areas. Tropical orchids grown in greenhouses are an important commercial plant in colder climates.

Orchid plants growing in tropical countries cling to the bark of trees, and their roots take food directly from the air.

In temperate climates, orchids usually grow from the ground. Some kinds, such as lady's slippers, grow as wild flowers in wooded areas. Most orchids in the temperate zone have green leaves. A few live in organic matter in the soil and have no green parts.

All orchid blossoms have irregular shapes. The 3 outer segments are sepals. They are usually dull in color. The 3 inner segments are brighter-colored petals. One petal is called a lip. The lip on each orchid has a shape that serves to guide insects to the pollen. The fruit is a 3-valved capsule that contains dust-like seeds.

For members of the orchid family, see *cattleya, lady's slipper* and *vanilla*.

oribi \ 'or-ə-bē \

The oribi is a small antelope belonging to the same family as cattle, oxen, sheep and goats. Like the larger antelopes, it is able to run extremely fast. The oribi is native to South and East Africa.

The oribi is sometimes called a pygmy antelope because of its small size. It is a little over 3 feet long, not including its short, thick 3- to 4-inch tail. The oribi stands only 20 inches high at the shoulder and weighs about 40 pounds.

The smooth, glossy hair is yellow-brown, sometimes touched with red. The underparts are white. There are tufts of long hair on the knees. Oribis have large ears and thin legs. The male has ringed horns which are short and straight. The female has a dark patch on the head.

Oribis like bush country and tall grass. They graze freely in the open plains. They usually live in pairs or small groups but may graze in herds of a dozen. Easily frightened, they scatter widely when alarmed.

The young are born in late fall or early winter. The life-span is about 11 years.

oriole \ 'ōr-ē-,ōl \

Orioles are brightly colored birds of 2 different families. In all kinds, the males are more colorful than the females. All orioles weave nests that hang from tree branches. They eat mostly insects, along with some fruits and berries.

The Old World orioles are a family of long-winged, medium-sized birds that live in Europe, Asia, Africa and Australia.

ORIBI

ORIOLE

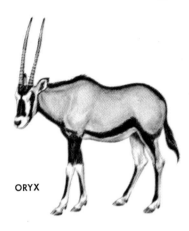

ORYX

They are related to the crow. The American orioles are birds of a family that includes the grackles, the bobolink, the cowbird, the American blackbirds and the meadowlarks.

The Baltimore oriole (illustrated) is one of America's best-known birds. The length is 7 to 8 inches. The male is orange and black, while the female is greenish-brown with yellowish underparts. Both have white bars on their wings. The song is a soft, cheerful whistle.

The nest of the Baltimore oriole is skillfully woven from strings, bits of cloth, grass and bark fibers. The nest usually swings from the end of a high branch, and it is often so strong that it lasts several years. The 4 to 6 eggs are white, marked with speckles or scrawling lines.

The Baltimore oriole is the state bird of Maryland. It nests throughout the eastern half of North America and winters in Central America.

oryx \ 'ōr-iks \

The oryxes are large, hoofed mammals that belong to the antelope family. They roam the deserts and dry plains of Africa and Arabia, often in herds that number up to 400.

Oryxes stand 3 to 4 feet tall at the shoulder. The body is about 4 feet long. The color is gray or pale brown, marked with white and dark brown or black.

Both male and female oryxes have horns 3 to 4 feet long. Females generally have longer horns than males. Young oryxes are born with 2-inch horns.

While most kinds of oryxes have straight horns, 1 kind native to northern Africa has horns that curve widely backward.

Shy animals, oryxes run fast to escape their enemies. If cornered, they use their horns to defend themselves and their young. They feed on grasses.

The gemsbok (illustrated) is the largest of the oryxes and the kind with the longest horns. It lives in southern Africa.

The gemsbok is pale pinkish-gray, with black and white markings on the face. The short mane is black, and black stripes run along the back and sides. The tail is tufted and there may be a dark beard on the chin.

osage \ ō-'sāj \ orange (hedge apple)

Osage orange is a thorny tree of the mulberry family. Its large, round fruit is not good to eat, but it is not poisonous as it was once thought to be. The milky juice is irritating to the skin.

American Indians used the tough wood of the osage orange to make bows and war clubs, and they made yellow dye from the roots. Today the wood is sometimes used for fence posts and for railroad ties.

Osage orange is usually a broad-crowned, spreading tree 20 to 60 feet tall. The leaves are 3 to 5 inches long, broadest near the base and pointed at the tip. They turn yellow in autumn.

Small green flowers appear on the twigs in late spring, after the leaves. The yellow-green fruit is 2 to 5 inches across and has a wrinkled surface.

The osage orange is native to Texas and Oklahoma, the territory of the Osage Indians. It has been planted in many other parts of North America, as a hedge or as a windbreak. It now grows wild throughout the central U.S.

ostrich

The ostrich is the world's largest living bird. It is unable to fly, and is the only bird with 2 toes.

Fossils show that the ostrich lived in Europe and Asia 60 million years ago. Today it is found largely in South Africa. Many birds are raised for their feathers, on ostrich farms.

A full-grown male ostrich stands 7 to 8 feet tall, when measured to the top of its head. Its back is about 5 feet from the ground. It weighs over 300 pounds and can run at speeds up to 50 miles an hour.

The male is much larger than the female. The male has pink or blue down on the neck and legs. The body plumage is black, with white wings and tail

OSTRICH

OTTER

feathers. The wing and tail plumes were once widely used on ladies' hats. They can be removed without harming the bird. The female ostrich is usually gray.

The ostrich does not bury its head in the sand when frightened, as some people believe. Instead, it will fight fiercely, kicking with its strong legs and large feet. It has keen eyesight, and it can live for long periods without water. It eats seeds, fruits and green plants, along with insects, small mammals and reptiles.

The ostrich egg is the largest bird egg. It weighs 3 pounds and measures 8 inches long. The female lays 10 to 12 eggs in the nest that the male builds by kicking a cavity in the sand. The male sits on the eggs each night for about 6 weeks until the young are hatched.

otter \ 'ät-ər \

Otters are mammals belonging to the weasel family. Their sleek, shiny fur is very valuable.

The otter, like the beaver, has 2 coats of hair. The undercoat is soft and thick. The outer coat is longer and darker in color. Both male and female have dark brown backs and lighter underparts. The lips and cheeks are gray.

Otters have short, powerful legs with webbed feet and clawed toes. They are expert swimmers, but on land appear awkward and playful. They often make mud or snowslides on river banks. They seem

OVENBIRD

to enjoy sliding down the banks into the water. Their homes are burrows or caves along the banks of streams. Otters live on fish and small animals found near water.

The male river or Canadian otter (illustrated) is 3½ to 4 feet long. The female is somewhat smaller. The river otter ranges throughout much of North America from central Canada south to the middle of the U.S. The finest skins come from Labrador, Newfoundland and the Hudson Bay area.

For another kind of otter, see *sea otter*.

outcrop \ˈau̇t-ˌkräp\

An outcrop is a piece of bedrock which has been uncovered by erosion. The bedrock has weathered more slowly than the material around it. Running water, wind or a glacier has carried away nearby soil or sand. The bare outcrop remains.

Over a long period of time, thin soil may form on an outcrop. Plants take roots. As these plants die and decay, they add material to the soil. Their roots help to break up the rock into particles which turn into more soil.

Outcrops are always made up of the rock native to the area in which they are found. They are often made of granite. One large granite outcrop is Half Dome in Yosemite National Park in California. This piece of bedrock towers 4,892 feet above the meadow around it.

OUTCROP

ovenbird \ˈəv-ən-ˌbərd\

The ovenbird of North America (illustrated) is really a member of the wood warbler family. The true ovenbirds are found only from Mexico to the tip of South America.

The North American ovenbird is sometimes called the "teacher bird" because of its call. Its song sounds like the word "teacher" repeated 3 times, each call louder than the last.

About 6 inches long, the North American ovenbird is olive-colored above and white beneath. Its breast and sides are streaked with black. Its golden crown has a black border and its long thin legs are pinkish.

The North American ovenbird hides its nest on the forest floor by covering it with dead grasses. The female lays 3 to 6 cream-colored, spotted eggs. She incubates them for about 2 weeks. The male helps feed the young until they leave the nest.

The North American ovenbird is valuable to man because it lives largely on insects. It breeds mostly in eastern and plains states south to Tennessee and Oklahoma, but it may nest in Canada as far north as Hudson Bay. It winters in Florida, the West Indies and from Mexico to Colombia.

owl

Owls make up 2 families of birds found in nearly all parts of the world. They are birds of prey that help man by killing mice and other rodents that destroy farm crops and stored foods.

Owls look quite different from most birds. Their large eyes, adapted to seeing in dim light, face forward as man's eyes do. Stiff feathers frame the face, forming a saucer-shaped disk that may receive and focus sound waves. Owls' hearing is very sharp, though their ears are concealed under the feathers.

Very soft, fluffy feathers cover owls' wings and make their flight noiseless. All but a very few owls roost during the day and hunt at night.

Strong beaks and sharp talons help owls catch and kill their prey. Most owls eat frogs, lizards, snakes and small birds, as well as rodents. The smaller kinds eat some insects. Owls swallow their victims whole. Later they vomit up a neat pellet that contains such indigestible parts as bones, fur and feathers.

Owls have very flexible necks that are longer than they appear to be. They can turn their heads so as to look directly behind them. Female owls are nearly always larger than males.

Most kinds of owls nest in hollow trees, but some nest on the ground or in burrows. Some kinds nest in little-used or abandoned buildings.

The 1 to 10 eggs are white and almost perfectly round. Usually, both male and female owls incubate the eggs. Both parents feed the young birds and will fight fiercely to defend the nest from enemies.

The barn owls, which have heart-shaped, monkey-like faces, are usually said to make up 1 family of owls. All other kinds make up the other family.

The common barn owl, 13 to 18 inches long, is less shy than most owls. It often nests in haylofts, church steeples and other buildings. Male and female seem to mate for life and return to the same nesting place year after year.

The common barn owl lives in most parts of North America and many other parts of the world. The other owls of the barn owl family live only in the Old World and nest in burrows in the ground.

The barred owl, the long-eared owl and the short-eared owl are all medium-sized birds up to 18 inches long. They live in forests in most parts of North America, and nest in hollow trees.

The great horned owl is the largest and most powerful of the owls common in the U.S. It is up to 25 inches long, and it kills animals as large as cats and chickens. It lives in forests, and it often hunts during the daylight hours.

The screech owl, about 10 inches long, lives on farms and in small towns, and it sometimes nests in birdhouses. It is active only at night, and its call is like a sad, trembling wail.

The saw-whet owl, 8 inches long, is the smallest of all the North American owls. Its call, heard only in spring, sounds like a saw being sharpened.

The burrowing owl, 8 to 10 inches long, lives only in open country, mostly in the southwestern states. It feeds on the ground and seldom flies. Its nest is a grass-lined burrow at the end of a long tunnel. It eats insects and small reptiles.

The snowy owl, 25 inches long, nests on the arctic tundra, north of the tree line. The female incubates the 3 to 10 eggs laid in a slight hollow on the ground, and the male brings her food. The male is mostly white. The female and young birds are marked with black and dark brown.

The snowy owl kills and eats lemmings, ducks and the arctic hare. In winter, when food is scarce, this bird is sometimes seen as far south as New England.

Owls—Birds of the Night

COMMON BARN OWL

BARRED OWL

BURROWING OWL

GREAT HORNED OWL

LONG-EARED OWL

SAW-WHET OWL

SCREECH OWL

SHORT-EARED OWL

SNOWY OWL

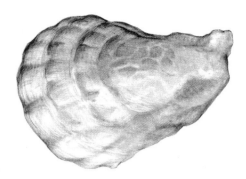

OYSTER

oyster

The oysters make up a family of bivalve mollusks that live in the ocean. They are usually found in shallow, fairly warm waters, near the mouth of a river or bay.

Pearls are produced by oysters when a grain of sand or a tiny animal inside the shell irritates the oyster. The particle then becomes covered with the same smooth material which lines the oyster shell. Oysters mature in 3 to 5 years.

The North American oyster (illustrated) is a valuable seafood. Great numbers of these oysters are cultivated and harvested for sale. The female produces many millions of eggs in 1 season.

The heavy, thick shell of the North American oyster is dull gray and rough on the outside. The inside is chalky-white and smooth, with a purple spot where the muscle is attached. The shell is usually 2 to 6 inches long. Some shells may reach a length of 10 or more inches.

North American oysters live on the ocean bottom attached to a solid object. They are found along the Atlantic coast from Maine to Florida. Oysters growing in some areas are more valuable as food than others. For example, the Blue Point oyster found near Blue Point, Long Island, is highly prized.

See *pearl*.

oyster drill

The oyster drills are gastropod mollusks that live in the ocean. They have snail-like bodies and live inside spiral, 1-piece shells.

Oyster drills are the worst enemies of young oysters. The oyster drill uses its rasp-like tongue to drill a tiny hole in the oyster's shell. It sucks the soft parts of the oyster's body out through the hole, which may be as small as a pinhole. Many valuable oysters are destroyed this way, each year.

Most oyster drills are less than 1 inch long. The largest ones are 3 inches long.

The outside of the shell is dull gray or yellowish. The surface bears spiraling, wavy lines crossed by raised ribs or ridges. The opening is oval, with a sharp-edged lip, and the inner surface is purplish.

The oyster drill has 2 small, black eyes on stalks. The fleshy foot it uses for creeping over the sea floor is the largest part of its body.

The female oyster drill lays eggs in capsules or cases. Each case contains as many as 12 eggs. The female may lay 100 cases in a few weeks.

Oyster drills are found in shallow, fairly warm parts of the oceans, among rocks and in tidal pools. One kind (illustrated) is common in the North Atlantic and in Chesapeake Bay.

OYSTER DRILL

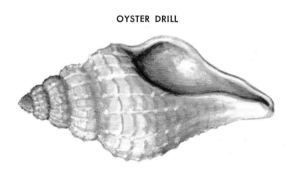

p

Pacific viperfish \ pə-'sif-ik 'vī-pər-ˌfish \

The Pacific viperfish belongs to a small family of fish that live only in very deep, dark water. This odd-looking fish has light organs on each side of its body. The light organs give off a pale light.

The head of the Pacific viperfish is large in relation to the rest of its body. Its long neck area makes it possible for the fish to bend its head backward. It spears its prey or enemies with its large, needle-sharp teeth.

The round body is usually less than 10 inches long. It ends in a slightly rounded tail fin. The first dorsal fin is very long and shaped like a triangle. The ventral fin is large and fan-shaped. The pectoral fins are small and near the head. The anal and second dorsal fins are near the tail.

The body is covered with dark, dull scales that are quite large, compared to the small size of the fish.

At night, the Pacific viperfish live at about 1,500 feet below the surface of the water. During the day they go down as far as 7,500 feet. They never come to the surface.

Pacific viperfish range from Alaska south to California.

PACIFIC VIPERFISH

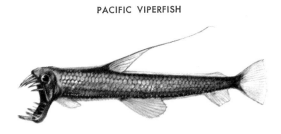

PADDLEFISH

paddlefish \ 'pad-ᵊl-ˌfish \

Paddlefish make up a family of freshwater fish. There are only 2 members of the paddlefish family. The North American paddlefish (illustrated) lives in the waters of the Mississippi valley. The other paddlefish is found in China. Paddlefish and their eggs are sometimes used for food.

The skeleton of the paddlefish is made entirely of cartilage. The skin is smooth. The fish is usually about 3 feet long and weighs 30 to 50 pounds. Large paddlefish 6 feet long and weighing 150 pounds have been caught.

The long, paddle-shaped snout makes up about ⅓ of the length of the fish. There are 4 small barbels under the snout. The large, toothless mouth is below the paddle. The small eyes are directly above the base of the paddle.

Paddlefish travel in schools as they search for food. They swim about with their large mouths wide open, taking in crustaceans and plankton which are strained through the gills.

palm tree

Palm trees are tropical evergreens that make up a large and important family of useful trees. They grow in the warmer areas of the world. Next to grains and grasses, the palm is considered the family of plants most valuable to man.

Palm trees provide man with food, drink, oil, fibers for rope and cloth, fuel and timber. Leaves of palm trees are sometimes made into baskets, mats, hats and roofs for tropical homes.

The large fan-like or feather-like compound leaves are grouped at the top of a slender, branchless trunk. The wood is soft and pithy. New leaves develop from a single seed leaf.

Clusters of small yellow flowers droop from the foliage crown. The fruits of the different kinds of palm trees differ greatly in shape and color.

The coconut palm (illustrated) is native to western Pacific islands and tropical America. It grows 60 to 100 feet tall. The trunk bends easily and the tree seldom stands erect. This palm has shallow roots.

The 8- to 10-inch coconut is the largest seed produced by any plant. One tree may produce 40 to 100 nuts a year. The bud is eaten as a vegetable, and the sap is used as a beverage. The dried meat of the coconut contains oil that is used in soap, salad oil and margarine.

The date palm, native to deserts of eastern Asia, also bears edible fruit.

For another kind of palm, see *cabbage palmetto*.

PALM TREE

PALOVERDE

paloverde\ ˌpal-ə-'vər-dē\

Paloverdes make up a group of thorny plants belonging to the pea family. The word paloverde means "green tree" in Spanish and paloverde bark is greenish. The paloverde grows as a tree or a shrub in the American desert and in Mexico.

The compound leaves of the paloverde are made up of 4 to 12 leaflets attached in opposite pairs. The leaves fall early and photosynthesis continues in the tree's smooth bark.

Paloverde seedpods dangle from the branches. Each round, bean-like pod contains 1 to 8 seeds. The small flowers are yellow and have 5 petals.

The yellow paloverde (illustrated) grows 15 to 25 feet tall. It has twisted, crooked twigs and branches. There is a tough spine at the tip of each twig.

The yellow paloverde grows in warm areas where there is dry, sandy or rocky soil. It is native to southern California, Arizona and New Mexico. It is the state tree of Arizona.

pangolin\ pan-'gō-lən\ (scaly anteater)

The pangolins make up a family of scaly mammals. They are toothless animals that look very much like reptiles. Pangolins have tough, sharp-edged scales that

PANGOLIN

cover them on the upper side from nose to tip of tail.

All pangolins are nocturnal animals. They make their homes in shallow burrows that they dig, or they take over the burrows of other animals. A pangolin can curl itself into a tight ball, even hooking the tip of the tail over a scale on the back. It is almost impossible to unroll a pangolin from this locked position. Pangolins curl up both to sleep and when they are in danger.

Large sharp claws on the front feet are used to tear open ant or termite nests. With their long, sticky tongues, they lick up the insects. Pangolins can extend their tongues almost half the length of their long, low bodies.

The largest pangolin is the giant pangolin (illustrated), which is native to equatorial Africa. Although some kinds live in trees, the giant pangolin lives on the ground.

This extremely powerful pangolin is 5 to 6 inches high and up to 6 feet long. It has 3- to 4-inch curved foreclaws. Its largest scales are about 3 by 5 inches.

papaw \ˈpäp-ˌȯ\ (pawpaw)

The papaws make up a group of trees and shrubs native to the eastern half of the U.S. They bear fruit that is edible but not very tasty. Some describe the papaw fruit as like a banana, while others say it tastes like an old, soft potato.

The papaws have broad, glossy leaves. The leaves and twigs give off an unpleasant odor when crushed. Small flowers appear on the twigs in spring, at the same time as the new leaves. Each flower has 3 outer petals that curve downward, set around 3 inner petals that stand erect. The smooth-skinned fruit ripens in early autumn.

The common papaw becomes a tree 20 to 40 feet tall. Its flowers (illustrated) are yellowish-green, later turning dark purplish-brown or red. The leaves are 10 to 12 inches long and 6 to 8 inches wide.

The fruit of the common papaw is 3 to 5 inches long. The skin is yellow at first, turning brown as the fruit ripens. Inside is a soft pulp containing large seeds.

The common papaw grows throughout the Mississippi Valley and as far west as Nebraska. A smaller, bush-sized papaw grows only along the Atlantic and Gulf coasts.

papaya \pə-ˈpī-ə\

The papaya is a fruit tree native to the American tropics. It looks much like a palm tree, as it has a slender trunk that is topped by 1 cluster of very large leaves. Flowers and fruit dangle below the leaves, at different times during the year.

PAPAYA

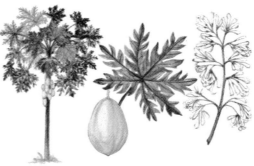

Papaya trees grow fast but live only a few years. They begin to bear fruit when only about 12 feet tall. They never become taller than about 30 feet.

The trumpet-shaped flowers are yellow or whitish and very fragrant. The fruit is 3 to 6 inches long and looks like a melon. The edible part is the soft, sweet pulp just inside the yellow or orange skin. The center is hollow. Black, wrinkled seeds the size of peas cling to the inner surface of the pulp.

Papaya fruit spoils quickly, so most of it is sold and eaten in the areas where the trees grow. Some fruit is used to make a juice or powder that is sprinkled on meat to make it more tender.

The papaya tree has been planted in Hawaii and in southern Florida. Some trees grow in southern California, but the fruit does not ripen well there. Even a slight frost will kill the papaya tree.

paper mulberry \ 'məl-ˌber-ē \

The paper mulberry is a tree belonging to the mulberry family. The fruit is not good to eat. The Polynesians use the bark to make a cloth called tapa. The Japanese use the inner bark to make paper.

The paper mulberry is native to China, Burma and the islands of Polynesia. It has been planted in many other parts of the world as an ornamental tree. It will grow almost anywhere, so long as the winter is not too severe.

In the U.S., the paper mulberry grows mostly in the southeastern states.

The paper mulberry is usually a small tree, growing to 25 to 30 feet tall. The leaves are 4 to 11 inches long, larger than the leaves of the other mulberry trees. Some leaves are heart-shaped while others are divided into several pointed lobes. Both leaves and twigs are hairy and rough to the touch.

The flowers are small tassels that dangle from the twigs in spring. Staminate and pistillate flowers are borne on separate trees. The fruit that ripens in September is a bristly ball about ¾ inch across.

parakeet \ 'par-ə-ˌkēt \

Parakeets are small, colorful parrots that live in the tropics. They are kept as cage birds in all parts of the world. Most wild parakeets are green or blue, and about 9 inches long. Yellow and white parakeets have been bred in captivity.

In Africa, India, Malaysia, Australia, Central and South America and the Caribbean islands, noisy flocks of wild parakeets feed on grain and seeds. Some nest on the ground, some in hollow trees. They make a variety of chirping and whistling noises, and scream when angry.

The Carolina parakeet, once common, became extinct about 1921.

PAPER MULBERRY

PARAKEET

The Australian budgerigar (illustrated) is the kind of parakeet most often seen in pet shops. It is about 7 inches long. This kind breeds well in captivity, the female laying as many as 9 eggs twice a year.

Like many other birds of the parrot family, the budgerigar can be taught to do simple tricks, to imitate human speech and to whistle short tunes.

paramecium \ˌpar-ə-ˈmē-sh(ē-)əm\

The paramecia are among the most common of the microscopic, 1-celled animals known as protozoans. Paramecia are almost always present in stagnant water.

Paramecia are among the smallest and simplest animals that have different body parts to serve different purposes. Their cell walls are covered with hair-like cilia that move in waves as they swim. They feed on bacteria, algae and floating animals smaller than themselves. They reproduce by fission.

The common, slipper-shaped paramecium (illustrated) has a groove along 1 side that funnels bits of food into a special mouth opening. On the opposite side is a smaller opening where waste materials are put out of the cell. Near the 2 ends are pump-like structures that let water into the cell or push it out. Food is stored in special cell parts called vacuoles. Near the center are 2 nuclei, 1 large and 1 small.

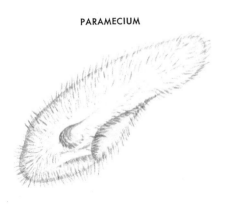

PARAMECIUM

PARROT

parrot

Parrots make up a large group of intelligent and colorful birds. There are 300 or more different kinds living in all parts of the tropics. Since about 400 B.C., parrots have been kept as pets and taught to imitate human speech.

All parrots have unusually strong, hooked beaks. The males and females usually look just alike. The smallest are 3½ inches long while the largest are 40 inches long.

Parrots feed on nuts, seeds, fruit and grain. Except while nesting, they travel and feed in large, noisy flocks. They are a nuisance in some places where they damage farmers' crops.

Some parrots nest in hollow trees, and some nest in burrows on the ground. They mate for life. The largest kinds lay 1 egg at a time, while the smaller kinds lay as many as 9. The young birds are blind and helpless.

The African gray parrot (illustrated) is the most expensive pet parrot. It is popular as a pet because it can be taught to imitate human speech very clearly. It is a medium-sized parrot about 13 inches long.

For other kinds of parrots, see *cockatoo, macaw* and *parakeet.*

PARSLEY

parsley \ 'pär-slē \

The parsley family is made up of about 2,000 different plants. Most are weeds and wild flowers, but some are vegetables and some are herbs used for flavoring foods. Celery, carrot, parsnip, dill and anise are all plants that belong to the parsley family. All are native to Europe and the Mediterranean region of Asia.

All plants of the parsley family have tiny flowers borne in umbrella-shaped clusters. Most have ragged-edged, compound leaves. Many have fragrant seeds.

The garden plant called parsley (illustrated) is used to decorate and season many different foods. Its dainty, ruffled leaves are a deep green color and have a mild, peppery flavor. They are a good source of vitamins.

The ancient Greeks and Romans grew garden parsley and used its leaves for both flavor and decoration. They also used wreaths made of the leaves in some ceremonies to honor heroes.

Garden parsley grows 10 to 15 inches tall. It is a biennial that lives through 1 winter and produces greenish-yellow flowers and tiny seeds the second summer. Parsley may be grown from seed or roots.

For other members of the parsley family, see *carrot, celery, dill, parsnip* and *poison hemlock*.

parsnip \ 'pärs-nəp \

The parsnip is a vegetable belonging to the parsley family. It has a fairly strong taste and smell, and it is very nutritious. This useful food plant, along with many other vegetables and herbs, was brought to America by European settlers.

The edible part of the parsnip is an enlarged taproot something like a carrot. The parsnip root may be 18 inches long and 3½ inches across at the widest point.

The parsnip plant is a biennial that produces flowers and seeds the second summer, if the root has not been harvested. The plants grow 3 to 5 feet tall. The compound leaves are dull green. Small, greenish-yellow flowers are borne in umbrella-shaped clusters at the tops of the branching stems.

Parsnips grow well in a cool climate. They taste best if they are left in the ground until midwinter. A hard frost improves their flavor.

partridge \ 'pär-trij \

Partridges are plump, swift-flying game birds that belong to the same family as pheasants and quail. They are native to the grasslands and cool, dry forests of the Old World. Two kinds, the chukar and Hungarian partridges, have been introduced successfully to North America.

PARTRIDGE

Partridges are gray and brown birds larger than quail but smaller than chickens. Except during the nesting season, they feed and travel in small flocks called coveys. They eat mostly seeds, berries and insects. Some sleep on the ground, the covey forming a circle with each bird facing out.

The Hungarian partridge (illustrated) was brought to the U.S. in 1800 and is now fairly common in the northern states and southern Canada. It is a favorite with hunters because it flies as fast as 50 miles an hour and makes a difficult target.

The female Hungarian partridge lays 9 to 20 eggs in a grass-lined nest on the ground. She incubates them for 24 days, while the male stands guard.

passenger pigeon

The passenger pigeon was a large North American bird of the dove family. It was once so common that large flocks sometimes darkened the sky. Passenger pigeons were hunted to extinction because they were a popular food and easily killed. The last wild birds were seen in 1899. The last passenger pigeon in captivity died in a Cincinnati zoo in 1914.

The passenger pigeon was about 17 inches long. It fed on berries and nuts, particularly beechnuts. The birds wintered in the southern U.S., from Arkansas and North Carolina south to Texas and Florida. In spring they migrated to crowded nesting grounds in the northeastern states and southern Canada.

At nesting grounds in Michigan and Wisconsin, millions of the birds were killed and shipped to cities where they were sold as food. As late as 1878, hunters used clubs, nets and smoke from burning sulfur as well as guns to kill the birds. So many were killed that some were used to feed pigs.

Passenger pigeons did not reproduce rapidly, as each female laid not more than 2 eggs a year. In small scattered flocks and in captivity they did not nest at all.

pea

The pea plant that grows in vegetable gardens belongs to a large family called the pea or legume family. Like many other vegetables, the garden pea (illustrated) was developed from a wild plant native to southern Europe. It was brought to America by the early settlers. The garden pea is nutritious and is a good source of vitamins A, B and C.

Pea plants have curling tendrils. The tall-growing varieties need some support to cling to. The leaves are compound and the leaflets are smooth and rounded. The butterfly-shaped flowers are usually white.

PASSENGER PIGEON

PEA

The fruit is a flat pod 2 to 4 inches long containing a number of round seeds called peas. In Europe, and in China and Japan, the young, tender pods are often eaten along with the seeds.

Peas need cool weather, so in most parts of the U.S. they are planted very early in spring. Light frost does not damage the plant, but hot weather kills it. Peas are ready to eat in 6 to 8 weeks.

For other members of the pea family, see *acacia, alfalfa, bean, clover, lentil, licorice, locoweed, locust, lupine, mesquite, mimosa tree, paloverde, peanut, poinciana* and *redbud*.

peach tree

The peach is a fruit tree from China. It belongs to the rose family and is related to the plum, cherry and apricot trees.

The Chinese value the peach tree for its deep pink flowers as well as for its sweet, juicy fruit. The flowers appear early in spring, before the leaves. The peach blossom is the state flower of Delaware.

Peach trees are usually 15 to 25 feet tall. They seldom live to be more than 20 years old. The leaves are narrow and pointed, and are about 5 inches long. The fruit turns yellow, shaded with red, as it ripens. The skin of the fruit is fuzzy. The 1 large seed inside the fruit is rough and pitted.

Peach trees will grow almost anywhere in the temperate zone, but they bear the most fruit only where the winters are mild and the summers warm and not too dry. Late frosts are likely to damage the flowers so that little or no fruit develops. Sandy, well-drained soil is best for peach trees. California, South Carolina, Georgia and Michigan are the states that lead in the production of peaches.

peafowl \ 'pē-ˌfau̇l \

Peafowl are large birds belonging to the same family as pheasants and quail. They are among the most beautiful of all birds, but they are usually cross and quarrelsome. The sounds they make are harsh cackles and loud screams.

Wild peafowl live in southeastern Asia and in some parts of Africa. They eat mostly seeds and grass. Each male is accompanied by a harem of 2 to 5 females. He attracts the females by strutting and showing off his colorful feathers.

The males, which are called "peacocks," measure 6 to 8 feet long, from beak to the end of the trailing feathers. The females, called "peahens," are dull-colored and smaller. Each female lays 3 to 5 buff-brown eggs once a year.

Peafowl have been kept as ornamental birds since about 1000 B.C. In spite of this, they are not entirely domesticated.

PEACH TREE

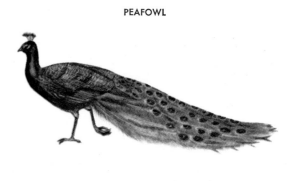

PEAFOWL

The common peafowl (illustrated) is the one most often seen in zoos and parks, and on private estates. It is native to India and Ceylon.

peanut

The peanut is an unusual plant that belongs to the pea family. It produces its fruit underground. The peanut is native to the American tropics.

The plant has 2 sets of yellow flowers. The larger set is near the top of the plant and the smaller set is near the ground. The smaller flowers bend over until they touch the ground and grow down into it, where the seedpod or peanut shell forms.

The peanut plant is a low-growing, sprawling or bushy plant with compound leaves. Each leaf is made up of 4 broad leaflets about 2 inches long.

The seeds, called peanuts, ripen only where the summer is very long and hot. In the U.S., peanuts are an important farm crop in Georgia, North Carolina, Virginia, Texas and Alabama. The whole plant is dug up in the fall and dried in the sun. The leaves and stems are made into hay for livestock. The seeds that are to be eaten as nuts are roasted and usually salted. Other seeds are made into peanut butter, cooking oil, margarine, soaps, cosmetics and many other products. Peanut shells can be made into wallboard.

PEANUT

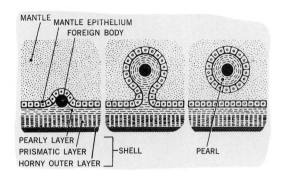

FORMATION OF A PEARL

pearl

The pearl is a gem, greatly valued for its beauty. It is created by a living animal, the oyster. An oyster makes a pearl by surrounding an object such as a grain of sand with layers of the same material that lines its shell. The material is called mother-of-pearl. It contains aragonite, a mineral that the oyster manufactures from calcium and other substances in sea water. The tiny crystals of aragonite are held together by a material like cartilage. Pearls are softer than other gems and are easily scratched.

The part of the oyster's body that lies nearest the shell, and that manufactures both the shell lining and pearl, is called the mantle.

Pearls show faint rainbow colors because light rays are bent as they pass through the thin, translucent layers of aragonite.

Natural pearls are not always round. Their shape depends on the shape of the object around which they are built.

Cultured pearls are round beads cut from mother-of-pearl and placed inside the shells of living oysters. The oysters are then placed in the sea, inside metal cages, for several years. During this time, the oysters coat the beads with a thin layer of true pearl.

PEAR TREE

pear tree

The pear tree is an important fruit tree from Europe. It belongs to the rose family, and is related to the apple tree.

Pears were known to the ancient Greeks and Romans. For many centuries, France was the chief center of pear growing. Most varieties of pears planted in America today were developed in France.

The pear tree grows as tall as 40 feet and lives as long as 60 years. Its white flowers appear fairly late in the spring. The leaves are broad but taper to a sharp point at the tip.

The fruit of the pear tree is bell-shaped. It contains a core like that of an apple, with 1 to 10 hard seeds. The edible part of the fruit is mild-flavored and juicy. It may contain a few gritty particles called stone cells. The thin, smooth skin of the fruit is yellow, brown or reddish.

Pear trees grow best where the climate is mild but where there is some cool winter weather. In the U.S., California, Washington and Oregon lead in the production of pears. About half the U.S. crop is eaten as fresh fruit. The other half is canned.

peat \ 'pēt \

Peat is a dark brown or black material soft enough to crumble in the hand. It is made up of partly rotted plants, along with some bits of sand and clay. Most peat contains visible traces of leaves, moss or wood.

In the U.S., peat is used to enrich and loosen the soil of lawns and flower gardens. In Ireland and other parts of Europe, it is cut into blocks, dried and used as fuel for heating houses.

Peat is found where there was once a shallow lake or pond. Leaves, twigs, moss and ferns sank to the bottom and decayed. In time, plant materials filled the pond. The water disappeared, and a bed of peat remained. Such peat beds are common in Canada, the northern U.S. and northern Europe, where glaciers scraped out many shallow lakes.

Coal is very old peat that has been changed by heat and pressure, deep underground. When coal or peat are burned, they release energy from the sun that was stored up by plants that grew long ago.

See *coal*.

peccary \ 'pek-ə-rē \

The peccaries are wild mammals belonging to the swine family. They are the only wild pigs native to America, and were once common from Arkansas through Central and South America to Argentina.

PECCARY

PELICAN

Peccaries are thinner and longer-legged than domestic hogs, and they have longer hair. They are 3 to 4 feet long, and weigh 40 to 65 pounds. On the peccary's arched back is a musk gland that gives off a strong smell when the animal is excited.

Peccaries are usually shy and run from danger. When cornered, they fight fiercely, biting savagely with their sharp teeth.

Plant materials, such as roots, nuts and grain, make up most of the peccary's diet. They may also eat some small animals, such as mice and snakes.

The collared peccary (illustrated) is the kind that still lives in wild, forested parts of Texas, Arizona and New Mexico. It is brownish-black, with a yellowish-white band around the shoulder. The young are reddish, with a black stripe down the back.

pelican \ 'pel-i-kən \

Pelicans make up a family of large, heavy-bodied water birds. They have unusual throat pouches. Loose skin under the bill and along the front of the throat stretches so that the bird can scoop up and hold about 3 gallons of seawater. When it tips its bill down, the water drains out, leaving fish and other bits of food ready for swallowing.

Pelicans look awkward on the ground, but they swim well and fly fast. They dive underwater to scoop up fish.

Pelicans are white or brown, with crested heads and webbed feet. Males and females look alike. Both incubate the 1 to 4 white eggs, and feed the helpless young birds on partly digested fish.

The brown pelican (illustrated) is about 50 inches long, with a wingspread of 6 feet. It lives in marshy areas and along seacoasts, as far north as the Carolinas and the middle of California. Large flocks winter in Florida, along the Gulf coast and along the Atlantic coasts of Central and South America.

The eastern brown pelican is the state bird of Louisiana.

penguin \ 'pen-gwən \

Penguins are birds that cannot fly. They spend their time in water except during breeding and molting seasons. They live in Antarctica, on nearby islands and along the southern coasts of Africa, South America and Australia.

Swimming underwater, penguins feed on fish, shrimp and squid. The birds swim very fast, using their stiff flippers as paddles and their feet as rudders. On land they often slide along over snow on their bellies.

PENGUIN

Penguins feed and nest in large, noisy flocks. They usually mate for life. The females lay 1 or 2 eggs. The young birds are often left in nurseries, cared for by a few adult baby-sitters, while the parents go to sea to feed.

The largest kind of penguin is the emperor penguin (illustrated). It stands 4 feet tall and weighs 75 pounds. The male incubates the single egg for about 60 days during the coldest part of the polar night. He holds the egg on top of his feet, where it is protected by a flap of warm, feathered skin.

penicillium \\,pen-ə-'sil-ē-əm\\

The penicillia are molds, tiny plants that grow from airborne reproductive cells called spores. Some kinds form patches of green or blue fuzzy growth on foods left uncovered. One kind is used to make a valuable medicine called penicillin.

Some kinds of penicillia have been used for centuries by cheese makers. Roquefort, Gorgonzola and Camembert cheeses all owe their special flavors to penicillium molds that act on milk.

In 1929 an English scientist, Sir Alexander Fleming, noticed that some bacteria disappeared when a certain penicillium grew near them. The mold was making an unknown substance that killed bacteria.

PENICILLIUM

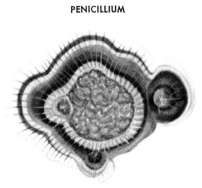

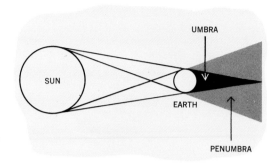

PENUMBRA

From this discovery came penicillin, the first antibiotic medicine. Penicillin cures many infections by attacking certain harmful bacteria in living things.

Most penicillin is produced from 1 kind of penicillium (illustrated), grown in huge vats in laboratories.

penumbra \\pə-'nəm-brə\\

A penumbra is a partial shadow, surrounding the cone of darkness created by an eclipse. The word "umbra" means shadow, while the word "penumbra" means partial shadow.

In both solar and lunar eclipses, the sun is larger than the earth or the moon, which are the objects casting the shadow. This produces a tapering umbra and a widespreading penumbra.

In a lunar eclipse (illustrated), the earth moves between the sun and the moon. The moon passes from sight if it goes through the umbra. Only a part of the moon vanishes if it passes through the penumbra.

In a solar eclipse, the moon moves between the earth and the sun. Where the umbra falls on the earth's surface, the eclipse is total. The sun passes from sight and the sky turns dark. Where the penumbra falls on the earth's surface, a partial eclipse is seen. Part of the sun disappears, and it may look like a crescent moon.

The partly dark border around the dark center of a sunspot is also called a penumbra.

See *eclipse*.

peony \ 'pē-ə-nē \

Peonies are perennial plants that bear very large, showy flowers. They have been cultivated for their flowers for several hundred years, and many different kinds have been produced. Some come from Europe, while others come from China, Japan and other parts of Asia.

Peonies have leaves cut into narrow, pointed segments so that they form a pattern that looks something like a bird's foot. Peony plants have thickened or tuberous roots. They can be grown from seed, but are usually planted by burying roots.

Most peonies grow 2 to 4 feet tall. A few are tree-like. All bloom in the spring. Single-flowering kinds have 5 to 10 broad petals around a cluster of narrow stamens. Double-flowering kinds have broad stamens that look like more petals.

The old-fashioned garden peony (illustrated) has red, cream-colored or white flowers about 4 inches across.

The peony has been adopted as the state flower of Indiana.

PEONY

PEPPERCORNS AND ENLARGED
CROSS SECTION

pepper

"Pepper" is the name given to 2 different groups of plants. Both groups grow in the tropics, and both groups are used to make spices and seasonings for food.

Bell peppers, green and red peppers, chili peppers, cayenne and paprika all come from plants of the nightshade family that is native to tropical America. Their fruits are large, pod-like berries that are hollow or spongy inside, where the seeds form. The hot-tasting kinds, like the chili pepper, are usually slender and pointed. Mild-flavored kinds, like the bell pepper, are more nearly round. The fruit turns red as it ripens.

Black and white pepper come from a vine of the pepper family native to Asia. Peppercorns (illustrated) are the dried berries of the pepper vine. Black pepper is produced when the whole peppercorn is ground. Milder-flavored white pepper is made from the inside part only.

The pepper vine has pointed or heart-shaped leaves. Tiny red flowers are borne in slender, pointed clusters.

peppermint

The peppermint is a perennial plant belonging to the mint family. Tiny glands in the leaves contain an oil used to flavor

PEPPERMINT

chewing gum, candy and medicines. A strong, pleasant mint smell is given off when the leaves are crushed.

Peppermint plants grow 1 to 3 feet tall. The leaves taper to a point, and have fine saw-toothed edges. The stems are squarish. Slender spikes of small, purplish-blue flowers appear at the tops of the plants throughout the summer. New plants grow from spreading roots as well as from seed.

Like many other useful plants, peppermint was brought to America by settlers from Europe. It now grows wild in parts of the eastern U.S., usually along streams where the soil is moist.

Peppermint is an important farm crop in parts of Indiana, Michigan, Washington and Oregon. The leaves are harvested and taken to mills where the oil is removed by distillation under pressure.

perch \ 'pərch \

The perch make up a large family of about 100 kinds of fish. All live in freshwater streams and ponds. Most are fairly small. Some kinds of perch are popular as both game fish and as food.

Perch have pointed snouts and forked tailfins. The 2 fins on the fish's back are separated, and only the front fin is spiny. A dark, curving lateral line shows up clearly on each side of the fish's body.

Perch are most common in the cooler parts of the Great Lakes area and the Mississippi Valley. They usually feed near the bottom. They eat smaller fish, insects, plankton and crayfish.

Spawning takes place in April and May, in shallow water near shore. The females lay 8,000 or more eggs, in long sticky strings that cling to stones on the bottom. The eggs hatch 7 to 10 days later.

The yellow perch is valued as both a food and game fish. It grows to about 12 inches and weighs about 1 pound.

For another member of the perch family, see *walleye*.

persimmon \ pər-'sim-ən \ tree

The persimmons are a group of useful, fruit-bearing trees. All are tropical except 1 kind which is common throughout eastern North America, as far north as New York.

Persimmon wood is hard and strong. It is used to make tool handles, shuttles for weaving cloth, billiard cues and golf club heads.

Persimmon trees have very small, white or green flowers that appear in the spring, after the leaves. The leaves are broad and glossy.

The common persimmon (illustrated) grows 30 to 50 feet tall, in wooded areas where the soil is fairly dry. The trees of-

PERSIMMON TREE

ten sprout from spreading roots and form dense thickets.

The fruit is yellow, orange or dark brown. It is round or slightly flattened, and 1 to 3 inches across. Each fruit contains 1 to 8 large seeds.

Persimmon fruit becomes edible only when it turns soft after the first frost. Before that it is very sour.

petrel \ 'pe-trəl \

The petrels are a group of sea birds closely related to the albatross. All petrels fly far away from land. They breathe through nostril tubes in the upper part of the hooked bill. Petrels feed on small fish and floating plankton, scooping them up from the surface of the water. Some petrels follow ships for the food scraps thrown overboard.

Petrels alight on land only during the breeding season. Large flocks return each year to nesting grounds on offshore islands, mostly south of the equator. Their nests are underground burrows.

Male and female petrels take turns incubating the 1 egg for 5 to 8 weeks. The young bird must be fed for about 7 weeks, an unusually long period.

The giant petrel is 3 feet long, with a wingspread of 8 feet. The storm petrels, called Mother Carey's chickens by sailors, are the size of sparrows.

PETREL

PETRIFIED WOOD

The diving petrel (illustrated) ducks underwater to capture bits of food, and often appears to swim through a tall wave. It is 6 to 10 inches long.

petrified \ 'pe-trə-ˌfīd \ wood

Petrified wood is wood that has become stone. Over a long period of time, minerals were deposited in the wood cells and hardened. The hardening preserved the shapes and structures of parts of ancient trees.

Petrified wood is found where mud or wet sand covered stumps and fallen tree trunks. Since the wood was not exposed to the air, it did not decay rapidly. Water carrying dissolved silica and other minerals trickled down through the sand and mud and seeped into the wood.

In time, deposits of the minerals replaced the cell walls. What had been wood became solid rock.

Petrified wood is mostly silica, in such forms as chalcedony, opal and agate. Most of it is gray or brown, but traces of iron oxide and other materials give it streaks or spots of red, yellow, black or purple.

Thousands of petrified logs lie on the ground at Petrified Forest National Park in Arizona. They are the trunks of pine trees that grew 150 million years ago.

PETUNIA

petunia \ pǝ-'tün-yǝ \

Petunias are flowering plants of the night-shade family. Once started, petunias require little care. They bloom all summer.

The wild petunias native to South America were probably perennials. The cultivated kinds developed from them are annuals killed by even a light frost. The seeds are often planted indoors, in wooden boxes or flowerpots, in early spring. The plants are moved outdoors when all danger of frost is past.

Petunia plants have fuzzy, sticky leaves and stems. Some are low-growing, bushy plants. Some have long but weak stems and sprawl on the ground.

The flower petals are joined together in a funnel-shaped corolla. It is twisted in the bud and unrolls as it opens.

The common garden petunia (illustrated) has white, pink, red or purple flowers. Some are double, ruffled or fringed at the edge. The fruit is a dry pod containing a number of tiny, black seeds.

pheasant \ 'fez-ᵊnt \

Pheasants are game birds belonging to the same family as peafowl and quail.

The largest males measure 8 feet long, counting tail feathers. The females are smaller, speckled brown and gray birds.

Pheasants are native to Asia, but they live in many other parts of the world. They were first released in North America about 1790 by Richard Bache, Benjamin Franklin's son-in-law.

Birds of open country, pheasants feed on grain, weed seeds, insects and green plants. Males stand guard over breeding territories where the several females of their harems nest. Each hen lays 8 to 15 eggs, once a year, in a nest on the ground.

The ring-necked pheasant (illustrated) is the kind now fairly common in the U.S. and southern Canada. Its original home was China. This pheasant is the state bird of South Dakota.

phlox \ 'fläks \

Phlox make up a family of many kinds of wild flowers and cultivated garden plants. Some are annuals and some are perennials. A few kinds are native to Asia. All the rest are native to North America.

Kinds of phlox vary from a few inches to 4 feet tall. All have narrow, hairy leaves. Clusters of flowers appear at the tops of the stems, at different times during the summer. The flower petals are joined together in a tube-shaped corolla that opens out into 5 round or pointed sections. The corolla is white, lavender, pink, red or purple. The fruit is a 3-part seedpod.

Most plants of the phlox family are

PHEASANT

PHOEBE

hardy and will grow in a variety of soils and climates.

Wild sweet William (illustrated) is a wild phlox fairly common in the eastern half of North America. It grows 1 to 3 feet tall, in open fields or along riverbanks. The leaves are 3 to 5 inches long. The pink or purple flowers are about ½ inch across. It blooms in April or May.

For another member of the phlox family, see *Jacob's ladder*.

phoebe \ 'fē-bē \

The phoebes are medium-sized, dark-colored birds belonging to the flycatcher family. They are swift and skillful flyers, and feed entirely on insects they capture in the air. Phoebes live in both North and South America.

Phoebes usually live near water where there are plenty of flying insects. Wet mud is used for the unusual, pocket-shaped nest, along with some feathers and grass. The nest is fastened to a vertical surface protected from rain. Western phoebes build nests in caves and on canyon walls. Eastern phoebes build under bridges or under the eaves of barns.

Three to 8 eggs are laid once a year and are incubated for about 12 days.

The black phoebe (illustrated) is about 7 inches long. It has a fairly large head and small, weak feet that are used only for perching. It is a year-round resident of California, the southwestern states, Mexico and part of South America. The black phoebe builds its nest against cliff faces, canyon walls and, sometimes, inside deserted buildings.

phosphorite \ 'fäs-fə-ˌrīt \

Phosphorite is a kind of rock used to make fertilizer. Phosphorite contains phosphates, which are minerals made up of phosphorus combined with oxygen.

When fields are used year after year for growing crops, the supply of phosphates in the soil is used up. Fertilizer made from crushed phosphorite is often added to the soil to renew the phosphates.

Phosphorite is a sedimentary rock that occurs in thin, flat beds, where minerals were deposited by water. The phosphorite is largely made up of once-living materials, such as bones, shells and birds' droppings, and also contains some clay particles.

Phosphorite is usually gray, or sometimes black, reddish or brown. It may occur in solid, hard blocks, in loose grains or in fibrous masses.

Large deposits of phosphorite have been mined in France, Belgium, Spain, Africa and, in the U.S., in Florida, Tennessee, South Carolina and the northern Rocky Mountains.

PHOSPHORITE

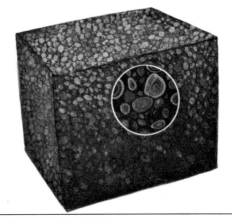

PIKA

pickerelweed \ 'pik-(ə-)rəl-ˌwēd \

Pickerelweeds are wild, flowering plants that grow in wet soil. They are 1 to 3 feet tall, with pointed or arrow-shaped leaves. Flowers bloom all summer long, but they fade quickly.

The flowers are blue, purplish-blue or white, and are shaped something like snapdragons. Each has a tube-shaped corolla that spreads open in 2 parts something like upper and lower lips. Each lip is cut into 3 pointed sections. The upper lip is usually spotted with white or yellow.

The pickerelweeds are fairly common in eastern North America. They usually appear in clumps, as new plants grow up from spreading, horizontal roots.

Common pickerelweed is sometimes called alligator wampee. It is an attractive wild flower that grows in shallow ponds and marshy places. Its purplish-blue or white flowers bloom from slender, pointed spikes about 4 inches long at the tops of the plants. The plants are from 2½ to 3 feet tall. The leaves are from 6 to 10 inches long.

pika \ 'pī-kə \

Pikas are small, furry mammals with short ears and no visible tails. They are closely related to rabbits, but they look more like guinea pigs. They are mainly nocturnal animals that live only on mountains in North America and Asia.

Pikas eat only plant foods. Because the winters are long and cold where they live, and they do not hibernate, it is necessary for them to store up a large supply of food during the summer. They pile grass and leaves in the sun to dry and then hide it under rocks or in their burrows.

Pikas are social animals, usually seen in groups. Their calls are high-pitched, whistling sounds. The females give birth to litters of 2 to 4 young, twice a year.

The most common kind of American pika (illustrated) is about 8 inches long and weighs 6 to 7 ounces. It is brown, shading toward yellow on the head, with whitish feet. It lives in the Rocky Mountains, 2,000 to 6,000 feet above sea level, in both the U.S. and Canada.

pike \ 'pīk \

Pike make up a family of long, slender game fish that includes the pickerel and muskellunge. They are favorites of sportsmen who catch them in the cooler lakes and streams of Europe, Asia and North America.

Pike have round rather than flat bodies. The long mouth contains many sharp teeth, and the lower jaw sticks out beyond

PIKE

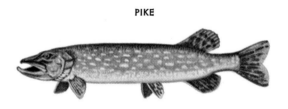

the upper jaw. The dorsal fin is near the tail. None of the pike's fins have sharp spines in them, and there is no marked lateral line along the sides of the body.

When hooked, pike are usually fierce fighters. They kill and eat frogs and young ducks as well as other fish. They usually swim singly, rather than in schools. Pike spawn very early in the spring.

The northern pike (illustrated) is an active, long-lived fish that averages 3 feet in length and weighs 12 pounds or more. Some weigh up to 40 pounds. The northern pike is found from New England and the Great Lakes west to Alaska.

For another member of the pike family, see *muskellunge*.

pilot fish

The pilot fish is a fairly small ocean fish that was named by sailors who saw it swim with sharks. They guessed that it led the shark to food. Actually, the pilot fish follows rather than leads the shark, to share its meals.

Pilot fish are 1 to 2 feet long. They are bluish, with 5 to 7 dark, vertical stripes.

Spawning takes place at sea, and the tiny eggs float. Newly hatched pilot fish look quite different from the adults. The young are short, with large eyes. Spines stick out from their heads. They are not

PILOT FISH

LEAVES AND BERRIES OF PIMENTO TREE

harmed by the poisonous tentacles of jellyfish and the Portuguese man-of-war, and they often hide under them for protection from enemies.

Pilot fish live in the warmer parts of all the oceans. In the Atlantic, they are found from Cape Cod south to Brazil.

pimento \pə-'ment-ˌō\ tree

The pimento tree is a tropical evergreen of the myrtle family. It is native to the West Indies and Central America.

The berries of the pimento tree are harvested when green. They are dried and ground to make allspice, which combines the flavors of clove, cinnamon and nutmeg. Jamaica leads in the production of allspice.

The pimento tree grows 20 to 40 feet tall. The bark is smooth and gray. The pointed leaves are dark green and glossy. Small white flowers are borne in clusters at the ends of the branches. The round berries turn purplish-black as they ripen, but they have a better flavor if picked before they turn dark. The leaves, twigs and berries have a pleasant, spicy smell.

The fruit of a sweet pepper plant is also called pimento, or pimiento. It is bright red, and is often used to stuff olives and decorate salads.

pineapple

The pineapple is a tropical, perennial plant. It is unusual because its stem grows through its fruit. Some leaves grow below the fruit, while others grow above.

The pineapple is native to Central and South America. It has been cultivated since the time of the Spanish Conquest, and now grows all through the tropics. Hawaii, Puerto Rico, the Philippines and Cuba lead in production of pineapples.

In the Philippines, a kind of cloth is made from fibers in the leaves of the pineapple plant. The leaves are thick and stiff, with sharp spines along the edges. From the center of each plant a flowering stem grows 2 to 4 feet tall. Purple or reddish flowers grow all around the stem, which becomes thick and pulpy as the fruit ripens. At the top of the stem grows the cluster of leaves called the crown. It may be left on the ripe fruit.

On pineapple plantations, new plants are started by burying crowns, or by burying roots or suckers cut from growing plants. Pineapple plants seldom produce seed.

pine tree

Pines make up a large group of beautiful and useful trees. Some kinds are used to

PINEAPPLE

make lumber for building. Others are the source of turpentine.

Pines grow in nearly all parts of the northern hemisphere. Some live to be 2,000 years old.

The leaves are narrow needles that are grouped in bundles of 2, 3 or 5, depending on the kind of pine tree. The fruit is a brown, woody cone. Winged seeds fall from between the scales of the cones when they are ripe, usually at the end of the second summer.

The eastern white pine (illustrated) is a valuable lumber tree that grows 80 to 150 feet tall. The masts of sailing ships were once made from the trunks of these trees.

The dark, blue-green needles are 3 to 5 inches long. There are 5 needles to a bundle. The cones are fairly slender. They are 4 to 8 inches long and are made up of thin, smooth scales. The eastern white pine grows mostly in New England and in the Great Lakes region. It is the state tree of Maine.

Other kinds of pines are the state trees of Alabama, Arkansas, Idaho, Michigan, Minnesota, Montana, New Mexico, Nevada and North Carolina.

pinworm \ 'pin-ˌwərm \

Pinworms make up a family of parasitic roundworms which live inside the human

PINE TREE

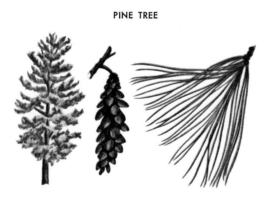

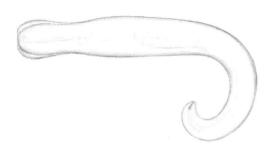

PINWORM

body. They are closely related to other parasitic worms that live in sheep, rabbits, horses, rats and mice. They cause discomfort, but no serious diseases.

Because they are white or colorless and very small, pinworms are not easy to see. The largest females are ½ inch long. The largest males are ⅕ inch long. The male pinworm (illustrated) has a hook-like, curved tail.

Pinworms live in the intestines, but lay their eggs outside the body. One female may lay thousands of eggs so small and light that they float through the air. Some people are infected by eating food the eggs have fallen onto. Others are infected by breathing eggs into their lungs. Eggs that reach the intestines hatch there.

Pinworms usually infect children rather than grownups. They are fairly common in both warm and cool parts of the northern hemisphere.

pipevine \ 'pīp-ˌvīn \

Pipevines are a group of perennial vines or shrubs. All have unusual flowers shaped something like old-fashioned tobacco pipes. The plants grow from seed.

Wild pipevines, or plants that have escaped from cultivation, are found from Pennsylvania south to Florida. They grow in rich soil, usually along the edges of streams.

Some pipevines grow only in the tropics or in greenhouses. Some are planted for their handsome leaves, rather than for their flowers. Some kinds have bad-smelling flowers. The fruit is always a pod containing flat seeds.

Dutchman's pipe is a tall, fast-growing pipevine that is native to eastern North America. Its heart-shaped leaves are sometimes 14 inches wide. The purplish-brown flowers are about 1 inch wide and 1½ inches long.

Dutchman's pipe is often planted in gardens where quick growth is needed to cover something unsightly.

pipit \ 'pip-ət \

Pipits make up a family of small, dark-colored songbirds. They live in nearly all parts of the world. They nest on the Arctic tundra and near the Antarctic Circle. In winter, they migrate to regions nearer the equator.

Pipits are 6 to 7 inches long, with slender bodies and fairly long legs. All have dark streaks on the breast, and white on the outer tail feathers. They feed and nest on the ground, and they wag their tails as they walk about.

Pipits eat mostly insects, grubs and seeds. The 5 to 7 grayish, speckled eggs are laid in a cup-shaped nest made of grass. The song is a clear twittering.

PIPIT

PIRANHA

The rock or water pipit (illustrated) lives in nearly all parts of the northern hemisphere. Its back is solid brown and its legs are dark.

In America, this pipit nests north of Hudson's Bay and winters south of New Jersey and Ohio. It lives in open fields and on seashores. When near water, it eats small crustaceans and mollusks.

piranha \ pə-'ran-yə \ (caribe)

Piranhas are small, bloodthirsty tropical fish. Sometimes 1,000 or more piranhas swim and feed together. They are attracted by splashing in the water and by blood. Piranhas have been known to attack animals such as deer or human beings that fall into the rivers where they live. After a few minutes, only a skeleton remains. Usually, however, piranhas feed on smaller fish.

The razor-sharp teeth in the piranha's upper and lower jaws fit together like scissors' blades. The fish can bite through steel fishhooks, or nip the fingers off a careless fisherman.

Most piranhas are 4 to 12 inches long. A few kinds are 18 to 24 inches long. All have narrow, flattened bodies and large heads. They are silvery-blue, greenish, yellow or black.

Piranhas live in the rivers of eastern South America, from Venezuela south to Argentina. The black piranha (illustrated) is common in streams of the Amazon basin, in Brazil.

pitchblende \ 'pich-ˌblend \

Pitchblende is a very valuable mineral that is the chief source of the uranium used in the production of atomic energy. Pitchblende is 50 to 80 percent uranium.

Pitchblende may also contain other rare elements, including radium, zirconium and helium, along with some lead. Madame Curie was studying a sample of pitchblende from what is now Czechoslovakia when she discovered radium, in 1898.

Usually black, pitchblende may have a slight green or grayish tint. It is usually found in rounded masses that look like lumps of pitch. Such masses are heavier than iron and harder than steel.

Pitchblende is found in coarse-grained granites, sandstones and other kinds of rocks. It is always found in areas where there are other metallic ores.

Nearly all the world's pitchblende comes from Canada, Czechoslovakia and the Republic of the Congo in Africa. Some pitchblende is found in southwestern England. In the U.S., small amounts have been found in Colorado, Arizona, Montana, New Mexico and Utah.

PITCHBLENDE

PITCHER PLANT

pitcher plant

Pitcher plants are a group of perennial plants native to North America. They are named from the shapes of their leaves, which grow up from the ground and are usually filled with water. Insects attracted to pitcher plants are trapped in the leaves and die.

The decaying insects provide nitrogen which the plants need, since they grow in peat bogs or other wet ground where there is little or no nitrogen in the soil.

Ball-shaped flowers and seedpods are borne at the tops of bare stems. The plants spread from creeping, horizontal roots.

Each leaf is rolled into a tube and has a kind of hood at the top. Under the hood are glands that attract insects. Inside the leaf are down-pointing hairs that keep insects from crawling out again, once they are inside. The insects drown in rainwater that collects at the bottoms of the tubes.

The common pitcher plant (illustrated) has flowers that are red on the outside and greenish on the inside. The flowering stems are about 12 inches tall. The leaves are greenish, marked with purple and red.

pit viper \ 'vī-pər \

The pit vipers make up a family of snakes which include the rattlesnakes, the copperhead and the cottonmouth moccasin. These snakes kill their prey by ejecting poison through their fangs. Large pit vipers can kill a man or a deer.

Pit vipers are named for sense organs located in pits on either side of the head. The pit is sensitive to heat, and it helps the snake locate warm-blooded animals to feed on. Pit vipers eat birds, rats and mice, as well as frogs, toads and insects.

Pit vipers live in North and South America, in Asia and in southeastern Europe. They are 2 to 8 feet long. Most have a fairly stout body, a triangular head and a slender tail.

Nearly all pit vipers give birth to living young. The young snakes develop inside eggs, as other reptiles do, but the female carries the eggs inside her body until they are ready to hatch.

For members of the pit viper family, see *snake* (copperhead, cottonmouth and rattlesnake).

plain

A plain is a fairly level part of the earth's surface. Plains are not perfectly flat, but they look flat when compared with mountains. River valleys often cut across

COASTAL PLAINS

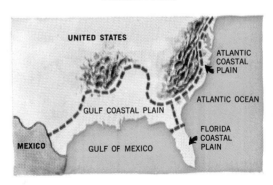

FLOOD PLAIN

plains, and there may be ranges of low hills on them.

Most plains were once covered with water. They are level because flat layers of sediments were deposited by water. Some were beds of ancient lakes.

Coastal plains were once under the ocean. They are a part of the continental shelf that extends out from the shore. The land has risen slightly, so that a part of what was once sea floor is now dry land. In the U.S., coastal plains (illustrated) extend along the Atlantic, south of New York, and along the Gulf of Mexico.

Flood plains are the level floors of broad valleys. The flood plain of the Mississippi River (illustrated) is 80 to 100 miles wide. Its fertile soil is made up of sediments that are deposited each time the river floods.

Most great civilizations have developed on plains, where travel is easy and the soil is good for farming.

planarian \ plə-'nar-ē-ən \

Planarians make up a family of flatworms living at the bottom of lakes and streams. They move about only at night. During the day they hide under rocks or leaves.

Planarians in most parts of the U.S. are brown on the back and cream-colored underneath. They are ¼ inch to 3 inches long. Kinds found near the tropics are larger and more colorful.

All planarians have very thin, flat bodies. Near the head end are 2 eyespots sensitive to light. A tube-shaped mouth is located near the middle of the body, on the underside. Planarians eat smaller worms, tiny snails and other animal foods. They reproduce by laying eggs, or by splitting into 2 parts. Planarians can be cut apart into several pieces and each part will grow into a whole animal.

One common planarian (illustrated) is usually about 1 inch long. It lives in the cooler ponds and streams of the U.S., from Wisconsin and Missouri to California.

planet \ 'plan-ət \

The planets are 9 rounded, mostly solid heavenly bodies that travel in regular orbits or paths about the sun. They are much smaller than most stars. Unlike stars, planets do not give off light but reflect light from the sun.

Venus, Mars, Jupiter and Saturn are the planets that can be seen easily without a telescope. Their light is a steady glow rather than the twinkling light of stars. Ancient sky watchers named them "planets" because they moved around the sky, appearing in different constellations at different times of the year. "Planet" means "wanderer."

PLANARIAN

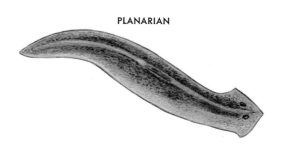

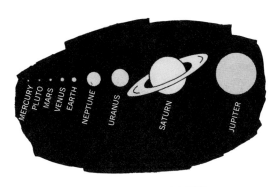

PLANETS IN ORDER OF SIZE

All the planets move in a counterclockwise direction as they circle around the sun. They take from 3 months to 248 years to complete 1 orbit. At the same time, each planet is turning on its own axis. The earth completes 1 orbit a year, and turns on its axis once a day.

Mercury, the smallest planet, is about 3,100 miles in diameter. Jupiter, the largest, is nearly 89,000 miles in diameter. The earth, 7,913 miles in diameter, is 1 of the smaller planets.

See *earth, Jupiter, Mars, Mercury, Neptune, Pluto, Saturn, Venus* and *Uranus.* See also *The Sun, the Moon and the Planets* on p. 502.

plankton \ 'plang(k)-tən \

Plankton is the mass of tiny floating plants and animals to be found in water. Most of the plants are too small to be seen without a microscope. Plankton is the chief food of fish and other water animals.

The plants that help to make up plankton are 1-celled algae, such as the diatoms and dinoflagellates. They live mostly near the surface, as they need light from the sun in order to use the food materials dissolved in the water.

The animal life in plankton is more varied. It includes protozoans, tiny crustaceans and jellyfish, as well as the eggs

and larvae of some fish and insects. These animals feed on the algae and on each other.

Plankton occurs in ponds, lakes and streams as well as in the ocean. It is most common in water that is rich in minerals. In the temperate and arctic zones, most plankton appears in the spring and early summer.

plantain \ 'plant-ən \

The plantains are a group of study plants that are mostly weeds. One kind, called seaside plantain, is used to make some medicines. The seed clusters of another kind are dried and sold in pet shops as a treat for cage birds.

The leaves of plantain are fairly coarse, with parallel veins. All the leaves grow from the ground level. The flowers and seeds grow on leafless stalks 6 to 18 inches high that rise from the centers of the plants.

Common plantain (illustrated) is a troublesome weed in lawns and flower gardens. It has broad leaves that are rough to the touch. Very tiny greenish flowers are crowded close together in slender clusters. In late summer the flowers are replaced by tiny pods holding 2 or more seeds. Wild birds eat the seeds, and they help to spread the plants.

PLANTAIN

PLATEAU

plateau \pla-'tō\

A plateau is a level area that is higher than the land on at least 1 side of it.

Some plateaus are very old mountain ranges worn nearly level by centuries of rain and wind. They are not steep or rugged mountains any longer, but they are still higher than the land around them. In the U.S., the Appalachian Plateau is an area of this kind. It is about 3,000 feet above sea level.

Other plateaus are level beds of hard rock that resisted erosion. Softer rocks and loose materials nearby were washed away, leaving a level plain with cliff-like edges. The mesas or tablelands of the western U.S. are plateaus of this kind.

The Colorado plateau is a large area of hard, level rock about 8,000 feet above sea level. The Grand Canyon of the Colorado River is a steep-sided valley that cuts through the Colorado plateau.

Plateaus usually have cool, dry climates and are seldom good for farming.

platy \'plat-ē\

Platys are small, bright-colored tropical fish that bear living young. They are popular aquarium fish, and they have been used in scientific research projects.

Platys have slender bodies, pointed snouts and large eyes. Many different kinds and colors have been developed through crossbreeding. The males are smaller than the females. The largest females are about 2 inches long.

Platys are native to Central and South America. They are most common in Mexico and Guatemala, in streams that empty into the Atlantic Ocean.

The young develop inside eggs, as all fish do, but the female carries the eggs inside her body until they hatch. She may produce as many as 300 young after 1 mating. The live young appear in bunches, at intervals of about 3 weeks.

The very colorful swordtail platy is a hybrid platy developed by crossbreeding the platy with a related fish called a swordtail.

plover \'pləv-ər\

Plovers make up a group of shorebirds with plump bodies and fairly short legs. They have stout, blunt-tipped bills something like the bills of pigeons. Their colors change with the seasons, and male and female birds always look alike. The largest plover is about 11 inches long. The smallest is 6 inches long.

Plovers live in nearly all parts of the world. Some kinds spend most of their time inland. Some kinds migrate long distances, from summer homes in the

PLOVER

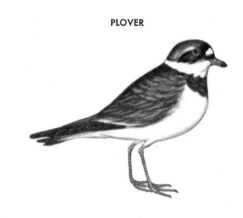

Arctic to winter homes in Argentina and New Zealand.

Inland, plovers eat mostly insects. Along seacoasts, they feed on crustaceans, worms and small fish. Plovers nest on the ground, usually on sand or pebbles where the 3 to 4 speckled eggs are nearly invisible. When an enemy comes near the nest, the adult birds pretend to be hurt. Flopping on the ground as if their wings were broken, they lead the enemy away from the nest.

The ringed or semipalmated plover (illustrated) is 6½ to 8 inches long. It nests in Alaska and northern Canada, and winters in Florida and along the Gulf coast.

plum tree

The plums are trees and shrubs belonging to the rose family. They are related to the cherries, peaches and apricots. All plums bear fruit that contains just 1 large seed.

Some plums were developed in Europe, while others were developed in China and Japan. Most plums are planted for their fruit, but some are ornamental shrubs planted for their flowers or foliage.

Plum trees grow 8 to 30 feet tall. The leaves are 1 to 3 inches long, and have fine, saw-toothed edges. The 5-petaled flowers are white, pink or red. The fruit is 1 to 2½ inches long. Some kinds of plums are red when ripe. Others are blue or purple.

The common or garden plum (illustrated) was brought to America from Europe. It grows best in a cool, fairly dry climate. In the U.S., California, Oregon, Washington and Michigan lead in the production of plums.

Some plums are marketed as fresh fruit and some are canned, while a great many are dried and sold as prunes.

Pluto \ ˈplüt-ˌō \

Pluto is 1 of the 9 planets which orbit the sun. It is the planet most distant from the sun, and was not discovered until 1930. Pluto was first seen in photographs taken through a very powerful telescope at the Lowell Observatory.

Once each 248 years, Pluto completes 1 trip around the sun. When it is nearest the sun, it is about 3 billion miles away. At its farthest point from the sun, it is 4½ billion miles away. Its day is believed to be about 150 hours long.

Pluto is so small and far away that astronomers have not been able to learn much about it. They believe it is about 3,600 miles in diameter, a little less than half the size of the earth. It is probably very dry and very cold, perhaps —370° F. It seems to have no moons. Its color is yellowish.

LEAF, FLOWER AND FRUIT OF PLUM TREE

DISCOVERY OF PLUTO (1930)

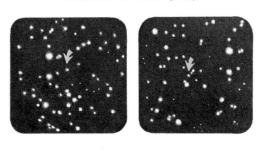

The other 8 planets all orbit the sun in about the same plane. The plane of Pluto's orbit lies at an angle to the others, so that it is sometimes above them and sometimes below.

See *The Sun, the Moon and the Planets* on p. 502.

poinciana \ ˌpȯin(t)-sē-'an-ə \

The poincianas are tropical trees and shrubs belonging to the pea family. They are native to the West Indies and to California and Florida. Poincianas bear showy red and yellow flowers all during the summer. Some kinds are shrubs, while some are trees up to 40 feet tall.

All poincianas have compound leaves made up of many, very small leaflets that grow opposite each other, with no leaflets at the ends of the stems. The fruit is a bean-like pod 4 to 24 inches long. In some places the seedpods are dried and used as fuel for cooking or heating houses. The flowers have 5 petals surrounding 10 very long stamens.

Dwarf poinciana (illustrated) grows 6 to 10 feet tall. It is usually planted as a flowering hedge. Its leaflets are about ½ inch long. The flowers have yellow or yellow-orange petals, and red stamens about 2 inches longer than the petals. The seedpods are about 4 inches long.

POINCIANA

POINSETTIA

poinsettia \ pȯin-'set-ē-ə \

The poinsettias are colorful, winter-blooming plants native to tropical America. In most parts of the U.S., they are cultivated in greenhouses and sold as potted plants at Christmas.

The true flowers of the poinsettias are very small. They are borne in clusters at the tops of the stalks. Around each cluster are 8 or more colored bracts that are often mistaken for flower petals. The bracts are usually red but may be white or pink.

Most poinsettias grow 2 to 4 feet tall. The leaves are 3 to 6 inches long, with irregularly notched edges. Some of the leaves near the top of the plant may have the same color as the bracts. The plants produce seeds in small pods, but plants are usually started by planting cuttings in damp sand.

The common poinsettia (illustrated) is the kind most often sold by florists. It can be planted outdoors only where temperatures do not drop much below 60° F.

poison hemlock \ 'hem-ˌläk \
(winter fern)

Poison hemlock is a biennial plant belonging to the parsley family. It is a common weed in Europe and Asia and now grows in much of North America.

POISON HEMLOCK

Persons eating any part of the plant or the seeds are likely to die. The poisonous drink given to the Greek philosopher Socrates about 400 B.C. was made from poison hemlock. Small children should be taught to recognize the plant and stay away from it.

Poison hemlock grows 2 to 5 feet tall. It has fern-like, compound leaves made up of many small, ragged-edged leaflets. All during the summer, tiny white flowers are borne in umbrella-shaped clusters at the tops of the stalks. The small, flattened seeds are marked with 5 light brown ribs.

poison ivy

Poison ivy is a poisonous plant belonging to the sumac group of trees and shrubs. It may be a shrub or a climbing vine. Poison ivy grows throughout North America and in the West Indies.

The 3 leaflets that make up each leaf are usually pointed, but are sometimes rounded at the tip. They are sometimes notched along the edges. The leaves turn a rich red in autumn, and the stems may show some red during the summer. The small flowers and berries are borne in loose, pointed clusters. The flowers have 5 greenish-yellow petals. The berries are white, and each contains 1 seed.

The roots, stems and leaves of poison

ivy all contain a poisonous oil that irritates the skin. When the plants are burned, smoke may carry the poison through the air.

Poison ivy is sometimes mistaken for Virginia creeper. Though the leaflets of the 2 plants look somewhat alike, Virginia creeper is not poisonous, and has 5 rather than 3 leaflets.

Poison oak is much like poison ivy, but its blunt-tipped, lobed leaflets look like oak leaves.

pompano \ˈpäm-pə-ˌnō\

Pompanos are a group of commercially valuable, ocean food fish. They are graceful fish, with deep bodies and smooth sides. The snout is blunt. The mouth contains small, useless teeth that often drop out as the fish matures. Fairly long, pointed fins are placed far back on the body. The 2 pointed lobes of the tail fin are spread wide apart.

Pompanos swim in schools, usually near the bottom where the water is fairly warm. They feed on smaller fish and on certain crustaceans.

The common pompano (illustrated) lives along the Atlantic coast, from Cape Cod to the Gulf of Mexico. It may become 18 inches long and weigh as much as 8 pounds.

POMPANO

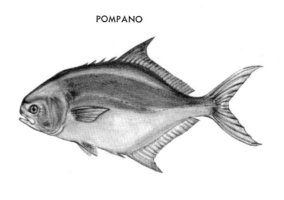

PONY

POORWILL

pony

Ponies are small, stocky breeds of horses. They are usually less than 4½ feet tall at the shoulders. Ponies serve chiefly as children's pets, but they also work at some jobs such as pulling carts in mines.

Ponies usually have short necks, stocky legs and stout bodies. They are sturdy animals, able to live on poor food that would not support other horses. They grow thick, shaggy coats in winter and need little shelter.

The Mongolian pony of northern Asia is the only wild horse living today. The Mongolian pony is also called Przhevalski's horse.

The Shetland pony (illustrated) is usually 3 to 3½ feet tall at the shoulders. Males weigh 300 to 700 pounds. Shetland ponies are brown, black, white or spotted. These ponies come from the Shetland Islands north of Scotland. The soil there is poor and rocky, and the winters are long and cold. Only a small, tough breed of horse could survive there.

poorwill\ 'pu̇r-ˌwil\

The poorwill is a bird belonging to the goatsucker family. It lives only in the western U.S. and is one of the few birds known to hibernate.

At first, naturalists did not believe Indians who said that some poorwills sleep through the winter months rather than fly south, as other insect-eating birds do. Only since 1950 has it been known for certain that while some poorwills migrate to Mexico, most hibernate in caves or in cracks between rocks. During this sleep the heartbeat of the bird is slow, its body temperature is low and it does not eat.

The poorwill is about 8 inches long. Its gray or brown feathers make it nearly invisible when on the ground, or clinging to a tree trunk. It lives in open brushland or sparse forests.

Poorwills never build nests. The 2 eggs are laid on the ground. Male and female take turns incubating them.

The loud, harsh cry of the poorwill is heard only at night.

poplar\ 'päp-lər\

Poplars are a group of fast-growing trees belonging to the willow family and closely related to cottonwoods and aspens. Poplar wood is soft and not very strong. It is used to make paper pulp, and for packing boxes. Poplars are valued as shade trees and windbreaks in areas where many trees will not grow.

Poplars are usually tall, fairly slender trees. The bark on young trees is light-

POPPY

tall. Its orange or yellow flowers wither quickly, but many appear all during the summer months. It is the state flower of California.

The opium poppy is a tall-growing plant cultivated mostly in Asia. Its seeds are used for decorating and flavoring some breads and cookies. The drug opium is made from milky juice that drips from unripe seedpods when they are cut.

porcupine \ ˈpȯr-kyə-ˌpīn \

Porcupines make up 2 different families of rodents. One family lives in the New World, from Alaska south to Central America. The other lives in warm parts of Europe, Asia and Africa.

Porcupines are best known for their quills, which are stiff, hollow bundles of hair tipped with barbs. The quills lay flat along the body, except when the animal is excited. The porcupine cannot throw its quills, but it can swing its tail so that quills stick in the flesh of an enemy.

All porcupines eat plant foods, such as roots and buds and the bark of trees. The females bear litters of 1 to 4 young, once a year.

New World porcupines are about 3½ feet long and weigh as much as 40 pounds. They are quiet, slow-moving animals that spend most of their time in trees. Some

colored and smooth. The flowers are grouped on tassels that dangle from the twigs in early spring. The leaves are broad at the base but taper to a sharp point. They have wavy or saw-toothed edges. They turn yellow in autumn.

Poplars grow throughout the northern hemisphere, from the Arctic Circle south to Mexico and parts of Africa. They are most plentiful where the climate is cool and the soil moist. They sprout quickly from roots or from cuttings. Any branch broken from a poplar tree and stuck in moist soil is likely to take root and grow.

See *cottonwood* and *quaking aspen*.

poppy

The poppies make up a family of flowering plants native to Europe, northern Asia and western North America. Some kinds of poppy bloom the first summer, while others bloom the second.

Poppies grow 6 inches to 4 feet tall. Most have hairy stems and leaves. Five-petaled flowers are borne singly, at the tops of tall stems. The flowers are red, yellow, orange, pink, white or violet.

The fruit is a seedpod that looks like a saltshaker. Small black seeds are scattered from holes in the top.

The California poppy (illustrated) is a fairly bushy perennial plant 12 to 20 inches

PORCUPINE

swing by their tails. Their quills are about 4 inches long.

Old World porcupines are about 2½ feet long, but they have quills up to 12 inches long. They live in holes in the ground and seldom climb trees.

The Canadian porcupine (illustrated) is brown or black, with white-tipped hairs and quills.

porcupine \ 'pȯr-kyə-ˌpīn \ fish (balloonfish)

Porcupine fish are a group of tropical ocean fish related to puffers. They can inflate their bodies with either water or air so as to appear much larger.

The loose skin of the porcupine fish is covered with pointed spines. When the fish swims, the spines lay flat against its sides. When the fish is attacked, it puffs up its body and the spines stick out stiffly in all directions.

Porcupine fish are 1 to 2 feet long. They have·beak-like mouths. On either side of the body are large, fan-shaped pectoral fins. The tail is not divided into lobes.

Porcupine fish are most common in shallow, warm parts of the ocean. They feed chiefly on crustaceans.

One fairly common kind of porcupine fish (illustrated) is almost ball-shaped when inflated.

PORCUPINE FISH

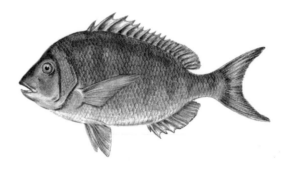

PORGY

porgy \ 'pȯr-gē \

The porgies make up a family of ocean fish that are valued both as food and game fish. There are about 100 different kinds. The fish known as sheepshead, pinfish and scup are porgies.

The largest part of the porgy's body is just behind the head. The eyes are fairly small and high on the head. The small mouth contains strong, sharp teeth. The 2 pointed lobes of the tail fin spread wide. Most porgies are about 16 inches long.

Porgies live near shore, in shallow, fairly warm parts of the ocean. In the North Atlantic, they are found from Cape Cod south to the Carolinas. They swim in schools, feeding on shellfish, small crustaceans and some seaweeds.

The northern porgy or scup (illustrated) is a popular North Atlantic game fish. It is sometimes 18 inches long, and it may weigh as much as 4 pounds.

porpoise \ 'pȯr-pəs \

Porpoises are small, toothed whales closely related to the dolphins. Like all whales, they are warm-blooded mammals that bear living young. They live in the sea, but they must regularly come to the surface to breathe air.

Porpoises are 4 to 8 feet long, with

PORPOISES LEAPING

streamlined bodies that are widest between the 2 blunt flippers. The largest porpoises weigh about 120 pounds. They have 1 low, triangular fin on the back, and their tails end in horizontal flippers.

These swift and graceful swimmers often leap out of the water before diving. They usually travel in groups, sometimes as many as 100 swimming together. They eat mostly fish and crustaceans and sometimes plants.

Porpoises mate in late summer. One young about 3 feet long is born the following summer.

Porpoises live in the northern parts of the Atlantic and Pacific oceans and in the Black Sea. The harbor porpoise (illustrated) is common in the Atlantic, as far south as New Jersey and the British Isles. It is often seen near shore, in bays and in the mouths of rivers.

Portuguese man-of-war \ ˌpōr-chə-ˈgēz ˌman-ə(v)-ˈwȯr \

Portuguese men-of-war are a group of odd sea animals related to the hydra and jellyfish. Below the shimmering float hang long tentacles that cause painful stings or even death to swimmers.

The part that shows above water is called the disk. It is a gas-filled bag 3 to 12 inches across. It may look like colorless jelly, or it may show iridescent tints of pink, violet or blue. On top of the disk is a ruffled, red-edged crest that catches the wind like a sail.

Hanging below the disk are hollow parts called polyps. There are 4 different kinds of polyps, serving different purposes. Stinging polyps that paralyze fish and other prey are up to 60 feet long. Feeding polyps are hungry mouths that digest the prey. Reproductive polyps produce eggs. The fourth kind of polyp helps the disk float, so the animal can travel with the wind.

Portuguese men-of-war are found in all tropical seas. One kind (illustrated) is common in the warm waters of the Gulf Stream as far north as New Jersey.

potato

One of the most useful of all food plants, the potato is an annual plant of the nightshade family. It is native to the Andes Mountains of South America.

Spanish explorers returning from the New World first planted the potato in Europe about 1570. Today the potato is an important staple food in most of the north temperate zone.

The edible part of the potato plant is an enlarged underground stem or tuber which stores food for the plant. Most of this food is in the form of starch.

PORTUGUESE MAN-OF-WAR

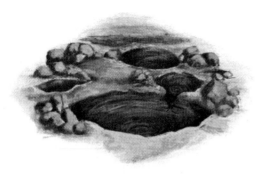

POTHOLES

The leaves of the potato plant are compound. Each is made up of pointed leaflets of different sizes. Loose clusters of white or purplish-pink flowers appear at the tops of the stalks. The fruit is a round, yellowish-green berry about ¾ inch across.

Cultivated potatoes seldom produce fruit or seeds. They are planted by burying a piece of the tuber that has on it 1 bud or "eye."

Potatoes can be grown almost anywhere, but they produce the best crops where the summer is cool. In the U.S., potatoes are grown commercially in Maine, Michigan, Colorado and Idaho.

pothole \ 'pät-ˌhōl \

Potholes are rounded depressions in stream beds. They were made by swift-running water that was caught and whirled by rocks, sand or gravel. Repeated grinding and bumping action of the rocks, sand or gravel wears the hole larger and deeper. A pothole is usually round and flat-bottomed, like the inside of a kettle.

Potholes are found in rocky stream beds where the current is swift, and below waterfalls.

Potholes on dry land often mark places where a glacier melted rapidly. Water from glacial ice melted by the sun may have drained down through a hole in the ice. Whirling around like water pouring down a bathtub drain, such water carried with it some rocks and gravel. Circular scouring action of the rocks and gravel created a pothole beneath the hole in the ice.

prairie \ 'prer-ē \ dog

Prairie dogs are a group of small rodents belonging to the squirrel family and are related to chipmunks, marmots and woodchucks. They are 12 to 17 inches long, with plump bodies, rounded heads and short tails.

Prairie dogs are social animals that live together in large groups. Their large underground burrows are called prairie dog towns. Some kinds build mounds at each entrance to the burrow and use them as observation posts. There, certain prairie dogs act as sentries while the others feed on grasses. If an enemy comes near, the sentries bark signals and all dash into the burrow.

Coyotes, ferrets, hawks and badgers are all natural enemies that kill and eat prairie dogs.

Prairie dogs were once common on the open plains of western North America. They are becoming rare, as much of their

PRAIRIE DOG

range has been taken over by farmers and ranchers.

Females bear litters of 4 to 8 young, in early May. The young prairie dogs remain inside the burrow for 3 to 4 weeks.

The white-tailed prairie dog (illustrated) is most common near mountains, from Wyoming south to Arizona. It is 12 to 15 inches long, and it looks something like a fat chipmunk.

primate \ 'prī-ˌmāt \

The primates are a group of mammals that have developed high intelligence. All primates have nimble hands that they use for grasping. The eyes of primates are in the front of their heads, and both eyes look forward. The best-known primates are man, the monkeys and the apes.

Other animals usually classified as primates are the tree shrews, lorises, lemurs and tarsiers. All are furry, squirrel-like animals that live in trees, in tropical Asia and Africa. Most are the size of rats and squirrels. The largest loris is about 16 inches long.

All primates hold their bodies more or less upright, and use their forelimbs to lift food to their mouths. They have more complex nervous systems than any other animals.

Most of the primates have flat nails on

THE OLDEST LIVING PRIMATE
(TREE SHREW)

PRIMROSE

their fingers and toes rather than claws. Man and some other primates can turn the thumb so that it is opposite to the fingers.

See *baboon, chimpanzee, gibbon, gorilla, lemur, loris, man, monkey, orangutan* and *tarsier*.

primrose \ 'prim-ˌrōz \

Primroses are perennial plants that bear bright-colored flowers in early spring. Some are wild flowers, and some are cultivated garden plants. All are native to the cooler parts of the northern hemisphere, and especially to the mountains of central Asia.

Primroses seldom grow taller than 12 inches. Their many leaves are rounded at the tip and have thick midribs along the undersides.

Loose, rounded clusters of flowers bloom at the tops of separate, leafless stalks. Each flower has a tube-shaped corolla that opens out into 5 petal-like lobes. The flowers are usually red, purple, pink, blue, yellow or white. The fruit is a dry pod that contains many seeds.

One kind of primrose (illustrated) is easy to grow in flower gardens. It blooms in May, the year after it is planted. The flowers are very fragrant, and they may be almost any color.

protozoan \ ˌprōt-ə-'zō-ən \

Protozoans are very small, 1-celled animals that live in water, in moist soil and in the bodies of larger animals. The largest are less than ¼ inch long.

Protozoans differ greatly in appearance and habits. Some are round or cigar-shaped. Others have irregular shapes that change as they move. Many kinds can swim by waving whip-like flagella. Some anchor themselves to a solid surface. Most live singly, but a few kinds cling together in colonies.

Most protozoans reproduce by simple fission, the process of splitting into 2 parts. They feed on bacteria, yeast cells and smaller protozoans.

The most useful of the protozoans are the ones that float in fresh and salt water. They help to make up plankton, which is the food supply of small fish and some other aquatic animals. The protozoans that live as parasites in animals may cause diseases.

The amoeba and the paramecium are 2 common protozoans that have been carefully studied by scientists.

For kinds of protozoans, see *amoeba, ciliate, flagellate, paramecium* and *radiolarian.*

PROTOZOAN REPRODUCING BY FISSION

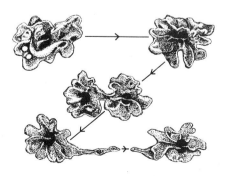

PTARMIGAN

ptarmigan \ 'tär-mi-gən \

The ptarmigans are plump game birds belonging to the grouse family. They live only in the far north and on high mountains, where in winter the ground is always covered with snow. Their legs and feet are completely covered with feathers.

Ptarmigans vary from about 12 to about 17 inches in length. They are white in winter and brown in summer. In spring and autumn they are a mixture of brown and white.

Ptarmigans winter in flocks, huddling under trees and bushes or burrowing in the snow for shelter. During the winter they eat the twigs of willow and alder trees.

In spring, ptarmigans move into open, treeless country, and the males fight fiercely to win mates. Pairs stay together until autumn. The female lays 6 to 10 spotted eggs in a hollow on the ground. The male guards the eggs during the incubation period, and he helps feed the young birds.

During the summer, ptarmigans eat insects, green plants and berries.

The rock ptarmigan (illustrated) lives near the Arctic Circle and in high mountains of Spain, Switzerland and Japan.

The Alaska willow ptarmigan is the state bird of Alaska.

PUFFBALL

PUFFER

puffball \ 'pəf-,bȯl \

The puffballs are fungus plants related to the mushrooms. Their round spore-producing parts appear in spring and summer, on the forest floor. Young puffballs can be cooked and eaten but are fairly tasteless. Old puffballs are dry and break apart when touched, releasing a cloud of tiny spores.

Like other fungi, the puffballs are plants that lack chlorophyll and cannot manufacture their own food from minerals in the soil. They absorb food from dead, decaying plants. Most of the puffball plant is hidden under the soil or among dead leaves and bits of rotting wood. Only the round spore-producing part can be seen above ground. The spores that ripen inside it are reproductive cells that can grow into new puffball plants.

The giant puffball (illustrated) may be as large as 4 feet across. It is yellowish-white or light brown, and its surface is usually marked with warts or scales.

puffer \ 'pəf-ər \ (blowfish, snowball)

The puffers make up a family of carnivorous ocean fish that can swallow either air or water until their bodies swell to 3 times normal size. Puffers inflate themselves to frighten their enemies.

Most puffers are about 18 inches long, with a rather large head and a tapering body. The largest are about 36 inches long. Most kinds have no scales. Their tough skin is covered with short but stiff spines. Their mouths are beak-like.

The flesh of many puffers is a popular food in Japan, but the internal organs and eggs are deadly poisonous. In some kinds the flesh is also poisonous.

Puffers live in warm and temperate parts of the ocean, near sandy bottoms or coral reefs. They eat crustaceans and other invertebrates.

The flesh of the northern puffer (illustrated) is sometimes marketed under the name "sea squab."

puffin \ 'pəf-ən \

Puffins are penguin-like seabirds with large, bright-colored beaks. They live on land only during the nesting season. The rest of the year they live at sea, in the northern parts of the Atlantic and Pacific.

Puffins are good swimmers, with short legs and webbed feet placed far back on the body. Unlike penguins, they can also fly. They walk awkwardly. The largest puffins are about 15 inches tall.

Flocks of puffins return from the open sea each spring to rocky islands and cliffs from Norway to Maine. Their nests are

PUFFIN

underground burrows 3 to 4 feet deep. Many pairs return to the same burrows year after year.

The female lays 1 egg. She incubates it for 6 weeks, with some help from the male. Both parents feed the young bird for 6 weeks, on fish they catch and carry to the burrow. Then the adults return to the sea. The young puffin remains in the burrow for another week, living on fat stored in its body, before taking to the sea to fend for itself.

pumice \ 'pəm-əs \

Pumice is an unusual kind of igneous rock. It contains many small airholes or openings and is so light in weight that it will float on water.

Pumice was formed from a kind of volcanic lava that cooled very quickly, while gas bubbles were trapped inside it. It is found in many different parts of the world wherever volcanoes have erupted in recent times. If the same lava had cooled under pressure, without bubbles, it would have turned into the hard, glass-like rock called obsidian.

Many scouring powders and polishing compounds contain pumice. Pumice is also used to make lightweight concrete and plaster for buildings.

Pumice is usually gray in color, but may be white, light brown or black. It contains mostly silica, the mineral used to make glass.

In the U.S., pumice is mined in the states of Arizona, California, Nevada, New Mexico and Wyoming.

pumpkin

The pumpkin is a vine-like annual plant belonging to the gourd family. It once grew only in the tropics.

Its fruit is used in pies and in making jack-o'-lanterns at Halloween. It is also used as feed for livestock. Pumpkin seeds are eaten in some parts of the world.

The pumpkin vine sprawls on the ground. The plant needs rich soil, a lot of space and a fairly long growing season. Pumpkin seeds are planted in early spring, 2 or 3 together, in hills at least 6 feet apart. The fruit ripens in autumn.

Pumpkin plants have very long stems that are rough and hairy. The deeply lobed leaves are 6 to 12 inches long. The yellow, bell-shaped flowers spread open in pointed segments.

The edible part of the fruit is the thick rind just inside the smooth skin. In the center is a stringy pulp that contains many flat seeds.

The pumpkin is rich in Vitamin A and is a good source of food energy.

PUMPKIN

PUSSY WILLOW

pussy willow

The pussy willow is a small, hardy tree belonging to the willow family. It is known for the furry, silver-gray catkins borne on its twigs in March or April. The catkins are flowers that appear very early, before the tree's leaves.

Branches of pussy willow can be cut and placed in water, in a warm room, any time after mid-January. Florists grow special kinds of pussy willows with very large catkins for use in spring bouquets.

The pussy willow grows to 15 to 25 feet in height. The trunk is covered with reddish-brown, scaly bark. The oval leaves are 2 to 5 inches long. The smooth upper surface of the leaf is dark green. The underside is covered with tiny white hairs.

As on other willows, staminate and pistillate flowers grow on different trees. Pollen from staminate catkins is carried by the wind or by insects to pistillate catkins on other trees. Only the trees with pistillate catkins bear seeds.

The pussy willow grows as far north as Newfoundland and Manitoba, and is common in the northern half of the U.S., as far west as the Dakotas. It usually grows in moist soil, along streams.

Cut-off branches buried in wet soil quickly take root and become new trees.

pyrite \ 'pīr-ˌīt \

Pyrite is a fairly common yellowish mineral and a valuable ore. Sulfur and sulfuric acid, both widely used in industry, are made from it. Pyrite also contains some iron, but it is hard to separate the iron from the rest of the mineral.

Pyrite is 1 of several minerals that are called "fool's gold," because of their color. Some pyrite does contain a small quantity of gold.

Like flint, pyrite gives off sparks when it is struck by steel. Prehistoric men may have used pyrite to make fire. Wheel lock guns, used before flintlock guns, were fired by turning a toothed metal wheel against a piece of pyrite.

Freshly broken surfaces of pyrite are usually a light yellow. When exposed to air, the surfaces often tarnish to a dark, brownish yellow.

Crystals of pyrite are cube-shaped and have a metallic luster. Other forms of pyrite are rounded lumps and small grains.

Pyrite is found in many different parts of the world. Large deposits are mined in Spain and Portugal. In the U.S., it is found in Virginia, Massachusetts, New York, Colorado, Arizona and California.

PYRITE

q

quail \ 'kwāl \

Quails are medium-sized game birds belonging to the same family as peafowl and pheasants. All quails have small heads, plump bodies and short tails. Most have a plume or crest on the head. The females are less colorful than the males, and they have smaller crests.

Quails feed and nest on the ground. They can run fast, and can fly rapidly for a short distance. When frightened they "freeze" for a moment, then dash for cover.

The female builds a neat nest, under a bush or low tree. She lays 6 to 15 eggs, as often as 3 times a year. The male helps incubate the eggs. The young birds can run soon after they hatch, and they fly when about 1 week old.

Quails eat seeds, berries, insects and some green plants. They do not migrate.

The California quail (illustrated) lives along the Pacific coast, from British Columbia to Mexico. It is about 11 inches long. Only the male has black and white markings on head and throat. This bird is the best known of the western quails and is the state bird of California.

For another kind of quail, see *bobwhite*.

QUAIL

QUAKING ASPEN

quaking aspen \ 'kwā-king 'as-pən \

The quaking aspen is a kind of poplar belonging to the willow family. Its leaves twist and tremble in the slightest breeze, when the leaves of other trees are still.

The quaking aspen grows 20 to 40 feet tall. Its yellow-green leaves are 2 to 4 inches long. They are glossy on the upper surface and dull underneath. Small greenish flower are clustered on tassels 1 to 4 inches long that dangle from the twigs in spring. The leaves turn bright yellow in autumn.

Fast-growing and hardy, the quaking aspen is often the first tree to reappear after a forest fire. It is found throughout the cooler parts of North America, from Labrador and Hudson's Bay south to Indiana and Pennsylvania. It grows along streams and on hillsides, often in sand or gravelly soil.

quartz \ 'kwȯrts \

Quartz is a form of silica and is one of the most common of all minerals. Sand is largely made up of grains of quartz, and such rocks as sandstone, quartzite and granite all contain large amounts of it.

Quartz is used in electronic and optical equipment. Quartz sand goes into glass and many other building materials.

Quartz is very hard but not very heavy. When perfectly pure, it is colorless and transparent.

Quartz crystals are 6-sided and have pyramid-shaped ends. Clear crystals, which are rare, are called rock crystal. Milky, grayish or yellowish crystals are most common.

Certain colored quartz crystals are valuable gems used in jewelry. Among these are amethyst, citrine, rose quartz and smoky quartz. Chalcedony, cat's eye, onyx, agate and flint are also forms of quartz.

Quartz is found in nearly all parts of the world. The largest and finest crystals come from Brazil, Switzerland, Japan and Madagascar.

quartzite \ 'kwȯrt-ˌsīt \

Quartzite is the hardest of all metamorphic rocks. It was originally sandstone. The cementing material that held the grains of sand together were changed by heat or pressure into interlocking crystals of quartz.

Sandstone and quartzite look much alike, but a broken surface of sandstone feels grainy, while a broken surface of quartzite feels smooth.

Quartzite is 90 to 99 percent silica. It is usually brown, like sandstone, but it may be white, gray or reddish.

Like other metamorphic rocks, quartzite is found where the earth's crust was folded and squeezed into mountains. In the U.S., quartzite is most common on the Appalachians, around Lake Superior and in the far western states.

Large beds of quartzite are likely to form plateaus or mountain ridges, as they are hard enough to resist erosion.

quince \ 'kwin(t)s \ tree

The quince tree is a fruit-bearing tree belonging to the rose family. It is related to the apple and the pear. Its fruit is eaten only after it is cooked. The cooked fruit is used to make jelly and preserves.

Although the quince tree is native to Persia, it has been cultivated for 2,000 years in both Europe and Asia. It is not widely planted in the U.S.

Quince trees live for about 30 years but seldom grow more than 25 feet tall. The branches are crooked, and the trees have irregular shapes. The leaves are 2½ to 4 inches long and have smooth edges.

Flowers and fruit are borne at the ends of the branches. The flowers have 5 white or pink petals.

The fruit is round or pear-shaped and slightly hairy. When ripe, it is a bright golden-yellow. It has a spicy fragrance when cooked and tastes a little like guava. The raw fruit is too sour to eat.

QUARTZITE

QUINCE TREE

r

rabbit

Rabbits and hares make up a family of fur-bearing mammals that live in nearly all parts of the world. Rabbits are generally smaller and plumper than hares, and their ears are not so long. Newborn hares have fur, and can hop when only a few hours old. Rabbits, on the other hand, are born naked, blind and helpless.

Rabbits eat green plants and the bark of trees. They are a nuisance in some areas where they damage garden crops and orchards.

Female rabbits bear litters of 3 to 10 young several times a year. The young are mature at 3 months.

Rabbits are hunted by man and are killed and eaten by many wild animals. If they did not reproduce so rapidly, they would probably become extinct.

The domestic rabbit (illustrated) has been raised in captivity for hundreds of years, for its meat and for its fur. It is widely used in scientific research, and is a popular pet. Domestic rabbits are gray, brown, white or spotted. The largest ones are about 30 inches long and weigh about 25 pounds.

RABBIT

RACCOON

raccoon

The raccoon is a fur-bearing mammal native to North America. Raccoons are easily recognized by the black mark around their eyes.

Fully grown raccoons are about 30 inches long, including the bushy, striped tail. The fur is a mixture of gray, brown and black. A raccoon's head is round with a pointed snout.

Good swimmers and climbers, raccoons live mostly in wooded areas near streams. They have also learned to live in city parks and in other suburban areas. They stay hidden during the day but roam widely at night, often raiding garbage cans and trash barrels for food scraps.

Raccoons eat a wide variety of both plant and animal foods, including fish, frogs, grain, vegetables, fruit and honey. They often carry their food to a running stream and wash it carefully before they eat it.

Raccoons normally mate for life. The female bears a litter of 3 to 6 young in early spring. The young, called kits, are born naked and blind. They remain with the parents for about a year.

Raccoons live in all parts of North America except the Rocky Mountains and the deserts. Their dens are cracks

RADIOLARIAN

between rocks, or hollow trees. The raccoon does not hibernate in very cold weather, but simply "holes up" and sleeps.

radiolarian \ ,rād-ē-ō-'lar-ē-ən \

Radiolarians are microscopic floating animals belonging to the large group of 1-celled animals called protozoans. Radiolarians live only in the ocean.

Radiolarians build lacy shells around their soft bodies. The shells are made of silica or other materials that the animal takes from seawater. The shell is usually round, and it always has many holes in it.

The living animal has a shapeless, soft body. It can stretch parts of its body out into slender rays that reach through the holes in the shell. These arm-like rays grasp bits of food that float by.

Radiolarians reproduce by simple fission, the process of splitting into 2 parts.

When radiolarians die, the empty shells fall to the bottom of the sea. Some parts of the ocean floor are covered with a thick layer of shells that have piled up there for millions of years. These shells form a material called "radiolarian ooze."

radish

The radish is a garden vegetable belonging to the mustard family, and related to the cabbages and turnips.

The radish plant has been cultivated for hundreds of years, in many areas. It was probably developed from a plant that once grew wild in southern Europe.

The edible part of the plant is a thickened root. It may be round, like a small beet, or long, like a carrot. It may be red, white, pink or purplish. The root is ready to eat 3 to 4 weeks after the seed is planted. Later, the root becomes soft and pithy, and is no longer eaten.

The leaves of the radish plant are irregular in shape but always rounded at the tip. Most of the leaves grow up from ground level in 1 cluster.

Most radish plants are harvested for their roots before flowers and seeds appear at the tops of the plants. The flowers have 4 purple petals. The seeds ripen inside a spongy pod 1 to 3 inches long.

ragweed \ 'rag-,wēd \

Ragweeds are a group of coarse weeds native to North America and Africa. Their pollen is a common cause of hayfever. The ragweeds are sometimes called wild tansy, hogweed, bitterweed or black weed.

Some ragweeds are annual plants that bear flowers the first year. Others are perennials that live through the winter and bloom the second year of growth.

RAGWEED

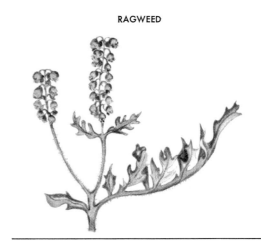

All ragweeds are fast-growing plants with rough, hairy stems. The leaves are irregular in shape but always ragged along the edges. Spike-shaped clusters of tiny, greenish flowers are borne at the top of the stalks, from midsummer through autumn.

Common annual ragweed (illustrated) grows 12 to 60 inches tall. Its leaves are divided into many pointed segments, and they grow either opposite each other or alternately along the stalks. This kind of ragweed grows along roadsides and in uncultivated fields throughout the eastern half of North America.

rail

The rails make up a family of birds that live in nearly all parts of the world. Most rails live in marshes. A few kinds live on grassy plains, away from water, and some live in tropical forests. Most make long migratory flights, but some kinds cannot fly at all.

Rails are mostly brown. Some have fairly long legs and bills, like cranes, while others look more like chickens. All rails have very narrow bodies so that they can run fast through tall grass or dense brush. Long toes keep them from sinking down into the mud.

Rails eat a wide variety of both plant

RAIL

RAINBOW

and animal foods. They nest on or very near the ground. Male and female share the task of incubating the 6 to 16 speckled eggs. Able to run and hide a few hours after they hatch, the young birds soon leave the nest.

The king rail (illustrated) is a long-billed, long-legged marsh bird with a body about 16 inches long. It nests throughout the eastern U.S., and it winters along the Atlantic and Gulf coasts.

For other members of the rail family, see *coot* and *gallinule*.

rainbow

A rainbow is an arch of colored light in the sky. It is actually part of a circle, but the rest of the circle is below the horizon where it cannot be seen.

A rainbow usually includes the colors red, orange, yellow, green, blue, indigo and violet. Red is always on the outside of the band of colors. Violet is always on the inside of the arch.

A rainbow is caused by the passing of the sun's light rays through water drops suspended in the air. Each drop acts as a tiny prism, bending the light rays and separating them into different colors.

Rainbows are most often seen on summer afternoons when the sun reappears after a brief rain. The raincloud usually moves from west to east with the winds, and the rainbow usually appears in the eastern sky, where the air is still full of raindrops. Morning rainbows, seen in the western sky, are more rare. None appear at noon, when the sun is directly overhead.

Rainbows almost never appear in winter, because there is seldom a quick change from rain to sunshine. They sometimes appear in spray or mist, where the air is full of water drops.

rain shadow

A rain shadow is an area that receives very little rainfall because it is on the side of mountains that is away from the prevailing wind. Most rain falls on the side of the mountain range that faces the wind.

Air is cooled as it blows up a mountainside. Cool air can hold less moisture than warm air, so water droplets condense and fall as rain from the rising current of air on the side of the mountain that faces the wind. Only cool, dry air passes over the mountaintops, to the rain shadow on the other side.

The deserts of northern Nevada lie in the rain shadow of the high Sierra Nevada range. The deserts of Tibet lie in the rain shadow behind the Himalayas.

On the island of Kauai in Hawaii, about 472 inches of rain fall on one side of a mountain peak each year, and only 20 inches on the other side, within the rain shadow.

raspberry \ 'raz-,ber-ē \

Raspberries are prickly shrubs belonging to the rose family. Both wild and cultivated raspberries grow in nearly all parts of the northern hemisphere.

The roots and base of the raspberry plant live for many years. The stems are biennial, and are usually cut back after the second year.

The first year's growth is an unbranched stem, or cane, that becomes 3 to 9 feet long. Short canes stand erect. Longer ones arch over and touch the ground. During the second season, short branches grow out from the cane.

Flowers and fruit are borne in small clusters, at the ends of the branches. The flowers are about ½ inch across. They have 5 white or greenish petals. The fruit is a dome-shaped cluster of tiny, juicy berries. Each berry contains 1 small, hard seed. The berries are eaten fresh, frozen or canned, or are made into jam and jelly.

Both red and black raspberries grow wild in North America, along roadsides and in open fields. The red raspberry grows as far north as Labrador and Alaska. The black raspberry (illustrated) grows as far north as Quebec and the Dakotas, and as far south as Georgia.

RAIN SHADOW

RASPBERRY

rat

Rats are gnawing rodents belonging to several different families. All rats sleep during the day and seek food at night. They do not hibernate, and most kinds of rats breed all during the year.

The Old World rat family includes the largest kinds of rats and the worst pests. The black rat and the common domestic rat, also called the brown or Norway rat, are both Old World rats from Asia. Traveling on ships, these animals have spread all over the world and they now live wherever man lives. They carry diseases, and they destroy huge amounts of stored grain. They will eat almost anything.

The black rat is 15 to 17 inches long, including the 8-inch tail. It is a good climber and lives on the roofs and upper floors of tall buildings. It is sometimes found in trees.

The common domestic rat is up to 19 inches long, including the 6- to 7-inch tail. A digger rather than a climber, it lives in cellars, sewers and trash dumps.

The black rat arrived in North America first, with the earliest settlers. The common domestic rat arrived later but it is larger and fiercer. It drove the black rat out of many areas. Today the common domestic rat lives all over North America, while the black rat lives only along the Atlantic coast, in the south and in Mexico.

The Old World rats are difficult to control because they reproduce very rapidly. A female rat may give birth to 6 litters a year, with as many as 20 young in each litter. Young rats are mature and ready to breed at about 2 months.

The white rat that is sold in pet shops and used in scientific experiments is a common domestic rat that is an albino.

The cotton rat, the rice rats and the wood rats all belong to the New World rat family. They are generally neater and cleaner than the Old World rats, and they seldom carry diseases.

The cotton rat, 13 inches long, and the rice rats, 11 inches long, are pests that destroy farm and garden crops. They live in the southern U.S. and Central America.

The cotton rat lives in dry, grassy places. The rice rats are good swimmers and live in swamps. The common rice rat lives from New Jersey and Kansas south to Florida and Texas.

The wood rats, up to 18 inches long, are also called pack rats or trade rats. They collect in their large nests colorful or shiny things, such as buttons, tin cans and bits of jewelry. They often enter houses to steal such things. Sometimes they leave pebbles or bits of trash behind them, as a kind of payment.

Wood rats live in western North America, mostly in the Rocky Mountains. The bushy-tailed wood rat lives in the Canadian Rockies and as far south as Nevada.

The kangaroo rats belong to still another rat family, the pocket rats. They have fur-lined cheek pouches and very long, tufted tails. On their long, strong hind legs, they can jump as far as 8 feet.

Kangaroo rats are up to 18 inches long. They live on deserts and dry plains. The moisture they need comes from the plants they eat, and they can live for a long time without water. The Ord kangaroo rat lives in western North America, from Manitoba south through Mexico.

The Florida water rat belongs to the same animal family as the muskrat. It lives in swamps and eats only wild plants that grow near water. Its home is a round-topped pile of plant materials surrounded by water. Two tunnels lead to the nest inside, just above water level.

The Florida water rat is about 14 inches long, including the rather short, scaly tail. The dark brown fur is soft and silky. It lives in Florida and in Georgia.

Rats—Gnawing Rodents

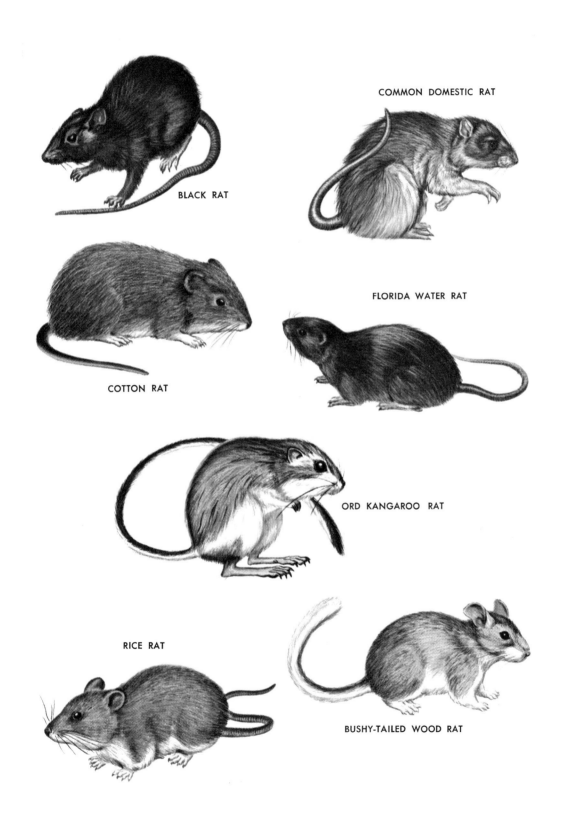

COMMON DOMESTIC RAT

BLACK RAT

FLORIDA WATER RAT

COTTON RAT

ORD KANGAROO RAT

RICE RAT

BUSHY-TAILED WOOD RAT

RAVEN

raven \ ˈrā-vən \

The raven is a large, hardy bird related to jays, magpies and crows.

Very intelligent birds, ravens make good pets if they are captured young and raised in captivity. They can be taught to imitate human speech. Wild ravens make a wide variety of croaking and gurgling sounds.

The raven looks like the common crow but it is much larger, and it has a larger, thicker bill. Ravens are 22 to 26 inches long, with a wingspread of 3 to 4 feet.

Ravens eat mostly dead fish and animals. During the summer, they also eat some seeds and insects. They usually mate for life and return each year to large, untidy nests of sticks on cliff ledges or in tall trees. Three to 7 spotted eggs are laid once a year. Young birds are fed in the nest for about a month.

Ravens once lived in all parts of the northern hemisphere. Today they are found only in wilderness areas, on the arctic tundra, in the desert and along rocky coasts.

ray

Rays make up a large group of odd-shaped ocean fish, closely related to sharks and skates. Rays have skeletons of cartilage rather than bone, and the females give birth to living young.

All rays have large, wing-like fins that extend out from the flattened body, and long, slender tails. The largest kinds of ray are up to 20 feet across and weigh as much as 3,000 pounds. The kinds called stingrays have a poison spine on the tail. Rays may seem to be slow-moving, sluggish animals, but they fight fiercely when disturbed.

Rays live in the warmer parts of the oceans. They move about mostly at night, seeking the small fish and invertebrates on which they feed. They breathe by drawing in water through 2 holes on the upper surface of the head, near the eyes. The water is then forced out through gill slits on the underside, near the mouth.

The stingaree (illustrated) is a small stingray that lives in the Atlantic Ocean and the Gulf of Mexico. It is usually about 18 inches long.

razor \ ˈrā-zər \ fish

Razor fish make up a group of colorful, tropical ocean fish.

The length of razor fish varies from 6 to 18 inches. Their bodies are deep and very narrow, with large heads and small tails. The eyes and the lateral line that runs from head to tail are very near the top of the body. Some have sharp teeth that stick forward, out of the mouth.

RAY

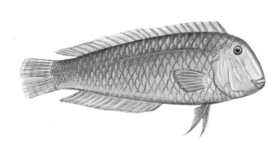

RAZOR FISH

Razor fish live in warm, shallow parts of the sea, near coral reefs. They build nests of a variety of materials, and spend a good deal of time repairing them.

At night, razor fish wriggle down into the sand until their bodies are completely covered. They may also burrow into sand during the day, to hide from their enemies. They feed on crustaceans and other small invertebrates.

The pearly razor fish (illustrated) is 15 to 18 inches long. It lives in the Atlantic. The pearly razor fish builds a nest from bits of coral.

redbud \ 'red-ˌbəd \ tree

The redbud is a small tree that belongs to the pea family. It bears many small purplish-pink flowers in early spring, before the leaves appear. The redbud is native to the eastern half of the U.S.

The redbud is usually 15 to 30 feet tall, with a broad, rounded crown. The trunk is short, and divides into spreading branches fairly near the ground. The bark is dark reddish-brown.

Unlike most plants of the pea family, the redbud tree has simple rather than compound leaves. They are heart-shaped and 3 to 5 inches long.

The flowers, about ½ inch long, are something like tiny sweet peas. They are borne in clusters of 4 to 8.

The fruit of the tree is a flat pod 2½ to 3½ inches long, containing a row of bean-like seeds. The seeds ripen in midsummer but the dangling pods remain on the tree until late autumn.

The redbud usually grows in moist soil, in wooded places partly shaded by taller trees. Because it blooms in early spring, the redbud is often planted in parks and gardens, as an ornamental tree.

The redbud tree is the state tree of Oklahoma.

redwood

The redwood is a huge evergreen tree related to the pines and closely related to the sequoia. The redwood lives for 1,000 years or more and grows as tall as 360 feet. Although it is usually taller than the sequoia, it does not live as long.

Redwoods grow only along the Pacific coast of North America, in a narrow area 500 miles long and about 30 miles wide. Fogs that move in from the ocean give this area the moist, cool climate that the trees need.

The leaves of the redwood tree are dark, yellowish-green needles less than 1 inch long. The branches are short, compared to the height of the tree, and they droop down toward the ground. Cones about 1 inch long are borne at the ends of the branches. The seeds ripen and fall from the cones in autumn, but few seeds man-

REDWOOD

age to grow into trees. Most young trees sprout from the roots of fallen or cut trees.

The tall, straight trunk is covered with thick bark that protects the tree from fire and from insects. The red-brown wood is soft but very useful because it does not decay and is not damaged by termites. It is made into shingles, siding, fences and outdoor furniture.

The redwood has been adopted as the state tree of California.

reef \ 'rēf \

A reef is a wall-like ridge of rock under the sea. If it is large enough to be partly above the water, it forms an island or a series of islands. The atolls of the Pacific are islands of this type.

Most reefs are in warm, shallow parts of the sea. They are usually made up of coral rock, the cemented-together skeletons of coral animals. Some algae and sea snails help to construct reefs. All of these forms of life take calcium from seawater and use it to build shell-like skeletons around their soft bodies. When the animals die, their skeletons remain and other creatures build on top of them.

Coral reefs are found only where the water is 68° F. or warmer, and where it is less than 200 feet deep.

A barrier reef (illustrated) is a long ridge that runs parallel to a shoreline. Between the barrier reef and the shore is a

REEF

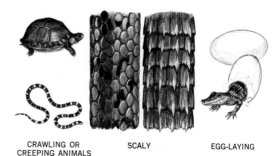

CRAWLING OR   SCALY   EGG-LAYING
CREEPING ANIMALS

REPTILES
(SOME TYPICAL CHARACTERISTICS)

quiet body of water called a lagoon. Running along the northeastern coast of Australia is a barrier reef 12,000 miles long. It is 20 to 30 miles from the shore.

reptile \ 'rep-t°l \

The reptiles make up a large group of cold-blooded animals with short legs or no legs at all. They include the alligators and crocodiles, the lizards, the snakes and the turtles. The dinosaurs, now extinct, were reptiles.

All reptiles have dry skin that is protected by horny plates or scales. All have lungs and breathe air, though some spend most of their time in water.

Only a few small reptiles live in the coolest parts of the temperate zone, and they hibernate in winter. Reptiles are most numerous in the tropics, and the largest ones live there.

All reptiles develop inside eggs that have soft, leathery shells. Some kinds of female snakes carry the eggs inside their bodies during the incubation period. Other reptiles lay their eggs on land.

Reptiles are among the oldest of all living animals. Some kinds have survived, almost unchanged, for 150 million years.

rhinoceros \ rī-'näs-(ə-)rəs \

The rhinoceroses make up a family of very large mammals that once lived in most parts of the northern hemisphere. Now they are found only in Africa and India.

RHINOCEROS

All rhinoceroses have short legs, thick skin, and 1 or 2 horns on the snout. They have weak eyesight but keen smell and hearing, and they can run very fast.

Singly or in pairs, rhinoceroses roam brushy country and grasslands, mostly at night. They eat only plants. Rhinoceroses usually sleep during the day. As they often bathe and wallow in the mud, they never stray far from streams.

The calves weigh about 75 pounds when they are born. Adults are 10 to 16 feet long, and weigh up to 6,000 pounds. The largest adults are 6½ feet tall.

The black rhinoceros (illustrated) lives in Africa, mostly in game preserves. It has a pointed upper lip that is used for grasping fruit, leaves and twigs. Other kinds of rhinoceroses eat mostly grasses. The Indian rhinoceros has very thick, stiff skin, folded so it looks like armor, and only 1 horn on its snout.

rhododendron \ ˌrōd-ə-'den-drən)

The rhododendrons are flowering shrubs related to heather. They are native to North America and eastern Asia. Some of them are called azaleas.

Some rhododendrons are low, creeping shrubs, and some are trees 30 feet tall. Their leaves are 1 to 12 inches long. Most kinds are evergreens that bear attractive flowers in early spring. The flower has a tube-shaped corolla that opens into 5 points. The flowers are white, pink,

orange or reddish, with long, slender stamens. The seeds ripen inside dry pods.

Rhododendrons grow only in rich, acid soil, where the summer is cool and moist. In the U.S., rhododendrons grow wild on mountain slopes in the Appalachians and along the Pacific coast ranges.

One kind of rhododendron (illustrated) loses its leaves in autumn and bears flowers in the spring before the new leaves appear.

The coastal rhododendron is the state flower of Washington, and the big rhododendron is the state flower of West Virginia.

rice

Rice is an important cereal plant that belongs to the grass family. It is native to China, where it has been cultivated for 4,000 years or more. Its seeds are the basic food of ⅓ of the earth's people.

The rice plant grows 3 to 4 feet tall. The leaves are 6 to 12 inches long, and about ½ inch wide. The leaves hide most of the slender stems. Flowers and seeds are borne at the tops of the stems.

Most kinds of cultivated rice are grown in flooded fields called paddies. Water 2 to 8 inches deep stands in the fields while the young rice plants are growing. Late in summer, when the grain is ready to ripen, the fields are drained.

RHODODENDRON

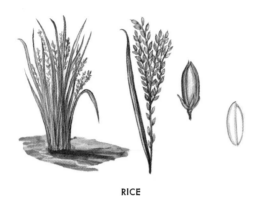

RICE

RINGTAIL CAT

Rice grows in the tropics and in the warmer parts of the temperate zone. It needs a long growing season and a great deal of water. Asia produces 90 to 95 per-cent of the world's supply of rice. In the U.S., rice is grown in Texas, Arkansas, Louisiana and California.

rill\ 'ril\

Rills are cracks or clefts on the surface of the moon. Most appear to be about ½ mile wide, and are visible only through a fairly powerful telescope. Rills appear mostly on the floors of the larger craters.

Some rills are narrow and deep, while others are broad and shallow. Many are straight, while others are curved or irregular.

No one is certain how rills were orig-inally formed, but several explanations have been suggested.

Rills may result from earthquake-like disturbances of the moon's crust. They may result from the shrinking of some mol-ten material, like lava, as it cooled and hardened.

ringtail\ 'ring-ˌtāl\ **cat** (cacomistle, civet cat)

The ringtail cat is not a cat, but a slender-bodied mammal related to the raccoon. It is named for its bushy, striped tail. This animal is fairly common in the southwest-ern U.S., though it is not often seen. It sleeps during the day, hidden in a hollow tree or between rocks, and prowls about seeking food at night.

The length of the ringtail cat is about 32 inches but the tail takes up about half of that length.

This animal is swift-moving and a fierce fighter. It kills and eats rats, mice and insects. It may climb trees to kill birds while they sleep. When angry, it arches its tail and barks.

Ringtail cats live in the forests and rocky canyons of western North America, from Oregon south to Costa Rica. In some areas they are trapped for their fur, which is thick and soft. It is sold as civet cat or California mink.

The female ringtail cat gives birth to 3 or 4 young in May or June.

river

Rivers are fairly large streams of fresh water. Together with smaller streams called creeks and brooks, rivers carry rain-water or water from melted snow from high places to lower places. Rivers empty into lakes, larger rivers or the sea.

Rivers are the most important of the natural forces that change the face of the earth. They are constantly moving rocks, sand and bits of soil.

Swift-flowing rivers move large rocks and constantly wear their channels deeper. Slow-flowing rivers drop the

ROADRUNNER

sediment they carry and build up fertile plains.

Rivers are important to man because they provide water power and transportation routes. They provide water for cities and industries, and for irrigation in areas where there is little rainfall.

Braided streams and yazoo streams are kinds of rivers found where slow-flowing water moves along broad, nearly level valley floors.

A braided stream is one that cannot carry its heavy load of sediment in 1 channel. It divides and then rejoins, forming a network of shallow streams between sandbars and low islands.

A yazoo stream flows parallel to a larger river. The 2 are unable to join because the larger river has built up high banks or natural levees along its channel. The name comes from the Yazoo River that flows parallel to the Mississippi River near Vicksburg.

See *meander*.

roadrunner \ 'rōd-ˌrən-ər \

The roadrunner is an odd-looking member of the cuckoo family. It is a fast runner and a poor flier. It lives only on the desert, in the southwestern U.S. and Mexico.

The roadrunner is about 23 inches long, including the long tail. Male and female birds look just alike. Both have crests on

their heads and patches of blue and red skin behind their eyes.

These birds kill lizards, snakes and large insects. Using their heavy bills as hammers, they pound their prey to death and then swallow them whole. They can run as fast as 15 miles an hour.

The nest of the roadrunner is about 1 foot across, and is lined with snakeskin, feathers or bits of bark. It is built in a cactus or mesquite bush. Four to 9 white eggs are laid once a year.

The roadrunner is curious and not at all shy. It often pokes about the tents of campers. It is the state bird of New Mexico.

robin

There are several kinds of birds called robins in different parts of the world. The original robin is a sparrow-sized European thrush common in England. English colonists carried its name with them, and used it for birds that reminded them of the robin back home.

The European robin has dark brown on the back and wings, white underparts and bright red on the throat and face. The American robin (illustrated) is a much larger bird, differently marked, but it is also a thrush and its habits are like those of the European robin.

Both European and American robins are friendly birds that nest near houses

ROBIN

and hop about city lawns looking for worms and insects. Both males and females feed the young birds, and they raise several families each summer.

In summer, the American robin nests as far north as Alaska. It spends the winter in the southern U.S. and in Central America.

The robin is the state bird of Connecticut, Michigan and Wisconsin.

roches moutonnées \ 'ròsh ˌmüt-ᵊn-'ā \

Roches moutonnées are outcroppings of hard bedrock smoothed and rounded by a glacier that passed over them. Glaciers did not carry these outcroppings away, because they are part of a larger rock mass that extends down under the earth.

The name "roches moutonnées" is a French phrase meaning sheep-shaped rocks. They often occur in groups. From a distance, roches moutonnées look a little like sheep lying down in a pasture.

Roches moutonnées may be marked with parallel scratches that show where the glacier carried rocks over them. Often one side slopes more steeply than the opposite side. The gently sloping side marks the direction from which the glacier moved.

Roches moutonnées are fairly common in northern Europe, in southern New England and in parts of New York State.

ROCHES MOUTONNÉES

SEDIMENTARY (Example: Oölitic Limestone) METAMORPHIC (Example: Granite Gneiss) IGNEOUS (Example: Obsidian)

ROCK (THE THREE MAJOR CLASSIFICATIONS)

rock

Rock is a compact, usually hard mass of minerals. The weight, color and hardness of rock depend on what minerals are in it, and the way in which the rock was formed. Some rocks contain just 1 mineral while others are mixtures of many different minerals.

Sedimentary rocks are made up of particles deposited by wind or water and bound together by some natural kind of cement. They usually show horizontal layers and flat surfaces. Sandstone, shale and limestone are all sedimentary rocks.

Metamorphic rocks are sedimentary or igneous rocks that were changed by great heat or pressure, or by both. Marble is a metamorphic rock that was once limestone. Slate was once shale. Gneiss was once granite.

Igneous rocks are made of magma or molten rock that was once deep under the earth's surface. It hardened as it cooled. Granite, basalt and obsidian are all igneous rocks.

See *stratified rock*.

rock crystal \ 'krist-ᵊl \

Rock crystal is a valuable mineral and is the purest kind of quartz. It looks like glass, but it is much harder. Rock crystal occurs as large, clear crystals.

Like all quartz, rock crystal is made of silicon combined with oxygen. While ordinary quartz is a common mineral found in most rocks and in sand, rock crystal is rare.

Flawless, perfect pieces of rock crystal are used to make lenses for optical equipment and as parts of radio transmitters.

The finest natural rock crystal comes from Brazil, Japan, Switzerland and Madagascar. When it was first discovered in Switzerland, men thought that rock crystal was ice, permanently frozen by extreme cold.

Like other forms of quartz, rock crystal is not affected by acids and it does not conduct electricity.

rockfish \ 'räk-ˌfish \

The rockfish are important food fish that belong to the scorpion fish family. They are closely related to the sculpins and sea robins. The flesh of 1 kind of rockfish is sometimes sold as ocean perch.

All scorpion fish have bony cheek plates, but those of the rockfish are not as spiny as most of the others.

Rockfish are usually 1 to 2 feet long. Some are brightly colored, while others are dull. Most are spotted or mottled and match the colors of rocks and seaweed where they feed.

These fish live in the cooler parts of all the oceans. They are most plentiful in the Pacific Ocean.

Female rockfish bear living young. The young fish develop inside eggs that the female carries inside her body during the incubation period. One female may bear as many as 20,000 young.

The copper rockfish (illustrated) is 1 of several kinds that have a reddish color.

rose

Nearly 3,000 different trees and plants make up the large rose family. The plants commonly called roses are flowering shrubs and vines with prickly stems. They are native to nearly all parts of the north temperate zone. Some grow farther north, and some on mountains in the tropics.

Roses have compound leaves made up of 5 or more leaflets. The leaflets are always uneven in number since there is 1 at the end. Wild roses have 5 petals. Double-flowering cultivated roses have many more. The seeds are inside a berry-like fruit called a rose hip.

Roses were cultivated by the Babylonians and ancient Persians. Over the centuries, many different kinds have been developed.

The cultivated tea rose (illustrated) was developed from a wild rose native to China. Its branching stalks grow 2 to 4 feet tall. The large, fragrant flowers are usually white or pink. Other kinds of roses have yellow or red flowers.

Various kinds of roses, both cultivated and wild, have been adopted as the state

ROCKFISH

ROSE

flower of the District of Columbia, Georgia, Iowa, New York and North Dakota.

For other members of the rose family, see *almond, American mountain ash, apple tree, cherry tree, pear tree, plum tree, quince tree, raspberry* and *strawberry.*

rosefish\ 'rōz-ˌfish\ (ocean perch, redfish)

The rosefish is an ocean fish that belongs to the scorpion fish family. It is related to the rockfish.

Rosefish are an important food fish. Commercial fishermen sell the fish to frozen food companies that make frozen fillets and fishsticks.

The largest rosefish are 20 to 24 inches long. They weigh as much as 13 pounds.

The rosefish has large eyes, and a bony cheek plate extends from the eyes to the gills. The mouth is large, and the lower jaw sticks out beyond the upper jaw. The spiny part of the dorsal fin extends farther along the fish's back than the soft part. The pectoral fins on either side are unusually large, and the tail is small and short.

The rosefish lives in the cooler waters of the Atlantic Ocean, as far south as Cape Cod. It feeds near the bottom on crustaceans and small fish. The young hatch from eggs inside the female's body. One female may bear 20,000 to 40,000 young.

ROSEFISH

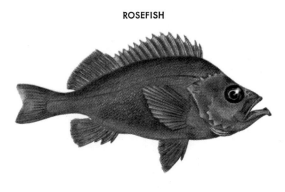

ROSEMARY

rosemary\ 'rōz-ˌmer-ē\

Rosemary is a fragrant evergreen shrub that belongs to the mint family. The leaves are dried and used as a kitchen herb, for flavoring such foods as lamb and veal stews. Dried rosemary leaves smell a little like pine needles. Oil from the leaves and flowers is used to make medicines and perfumes.

Rosemary is native to southern Europe and the Mediterranean region. It was brought to America by the early settlers. In the southern U.S., it becomes a bushy shrub up to 6 feet tall, and it is sometimes planted as a hedge. In cold climates, smaller plants are sometimes kept indoors, in flowerpots, during the winter.

The narrow leaves are about 1 inch long. They are gray-green, and covered with tiny white hairs. Pale blue, tube-shaped flowers are borne in clusters along the stems. The seedpod splits apart into 4 sections when the seeds are ripe.

ruby\ 'rü-bē\

A ruby is a red-colored crystal of corundum. Rubies are very rare, and they are among the most valuable of all the gem stones used in fine jewelry. A perfect ruby may be worth 3 times as much as a diamond the same size.

In ancient times rubies were believed to bring their owners love and good fortune.

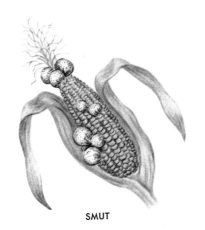

SMUT

Some thought the ruby had magic power that would keep bad dreams from coming true.

Rubies range in color from rose-red to a deep purplish red that is called "pigeon's blood." The darker rubies are usually more valuable than the lighter ones.

Most rubies come from Burma, Ceylon, Thailand, India and Afghanistan. A few small stones have been found in the U.S., in North Carolina, Georgia and Montana.

Corundum in natural rubies is aluminum oxide. Synthetic rubies are made by heating purified ammonium alum and chromium sulfate to 1,000° C.

rust and smut \ 'smət \

Rust and smut are parasitic fungi that cause plant diseases, damaging farm crops and trees. At first, the fungus is invisible. It lives inside the leaves and stems of the plant. Later, the spore-producing part of the fungus appears on the surface of the diseased plant.

The rust that infects wheat and white pine trees is a fungus that lives during the winter in wild barberry bushes. This fungus has a very complicated life cycle. It passes through several stages, and produces 5 different kinds of spores at different times.

Wheat rust usually disappears when all the wild barberry bushes in an area are destroyed.

Corn smut (illustrated) is a fungus that lives in the soil from one season to the next. In spring, it enters young corn plants through their roots. In late summer, smut appears on the corn ears and tassels.

rye

Rye is an important cereal plant that belongs to the grass family. It looks something like wheat but it grows taller, up to 5 feet high, and it has stiffer, stronger stems.

Rye will grow on poorer soil than oats or wheat, and in a cooler climate. About half of the world's rye is grown in Russia. Some rye is grown as far north as the Arctic Circle.

The seeds, or grain, of rye are used to make flour for bread, and as food for livestock. Bread made entirely from rye flour is the coarse black bread of European peasants. Most rye bread is made of a mixture of wheat and rye flours.

Rye is an annual that usually is planted in the fall. The young plants live through the winter and bear seed the next summer, in June or July.

Like the other grasses, rye has slender, jointed stems. The first leaf put out by the seedling is reddish. The other leaves are dark blue-green and about 18 inches long. Tiny green flowers and seeds are borne in spike-shaped clusters at the tips of the stems.

RYE

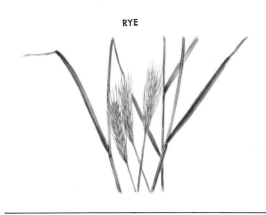

S

sable \ 'sā-bəl \

The sable is a fur-bearing mammal belonging to the weasel family and native to northern Asia. It is related to the American sable.

The sable has been hunted and trapped for its fur until it is now rare.

Sables are 14 to 20 inches long, with bushy tails 5 to 7 inches long. They range in color from brown to black, with a lighter patch on the throat. The animals most valued for their fur are blue-black with silver-tipped hairs.

Like the other weasels, the sable is quick-moving and a savage fighter when cornered. It kills and eats a wide variety of small animals and birds.

The female sable gives birth to a litter of 1 to 5 young, called kits, once a year. They are mature at about 3 months.

For another kind of sable, see *American sable*.

sage \ 'sāj \

Sage is a useful plant that belongs to the mint family. The stuffing that goes into most Thanksgiving turkeys owes much of its flavor to the leaves of this plant. The leaves are also used in many other recipes, and a fragrant oil from the plant is used in some cosmetics.

Sage is native to southern Europe. It

SABLE

SAGE

has been cultivated as a kitchen herb for about 300 years.

A shrubby perennial, sage lives through the winter in all but the coldest climates. It grows about 2 feet tall.

The leaves are 2 to 3 inches long and grow in opposite pairs. They are slightly wrinkled and are covered with tiny white hairs. Tube-shaped flowers are borne in spike-shaped clusters at the tops of the stalks. The flowers are usually purplish-blue but sometimes white. The small seedpod splits into 4 sections when ripe.

salamander \ 'sal-ə-,man-dər \

Salamanders are short-legged, long-tailed amphibians. Although they are fairly common in most parts of the northern hemisphere, they are seldom seen. Shy and silent, they hide under fallen leaves or at the bottoms of streams.

Salamanders are harmless. Some have brightly colored, nearly transparent skin. They eat insects and worms, and they absorb water through their skins instead of drinking.

Most salamanders live on land as adults, but they stay under cover to keep their bodies cool and moist. Most enter streams in spring, to mate and lay eggs. The young live in water and breathe through feathery gills.

The red-backed woodland salamander (illustrated) is usually 3 to 4½ inches long.

SALAMANDER

It is 1 of the few salamanders that mate and lay eggs on land. The young pass through a larval stage before hatching out of the eggs. The salamander does not develop true lungs, but breathes through tissues of the skin and mouth lining.

For other kinds of salamanders, see *mud puppy, newt* and *siren.*

salmon

The salmon and their relatives, the trout, make up the salmon family of fish. They are among the most important of all food and game fish. All spawn in freshwater streams, but most live in the ocean as adults. A few remain landlocked.

All salmon have long, rounded bodies, scale-less heads, and large mouths with well-developed teeth. The largest kinds are 3 to 5 feet long and weigh up to 100 pounds. Most salmon are 10 to 28 inches long. They are silvery, sometimes tinted with red or pink. Salmon live in cool water, and feed on other, smaller fish and crustaceans.

When they are ready to spawn, salmon migrate up coastal rivers. Some return to their birthplaces.

The Pacific or true salmon usually spawns in spring, and the adults nearly always die after the eggs are laid. The Atlantic salmon, actually a kind of trout, spawns in autumn and usually lives to return to the sea.

The pink salmon (illustrated) is a small Pacific salmon that usually weighs 5 to 7 pounds.

For other members of the salmon family, see *trout.*

sandbar \ˈsan(d)-ˌbär\

A sandbar is a long, low ridge of sediments deposited by water. A sandbar develops where swift-flowing water is slowed. Slow-moving water cannot carry as much sediment with it as swift-moving water can, so some is dropped at this point.

Sandbars sometimes develop along rivers, where the faster current moves to the outsides of curves. Sandbars also develop at the mouths of rivers, where the river water is slowed as it flows into a larger, quieter body of water.

A sandbar is likely to change its shape and size from one season to another. A storm or flood may carry it away entirely, but it will probably re-form during the next period of low water.

sand dollar

Sand dollars make up a group of sea urchins, and are related to the starfish. Sand dollars are named for their flat, rounded shells which are sometimes washed up on beaches.

The living sand dollar has short, velvety spines that entirely cover the shell. The animal crawls about in the sand by

SAND DOLLAR

SAND DUNE

SANDPIPER

waving these spines. Tube feet that serve as breathing organs stick up through rows of tiny holes. The tube feet form a 5-part pattern on the upper surface of the animal. Its mouth is in the middle of the lower surface. It feeds on tiny plants and animals it finds in the sand or drifting along the sea floor.

The Atlantic sand dollar (illustrated) lives along the eastern coast of North America, as far south as Long Island. The animal is usually blue or purplish, and 4 to 5 inches across.

sand dune \ 'dün \

Sand dunes are rounded hills of sand piled up by the wind. They are made up of loose, very tiny rock fragments that are mostly grains of quartz.

Sand dunes up to 100 feet tall are found on the shores of Lake Michigan. Dunes up to 400 feet tall are found on the Sahara Desert, in Africa.

Unless sand dunes are anchored in place by the roots of grass and other plants, the dunes constantly move and change their shape. They usually move slowly, in the direction of the prevailing winds, as grains of sand are pushed up one side and over the top.

The shape of a dune tells which way the prevailing winds blow. The side facing into the wind is sloped more gently. The side away from the wind is steeper. In open country, dunes often become crescent-shaped, with the horns of the crescent pointing away from the wind.

sandpiper \ 'san(d)-ˌpī-pər \

The sandpipers are streaked and speckled shorebirds related to snipes, curlews and yellowlegs. Sandpipers run rapidly along the beach, sometimes stopping to probe the wet sand with their long, slender bills. These birds are 5 to 11 inches long.

Sandpipers migrate long distances, always in large flocks. Some nest on the arctic tundra and winter as far south as Argentina and New Zealand.

Along the seashore, sandpipers eat marine worms, small crustaceans and insect larvae. Inland, they eat a variety of insects and some berries.

Nests are built on the ground. The female lays 4 speckled, pear-shaped eggs.

The spotted sandpiper (illustrated) is fairly common around lakes in the U.S. It sometimes nests as far south as Virginia. The spotted sandpiper has an odd, teetering walk. As it walks, it constantly twitches its tail up and down.

For another kind of sandpiper, see *upland plover*.

sandstone \ 'san(d)-ˌstōn \

Sandstone is a common kind of sedimentary rock that is made up of grains of sand bound together by a natural cement.

SANDSTONE

Hard sandstone is sometimes used as a building material.

Quartz grains make up most of sandstone. The color and hardness of sandstone depend on the kind of mineral that binds the grains together. Very hard sandstone that is reddish or brown is held together by iron oxide. Hard sandstone that is white or gray is held together by silica. If calcium is the only natural cement present, the sandstone is white or gray and quite soft.

Sandstone can be identified by the grainy look and feel of its broken surfaces. It breaks apart through the cementing material and around the grains of sand. Most sandstone was formed under water, so it is likely to contain fossil shells.

Fine-textured, earthy sandstone is very much like shale. Coarse-textured sandstone that contains very large grains of sand and tiny pebbles is like conglomerate.

sapphire \ 'saf-ˌīr \

Sapphires are precious stones used in jewelry. They are crystals of the very hard mineral corundum, which is aluminum oxide. Small amounts of other minerals give sapphires different colors.

Long ago, sapphires were considered good luck charms that brought happiness and protected the wearer from eye diseases and snakebite.

Sapphires are deep blue, pink, yellow or colorless. Most sapphires come from Ceylon, Burma, Thailand and India. A few small stones have been found in the U.S., in Montana and North Carolina.

Star sapphires reflect light along 6 ray-like lines, because of impurities and tiny air bubbles inside the crystal.

Synthetic sapphires made in laboratories are used by industry and as gem stones. The tips of phonograph needles and the jeweled bearings in fine watches are made of synthetic sapphires. Like true sapphires, they are very hard.

sapsucker \ 'sap-ˌsək-ər \

The sapsuckers make up a group of birds related to woodpeckers. Sapsuckers bore holes in living trees and then use their brush-tipped tongues to drink the sap. They eat more plant materials than woodpeckers do, and often damage shade and fruit trees. They also eat ants and other insects.

Sapsuckers are 8 to 9 inches long. Only the males have red on the head or breast. They are noisy birds, particularly in spring when the males tap on hollow trees to attract the females.

In summer, sapsuckers range as far north as Alaska. They spend the winter in the southern half of the U.S., Mexico and Central America. They nest in holes in trees. Four to 7 white eggs are laid once a year.

SAPSUCKER

SATURN

The yellow-bellied sapsucker (illustrated) is common in woodlots and orchards in nearly all parts of the U.S. The other 2 kinds, Williamson's sapsucker and the red-breasted sapsucker, are seen only in the western states.

sardine

The sardines are several different kinds of small edible fish of the herring family. They are closely related to the American shad and the alewife.

Most sardines are a silvery blue or green color, and are 6 to 8 inches long. They swim in large schools, off both coasts of North America.

One female sardine may lay as many as 300,000 eggs in the spring. The eggs hatch in about 3 days. In about 2 years, the fish grow to full size.

Commercial fishermen catch large numbers of sardines in bag-like nets called purse seines, or in underwater traps. Some sardines are used as bait. Others are made into fish meal, for poultry and cattle food, or into oil. Many sardines are dried or canned in oil as food for humans.

sassafras \ 'sas-(ə-),fras \

The sassafras is a North American tree related to the laurel. It has leaves of different shapes. Some leaves are oval, some are mitten-shaped, and some are divided

SASSAFRAS

into 3 lobes. All 3 kinds of leaves appear on all trees.

The bark-like outer layer of sassafras roots makes a fragrant tea, used as medicine by the pioneers. Sassafras tea was once popular as a spring tonic. An oil made from the roots is used to perfume some soaps and cosmetics.

Sassafras grows only in the eastern half of the U.S. The tree seldom becomes taller than 50 feet, and it is often a bushy shrub that grows under larger trees. The leaves are 3 to 9 inches long.

Drooping clusters of yellowish-green flowers hang from the twigs in early spring. The fruit is a glossy blue berry.

Sassafras trees grow quickly but they do not live very long. They are most common in sandy soil or on hillsides.

Saturn \ 'sat-ərn \

Saturn is the second largest of the 9 planets in the solar system and the sixth most distant from the sun. It is the only planet surrounded by rings, which are made up of millions of small particles. The rings are about 171,000 miles wide and somewhat less than 10 miles thick.

Galileo studied Saturn through a weak telescope in 1610 and reported that there was something strange about its appearance. Forty-five years later Christian Huygens first saw the rings clearly through a stronger telescope.

Saturn is about 74,100 miles in diameter. It is about 886 million miles from the sun. It turns on its axis once every 10 hours, and it requires 29½ years to complete 1 orbit around the sun.

In addition to the rings, Saturn has 9 satellites, the largest of them larger than the earth's moon. One of the satellites revolves in a direction opposite to that of the others.

The surface of Saturn is always covered with bands of clouds. It seems likely that the surface is not solid. The planet may have a solid core surrounded by ice and dense gasses.

The temperature of Saturn is probably below -240° F.

See *The Sun, the Moon and the Planets* on p. 502.

sawfish \ 'sȯ-ˌfish \

The sawfish make up a family of ocean fish related to the sharks, skates and rays. They have skeletons of cartilage.

The sawfish's weapon is a hard, flat snout that is edged with many sharp teeth. The fish uses this saw as a club, to attack its enemies or to stun the smaller fish it feeds on.

The largest sawfish are 20 feet long and weigh as much as 1,200 pounds. They live in warm, shallow parts of the ocean.

The young develop inside eggs that remain inside the female's body during a long incubation period. They are born alive, in litters of 15 to 20. Newborn sawfish are about 2 feet long. They look like the adults, but their saws are covered by a protective membrane.

Sawfish are good to eat but commercial fishermen prefer not to catch them, as their saws damage nets and lines.

The most common kind of sawfish is the smalltooth sawfish (illustrated). It grows to about 19½ feet in length.

scale insect

The scale insects are a family of very small insects that cling to the leaves or stems of living plants and suck out sap. The females are blind, wingless and nearly legless. They live under a scale-like protective covering. The males are smaller than the females, and have 1 pair of wings.

Shellac and some dyes and waxes are made from the coverings secreted by female scale insects. Most kinds are pests that damage or kill fruit trees and garden plants. Ladybugs and certain small wasps feed on scale insects and help to control them.

The female of most kinds of scale insects lays eggs under her covering before she dies in autumn. The young insects hatch out the following spring.

The female oystershell scale insect (illustrated) is about $\frac{1}{10}$ inch long. It clings to the bark of trees.

SAWFISH

SCALE INSECT

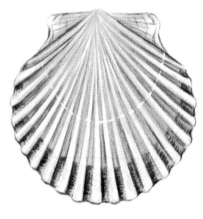

SCALLOP

scallop \ 'skäl-əp \

The scallops are a family of marine mollusks that live inside pairs of fluted, fan-shaped shells. Scallops are a popular food. The edible part is the strong muscle that opens and closes the shells.

Scallops are among the very few mollusks that can see and swim. They have eye-like organs around the edge of the mantle, and a fringe-like row of short tentacles. They swim by opening and closing the shells rapidly so that a jet of water is forced out behind them.

Scallop shells are often washed up on beaches, and they are favorites of many shell collectors. They are 1 to 6 inches across, and have a variety of colors and patterns. The 2 shells of a pair are not exactly alike. The upper shell is larger and flatter than the lower shell.

The bay scallop (illustrated) lives in shallow water along the Atlantic coast, from New England south to North Carolina. Its shells are gray, rusty-red, yellow or white. They are 2 to 3 inches across.

schist \ 'shist \

Schist is a common kind of metamorphic rock that looks scaly or flaky, and that will break apart in flat sheets. The mineral crystals within schist were forced into parallel layers as the rock formed.

Schist varies in appearance and composition. It may be white, gray, black, green or brown. It is made up of quartz and mica combined with different amounts of chlorite, talc, hornblende and other minerals. The particles of these different minerals cannot easily be seen.

Like most other metamorphic rocks, schist occurs where the earth's crust has been folded up into mountains. It is fairly common in Scotland, Norway, Sweden and the Himalaya mountains in Asia. In North America, schist occurs in eastern Canada, New England, New York, the Piedmont plateau and the far western states.

scoria \ 'skōr-ē-ə \

Scoria is a cinder-like rock that is full of airholes. It is 1 of the many different kinds of lava. Scoria formed at the top of a lava flow in which gas bubbles were trapped. As the lava flowed onto the surface of the earth and hardened quickly, the holes remained.

Black or dark reddish-brown, scoria looks a little like a sponge. The holes in it are of different sizes, some large and some small.

Scoria is something like pumice but not so light in weight. Pumice floats on water, while scoria sinks. Pumice is lighter colored than scoria, and the holes in it are all about the same size.

SCORIA

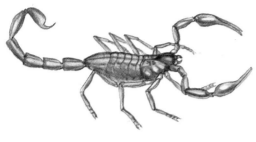

SCORPION

SCORPION FISH

scorpion \ 'skȯr-pē-ən \

Scorpions are arachnids like spiders, ticks and mites. They look a little like large insects, but they have 4 pairs of jointed legs rather than 3 pairs as insects have.

The scorpion's weapons are pincers that look like a lobster's claws, and a poison stinger on the end of the tail. The scorpion uses its sting to paralyze the insects, spiders and worms it feeds on. Only a few large scorpions that live in the tropics are dangerous to humans.

The head and thorax are combined to form the front part of the scorpion's body. The rest is abdomen that stretches out to form the tail. The tail curves downward, under the body, except when the scorpion is about to use its stinger.

The female often stings and kills the male after mating. She bears living young and carries them about with her for a week or so. They ride on her abdomen, holding fast with their pincers.

Scorpions live only in the warmer parts of the world. The largest kinds, up to 8 inches long, live only in the tropics. The common scorpion (illustrated) lives in the southern part of the U.S.

scorpion \ 'skȯr-pē-ən \ **fish**

The 250 different kinds of scorpion fish make up a family of ocean fish with poisonous spines along their dorsal fins. The poison can cause extreme pain or even death. Because of their protective coloration, scorpion fish are hard to see among rocks and seaweed on the ocean floor.

Scorpion fish are 3 to 12 inches long. Most live in tropic or temperate parts of the sea. A few live in very cold water. All feed near the bottom, on smaller fish and invertebrates.

In most kinds of scorpion fish, the female gives birth to living young. The young fish develop inside eggs, but the eggs remain inside the mother's body during the incubation period.

The California scorpion fish (illustrated) is fairly common along the coast of southern California.

For other members of the scorpion fish family, see *rockfish* and *rosefish*.

sea anemone \ ə-'nem-ə-nē \

Sea anemones are unusual animals that look something like flowers. They are related to jellyfish and corals.

The sea anemone's body is a muscular tube that spreads out into a disk at each end. The lower disk is a flattened foot that clings to some solid surface such as a rock or shell. The upper disk has a mouth opening surrounded by tentacles.

Poison cells in the tentacles paralyze small fish and other animals that swim within reach. Then the tentacles wave the victim into the mouth opening, where it is digested.

Some sea anemones can swim, and some can creep slowly. Some live singly, while others live in colonies. The largest are about 12 inches across. The kinds that live in tropical seas are often brightly colored.

The green anemone is fairly common in shallow water along the coast of California. Its green color is due to algae that live inside its body tissues.

sea cucumber \ 'kyü-ˌkəm-bər \

Sea cucumbers belong to a very large group of marine animals that also includes starfish and sea urchins. About 500 kinds of sea cucumbers are known. They are greatly prized as food in oriental countries. In China they are used in soups.

Some of the sea cucumbers have simple worm-like shapes. Others are round, with parts of the body branching out from a central point. All have thick, leathery skins. Their spiny exoskeletons are made of small bony plates embedded in the skin. Some kinds have small, tube-like feet. Around their mouths are many tentacles that look something like seaweed. These tentacles are used for breathing and for trapping the small sea animals on which the sea cucumber feeds.

Sea cucumbers vary from ½ inch to several feet long. Some kinds are common

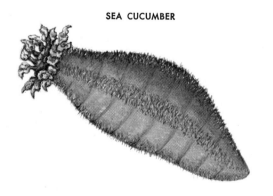

SEA CUCUMBER

SEA FAN

along cooler Atlantic and Pacific shorelines. They attach themselves to rocks or bury themselves in sand. Other kinds live in the deepest parts of the ocean.

Sea cucumbers are usually reddish-brown, gray, brown or black.

The northern sea cucumber (illustrated) is a common kind. It lives on the northern Atlantic coast. Six to 12 inches long, it has 10 branched tentacles and 5 rows of tube feet.

sea fan

The sea fans are marine animals belonging to a group of corals. Sea fans live in colonies that look much like plants or trees. Each colony is a flexible, fan-shaped form that waves gracefully in the current. A colony is started when one animal builds on top of another, forming a central stem and then branching out to take the shape of a fan. Dried sea fan skeletons are often used as ornaments.

The body of each sea fan animal is shaped like a tube. It is closed at the top and bottom by tissue disks. The top disk has a slit-shaped mouth surrounded by 8 hollow tentacles.

Sea fans live in warm, shallow waters along both the Atlantic and Pacific coasts. They are especially common around coral reefs. One kind (illustrated) lives off the coasts of Florida and the West Indies. The colony grows to about 2 feet in height.

SEA HORSE

sea horse

Sea horses are small ocean fish that do not look like any other fish. Instead, a sea horse looks very much like the knight in a chess set. There are nearly 50 different kinds.

The bodies of sea horses, which are covered with scales, are 2 to 12 inches long. The head tilts to 1 side. The snout is long and the pectoral fins are ear-shaped. The strong, flexible tail is used for clinging. By waving its dorsal fin back and forth, the sea horse is able to swim in an upright position.

Sea horses live along shorelines from Cape Cod to Florida. They are most common in shallow water in which they can cling to reeds and other plants. They feed on shrimps and other small marine animals.

In summer the female sea horse lays from 150 to 200 eggs in a pouch on the male's abdomen. The eggs hatch in about 45 days and the young then are expelled.

The northern sea horse (illustrated) is about 5 inches long.

seal

Seals make up a group of fur-bearing, carnivorous mammals that live mostly in the coldest parts of the sea. A few kinds live in the tropics.

Seals have been hunted for their valuable fur and body oil until some kinds are nearly extinct.

Powerful flippers and streamlined bodies make the seals good swimmers. They are slow and clumsy on land. Some kinds come on shore only to breed. Other kinds spend about half their time on ice, or on rocky islands.

Seals eat mostly fish, along with some squid and other marine animals.

The smallest seals are about 6 feet long. The largest kind is about 18 feet long. Females are much smaller than males. One or 2 pups are born, usually in the spring.

The gray seal lives in the North Atlantic. It is most common off the coast of northern Europe, but it is sometimes seen along the coast of North America, as far south as New Jersey.

The male gray seal is about 12 feet long. The female is about 7 feet long. Long hair grows on the nose of the male during the breeding season. The young are born in autumn.

For another kind of seal, see *sea lion.*

sea lion

Sea lions make up several groups of large, intelligent seals with visible ears. They are related to the fur seal, but their pelts are not valuable. Sea lions can balance objects on their noses, and are the trained seals seen in circuses.

Bull sea lions average 13 feet long and

SEA LION

weigh as much as a ton. Cows are about 8 feet long and weigh about 600 pounds. Sea lions have dog-like faces and long necks. They have longer and more flexible flippers than other seals, and are thus better able to move on land.

Sea lions live along the Pacific shores of North and South America, Australia and New Zealand. They eat squid, octopuses and fish.

The breeding ceremony of sea lions is something like that of elephant seals and the fur seals. One young is born each year and is guarded and cared for by both parents.

The California sea lion (illustrated) is the smallest kind of sea lion. The bull is about 8 feet long and weighs about 600 pounds. These sea lions are yellowish-brown but look black when wet. They live off the California coast north to San Francisco.

seamount \ 'sē-ˌmaůnt \

A seamount is an underwater mountain that has been formed of volcanic materials. It stands alone, and is not a part of submerged mountain ranges.

Seamounts were formed billions of years ago. They were unknown until modern times. Since World War II several hundred seamounts have been discovered by means of electronic soundings. Many seamounts rise to within a mile of

SEAMOUNT

SEA OTTER

the sea's surface. Some volcanic islands are really the peaks of seamounts.

One type of seamount called a guyot has a flat top. Many of these are in the Pacific Ocean. They lie from 2,500 to 6,000 feet below sea level. Guyots are thought to be islands which sank below sea level as their weight caused the earth's crust to give way beneath them.

sea otter \ 'ät-ər \

The sea otter is a water mammal belonging to the weasel family. At one time the pelt of the sea otter sold for more than $2,000. For this reason, the sea otter was widely hunted in its North Pacific waters. By 1911 it was almost extinct.

Although the sea otter is now protected by a treaty among nations, it is still quite rare. It lives only among seaweed in isolated bays from Alaska to California.

The sea otter is 4 or 5 feet long and is larger than land otters. It is often mistaken for a seal. It has webbed hind feet that look like fins and short forelimbs with claws. The head is flat, with bulging eyes and white whiskers. The velvety fur is black or brown and is sprinkled with white-tipped hairs.

These otters swim in herds called "pods." They almost never leave the sea, and they may dive 300 feet for fish and shellfish. The sea otter spends a great deal of time floating on its back. It eats in this position, often with a stone on its flat chest. It cracks shells and other hard foods against the stone. At night the sea otter floats on its back and sleeps.

About 8 or 9 months after mating, in April or May, a single pup is born at sea. While floating on her back, the female holds her pup to her chest. Sea otters are full grown at 4 years.

sea raven \ 'rā-vən \

The sea raven is a strange-looking ocean fish that is fairly common off the North Atlantic coast of North America. It has no commercial value except as a lure for lobster traps. The body swells when the fish is handled.

Averaging 12 inches in length, the sea raven may grow to 24 inches and 7 pounds. It has a broad head with large teeth. The head is covered with fleshy tabs. The skin on the body is prickly. The spiny dorsal fin is higher and longer than the soft dorsal fin, and is jagged. The pectoral fins are large and fan-like. Skin color is dingy red to purplish and, sometimes, bright yellow. The underside is yellowish.

The sea raven is most common from Labrador to Cape Cod. It lives in fairly deep water over rocky, pebbly or sandy bottoms. The sea raven feeds on fish and invertebrates, and can swallow a fish nearly as large as itself.

Spawning occurs in winter. A single female may lay up to 40,000 sticky eggs.

SEA RAVEN

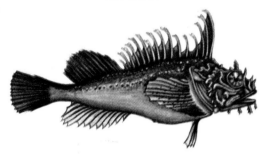

SEA URCHIN

sea urchin \ 'ər-chən \

Sea urchins make up a group of small marine animals with hard, spiny shells and radial bodies, like those of the closely related starfish. They live in seas all over the world. In some European countries the eggs are used for food.

The sea urchin looks something like its relative, the starfish. Its round body is completely covered with many thin plates, like a suit of armor. The plates are covered with sharp spines which vary in size according to the kind of sea urchin. Some kinds have poison-tipped spines.

The sea urchin's mouth is on the underside and has 5 teeth. Around the mouth are 5 bands of holes. Tube-like suckers stick out of the holes. The sea urchin uses these suckers to attach itself to rocks.

Sea urchins are 1½ to 10 inches across. Colors may vary from red to purple to green to black. They move slowly on the ocean bottom, using both their spines and sucker feet. They feed on plants, and reproduce in much the same way as starfish.

The purple sea urchin (illustrated) lives in tidal pools from Cape Cod south. It is about 2 inches wide and is purplish-brown, with red feet.

For another kind of sea urchin, see *sand dollar*.

SELENITE

selenite \ 'sel-ə-,nīt \

Selenite is a clear crystal form of the mineral gypsum. It is found in caves, in the cracks of limestone rocks and as free crystals in clay beds.

The ancient Greeks were familiar with this mineral. Its name comes from a word meaning moon, because the Greeks thought its pale, smooth surface looked like the moon. At one time they believed that its luster became brighter or dimmer along with the changes in brightness of the moon.

Selenite has a glassy or pearly luster. It sometimes splits into smooth, flat sheets. Rare double or twinned crystals sometimes look like arrowheads or fishtails.

Like other forms of gypsum, selenite is soft enough to be scratched with a fingernail. It contains the elements calcium, sulfur, hydrogen and oxygen.

Very fine crystals of selenite up to 5 inches long have been found in Mexico.

sequoia \ sē-'kwȯi-ə \

Sequoias are enormous evergreen trees related to pines and closely related to the redwood. They are the largest and oldest of all living things. Sequoias do not die of old age, and disease and insects do not affect them. The wood is not very useful, as it is weak and brittle.

The giant sequoia (illustrated) grows 200 to 290 feet tall and lives to be about 4,000 years old. The very large trunk may sometimes measure 35 feet across at the base. Because the branches are short, the tree has very little foliage for its size.

The reddish-brown bark, from 1 to 2 feet thick, divides into rounded vertical ridges. The leaves, which are pointed scales from ⅛ to ½ inch long, cling tightly to the twigs. They are blue green for about 3 years, then turn brown and stay on the tree several years longer.

The dark brown cones, 2 to 3½ inches long, ripen at the end of their second year. They may remain on the tree for 20 years before opening to release their seeds.

The giant sequoia grows only in the Sierra Nevada Mountains of California at altitudes of 5,000 to 8,400 feet above sea level.

serpentine \ 'sər-pən-,tēn \

Serpentine is a common mineral found in several different forms. It has many uses. Attractively colored masses of serpentine are used as building stones or for carving. One form, chrysotile, is used to make asbestos. Other forms are used to make heat-resistant bricks to line fireplaces and furnaces.

Usually some shade of green, serpentine is spotted or striped with white or black. The solid masses sometimes look like green marble and have a waxy luster. Grains of serpentine are sometimes embedded in

SEQUOIA

rocks. Serpentine may also occur in flaky masses like mica. Chrysotile is made up of fine, flexible fibers.

Serpentine occurs in most parts of the world. It results from the changing of rocks through the chemical action of water. Serpentine is made up of magnesium and silicon, combined with oxygen and hydrogen.

Serpentine is quarried in England, France, Italy and Greece and, in the U.S., in Vermont. Chrysotile is found in Quebec and Africa, and, in the U.S., in Vermont and Arizona.

serpent \ 'sǝr-pǝnt \ star (brittle star)

The serpent stars are small marine animals closely related to the starfish. They are named for their long, waving arms. There are about 2,000 different kinds of serpent stars.

The body of the serpent star is a disk with 5 to 8 long, slender, jointed arms. These arms break off easily, but the serpent star often grows new ones.

The mouth opening of the serpent star is on the underside. It is covered with rows of spines which strain out the small organisms and decaying plants that the serpent star eats. Some serpent stars have 2 rows of tube-like feet. These feet serve mainly to direct food into the mouth, and as breathing and sense organs.

Serpent stars live in deep water or rocky

SERPENT STAR

SHALE

tide pools. They hide in seaweed or sand during the day and feed at night. They can move quickly up and down as well as sideways.

One kind of small serpent star is the green brittle star (illustrated). It may be green, brown or striped. It lives near the shore, from Cape Cod south. Its disk is about ½ inch across and it usually has 5 arms.

shale \ 'shāl \

Shale is a common sedimentary rock made up of hardened clay. Sometimes the clay contains sand, iron oxides, calcite and other materials. Some shale is a source of oil.

Shale is found in nearly all parts of the world. In some places it is used to make brick, tile and cement.

Shale is formed under water. It occurs farther from shore than sandstone because the tiny clay particles are lighter than sand and drift farther before settling to the bottom.

Shale is usually gray, but may be white, yellow, green or black. It has a dull luster and an uneven texture. Shale sometimes shows the pattern of the layers in which it was formed. It may break apart into flat sheets. It may contain fossils of plants or shells. Some shale is soft enough to be cut with a knife.

Sharks of the World

BASKING SHARK

BLUE SHARK

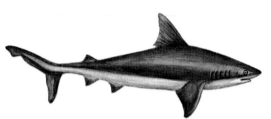

BROWN SHARK

SMOOTH HAMMERHEAD SHARK

NURSE SHARK

SOUPFIN SHARK

COMMON THRESHER SHARK

TIGER SHARK

WHALE SHARK

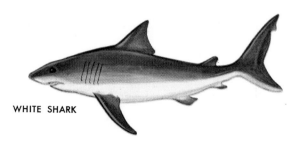

WHITE SHARK

shark \ 'shärk \

The sharks and their close relatives, the skates and the rays, make up a group of fish quite different from all others. Their skeletons are made of flexible cartilage rather than hard bone.

Sharks are older than most other kinds of fish. Some sharks have existed unchanged for millions of years.

Most sharks live in the warmer parts of the oceans. A few kinds live in rivers, and 1 kind lives in lakes in Central America.

All sharks have streamlined, powerful bodies. Most kinds have pointed snouts above crescent-shaped mouths.

On the sides of the body, well behind the head, are 5 to 7 pairs of gill slits. Set into the tough skin are small, sharp-pointed scales. Inside the mouth, larger scales serve as teeth.

The tail is always divided into 2 pointed lobes. The upper lobe is always larger than the lower one.

Sharks have weak eyesight but a keen sense of smell. They may also have a special way of sensing movements in water.

Most sharks, but not all, are greedy feeders. They eat mostly fish, but some kinds will also attack and kill sea lions, turtles and humans.

Like the largest whales, the largest sharks eat only very small tidbits of food. As they swim, these large sharks use gill rakers to strain tiny fish and floating animals such as shrimp from seawater.

Most kinds of sharks bear living young. The sharks develop inside eggs, as other fish do, but the eggs are fertilized inside the female's body and they remain there during the incubation period. Small sharks have litters of 2 to 6 young. Larger kinds bear 20 or more young at a time.

Some kinds of sharks are hunted for their edible flesh, or for their oil. The skin of some kinds is made into leather.

The basking and whale sharks are the largest of the sharks and the largest of all fish. The basking shark is up to 45 feet long, and the whale shark is up to 60 feet long. The whale shark has a broad, flat snout. The upper surface of its body is black, speckled and striped with white. Basking and whale sharks eat only tiny fish and plankton. They are lazy, slow-swimming fish that live in mid-ocean.

The blue, brown, nurse, soupfin and tiger sharks are all fast-swimming, medium-sized sharks 6 to 14 feet long. They eat mostly fish, along with some squid and other invertebrates. The soupfin shark, found only in the Pacific, is the most valuable of the sharks since its flesh is prized as food. The nurse and tiger sharks are sometimes hunted for oil or skins.

The hammerhead sharks are a family of odd-looking sharks with very wide heads. Their eyes and nostrils are set at opposite sides of the head, and may be 36 inches apart. Hammerhead sharks are usually about 12 feet long. The smooth hammerhead (illustrated) is sometimes hunted for its liver which contains oil rich in vitamins, and for its skin.

The thresher sharks are a family of sharks with unusually long and powerful tails that they use as weapons. Often 2 thresher sharks work together, rounding up a school of smaller fish. Then, they thresh with their tails until the smaller fish are stunned or killed.

Thresher sharks are usually 12 to 20 feet long, including the tail. The common thresher shark (illustrated) is sometimes called the fox shark.

The white shark, sometimes called the man-eater shark, attacks humans more often than other sharks. It is a powerful, fast-swimming shark up to 40 feet long. Though fairly rare, it is found in all tropic seas. It often swims quite near shore.

For another kind of shark, see *smooth dogfish*.

SHEEP

sheep

Sheep are hollow-horned, ruminant mammals related to antelopes and goats. Male sheep, unlike goats, do not have beards, or scent glands on their tails. Some kinds of sheep are wild, while others are domestic.

Kinds of sheep vary widely in appearance. The fleece may be long or short, curly or straight. Males, called rams, are always larger than females, called ewes. In some kinds, both rams and ewes have horns. In other types, only rams have horns. Sheep mate in the fall and lambs are born in the spring. Wild sheep bear 3 or 4 young.

Sheep feed mostly on grass. At times, they cause soil erosion because they pull up the whole plant, leaving the soil bare.

The domestic sheep (illustrated) exists in several breeds. They were tamed by man, and many were tamed in very ancient times. Most domestic sheep have long, curved horns, but some have none at all. Domestic rams may weigh up to 285 pounds. Some types of domestic sheep are specially bred to produce twins.

Today, domestic sheep are bred for meat, wool and hides. Roquefort cheese is made from the ewe's milk.

shell

Shells are the hard coverings that mollusks make to protect their bodies. The part of the body called the mantle puts out a limy substance that becomes the shell.

Each shell is made up of 3 layers. The thin, fairly hard outer layer protects the limy substance from dissolving in water. The thicker middle layer, usually white and chalky, is made up of crystals of calcium carbonate. The inner layer that touches the mollusk's body is smooth and pearly.

Most common shells belong to 3 groups of mollusks. The gastropods have twisted spiral shells, like the shells of snails, whelks and conchs. The bivalves have double or hinged shells with 2 parts, like the shells of clams and oysters. The third group, the tooth shells, are tube-like and open at both ends.

Boat shells are gastropod shells that are rounded, with flattened spirals. A shelf or plate extends across about half the opening. The common boat shell is usually gray-white and about 1½ inches long. It is found along the Atlantic coast of North America, as far north as Canada.

shiner \ 'shī-nər \

Shiners are small freshwater fish related to carp and goldfish. Along with many other kinds of small fish, they are often called minnows. Such fish are important as food for larger fish, and they are often used by fishermen as bait.

Most shiners are 2 to 4 inches long. About 50 different kinds are known. They live in ponds, lakes and quiet streams, in most parts of North America.

SHINER

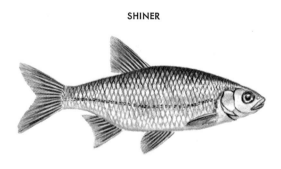

The mouths of shiners slant downward, and a groove separates the upper jaw from the snout. The single dorsal fin, which is triangular, begins at the highest curve of the fish's back. The anal fin is sail-shaped, and nearly as large as the dorsal fin.

Shiners eat mostly plankton. Some eat snails and smaller fish.

The golden shiner (illustrated) is fairly common in southeastern Canada and the eastern half of the U.S. It is yellowish, and its scales seem large for the small size of the fish. A clearly marked lateral line marks the sides of the body.

Most golden shiners are 3 to 4 inches long but a few, in lakes, grow to 12 inches.

shrew \ 'shrü \

Shrews are a family of insect-eating mammals. One kind found in Borneo grows 2 feet long, while another kind found in Europe is less than 2 inches long.

Shrews look something like moles, but they spend most of their time above ground and do not dig well. They are active day and night. They have silky, brown fur, short-haired tails and hooked teeth. Shrews are nearly blind and have very delicate skeletons.

Most shrews eat 3 times their weight in food daily, and they can starve in a few hours. They will eat almost anything, including their own young or each other. They will attack animals much larger than themselves. Some kinds of shrews paralyze their victims with poison.

Shrews produce 4 litters of up to 10 young each year. They are mature at 4 weeks, but live only about 2 years.

The rare pigmy shrew (illustrated) is the smallest North American mammal. It is only 3 inches long, including its 1-inch tail. Because its scent glands give its flesh an unpleasant taste, the pigmy shrew is seldom eaten by other animals. This shrew is found in a few places from the Carolinas north to Canada.

shrike \ 'shrīk \

Shrikes make up a family of birds that resemble songbirds, except that they feed like birds of prey. They often capture field mice, lizards or smaller birds and pin them on thorns. The thorns hold the victim in place while the shrike tears it apart and eats it. If the shrike cannot find a thorn for its prey, it may use a twig or a barbed wire fence. Shrikes are sometimes called butcher birds because they seem to kill more victims that they can eat.

Dull-colored birds 9 to 12 inches long, shrikes have large heads, long hooked bills and long tails.

Shrikes live mostly in the Old World but 2 kinds live in America. The northern shrike (illustrated) is about the size of a robin. It breeds in Canada and Alaska and winters in the northern half of the U.S. It usually nests in a shrub or low

SHREW

SHRIKE AND
IMPALED VICTIM

tree. The 4 to 6 eggs are bluish-green, spotted with purple and brown.

The loggerhead shrike looks like the northern shrike but is a little smaller. It nests in the northern half of the U.S. and winters in the southern states and Mexico.

shrimp \ 'shrimp \

The shrimps are a group of crustaceans related to the lobsters and crabs. Most kinds of shrimps live in the sea, but a few tropical kinds live in rivers. Some kinds are in great demand as food.

The smallest shrimps are microscopic. The largest ones become 9 inches long. Like other crustaceans, shrimps have shell-like, jointed exoskeletons. Five pairs of legs are attached to the thorax of the fairly narrow body. Shorter swimmerets are under the abdomen, which ends in a fan-like tail fin. On the head are very long, slender antennae.

Shrimps swim backward, very rapidly. They eat both small animals and plants. Shrimps live in both shallow and deep water, in both warm and cool parts of the oceans. Females fasten their eggs to their swimmerets and carry them until they hatch. The young shrimp pass through several larval stages. Some kinds change from male to female as they mature.

One kind of edible shrimp (illustrated) is up to 6 inches long, with antennae up to 12 inches long. The shell is thin and

SHRIMP

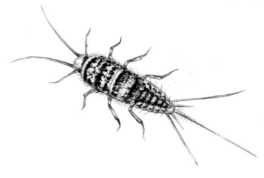

SILVERFISH

flexible, and a brownish-green color. This shrimp lives all along the east coast of North America and in the Gulf of Mexico.

silverfish \ 'sil-vər-ˌfish \

Silverfish are small insects that have small silvery scales on their bodies. They have no wings, and they belong to a very primitive group of insects. Silverfish hide during the day and move about at night.

Silverfish have slender bodies, about ½ inch long. There are 2 or 3 thread-like, jointed extensions at the tail, and 2 long antennae.

Silverfish are often found around books and papers in homes and libraries. They are also found outdoors under stones or the loose bark of trees. Those living indoors feed on the glued edges of books and eat holes in the paper. Those living outdoors feed on decaying leaves.

Scientists believe that young silverfish pass through as many as 6 stages before they become adults. They probably take about 2 years to grow into adults. It is thought that the eggs are very small and are laid in cracks or places where dust gathers.

The common silverfish (illustrated) is found in most parts of North America.

siren \ 'sī-rən \

The sirens are a family of salamanders that look like eels. Although they are amphibians, they spend all their lives in wa-

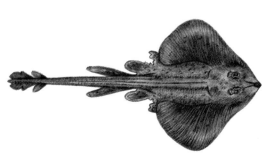

SKATE

ter. Sirens have very short forelegs, and no hind legs at all.

Sirens live only in the southeastern U.S. and parts of Mexico. They are from 4 to 36 inches long. They have feathery gills just behind the head. The 2 tiny legs are close to the head.

Shy and wary animals, sirens burrow in mud at the bottom of streams or marshes, or hide among water plants. They feed on insects or insect larvae, and small fish.

Sirens are brown or dark gray marked with lighter spots or stripes. They mate and lay their eggs in water.

The slender dwarf siren is sometimes called the mud siren. It is 4 to 6 inches long, and a dull greenish-brown. It lives in Florida and Georgia.

skate

Skates make up a family of marine fish related to the sharks. Like sharks, they have skeletons of flexible cartilage rather than bone. Large, wide fins extend along both sides of the head and upper body. In some places, these fins are a popular food. Some kinds of skates are used to make fish meal.

Skates have flat bodies and long tails. Their eyes are on top of their heads. The skin is covered with spiny bumps. Some skates grow to be 6 feet long and weigh 60 pounds, although skates 2 to 3 feet long are more common. The females are larger than the males.

By waving the wide fins along either side of the head and body, skates swim. They live mostly at the bottom of the sea, and feed on small fish, shrimps and other sea animals. They are sometimes seen at the surface of the water, basking in the sun.

Skates are found in temperate to cold waters along the Atlantic coast. They can live at depths of several hundred feet. Skate eggs are protected by flat, rectangular cases with hooks at either end. The young hatch in about 6 months.

The common skate (illustrated) is 1 to 2 feet long.

skink\ 'skingk\

Skinks are a family of small, long-tailed lizards covered with smooth, glossy scales. They live in nearly all parts of the temperate and tropic zones.

Most skinks are less than 8 inches long, and half of this length is the tail. Most kinds of skinks live on the ground, but some kinds burrow and others climb trees. Still others have no legs.

Like many lizards, skinks can lose their tails to confuse an enemy when attacked. New but smaller tails then grow in place of the old tail. Skinks usually feed on insects and worms. In cold climates, they hibernate under rocks or in burrows.

The 5-lined skink (illustrated) is sometimes called the blue-tailed skink. It lives in the eastern half of the U.S., except for

SKINK

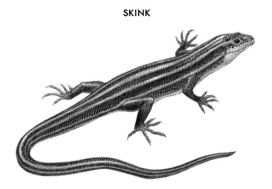

SKUNK

New England and Florida. Its coloring differs with sex and changes with age. The young are black with 5 lines of white or yellow down the back. The tip of the tail is bright blue. In adults the tail turns gray, while the body of the adult male turns greenish-brown. The female may keep dull lines.

Five-lined skinks usually live in trash piles or among stumps or rocks. The female lays 2 to 15 eggs in summer and guards them during the 5- to 6-week incubation period.

skunk (polecat)

Skunks are mammals that belong to the weasel family, and are closely related to badgers. Skunk oil is used in making perfume, and the fur is widely used for coats.

Skunks are best known for the foul-smelling liquid which they spray at an enemy when they are attacked. This liquid comes from scent glands under the tail. The sprayed fluid clings for months, and can burn the eyes badly. Most skunks do not use this weapon unless they are really in danger. Most pet skunks have had their scent glands removed.

The striped or common skunk (illustrated) roams meadows, woods and plains in Canada, the U.S. and Mexico. These skunks have 2 white stripes down their sides and flanks. The stripes meet at the top of the head and continue down to the snout.

Striped skunks are about the size of cats. They have a plume-like tail and long, glossy black fur which is much used by furriers. They sleep in holes in the ground by day and feed at night. Half of their diet is insects, and the rest is small animals such as snakes and frogs.

The young are born in April or May. There are usually 4 to 6 young in the litter.

skunk cabbage (polecat weed, swamp cabbage)

Skunk cabbage is a perennial plant closely related to jack-in-the-pulpit. In many areas of North America, skunk cabbage is the first wild flower to appear in the spring. It often blooms when there is still snow on the ground.

Skunk cabbage is named for the bad smell given off when any part of the plant is crushed.

Like jack-in-the-pulpit, skunk cabbage has small flowers that are hidden inside a hood-shaped bract. The flowers are clustered on a thumb-shaped spike about an inch thick. The bract, 4 to 8 inches long, is mottled green, purple and brown.

The large leaves appear after the flowers. At first they are tightly rolled around the stalk. When full-sized, the leaves are 1 foot wide and up to 3 feet long. The fruit is a cluster of red berries.

Skunk cabbage grows only in moist soil. It lives in damp wooded places and swamps, through eastern North America.

SKUNK CABBAGE

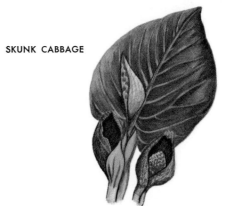

SLATE

SLIME MOLD

slate

Slate is a common and useful kind of rock that can be split into smooth, flat sheets. A metamorphic rock, slate is shale that has become harder and more compact. This change took place under great pressure, usually when the earth's crust was being folded into mountain ranges.

Pioneer children used wood-framed sheets of slate rather than paper for their school work. Wall chalkboards made of larger sheets of slate are still used in some schools.

Today slabs of slate are used for floor tile, laboratory tabletops and electrical switchboards. Crushed slate is used in making roof shingles.

Slate is fine-textured, hard and durable. It is always dark-colored, usually gray or brown, but sometimes reddish or green. It contains quartz and mica, along with other minerals. Reddish slate contains iron oxide, while greenish slate contains chlorite.

Slate is found mostly in very old mountain ranges. In the U.S., most slate is quarried in Vermont, Pennsylvania, Maine, New York and some other states. Most of the slate used in Great Britain comes from Wales.

slime mold \ 'slīm 'mōld \

Slime molds make up a group of unusual plants related to fungi. They form shapeless, slippery masses that cover dead leaves and decaying wood. The color may be white, bright yellow, red, purple or black. Some are up to 12 inches wide.

Like fungi, slime molds have no chlorophyll and cannot produce their own food. They feed on dead plant matter and grow from spores, rather than from seeds.

The slime molds are unusual because they can move about at certain stages in their development. The soft, formless cells flow. In the first part of the life cycle, the slime mold lives in moist, dark places. Later it moves to a lighter, drier surface and stays there. Spore-producing organs are raised up at this time. One common kind (illustrated) has spore-producing parts that are club-shaped and look something like mushrooms.

sloth \ 'slȯth \

Sloths are toothless mammals that spend most of their lives hanging upside down from trees. They eat, sleep, mate and give birth in this position. They come to the ground only to climb another tree. Sloths live mostly in rain forests of Central and South America.

Sloths hang by their long, strong legs. All sloths have 3 toes on their hind feet, but some types have 2 toes and others 3 on their forefeet. Blue or green algae grow in their shaggy hair.

During the day, sloths sleep. At night, they munch leaves and berries. The young

SLOTH

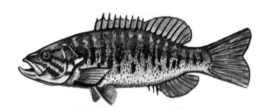

SMALLMOUTH BLACK BASS

are born 4 to 6 months after mating. A young sloth clings to the hair on its mother's belly.

The common 2-toed sloth (illustrated) grows to about 28 inches in length, and has yellowish-gray fur. Like most sloths, it seems lazy, but it can move quickly when it is disturbed and can even swim well.

Two-toed sloths are unusually hardy. They can live through attacks from enemies that would kill other animals their size. Two-toed sloths live in Central America, from Costa Rica to Panama.

smallmouth black bass \ 'smȯl-ˌmaúth 'blak 'bas \

The smallmouth black bass is a popular freshwater food fish and a favorite game fish. It belongs to the sunfish family, and lives in cooler water than its close relative, the largemouth black bass.

This fish has a long body with a long, low dorsal fin that is notched in the middle. The anal fin is a little shorter than the second dorsal. The tail fin is slightly forked. The mouth extends as far back as the eye, and the lower jaw protrudes. The usual size is 3 to 6 pounds, but much larger ones have been caught.

The smallmouth black bass is native to the northern and eastern part of the U.S. and Canada. It has been introduced into many other areas. It is most common in deep, clear, moving waters of lakes and streams. It feeds on other fish, shellfish and insects.

The male builds a shallow nest on gravelly bottoms in the late spring or early summer. Several females lay their eggs in the nest until about 2,000 eggs are in the nest. The male then guards the nest until the young hatch.

smelt \ 'smelt \

Smelts make up a family of fish that live mostly in the ocean. They are related to salmon and trout. Some freshwater kinds of smelts are commercially fished in the Great Lakes. The saltwater smelts have little commercial value, but they provide food for other fish.

The smelt is small, averaging 7 to 9 inches and less than ½ pound. The body is slim and salmon-shaped. The short adipose fin is opposite the anal fin.

Smelts are found in cold or temperate waters of the northern hemisphere. They swim in schools, in shallow waters near shore. They feed on smaller fish and shellfish.

Like their larger relatives, the salmon and trout, smelts swim up freshwater streams to spawn. Their small, sticky eggs cling to rocks or plants underwater.

Some adults return to the sea after spawning. Others remain in freshwater streams and lakes.

The American or Atlantic smelt is common all along the east coast of the U.S. and in the Great Lakes. It sometimes grows to 15 inches in length.

smooth dogfish \ 'dȯg-,fish \

The smooth dogfish is a shark that is fairly common along the Middle Atlantic Coast. It is a game fish valued by shallow-water boat fishermen and surf casters. Its oil has some commercial use.

The slender body of the smooth dogfish has a flattened lower surface. The snout is blunt and the sharp teeth can crush shells. The 2 dorsal fins are far apart and the pectoral fins are large. The tail slants upward. The smooth dogfish is usually 3 to 4 feet long. It sometimes becomes as long as 5 feet.

Body color may be dark gray or greenish-brown. The lower body is white, tinged with yellow or gray. The smooth dogfish is one of the few sharks that can change its color to a paler shade. The change takes about 2 days.

The smooth dogfish is found as far north as the Bay of Fundy. It is more common in the Middle Atlantic regions than in tropical waters. It is usually found in shallow water along beaches. This shark feeds chiefly on large crustaceans and small fish. It also eats dead plant and animal materials.

The smooth dogfish mates in summer. Ten to 20 live young are born about 10 months after mating.

snail

Snails make up many groups of small, soft-bodied, gastropod mollusks with spiral shells. There are several thousand kinds of snails. Some kinds live on land while others live in the sea or in freshwater streams. Slugs are a form of snail, but do not have shells.

The snail's body includes a distinct head, a radula used for chewing food, tentacles and a large foot. Water snails breathe through gills, while land snails have a lung-like air chamber. Snails feed chiefly on plants, though some water snails eat other marine life.

The white-lipped land snail (illustrated) is usually about 2 inches long. Land snails have 2 pairs of tentacles. One pair has eyes at the tips or at the bases, and the other pair has sense organs at the tips.

Some kinds of land snails are used for food, and are raised commercially in Europe. Other kinds destroy crops, and some carry parasites that live on the bodies of domestic animals.

Land snails are found in all parts of the world, most often where the soil contains lime, a chemical that the snail needs to make its shell.

SMOOTH DOGFISH

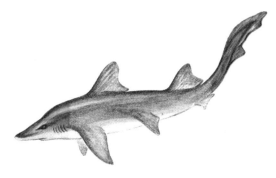

SNAIL

snake

Snakes are legless reptiles with long, slender bodies. They live in all but the coldest parts of the world. Like other reptiles, they are most common in the tropics. They are fairly rare in the cooler parts of the temperate zone. Since they are cold-blooded, snakes hibernate wherever the temperature goes below freezing.

Poisonous snakes are common in only a few parts of the world. Most snakes are harmless to man. They help to control the rats and mice that damage farm crops.

Snakes also eat frogs, lizards, birds, eggs and smaller snakes. They swallow their victims whole, sometimes while they are still alive. Snakes' mouths and throats stretch open so widely that they can swallow objects larger than themselves.

Snakes develop inside eggs, as other reptiles do. In some kinds of snakes, the eggs are incubated inside the female's body and the young are born alive. The copperhead, cottonmouth, garter snake and rattlesnake all bear living young.

Other kinds of snakes lay 6 to 24 oval-shaped eggs at a time. The eggs have leathery shells and are usually buried in sun-warmed sand. Some eggs are laid under dead plants or rotting wood, where the heat of decay will incubate them.

The pythons are among the few snakes that lay eggs and incubate them. The female python lays as many as 100 eggs. She pushes them into a cone-shaped pile and wraps her body around them.

Snake eggs hatch in 6 to 8 weeks. The adults never care for the young.

The garter snakes, the milk snake and the coachwhip snake are all harmless. Garter snakes live in southern Canada, northern Mexico and almost all parts of the U.S. They are 1 to 4 feet long. The common garter snake found in the eastern U.S. has 3 yellow stripes.

The milk snake, 2 to 4½ feet long, lives east of the Rocky Mountains. The slender, long-tailed coachwhip snake, 4 to 8 feet long, lives only in the southeast.

The coral snakes, the copperhead, the cottonmouth and the rattlesnakes are all poisonous snakes. They kill their prey by shooting venom through sharp, hollow teeth called fangs.

The bright-colored coral snakes, 1 to 5 feet long, live mostly in the tropics. The only kind found in the U.S. is the North American coral snake (illustrated). It lives in or near water, from the Carolinas west to Texas, and is poisonous.

The copperhead, the cottonmouth and the rattlesnakes all belong to the pit viper family. All have wedge-shaped heads and all are poisonous. Near their nostrils are pits or hollows sensitive to heat. These sense organs help them follow the trails of warm-blooded animals.

The copperhead is about 2½ feet long. It lives from Massachusetts west to Illinois and south to Florida and Texas.

The cottonmouth is usually about 3 feet long. White shows inside its mouth when it prepares to strike. This snake lives in swamps and along rivers, in the southeastern part of the U.S.

Rattlesnakes, 2 to 8 feet long, live in nearly all parts of the U.S. Before striking, they coil the body and raise both head and tail. Rattles on the tail make a dry, buzzing sound. The eastern diamondback rattlesnake (illustrated) weighs up to 15 pounds and is the largest poisonous snake native to North America.

The sidewinder is a small desert rattlesnake, 18 to 30 inches long, found in the southwestern U.S. and in Mexico. Unlike other rattlesnakes, it moves by throwing loops of its body ahead and to the side.

Pythons, 10 to 30 feet long, kill animals as large as wild pigs and deer. They live in Africa and southern Asia. The Indian python (illustrated) is often seen in zoos.

Snakes—Legless Reptiles

COACHWHIP SNAKE

COPPERHEAD

NORTH AMERICAN CORAL SNAKE

COTTONMOUTH

GARTER SNAKE

MILK SNAKE

PYTHON

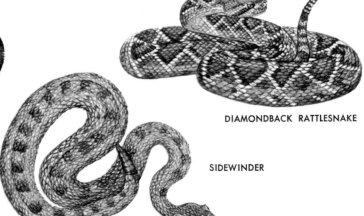

DIAMONDBACK RATTLESNAKE

SIDEWINDER

SNAPPER

snapdragon \ 'snap-,drag-ən \

Snapdragons make up a group of about 32 annual and perennial plants native to the northern hemisphere. Some are garden plants, while others are wild flowers.

The snapdragons include erect, climbing and creeping plants. The flowers are usually clustered in slender spikes at the tops of the stalks. The flowers are white, yellow, pink, red or purple. Each flower is tube-shaped, ending in 2 parts that are like upper and lower lips. The fruit is a dry capsule from which tiny seeds fall.

The common garden snapdragon is native to parts of Europe and Asia near the Mediterranean Sea. It grows 12 to 24 inches tall. The alternate leaves that grow close together along the stalks are bright green and 2 to 3 inches long. The flowers, usually white or reddish-purple, are about 1½ inches long.

snapper \ 'snap-ər \

Snappers make up a widespread family of tropical ocean fish. They are important food fish, and some types are valued as game fish. The snout is flat on top. The large mouth has sharp jaw teeth. Snappers average about 15 to 20 pounds, but some grow to twice that weight.

Snappers are common in the tropical Atlantic and Gulf of Mexico regions. Some are found as far north as Cape Cod. Snappers travel in large schools near the surface and eat smaller fish and marine animals, such as shrimp and crabs. Little is known about the breeding habits of snappers, but they probably spawn in summer.

The kind of snapper called red snapper, or Pensacola red snapper (illustrated), is a well-known food and game fish. It lives in the Gulf of Mexico and along the Atlantic Coast as far north as Long Island. It may grow to 3 feet in length.

snipe \ 'snīp \

Snipes make up a group of wading birds related to sandpipers, curlews and yellowlegs. They live in wet forests and marshy places, in nearly all parts of the world. The smallest kinds are about 10 inches long, while the largest are about 16 inches long. They are popular game birds.

Snipes have long, slender bills covered with skin. The bodies are marked with spots or streaks of buff and brown. The legs are short and the toes are long.

Skillful fliers, snipes zigzag back and forth through the air, near the ground. Snipes eat mostly worms and small crustaceans that they find in wet mud. During the mating season, the male snipe performs an acrobatic courtship flight.

The nest is a hollow on the ground, or on a tuft of grass surrounded by water. The 4 eggs, laid once a year, are a speckled olive color.

The common snipe (illustrated) is 10 to 11 inches long. It lives throughout the

SNIPE

northern hemisphere. In the New World, it breeds from the Arctic south to Pennsylvania and southern California. In the winter, the common snipe ranges as far south as Brazil.

snow

Snow is crystallized water vapor. When a rising mass of moist air is cooled rapidly to a temperature below freezing, moisture condenses from the air and is changed directly from a vapor to a solid. The solid is the snow crystal. Snowflakes are groups of snow crystals that clump together as they fall through the air.

Snow crystals have different sizes and patterns, but they are always 6-sided or have 6 equal and similar parts extending out from the center. Their sizes and patterns depend on the amount of moisture in the air, and on the temperature.

If the air contains much moisture and the temperature is just below freezing, snow crystals form quickly and are likely to be large. Drier air and colder temperatures produce smaller crystals.

Once on the ground, snow sometimes melts slightly and then refreezes, so that it loses the delicate pattern of crystals.

soil

Soil is the loose material that covers much of the surface of the earth. It is made up of bits of rock mixed with decaying plant and animal matter, water and air.

Soil is a valuable natural resource, since it provides the things plants need to grow.

Topsoil is the thin, upper layer of soil that is rich in plant foods, oxygen and moisture. It is usually 6 to 8 inches thick, and is fairly dark in color and fine-textured. About half of it is rock and mineral material. The other half is water, air and decaying plant matter.

Below the topsoil lies a thicker layer of subsoil that is usually lighter in color and coarser in texture than the topsoil. Nearly all of the subsoil is made up of large and small bits of rock. Subsoil is much less fertile than topsoil. Under the subsoil lies solid rock.

In warm areas where there is much rainfall, soil is dark brown or black because it contains much decaying plant material.

solar flare \ 'sō-lər 'flar \

A solar flare is a large, bright outburst of burning gas from the sun. Solar flares come from the outer portion of the sun, but they are caused by bursts of energy from within the sun. They usually appear above groups of sunspots.

A solar flare looks like a giant tongue of flame that rises quickly and fades more slowly. Solar flares stream out great distances, up to a million miles from the sun's surface. They push free atoms out into space at great speed. Some of the atoms reach the earth's atmosphere, where they cause magnetic storms and other electri-

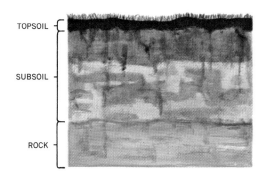

TOPSOIL AND SUBSOIL

TOPSOIL

SUBSOIL

ROCK

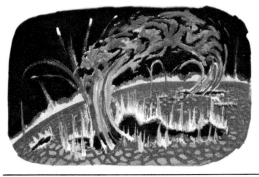

SOLAR FLARE

SOLE

cal disturbances. These disturbances interrupt short wave radio, telephone and telegraph operations. Solar flares often cause an increase in the bright streamers of light that make up auroras.

Solar flares do not occur very often, and they usually last only a few minutes. They can be seen only by astronomers using special telescopes.

sole

The true soles are ocean flatfish. The "filet of sole" listed on American restaurant menus is usually flounder or some other kind of fish.

Like the flounders, soles have both eyes on 1 side of the body. They swim on 1 side, and lie flat on the sea floor with the eyed side up. The eyes are quite small. Soles have short, crooked mouths and rounded snouts.

Most soles are small fish about 6 inches long. They live in shallow, warm water near shore. They feed near the bottom.

Newly hatched soles swim upright, and have 1 eye on each side. As they grow larger, they begin to turn onto the left side, and the left eye moves around to the right side. The right or top side is usually a darker color than the left or bottom side.

The naked sole (illustrated) lives along the southeast coast of North America, from Georgia south to the Florida Keys and along the Gulf coast.

sorghum \ˈsȯr-gəm\

Sorghums are corn-like plants belonging to the grass family. Probably native to Africa, sorghums have been cultivated for hundreds of years.

Sorghum grows best in hot countries where there is little rainfall. It is an important food crop in southern Africa, where the grain is ground and made into cakes called mealies.

In the U.S., the grain, stems and leaves of sorghum are used as food for livestock. Some kinds of sorghum contain a sweet juice that is made into syrup.

The sorghums have thick, pithy stems and long, corn-like leaves. The flowers and seeds are grouped in tight clusters at the tops of the stalks. The seeds are round, and smaller than grains of wheat. They are yellow, brown, white or red.

Sweet sorghum has been planted widely in the southeastern U.S. It is used as food for cattle, and for making syrup. It grows up to 15 feet tall.

sowbug and pillbug \ˈsau̇-ˌbəg ənd ˈpil-ˌbəg\

The sowbugs and pillbugs are small crustaceans that live on land. They look much alike, but only the ones called pillbugs curl up in a ball (illustrated) when disturbed.

When not curled up, sowbugs and pillbugs have flattened, oval bodies. Most are less than 1 inch long. The body is

SOWBUG

PILLBUG COILED UP

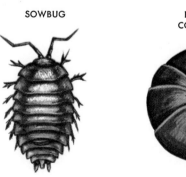

414

made up of jointed sections. The short head is joined with the first section and bears a pair of wide-spreading antennae.

Sowbugs and pillbugs live only in damp places, as they breathe through gills. They hide under logs or rocks during the day, and move about seeking food at night. They eat mostly dead leaves and rotting wood, but they sometimes damage growing plants in greenhouses.

Females lay eggs and carry them in a pouch during the incubation period. Young sowbugs and pillbugs look like the adults but are much smaller.

sparrow

Sparrows are small, streaked birds common in many different parts of the world. The English sparrow and the European tree sparrow are not closely related to the sparrows native to North America, which belong to the finch family.

All of the North American sparrows are brown and gray, marked with some black and white. They have short but strong, cone-shaped bills for cracking seeds. They also eat fruit, berries and insects.

The true sparrows of North America nest on the ground, in fields and brushy places. The cup-shaped nest is made of grass and roots and lined with soft hair. Male and female birds share the tasks of nest building and incubating the eggs. They usually raise several broods during the nesting season.

SPARROW

SPEARMINT

The field sparrow (illustrated) is 5 to 6 inches long. In summer it lives from North Dakota and Texas east to the Atlantic coast. It is a year-round resident as far north as New York.

spearmint \ 'spir-,mint \

Spearmint is a perennial plant that belongs to the mint family. Oil distilled from spearmint is used to flavor chewing gum, toothpaste, candy and medicines. Spearmint is native to southern Europe and eastern Asia.

Spearmint grows 12 to 14 inches tall. Its leaves grow in opposite pairs along the smooth stems. The leaves are 1 to 2½ inches long, with toothed edges. The leaves contain oil glands, which give off a strong but pleasant smell of mint when cut or bruised.

The small flowers are pink, white or purplish. They are borne in spike-shaped clusters at the tops of the stalks and at some places along the stems. The seeds are 4-lobed nutlets.

Spearmint grows from seed or from spreading roots. It does best in moist, rich soil. It is widely planted in herb gardens, and it is grown commercially in some areas.

Spearmint grows wild in many parts of North America. It is an important farm crop in some parts of Indiana, Michigan and Washington.

SPIDER

spider

Spiders are air-breathing animals with 2-part bodies and 8 legs. They are more closely related to ticks, mites and scorpions than to insects.

On the spider's head are jaw-like antennae with poison claws on the ends. These are used to kill and crush insects the spider eats. At the tip of the abdomen are spinnerets that produce silk for the web and for the cocoon-like case in which the eggs are placed. The female may fasten the egg case to a leaf or twig, or she may carry it with her until the eggs hatch. Newly hatched spiders look like the adults but are much smaller.

Not all spiders spin webs. Some hide in underground burrows, or under rocks or dead leaves.

The black widow spider (illustrated) is one of the few spiders that can bite through human skin and eject enough poison to cause serious illness. This spider is about ½ inch long, and is all black except for the underside. The black widow is fairly common in the tropics and in the southern U.S.

For another kind of spider, see *tarantula*.

spiderwort \ 'spīd-ər-ˌwərt \

Spiderworts make up a group of garden plants and wild flowers that grow mostly in the American tropics. A few kinds grow in the northern U.S.

All spiderworts have narrow, pointed leaves. The base of the leaf wraps around the stem, forming a knob.

Flowers appear on these plants all during the summer months, but the flowers last a very short time. They have 3 broad petals that are white, blue, purple or pinkish. The fruit is a 3-sectioned seedpod.

Common spiderwort (illustrated) grows wild in the northern U.S. It has blue or purple flowers 1 to 2 inches across. The flowers are borne in tight clusters, at the tops of the stalks. The stems stand erect, and are up to 16 inches tall. The leaves are 12 to 15 inches long, and up to 1 inch wide. Most of the leaves are marked with parallel grooves.

The common spiderwort grows in shaded places where the soil is moist, often along the edges of streams.

spinach

Spinach is an important garden vegetable that is native to Asia. It is closely related to beets and chard. The leaves of the spinach plant are rich in vitamins and iron.

Spinach is an annual plant that grows from seed. It is planted in late fall or early spring, as the plants do not grow well during hot summer weather. Spinach needs rich soil containing much nitrogen.

Most of the broad, ruffled leaves grow from the base of the spinach plant. A few smaller leaves grow on the flowering stalks

SPINACH

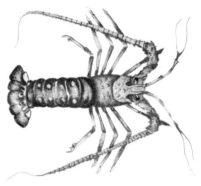

SPINY LOBSTER

that rise above the leaves in midsummer. Clustered at the tops of stalks are yellow-green flowers without petals. Staminate flowers are borne on some plants, while pistillate flowers grow on others. The pistillate flowers produce small seeds. Each seed is enclosed in a small, prickly capsule.

Spinach is grown in vegetable gardens in nearly all parts of the world.

spinel \ spə-'nel \

Spinel is a mineral that contains mostly magnesium, aluminum and oxygen. It occurs in both igneous and metamorphic rocks where minerals have been changed by great heat and pressure.

Clear, bright-colored crystals of spinel are classified as gems and they may be very valuable. Red crystals of spinel, called "ruby spinel," are sometimes mistaken for rubies. Blue crystals may be mistaken for sapphires.

The more common kinds of spinel are black, brown or green. Spinel is hard but not very heavy. It may be translucent so that light passes through its thin edges.

In the U.S., spinel is found mostly in New York and New Jersey. Gem quality spinel comes mostly from Ceylon and Burma.

spiny \ 'spī-nē \ lobster (rock lobster, sea crayfish)

The spiny lobster is a marine crustacean that lives in warm, shallow water near the coast. It is a popular seafood. It is not closely related to the common American lobster.

The spiny lobster is usually 8 to 16 inches long. It is named for the numerous sharp spines on its shell. The antennae are sometimes used as weapons.

Spiny lobsters live in both the Atlantic and Pacific oceans. They are most common around coral reefs and in weedy tidal pools.

When disturbed, male spiny lobsters make loud grating sounds. Females produce up to half a million eggs each year. The eggs are attached to the underside of the female's abdomen, where the newly hatched young cling for some time.

Young spiny lobsters are leaf-shaped and nearly transparent, with large eyes on stalks. They molt several times.

spittlebug \ 'spit-ᵊl-ˌbəg \ (froghopper)

Spittlebugs make up a family of small insects related to cicadas and aphids. They feed on juices they suck from plants, and they sometimes damage evergreens and garden plants. In most areas they are controlled by the many birds that kill and eat them.

Usually a dull brown color, spittlebugs are less than ½ inch long. They have flat, broad bodies. They usually hop rather than fly, so they are most often found on low-growing plants and shrubs.

The female spittlebug lays her eggs in

SPITTLE MASS AND SPITTLEBUG

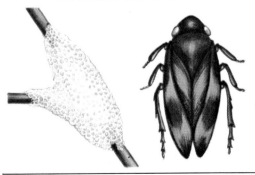

slits she makes in plant stems. The young insects produce a froth that covers them and hides them from their enemies. It may also help to keep their bodies from drying out. They remain under the froth until they are mature adults.

Spittlebugs live in all parts of the U.S. and in southern Canada. The meadow spittlebug (illustrated) is a common kind that lives in grassy fields.

sponge \ 'spənj \

The sponges make up a large group of mostly marine animals. They are among the simplest of many-celled creatures. One small family of sponges lives in freshwater streams. All the rest live on the ocean floor, anchored to rocks or shells.

Some sponges are vase-shaped or tube-like, while other kinds look like branching fingers. Some kinds form a flat or rounded mass. The many different kinds grow in nearly all warm, shallow parts of the sea.

Sponges have jelly-like bodies, but they secrete a kind of skeleton made of interlocking fibers. This tough skeleton remains after the animal dies. The skeleton is tough, absorbent and elastic.

The smallest sponges are less than 1 inch across. The largest ones are about 6 feet across. All have many holes in them. Seawater flowing through the holes carries bits of food to the sponge's many cells.

SPONGE

SPOONBILL

Sponges feed on tiny plants and animals.

A sponge has no special parts such as mouth or stomach. Sponges reproduce asexually or by budding.

The skeleton of the common horse sponge (illustrated) is the one most commonly used for washing walls, windows and automobiles. Plastic sponges have largely replaced natural sponges.

spoonbill \ 'spün-,bil \

The spoonbills are large wading birds that live along seacoasts and in marshy places in the warmest parts of the world. Their long bills are broad and rounded at the tip. When feeding, they dip the bill into the water and swing it from side to side.

Spoonbills have a body length of 20 to 40 inches.

All spoonbills eat small fish, along with crustaceans and small mollusks, such as snails. All build large nests of sticks, placed in the ground near water or in a low tree. The 3 to 5 eggs are white, spotted with brown.

Old World spoonbills are white, with yellow or black bills. The roseate spoonbill (illustrated) is the only kind found in America.

The roseate spoonbill has been hunted for its feathers, and as food, until it is now quite rare. It breeds in a few parts of the southeastern U.S. and in the West Indies and Mexico. It winters in South America.

SPOTTED HYENA

sporozoan \ ˌspōr-ə-'zō-ən \ (plasmodium)

Sporozoans are tiny 1-celled animals that live as parasites inside the bodies of larger animals. Some kinds of sporozoans cause diseases.

Seen under a microscope, sporozoans are round or oval, without special parts to their bodies. They absorb food through their cell coverings. They reproduce by simple fission, or by producing 2 different kinds of cells that join.

The many different kinds of sporozoans live in the blood and in the glands and organs of animals such as earthworms, insects, birds, sheep and human beings. Some live in 2 different hosts during their stages of development.

Malaria is a disease caused by certain kinds of sporozoans called plasmodia. These live in the salivary glands of certain female mosquitoes. When the mosquito bites a human, the plasmodium may pass into the human's bloodstream.

Other diseases caused by sporozoans infect cattle, poultry and silkworms.

spotted hyena \ 'spät-əd hī-'ē-nə \ (laughing hyena)

The spotted hyena is a carnivorous mammal that lives only in Africa. Its closest relative is the striped hyena found in India and certain other parts of western Asia.

About the size of a large dog, the spotted hyena is 4½ feet long and about 2½ feet tall at the shoulder. The forelegs are longer than the hind legs, and there are 4 toes on each foot.

Though they fight fiercely when attacked, hyenas are generally cowards that attack only injured or weak animals. When hungry, they will sometimes attack a child or a lone man. In many areas they are scavengers that eat what is left of animals killed by lions and other beasts. Their strong jaws can easily crush the largest bones of elephants and cattle.

Spotted hyenas feed and travel in large, noisy packs. They make a wide variety of sounds, including barks, howls and cries like insane human laughter. Though they look awkward, they can run very fast.

Female spotted hyenas bear litters of 2 to 6 pups.

spruce \ 'sprüs \

The spruces are trees closely related to the pines, and are native to the cooler parts of the northern hemisphere. Some kinds of spruce are planted as ornamental trees. Others are grown commercially and sold as Christmas trees. The wood of spruce trees is not strong, but it has some uses as lumber and for making paper pulp.

All spruces are pyramid-shaped and taper to a pointed spire at the top. They have stout branches that grow out from the straight trunk like the spokes of a

SPRUCE

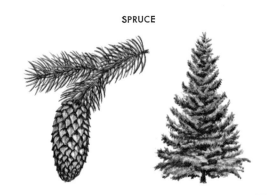

419

wheel. The bark is thin and scaly. The needles grow singly, rather than in bundles, and they stick out from all sides of the twigs.

Spruce cones are fairly small. Tiny winged seeds fall from between the thin, smooth scales that make up the cones.

The blue spruce (illustrated) is native to the Rocky Mountains, from Wyoming south to New Mexico. It is the largest American spruce, and it has been planted in many other parts of the world. It grows 80 to 150 feet tall. The needles are ½ to 1 inch long.

squash

Squashes make up a group of useful plants that are grown for their edible fruit. They belong to the gourd family, and are closely related to pumpkins, cucumbers and melons. Squashes are native to the tropics, and they need a long growing season. Even a light frost will kill them.

The squash plant was cultivated by the Indians of Central and South America before the arrival of European explorers. It is now grown in many parts of the world, and many different kinds have been developed.

Squash stems are nearly always thick and hairy. The large leaves are divided into several pointed sections. The flowers are yellow and bell-shaped, opening out into 5 petal-like segments. The fruit is a

SQUASH

SQUID

very large berry containing many flat seeds. The skin and thick rind of the fruit are yellow, orange or green. Some kinds of squash have odd-shaped or striped fruit.

Summer squashes grow on erect, bushy plants. They are harvested before the seeds ripen. The entire fruit is cooked and eaten. Crookneck, pattypan, zucchini and scallop squashes are all summer squashes.

Winter squashes grow on sprawling vines. They are harvested in autumn, and they can be kept for months in a cool, dry place. Acorn (illustrated), Hubbard and butternut squashes belong to this group.

squid \ 'skwid \

Squids make up a group of marine mollusks closely related to cuttlefish and octopuses. Squids that live near coasts are 1 to 2 feet long. The giant squid, found only in deep water, is up to 60 feet long and is the largest known invertebrate animal.

Squids have long, tapering bodies covered with a muscular mantle that contains gills for breathing. Hidden in a pocket or groove along the back is a transparent horny shell that stiffens the body.

At the head end are large eyes and a beaked mouth surrounded by 10 tentacles. Two of the tentacles are longer than the others. All end in suction disks.

Squids change color to match their surroundings. They may appear yellow, purple, blue, red or gray. When disturbed, they release an inky fluid that forms a black cloud in the water.

Swimming either forward or backward, squids move through the water with quick, darting motions. They often swim and feed in schools. They eat mostly fish that they capture and kill with their tentacles.

Female squids lay numerous eggs enclosed in finger-shaped capsules. These capsules cling to rocks in shallow water.

The Atlantic squid (illustrated) is fairly common along the east coast of North America.

squirrel

Squirrels make up a family of small rodents found in nearly all parts of the world except Australia. They eat mostly seeds and nuts, along with some buds, leaves and insects. Most kinds of squirrels gather seeds and nuts in autumn and store them for the winter.

The squirrels that live in trees have long, bushy tails that help them balance as they run along branches or leap from tree to tree.

Most kinds of squirrels raise 2 litters of young during the spring and summer. Newborn squirrels are naked and helpless, and remain in the nest for about 6 weeks.

The flying squirrel has flaps of skin that extend from its forelegs to its hind legs. Spreading these flaps like wings, this squirrel glides long distances through the air. Its flattened tail serves as a rudder.

Ground squirrels have short, slender tails. They live in burrows, or under rocks. Most ground squirrels hibernate.

The gray squirrel (illustrated) is native to the eastern half of the Rocky mountains. It builds a nest of leaves and twigs.

For other members of the squirrel family, see *chipmunk, marmot, prairie dog* and *woodchuck.*

star

Stars are celestial bodies that give off light. Scientists believe that they are globe-shaped masses of very hot gases. Nuclear reactions taking place within these gases produce energy that is given off as light and heat.

Billions of stars are visible through telescopes. Some stars are about the size of our sun. Some are nearly 400 times as large as our sun.

All stars are moving, but because they are very far away they appear to stand still. The nearest star is so far away that it takes 4 years for its light to reach the earth.

The colors of stars depend on their temperatures. The hottest ones are blue-white, while the cooler ones are yellow or red. The colors are usually faint and not easy to see.

The brightness of stars is measured in magnitudes. The brightness as seen from the earth depends on how far away a star is, as well as on its size.

SQUIRREL

STAR TRAILS AROUND POLARIS

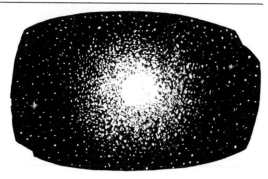

STAR CLUSTER

STARFISH

star cluster \ 'kləs-ter \

A star cluster is a group of stars that are relatively close to each other and that are moving together in the same direction. Star clusters can be divided into 2 groups, globular clusters and open clusters.

The stars in a globular cluster are so close together that it is hard to see the single stars that make up the cluster. Only about 100 globular clusters are known, and they are all very far away from the earth. None can be seen clearly without a telescope.

The globular cluster M 13 (illustrated) is located in the constellation Hercules. It is 100 light-years across, and it may contain millions of stars.

Open star clusters are also called galactic clusters or nebulae. They are loose, irregular groupings of stars. Open star clusters are closer to the earth than the globular clusters.

Five of the stars in the Big Dipper belong to another open cluster. They are moving slowly in one direction, while the other 2 stars in the Big Dipper are moving in the opposite direction.

starfish \ 'stär-ˌfish \

Starfish make up a group of marine animals that live on the ocean floor. They are related to the sea urchins. Starfish are most common in shallow water, near shore, where the bottom is rocky.

Most kinds of starfish have 5 arms or tentacles. Arms that are damaged or destroyed are replaced by new ones.

The upper surface of the starfish's body is covered with jointed plates. At the tip of each arm is an eyespot sensitive to light. On the undersides of the arms are rows of tube feet used for walking and for grasping food. In the middle of the underside is the mouth.

The smallest starfish are about ½ inch across, while the largest ones are 32 inches across. They are yellow, red, brown or green.

Starfish eat mostly mollusks and crustaceans. They can force open clams and oysters by grasping the 2 shells and pulling them apart.

Female starfish lay eggs in spring. The newly hatched young do not look like the adults.

The common or eastern starfish (illustrated) is 6 to 12 inches across. It lives along the Atlantic coast of North America, as far north as Maine.

starling \ 'stär-ling \

Starlings make up a family of birds native to the Old World. They are most numerous in the tropics. The common starling (illustrated) was introduced into North America in 1890. It is now a nuisance in many areas.

The common starling is 7½ to 8½ inches long, with a plump body and a short tail.

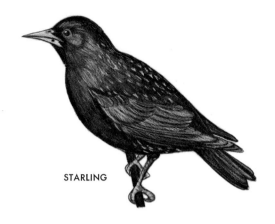

STARLING

Its glossy black feathers show iridescent green or purple, and are speckled with small white and brown spots. The bill is yellow in summer and black in winter.

Usually seen in large flocks, common starlings are equally at home in farming country and in large cities. They build bulky nests on the ledges of city buildings or in hollow trees.

Common starlings eat mostly fruit and insects. Quarrelsome birds, they often drive other birds away.

Female starlings lay 4 to 7 greenish-blue eggs, twice a year.

For another member of the starling family, see *mynah bird*.

star-of-Bethlehem \ 'beth-li-ˌhem \

Star-of-Bethlehem is a flowering plant of the lily family. It is native to Europe. In May or June, star-of-Bethlehem bears white flowers. Like other lilies, it is a perennial that grows from a bulb.

The star-of-Bethlehem has narrow leaves that look something like grass-blades. They are 6 to 12 inches long, and ¼ to ½ inch wide.

Three to 7 flowers are borne in a loose spray at the top of a separate stalk 8 to 12 inches tall. Each flower has 6 pointed petals that are pure white on the upper surface and striped with green on the underside. The fruit that appears later in the summer is a small 3-sided seedpod.

Star-of-Bethlehem has been planted in many flower gardens in North America, and now grows wild in some parts of the eastern U.S. It is most commonly seen along roadsides and in grassy fields.

In gardens, star-of-Bethlehem bulbs are planted between September and February, about 1 inch deep in rich, sandy soil.

stegosaur \ 'steg-ə-ˌsȯr \

The stegosaurs were dinosaurs that lived about 130 million years ago, during the late Jurassic and early Cretaceous period. They were odd-looking reptiles with long hind legs, short forelegs and very small heads.

Two rows of pointed bony plates stood up along the spine. The largest plates, near the hips, were about 2 feet tall. The powerful tail, armed with 2 pairs of sharp spines 6 inches to 3 feet long, was probably used as a weapon. Inside this dinosaur's small, beaked head was a brain about the size of a walnut.

The shape of the stegosaur suggests that it may have developed from an earlier dinosaur that stood erect on its hind legs.

The stegosaur was probably a slow-moving animal well able to defend itself in a fight. It ate only plants. The young developed inside eggs laid by the females.

One kind of stegosaur (illustrated) was about 30 feet long and stood 10 feet tall at the hips. It weighed about 10 tons.

STEGOSAUR

STILT

stickleback \ 'stik-əl-ˌbak \

Sticklebacks make up a family of small fish found in both fresh and salt water. Some kinds are popular aquarium fish, while others are of particular interest because of their nesting habits.

The largest sticklebacks are about 7 inches long. Most are less than 4 inches long. All have sharp, stout spines along their backs. Bony plates protect their heads and the sides of their bodies. The largest stickleback, found along the coast of northern Europe, has 15 spines on its back.

The 3-spined stickleback (illustrated) is common in the cooler parts of the northern oceans. In the Atlantic, it is found as far south as Virginia.

When the spawning season begins in spring, the belly of the male 3-spined stickleback turns bright red. He builds a deep, rounded nest of underwater plants, binding them together with a sticky thread he produces. While inviting females inside to lay their eggs, he fights fiercely any other males that approach the nest. He guards the nest until the eggs hatch, about 10 days later, and protects the young fish until they are several days old.

stilt \ 'stilt \

Stilts make up a group of wading birds with unusually long legs and long, slender bills. There are several different kinds, but they all look much alike. They are usually seen in small flocks, on mud flats

STICKLEBACK

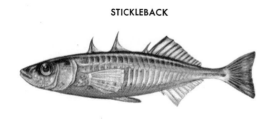

and sandy beaches in the warmer parts of the world.

Stilts feed on insects, worms and small crustaceans that they find in wet sand and mud. Their calls are sharp, yipping sounds.

Nesting near inland lakes or marshes, stilts make hollows in the sand and line them with grass and other plant materials. The nest is usually hidden among tall reeds. The 3 or 4 eggs are light brown speckled with darker brown.

The black-necked stilt (illustrated) is the only kind of stilt native to North America. It spends the summer in the western states as far north as Oregon and along the Gulf coast. It winters in southern California, Louisiana and Florida, and in Central and South America.

The black-necked stilt has a body length of 14 to 15 inches.

stratified \ 'strat-ə-ˌfid \ rock

Stratified rocks are those that show parallel lines or layers. The layers may be of different colors and textures. Sometimes there are cracks separating the layers.

Nearly all stratified rocks are sedimentary, and are made up of particles dropped by wind or water and then cemented together. Limestone, shale and sandstone are likely to be stratified rocks.

Layers of different thicknesses in stratified rock may mark seasons of the year, as wind and water carry different materials

STRATIFIED ROCK

at different times of the year. Thick layers may mark different climates that existed over very long periods of years.

The layers of stratified rock were horizontal when the rock was formed. Where the earth's crust has been disturbed, the layers are often tipped and bent.

Stratified rock is most commonly seen where it has been laid bare by erosion or road cuts. It is often visible along stream banks, and in gorges and canyons.

strawberry

Strawberries are low-growing perennial plants of the rose family. They grow wild in most parts of the north temperate zone, and in the mountains of South America. Strawberries have been cultivated for hundreds of years, and many different kinds have been developed.

All strawberries have compound leaves made up of 3 broad, hairy leaflets. The leaves and separate flowering stems all grow up from ground level. New plants develop from creeping runners that grow from the sides of the plants and take root.

Five-petaled, white or pinkish flowers are borne in early spring. The true fruit of the plant is a small, dry seed envelope inside the mass of juicy flesh that is eaten. The fruit ripens about 5 weeks after the flowers appear.

The common wild strawberry grows in meadows and along roadsides throughout eastern North America. Its flowers and fruit are borne in loose clusters on short stems, and are usually hidden under the leaves. Its berries are sweet and juicy, but not so large as cultivated kinds.

sturgeon \ 'stər-jən \

Sturgeons make up a group of large fish that live in the cooler parts of the northern hemisphere. Their flesh is eaten fresh, pickled or smoked. Their eggs are eaten as caviar.

The largest sturgeons are 18 feet long and weigh 300 to 400 pounds. Some kinds may live to be 300 years old.

All sturgeons have long, tube-like snouts. The toothless mouth is located under the snout, behind the whisker-like barbels. Bony plates cover the head and the sides of the body.

Sturgeons feed on the bottom. Their eyesight is poor, but their sensitive barbels feel for bits of food in the mud and sand. They eat mollusks, crustaceans and insect larvae, along with some fish and underwater plants.

Female sturgeons lay many small eggs over a period of time, scattering them over a wide area. The newly hatched fish, which do not resemble the adults, have suction disks for clinging to plants.

Most kinds of sturgeons live in the ocean as adults but swim up large rivers to spawn. The lake sturgeon (illustrated) lives entirely in fresh water and is the largest fish in the Great Lakes. It also lives in the smaller lakes and rivers of Canada and the upper Mississippi Valley.

STURGEON

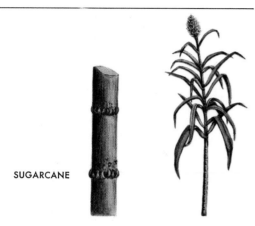

SUGARCANE

sugarcane \ˈshu̇g-ər-ˌkān\

Sugarcane is a tropical plant that belongs to the grass family. It is probably native to the island of New Guinea. In prehistoric times, sugarcane was carried to many parts of southern Asia. It was later introduced into Europe, Africa and the Americas.

More than half the world's supply of sugar comes from the sweet juice of this plant. In the U.S., sugarcane is grown mostly in Louisiana and Florida. It is an important crop in Brazil, Cuba, Hawaii, the Philippine Islands and many other parts of the world. Sugarcane requires a long growing season and much water.

Sugarcane grows 10 to 15 feet tall and looks much like corn. Its leaves are about 3 feet long, and have rough edges. The bases of the leaves wrap around the stems, which are 1½ to 2 inches across. The many, very small flowers are grouped in feathery clusters about 2 feet long. Sugarcane is usually planted by burying pieces of the stem. New plants grow up from each of the ring-like joints in the stem.

sulfur \ˈsəl-fər\

Sulfur is a common and very useful chemical element found in many different parts of the world. Pure sulfur is pale yellow, heavy and fairly hard. It occurs near hot springs and volcanoes, and with underground salt domes.

Sulfur burns easily, with a clear blue flame. Ancient peoples called it "brimstone" or burning stone, and they used it in religious ceremonies.

Today, sulfur is widely used in making many different products. It goes into matches, gunpowder, fireworks, insect poisons, vulcanized rubber, fertilizers and photographic chemicals. As sulfuric acid it is used in many manufacturing processes.

Small amounts of sulfur are found in all living plants and animals. Eggs and cabbage are foods rich in sulfur. Spoons and forks used in these foods are likely to tarnish quickly because sulfur combines with silver to form a dark-colored compound.

Most of the sulfur used in American industry comes from huge underground deposits in Texas, Louisiana and Mexico. Sulfur is also mined in Sicily, Chile, Japan and Indonesia.

sumac \ˈs(h)ü-ˌmak\

Sumacs make up a group of shrubs and small trees with leaves that turn a clear bright red color in autumn. Sumacs grow wild in many parts of the north and south temperate zones. They are related to poison ivy, and some kinds irritate the skin as poison ivy does.

Sumacs grow 10 to 40 feet tall, with wide-spreading, slender branches. They have compound leaves made up of 7 to 31 pointed leaflets. Small, white or greenish

SUMAC

flowers are borne in spike-shaped clusters. The fruit is a small, dry berry.

Poison sumac (illustrated) is a shrub that grows in swampy places throughout eastern North America. Its leaves are 7 to 14 inches long. During the summer the leaves are pale green on the undersides, and they may show red lines along the midribs. Poison sumac has glossy white or yellowish berries that remain on the branches all winter.

Two other sumacs that are not poisonous grow in eastern North America, but in dry soil. The kind called smooth sumac has red berries. The kind called staghorn sumac has reddish-brown berries.

sun

The sun is a medium-sized star about 5 billion years old. It is the center of the solar system, and the source of all energy on the earth. About 93 million miles away, the sun is much closer to the earth than any other star.

Like other stars, the sun is a globe-shaped mass of very hot, glowing gases. Scientists believe that these gases contain at least 66 of the 92 elements that make up the earth. Hydrogen, the most common element, makes up about ¾ of the sun.

The sun produces its energy by a nuclear reaction that is like that of an H-bomb. In this reaction, hydrogen atoms are changed into helium atoms. A by-product of this reaction is energy, which

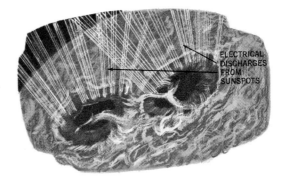

ACTIVE SUN

is released as heat and light. Without the sun's heat and light, there would be no life on earth.

The sun is about 864,000 miles across. The temperature of the surface is about 10,000° F.

The surface of the sun is called the photosphere. A layer of cooler, lighter gases surrounding the sun forms the chromosphere. The outermost part is the corona.

See *chromosphere* and *corona*. See also *The Sun, the Moon and the Planets* on p. 502.

sundew \ 'sən-,d(y)ü \

Sundews make up a group of unusual plants with bristly leaves that trap and digest insects. The decaying bodies of the insects provide nourishment that is lacking in the acid bog soils where these plants grow.

Sundews are found in many different parts of the world, but they are most common in Australia. Most kinds are low-growing perennials. Their small, white or pinkish flowers have 5 petals. The flowers dangle from 1 side of a slender stalk.

The leaves all grow up from the base of the plant, at ground level. The rounded tip of the leaf is covered with stiff hairs that produce a sticky liquid attractive to insects. When an insect touches one of the hairs, it sticks fast, and the leaf closes around it until the insect dies.

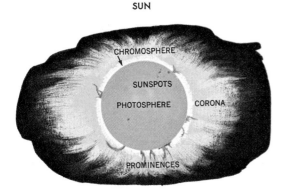

SUN

CHROMOSPHERE

SUNSPOTS

PHOTOSPHERE   CORONA

PROMINENCES

SUNFLOWER

Several different kinds of sundews grow in North America. The most common kind of sundew has purplish hairs on its leaves, and fuzzy stalks. Its white or pink flowers are about ½ inch across. The fruit is a slender, 3-sectioned seed-pod. This sundew grows in bogs and swampy areas, in the eastern U.S., in California and in southern Canada.

sunfish \ 'sən-ˌfish \

Freshwater sunfish make up a family that includes many kinds of popular game fish. They are native to North America and are not closely related to the ocean sunfish.

Most sunfish are 3 to 10 inches long, but some kinds grow to 14 inches. Most kinds are greenish, marked with yellow or orange. Nearly all have a dark spot on the upper corner of the gill cover.

Sunfish live in ponds, lakes and quiet streams where the water is clear and clean, throughout eastern North America.

Spawning takes place all during the summer, in shallow water where the bottom is sandy. The fish swim in circles, fanning the sand with their tails, till they hollow out a bowl-shaped nest about 2 feet across. The females lay eggs in the nests, and the males guard the eggs until they hatch 3 to 6 days later.

The male fish may care for the young fish for several weeks.

The pumpkinseed (illustrated) is a small sunfish that averages about 5 inches

SUNFISH AND NEST

in length. It feeds on other fish, insects and its own kind. It is most common in the northeastern states.

For other members of the freshwater sunfish family, see *bluegill, crappie, largemouth black bass* and *smallmouth black bass.*

sunflower

The sunflowers are tall-growing plants valued for their showy flowers and useful seeds. The flowering heads of most kinds of sunflowers turn from east to west during the day, to follow the sun across the sky.

Most kinds of sunflowers are native to the prairies of western North America. The Indians cultivated them for their seeds, which are rich in oil and protein, and for fibers of the stalks.

Today, sunflowers are planted as a farm crop in many parts of the world. The stems and leaves are fed to livestock. The seeds are used as food for humans, wild birds, poultry and livestock, or are made into oil.

All sunflowers have coarse, hairy stems. The leaves are heart-shaped, with saw-toothed edges. The flowering head, 2 to 12 inches across, is made up of a flat cluster of brown or purplish disk florets, surrounded by petal-like, yellow ray florets.

The common sunflower (illustrated) grows to 12 feet tall. Its flowering heads are up to 12 inches across.

SUNSPOTS

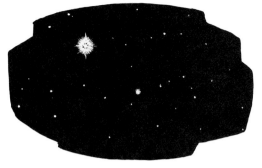

SUPERNOVA

sunspot \ 'sən-,spät \

Sunspots are dark areas that appear on the surface of the sun. Because of the sun's brightness, they cannot be seen with the naked eye.

Astronomers believe that sunspots are violent eruptions of gases bursting out from the sun's interior. They appear dark only because they are cooler than the sun's very hot surface.

Sunspots usually appear in groups. They are seldom near the sun's poles, or near the sun's equator. Some last only a few days, while others last a month or so. The smallest sunspots are only a few hundred miles across, while the largest ones may be 150,000 miles across.

Powerful magnetic fields are produced by sunspots. They disturb radio and telephone communications on the earth, and they seem to be connected with displays of the auroras.

The number of sunspots varies according to a regular cycle. The greatest number of sunspots occurs about every 11 years. The fewest sunspots appear between cycles.

supernova \ ,sü-pər-'nō-və \

A supernova is a rare and unusual kind of star that becomes extremely bright for a time and then disappears. A nova is a faint star that becomes brighter for a short time and then faint again. It is never as brilliant as a supernova, and it does not disappear.

Astronomers believe that supernovae may be stars that explode and disintegrate. A cloud of expanding gas may be all that is left.

Three supernovae are known from historical records. All were located in the Milky Way. The first was observed by Chinese and Japanese astronomers A.D. 1054. The remains of this supernova probably form the still-glowing cloud of gas called the Crab Nebula.

A supernova located in the constellation Cassiopeia appeared in 1572. It is called Tycho's star, because it was observed by the Danish astronomer Tycho Brahe. It was brighter than the planet Venus, and could be seen in daylight.

Kepler's star was a supernova that appeared in 1604. It is named for the German astronomer Johannes Kepler.

In recent years other supernovae, farther from the earth, have been observed by astronomers using powerful telescopes.

See *nova*.

swallow

The swallows and their close relatives, the martins, make up a family of birds that spend most of their time flying. They feed entirely on insects that they catch in the air. Most kinds make squeaking and twittering sounds as they swoop and dive.

SWALLOW

SWAN

All swallows have small, triangular bills surrounded by bristles. Their bills are wide open when they fly, and the bristles help to funnel insects inside their mouths. Their feet and legs are small and weak, and are used only for perching. The wings are long and tapering. The tails of most swallows are long and notched.

Some swallows nest in hollow trees. Others burrow into mudbanks or cliffs. Still other kinds build cup-shaped nests of mud and grass against the sides of farm buildings and under bridges.

Most kinds of swallows raise 2 or 3 broods of young birds during the summer. The female incubates the 3 to 7 eggs, and both parents feed the young.

In the U.S., the barn swallow (illustrated) is a slender bird about 7½ inches long. It can be identified in flight by its V-shaped tail. It is most often seen near farm buildings, where it often nests, and over open fields, near streams. It spends the summer from southern Canada to Mexico. In autumn, when insects become scarce, it migrates to South America.

swan

Swans are large water birds with very long, slender necks. They belong to the same family as ducks and geese. The largest swans measure 6 feet from bill to tail. Most kinds are white, but a few kinds are black or white marked with black.

Swans live mostly in the northern hemisphere. They spend the summer on freshwater streams and lakes, sometimes north of the Arctic Circle. Most swans winter along seacoasts south of New Jersey.

Like ducks and geese, swans feed on aquatic plants, grass and seeds. Their nests, built on the ground, are large piles of reeds and other plant materials. Both male and female incubate the eggs and guard the nest. Swans usually mate for life, and they often live to be 80 years old.

The mute swan (illustrated) is native to Europe and Asia where it has been domesticated for hundreds of years. It is the swan most often seen in parks and zoos, in all parts of the world. Both male and female adults have round knobs at the bases of their bills. The male's bill is orange-red, while the female's bill is pinkish.

sweet basil \ 'baz-əl \

Sweet basil is a plant of the mint family that is often planted in herb gardens. Its fragrant leaves are dried and used to flavor foods.

Sweet basil is native to tropical Asia and Africa. It has been planted in many other parts of the world, and it now grows wild in some parts of Europe and Asia. It is an annual or a perennial, depending on the climate.

The branching stems of this plant grow 12 to 24 inches tall. The leaves, which are

SWEET BASIL

sometimes purplish, are 1 to 2 inches long. They grow in opposite pairs.

Small, white or purplish flowers are grouped in irregular, sometimes branching clusters at the tops of the stalks. Each flower is about ¼ inch long. The fruit is a cluster of 4 nutlets, each containing 1 seed.

sweet gum (red gum)

The sweet gum is an attractive shade tree that is also valued for its wood. It is related to the witch hazel. The wood of the sweet gum is reddish-brown. It is used as veneer for fine furniture.

The sweet gum is usually a slender, erect tree 80 to 120 feet tall. Some of its twigs have odd, wing-like ridges running along them.

The leaves are 3 to 5 inches long. They are a bright, glossy green during the summer. In autumn, they turn varied shades of gold, rust and red.

Round clusters of tiny green flowers appear on the smaller branches in April and May. The fruit that ripens in autumn is a dry, prickly ball that dangles from a long stalk. The ball is made up of many horn-shaped capsules, each containing 1 seed.

The sweet gum is native to the eastern half of the U.S., as far north as Illinois and Connecticut. In recent years it has been planted as a shade and ornamental tree in many other parts of the world. It grows best in rich, fairly moist soil.

sweet potato

The sweet potato plant is a creeping vine that belongs to the morning glory family. It is native to the American tropics, and it needs a long growing season.

The sweet potato is sometimes called a yam, but the true yam is a different plant native to the Old World. The sweet potato is an important crop in the southern part of the U.S. The true yam is grown mostly in Asia and in the West Indies.

The edible part of the sweet potato plant is an enlarged root. It is cream-colored, orange or reddish-brown. It contains more protein and vitamins than the white potato.

The stems are very long, so that the plants cover the ground with a dense mat of foliage. The leaves are 4 to 6 inches long and irregular in shape. The funnel-shaped flowers are pink or purplish. The fruit is a round pod containing 4 to 6 seeds.

In the temperate zone sweet potato plants seldom produce seeds. They are planted by burying sprouts that grow from old roots.

In the U.S., Louisiana, North Carolina and Virginia lead in the production of sweet potatoes. Other countries that grow sweet potatoes include China, Japan, India and Brazil.

SWEET POTATO

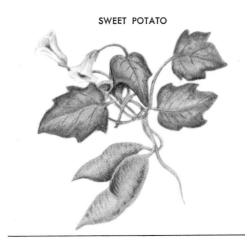

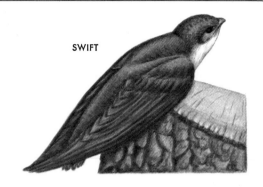

SWIFT

swift

Swifts make up a family of birds that spend more time in the air than most other land birds. They fly high and fast, eating only insects that they catch in the air. They build their nests of twigs that they pluck from trees as they fly past.

Swifts' legs and feet are weak. Some kinds use their short, stiff tails to help them perch on vertical surfaces such as the inside walls of chimneys.

All swifts are dull brown or gray birds 4 to 7 inches long. They have long, crescent-shaped wings. Some kinds have V-shaped tails.

The twigs on the nests are glued together with saliva and fastened inside chimneys, caves or hollow trees. Most kinds of swifts lay 2 or 3 white eggs. The young birds remain in the nest for a long time, often 4 to 6 weeks, until they are fully feathered and able to fly well.

Swifts live in nearly all parts of the world. The chimney swift (illustrated) spends the summer in most of the U.S. east of the Rocky Mountains. Flocks of chimney swifts migrate to South America in autumn, roosting at night in chimneys and hollow trees along the way.

swine \ 'swīn \

The swine make up a family of short-legged, hoofed mammals native to Asia, Europe and parts of Africa. The barnyard pig is descended from swine domes-ticated in China about 2900 B.C. Many breeds of pigs have been developed.

Wild boars that roam the forested parts of the Old World belong to this family. The wild pigs native to the New World belong to another family and are properly called peccaries.

Swine have 4 toes on each foot but only the middle 2 touch the ground. They have heavy, barrel-shaped bodies.

Wild swine are more muscular than the barnyard pig, and they have longer legs. Their bodies are covered with thick, coarse hair, and their tails are straight rather than curly. The males have long, sharp tusks that they use as weapons.

The domestic pig will eat almost anything. Wild swine eat mostly roots, earthworms, snails and fungi that they dig from the forest floor with their snouts.

Swine breed once a year. Wild swine generally give birth to 2 or 3 piglets. The domestic pig has much larger litters.

For other members of the swine family, see *bushpig, European wild boar, peccary* and *warthog*.

swordfish \ 'sōrd-,fish \ (broadbill)

The swordfish is a large and unusual fish that is not closely related to any other kind of fish. It lives in the warmer parts of the oceans, usually in deep water far from shore.

The largest swordfish are 20 feet long and weigh half a ton. Most are 6 to 10

SWORDFISH

feet long and weigh 100 to 250 pounds.

The upper jaw extends out to form a long, pointed bill that is about ⅓ the length of the body. This is used as a weapon, to stun the smaller fish and squid the swordfish eats. When harpooned or hooked, large swordfish have been known to thrust their bills through small boats.

The swordfish swims by powerful sweeping movements of its large, forked tail. It has 2 dorsal fins, 1 tall and very near the head, and the other small and near the tail. The eyes are very large. The large mouth is toothless.

Swordfish are favorites of deep-sea fishermen because they fight fiercely and are also popular as food. They are caught in the Atlantic and Pacific oceans and in the Mediterranean Sea. In summer, some wander as far north as Nova Scotia.

sycamore \ 'sik-ə-ˌmōr \ (plane tree)

Sycamores make up a group of hardwood trees that are easy to identify. All have gray-brown bark that peels off the branches and upper trunk, exposing a smooth, white underbark. Sycamores are native to Asia and to North and South America.

The wood of sycamore trees is hard and strong. It is used mostly for making boxes and furniture.

The American sycamore (illustrated) is fairly common in the eastern half of the U.S. One of the largest of all hardwood trees, it grows 140 to 160 feet tall, with a thick trunk 8 to 11 feet across. It usually grows along the banks of streams.

The broad leaves, 4 to 8 inches long, are divided into 3 or 5 short, pointed sections. Round clusters of green flowers dangle from the twigs in spring. In autumn, the seeds ripen in dry brown balls.

The sycamores native to the western U.S. and Asia are similar but smaller trees. Their leaves are more deeply cut into pointed sections.

syncline \ 'sin-ˌklīn \

A syncline is a U-shaped rock formation. It occurs where layers of sedimentary rock that were once level have been folded and bent under great pressure. The same forces that created synclines formed mountain ranges.

A rock formation that curves upward is called an anticline. Together, synclines and anticlines form patterns like waves.

Synclines are visible where the insides of old mountains have been exposed by erosion, or where highways and railroads have been cut through mountain ranges.

Synclines are found in the Alps and in the Rocky Mountains and Appalachian Mountains of North America. In the Appalachians, most synclines are 1 to 10 miles across, and 2 to 5 miles deep. In the Rockies, some synclines are 10 to 50 miles across.

See *anticline* and *geosyncline*.

SYCAMORE

SYNCLINE

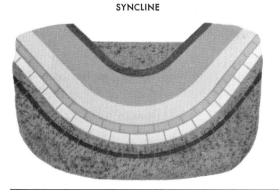

t

talc \ 'talk \

Talc is the softest of all common minerals and can be easily scratched with a fingernail. It is soft because its crystals are flat plates loosely bound together. Under slight pressure, the crystals slip and slide apart. Talc is nearly always found among metamorphic rocks.

Talc is used to make talcum powder and cosmetics, but it also has many other uses. Large quantities of talc go into paper, paint, ceramic products, insect poisons, rubber and roofing.

Soapstone is the most solid kind of talc. It is split into flat slabs that are used to make laboratory tabletops and sinks, and electrical switchboards.

Most talc is white, light gray or light green. Soapstone is often a dark greenish-gray. All forms of talc feel greasy or soapy to the touch. Some forms are translucent. All forms of talc are poor conductors of heat and electricity.

Talc is made up of magnesium and silicon, combined with oxygen and hydrogen.

In the U.S., talc is found in the Appalachian Mountains and in some parts of the Rockies and the Cascade Range. Talc mines are located in Vermont, New York, North Carolina and California. Talc is also mined in South Africa, Japan, Canada and several European countries.

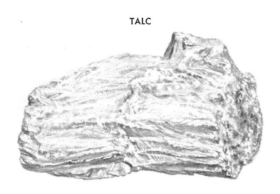

TALC

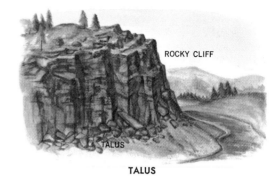

ROCKY CLIFF

TALUS

TALUS

talus \ 'tā-ləs \

Talus is loose rock material that piles up at the foot of a steep mountain or cliff. A tall, pointed pile of such material is called a talus cone.

Erosion and weathering are the chief forces that create talus. Weathering is the action of alternate freezing and thawing. Water seeps into cracks between rock masses, high on a mountainside or cliffside. As it freezes, the water expands, and the rocks break apart. Some rocks fall in response to gravity. As they tumble down the slope, they often knock other rocks loose.

A talus slope is generally steep and rugged, because it is made up of different sizes and shapes of rock fragments. Finer materials such as gravel or sand would slide farther, and form a gentler slope.

Talus is seen only in rugged mountain country, as in western North America.

tanager \ 'tan-i-jər \

Tanagers make up a family of bright-colored woodland birds that live only in the New World. Most are year-round residents of tropical forests in Central and South America. A few kinds spend the summer in the U.S. and Canada.

Most tanagers are about the size of sparrows. The largest tanagers are less than 8 inches long. They are red, blue, green, yellow or black. Some change color with the season. All have cone-

434

TANAGER

shaped bills that curve down slightly.

Tanagers eat mostly fruit and berries, along with some insects. Most kinds raise 2 broods of young during the summer. The females incubate the eggs, but both parents feed the young birds. Newly hatched tanagers are blind and have a light covering of down on their bodies.

The tanagers that summer in North America build saucer-shaped nests in tall trees. The 3 to 5 eggs are greenish-blue, spotted with brown or purple.

The scarlet tanager (illustrated) nests as far north as Saskatchewan and Nova Scotia. The female is yellowish-green all year, and the male is yellowish only during the winter. In the summer, the male scarlet tanager is bright red, with black wings and tail.

The summer tanager, bright red all over, nests in the southeastern states. The western tanager is yellow and black with a red head.

tapeworm \ 'tāp-ˌwərm \

Tapeworms make up a group of parasitic flatworms. They live inside the bodies of larger animals such as crustaceans, fish, sheep, domestic pigs and humans. Tapeworms often pass from one animal to another. Humans get tapeworms from eating infected meat or fish that has not been thoroughly cooked.

All tapeworms have flat, ribbon-like bodies. They are white or yellowish.

Most kinds have a head-like end that clings to the lining of the host's intestines. Attached to this head are a large number of segments. New segments are constantly forming, just behind the head. Some tapeworms grow to more than 300 feet long.

Tapeworms do not have mouths. Each segment absorbs food through its cell walls. Each segment has both male and female parts, and can produce fertilized eggs.

The beef tapeworm is often 50 to 60 feet long. It reproduces inside the intestines of cows. Newly hatched larvae pass into the bloodstream and form tiny, hard cysts inside the cow's muscles. When undercooked beef containing these cysts is eaten by humans, tiny worms break out of the cysts and attach themselves to the intestines.

tapir \ 'tā-pər \

Tapirs make up a family of hoofed mammals with long, flexible snouts. Among the oldest of all living mammals, tapirs have not changed much for millions of years.

Tapirs live in the forests of southeastern Asia and Central and South America. The largest ones are powerful animals 8 feet long. Tapirs are plant eaters that sleep during the day and roam about seeking food at night.

When attacked, tapirs usually run

TAPIR

away. They can move very quickly, and their thick skins protect them as they crash through dense and prickly underbrush. They are also good swimmers.

When cornered, tapirs use their sharp teeth and strong jaws to protect themselves and their young. Leopards and jaguars are their chief enemies.

Adult tapirs native to the New World are dark brown. Asian tapirs are black, with a wide white stripe across the back.

The common South American tapir (illustrated) ranges from Venezuela south to Argentina. Adults are up to 6 feet long. They have manes or crests of stiff, bristly hair on their necks.

tarantula \ tə-'ranch-(ə-)lə \

Tarantulas make up a group of large, hairy spiders that are not nearly so dangerous as they look. Although the bite of a tarantula may be painful, it will not cause illness or death. Some kinds of tarantulas can be tamed and kept as pets.

Most tarantulas are dark-colored and slow-moving. The largest kinds are 4 to 5 inches across, including the legs. The bodies are up to 2 inches long. Tarantulas sometimes capture, kill and eat frogs and small birds, as well as the largest beetles and grasshoppers.

Most tarantulas live in burrows in the soil. Some line their tunnels with silk, and build a silken trapdoor to close the entrance. Some live in cracks in trees, or under rocks. Some spin funnel-shaped webs.

The Old World spider called tarantula was once greatly feared in Europe. Persons bitten by this spider were believed to go into a wild dance and then fall dead.

The New World tarantulas live in the southwestern U.S., Mexico, Central America and tropical South America. The one most common in the U.S. (illustrated) benefits man by killing and eating many harmful insects.

tarn \ 'tärn \

Tarns are lakes in high, rugged mountains that have been shaped by glaciers. Most tarns are oval and fairly small. High, steep cliffs rise behind them. The water that fills them is clear and very cold.

A tarn usually marks the point where a glacier began. Deep snows piled up on the mountainside at this point. When the weather turned warm, some water melted from the snow and trickled down into cracks in the rock. When it turned colder again, the water froze and expanded, breaking the rocks apart.

Eventually the snow became so thick and heavy that it began to move slowly down the mountainside. The loosened rocks traveled with it, leaving a bowl-shaped hollow on the mountainside. A tarn is the lower part of this hollow, filled with water.

TARANTULA

TARNS

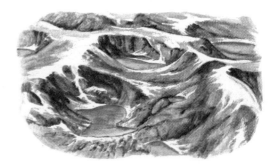

In the U.S., Iceberg Lake in Glacier National Park is a tarn at the foot of steep, rocky walls 3,000 feet tall.

tarsier \ 'tär-sē-,ā \

The tarsiers are small nocturnal mammals with very large, round eyes. They are primates distantly related to the apes and to man. Like other primates, they use their hands to raise food to their mouths, and both their eyes face forward.

About the size of rats, tarsiers are covered with woolly fur. They have tufts of hair at the ends of their long tails. Suction pads at the ends of their fingers and toes help them cling to twigs and branches.

Tarsiers live in the tropical forests of Sumatra, Java, Borneo and the Philippines. They spend their lives in the treetops, leaping from tree to tree as squirrels do. They sleep during the day and seek food in the late evening and at night. Tarsiers eat mostly insects, but they also eat some fruit.

Not much is known about the habits of tarsiers. It is believed that their young are born singly, with their eyes open, and that they are covered with fur.

The spectral tarsier (illustrated) has goggle-like rings around its eyes, and large ears that are constantly twitching. It is brownish-gray, with some black and greenish markings. The body is about 6 inches long.

TARSIER

TEA

tea

Tea is an evergreen shrub or small tree native to Asia. The world's most popular drink is made from its leaves. Tea was drunk as early as A.D. 400 in China. It was introduced into Europe in 1610.

The tea tree grows as tall as 30 feet, but on plantations it is usually cut back to a height of 6 feet or less. The small young leaves from the ends of the twigs are picked and dried to make commercial tea. Green and black tea come from the same kind of tree. The black tea leaves have been fermented.

If they are not picked, the leaves grow 4 to 10 inches long. They are oval and have fine sawtooth edges. The fragrant flowers have 5 white petals. The fruit is a woody pod containing 3 round seeds.

India, Ceylon, China, Indonesia, Japan and East Africa lead in the production of tea. The trees are usually planted on mountainsides. They need a warm climate and much rainfall.

Tea leaves contain caffein, the same stimulant that is in coffee berries. In most parts of the world, tea is a more popular drink than coffee. Great Britain imports about 11 pounds of tea per person, each year. Australia imports 8 pounds per person. The U.S. imports about ½ pound per person.

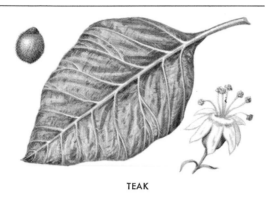

TEAK

teak \ 'tēk \

Teak is a valuable timber tree native to southeastern Asia. Its heartwood is very durable. It may remain strong and useful for 500 years or more. It does not warp or split, and it is almost never damaged by termites or borers.

The heartwood is yellow when freshly cut, but it seasons to a dark brown color. It is used for building ships and wharves, window frames, fine furniture and flooring. The sapwood is white.

When fully grown, teak trees are 100 to 150 feet tall. They have large, rough-surfaced leaves 1 to 2 feet long and up to 1 foot wide. The leaves fall from the trees when the dry season begins, in January. The branches remain bare until the rainy season begins in April.

The flowers are small and white. They are borne in large clusters, at the ends of the higher branches. The fruit has a wrinkled, papery shell and contains 4 seeds. It is about ½ inch in diameter.

Burma, Thailand and India lead in production of teak wood. In some places, the trees are grown on plantations.

teasel \ 'tē-zəl \

Teasels make up a group of thistle-like plants native to Europe and Asia. Most teasels are annual plants, but some kinds do not produce flowers and seeds until the second year.

Most kinds of teasel are coarse weeds with prickly stems. Teasels grow as tall as 6 feet. The edges of the leaves are joined near the base to form a kind of cup that holds moisture. The leaves grow in opposite pairs or in whorls.

Tiny, tube-shaped flowers are clustered on an oval flowering head. Hooked spines cover the head in autumn, when the seeds ripen.

Fuller's teasel was once cultivated for its prickly fruiting heads. They were used to raise the nap on woolen cloth. The flowers are pale lavender. The leaves are about 12 inches long. In autumn, the fruiting heads stand alone at the tops of the tall stems.

tent caterpillar

Tent caterpillars are a group of moth larvae that build ugly, web-like nests in the forks of trees. They feed on leaves, and do a good deal of damage to fruit trees. Many kinds of birds eat tent caterpillars.

The adult form of the tent caterpillar is a plump, hairy moth about ¾ inch long. It is yellowish or reddish-brown, with darker stripes on the forewings. The females lay masses of 300 to 400 eggs in the forks of tree branches, covering each mass with a protective, waterproof coating.

The larvae remain inside the eggs until the following spring. They hatch out as very small caterpillars that are fuzzy and usually bright-colored.

TENT CATERPILLAR

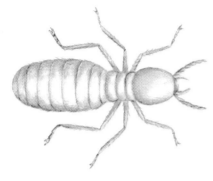

TERMITE

The tent caterpillars that hatch from 1 egg mass stay together and share 1 tent or nest for some time. As they grow larger, they spin silken threads and use them to enlarge the tent. They leave the nest to feed, but return for shelter.

When fully grown, the caterpillars crawl away from the tent and spin oval, white cocoons. In late summer they emerge as adult moths.

The eastern tent caterpillar (illustrated) is most often seen on apple, plum and wild cherry trees.

termite \ 'tər-ˌmīt \ (white ant)

Termites make up a group of insects that look like ants, although they are not closely related to them. Termites eat wood, and they do a great deal of damage to wooden houses and other wooden structures. They are most common in the tropics.

Termites are social insects that live in colonies. Each colony has 4 separate castes. Each caste has a different duty to perform.

Only termites of the royal caste have wings and can reproduce. The queen is a member of the royal caste. She loses her wings after mating, and her body becomes so large that she is nearly helpless. She lays thousands of eggs.

Most numerous are termites of the working caste. They are blind, and they have soft, white bodies. Termites of the

soldier caste are slightly larger, and they have stronger jaws and legs. They will fight to defend the queen or the colony.

The fourth caste is made up of immature nymphs that develop into termites of the royal class if more kings or queens are needed.

In the tropics, some termites build earth mounds up to 6 feet tall. In the temperate zone they live in underground burrows.

The common termite (illustrated) is found in most parts of the U.S.

tern \ 'tərn \

The terns are long-winged seabirds that belong to the same family as gulls. Terns look much like gulls but are smaller and more streamlined, with thinner bills.

Coloring varies with the season and with the age of the birds. In winter, most adults are gray and white, with black on the head. Most adults have long, V-shaped tails, while young terns have short, stubby tails.

Terns live along coastlines and around large lakes, in nearly all parts of the world. Some kinds migrate long distances between summer and winter homes. They eat mostly small fish, diving underwater to catch them or scooping them up from the surface as they fly.

Most kinds of terns nest on sandy beaches. The 2 to 4 spotted eggs are placed in a slight hollow in the sand.

TERN

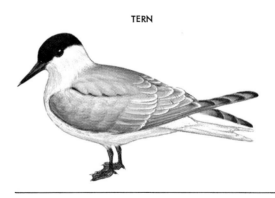

439

Both parents incubate the eggs. Young terns fly when about 1 month old.

The common tern (illustrated) spends the summer along the east coast of the U.S. and around the Great Lakes, and along the coastlines of Europe, Asia and North Africa. It winters along the coastlines of Baja California and on Atlantic and Gulf coasts from Maine to Central America.

tetra \ 'te-trə \

Tetras are freshwater tropical fish that are popular with aquarium owners. Tetras are hardy and easy to care for, and they live peacefully with other kinds of tropical fish.

Most tetras are about 2 inches long when fully grown. They have squared-off dorsal fins and notched tails. Males and females look just alike, but males are more slender than females.

The many different kinds of tetras are marked with a variety of bright colors. Some have stripes and spots that show only under artificial light.

In their natural state, tetras live in Central and South America and in Africa. They are found both in running streams and in ponds and lakes. They eat mostly insect larvae and tiny crustaceans.

Spawning females drop their eggs wherever they happen to be. Some of the eggs cling to underwater plants.

TETRA

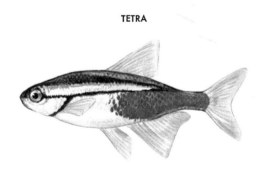

THISTLE

The neon tetra (illustrated) is a lively fish that does well in an aquarium but usually will not breed there. It is native to the headwaters of the Amazon River. It is seldom more than 1½ inches long.

thistle \ 'this-əl \

Thistles make up a group of prickly weeds that grow in nearly all parts of the north temperate zone. Some kinds that once grew only in Europe or Asia now grow wild throughout North America.

Most thistles are biennials. The first summer, they produce only a rosette-like cluster of leaves at ground level. The second summer, a flowering stalk grows up to 6 feet tall. Flowers and seeds are borne in heads at the tops of the stalks.

The tiny, tube-shaped flowers are blue, purple, yellow or white. The seed is a dry achene. In many kinds of thistles, the seeds are attached to tufts of down.

The leaves are cut into pointed lobes. The leaves of most kinds of thistle have sharp spines along the edges.

The bull thistle (illustrated) is native to Europe but has spread throughout the U.S. and southern Canada. It is a coarse, sturdy weed that develops a strong root system and is not easy to kill. The flowers are pinkish-purple. The leaves are irregular in shape and very prickly.

The bull thistle grows mostly in open fields and along roadsides, where the soil is rich and moist.

THRASHER

thrasher \ 'thrash-ər \

Thrashers make up a group of New World songbirds with very long tails. They are closely related to the catbird and the mockingbirds.

Thrashers are 8 to 12 inches long. Most are brown or dark gray, with lighter underparts. They have loud songs, and usually repeat a phrase 2 or 3 times before going on to another phrase. Thrashers are named for the way they twitch their tails from side to side while perching.

Mostly woodland birds, thrashers eat insects, grubs and worms, along with some fruit and berries. They nest near the ground, in bushy shrubs. Both parents incubate the 3 to 5 speckled eggs and feed the young birds. Adults attack any intruder who comes near the nest. Young thrashers have spotted breasts.

Thrashers live in North and South America and in the West Indies. The brown thrasher (illustrated) is the kind best known in the eastern U.S. It nests from the Atlantic coast west to the Rockies, and north to Quebec. It winters in the southern states and in Central America.

The brown thrasher is 10½ to 11½ inches long. The spots on the adult bird's breast are arranged in vertical rows.

thrush \ 'thrəsh \

Thrushes make up a family of birds that includes many songbirds. They live in all parts of the world except near the poles and on some ocean islands. All are strong fliers, and some kinds of thrushes migrate long distances.

Most thrushes are plump-bodied birds 6 to 10 inches long. They have large eyes, with light-colored rings around them.

Though they are chiefly insect eaters, thrushes also eat some fruit and berries. They build saucer-shaped nests of twigs and grass, sometimes strengthened with mud. Most kinds nest in trees and bushes, but some kinds nest on the ground. The 3 to 6 eggs are white or bluish, sometimes speckled with dark brown.

The hermit thrush (illustrated) is about 7 inches long. It has a bell-like song. Seldom seen in open fields or near cities, the hermit thrush usually lives in deep woods.

In summer, the hermit thrush lives in the far western U.S., Canada and Alaska. It winters in the southern U.S., Mexico and Central America.

For other members of the thrush family, see *bluebird, nightingale* and *robin.*

thyme \ 'tīm \

Thymes are perennial creeping plants that are native to the Mediterranean regions of Europe. They belong to the mint family. The leaves and flowers contain a fragrant oil, and they are often used for seasoning soups and meats. The oil is also used in perfumes and in the drug, thymol.

THRUSH

There are about 50 kinds of thyme. The small, lilac or purplish flowers appear in summer in small clusters or loose spikes where the leaves join the stem. The leaves are small and opposite. The fruit is a collection of 4 nutlets.

Common thyme grows 6 to 8 inches high. The square stems are covered with fine white hairs. The flowers are about ¼ inch long and grow in short spikes.

Thyme is often grown in herb gardens. Creeping thyme is sometimes used as a ground cover in rocky areas.

Thyme is now grown commercially in northeastern U.S. and southern Canada.

tick

Ticks make up a group of small invertebrate animals related to spiders. Ticks are parasites that feed on the blood of reptiles and warm-blooded animals. Some kinds carry diseases such as tularemia and Rocky Mountain spotted fever.

Ticks have head, thorax and abdomen all joined together in an oval-shaped body. There are 4 pairs of jointed legs and no antennae. The mouth is beaklike, with strong teeth used for piercing the skin of larger animals.

At 1 feeding, ticks may suck blood until they swell up to many times their original size. They can live for as long as a year before feeding again.

Ticks lay their eggs on the ground,

TICK

TIGER

among dead leaves and grasses. The 6-legged larvae that hatch from the eggs climb up onto trees and plants. Like adult ticks, they cling there until an animal passes by. After feeding, the larvae drop to the ground and molt, becoming larger and 8-legged. After a second molt, they are adults.

The American dog tick (illustrated) fastens itself to dogs and also to horses and cattle. It is about ⅕ inch long, but after feeding it may appear much larger. Although most kinds of ticks live in woods and fields, the American dog tick sometimes becomes a household pest.

tiger

Tigers are large, flesh-eating Asian mammals belonging to the cat family. They are very much like lions in size and shape. Tigers are native to Java and Sumatra.

About 3 feet at the shoulder, tigers weigh up to 500 pounds. They are yellowish-brown with black stripes and white underparts. Albino tigers are not uncommon. The Bengal tiger of India (illustrated) measures 10 feet long. It is considered to be the most beautifully marked tiger.

Tigers live in damp jungles and grassy plains. They are not good climbers. Their eyesight and sense of smell are poor. They hunt other mammals mostly at night, by ear. They usually drag their prey to their lairs, and eat them slowly.

Man-eating tigers are rare, and live only in India.

Except at breeding time, tigers live alone. They wander widely, especially in cold weather. Females mate every other year in any season. Litters of 4 to 5 cubs are born, but usually only 2 survive. The cubs leave the mother at 2 years.

Tigers range from the Caucasus Mountains to Siberia. In the Himalayas, they live as high as 7,000 feet above sea level.

timberline \ 'tim-bər-ˌlin \

A timberline is the limiting line above which trees do not grow, mostly because of the altitude. Usually, a timberline can be seen as a ragged fringe of trees circling a mountain. Below the line, trees and bushes grow. Above the line are meadows. If the mountain is very high, only bare rocks, snow and ice are near its peak.

Because very cold weather is one cause of timberlines, they are most common near the north and south polar regions. Wind, soil and water conditions also help to determine where the timberline will be. A timberline does not often have a well-marked boundary. Near the line, the trees are widely spaced, and are often poorly formed and shrub-like.

The altitude of a timberline depends upon local climate. In the mountains of New Mexico, no timberline is above an altitude of 12,000 feet. In northern Canada, the timberline occurs at sea level.

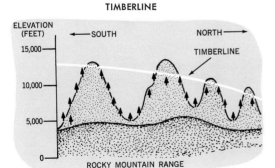

TIMBERLINE

ELEVATION (FEET)
←— SOUTH   NORTH —→
15,000 —   TIMBERLINE
10,000 —
5,000 —
0 —
ROCKY MOUNTAIN RANGE

titmouse

TITMOUSE

titmouse \ 'tit-ˌmaus \

Titmice make up a group of small, quick-moving birds closely related to chickadees. They live in North America, Europe, Asia and Africa. In most parts of their range they are year-round residents.

Titmice are 4 to 8 inches long. Most are gray and white, but some are bluish or yellow. Their calls are soft whistling sounds.

In summer, titmice eat mostly insects that they pick from tree leaves and bark. In autumn and winter, they eat berries, seeds and thin-shelled nuts. Most kinds nest in hollow trees. Both parents incubate the eggs and feed the young birds.

The kind of titmouse best known in eastern North America is the tufted titmouse (illustrated). It is fairly common from the Atlantic coast west to Kansas and Oklahoma, in city parks and small towns as well as in forested places. In winter, the tufted titmouse often visits bird feeders, along with nuthatches and chickadees.

The tufted titmouse is about 6 inches long. Male and female are colored alike, gray and white with patches of rust on the sides of the body. The 5 to 6 eggs are white, speckled with brown. The nest is often an abandoned woodpecker hole lined with soft grass, hair or fur.

443

toad

Toads and frogs together make up a group of amphibians that have long hind legs and no tails. In general, the ones that have warty skin and that spend most of their time on land are called toads. The ones that have smooth skins and spend most of their time in water are called frogs.

Toads are harmless. They eat only insects and worms that they catch by flicking out long, sticky tongues. They aid man by helping to control many insect pests. Toads hibernate underground when temperatures go below freezing.

All but a very few toads mate and lay their eggs in water. The young toads that hatch from the eggs are tiny black tadpoles. They live in ponds and streams, and breathe through gills. They eat plants that grow in water. Through metamorphosis, the tadpoles turn into tail-less adults with lungs for breathing air.

Some kinds of toad tadpoles take 2 seasons to turn into adults. Kinds that live in deserts develop very quickly, before the puddles where the eggs are laid dry up.

The American toad, Fowler's toad, the great plains toad, the green toad and the western toad all have squat bodies and bowed forelegs. Their hind legs are long, but not so long as frogs' legs. Their bodies are 1½ to 4½ inches long.

The American toad, common throughout the eastern half of the U.S., may be gray, greenish or brown. Fowler's toad, which lives only along the Atlantic coast, is brown or dark gray, with a light yellowish line down the center of its back.

The great plains toad lives from Montana and North Dakota south to New Mexico and Arizona. It is light gray or yellowish, with clearly marked dark spots.

The green toad, seldom more than 2 inches long, lives in dry parts of the southwestern U.S. and northern Mexico. The gray or greenish-brown western toad lives near mountain streams in the far western U.S.

The bell toad, only 1 to 1½ inches long, lives along cool mountain streams in the northwestern U.S. and western Canada. It may be pinkish, gray, green, brown or nearly black, marked with spots and stripes.

The narrow-mouthed toads live in nearly all parts of the world, but they are shy and are seldom seen. They hide under rocks or under rotting logs. They have very small, pointed heads.

The eastern narrowmouth toad (illustrated) is only ¾ to 1½ inches long.

Spadefoot toads are also common in many parts of the world but are seldom seen. They leave their burrows only at night. Horny spurs on their feet make them good diggers. In sandy soil they burrow straight down and quickly sink out of sight.

The eastern spadefoot toad (illustrated) lives in the U.S. from New England south to Florida and Texas.

The midwife toad lives only in Europe. The male (illustrated) wraps the strings of sticky eggs around his body and carries them until they hatch. At night he hops into a stream or pond to wet the eggs. During the day he hides from the sun, so the eggs will not dry out. After about a month he enters water and stays there until all the tadpoles hatch out and swim away.

The flat-bodied Surinam toad lives only in South America. Unlike most toads, it lives in water as an adult. The hind feet are webbed for swimming. The front feet end in slender, branching fingertips that feel in river-bottom mud for bits of food.

The male Surinam toad (illustrated) places the female's eggs on his back, where pockets form and hold them until they hatch.

Toads—Land Amphibians

AMERICAN TOAD

BELL TOAD

FOWLER'S TOAD

GREAT PLAINS TOAD

GREEN TOAD

NARROWMOUTH TOAD

MIDWIFE TOAD

SPADEFOOT TOAD

SURINAM TOAD

WESTERN TOAD

TOBACCO

tobacco

Tobacco is a member of the nightshade family. It may be an annual or a perennial. It is native to tropical America except for 1 kind which grows in Asia. Tobacco has been cultivated in the U.S. since 1612.

There are about 50 kinds of tobacco plants. Some are grown only for ornament. Most tobacco plants are grown for their large leaves which are dried and cut for use in smoking products and snuff.

Tobacco plants grow 2 to 20 feet high. Some look like trees, while others are shrubs. All are covered with short, sticky hairs. The flowers are white, greenish-yellow or purple. The thick leaves contain a juice that may be poisonous or habit-forming.

Commercial tobacco (illustrated) is an annual plant grown in warm climates. It reaches a height of 6 to 8 feet. The stems are erect and bear leaves up to 2 feet long and 1 foot wide. The edges curl somewhat downward.

The sweet-smelling flowers of commercial tobacco grow in loose, open clusters at the tops of the branches. The blossoms have a calyx composed of 5 green sepals and a tube-like corolla. The flowers remain open only during the daylight hours. The fruit is a dry capsule containing many small seeds that look like finely ground pepper.

tokay \ tō-'ka \

The tokay is a harmless, brightly colored lizard. It is the largest of the geckos and is native to southeastern Asia. Many Malayans believe the tokay to be a symbol of good luck.

The tokay measures 10 to 14 inches long. The skin is covered with small scales and is gray with yellow or orange spots. The head is flat with large, bulging eyes. The tail is slightly flattened.

The feet of the tokay have a pattern of scales or plates under the toes. Many small, hook-like cells on the plates make it possible for the tokay to climb on smooth surfaces, even glass. There are also sharp claws, which the tokay uses to cling to rough stone or tree bark.

Tokays often live inside houses. During the day, they hide in cracks in the wall or behind furniture. At night, tokays run about over the walls and ceiling, where they feed on insects attracted by the lamplight. Tokays sometimes make a loud barking sound.

Usually a gentle animal, the tokay will bite and hang on with a firm grip if it is annoyed.

The female tokay lays 2 eggs at a time. She hides them in a crack in the wall or under the bark of a tree. They hatch in 2 to 8 weeks.

TOKAY

tomato

The tomato is an annual garden plant related to tobacco, potato and eggplants. It is native to South America. The fruit of the tomato is eaten throughout the world. It is rich in vitamins A and C.

In the U.S., tomatoes were once thought to be poisonous. They were cultivated only as ornamental plants known as love apples.

Many cultivated forms of tomatoes have been developed. The round, juicy fruit may be either red or yellow. The shape may be rounded, flattened or oblong. Some forms are very small, less than 1 inch across.

The garden tomato (illustrated) stands erect when young. As it grows, the stems and branches begin to trail. They reach a length of 6 to 8 feet. The compound leaves have a strong odor. A single leaf may measure up to 12 inches and is made up of many lobed or toothed leaves. The small, yellow flowers are bell-shaped. They grow in clusters of 3 to 7. The fruit is a berry containing 2 or more seeds surrounded by juicy pulp.

Tomatoes grow best where night temperatures do not go below 60°. They are often grown in greenhouses. In the U.S., tomatoes are grown commercially in every state but Alaska.

TOMATO

TOPAZ

topaz \ 'tō-,paz \

Topaz is a hard, glassy mineral that is prized by rock collectors. Clear topaz is used in jewelry. Topaz crystals may be colorless, yellow, white, pale blue, brown, yellow-brown or pink. They are most valuable as gem stones when they have a brown or pink tint. Topaz also occurs as a solid mass, either gray or white.

The mineral topaz contains aluminum, silica and fluorine combined with oxygen and hydrogen.

Topaz is usually found with granites. It was formed as igneous rocks cooled. Topaz crystals were the last part of the rock to cool because they contained the water and vapors given off by the surrounding rock.

Some colors of topaz fade when exposed to sunlight. Brown topaz turns pink when heated. Most pink topaz used in jewelry is brown topaz that has been heated.

The finest yellow gem topaz comes from Brazil, where pink, blue and brown crystals occur. Other valuable topaz is found in Russia and Saxony. Large topaz crystals are fairly rare in the U.S. The biggest white crystals have been found in Virginia. Clear topaz crystals have come from Colorado and blue crystals in New England. Others have been found in Texas and California.

tourmaline \ ˈtur-mə-lən \

Tourmaline is a very hard mineral that occurs in many different colors. Some crystals of tourmaline are prized as gem stones and used in jewelry. Because they conduct electricity, tourmaline crystals are used in electrical equipment.

Tourmaline crystals usually have 6 sides. Some crystals are 3 feet in length. Like topaz, tourmaline occurs in granite. The crystals were formed by vapors given off as the igneous rock cooled.

Tourmaline is commonly black or brown, but may be pink, red, green, blue or yellow. Two colors are sometimes found in 1 crystal. "Watermelon tourmaline" is pink in the center and green at the edges. Black tourmaline looks very much like coal.

When used as gems, tourmaline has several names. Only the green crystals are called tourmaline. Red tourmaline is known as rubellite. Blue is indicolite.

The finest tourmaline gems come from Brazil, Russia, Madagascar and the island of Elba. In the U.S., tourmaline occurs in the New England states, New York and California.

towhee \ tō-ˈ(h)ē \

Towhees are shy, woodland birds belonging to the finch family. They are native to most parts of North and South America.

Towhees are 7½ to 9½ inches long, and they have long tails that are rounded at the tip. Most are brownish, streaked birds that look like large sparrows.

Towhees feed mostly on the ground. They eat grubs, beetles and seeds, along with some fruit and berries. Their cup-shaped nests are built on the ground in a sheltered place, or in a low shrub. Usually, both male and female incubate the 3 or 4 eggs and bring food to the young.

The name "towhee" comes from the call of the kind most common in the U.S., the rufous-sided towhee (illustrated). It is the most colorful towhee, and is sometimes mistaken for a robin. Both male and female have patches of bright reddish-brown on the sides, but the female is dark brown where the male is black.

The rufous-sided towhee always nests on the ground. It breeds in southern Canada and in the U.S. as far west as Manitoba, the Dakotas and Kansas. It winters in the southern half of the U.S. and in Mexico and Central America.

travertine \ ˈtrav-ər-ˌtēn \

Travertine is an ornamental stone that is one of the many forms of the mineral calcite.

Travertine may be banded or mottled in shades of cream, yellow, pink and red.

TOWHEE

TRAVERTINE

It is usually found around hot springs or in caves, where water containing calcium cooled or evaporated. The red and yellow coloring is caused by iron oxides and other materials that were in the water.

When first cut, travertine is soft and easily worked. It hardens after it has been exposed to air, and is often used as a trim on the inside of buildings. It can be highly polished and, indoors, is long lasting. Because travertine is porous, it is not often used on the outside of buildings in cold climates. Ice forming and melting in the porous stone causes it to crumble.

The best-known bed of travertine is in Italy, near Rome. Many of Rome's famous buildings, such as the Colosseum and St. Peter's Church, were built of travertine. In the U.S., travertine occurs in Montana, Florida and California.

trench \ 'trench \

A trench is a deep, narrow, V-shaped canyon on the floor of the ocean. Trenches make up the deepest parts of the oceans. Many trenches in the Atlantic and Pacific oceans have been discovered recently through the use of new instruments.

Oceanographers are puzzled as to the formation of trenches. They believe the deep canyons were caused by the downward pull of some force beneath the earth's crust.

Trenches are of different lengths, but

TRENCH

TRICERATOPS

they are always on the seaward side of a chain of volcanic islands or off-shore from a range of mountains. All trenches seem to have been about 35,000 feet deep when first formed. Some old trenches are slowly filling with sediment from land nearby. Once a trench has filled with sediment, it is pushed up, forming a new chain of islands.

The Puerto Rico Trench, north of Puerto Rico, is the deepest known trench in the Atlantic Ocean. Fourteen trenches have been found in the Pacific Ocean. At 35,800 feet, the Mariana Trench in the Pacific Ocean is the deepest trench known. It is at the western edge of the Pacific Ocean, near the Philippines. Other deep trenches are located east of Japan and south of the Aleutian Islands.

triceratops \ trī-'ser-ə-,täps \

The triceratopses were horned dinosaurs that lived about 100 million years ago. They were among the last of the dinosaurs. Probably because of their small brains, their stay on earth was shorter than that of other giant reptiles.

The most common kind of triceratops (illustrated) stood about 8 feet high at the hips. It measured 25 to 30 feet in length. A huge rhinoceros-like head made up about ⅓ of this length. A bony crest fanned out behind the huge skull.

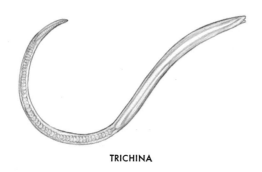

TRICHINA

It protected a short, stocky neck. The body was barrel-shaped. There were 5 hoofed toes on each front foot, and 3 on each hind foot.

The triceratops had 3 sharp horns. One was on the snout. The other 2 were over the eyes and were 3 to 4 feet long. The mouth had a parrot-like beak. The triceratops probably fought by charging head down at its enemies, much as the rhinoceros does. The triceratops ate green plants and laid eggs.

Bones found in Wyoming show that the triceratops once lived there. At that time, the region had a tropical climate.

trichina \ trik-'ī-nə \

The trichina is a tiny, parasitic roundworm that causes the disease trichinosis. Pigs, rats, cats and bears often carry this parasite. Humans get the disease by eating infected meat that has not been thoroughly cooked.

Barnyard pigs become infected when they are fed on garbage that contains infected meat.

The mature female trichina is about ⅛ inch long. The male is still smaller. As adults, trichinas live in the intestines of the host animal. After mating, the female burrows into the intestinal wall and gives birth to 1,000 or more live young. The microscopic larvae travel in the host's

bloodstream to muscle tissue. There they form tiny, hard-shelled capsules called cysts.

When another animal eats flesh containing trichina cysts, the larvae hatch out in the new host's stomach and intestines.

Thorough cooking kills the larvae inside the cysts, and makes the meat safe to eat.

Humans infected with trichinosis suffer from headaches, swollen eyes, fever and sore muscles. A severe infection may cause death.

trillium \ 'tril-ē-əm \

Trilliums are hardy flowering plants that belong to the lily family. The name trillium comes from the Latin word for 3. The trillium's leaves, flower petals and sepals grow in 3's. Some kinds of trilliums are called wake-robins because they bloom early in the spring. Trilliums are native to North America and Asia.

Trilliums grow from thick, short rhizomes under the ground. Each flower grows at the top of a short stalk, above a cluster of 3 leaves. The plants are 6 to 24 inches tall. The 3 spreading petals are pink, white, greenish-white or purple. Between the petals are 3 green sepals. Trilliums bloom from early spring to summer.

The leaves near the top of the stalk are

TRILLIUM

broad ovals with clear veins. A few scale-like leaves occur at the bottom of the stalk. The fruit is a 3-celled berry.

The trillium grows in moist woodlands. It does not do well in direct sunlight.

The red or purple trillium (illustrated) is a sturdy early-spring plant. The petals measure up to 1½ inches long. They may be brown to purplish red. The flower has an unpleasant odor. This trillium is fairly common in eastern North America.

trilobite \ 'trī-lə-ˌbīt \

Trilobites make up a large group of marine invertebrates known only from fossils. About 500 million years ago, they were the most important form of animal life on earth.

Trilobites looked something like large insects. Their shells were much like the exoskeletons of modern insects. They molted from time to time, and many of their discarded shells became fossils. Young trilobites passed through a larval stage, and many fossil larvae have been found.

Mature trilobites were mostly 1 to 2 inches long, but a few grew to 2 feet long. Trilobite bodies were divided into head, thorax and abdomen. On the head were 2 long antennae and eyes that were usually compound. The thorax was made up of a number of jointed segments, with a pair of short legs on each segment. Each leg branched into 2 parts. The front branch was probably used for crawling on the sea floor or for burrowing. The feathery rear branch was probably used for swimming or for breathing.

Most trilobites could curl up in a ball, so that the softer underparts of the body were protected by the shell. Most ate smaller animals, both living and dead, but some kinds ate plants.

tropical \ 'träp-i-kəl \ fish

This term is used for a great number of small fish native to tropical waters. The raising of brightly colored tropical fish is a popular hobby. About 300 kinds of tropical fish are kept in home aquariums.

For kinds of tropical fish, see *betta, black mollie, guppy, platy* and *tetra*.

trough \ 'trȯf \

A trough is a rounded, U-shaped valley on the earth's surface. Some troughs were formed by synclines. Other troughs were formed by glaciers. Ice and the rocks carried by the glacier scraped away the soil, leaving a long, round-bottomed valley.

The shape of troughs differs from the shape of valleys cut out by running water. Valleys made by running water are usually narrow and V-shaped.

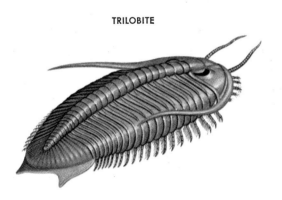

TRILOBITE

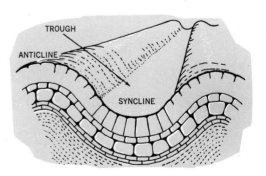

TROUGH

451

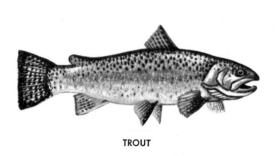

TROUT

The term trough is also used for the low place between the crests of 2 waves. One complete wave includes a crest and a trough. The length of a wave is measured from crest to crest or trough to trough. Crests and troughs exist in all kinds of waves, including water, sound and electromagnetic waves such as radio and light.

trout

Trout are freshwater fish belonging to the salmon family. They are among the most popular of all freshwater fish, both as food and as game fish.

Trout have long, slim bodies. Their large mouths have well-developed teeth. Most kinds have forked tails. The fins are fairly small and all are soft-rayed rather than spiny. Scales are small and smooth. Usually there are no scales on the head. Most kinds of trout are speckled or striped. Some are quite colorful.

The rainbow trout (illustrated) lives in cold, clear streams where the current is swift. A fast swimmer and a fierce fighter when hooked, it often leaps out of the water.

Rainbow trout measure up to 3 feet in length, but are usually smaller. They generally weigh 2 to 8 pounds. Unlike most trout, the rainbow trout has a squared-off tail. There is a wide rose stripe along its side. The entire body is spotted with irregular dark dots. Its body color varies from silver to dark olive.

The rainbow trout eats water insects and their larvae, crustaceans and worms. The nest is made on the gravel in the bottom of a stream. From 400 to 3,000 eggs are laid, in spring or early summer.

The rainbow trout is native to Pacific coast streams. Because of its popularity as a game fish, this trout has been introduced into many streams in the eastern U.S. and the Great Lakes area.

trypanosome \ trip-'an-ə-,sōm \

The trypanosomes are a group of parasitic, 1-celled animals that are microscopic in size and have flagella. Some cause diseases. They live in the bloodstreams of many different animals, and in the digestive tracts of some insects and leeches.

Trypanosomes have flattened, slender bodies. Most kinds have a fin-like wavy membrane along 1 side and a single whiplike flagellum at 1 end. Very simple organisms, they take in food and give off wastes through any part of the cell wall. They reproduce by fission.

Some kinds of trypanosomes infect warm-blooded animals. They are carried from one host to another by blood-sucking insects such as fleas, mosquitoes and the tsetse fly. These kinds are most common in warm or tropical climates.

TRYPANOSOME

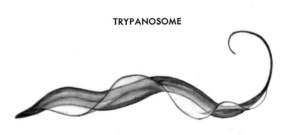

One troublesome kind of trypanosome (illustrated) causes African sleeping sickness in humans. Others cause Texas fever of cattle and a number of skin diseases.

Other kinds of trypanosomes infect cold-blooded animals such as fish, reptiles and amphibians. Such kinds are carried by blood-sucking leeches.

A few kinds of trypanosomes live in the cells of plants.

tsunami \ (t)sü-'näm-ē \

A tsunami is a series of giant waves caused by a movement of the earth beneath the sea. The movement may be an earthquake or a volcanic eruption. Tsunamis are sometimes incorrectly called tidal waves, but they are not caused by tides. The word "tsunami" is Japanese. "Tsu" means port or harbor and "nami" means wave or sea.

Tsunamis sometimes travel over long distances at great speeds. They have moved at 500 miles an hour with single waves about 15 minutes apart.

As the waves of a tsunami reach shallow water, they may rise to heights of 100 feet or more. The waves roll far up on shore, destroying everything in their path. They may cause great loss of life, as well as damage to docks and shipping.

New methods of recording movements of the earth now make it possible to warn

TSUNAMI

TULIP TREE

people that a tsunami is coming. The warnings permit people to leave areas near the shore before the wave strikes.

More than 200 tsunamis have been recorded. They occur more often in the western Pacific than in other parts of the world. Japan has recorded the most tsunamis. They have also reached islands in the Caribbean and the coasts of Alaska, Mexico and South America.

tulip tree (yellow poplar)

The tulip tree is a large tree related to magnolias. Tulip trees have broad leaves and easily worked wood used in plywood, furniture and other products. The tree is native to eastern North America.

The tulip tree is fast-growing and long-lived. It has a straight trunk, 4 to 9 feet across. It reaches a height of 80 to 200 feet. The slender branches are fairly high on the trunk. The bark on old trees is gray-brown with deep grooves.

The smooth leaves of the tulip tree are dark green and are 4 to 6 inches long. Each leaf is cut into 4 pointed lobes. In autumn, the leaves turn yellow.

The flowers of the tulip tree are 1½ to 2 inches long. They appear on the smaller branches in May or June. Each flower has 6 pale green petals marked with orange. The seeds mature in an erect, cone-like cluster 2½ to 3 inches long.

The tulip tree grows in rich, moist soil in river valleys and on the lower slopes of mountains. It has been planted as a shade tree in many parts of the world. The tulip tree is the state tree of Indiana.

tuna \ 't(y)ü-nə \

Tuna are large ocean fish related to mackerel. Popular both as food fish and game fish, tuna are caught by lines and nets. Large amounts of tuna are canned each year in the U.S. and in southern Europe.

Like mackerel, tuna are streamlined in shape and are swift swimmers. The lobes of the tail fin are widely separated. The fins on the body are small. The soft dorsal and anal fins are followed by a row of smaller fins reaching to the tail.

Tuna weigh from 20 to 1,800 pounds. Some kinds measure 2 feet when mature, while other kinds reach 14 feet.

Tuna live in nearly all parts of the world, in tropical and temperate waters. They travel in large schools, eating smaller fish and squid. They spawn in the open sea and migrate over large areas.

The skipjack or striped tuna (illustrated) has 4 long stripes on its sides. This tuna averages 2 to 2½ feet in length and weighs about 20 pounds. It lives in both the Atlantic and Pacific oceans in tropical waters. The skipjack often feeds on flying fish.

TUNA

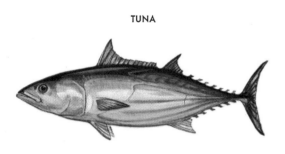

TURKEY

turkey

The wild turkeys are the largest game birds in North America. They are related to pheasants. Wild turkeys were once so common that they were suggested as the national bird of the U.S. Today, they are fairly rare. Many have been killed by hunters, and most of the deep forests where wild turkeys once lived have disappeared.

Wild turkeys are over 4 feet long and have a 5-foot wingspread. Their heads and necks have no feathers. The tail and upper tail feathers of the North American wild turkey are reddish-brown. Mexican wild turkeys have white-tipped feathers. Male wild turkeys have spurs and a bright red, fleshy growth called a wattle that hangs from the front of the throat.

Wild turkeys nest on the ground and roost in trees. One male, or gobbler, usually mates with about 15 females. Wild turkeys eat seeds, nuts, insects and grain that they find on the ground.

Turkey eggs are about twice the size of chicken eggs. They are creamy tan, spotted with brown.

The North American wild turkey (illustrated) is the ancestor of today's domestic turkeys. In many parts of the world, the raising of domestic turkeys is an important part of the poultry industry. Although legend says that turkeys were first seen by Pilgrims in America, turkeys were known much earlier in Europe. They were introduced there by the Spaniards.

turnip \ 'tər-nəp \

The turnip is a hardy, perennial plant that has been cultivated as a vegetable for hundreds of years. It is a member of the mustard family.

Although the turnip is mostly grown for its edible taproot, the tops are sometimes cooked and eaten as greens. The taproot is thick and usually white with some purple on the top. The yellow turnip is known as rutabaga.

Hairy, blue-green leaves rise from the top of the turnip root. The lower leaves have stalks and are somewhat lobed. The upper leaves are longer and toothed. Small, yellow flowers with 4 petals are borne on a separate flowering stem. The fruit is a seedpod 1½ to 2½ inches long.

Turnips grow best in cool climates. They mature late in the summer. Turnips are easy to grow in home gardens and keep well during the winter.

Turnips are probably native to Siberia and Russia where they grow wild. They were brought to Virginia in 1609. In some countries turnips are fed to livestock. In the U.S., they are grown mostly as a vegetable.

TURQUOISE

turquoise \ 'tər-ˌk(w)ȯiz \

Turquoise is a mineral that is popular as a gem stone. The color of turquoise ranges from blue through shades of green to greenish mixed with yellowish-gray. True turquoise is usually marked with veins of black, brown or white. The lines add to the value of the turquoise. They show that it is real turquoise rather than an imitation.

Early peoples believed that turquoise protected the wearer from bad luck. Turquoise found in ancient ruins shows that it has been used as a gem for more than 80 centuries. It has been found in very old jewelry and ornaments in Egypt, Asia Minor and the Orient. Turquoise was also used by American Indians of our Southwest.

Turquoise is usually found in warm, dry climates. Most turquoise veins are in volcanic or sedimentary rocks.

When used as a gem, turquoise is usually cut into round or oval shapes. Some turquoise is porous and may become greasy with use and fade if exposed to sunlight.

Turquoise is mined in many parts of the world, including Europe, Asia, Africa and Australia. The largest deposit in the U.S. is in New Mexico.

TURNIP

Turtles—Armored Reptiles

BOX TURTLE

DIAMONDBACK TURTLE

LOGGERHEAD TURTLE

MAP TURTLE

MUD TURTLE

PAINTED TURTLE

SNAPPING TURTLE

SPOTTED TURTLE

turtle

Turtles are egg-laying reptiles related to snakes and lizards. Fossils prove that turtles have been on the earth for a long time. Some kinds of turtles have lived on, almost unchanged, since the time of the dinosaurs 200 million years ago.

The backbone, ribs and breastbone of a turtle join together to form a shell that covers most of the body. The rounded, upper part of this shell is called the carapace. The flat, lower part of the shell is called the plastron.

Both carapace and plastron are divided into squarish or odd-shaped sections called shields. Sometimes there is a ridge along the center of the carapace.

The head, legs and tail are usually covered with small scales. There are hard, beak-like jaws but no teeth. Turtles are voiceless but sometimes make hissing or clicking sounds. Females are usually much larger than males.

All turtles have lungs and breathe air. Most kinds also have gill-like tissues that can absorb oxygen from water.

Turtles eat mostly animal foods, along with some green plants. Small turtles eat insects and worms. Larger turtles kill and eat fish, frogs and water birds.

Most turtles mate once a year, in spring. The female lays her eggs in a shallow hole and covers them with sand or dirt. They are incubated by the heat of the sun.

Young turtles are usually about 1 inch long when they dig their way up to the surface. Most kinds crawl straight toward the nearest water.

The box turtles are the only kinds that can close their shells tightly with all parts of the body inside. Both the front and back sections of the plastron are hinged like trapdoors. The shell length is 4 to 6 inches. The eastern box turtle (illustrated) makes a very interesting pet. Box turtles are most often seen on land.

The diamondback turtle, sometimes called the diamondback terrapin, lives along the edge of the ocean, in salt marshes and bays. Because its flesh is popular as food, it has been hunted until it is rare. The shell length is 4 to 8 inches.

The loggerhead is a large marine turtle that has flippers for swimming rather than feet for walking on land. Male loggerheads spend all their lives in the ocean. Females crawl up onto sandy beaches only to lay their eggs.

Loggerheads have heart-shaped, ridged shells 2 to 6 feet long. Some loggerheads weigh as much as 900 pounds.

Map, mud, painted, spotted and snapping turtles all live in ponds, lakes and quiet streams. They range from southern Canada through most parts of the U.S.

The map turtle is named for the pattern of lighter lines on its carapace. The shell length is 4 to 10 inches.

Mud turtles are small, dull brown turtles that give off an unpleasant smell when disturbed. They live at the bottoms of streams and ponds, and are seldom seen except by fishermen who catch them by accident. The eastern mud turtle (illustrated) has a shell length of 2 to 4 inches.

Painted turtles have red, yellow and black markings on head and legs and around the edge of the carapace. The turtles sold as pets are usually young painted turtles. The eastern painted turtle (illustrated) has a shell 4 to 8 inches long.

The spotted turtle has yellow spots on head and carapace. Young turtles have 1 spot on each shield. The shell length is 3 to 5 inches.

The bad-tempered snapping turtle has very strong jaws, and it can easily nip off a man's finger. The shell length is 12 to 18 inches.

For another kind of turtle, see *giant tortoise.*

TYRANNOSAUR

tyrannosaur \ tə'ran-ə-,sȯr \

The tyrannosaur is sometimes called the king of the dinosaurs, as it was the fiercest of the ancient dinosaurs. It lived late in the age of dinosaurs, probably about 120 million years ago.

The tyrannosaurs belong to the group of dinosaurs called theropods. They had lizard-like hip joints but they stood and walked on their hind legs. They used their smaller, weaker front legs only for holding or tearing food.

The tyrannosaur's front legs were probably too short to reach easily to the ground or to the animal's mouth.

About 20 feet tall, the tyrannosaur was about 50 feet long. The neck was short, and the tail long and heavy. The large head was about 4 feet long. The strong jaws were lined with sharp, dagger-like teeth 3 to 6 inches long. There were spurs on the hind legs and long, sharp claws on the 3-toed feet.

Carnivorous dinosaurs, tyrannosaurs killed and ate other animals. They are believed to be the largest flesh-eating animals that ever lived on earth. They could probably run very fast on dry land, but they were probably unable to swim. Like other reptiles, tyrannosaurs reproduced by laying eggs.

Tyrannosaurs are known mostly from fossils found in Wyoming and Montana.

u

upland plover \ 'pləv-ər \

The upland plover is not a true plover but a bird related to sandpipers. Although a shore bird, the upland plover usually lives inland, away from water.

True plovers have short necks and large heads close to the body. The neck of the upland plover is fairly long and slender and the head is small.

The upland plover is dark brown, streaked with lighter shades. It has a long slender bill and a white line over the eye. The outer tips of its tail are white. The legs are yellow. Male and female are colored alike and are 11 to 12½ inches long.

The home of the upland plover is the open prairie or grassy fields, where it feeds on insects, grubs and cutworms. It often perches on fence posts. The nest is built on the ground, and is usually well hidden by grasses. The upland plover often builds nests in pastures. The young are sometimes killed by mowing machines. The eggs are buff, spotted with brown.

The upland plover is rare. It breeds in southern Alaska, Canada and as far south as Virginia, Illinois, Oklahoma and Oregon. In the winter, upland plovers migrate to South America.

UPLAND PLOVER

Uranus \ 'yŭr-ə-nəs \

Uranus is the third largest of the 9 planets and the third most distant from the sun. Only Jupiter and Saturn are larger, and only Neptune and Pluto are farther away from the sun.

Uranus was discovered by William Herschel in 1781. Astronomers were greatly surprised, as they had not guessed that there were more planets beyond Saturn, which had been known since very ancient times.

Uranus completes 1 orbit of the sun in 84 years. It rotates once on its axis in 10¾ hours. Its axis of rotation is nearly parrellel to the plane of its orbit, so that the poles face the sun at times. Five moons revolve around Uranus.

Although it is small and dim, Uranus can be seen without a telescope. Through a telescope, Uranus appears greenish, with lighter-colored bands running across it.

Scientists believe that Uranus, like Neptune, has a small core of rock surrounded by ice and solid hydrogen. The atmosphere probably contains methane.

Because it is nearly 1,782 million miles away from the sun, Uranus is very cold. The surface temperature is probably $-270°$ F.

See *The Sun, the Moon and the Planets* on p. 502.

V

valley

A valley is the long path made by a river or glacier as it moves downhill. A valley is always lower than the land around it because stones and soil from the land have been picked up by the water or ice and moved downstream. Valleys may be deep or shallow, narrow or wide. Deep, narrow valleys with steep sides are called canyons.

A drowned valley, or estuary, is a river valley partly filled by water coming in from the sea. The land may have sunk or the level of the sea may have risen.

Hanging valleys form where the bed of a stream ends suddenly at a point high above the valley it is entering. The higher stream has a hanging valley.

A U-shaped valley (illustrated) is sometimes called a trough. U-shaped valleys have rounded floors and nearly straight sides. Most U-shaped valleys were carved out by alpine glaciers.

A V-shaped valley (illustrated) has sloping sides and a narrow floor. It is a geologically young valley. When the same valley is old its sloping sides may be far apart and its floor may be a broad flood plain.

See *estuary* and *trough*.

U-SHAPED VALLEY

V-SHAPED VALLEY

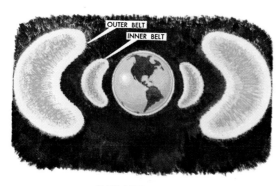

VAN ALLEN BELTS

Van Allen \ 'van 'al-ən \ belts

The Van Allen belts are a pair of dough-nut-shaped radiation zones that encircle the earth. The belts are made up of a mixture of high energy protons and electrons. The earth's magnetic field keeps the protons and electrons from escaping into space or reaching the earth's surface.

The protons and electrons that make up most of the belts come from the sun, cosmic rays and high altitude, man-made nuclear explosions.

The inner Van Allen belt is between 1,400 and 3,400 miles from the earth's surface. The outer belt is between 5,000 and 12,000 miles out. The 2 belts follow the magnetic lines of force around the earth. They are strongest and thickest near the earth's magnetic equator. They are thinnest over the poles, where they almost disappear.

Radiation in the Van Allen belts is very much like X rays. The rays are dangerous to life. For this reason, astronauts traveling through the belts must be shielded against them.

The Van Allen belts were not discovered until man began to send artificial satellites into space. They are named for James A. Van Allen, whose study led to the discovery of the belts in 1958. The belts were detected by a Geiger counter in Explorer I, the first U.S. artificial satellite.

vanilla

The vanillas make up a group of climbing vine plants which grow in tropical jungles. They belong to the orchid family. Vanillas have aerial rootlets as well as ordinary roots that extend down into the soil.

Vanilla is native to Central America and Mexico. It is now grown as a commercial crop in many tropical areas including the East and West Indies.

Vanilla pods are harvested while green. They are dried and put through a long process to remove the vanilla oil that is used as flavoring.

The best vanilla flavoring comes from a kind of vanilla (illustrated) that grows in southeastern Mexico. It was cultivated by the Indians long before Spanish explorers came to the New World.

This vanilla plant has thick, fleshy leaves, 6 to 8 inches long and about 2 inches wide. The white or greenish flowers are trumpet-shaped. The fruit is a pod 6 to 8 inches long and about ½ inch across. It contains many small seeds in a black, oily pulp. The pod shrinks and turns dark brown as it dries.

VANILLA

VELVET ANT

vein \ vān \

A vein is a crack or seam in a rock containing mineral matter different from the surrounding rock. Veins may run through a rock, somewhat as blood vessels run through a human body.

Some veins were formed when water carrying minerals seeped into the rock. The water evaporated, leaving the mineral. Other veins were formed as igneous rock cooled. Liquids containing metals and gases flowed toward the surface, cooling more slowly than the rock. Such veins, often found in granite, are sometimes called dikes.

Veins occur at different depths in the earth's crust and are of different thicknesses. Some are in thin sheets. Others are several feet thick. Veins may be a few inches long or miles in length.

Ores containing metals such as gold, silver, lead and zinc occur in veins. When several ore-bearing veins are found close together, the deposit is called a lode.

velvet ant

Velvet ants are not true ants, but wasps. They are covered with short, velvety hairs. They are called ants because the wingless females look something like ants.

About 200 kinds of velvet ants are known. Most kinds are less than ½ inch long. The males are larger than the females, and the sexes are marked differently. Only the females have stingers. Most velvet ants are bright colored. They may be red, orange or yellow, marked with black, brown or white.

Velvet ants usually live in open, sandy places. The males may fly around flowers. The females scurry about on the ground, as ants do.

Female velvet ants lay their eggs in the nests of other kinds of wasps, on top of larvae already in the nest. The velvet ant larvae feed on the other larvae. After feeding they spin silky cocoons. Adult velvet ants come from the cocoons 8 to 10 days after they are spun.

The cow killer (illustrated) is 1 of the largest kinds of velvet ants. It is so named because it was once thought that the sting of the female was fatal to cows and other large animals. The male is about 1 inch long, and the female about $\frac{7}{10}$ inch long. Both are marked with bright red and black. The cow killer is fairly common in the southeastern U.S.

ventifact \ 'vent-ə-ˌfakt \

A ventifact is a stone or pebble that has been shaped and polished by the wind. Dust and sand carried by the wind have

VENTIFACT

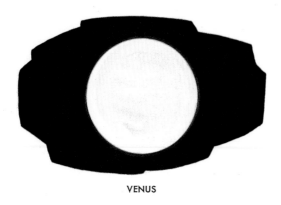

VENUS

scraped against the rock for a long time. As a result, its shape is different from its original form. The word ventifact comes from Latin words meaning "made by the wind."

Some ventifacts have ridges or look like pyramids or fans. Others look like Brazil nuts and are 3-sided.

Ventifacts are usually found on ocean beaches or on deserts. They are sometimes found where there is no sand, and where plants and grasses grow. Such ventifacts show that the climate in the region has changed.

Venus \ 'vē-nəs \

Venus is the earth's nearest neighbor in the solar system. Because of its nearness to the earth, Venus is the brightest natural object in the sky except for the sun and moon. It is sometimes called the Morning Star or the Evening Star, depending on when it appears.

In size, mass and surface gravity, Venus is very much like the earth. Venus is about 7,700 miles in diameter, while the earth is 7,927 miles in diameter. Venus is about 67 million miles from the sun, and it completes 1 orbit around the sun every 225 days. Once every 19 months it passes within 26 million miles of the earth.

Because Venus is inside the earth's orbit, it passes through phases as the moon does. It appears brightest when crescent-shaped, since at that time it is nearest to the earth.

The surface of Venus is hidden by thick, dense clouds. The clouds are mostly carbon dioxide, and they are yellowish-white. U.S. and Russian space probes indicate that the surface temperature is about 536° F. The probes also indicated that Venus rotates once every 244 days, and that it always presents the same face to the earth.

See *The Sun, the Moon and the Planets* on p. 502.

Venus's-flytrap \ ˌvē-nə-səz-'flī-ˌtrap \

Venus's-flytrap is a carnivorous plant that captures and feeds on insects, insect larvae and other small animals. It is a perennial that grows only in North and South Carolina. There is little or no nitrogen in the acid bog soil where Venus's-flytraps grow.

The rounded, fringed end of the leaf is hinged along the midrib and it folds shut when an insect lights on it. Sensitive hairs on the surface of the leaf trigger this action, which takes 10 to 20 seconds. Very small insects have time to escape as the leaf closes. Larger ones are trapped inside. Glands on the leaf produce a digestive juice that breaks down the insect's body. From it, the plant obtains needed

VENUS'S-FLYTRAP

nitrogen that is lacking in the acid bog soil where the plant grows.

Five to 10 days after the leaf has closed on a victim, the leaf reopens. Animals as large as small frogs may be trapped and killed by the plants.

Venus's-flytrap grows from a bulb-like rootstock. Its leaves are 3 to 6 inches long. A cluster of small white flowers is borne at the top of a stem 8 to 12 inches tall.

verbena \ vər-'bē-nə \

Verbenas make up a group of flowering plants that grow mostly in North and South America. One kind grows in Europe and Asia.

Some verbenas are low-growing, creeping plants, while some stand erect. Some are annuals and some perennials. All bear clusters of slender, tube-shaped flowers that open out in 5 rounded lobes. The flowers are white, pink, red or purple. The fruit is a seedpod that separates into 4 parts, each containing 1 seed. The leaves are usually wedge-shaped, with ragged edges.

The verbena most common in the U.S. (illustrated) is a wild flower that grows on rocky ledges and in dry, sandy fields. Its stems are 8 to 20 inches long. They usually lie flat on the ground except for the tip end and the short branches which

VERBENA

VERMICULITE

bear the flower clusters. The flowers are about 1 inch long, and they are white, pink or lavender. The leaves are 3 to 4 inches long. This kind of verbena grows from Pennsylvania and Illinois south to Florida and Texas and as far west as Colorado.

vermiculite \ vər-'mik-yə-ˌlit \

Vermiculite is an unusual and useful mineral that expands rapidly when heated, increasing to about 20 times its original volume.

Something like mica, vermiculite contains magnesium, silica, oxygen and hydrogen. It is light brown in color. It sometimes has a bronze metallic luster on smooth surfaces.

Expanded vermiculite is a lightweight material that flakes apart in flat, smooth sheets. It is used as an insulating material, and for packing delicate objects. Plant seeds are sometimes started in vermiculite rather than in soil. Filters for purifying oil may contain vermiculite. Lightweight cement and plaster sometimes contain vermiculite instead of sand or gravel.

Large deposits of vermiculite have been found in the western U.S., mostly in Montana and in North and South Dakota. Deposits also occur in Russia, South Africa and Brazil.

VICUNA

vicuna \ vī-'k(y)ü-nə \

Vicunas are South American ruminant mammals related to camels, and closely related to llamas. They are a little smaller than llamas, and they have never been successfully domesticated as llamas have.

Vicunas are shy, alert animals that travel and graze in small herds. They live only on the higher slopes of the Andes Mountains, from Ecuador south to Chile. Hunted extensively, they are now quite rare and are protected by law in most areas.

The silky but thick wool of the vicuna is valuable as it can be spun and woven into soft, warm cloth. The vicuna is also a source of meat and of hides for leather.

The vicuna stands about 3 feet tall at the shoulders. It has a long neck, a stumpy head and long ears. The shaggy wool sometimes hangs down below the animal's knees.

Male vicunas usually collect a group of 12 to 16 females. The male is leader of this herd. He acts as lookout while the females feed on grass and other green plants. Usually, each female bears 1 young every other year, in February. The young vicuna stays with its mother for about 10 months.

violet

Violets make up a family of perennial flowering plants that grow in nearly all parts of the tropic and temperate zones. All have 5-petaled flowers borne singly at the tips of slender stems. The flowers are purple, blue, yellow or white. The fruit is a seedpod that divides into 3 sections, each containing many tiny seeds.

The violets most common in the U.S. are delicate wild flowers that grow 3 to 6 inches tall. They are most common in wooded areas or along the edges of fields, where they have some protection from the sun.

The common blue violet (illustrated) grows wild in the eastern half of North America. Its flowers may be either dark blue or purple, and they usually hang down from the tips of their stalks. The 5 petals are uneven, with the lowest petal the largest.

Both leaves and flowering stems grow up from ground level. The leaves are heart-shaped or oval.

Although the violets best known in the U.S. are low-growing plants, some kinds that grow in the tropics look like bushes or small trees.

Pansies are cultivated garden plants developed from violets.

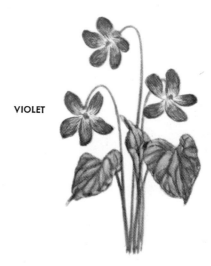

VIOLET

vireo \ 'vir-ē-ˌō \

Vireos are small, greenish-gray birds that live in the tops of trees and are rarely seen on the ground. They are not easy to identify, as they have no markings that can be seen from a distance. Males and females look just alike.

Ranging from central Canada south to Brazil, vireos live only in the New World. They eat mostly insects that they pick from the leaves and twigs of trees, along with berries that grow on trees or tall shrubs.

The female vireo builds a neat basket-like nest that is always hung from a forked tree branch. The outside of the nest is often covered with lichens, cocoons or such things as scraps of newspaper, all fastened on with bits of spider web.

Both male and female birds incubate the 3 to 5 eggs. In warm areas vireos raise 2 broods of young birds during the summer. In cooler areas they raise 1 brood.

The red-eyed vireo (illustrated) is 5 to 6 inches long. In summer, it ranges through most parts of the U.S., as far north as Nova Scotia and British Columbia. In autumn, it migrates to southern Florida, the Bahamas and Central and South America.

VIREO

VIRGINIA BLUEBELL

Virginia bluebell \ vər-'jin-yə 'blü-ˌbel \

The Virginia bluebell is a wild flower that grows in nearly all parts of eastern North America.

The flowers are unusual because they change color as they open. In the bud, they are pink. When fully open, they shade from purple to a clear, bright blue. The flowers are about 1 inch long. Each has a tube-shaped corolla that opens out into a flaring bell-shaped mouth.

Virginia bluebell grows 12 to 20 inches tall. The leaves are 3 to 7 inches long, and are marked with a strong pattern of veins. The flowers appear in a loose cluster at the tops of the stalks, in April or May. The fruit is a dry pod containing 4 fairly large seeds that ripen in midsummer. By August, the leaves and stalks die back to the ground. The roots live through the winter and send up new stalks and leaves the following spring.

Virginia bluebell grows in wooded areas where the soil is rich and moist, and where it is shaded from the sun.

volcanic \ väl-'kan-ik \ **cone**

A volcanic cone is a hill or mountain built up by an active volcano. It surrounds the vent of the volcano. The cone is made of materials thrown out of the vent during eruptions of the volcano.

A volcano that produces only flows of liquid, molten rock creates a broad, gently-sloping lava cone.

A volcano that throws out rock fragments, cinders and dry ashes creates a steeper, more pointed cone.

Alternating eruptions of molten rock and dry cinders create a composite cone that slopes gently near the base but has a steep point at the top. Mt. Ranier in the U.S. and Fujiyama in Japan are composite cones.

See *composite cone*.

volcanic \ väl-'kan-ik \ neck

A volcanic neck is a stump-like, vertical mass of some hard, igneous rock such as basalt. It is lava that hardened inside the vent of a volcano after the volcano stopped erupting.

A volcanic neck is usually harder than the cone of volcanic material that piled up around the vent. It may remain after erosion has worn away the softer, looser material of the cone.

Small volcanic necks are 20 to 30 feet across. Very large ones are several miles across. Some are irregular in shape, while others have nearly vertical sides and flat tops so that they look like sawed-off tree trunks.

Devil's Tower in Wyoming is an exposed volcanic neck that stands 865 feet tall.

volcano

A volcano is a chimney-like opening in the earth's crust. This opening connects with some part of the earth's interior where there is great heat.

A volcanic eruption takes place when steam and other gases trapped deep underground become heated and expand. They force their way upward through the opening, carrying with them cinders and lava that are thrown out onto the earth's surface. Repeated eruptions build up a cone-shaped hill or mountain that surrounds the opening.

At one time or another there have been active volcanoes in nearly all parts of the world. The volcanoes that are active today, and have been active in the recent past, are grouped in limited areas. Most are in a circular band that surrounds the Pacific Ocean. A few are in the Mediterranean area and some are in a belt that extends through Indonesia and New Guinea.

Volcanoes are named for Vulcan, the Roman god of fire.

VOLCANIC NECK

VOLCANO

vole \ 'vōl \ (meadow mouse)

Voles make up a group of small rodents common in northern Europe, Asia and North America. They look very much like mice but they have plumper bodies and shorter tails. Their eyes and ears are small, and their snouts are fairly short and blunt.

Living mostly in open fields, voles eat grasses, seeds, nuts and sometimes insects. They are pests in some areas where they damage farm crops. Some kinds of voles collect large amounts of food and store it for the winter. Some nest in tufts of grass, while others dig snug underground burrows.

Voles reproduce very rapidly, but they do not live long and they have many natural enemies. Snakes, hawks, owls and shrews are some of the animals that kill and eat large numbers of voles.

The meadow vole (illustrated) is fairly common in North America, from Alaska and Labrador south to New Mexico and Georgia. It usually builds a globe-shaped nest of grass. It may also use burrows in summer, for protection from the hot sun.

A female meadow vole may bear litters of 5 to 7 young every 2 weeks during the warmer parts of the year. The young grow to full size in 3 weeks.

VOLE

VULTURE

vulture \ 'vəl-chər \

Vultures are large birds with bare, featherless heads and long wings. They are scavengers, animals that feed on garbage and the flesh of dead animals.

The vultures of Asia, Europe and Africa are related to eagles, hawks and kites, while the vultures of America make up a separate family. The New World vultures are larger and have longer legs than the Old World vultures. They usually nest on the ground, while Old World vultures nest in trees. The turkey vulture (illustrated), the black vulture, the California condor and the Andes condor all belong to the New World vulture family.

The turkey vulture is up to 2½ feet long, with a 6-foot wingspread. It soars gracefully in wide circles, rarely flapping its wings, as its keen eyes scan the ground for food.

This bird nests among rocks, or on mountain ledges. The female usually lays 2 eggs, sometimes 3 or 4. The eggs are incubated for about 6 weeks. Young turkey vultures have white down on their heads as well as on their bodies and wings.

The turkey vulture ranges from southern Canada and New England south to Chile and Argentina. In the U.S., it is most common in the southern states.

W

wahoo \ 'wä-ˌhü \

The wahoo is a kind of mackerel. It is a valuable food and game fish found mostly in tropical parts of the oceans.

Very large wahoos are 6 feet long and weigh up to 125 pounds. Most weigh 20 to 30 pounds.

Like all mackerel, the wahoo has a streamlined body that is narrow at the base of the tail. Rows of tiny finlets run from the second dorsal fin to the tail, and from the anal fin to the tail. The sides of the body are marked with dark vertical bands that extend down below the lateral line.

The wahoo has a longer, more pointed snout than most mackerel. Because of its large teeth and the shape of its mouth, the wahoo is sometimes mistaken for the great barracuda.

The wahoo is fairly common in the Atlantic near the West Indies. Sometimes it follows the Gulf stream as far north as Cape Hatteras.

walkingstick \ 'wȯ-king-ˌstik \

Walkingsticks make up a family of slow-moving insects with long, narrow bodies that look like twigs. The antennae and legs are very slender. The kinds of walkingsticks common in the U.S. and Canada are wingless. Some tropical kinds have

WAHOO

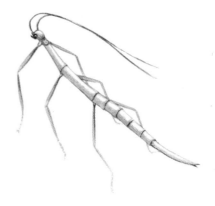

WALKINGSTICK

wings and are called walking leaves. All kinds depend on their appearance for protection from their enemies. On certain shrubs or trees they are nearly invisible.

Walkingsticks are gray, green or yellow. Some kinds give off an unpleasant smell. In the temperate zone, female walkingsticks are 2 to 3 inches long and the males are smaller.

All walkingsticks have chewing mouthparts and feed on the leaves of trees. They are seldom serious pests, as many birds eat them and keep their numbers under control.

The female walkingstick lays 100 or more eggs in late summer, 1 egg at a time. The eggs fall to the ground and remain there, among dead leaves, until they hatch the following spring. Young walkingsticks look like adults but are usually yellowish. They molt 5 or 6 times as they grow to full size.

The common walkingstick (illustrated) ranges from the Atlantic coast west to the Rocky Mountains, and from Ontario and Manitoba south to Texas.

wallaby \ 'wäl-ə-bē \

Wallabies make up a group of pouched mammals that belong to the kangaroo family. They are much like kangaroos but they are usually smaller and more

WALLABY

brightly colored. Wallabies live in Australia, New Guinea and Tasmania.

The smallest wallabies are about the size of rabbits. The largest are about 6 feet long, including the tail. All have large ears and hand-like forepaws. Their hind feet are long and narrow. Their round, furry tails taper gradually toward the end.

Wallabies are mostly gray or reddish-brown, but many are marked with black, white, dark brown or yellowish-brown. Some kinds are hunted for their fur or hides.

Traveling in large herds, wallabies move from place to place feeding on grass and leaves. Some dig for roots. They do not build dens or nests, but they sometimes rest in gullies or ravines where they are sheltered from the sun. Some kinds live on open, grassy plains, while other kinds live on rocky hillsides.

About 6 weeks after mating the female bears 1 young. Blind, helpless and about 1 inch long, the young wallaby creeps into the mother's pouch and remains there for as long as 8 months.

The pretty-faced wallaby (illustrated) has thick, shaggy fur. It is mostly gray, with white markings on the cheeks and ears. The long, round tail is furred all the way to the tip.

walleye \ 'wȯ-ˌlī \ (walleyed pike)

The walleye is not a pike, but a freshwater fish of the perch family. It is a favorite of fishermen in the eastern half of the U.S. and Canada. It is the largest of the perches. It may grow to 3 feet in length and weigh as much as 25 pounds. Most walleyes weigh 3 to 5 pounds.

The walleye spends most of the year in deep water. Walleyes swim in schools. They feed mostly at night, on smaller fish, crayfish and insects. Walleyes have large eyes, adapted to seeing in dim light.

The head and jaws of the walleye are long, and the mouth contains strong, sharp teeth. The first dorsal fin is stiff and spiny, while the second is soft. The scales have tiny barbs on them and feel rough.

In spring, walleyes move into shallow water to spawn. The female lays up to 50,000 eggs in a long, sticky string that clings to underwater rocks or plants. The eggs hatch about 10 days later. The young fish grow very quickly, and usually stay together until autumn. They probably begin to eat smaller fish, such as tiny minnows, when only about 3 inches long. The females first lay eggs when they are 3 years old and about 14 inches long.

Walleyes live in lakes and in clean, fairly deep streams, from Hudson Bay south to Georgia and west to the upper Mississippi Valley.

WALLEYE

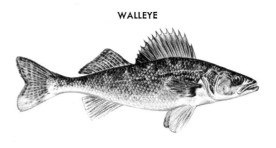

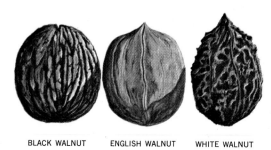

BLACK WALNUT   ENGLISH WALNUT   WHITE WALNUT

WALNUTS

walnut tree

Walnuts make up a group of fast-growing trees valued for their wood and for their edible nuts. Walnuts grow in North America, the West Indies and in parts of South America and eastern Asia.

All walnuts have compound leaves made up of pointed leaflets. The number of leaflets is always uneven. One leaflet stands alone at the tip of the leaf. Small greenish flowers are borne on the twigs in spring. The sweet, oily seeds ripen in autumn, inside a hard, woody shell and a thick husk.

The black walnut, one of America's most valuable timber trees, grows to 150 feet tall with a straight trunk 3 to 6 feet across. It ranges throughout eastern North America and as far west as Kansas. Its wood is hard and strong, and is used for fine furniture and veneer. The nut (illustrated) is sweet and oily.

The English walnut is native to southern and eastern Asia, rather than to England. Cultivated since Roman times for its large, thin-shelled nut (illustrated), this tree is grown commercially in California and Oregon.

The white walnut, also called butternut, grows in eastern North America as far south as Virginia. Its wood is not strong. Pioneers used the hull from the nut (illustrated) to make yellow dye for cloth.

walrus \ 'wȯl-rəs \

The walrus makes up a family of large aquatic mammals related to the seals. Males are up to 16 feet long and weigh as much as 3,000 pounds. Females are smaller, about 8 feet long. Both sexes have tusks. The tusks of the male may grow 2 feet long.

Walruses once ranged along all arctic coastlines. They are now rare in most areas, as they have been widely hunted for their ivory tusks, their oil and their thick, tough hides. Walruses are now protected by law.

Awkward on land, walruses are expert swimmers and divers. They use their tusks to dredge the ocean floor for the mollusks and crustaceans they eat. Stiff bristles around their mouths strain smaller bits of food from the mud and sand they dredge up. When attacked, walruses fight fiercely and make loud bellowing sounds.

In herds of 50 to 100, walruses migrate south to warmer waters in winter. They spend most of their time in the sea, but sometimes drag themselves onto ice floes or rocks to sleep. Males may mate with several females. Females bear 1 or 2 young every other year.

A young walrus is gray and has no tusks and bristles. It rides on the mother's

WALRUS

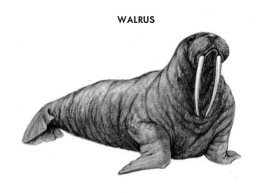

neck when small, and stays with the mother for about 2 years.

The Atlantic walrus (illustrated) lives in the colder waters north of Labrador.

wapiti\ 'wäp-ət-ē \ (American elk)

The wapiti is a large mammal of the deer family. It stands about as tall as a horse. Mature bulls weigh up to 1,000 pounds. In the deer family, only the moose is larger and heavier. Early settlers called the wapiti an elk, since it looked much like the true elk of Europe.

The wapiti is reddish brown, with darker, shaggy fur around the neck and white on the tail. Bulls have sharp-pointed, branching antlers up to 5 feet long.

Once common throughout much of North America, the wapiti now lives only in wilderness areas of Canada and Alaska and on game preserves in the western states.

Wapiti travel longer distances than deer or moose. They usually move onto higher mountain slopes in summer, and spend the winter in sheltered valleys. They eat mostly grass, moss and lichens. Bulls spend most of the year alone, while females and young animals feed and travel in herds.

In autumn, bulls make loud, trumpet-

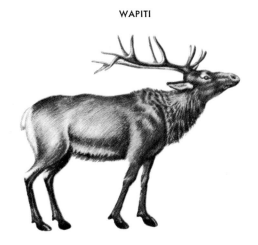

WAPITI

WARBLER

ing sounds and fight fiercely for females. Young wapiti are yellowish and spotted. They are born in May or June, and they stay with their mothers until autumn.

warbler\ 'wȯr-blər \

Warblers are small, very active birds that make up 2 different families, the Old World warblers and the New World or wood warblers. Warblers live in nearly all parts of the world. They are nearly all tree dwellers that eat insects they pick from leaves and twigs. Some kinds also eat seeds and berries.

About 50 different kinds of New World warblers spend the summer in North America. They are black and white, brown or olive green. Some are marked with yellow, red or blue. The males are usually more colorful than the females. Some change color with the season, losing their brightest markings before they fly south in autumn.

Warblers migrate in large flocks, flying at night. They are often confused by bright lights or high winds, so that they collide with each other or fly into the sides of buildings.

Most warblers build neat, cup-shaped nests in trees. The female does most of the nest building. She incubates the 4 or 5 eggs for about 12 days.

The black-throated blue warbler (illustrated) is a wood warbler about 5 inches long. It nests from New England west to Minnesota and, in the eastern mountains, as far south as Georgia.

For members of the Old World warbler family, see *gnatcatcher* and *kinglet*.

warthog \ 'wȯrt-ˌhȯg \

The warthog is a wild South African mammal that belongs to the swine family. It is named for the 3 pairs of large wart-like knobs on its face.

The warthog is about 5 feet long and stands 28 to 30 inches high at the shoulder. It may weigh 200 pounds. There is little hair on its thick gray hide except for a mane of long bristles along its spine. The thin tail looks something like a piece of old rope.

The large head has white side whiskers and a shovel-like snout. The upper pair of tusks is dull and curves backward. The sharp lower pair helps the warthog defend itself and root for food.

The warthog can run as fast as 30 miles an hour. Each foot has 4 toes, with the 2 middle toes developed into hoofs.

A nocturnal animal, the warthog feeds on grass, other plants and roots. It lives in a burrow and usually backs in, so that its head and sharp tusks face any enemy.

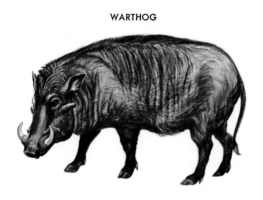

WARTHOG

WASP

The sow gives birth to 3 or 4 young at a time. Several sows and their young usually live together. Boars usually live alone.

wasp

Wasps make up several families of insects closely related to ants and bees. Most wasps are useful to man because they pollinate plants and eat the larvae of harmful insects.

Some kinds of wasps are solitary, while others are carnivorous or parasitic. A few kinds of female wasps sting if they are disturbed. All wasps have 4 wings. Length varies from very small to over 1 inch. All have biting mouthparts.

The blue mud dauber (illustrated) is a social wasp belonging to the family of thread-waisted wasps. This wasp is nearly an inch long and has a metallic blue body. The blue mud dauber lives near damp ground and is fairly common in the U.S.

Blue mud daubers do not build their own nests as true mud dauber wasps do. Instead, they use nests already built by true mud daubers. Blue mud daubers take out whatever is in the nests and fill the cells with spiders that they have paralyzed by stinging. The female then lays an egg on the last spider and seals the cell.

The larva feeds on the stored spiders and pupates over the winter. In the spring, it comes out of the cell as an adult wasp.

For other kinds of wasps, see *hornet, horntail, velvet ant* and *yellow jacket.*

waterbuck \ 'wȯt-ər-ˌbək \

Waterbucks make up a group of ruminant mammals that belong to the antelope family. Although they live in the warmest parts of Africa, their bodies are covered with long, shaggy hair. Like other antelopes, they are swift runners.

Waterbucks stand 4 to 5 feet tall at the shoulder. They are reddish-brown or grayish-brown, with white markings on the throat and face. The ears are large and spade-shaped. The tail is long and tufted at the end.

Only male waterbucks have horns 2 to 3 feet long. The horns are yellowish, ringed with brown, and they are ridged near the base. The tips curve slightly inward.

As the name suggests, these animals usually live near water. They feed on grasses and other plants, on open plains and along streams. When frightened, they sometimes plunge into the water. Waterbucks are almost never seen in deep forests.

Bulls collect a herd of about 20 females

WATER GAP

WATERBUCK

and young, and chase other males away. Females bear 1 or 2 young about 8 months after mating.

The common East African waterbuck (illustrated) stands about 4 feet tall at the shoulder.

water gap \ 'gap \

A water gap is a narrow opening cut by a stream across a mountain ridge. In places where the stream continues to flow, the opening is called a water gap. If the water is no longer there, the opening is called a wind gap.

In the U.S., water gaps made it easier for settlers to cross through the Appalachian Mountains. Roads and railroads are often routed through water gaps.

Harpers Ferry Gap was cut through the Blue Ridge Mountains by the Potomac River. Cumberland Gap in the Appalachians is on the border of Kentucky, Tennessee and Virginia. It is now a wind gap. South Pass in Wyoming is the gap by which travelers on the Oregon Trail crossed the Rockies.

water lily

Water lilies are not true lilies, but make up a separate family of perennial plants that grow in shallow, fresh water. They live in nearly all parts of the temperate and tropic zones, in ponds, lakes and slow-moving streams.

Water lilies grow from thick rootstocks or tubers buried in mud, under the water. These tubers contain starch and are eaten like potatoes in some parts of the world. The leaves and flowers are borne on separate stems that grow up from the roots. The stems and leaves contain air passages. In some kinds, both leaves and flowers float on the surface of the water. In other kinds, leaves and flowers are lifted up above the surface.

The large, fragrant flowers are white, pink, red, purple or blue. They are surrounded by green sepals that cover the petals when the flowers close. Some kinds have flowers that open only at night. Other kinds have flowers that open only during the day. The seeds are berry-like.

The common water lily has white or pinkish flowers from 3 to 5 inches across. The leathery leaves are broad and rounded, and the underside is purplish. The common water lily grows wild in ponds and lakes throughout eastern North America.

watermelon

The watermelon is a vine plant that belongs to the gourd family. Its juicy red fruit has been a popular food since the days of early Egypt. The watermelon is native to tropical Africa, but is now widely grown in many parts of the world.

The watermelon grows best in rich sandy soil and needs a long growing season. The vine may branch out 12 feet in several directions. The vine has many, yellow, 5-part flowers. Staminate and pistillate flowers grow separately on the same plant, and each flower produces either pollen or fruit. The broad, alternate leaves are divided into segments.

The fruit of the watermelon varies in weight from 2 to 50 pounds or more. The fruit has a hard green rind or outer covering. When ripe, the flesh inside is red, white, pink or yellow. The many seeds may be black or white. The fruit is 93 percent water. It has little food value, but is grown for its flavor.

In the U.S. watermelons are raised in many southern states, Arizona and California. The states that produce the most watermelons are Florida and Texas.

waterspout \ 'wȯt-ər-ˌspau̇t \

A waterspout is a narrow, twisting column of water that rises above a body of water. A waterspout may be formed when a funnel cloud forms at the base of a low-hanging cumulus or cumulonimbus cloud. The funnel circles rapidly and a low pressure area forms in the center. Moist air is

WATERMELON

WATERSPOUT

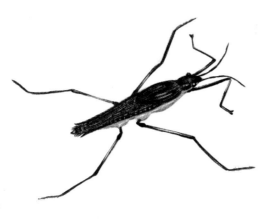

WATER STRIDER

drawn into the center. Water from the surface of the lake or ocean is also drawn up into the center.

Another kind of waterspout is caused when a tornado moves from the land to the sea or other body of water.

Algae and small fish may be lifted up by a waterspout. They are carried for a distance and dropped.

A waterspout may reach several hundred feet into the air. Waterspouts form most often in the tropics. They usually break up near land.

water strider \ 'strīd-ər \

Water striders make up a family of long-legged aquatic insects that can run rapidly on top of the water. They live on the surface of fresh or salt water.

The body of the water strider is usually less than ½ inch long. About half of the body is the thorax.

The 2 front legs are short. The middle and hind legs are long and slender. The hind legs have fine hairs, which allow the insect to skate on the surface of the water. To keep the hairs dry, the water strider lifts its legs often. If the hairs become wet, the insect may drown.

Some water striders have wings. Others do not. Winged kinds fly at night.

Water striders live on the juices of dead

or living insects which fall upon the water. They grasp their prey with their front legs.

The female water strider lays her eggs in a sticky mass on the leaves and stems of aquatic plants. The young hatch in 2 or 3 weeks. They look much like adults, but are smaller and have no wings. Adults hibernate in the winter under leaves or mud in dried-up streams.

A common kind of water strider (illustrated) lives throughout the northern part of the U.S. and in Canada.

waves

Waves are disturbances of the surface of the water. They are usually caused by wind, but they may also be caused by earthquakes.

When the wind blows against the surface of the water, it transfers its energy to the water. The particles of surface water in turn transfer the energy to the particles next to them. The energy of the wave travels along, but the water moves very little. The wind lifts the water up slightly, while gravity pulls it down. The water particles follow a fairly flat, circular path.

A cork dropped into a tub of water will show that the water moves little. When the surface of the water is disturbed, the cork stays with the water. It bobs up and

SHORT WAVES

LONG WAVES

down as the wave passes, but it does not travel with the wave.

The size of waves depends on the strength of the wind, the length of time it blows and the distance it travels over the water.

Newly formed waves are usually short waves (illustrated). They are choppy and often have whitecaps. They do not reach far below the surface of the water. Short waves are also called surface waves. They are most common in the open ocean bays and lakes. As short waves move out from the place where they were formed, they may become longer.

Long waves (illustrated) are also called swells. They have round tops and seldom have whitecaps. Long waves travel 15 to 35 miles an hour and may be 55 feet high. They are caused by high winds blowing continuously over large areas.

Long waves reach farther below the surface than can short waves. New winds may cause them to grow in size as they near land. When long waves break on the shore, they are sometimes called surf.

The largest waves are ones caused by violent windstorms such as hurricanes, or waves that have traveled across wide oceans. Some of the giant waves that break on the west coast of the U.S. have traveled all the way from New Zealand.

waxwing \ 'waks-wing \

Waxwings make up a family of brownish, crested birds that live in all parts of the northern hemisphere. They are named for the tiny red droplets of a wax-like substance that form at the tips of some wing feathers.

All waxwings have black around their eyes and on their throats, and a band of bright color at the tip of the tail. They are 6 to 8 inches long.

Waxwings feed and travel in flocks and usually nest near each other. They eat mostly fruit, including the berries of cedar and juniper trees. In summer they also eat flower petals and insects. The young birds are fed on insects.

Three to 6 grayish, speckled eggs are laid in a cup-shaped nest on a tree branch. The male bird helps to incubate the eggs, or brings food to the female while she is on the nest.

The kind best known in America is the cedar waxwing (illustrated). This bird is 6 to 7 inches long, and has a bright yellow band at the tip of the tail. It nests in Canada and in the northern U.S., and winters from the Great Lakes south to Central America.

The Bohemian waxwing lives in the far western U.S. and in Europe and Asia. It is slightly larger than the cedar waxwing and its color is more gray.

WAXWING

WEASEL

weasel \ 'wē-zəl \

Weasels make up a family of small, carnivorous mammals that live in nearly all parts of the world. They are fierce hunters that sometimes kill animals many times their own size. At times, weasels seem to kill for the love of killing.

Many animals of the weasel family are hunted or trapped for their valuable fur. Most have well-developed musk glands and give off a strong odor.

Most of the weasels that live in the northern hemisphere are about 18 inches long.

The least weasel (illustrated) averages about 7 inches long, including the 1½-inch tail. It is the smallest of the weasels, and one of the smallest of all carnivorous mammals. In summer, it is brown above and white below. In winter, it turns white all over.

The least weasel catches and kills mice, shrews, insects, snails and other small animals. It lives in woods and in open fields. Its den is a hole in the ground.

The female least weasel bears 2 or 3 litters a year, at different seasons. There are 3 to 10 young in a litter.

Most common in Canada and Alaska, the least weasel ranges as far south as Pennsylvania and Montana.

For other members of the weasel family, see *American sable, badger, ferret, fisher, mink, otter, sable, sea otter, skunk* and *wolverine.*

weevil \ 'wē-vəl \

Weevils make up a group of insect pests that destroy millions of dollars' worth of farm crops each year. Some live inside seeds such as peas and beans, nuts and acorns. Other kinds feed on the roots, stems and leaves of growing plants. The smallest kinds are about $\frac{1}{25}$ inch long. The largest kinds are about 3 inches long.

The weevils that damage growing plants belong to a family of beetles. They have hard bodies and long heads that taper to a pointed snout. In most kinds, the female lays eggs 1 at a time, in slits cut in plant stems or leaves. The worm-like, legless larvae live inside the plant, and pass through the pupal stage there.

A few kinds of weevils lay eggs in the soil, near plants the larvae can feed on. Some kinds pass through the complete life cycle, from egg to adult, in 3 weeks. Other kinds take 1 to 3 years.

The cotton boll weevil (illustrated) is usually about ¼ inch long. Its larvae live in the buds of cotton plants, destroying them from the inside so that no cotton fibers are produced. In winter, adults hibernate in dead plants or in the soil, near cotton fields.

The cotton boll weevil is native to Central America and Mexico but it is now common in all the cotton-growing states of the U.S.

WEEVIL

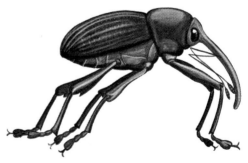

whale

Whales make up a group of large aquatic animals that includes the largest of all living animals. Although whales look like fish and spend all their lives in the sea, they are mammals. They are warm-blooded and breathe air. Their young are born alive and fed on milk.

The smallest whales are about 5 feet long. The largest ones are 100 feet long and weigh about 150 tons. Whales live in all oceans and in some rivers and lakes. Many kinds spend the winter fairly near the equator but move to feeding grounds near the poles in summer. Most kinds feed and travel in groups or schools.

Females give birth to 1 young, called a calf, every other year. Twins are rare. The young swim as soon as they are born.

A thick layer of fat surrounds the whale's body and insulates it from the cold water. Whale oil made from this fat has many uses. Ambergris, used in making perfume, and spermaceti, used in cosmetics and medicines, are other valuable products that come from whales. Some kinds of whales have been hunted until they are now nearly extinct.

Whales have powerful tails that they use for swimming. The small flippers that take the place of forelegs are used only for balance and steering.

These animals spend most of their time near the surface of the sea. They dive deep only to seek food, or to escape from their enemies. Some kinds can stay under water for about 30 minutes.

At the top of the head is a single nostril, or blowhole. When a whale exhales, warm, moist air from its lungs forms a steamy cloud called a spout.

Whales are divided into 2 groups called baleen or whalebone whales, and toothed whales.

Baleen whales eat floating plants as well as tiny fish and crustaceans such as shrimp. Inside their mouths are curtain-like fringes of tough baleen that strain plankton from seawater. The blue, finback, gray, humpback and right whales are all baleen whales. All have been widely hunted and are now rare.

Toothed whales kill and eat large fish, cuttlefish and squid. The killer, pilot and sperm whales are all toothed whales.

The blue whale, up to 100 feet long, is the largest of all animals. Newborn calves are 23 to 26 feet long. Now rare, the blue whale is found mostly in the coldest parts of the oceans.

The gray whale, 30 to 50 feet long, lives in the Pacific Ocean. The humpback whale, 40 to 50 feet long, and the finback whale, 60 to 80 feet long, live in both the Atlantic and Pacific oceans.

Old-time whaling men named the right whales, saying they were the "right" whales to capture. Their mouths contain very long slabs of whalebone which were once very valuable. Right whales are 50 to 70 feet long. The North Atlantic right whale (illustrated) is now quite rare.

The killer whale, 20 to 30 feet long, has 48 sharp teeth in its powerful jaws. Hunting in packs, killer whales attack almost anything alive. They kill seals, dolphins, large squid and other whales.

Pilot whales, 15 to 18 feet long, are named for their habit of following a leader. They swim in large schools, often 1,000 together. One kind (illustrated) is hunted in northern seas, for its oil.

The sperm whale, 30 to 60 feet long, is the largest of the toothed whales. Its diet is mostly squid. Its very heavy, squared-off head contains the valuable sperm oil which is like liquid wax. It was once used in lamps, and to make fine candles. The book *Moby Dick*, by Herman Melville, describes a giant sperm whale.

For other kinds of whales, see *dolphin* and *porpoise*.

Whales—Giants of the Sea

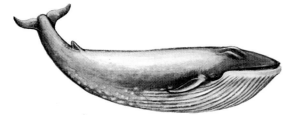

BLUE WHALE

FINBACK WHALE

GRAY WHALE

HUMPBACK WHALE

KILLER WHALE

PILOT WHALE

RIGHT WHALE

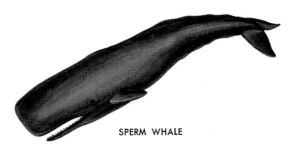

SPERM WHALE

WHEAT

wheat

Wheat makes up a group of about 10 kinds of plants belonging to the grass family. They are annuals and biennials that grow best in cool, fairly dry parts of the temperate zone. The grain, or seed, of wheat is the source of flour and has been important since ancient times.

Common wheat (illustrated) is probably native to Asia, but it is now the most important cereal grain in Europe, North America and Australia. Rice is more important in Asia.

Common wheat has been cultivated for about 6,000 years, and many different varieties have been developed. Some varieties are planted in the spring, while others are planted in the fall and live through the winter. Common wheat grows 20 to 48 inches tall.

The leaves of wheat look like grass blades. They are 12 to 16 inches long and about ½ inch wide. The slender stems are hollow. The flowers, borne in clusters at the tops of the stems, are tiny green spikes. The seed or grain is ⅛ to ¼ inch long. Each seed is enclosed in a tight outer husk. Some varieties have stiff hairs called beards on the husks.

Common wheat is green in spring, turning golden yellow when the seeds ripen in summer.

whelk \ 'hwelk \

Whelks make up a family of marine gastropods. They are carnivorous mollusks with spiral shells that live on the sea floor in many parts of the world. Whelks are used as human food, especially in European countries. In other places they are used as bait by fishermen.

Whelk shells are thick and heavy, and are 3 to 16 inches long. The outer surface, usually marked with ribs and ridges, is grayish or yellow-brown. The smooth inner surface is white or yellowish. The opening is wide and rounded.

Tropical whelks are usually more colorful than those found in cooler waters.

The living whelk has a muscular foot for creeping. A rasping radula, edged with rows of teeth, is used for boring holes in the shells of other mollusks the whelk eats. The radula is also used to force apart the shells of clams. The whelk also eats worms and some crustaceans and fish. Fish and starfish eat whelks.

Whelks lay eggs that are enclosed in hard capsules. Clusters or strings of whelk eggs cling to rocks or shells on the sea floor until they hatch.

The channeled whelk (illustrated) is 5 to 7 inches long. Its shell is found on beaches along the Atlantic coast of North America, from Cape Cod south to Florida.

WHELK

whippoorwill\ 'hwip-ər-ˌwil\

The whippoorwill is a bird that belongs to the goatsucker family. It is a nocturnal insect eater that sleeps during the day.

The whippoorwill is named for the loud, whistling call it repeats over and over, as many as 1,000 times without stopping. The call is heard mostly at dusk and at dawn, and on moonlight nights.

Both male and female whippoorwills are mottled brown birds. They are hard to see against a background of fallen leaves or tree bark. The male, about 10 inches long, has white outer tail feathers and a narrow white band on the throat. The female, a little smaller, has dark tail feathers and a buff line on the throat.

Like the nighthawk, the whippoorwill has strong wings but small, weak legs. It cannot walk or hop well. It eats only insects that it catches while flying with its large mouth wide open. Stiff bristles around the bill help to funnel the insects inside.

The 2 spotted eggs are laid on the bare ground, or among fallen leaves on the forest floor. They are incubated 16 to 20 days.

In summer, the whippoorwill is fairly common in the eastern U.S. and southern Canada. It winters in Florida and Central America.

WHIPPOORWILL

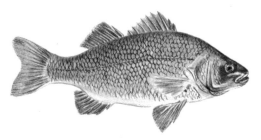

WHITE PERCH

white perch\ 'pərch\

The white perch is an edible fish most important to commercial fishermen in the Chesapeake Bay. It belongs to the sea bass family, but it lives in both salt and fresh water. It is found mostly in shallow water near shore, in bays and in the mouths of rivers that empty into the sea.

The white perch is 10 to 15 inches long and it weighs 2 to 3 pounds. It is dark olive or gray-green above, and silvery or yellowish below. Young white perch have horizontal stripes that fade as the fish become adults.

Swimming in large schools, white perch feed on smaller fish and crustaceans. In spring they enter rivers and travel upstream to spawn in fresh water. Some adults remain there, while others return to the sea. The eggs are sticky and cling together in clumps, or become attached to underwater plants or rocks.

White perch range along the Atlantic coast of North America, from Nova Scotia south to the Carolinas.

wild rice

Wild rice is an annual plant belonging to the grass family. Its grain is valued for its flavor and nourishment. American Indian tribes traveled long distances to harvest wild rice and store it for winter use.

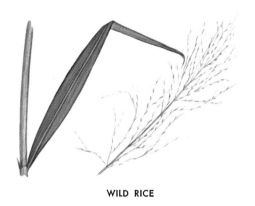

WILD RICE

Sportsmen plant it from seed as food for wild ducks and geese.

The plants are up to 10 feet tall, with leaves 18 inches long and about 2 inches wide. The small greenish flowers and the seeds are borne in loose, branching clusters 1 to 2 feet long. Each slender, purplish-black seed is about ¾ inch long.

Wild rice grows in quiet water 3 inches to 5 feet deep, where the bottom is muddy, along the edges of lakes and in marshy areas. It is found in scattered places throughout the eastern half of North America, but mostly in southern Canada and the northern U.S.

Some wild rice is produced commercially. Much of the crop is still harvested by Indians who paddle canoes among the plants and shake loose the ripe grain.

willow

Willows make up a family of fast-growing trees and shrubs. They grow in nearly all parts of the northern hemisphere and in some parts of Africa and South America. Some willows grow near the Arctic Circle, as far north as any trees grow.

About 70 different kinds of willows are native to North America. Most grow in moist soil, along the banks of streams.

The wood of willow trees is too soft and brittle to be very useful as lumber, but it is sometimes used for baskets and paper pulp. The leaves, buds and twigs provide food for such wildlife as birds, deer and elk. Willow trees are often planted along stream banks to control erosion.

All willows have narrow leaves that taper to a sharp point at the tip. The flowers are catkins or tassels ½ to 3 inches long that appear on the twigs in early spring. Staminate and pistillate flowers are borne on separate trees. Only trees with pistillate flowers produce seeds. Most willows are short-lived trees that seldom grow taller than 40 feet.

The weeping willow (illustrated) comes from China. It has slender, arching branches and limp twigs that hang down on or close to the ground.

The weeping willow has been widely planted as an ornamental tree, and it now grows throughout Europe and North America.

For other members of the willow family, see *poplar, pussy willow* and *quaking aspen.*

witch hazel \ 'hā-zəl \

Witch hazels are shrubs and small trees that bear spidery-looking yellow flowers in autumn or winter. The seeds ripen a year later, at about the same time new flowers appear on the trees.

WILLOW

WITCH HAZEL

WOLF

The leaves of witch hazels are irregular in shape and always uneven at the base. They have strongly marked veins. The flowers have 6 very narrow, curling petals. The seeds, about ¼ inch long, develop inside pointed, woody capsules. When the seed is ripe, the capsule bursts open and ejects it.

Witch hazels grow in eastern North America and in China and Japan. They are most common where the soil is moist, often along the edges of forests where they are partially shaded by taller trees.

The kind of witch hazel most common in the U.S. grows from Nova Scotia south to Georgia and as far west as Iowa and Minnesota. It is usually 10 to 25 feet tall. Its leaves (illustrated) are 4 to 6 inches long. The flowers (illustrated) appear between mid-September and November, usually 3 together near the ends of the branches. The seedpods are a dull orange-brown color. A soothing skin lotion is made from the leaves.

wolf

The wolves are wild, carnivorous animals of the dog family. Wolves once ranged throughout the northern hemisphere but they are now rare in civilized areas.

Men have always feared and hunted wolves. Actually, wolves seldom attack men, and they are useful in maintaining the balance of nature. Where there are no wolves, deer sometimes become too numerous for the available food supply, and die of starvation.

Wolves are 5 to 6 feet long, including the 16-inch tail. The largest ones weigh about 100 pounds. The shaggy fur is gray, blackish or reddish-brown.

Moving about mostly at night, wolves travel and hunt in small packs. Although they kill deer, cattle and sheep, their diet is mostly smaller wild animals such as rodents and rabbits. They live mostly in the brush, using burrows or rocky dens only while their young need shelter.

Wolves mate for life. The female bears 1 litter of 3 to 13 pups each year, in early spring. Newborn pups are blind and helpless. All members of a pack care for the pups.

The gray or timber wolf (illustrated) lives in western North America and in the wilderness areas of eastern Canada, Michigan, Wisconsin and Minnesota.

wolverine \ ˌwu̇l-və-ˈrēn \

Wolverines are the largest and most powerful members of the weasel family. Wolverines are 3½ feet long and stand about 1½ feet tall at the shoulders. They weigh

WOMBAT

up to 40 pounds. Indians and Eskimos kill wolverines for their fur, which is thick and very warm.

Although they look clumsy, wolverines are clever and savage hunters. They have been known to attack and kill animals as large as elk and deer. They are expert swimmers and catch fish with their long, sharp claws. Sometimes they climb trees and then drop down on their prey. They kill and eat animals caught in traps, and they steal food and other articles from hunters' cabins. Wolverines have no enemy except man.

Wolverines' dens are underground burrows or rocky caves. Solitary animals, they usually sleep during the day and prowl the woods hunting food at night.

Female wolverines give birth to a litter of 1 to 5 young in late spring. The newborn wolverines are almost entirely white. Until autumn, the young animals stay with the mother. By the following spring they are fully grown and ready to breed.

Wolverines once ranged throughout the cooler parts of the northern hemisphere, as far south as Maryland. They are now very rare.

The American wolverine (illustrated) lives only in wilderness areas of Alaska, Canada and the far northern U.S.

WOLVERINE

wombat \ 'wäm-ˌbat \

Wombats make up a group of Australian marsupials that look like small bears but in other ways resemble woodchucks. Unlike all other marsupials, wombats have front teeth that grow as long as they live.

Wombats are considered very good to eat, and their fur is used to make warm clothing and long-wearing rugs.

Most wombats are 2 to 4 feet long, with stocky bodies, stout legs and small tails or none at all. They weigh up to 80 pounds. Strong nails on the toes of the front feet are used for digging long tunnels that end in roomy dens lined with bark and grass.

Wombats usually sleep during the day and move about seeking food at night. They eat roots, tree bark, grass and fungi. The sound they make is a cough-like growl.

Usually 1 young is born at a time. It crawls into the mother's pouch and remains there for 5 to 8 months.

Now quite rare, wombats live only in southern Australia, Tasmania and on Flinders Island. The naked-nosed wombat (illustrated) lives in mountainous areas. It has fairly coarse fur and small ears. The hairy-nosed wombat lives on plains, near the coast. It has silkier fur and longer, more pointed ears.

WOODCHUCK

woodchuck (groundhog)

Woodchucks are rodents belonging to the squirrel family, and are related to chipmunks, gophers and prairie dogs. Their close relatives living in the western U.S. and in Europe are called marmots.

Woodchucks are about 26 inches long, including the 6-inch tail. Their heads are squirrel-like, with very small ears. The thick fur is usually dark reddish-brown.

The body is plump, and the legs are short. The small black paws are armed with sharp claws for digging.

Adult woodchucks live alone most of the year. Each has its own burrow, where it sleeps at night and hibernates during the winter months. The burrow is often dug at the edge of an open meadow. Woodchucks look all around them very carefully before they leave their burrows. Once outside, they are fearless and not at all shy. They eat green plants, and often damage valuable farm crops and garden vegetables.

In early spring, the female bears 1 litter of 2 to 6 young. Newborn woodchucks are furless, blind and helpless. They are mature when about 1 year old.

There is a superstitious belief that if a woodchuck sees its shadow on February 2, Groundhog Day, there will be 6 more weeks of cold weather.

woodpecker

Woodpeckers make up a large group of short-legged birds that perch upright on the trunks of trees, using their stiff tail feathers as props. On each foot are 2 toes that point forward and 2 that point backward. All woodpeckers have sharp, strong bills for pecking and boring into bark and wood. Nearly all have very long, sticky tongues with barbs on the end.

Woodpeckers eat mostly insects and insect larvae that they find in and under the bark of trees. Some kinds also eat ants and other insects that they find on the ground, and some eat seeds and berries or suck plant juices.

Some male woodpeckers peck on hollow tree trunks in spring, making loud drumming noises to attract females. Some kinds chisel large holes in dead trees to use as nests. The male often spends more time in the nest incubating the eggs than the female does.

Woodpeckers live in nearly all parts of the world where trees grow, except in Australia and Madagascar. Most woodpeckers native to North America are black and white, with some red or yellow markings.

The red-headed woodpecker (illustrated) lives throughout the eastern half

WOODPECKER

WOOLLY BEAR

of North America. It is 9 to 10 inches long.

For other kinds of woodpeckers, see *flicker* and *sapsucker*.

woolly \ 'wu̇l-ē \ bear

Woolly bears are plump, hairy caterpillars that appear in late summer or autumn. They are the larvae of tiger moths.

Woolly bears usually feed on grasses and other low-growing plants. Some kinds damage orchards by feeding on tree leaves.

Most kinds of woolly bears hibernate. In spring, they form cocoons and enter the pupal stage. In midsummer, woolly bears turn into moths with pale-colored, narrow wings and slender antennae.

Tiger moths are fairly common in most parts of the U.S. They lay their eggs on the undersides of leaves. The moths are most often seen clustered around outdoor lights at night.

The larva (illustrated) of the Isabella tiger moth is the hairiest of all woolly bears. It is reddish-brown in the middle and black at both ends. When disturbed, this larva rolls up into a ball.

worm

Worms make up a large group of limbless, crawling animals with long, soft bodies.

The smallest ones are microscopic, and the largest ones are many feet long. Some worms live in water, some live in soil, and some live in the bodies of other animals or inside plants.

Worms are generally divided into 3 large groups: flatworms, roundworms and annelid or segmented worms.

Flatworms include planarians and tapeworms. They are the simplest of all animals with 3 body layers and some kind of nervous system. Some have no digestive system and absorb food through the skin.

Roundworms include many parasites such as hookworms and guinea worms. They have a mouth at one end and a digestive tract running the length of the body. They also have a system of blood vessels.

Annelid worms are the most highly developed of the worms. Their bodies are nearly always divided into several segments. They have many different body organs, and a complex nervous system that includes a kind of brain. The earthworm is the best known of the annelid worms. The feather duster worm (illustrated) is a marine annelid that lives on the sea floor. It has around its mouth a cluster of tentacles that guide floating bits of food inside.

For other kinds of worms, see *annelid,*

WORM

ascaris, earthworm, filaria, flatworm, fluke, hookworm, leech, nereis, pinworm, planarian, tapeworm and *trichina.*

wren

Wrens make up a family of small perching birds. Most are brownish in color and are less than 6 inches long. The largest ones are 9 inches long. They nearly always hold their stubby tails tilted up when perching or hopping.

One kind, called the winter wren, lives throughout the northern hemisphere and is common in Europe and Asia. The others live only in North and South America.

Wrens live in brushy areas and thickets. They feed on insects and spiders. Some kinds of wrens use nesting boxes very near homes, in cities and suburban areas. Other kinds build dome-shaped nests with a small entrance on the side. The male does most of the nest building. Some kinds of wrens build a second nest to lure enemies away from the nest they are using. Females lay 2 to 10 eggs, several times during the summer.

The house wren (illustrated) spends the summer in nearly all parts of the U.S. and in southern Canada. It winters in Florida and along the Gulf coast, and throughout Mexico. The house wren has been known to nest in the pockets of coats left hanging outdoors.

y

yak \ 'yak \

The yak is a kind of cattle native to Tibet. Shaggy, very thick hair allows the yak to live on high mountain slopes and plateaus too cold for most animals. Because wild yaks have been widely hunted, they are now rare.

In Tibet, the yak has been domesticated since ancient times. The people of Tibet depend on the yak for milk, butter and meat. The hair is used for making ropes and cloth. The hide is made into leather. Dried yak dung is used for fuel. Yaks are sometimes ridden like horses, and they are also used as pack animals.

Like the American bison, the yak has a hump at the shoulder and a low head. The hollow, curving horns measure up to 40 inches long. Wild yaks are up to 6 feet tall at the shoulder. They are dark brown or grayish. Domesticated yaks are usually less than 5 feet tall. They are reddish-brown or spotted black and white.

Yaks feed on grass, and they sometimes obtain the water they need by eating snow. Females bear 1 or 2 calves in autumn. During most of the year, females and young feed and travel together in herds. The males live apart, in smaller herds.

WREN

YAK

YARROW

yarrow \ˈyar-ˌō\

Yarrows make up a group of perennial plants native to the north temperate zone. Most kinds bear flat-topped clusters of small white, yellow or pink flowers. The leaves are usually divided into narrow sections. In some, the leaves and stems are covered with short, white hairs.

Most yarrows are weeds, but some kinds are cultivated garden plants most often planted in rock gardens. Some low-growing yarrows are used as substitutes for lawn grass in dry, hot climates.

Common yarrow (illustrated) is a weed from Europe and Asia that is now fairly common in North America. It is a slender, erect plant with its branches near the tops of the stalks. It grows 12 to 24 inches tall. The lacy leaves are 1 to 7 inches long.

The flowers are usually white but sometimes pink. The leaves and stems give off a strong odor when crushed.

Common yarrow grows along roadsides, and in dry, open fields, in most parts of the U.S.

yeast \ˈyēst\

Yeasts make up a group of fungi. They include yeasts that live in the soil, on plants and in fruit, and the domesticated kind of yeast that is used in making bread. Yeasts have been used in making both bread and beer since about 2000 B.C.

Like other fungi, yeasts are primitive plants that lack chlorophyll and cannot manufacture their own food from minerals in the soil. They are saprophytes that feed on dead plant materials.

Unlike other kinds of fungi, yeasts do not develop any kind of plant body. They live only as single cells, and they reproduce mostly by budding.

Domesticated yeast is useful because it digests certain sugars, turning them into ethyl alcohol and carbon dioxide gas. Bread dough rises because the yeast in it produces tiny bubbles of carbon dioxide gas. Both the gas and the alcohol produced by the yeast disappear when the bread is baked.

Each cell of domestic yeast is about 1/3,000 inch wide. A small package of dry yeast contains billions of cells.

yellow daisy (black-eyed Susan, coneflower)

The yellow daisy is a tall, flowering weed that blooms from midsummer until autumn. It is a biennial that blooms the second year, and it is sometimes planted in flower gardens.

The branching stalks grow 1 to 3 feet tall. The pointed leaves are 3 to 4 inches long. Both stems and leaves are covered with short, stiff hairs, and they feel rough to the touch.

The flowering heads that are borne at

YELLOW DAISY

YELLOW JACKET

the tips of the stems are 3 to 4 inches across. The center is a round cluster of tiny, purplish-brown disk florets. The petal-like rays that surround the center are a bright yellow. The seeds are flat, dry achenes.

Yellow daisy grows in dry or moist soil, in full sunshine or partial shade. It is most common along roadsides, in open fields, and at the edges of woods, from New Jersey west to Colorado and from Ontario south to Georgia.

yellow jacket

The yellow jacket is a kind of social wasp belonging to a group known as paper wasps. Paper wasps live in colonies, in many-celled nests the females build. The nests are made up of bits of wood that have been chewed and moistened by the female. Yellow jacket nests are always built underground, or hidden between rocks or under logs.

Adult yellow jackets have black bodies striped with yellow, and are up to 1 inch long. They are most often seen near flowers or decaying fruit, or clustered around picnic tables. They feed on flower nectar and sweet plant juices. Workers and females can sting, but they usually do so only if disturbed, or if their nest is threatened.

Male and worker yellow jackets all die during the winter. The queens mate in autumn and then go into hibernation. In spring, each begins construction of a new nest and lays eggs there. The eggs laid by the queen early in the summer all develop into workers, who enlarge the nest and feed the larvae of later broods. In late summer, some eggs develop into males, while others develop into new queens.

Yellow jacket larvae are fed on dead insects. After about 2 weeks, they spin cocoons inside their cells and pass into a pupal stage that lasts about 2 weeks.

Although yellow jackets damage some orchard trees and garden plants, they help man by destroying harmful insects.

yellowtail \ 'yel-ō-ˌtāl \ (California yellowtail)

The yellowtail is an ocean fish closely related to the pompano. It is a game and food fish valued by both sportsmen and commercial fishermen. Its name is suggested by a yellow stripe that runs along both sides of the body and onto the tail.

The yellowtail is most common off the coast of southern California. Swift-moving and graceful, it swims alone or in schools. It feeds on smaller fish.

Average-sized yellowtails are 30 inches long and weigh 10 to 12 pounds. The largest ones are 5 feet long and weigh up to 60 pounds.

The rounded, streamlined body tapers to a narrow stalk at the base of the V-

YELLOWTAIL

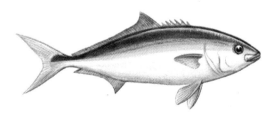

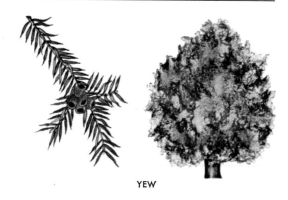

YEW

shaped tail. The first dorsal fin is small and spiny. The second dorsal is taller, and extends almost all the way to the tail.

The yellowtail probably spawns in summer, in deep water far from shore. About 7 million pounds are caught each year.

yew \ 'yü \

Yews make up a group of evergreen trees and shrubs that look much like the pines. They have narrow leaves that look like pine needles, but they are softer and bend more easily than pine needles. The seeds ripen inside cones that look something like berries.

In most kinds of yews, the fleshy part of the fruit can be eaten, but the leaves and seeds are poisonous.

Tree-sized yews are the source of hard, close-grained wood that is used to make archery bows and tool handles. Smaller kinds of yews are widely planted as ornamental shrubs.

Two kinds of yews are native to North America, but they grow only in California and Florida. The kind best known in the U.S. is the Japanese yew, a fast-growing bushy shrub from Asia. It has needles 1 inch long that end in short, blunt points. Its fruit is bright red.

The English yew (illustrated) is more widely distributed. It grows in Asia and North Africa as well as in Europe. It is a slow-growing but long-lived tree that becomes 30 to 60 feet tall. Its needles are 1 to 1¼ inch long, and they taper to a long, slender point. Its fruit is brownish-red and about ½ inch across.

yucca \ 'yək-ə \

Yuccas make up a group of unusual flowering plants belonging to the lily family. They grow in the southern U.S., in Mexico and in Central America, mostly on deserts.

In Mexico, tough fibers from yucca leaves are used to make rope. The roots of some kinds are used as soap. The buds and fruit of some kinds are eaten. Some kinds of yuccas are planted in flower gardens as far north as Massachusetts.

All yuccas have thick, sword-shaped leaves that taper to sharp points. Most kinds bear large clusters of bell-shaped white flowers.

The largest kind of yucca is the Joshua tree of the southwestern U.S., which grows 20 to 40 feet tall.

Spanish bayonet (illustrated) is the kind of yucca best known in the southeastern U.S. It grows in sandy soil near the Atlantic coast, from North Carolina and Florida west to Louisiana.

The leaves of Spanish bayonet are 18 to 32 inches long and about 2 inches wide. The flowers are white, tinged with purple, and 3 inches across. They bloom in midsummer, on a tall flowering stalk. The fruit is a dangling, 6-sided seedpod 3 to 4 inches long.

YUCCA

Z

zebra

Zebras are African mammals belonging to the horse family. They are marked with black and white stripes. The stripes on the neck and body are mostly vertical, while the stripes on the legs are horizontal.

Traveling in large herds, zebras live on the open plains south of the Sahara desert. They eat mostly grasses. Zebras can run as fast as 40 miles an hour.

Zebras are shy animals. They usually run from danger, but they may kick and bite fiercely to defend themselves. Some zebras have been broken to harness and used in circuses, but they have never been truly domesticated.

Mating may take place at any time during the year. The females bear young 11 to 13 months later. The normal life-span is about 25 years.

The several different kinds of zebras are much alike. They differ only slightly in size, and in the patterns of their stripes. The common zebra (illustrated) is usually about 3½ feet tall at the shoulder.

zebu \ 'zē-ˌb(y)ü \ (Brahman)

The zebu is a kind of domesticated cattle common in India. For about 6,000 years it has been kept as a work animal, and for its milk. In India it is generally believed

ZEBRA

ZEBU

to be sacred, and is seldom killed for its meat.

Scientists think the zebu may be native to tropical Africa. It no longer exists as a wild animal in any part of the world.

The zebu is better suited to life in hot countries than most cattle. The fatty shoulder hump and the loose folds of skin under the neck give it extra skin surface, helpful in regulating body temperature.

In size, the zebu is about like other kinds of cattle. The head is narrow, and the ears are large and drooping. The horns vary in size and shape. The body color is gray, brown or black.

Like other cattle, the zebu eats grain and grasses. The female bears 1 or 2 calves about 4½ months after mating.

Zebus were first brought to North America before the Civil War. In recent years, they have been crossbred with other kinds of cattle to produce new breeds of cattle that do well in the warm southern states.

zinnia \ 'zin-ē-ə \

Zinnias make up a group of flowering plants native to the New World. Wild zinnias are most common in Mexico, but some kinds grow as far north as Colorado, and others as far south as Chile.

The cultivated zinnias that have been developed from the wild kinds are among the most popular garden flowers. They are easy to grow, and they bear flowers from midsummer until the first frost. Garden zinnias are mostly annuals grown from seed, but some kinds of zinnias are perennials.

All zinnias have stiff, erect stems that are covered with short, bristly hairs. The oval or pointed leaves grow in opposite pairs.

One flower head is borne at the top of each stem. The flower centers are compact clusters of yellow, orange or brown disk florets. Around the centers are 1 or more rows of petal-like ray florets.

The different kinds of zinnias grow 10 to 36 inches tall. One common garden zinnia grows 24 to 36 inches tall. Its flower heads are 3 to 4½ inches across and have yellow or yellow-orange centers.

zircon \ 'zər-ˌkän \

Zircon is a mineral that occurs only as a crystal. When transparent, it is classed as a gem and is used in jewelry. Colorless, yellow or smoky zircon is most valuable.

Ordinary zircon crystals are darker in color and are translucent rather than transparent. They are usually some shade of brown, but are sometimes gray, green or red. Some blue-tinted zircon crystals have been produced artificially.

Most gem quality zircon comes from Ceylon, Russia, Australia and Canada. Ordinary zircon is found in small quantities in many other parts of the world, in granites and other kinds of rocks, and as grains of sand. In the U.S., zircon is most common in Maine, New York and North Carolina.

Zircon contains the elements zirconium and silicon combined with oxygen. It is sometimes mined as an ore of zirconium, which is used to make jackets for the uranium rods in nuclear reactors.

zodiacal \ zō-'dī-ə-kəl \ light

Zodiacal light is a cone-shaped or half-oval area of brightness sometimes visible in the night sky. It extends up from the horizon, about halfway to the center of the sky, along the yearly path the sun seems to make across the sky.

Zodiacal light is usually very faint, but on a clear, moonless night it may be about as bright as the Milky Way.

Astronomers believe that zodiacal light is sunlight reflected from tiny meteoric particles outside the earth's orbit. Such light is present in all parts of the sky, but it is visible only where the particles are most dense, and where they are in a position to reflect light toward the earth.

Zodiacal light is most often seen from the tropics. It cannot be seen at all from near the poles. In the north temperate zone, zodiacal light is most often seen in autumn, in the eastern sky before dawn, and in early spring, in the western sky after sunset.

See *counterglow.*

ZIRCON

ZODIACAL LIGHT

GEOLOGIC TIME CHART

ERA AND DURATION, MILLIONS OF YEARS	PERIOD AND DURATION, MILLIONS OF YEARS	EPOCH AND DURATION, MILLIONS OF YEARS*	MILLIONS OF YEARS AGO THAT INTERVAL BEGAN*	DOMINANT LIFE FORMS
CENOZOIC (63)	QUATERNARY	RECENT		Man; Modern mammals; Modern plants
		PLEISTOCENE (1)	1	
	TERTIARY	PLIOCENE (12)	13	Mammals; Temperate climate plants
		MIOCENE (12)	25	
		OLIGOCENE (11)	36	
		EOCENE (22)	58	Subtropical plants
		PALEOCENE (5)	63	
MESOZOIC (167)	CRETACEOUS (72)		135	Reptiles
	JURASSIC (46)		181	
	TRIASSIC (49)		230	Conifers, cycads, ginkgos
PALEOZOIC (370)	PERMIAN (50)		280	Amphibians
	CARBONIFEROUS	PENNSYLVANIAN (30)	310	Swamp forests
		MISSISSIPPIAN (35)	345	
	DEVONIAN (60)		405	Fishes; Scale trees
	SILURIAN (20)		425	
	ORDOVICIAN (75)		500	Invertebrates: brachiopods, bryozoans, trilobites, cephalopods
	CAMBRIAN (100)		600	
PRE-CAMBRIAN Eras	Began about 4,500,000,000 years ago, lasted about 3,900,000,000 years.			Bacteria; Fungi; Marine algae; Blue-green algae

* The periods of time for the various intervals are based upon isotopic age determinations as reported by J. Laurence Culp in Science, Vol. 133, No. 3459, pp. 1105–1114, April 14, 1961.
Copyright 1961 by the American Association for the Advancement of Science.

CLASSIFICATION OF THE
ANIMAL KINGDOM

Phylum Protozoa

20,000 species. One-celled animals or animals made up of loose groups of cells not forming tissues.

    Class Sarcodina — Have pseudopodia (amoeba).

    Class Mastigophora — Have one or more flagella (euglena).

    Class Ciliata — Move about by means of cilia (paramecium).

    Class Sporozoa — Have no means of locomotion (plasmodium).

Phylum Porifera

2,500 species. Two-cell-layer tubes closed at one end; penetrated by pores; radially symmetrical; aquatic; colonial, usually have skeleton (sponges).

Phylum Coelenterata

10,000 species. Body a double-walled sac that is tube-shaped or umbrella-shaped; tentacles with sting cells usually surround the mouth; colonial or solitary.

    Class Hydrozoa — (Hydra, Obelia)

    Class Scyphozoa — (Jellyfish, Portuguese man-of-war)

    Class Anthozoa — (Coral, sea anemone)

Phylum Platyhelminthes

6,500 species. Flattened, bilaterally symmetrical, unsegmented worms; three cell layers; without blood-circulatory and respiratory systems; no body cavity or alimentary canal.

    Class Turbellaria — (Planarians)

    Class Trematoda — (Flukes)

    Class Cestoda — (Tapeworms)

Phylum Nemathelminthes

3,500 species. Round, bilaterally symmetrical, unsegmented worms; have body cavity and complete alimentary canal (hookworm, vinegar eel).

Phylum Rotifera

1,500 species. Small aquatic animals having cilia around mouth that move in the manner of a rotating wheel; well-developed digestive system with mouth, pharynx, stomach and intestine.

Phylum Mollusca

90,000 species. Soft-bodied animals usually having a muscular foot; the body covering (mantle) in many groups may secrete a single or hinged shell; land, marine, and freshwater species.

    Class Amphineura — (Chitons)

    Class Pelecypoda — (Clams, oysters)

    Class Gastropoda — (Snails, slugs)

    Class Cephalopoda — (Octopuses, squids)

CLASSIFICATION OF THE
ANIMAL KINGDOM

Phylum Echinodermata	5,000 species. Marine; adults are radially symmetrical; exoskeleton of calcium carbonate plates; locomotion by tube feet (starfish, sea urchins, brittle stars, crinoids).
Phylum Annelida	5,000 species. Segmented worms with blood vessels, excretory organs and nervous system; appendages not jointed.
Class Oligochaeta	(Earthworms)
Class Hirudinea	(Leeches)
Class Polychaeta	(Sandworms)
Phylum Arthropoda	674,000 species. Animals with paired, jointed appendages, segmented bodies and chitinous exoskeletons.
Class Crustacea	Gill-breathing; two pairs of antennae; two body divisions (crayfish, crabs).
Class Insecta	Breathe by means of tracheae; one pair of antennae; three pairs of legs; three body divisions (ants, beetles, flies).
Class Arachnida	Breathe by means of book lungs or tracheae; no antennae; four pairs of legs; two body divisions (spiders, ticks).
Class Chilopoda	One pair of legs attached to each of 15 to 170 or more segments (centipedes).
Class Diplopoda	Two pairs of legs attached to each of 25 to 100 or more segments (millipedes).
Phylum Chordata	40,000 species. Internal skeleton with notochord present sometime during life history; temporary or permanent paired gill slits.
Subphylum Vertebrata	Chordates whose notochord is replaced by a backbone composed of vertebrae that contain dorsal nerve cord.
Class Cyclostomata	(Lampreys)
Class Elasmobranchii	(Sharks)
Class Pisces	(Bony fish)
Class Amphibia	(Frogs, salamanders)
Class Reptilia	(Snakes, lizards, turtles, alligators)
Class Aves	(Birds)
* **Class Mammalia**	(Mammals)

* The further classification of the mammal, man:

Order **Primate**—lemur, monkey, man
Family **Hominidae**—Peking, Neanderthal and Modern Man
Genus **Homo**—Neanderthal and Modern Man
Species **sapiens**—Modern Man

CLASSIFICATION OF THE
PLANT KINGDOM

Subkingdom Thallophyta	110,000 species. The simplest plants without true roots, stems or leaves; some have chlorophyll; others do not.
Phylum Cyanophyta	The blue-green algae. Chloroplasts and nuclei not clearly seen.
Phylum Chlorophyta	The green algae. Chloroplasts and nuclei clearly seen.
Phylum Chrysophyta	The diatoms, yellow-green and golden-brown algae; have a golden pigmentation.
Phylum Phaeophyta	The brown algae. Large, many-celled seaweed.
Phylum Rhodophyta	The red algae. Large, many-celled seaweed sometimes containing calcium carbonate.
Phylum Schizomycophyta	The bacteria. One-celled fungi.
Phylum Myxomycophyta	The slime molds. Many nuclei, no cell walls, amoeboid movement.
Phylum Eumycophyta	The true fungi.
Class Phycomycetes	Bread and leaf molds.
Class Ascomycetes	Yeasts, mildews and cheese molds.
Class Basidiomycetes	Mushrooms, toadstools and rusts.
Class Deuteromycetes	Imperfect fungi (athlete's-foot and ringworm fungi).

CLASSIFICATION OF THE PLANT KINGDOM

Subkingdom Embryophyta	283,700 species. Plants that form embryos in their development.
Phylum Bryophyta	23,000 species. Many-celled land plants without tissues specialized to transport food and water.
Class Hepaticae	The liverworts.
Class Musci	The mosses.
Phylum Tracheophyta	260,700 species. Plants having tissues adapted to carry food and water.
Subphylum Lycopida	Club mosses.
Subphylum Sphenopsida	Horsetails.
Subphylum Pteropsida	Complex conductive system and large leaves.
Class Filicineae	Ferns.
Class Gymnorospermae	Cone-bearing plants.
Class Angiospermae	Flowering plants.
Subclass Monocotyledonae	One seed leaf (grasses).
* **Subclass Dicotyledonae**	Two seed leaves (peas).

*The further classification of the dicot, white clover:

Order **Rosales**—rose, apple, clover

Family **Leguminosae**—pea, bean, clover

Genus **Trifolium**—clover

Species **repens**—white clover

THE EARTH

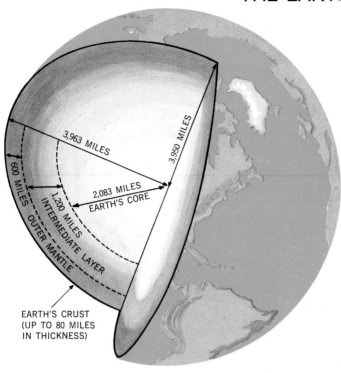

THE EARTH'S INTERIOR

The center of the earth is probably white-hot, and geologists believe that it is composed largely of nickel and iron. Much of the matter beneath the earth's surface is hot, molten rock. The surface is a relatively cool, solid crust. The force of gravity holds these solids and hot liquids rigidly together.

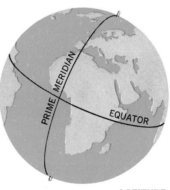

LATITUDE AND LONGITUDE

Latitude and longitude start from two imaginary lines, the equator and the prime meridian (left). The equator circles the earth halfway between the poles. The prime meridian, running from the North to the South Poles, passes through Greenwich, England. (Any north-south line running between the poles is called a meridian.) The picture at the right shows how the parallels of latitude and the meridians of longitude are laid out from these starting lines.

WESTERN

EASTERN

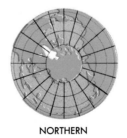

NORTHERN

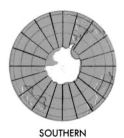

SOUTHERN

THE EARTH'S HEMISPHERES

Hold a globe even with your eyes so your right hand is over the western bulge of Africa. What you now see is the Western Hemisphere. The opposite half is the Eastern Hemisphere. Look straight down on the North Pole and you see the Northern Hemisphere. Look up at the South Pole and you see the Southern Hemisphere.

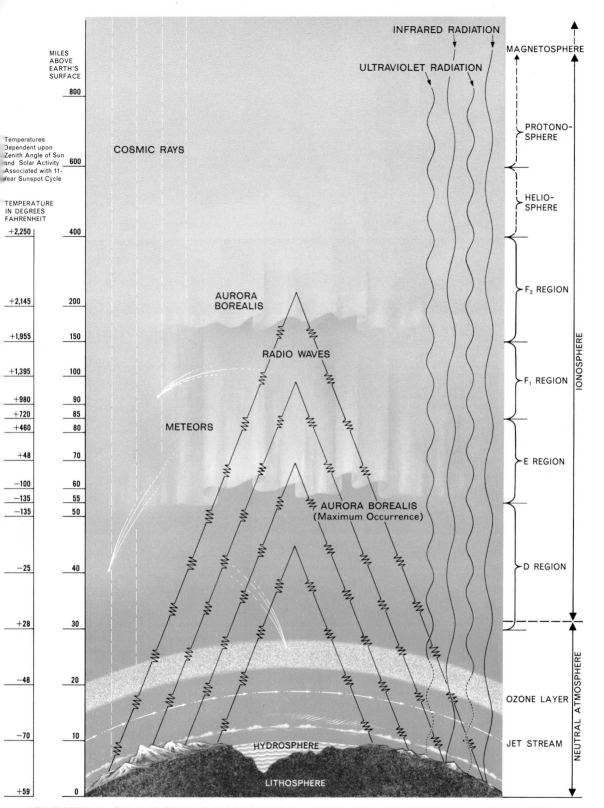

STRUCTURE OF EARTH'S ATMOSPHERE BASED ON ELECTRICAL PROPERTIES

The solid part of the earth is the lithosphere. All the water on the earth's surface makes up the hydrosphere. The atmosphere surrounding the earth may be divided into an almost neutral layer and the ionosphere. The ionosphere consists of regions which differ in their degree of ionization—D region, E region (Kennelly-Heaviside layer), F (F_1 and F_2) region (Appleton layer), heliosphere, and protonosphere. The magnetosphere is a teardrop-shaped band of ionized particles trapped by the earth's magnetic field. It extends to about 40,000 miles on the earth's sunlit side and to at least 120,000 miles on the earth's dark side.

Weather Extremes Around the World

WORLD'S HIGHEST MEAN MONTHLY DEW POINT **83° F** AUGUST, BAHREIN ISLAND

CHERRAPUNJI, INDIA HAD **150 INCHES** RAIN IN ONE 5-DAY PERIOD AUG., 1841

WORLD'S GREATEST RAINFALL IN ONE MONTH **366 INCHES** JULY, 1861 CHERRAPUNJI, INDIA

WORLD'S GREATEST RAINFALL FOR ONE YEAR **1042 INCHES** AUG., 1860-JULY, 1861 CHERRAPUNJI, INDIA

WORLD'S HIGHEST AV. ANNUAL TEMPERATURE **88° F** LUGH FERRANDI, SOMALI REPUBLIC

WORLD'S GREATEST 20-MINUTE RAINFALL **8 INCHES** 7 JULY, 1889 CURTEA-DE-ARGES, RUMANIA

EUROPE'S GREATEST AV. ANNUAL PRECIPITATION **183 INCHES** CRKVICE, YUGOSLAVIA

AVERAGE DAILY TOTAL SOLAR RADIATION **770 GM CAL/CM²** JUNE, DAVOS, SWITZERLAND

WADI HALFA, SUDAN, HAD NO RAIN IN A **19-YEAR** RECORD OF OBSERVATIONS

WORLD'S HIGHEST TEMPERATURE **136° F** 13 SEPT., 1922 EL AZIZIA, LIBYA

GREENLAND'S LOWEST TEMPERATURE **—87° F** AT 9820 FEET 6 DEC., 1949

WORLD'S HIGHEST SURFACE WIND SPEED **225 MPH** 12 APRIL, 1934 MT. WASHINGTON, N. H.

LARGEST OFFICIALLY RECORDED HAILSTONE **5.41-INCH CIRCUMFERENCE** POTTER, NEB., 7 JULY 1928

WORLD'S GREATEST 42-MINUTE RAINFALL **12 INCHES** 22 JUNE, 1947, HOLT, MO.

U. S. GREATEST 24-HOUR SNOWFALL **76 INCHES** 14-15 APRIL, 1921 SILVER LAKE, COLO.

U. S. UNOFFICIAL GREATEST 12-HOUR RAINFALL **32 INCHES** 9 SEPT., 1921, THRALL, TEX.

IQUIQUE, CHILE, HAD NO RAIN FOR **14 YEARS**

WORLD'S LOWEST TEMPERATURE **—127° F** AUGUST, 1960 VOSTOK, ANTARCTICA

U. S. LOWEST TEMPERATURE (Excluding Alaska) **—70° F** 20 JAN., 1954 ROGERS PASS, MONT.

U. S. GREATEST 2-MINUTE TEMPERATURE RISE **49° F** FROM —4° F TO 45° F 22 JAN., 1943 SPEARFISH, S. D.

NORTH AMERICA'S LOWEST TEMPERATURE **—81° F** 3 FEB., 1947, SNAG, YUKON

ALASKA'S LOWEST TEMPERATURE **—76° F** JAN. 1886, TANANA

U. S. HIGHEST TEMPERATURE **134° F** 10 JULY, 1913 DEATH VALLEY, CALIF.

SOUTH AMERICA'S GREATEST AV. ANNUAL RAINFALL **413 INCHES** QUIBDO, COLOMBIA

WORLD'S LOWEST AV. ANNUAL RAINFALL **.02 INCH** ARICA, CHILE

BAHIA FELIX, CHILE, HAS AN AVERAGE OF **325 DAYS/YEAR** WITH RAIN

U. S. GREATEST 24-HOUR TEMPERATURE FALL **100° F** FROM 44° F TO —56° F 23-24 Jan., 1916 BROWNING, MONT.

U. S. GREATEST AV. ANNUAL PRECIPITATION (Excluding Hawaii) **154 INCHES** WYNOOCHEE, WASH.

U. S. GREATEST SINGLE SEASON SNOWFALL **1000.3 INCHES** 1955-56, PARADISE RANGER STATION, WASH.

U. S. LONGEST DRY PERIOD **767 DAYS** OCT., 1912-NOV., 1914 BAGDAD, CALIF.

ANTARCTICA'S LOWEST AV. ANNUAL TEMPERATURE **—71° F** SOVIETSKAYA, 12,200 FEET

NORTHERN HEMISPHERE'S LOWEST TEMPERATURE **—90° F** OIMEKON (1933) AND VERKHOYANSK (1892), SIBERIA

NORTHERN HEMISPHERE'S UNOFFICIAL LOWEST TEMPERATURE **—108° F** OIMEKON, SIBERIA

FORMOSA'S GREATEST 2-DAY RAINFALL **66 INCHES** 18-19 JULY, 1913 FUNKIKO

WORLD'S GREATEST AV. ANNUAL PRECIPITATION **472 INCHES** MT. WAIALEALE KAUAI, HAWAII

AUSTRALIA'S HIGHEST TEMPERATURE **127° F** 16 JAN., 1889 CLONCURRY, QUEENSLAND

AUSTRALIA'S GREATEST 24-HOUR RAINFALL **35 INCHES** 17-18 FEB., 1958 FINCH HATTON

WORLD'S GREATEST 24-HOUR RAINFALL **46 INCHES** 14-15 JULY, 1911 BAGUIO, LUZON

AUSTRALIA'S LARGEST RECORDED HAILSTONE **12-INCH CIRCUMFERENCE** 26 JAN., 1858, BOWENVILLE

BUITENZORG, JAVA, HAS AN AVERAGE OF 322 DAYS/YEAR WITH THUNDERSTORMS

Compiled from various sources by **EARTH SCIENCES DIVISION LABORATORY** **U. S. ARMY NATICK LABORATORIES** **NATICK, MASS.**

Courtesy of the **Air Weather Service** *Observer*

OCEAN SURFACE CURRENTS

WARM CURRENTS
COLD CURRENTS

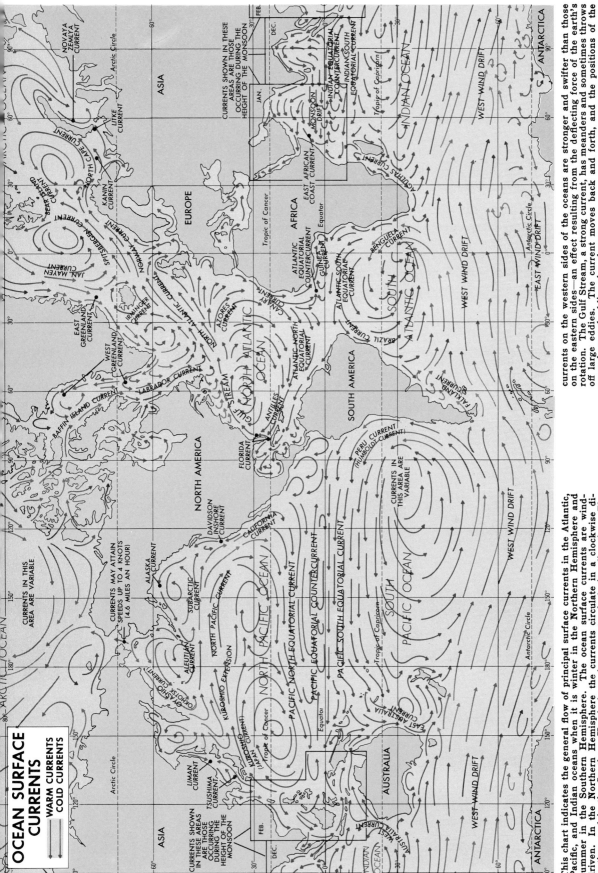

This chart indicates the general flow of principal surface currents in the Atlantic, Pacific, and Indian oceans when it is winter in the Northern Hemisphere and summer in the Southern Hemisphere. The ocean surface currents are wind-driven. In the Northern Hemisphere the currents circulate in a clockwise direction, and in the Southern Hemisphere, in a counterclockwise direction. The currents on the western sides of the oceans are stronger and swifter than those on the eastern sides—an effect resulting from the deflecting force of the earth's rotation. The Gulf Stream, a strong current, has meanders and sometimes throws off large eddies. The current moves back and forth, and the positions of the meanders and eddies also change.

501

THE STARS, SUN, MOON AND PLANETS
STARS VISIBLE FROM THE UNITED STATES
(listed in order of apparent brightness)

Common Name	Constellation	Color	Month When Visible on the Meridian at 9:00 P.M.
SIRIUS	Canis Major	Bluish	February
VEGA	Lyra	Blue-white	August
CAPELLA	Auriga	Yellow	January
ARCTURUS	Bootes	Orange-yellow	June
RIGEL	Orion	Blue-white	January
PROCYON	Canis Minor	Yellow-white	March
ALTAIR	Aquila	Yellow-white	September
BETELGEUSE	Orion	Reddish	February
ALDEBARAN	Taurus	Orange	January
POLLUX	Gemini	Yellow	March
SPICA	Virgo	Bluish	May
ANTARES	Scorpius	Reddish	July
FOMALHAUT	Southern Fish	White	October
DENEB	Cygnus	White	September
REGULUS	Leo	Blue-white	April
CASTOR	Gemini	Green-white	February
POLARIS	Ursa Minor (circumpolar)	Yellowish	Visible all year
MIZAR	Ursa Major (circumpolar)	Green-white	Visible all year

THE SUN, THE MOON AND THE PLANETS

Name	Distance from Sun, Millions of Miles	Equatorial Diameter, Miles	Period of Rotation	Period of Revolution Sidereal	Period of Revolution Synodic	Number of Satellites	Weight of Object Weighing 100 lbs. on Earth
SUN	——	864,000	24.7 days	——	——	——	2,800.0 lbs.
MOON	——	2,160	27.3 days	27.3 days	29.5 days	0	16.7 lbs.
MERCURY	36.0	3,100	88 days	88.0 days	115.9 days	0	25.0 lbs.
VENUS	67.2	7,700	244 days(?)	224.7 days	583.9 days	0	85.0 lbs.
EARTH	92.9	7,927	23^h 56^m	365.3 days	——	1	——
MARS	141.5	4,215	24^h 37^m	687.0 days	779.9 days	2	36.0 lbs.
JUPITER	483.2	88,640	9^h 50^m	11.9 years	398.9 days	12	264.0 lbs.
SATURN	885.9	74,100	10^h 14^m	29.5 years	378.1 days	9	117.0 lbs.
URANUS	1,782.0	32,000	10^h 45^m	84.0 years	369.7 days	5	92.0 lbs.
NEPTUNE	2,793.0	27,740	15^h 48^m (?)	164.8 years	367.5 days	2	112.0 lbs.
PLUTO	3,670.0	3,600 (?)	6.4 days(?)	247.7 years	366.7 days	?	0.8 lbs.(?)

PREFIXES AND SUFFIXES OF NATURAL SCIENCE TERMS

PREFIX	MEANING	EXAMPLE
aero-	air	aerobic
amphi-	both	amphibian
an-	absence of, without	anaerobic
ana-	up, back	anabatic
ante-	before	anterior
anthropo-	man	anthropoid
anti-	against	anticline
apo-	away from	apogee
aqua-	water	aquatic
astro-	star	astronomy
bacteri-	bacteria	bacteriology
baro-	weight	barometer
bathy-	deep	bathypelagic
bi-	two	biennial
bio-	life	biology
bryo-	moss	bryozoan
cata-	down, against	cataract
centro-	center	centrosphere
cephalo-	head	cephalothorax
chemo-	chemical	chemosynthesis
chloro-	green	chlorophyll
co-	together	coexist
cyto-	cell	cytoplasm
denti-	tooth	dentition
di-	two	diurnal
dors-	back, dorsal	dorsiventral
eco-	environment	ecology
ecto-	outside	ectoderm
embryo-	embryo	embryology
endo-	within, inside	endoderm
epi-	on, upon	epicenter
equi-	equal	equinox
ex-	out of, from	exfoliation
exo-	out of, from	exosphere
gastro-	ventral area	gastropod
geo-	earth	geotropism

PREFIX	MEANING	EXAMPLE
helio-	sun	heliocentric
hemi-	half	hemisphere
hetero-	abnormal, different	heterozygote
homo-	same, similar	homogeneous
hydro-	water	hydrosphere
hypo-	under	hypocotyl
inter-	between	interphase
intra-	within	intracellular
iso-	equal	isostasy
leuco-	white, colorless	leucoplast
litho-	stone	lithosphere
macro-	large, great	macronucleus
mega-	large, great	megaspore
meso-	middle, intermediate	mesoderm
meta-	between, beyond	metaphase
meteor-	high in the air	meteorology
micro-	small	microorganism
mito-	thread	mitochondria
mono-	one	monocotyledon
morpho-	form, shape	morphology
multi-	many	multicellular
myc-	fungus	mycology
nema-	thread	nematode
noct-	night	nocturnal
omni-	all	omnivorous
oo-	egg	oogenesis
ortho-	normal, regular	orthogenesis
ov-	egg	ovipositor
paleo-	old, ancient	paleontology
para-	beside, almost	parasite
patho-	disease	pathogenic
per-	throughout	perennial
peri-	around	pericarp
petri-	stone	petrified

PREFIXES AND SUFFIXES OF NATURAL SCIENCE TERMS *continued*

PREFIX	MEANING	EXAMPLE
photo-	light	photosynthesis
poly-	many	polymorphism
post-	after	posterior
pre-	in front of, before	prehensile
pro-	before	proboscis
proto-	first, original	protozoa
pseudo-	false	pseudopodium
retro-	backward, behind	retrograde
rhiz-	root	rhizome
sapro-	rotten, dead	saprophyte
seismo-	earthquake	seismology
semi-	half, imperfectly	semipermeable
sol-	sun	solstice
spor-	seed, spore	sporangium
strati-	layer	stratification
strato-	horizontal	stratosphere
sub-	under, below	subpolar
super-	above, beyond	supernova
sym-	with, together	symbiosis
syn-	with, together	synodic
tele-	distant, far off	telephase
therm-	heat	thermocline
trans-	through, across	transpiration
tri-	three	Triassic
trop-	turn, turning	tropism
uni-	one	unicellular
vivi-	alive	viviparous
zoo-	animal	zoology

SUFFIX	MEANING	EXAMPLE
-blast	formative	diploblast
-cardium	heart	pericardium
-centric	having a center or centers	geocentric
-cline	slope	syncline
-coccus	spherical cell	streptococcus
-cosm	world	microcosm
-cotyl	cotyledon	hypocotyl
-cyte	cell	leukocyte
-derm	skin	endoderm
-duct	guide, tube	oviduct
-ism	state, condition	polymorphism
-lith	stone	gastrolith
-logy	study of	geology
-morph	form	polymorph
-oid	resembling	desmoid
-phore	bearer, carrier	chromophore
-phyll	coloring matter in plants	chlorophyll
-phyte	possessed by a plant	gametophyte
-plasm	growth material	protoplasm
-pod	foot	pseudopod
-ptera	winged	homoptera
-sphere	round	atmosphere
-tropism	affinity toward	heliotropism
-vorous	devouring	carnivorous
-zoa	animals	protozoa
-zoic	of animals	Mesozoic
-zygous	yoked	heterozygous

a

aardvark p. 1

abalone p. 1

abdomen \'ab-də-mən\ The part of a human or animal body that contains the stomach, intestines and other internal organs.

abnormal \ab-'nor-məl\ Describing something that is not normal or that is unusual.

aboriginal \ab-ə-'rij-(ə-)nəl\ Describing animals or plants that first lived in a certain area of the earth. Aboriginal usually refers to man.

absolute magnitude \'ab-sə-,lüt 'mag-nə-,tüd\ The brightness of a star from a distance of 32½ light-years.

absorption \əb-'sorp-shən\ The taking in of dissolved substances by live tissues.

acacia p. 1

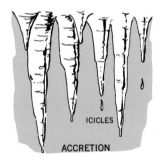

ICICLES

ACCRETION

accretion \ə-'krē-shən\ An increase in the size of organic substances by the addition of particles from another source.

achene \ə-'kēn\ A small, dry fruit containing just 1 seed.

acorn \'ā-,korn\ A round nut set in a woody cup, as the fruit of an oak tree.

acorn squash p. 420

acquired characteristics \ə-'kwird ,kar-ik-tə-'ris-tiks\ Characteristics that an organism receives from its environment rather than from its parents.

adaptation \,ad-,ap-'tā-shən\ Changes in structure, function or form of plants or animals which occur over a long period of time. These changes help the plant or animal survive more easily in its environment. Adaptation may also refer to a change in behavior that is not passed on to offspring.

adipose \'ad-ə-,pōs\ Having to do with an animal fat. Adipose also means fatty.

adrenal \ə-'drēn-əl\ Having to do with or being on or near the kidneys. Adrenal also means having to do with the adrenal glands.

adult \ə-'dəlt\ Describing an animal or plant that is fully grown.

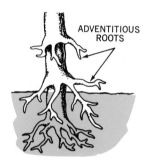

ADVENTITIOUS
ROOTS

adventitious \,ad-vən-'tish-əs\ **roots** Plant roots that do not grow at the bottom end of the stem. Corn has adventitious roots.

aerial \'ar-ē-əl\ **stems** Stems that grow above the ground, as the stems of the morning glory.

aerobic \,a-'rō-bik\ Describing something that can live only where there is free oxygen.

African elephant p. 140

African gray parrot p. 333

African jerboa p. 233

African marigold p. 275

African violet p. 2

agar-agar See *algae:* p. 6

agate p. 2

agave p. 2

age A period of time in the history of the earth. An age is usually known for certain features.

Age of Coal The Carboniferous Period, an age during which large deposits of coal were formed by decaying swamp forests.

Age of Crinoids \'krī-,noidz\ An age within the Paleozoic Era, during which there were a great many sea lilies.

Age of Dinosaurs \'dī-nə-,sorz\ An age during which dinosaurs were the main animals on earth. The Age of Dinosaurs occurred during the Mesozoic Era. The Age of Dinosaurs includes the Jurassic Period, during which flying reptiles appeared.

Age of Mammals \'mam-əlz\ An age during

which great numbers of mammals of various sizes and shapes appeared. The Age of Mammals began about 75 million years ago and is also called the Cenozoic Era.

agonic line p. 3

agouti p. 3

air A mixture made up mostly of oxygen and nitrogen and water vapor. Air has no color and no odor. Air is the earth's atmosphere.

air bladder \\'blad-ər\\ An air sac or pocket in the body of a fish. By filling the sac with air, the fish can swim nearer the surface. In fish that breathe air, an air bladder is a lung.

air mass \\'mas\\ A large body of air that has nearly the same temperature and humidity at any given level. There are 4 main types of air masses: arctic, polar, tropic and equatorial.

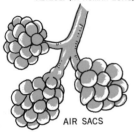

ALVEOLI (IN HUMAN LUNG)

AIR SACS

air sacs \\'saks\\ Pockets of air in the bodies of birds. Air sacs are part of every bird's breathing system. They are also found in some insects such as the honeybee. The air sacs in human lungs are called alveoli.

alabaster p. 4; see also *gypsum:* p. 202

Alaskan moose p. 295

Alaska willow ptarmigan p. 364

albacore p. 4

albatross p. 4

albino \\al-'bī-,nō\\ A plant or animal without the genes that would give it its natural color.

albumin \\al-'byü-mən\\ A protein substance found in plant and animal tissues and fluids. Albumin is made up of nitrogen, carbon, hydrogen, oxygen and sulfur.

alder p. 4

alewife p. 5

Alexander archipelago p. 19

alfalfa p. 5

alfalfa butterfly pp. 60, 61

algae pp. 6–7

alligator p. 8

alligator wampee See *pickerelweed:* p. 346

allspice See *pimento tree:* p. 347

alluvial \\ə-'lü-vē-əl\\ Describing matter made up of bits of rock, clay or sand left behind by running water.

alluvial fan p. 8

almond tree p. 8

alpaca p. 9

alpha \\'al-fə\\ A term used to name the brightest star in a constellation.

alphabet cone shell p. 101

Alpine ibex p. 224

alternate \\'ol-tər-nət\\ In plants, the way leaves grow at different points along a stem or twig, rather than opposite each other.

alternate \\'ol-tər-nət\\ **host** A host that is not the same host on which a plant or animal usually feeds.

alternation of generations \\,ol-tər-'nā-shən əv ,jen-ə-'rā-shənz\\ A cycle of reproduction in which an organism appears in two different forms. Each form gives rise to the other form by an alternation of asexual and sexual reproduction.

altitude \\'al-tə-,tüd\\ Height above a certain level of the earth, usually sea level.

altocumulus clouds pp. 90, 91

altostratus clouds pp. 90, 91

aluminum See *bauxite:* p. 32

amber p. 9

American alligator p. 8

American badger p. 26

American beech p. 35

American bison p. 9

American bittern p. 41

American chameleon See *anole:* p. 15

American chestnut p. 80

American cockroach p. 95

American coot p. 102

American cranberry p. 110

American crocodile p. 114

American dog tick p. 442

American eel pp. 137, 138

American egret p. 138

American elk See *wapiti:* p. 471

American elm p. 140

American goldfinch p. 187

American grasshopper p. 196

American holly p. 216

American lobster p. 260

American mink p. 287

American mistletoe p. 288

American mountain ash p. 10

American muskmelon See *melon:* p. 281

American pika p. 346

American robin p. 381

American sable p. 10

American shad p. 11

American smelt p. 409

American sycamore p. 433

American toad pp. 444, 445

American widgeon See *baldpate:* p. 26

American wolverine p. 484

amethyst p. 11

amoeba p. 11

amorphous \\ə-'mor-fəs\\ Without form.

amphibian p. 12

amphibole p. 12

anaerobic \\,an-ə-'rō-bik\\ Describing an organism able to grow without free oxygen or air, as certain bacteria. Such organisms need oxygen that has combined with another element such as carbon dioxide.

anal fin \'ān-ᵊl 'fin\ A single fin located below and to the rear of fish.

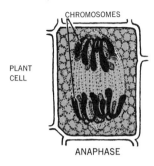

CHROMOSOMES

PLANT CELL

ANAPHASE

anaphase \'an-ə-ˌfāz\ A stage in the process of cell division called mitosis. During anaphase, the chromosomes move toward the opposite ends of the spindle in the cell.

anatomy \ə-'nat-ə-mē\ The science of plant and animal structure. Anatomy also means the physical structure of a particular kind of plant or animal.

anchovy p. 13

andalusite p. 13

Andean condor p. 100

Andromeda See *galaxy:* p. 170

angelfish p. 13

angiosperm \'an-jē-ə-ˌspərm\ A plant that has seeds in seedpods, such as nuts, berries and fruits. An angiosperm is also a flowering plant.

angular-winged katydid p. 14

animal Any living thing that moves from place to place, that is very sensitive to stimuli both inside and outside its body and that takes in plant or animal substances to stay alive. Animals do not have chlorophyll or carry on photosynthesis.

animal classification \ˌklas-ə-fə-'kā-shən\ The division of the animal kingdom into related groups and subgroups. See pp. 494–495.

annelid p. 14; see also *worm:* pp. 486, 487

annual \'an-yə-wəl\ A plant that lives for only one year or one season.

annual cicada See *harvest fly:* p. 207

annual \'an-yə-wəl\ **ring** Circular markings that can be seen in the cross section of a tree trunk or a shrub stem. An annual ring is formed by differences in wood growth in the different parts of the year. The age of a tree can be estimated from the number of rings.

anole p. 15

anopheles mosquito p. 297

ant p. 15

antarctic \(')ant-'är(k)t-ik\ Describing the South Pole or the south polar area.

ant bear See *aardvark:* p. 1

ant cow See *aphid:* p. 17

anteater p. 16

antelope p. 16

antenna \an-'ten-ə\ A movable, hair-like organ of touch. Antennae are usually found in pairs on the heads of insects.

anterior \an-'tir-ē-ər\ Toward the front or near the head.

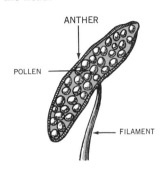

ANTHER

POLLEN

FILAMENT

anther \'an(t)-thər\ In a flower, the small tip of the stamen that produces and contains the pollen.

anthracite coal p. 93

anthropoid \'an(t)-thrə-ˌpoid\ Describing appearance or actions that are like those of man or of apes.

anthropology \ˌan(t)-thrə-'päl-ə-jē\ The science that deals with the study of man and his development. It includes where he has lived on earth and where he lives now, his physical structure, his different races, customs and religions and the things he has built and invented.

antibiotic \ˌant-i-bī-'ät-ik\ A chemical produced from living organisms such as bacteria, fungi and molds. Antibiotics are used as medicines to destroy or slow the growth of disease-causing organisms in man and animals.

antibody \'ant-i-ˌbäd-ē\ A substance that is produced in the bloodstream of an animal in order to destroy harmful bacteria. An antibody may be produced by immunization shots.

anticline p. 17

antigen \'ant-ə-jən\ A substance either in the blood, or put into the blood, that stimulates the production of antibodies.

anting \'ant-ing\ A habit of some birds of placing live ants among their feathers. Scientists do not know exactly why birds ant.

antiseptic \ˌant-ə-'sep-tik\ A substance that slows down or stops the growth of bacteria that cause infection or decay.

antlers \'ant-lərz\ Outgrowths of bone-like material, usually branch-shaped, on the heads of animals in the deer family. Antlers are shed each year. During the growing period, antlers are covered with a velvety layer of sensitive skin which peels off later in the year.

ant lion p. 17

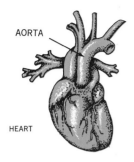

AORTA

HEART

aorta \ā-'ort-ə\ In vertebrates, the main artery that carries blood from the heart to the different parts of the body.

ape Any monkey. An ape is usually one of the larger tail-less monkeys.

aphelion \a-'fēl-yən\ The point on the orbit of a planet or comet that is farthest from the sun.

aphid p. 17

aphis lions See *lacewing:* p. 243

aphis wolves See *lacewing:* p. 243

apogee \'ap-ə-jē\ The part of a satellite's elliptical orbit that is farthest from the center of the earth or of any other planet.

appendage \ə-'pen-dij\ An extension of the main body of an animal, as an arm, a leg or a tail.

apple murex shell See *murex:* p. 304

apple tree p. 18

aquamarine See *beryl:* p. 38

aquatic \ə-'kwat-ik\ Having to do with water or things living in water.

arachnid \ə-'rak-nəd\ An arthropod animal with 4 pairs of legs and no wings, as a spider, scorpion, mite or tick. Arachnids have simple eyes and they have pincer-like organs instead of antennae.

arboreal \är-'bōr-ē-əl\ Having to do with trees or with things that live in trees.

archaeopteryx p. 18

archipelago p. 19

Arctic fox p. 165

Arctic hare p. 206

arête p. 19

argentite p. 19

arid region \'ar-əd 'rē-jən\ An area that does not get enough rainfall to grow plants. An arid region is a desert-like region.

Arizona cypress p. 119

arm In humans, the part of the upper limb between the shoulder and the wrist. In vertebrate animals, an arm is any structure like a human arm. In invertebrate animals, arms are structures used for grasping, as the arms of a starfish.

armadillo p. 20

artery \'ärt-ə-rē\ Any blood vessel that carries blood from the heart through the body.

artesian \är-'tē-zhən\ **well** A deep well, natural or drilled. Water is forced out of an artesian well by the natural pressure of the underground water.

arthropod \'är-thrə-,päd\ A group of invertebrate animals with external skeletons, such as centipedes, crustaceans, insects, millipedes and spiders. Arthropods have segmented bodies and jointed limbs.

artichoke p. 20

asbestos \as-'bes-təs\ A mineral made up of long fibers. Asbestos is found tightly packed in veins and pockets in rocks. It is often used in fireproof fabrics.

ascaris p. 20

asexual reproduction \(')ā-'seksh-(ə-)wəl ,rē-prə-'dək-shən\ A kind of reproduction such as budding or fission, that does not involve the union of male and female reproductive cells.

ash p. 21

Asiatic dayflower p. 122

asparagus p. 21

asparagus beetle pp. 36, 37

asparagus broccoli See *cabbage:* p. 62

ass See *donkey:* p. 130

assassin bug pp. 54, 55

assimilation \ə-,sim-ə-'lā-shən\ The changing of digested and ingested food into living tissue.

aster p. 22

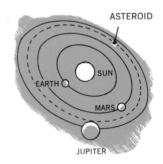

ASTEROID

SUN

EARTH

MARS

JUPITER

asteroid \'as-tə-rȯid\ A small unevenly shaped planet. Many asteroids orbit the sun between Mars and Jupiter.

astronomy \ə-'strän-ə-mē\ The study of the position, movements, sizes and makeup of planets, stars and other objects in space.

Atlantic bonito p. 22

Atlantic cod p. 96

Atlantic croaker p. 114

Atlantic hagfish p. 203

Atlantic halibut p. 204

Atlantic herring p. 214

Atlantic mackerel p. 265

Atlantic manta pp. 273, 274

Atlantic needlefish p. 310

Atlantic sailfish pp. 22, 23

Atlantic salmon p. 387

Atlantic sand dollar p. 388

Atlantic smelt p. 409

Atlantic squid pp. 420, 421

Atlantic tarpon p. 23

Atlantic walrus p. 470, 471

atmosphere \\'at-mə-,sfir\\ The mixture of gases that surround the earth and certain other planets. See p. 499.

atoll p. 23

auditory \\'ȯd-ə-,tōr-ē\\ Having to do with the sense of hearing or the organs of hearing.

auk p. 23

auricle \\'ȯr-i-kəl\\ One of 3 parts of the outer ear. The auricle receives sound waves from the air. An auricle is also the atrium, or small upper chamber of the heart. The blood enters the heart through the auricle.

aurora p. 24

aurora australis p. 24

aurora borealis p. 24

Australian budgerigar See *parakeet:* p. 332

Australian man pp. 270, 271

autonomic nervous system \\,ȯt-ə-'näm-ik 'nər-vəs 'sist-əm\\ In vertebrates, the part of the nervous system that includes the sympathetic and parasympathetic nerves. These nerves control certain involuntary activities of the body such as breathing.

auxin \\'ȯk-sən\\ A chemical substance in plants that functions somewhat the same way as hormones do in animals. Auxin regulates and controls the growth of plants. It is produced at the tips of stems and roots and works its way back to the living cells of the leaves, stems and roots.

axil \\'aks-əl\\ The angle between the bract and the stem of a flower. An axil is also the point where a leaf or branch grows from a stem or another branch.

axis \\'aks-əs\\ A straight line either real or imaginary. It goes through the center of an object that has the same size and shape on both sides of this line.

azimuth \\'az-(ə-)məth\\ Any part of the circle of the horizon, expressed in degrees. Azimuth usually measures the distance between some fixed point, such as true north, and an imaginary line running at right angles to the horizon and passing through some object such as a star.

Aztec marigold p. 275

azurite p. 24

b

baboon p. 25

bachelor's button p. 25

bacillus See *bacteria:* p. 25

backbone \\'bak-'bōn\\ The spine, a column of bones that forms the main support for the body of man and other vertebrates.

bacteria p. 25

bacteriology \\(,)bak-,tir-ē-'äl-ə-jē\\ The science having to do with the study of bacteria.

Bactrian camel p. 65

badger p. 26

badlands \\'bad-,landz\\ A nearly barren area, as in South Dakota, where erosion has cut the land into many sharp-topped hills and narrow gullies.

balanced diet \\'bal-ən(t)st 'dī-ət\\ A diet made up of certain amounts of different foods necessary to give an organism the nourishment it needs.

balance of nature \\'bal-ən(t)s əv 'nā-chər\\ The proportion of populations of different plants and animals in a certain area which enable all to live without great changes.

bald cypress p. 119

bald eagle p. 135

bald-faced hornet pp. 218, 219

baldpate p. 26

baleen \\bə-'lēn\\ A fringe of tough but flexible horny material that grows from the upper jaw of some whales. When sea water passes through the baleen, the tiny marine plants and animals which the whale eats are left in its mouth. Baleen is also called whalebone.

baleen whales pp. 478, 479

balloonfish See *porcupine fish:* p. 360

balsa p. 27

balsam p. 27

balsam fir p. 152

Baltimore oriole p. 323

bamboo p. 28

banana p. 28

banded gecko p. 175

banks p. 29

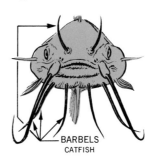

BARBELS
CATFISH

barbels \\'bär-bəlz\\ Soft, thin, whisker-like feelers around the mouths of such fishes as catfish, cod, drumfish, goatfish and sturgeon. Barbels contain sensitive nerve organs with which the fish senses food or other objects.

barberry p. 29

bark The cork-like, outer covering of trees. Bark is made up of dead cells that becomes rougher as time passes.

barking frog pp. 166, 167

barley p. 29

barnacle p. 30
barn owl p. 326
barn swallow p. 430
barracuda See *great barracuda:* p. 196
barred owl pp. 326, 327
barrier \'bar-ē-ər\ Something that blocks or hinders the movement of animals from one place to another. A barrier may be due to geography, climate, organisms or other causes.
barrier beach p. 30
basalt p. 30
base The part of an animal organ that attaches the animal to something else.
basement Crystalline rocks, probably from the pre-Cambrian Period. Such rocks are covered by flat or slightly dipping sediments called shield areas.
basin p. 31
basking shark pp. 400, 401
bass p. 31
bat p. 32
bauxite p. 32
bay An inlet of a sea or lake. It is smaller than a gulf and larger than a cove. A bay is also a chestnut-colored animal, usually a horse.
bay lynx p. 264
bayou \'bī-,(y)ō\ A small secondary river or stream with a slow or blocked current.
bay scallop p. 392
beach A nearly level stretch of pebbly or sandy shore washed by the high tides or high waters of a sea, lake or river.
beak \'bēk\ The bill of a bird or the projecting mouth of certain invertebrates and insects.
bean p. 33
bear p. 33

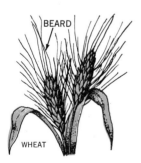

beard Bristly growth on some plants, as on the grain of wheat or barley. A beard is also a tuft of hair on some animals.
beaver p. 34
bed A layer of rock, or a layer of rock that contains several fossils.
bedbug pp. 54, 55
bedrock \'bed-'räk\ Solid rock, still in the position and place where it was formed. On most of the earth's surface, bedrock lies under loose rock material and soil. In some places it has been exposed by erosion.

bee p. 34
beech p. 35
bee fly pp. 160, 161
beef tapeworm p. 435
beet p. 35
beetle pp. 36–37
begonia p. 38
behavior \bi-'hā-vyər\ All the actions an organism takes in response to stimulation from inside or outside its body.
bell Any part or organ of an organism that has a bell-like structure, as the umbrella of a jellyfish. A bell is also the cup of a flower.
bellflower p. 38
bell pepper p. 341
bell toad pp. 444, 445
belly \'bel-ē\ The underside of an animal.
belted kingfisher p. 238
Bengal tiger p. 442
bent grass pp. 194, 195
Bermuda grass pp. 194, 195
berry A small fruit with seeds in the pulp.
beryl p. 38
beryllium See *beryl:* p. 38
betta p. 39
biennial \(')bī-'en-ē-əl\ A plant that completes its life cycle in 2 years. It grows leaves and roots the first year, and flowers, fruit and seed the second year.
big rhododendron p. 379

BILATERAL SYMMETRY

bilateral symmetry \(')bī-'lat-ə-rəl 'sim-ə-trē\ Having the right and left sides equal or the same. One side seems to be the reflection of the other, as the right and left halves of a dog or of the human body.
bile \'bīl\ A substance given off by the liver. Bile helps in the digestion and absorption of fats. It also carries some of the waste material from the body.
bill A beak, as the jaws of a bird, including the horny sheath.
billfish See *needlefish:* p. 310
binary division \'bī-nə-rē də-'vizh-ən\ The asexual reproductive process of most bacteria. A cell divides into 2 similar cells. This is followed by a second division of each of these cells, and so forth. Binary division is also called binary fission.

binocular vision \bə-'näk-yə-lər 'vizh-ən\ Vision with 2 eyes. In binocular vision, slightly different images form on each retina because each eye sees an object from a slightly different angle. As a result, an animal with binocular vision sees objects in depth rather than flat, as in a photograph.

biochemistry \,bī-ō-'kem-ə-strē\ A branch of chemistry. Biochemistry has to do with the makeup and life processes of all plants and animals.

biogenesis \,bī-ō-'gen-ə-səs\ The theory that living organisms are produced only by other living organisms.

biological \,bī-ə-'läj-i-kəl\ **community** The balance of nature in an area where different plants and animals have reached a steady relationship of dependence on one another.

biological control \,bī-ə-'läj-i-kəl kən-'trōl\ The destroying of unwanted plants or animals by upsetting their biological community. This is done by bringing in organisms that are unfriendly to the unwanted organisms.

biology \bī-'äl-ə-jē\ The science of living things.

bioluminescence \,bī-(,)ō-,lü-mə-'nes-ᵊn(t)s\ The giving off of light by living cells.

biome \'bī-,ōm\ The community of all the plants and animals in an area and the relationship between them.

biophysics \'bī-ō-,fiz-iks\ The study of the structures and processes of living things as related to the laws of physics.

biosphere \'bī-ə-,sfir\ The areas of the earth and the earth's atmosphere where plants and animals live.

biotic \bī-'ät-ik\ **community** An area where plants and animals depend on one another to live. In a biotic community, one or more kinds, or species, of plant and animal is stronger or more common than the others.

biotite p. 39
biotite mica p. 284

STARFISH

BIRADIAL SYMMETRY

biradial symmetry \(')bī-'rād-ē-əl 'sim-ə-trē\ Having a structure in which similar parts have both radial and bilateral symmetry, as a starfish.

birch p. 39

bird p. 40
bird louse p. 263
bird of paradise p. 40
birth rate The speed at which a species of mammal gives birth to its young. In the case of humans, it is the number of babies born every year for every 1,000 people.

bisexual \(')bī-'seksh-(ə-)wəl\ Having male and female organs in 1 organism.

bisexual reproduction \(')bī-'seksh-(ə-)wəl ,rē-prə-'dək-shən\ The production of young by the joining of the male and female reproductive cells.

biting louse p. 263
bittern p. 41
bituminous coal p. 93

BIVALVE

MUSSEL

bivalve \'bī-,valv\ Any animal, such as a clam, mussel or oyster, that has a 2-valved shell. See *shell*: p. 402. A bivalve is also a plant part having 2 valves, as a seedcase or capsule.

blackberry p. 41
black-billed cuckoo p. 116
black-billed magpie p. 267
blackbird p. 42
black bullhead p. 56
black-capped chickadee p. 80
black crappie p. 111
black duck pp. 132, 133
black-eyed Susan See *yellow daisy*: p. 488
black fly pp. 160, 161
black-footed ferret p. 42
black gum p. 43
black-headed grosbeak p. 198
black huckleberry p. 221
black jewfish See *grouper*: p. 199
black locust p. 261
black mica See *biotite*: p. 39
black mollie p. 43
black mustard p. 307
black-necked stilt p. 424
black nightshade p. 313
black oak p. 316
black opal p. 320
black pepper p. 341
black phoebe p. 345
black piranha p. 350
black raspberry p. 373
black rat pp. 374, 375

black rhinoceros p. 379
black sea bass p. 31
black-tailed deer pp. 122, 123
black-throated blue warbler p. 471, 472
black walnut p. 470
black widow spider p. 416
blackwing damselfly p. 120
bladder \\'blad-ər\\ In many animals, a sac of thin sheets of tissue that collects liquids or gases that are later discharged from the body.
bladderwort p. 44
blade The flat, enlarged part of a leaf or similar structure.

FROG EGG

BLASTULA

blastula \\'blas-chə-lə\\ An early stage in the development of the embryo in many animals.
bleeding heart p. 44
blenny p. 44
blight \\'blīt\\ Any condition of air or soil, or any insect or parasite, that harms, kills or slows the growth of plants. A blight is also a plant disease itself.
blizzard A long and heavy snowstorm, usually with a high wind.
block mountain p. 300
blood A fluid that circulates in the heart, arteries and veins of certain animals. It carries nourishment and oxygen to all body parts, and carries away waste products of metabolism.
bloodroot p. 45
blood vessel Any tube through which blood circulates in an animal.
bloom A flower or several flowers of a plant.
blossom The flower or bloom of a seed plant, especially a plant that bears fruit.
blowfish See *puffer:* p. 365
blowfly pp. 160, 161
blue anemone See *hepatica:* p. 213
blue-banded goby p. 186
bluebell See *bellflower:* p. 38
blueberry p. 45
bluebird p. 46
bluebottle fly pp. 160, 161
blue butterfly pp. 60, 61
blue cornflower See *bachelor's button:* p. 25
bluefish p. 46
bluegill p. 47
blue grass pp. 194, 195
blue-gray gnatcatcher p. 183

blue-green algae p. 6
blue gum p. 47
blue jay p. 232
blue marlin p. 276
blue mud dauber See *wasp:* p. 472
blue shark pp. 400, 401
blue spruce pp. 419, 420
bluet p. 48
blue whale pp. 478, 479
boat shell p. 402
bobolink p. 48
bobwhite p. 49
body The entire structure of a plant or animal.
body cavity \\'kav-ə-tē\\ The hollow inside of an organism. A body cavity usually contains the organs necessary for life.
body louse p. 263
bog \\'bäg\\ Wet, spongy ground that contains decayed moss and other plant matter. A bog is a swamp.
Bohemian waxwing p. 476

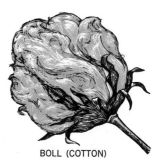

BOLL (COTTON)

boll \\'bōl\\ The seedpod of a plant, especially cotton or flax. See *cotton:* p. 106.
bone Any of the single pieces of a vertebrate skeleton. Bone is also the material that makes up a skeleton. Bone contains a soft tissue called marrow that makes blood cells and is surrounded by spongy or compact material. A thin membrane covers all the bones except at the joints, where there is a layer of cartilage.
bony gar p. 172
book louse p. 49
borax p. 50
bore \\'bōr\\ A fast-rising tide that moves up a river or a narrow inlet.
borer p. 50
boschvark See *bushpig:* p. 58
Boston fern pp. 148, 149
Boston ivy p. 50
botany \\'bät-ᵊn-ē\\ The branch of biology that deals with the life, structure, growth and classification of plants.
bottle-nosed dolphin p. 129
bottom fish Fish that live on or near the bottom of a body of water.
bougainvillea p. 51
boulder \\'bōl-dər\\ A large rock that has been rounded by weather and water.

box elder p. 51

box turtle pp. 456, 457

bracken See *fern:* pp. 148–149

bracket fungus p. 169

brackish \'brak-ish\ Having a small amount of salt, as brackish water.

bracts \'brakts\ The leaves in a flower cluster. Bracts are usually small and scale-like. In a few kinds of plants, such as the poinsettia and bougainvillea, the bracts are so large and colorful that they are often mistaken for flowers.

Brahman See *zebu:* p. 491

braided stream See *river:* p. 380

brain A large mass of nerve tissue that is the center of voluntary movement and coordination in man and other vertebrates. The brain is also the part of the nervous system where memory, reasoning and other mental processes occur. In vertebrates, the brain is located in a skull at the top of the spine.

branch herring See *alewife:* p. 5

breakers \'brā-kərz\ Waves that break in a foam against the seashore or against rocks that stick up out of the water. Breakers are also waves that break in a line at a distance from the shore.

BRECCIA

breccia \'brech-(ē-)ə\ A rock composed of sharp-cornered fragments that are cemented together by sand, clay or lime.

breed \'brēd\ A domestic animal or plant that differs from other animals or plants of the same kind by certain features that do not change in parents, young or future young.

Brewer's blackbird p. 42

bright nebula p. 309

brindled gnu pp. 184, 185

brine shrimp p. 52

bristle annelid p. 14

bristles \'bris-əlz\ Short, stiff, coarse hairs, found on animals such as hogs.

bristle-thighed curlew pp. 117, 118

brittle star See *serpent star:* p. 399

broadbill See *swordfish:* p. 432

broccoli See *cabbage:* p. 62

brontosaur p. 52

bronzed grackle p. 191

brood \'brüd\ A number of young birds hatched at the same time and cared for as a group.

brown algae p. 6

brown bullhead p. 56

brown hydra p. 223

brown lacewing p. 243

brown pelican p. 339

brown rat p. 374

brown shark pp. 400, 401

browntail moth pp. 298, 299

brown thrasher p. 441

Brussels sprouts See *cabbage:* p. 62

bryozoan \,brī-ə-'zō-ən\ A kind of very small water animal. Bryozoans live together in masses, or colonies, that look something like plants. Bryozoans are called "moss animals."

buckeye p. 53

buckeye butterfly pp. 60, 61

bud A small, undeveloped stem or shoot of a plant. Leaves or flowers develop from the bud.

budding \'bəd-ing\ In plants, a kind of grafting in which a bud from one kind of plant is attached to another kind of plant. Budding is also a kind of asexual reproduction, as in yeast.

budgerigar See *parakeet:* p. 332

buffalo p. 53

buffalo bird See *cowbird:* p. 108

buffalo grass pp. 194, 195

bug pp. 54–55

bulb A thickened, fleshy plant part that is usually underground. It has overlapping, scale-like leaves that contain 1 or more buds.

bullfrog pp. 166, 167

bullhead p. 56

bull thistle p. 440

bunting p. 56

burbot p. 56

burdock p. 57

burro See *donkey:* p. 130

burrowing owl pp. 326, 327

bush dog p. 57

bushpig p. 58

bushtit p. 58

bushy-tailed wood rat pp. 374, 375

buteo hawk pp. 208, 209

butte p. 59

buttercup p. 59

butterfly pp. 60–61

buzzard hawk pp. 208, 209

C

cabbage p. 62

cabbage palmetto p. 62

cacao p. 62

cacomistle See *ringtail cat:* p. 380

cactus p. 63

calcite p. 63

caldera p. 64

calf The young of some large mammals, such as the cow, elephant, hippopotamus, rhinoceros, whale and moose.
California condor p. 100
California flying fish p. 162
California grunion p. 64
California halibut p. 204
California laurel p. 64
California poppy p. 359
California quail p. 368
California scorpion fish p. 393
California sea lion pp. 395, 396
California yellowtail p. 489
calla lily p. 65

CALYX

calyx \'kā-liks\ All the sepals of a flower, usually in a ring.
cambium \'kam-bē-əm\ A layer of cells in the stem and roots of woody plants. New cells formed on the inside of the cambium add xylem, while new cells formed on the outside of the cambium add phloem.
Cambrian Period \'kam-brē-ən 'pir-ē-əd\ See Geologic Time Chart, p. 493.
camel p. 65
canary bird p. 66
Canada goldenrod p. 187
Canada goose p. 188
Canadian otter p. 325
Canadian porcupine pp. 359, 360
cankerworm p. 66
cannibalism \'kan-ə-bə-,liz-əm\ The tendency of certain animals to eat the flesh or eggs of their own kind.
cantaloupe See *melon:* p. 281
canyon A deep gorge with steep walls made by running water cutting down through the rock. A canyon is also a steep underwater valley.
cape A piece of land, or point, that sticks out into a large body of water.
Cape anteater See *aardvark:* p. 1
Cape buffalo p. 53
Cape hartebeest pp. 206, 207
Cape jasmine See *gardenia:* p. 172
capillary \'kap-ə-,ler-ē\ In many animals, any of the tiny blood vessels that form a network through most of the body.
capsule \'kap-səl\ A closed plant structure that has seeds in it.

capuchin monkey pp. 292, 293
capybara p. 67

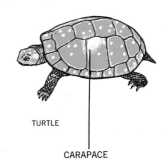

TURTLE

CARAPACE

carapace \'kar-ə-,pās\ A bony shield that covers all or part of the backs of such animals as crabs, armadillos and turtles.
carbohydrate \,kär-bō-'hī-,drāt\ A complex chemical compound containing carbon, hydrogen and oxygen. Sugars, starches and cellulose are all carbohydrates. Carbohydrates occur in plants and in the bodies of animals.
carbon cycle \'kär-bən 'sī-kəl\ The cycle that involves the carbon dioxide and water that is taken from the air by plants during their photosynthesis of carbohydrates. The carbon dioxide is later put back in the air during plant respiration, and by animals during breathing, and also by decaying plant or animal matter.
carbon dioxide \'kär-bən (')dī-'äk-,sīd\ A gas formed when carbon is combined with oxygen. It has no color or odor. Things cannot burn in it. Carbon dioxide is produced by plants and animals, as in breathing and decay.
carbon dioxide-oxygen cycle \'kär-bən (')dī-'äk-,sīd 'äk-si-jən 'sī-kəl\ A natural process of exchange that never stops. Carbon dioxide is taken from the air and used by green plants during photosynthesis. It is given off during plant respiration and animal breathing, and during the decay of plant and animal materials. Oxygen is used by plants and animals during respiration and during the decay of plant and animal materials. Oxygen is given off by plants while they are making carbohydrates by photosynthesis.
Carboniferous Period. \,kär-bə-'nif-(ə-)rəs 'pir-ē-əd\ The Age of Coal. See Geologic Time Chart, p. 493.
cardiac muscle \'kärd-ē-,ak 'məs-əl\ The main muscle tissue of the heart of both vertebrate and invertebrate animals.
cardinal p. 67
caribe See *piranha:* p. 350
caribou p. 68
carnation p. 68
carnivore \'kär-nə-,vōr\ An animal that eats flesh as its main diet. A carnivore is also a plant that absorbs animal materials as food.

Carolina blenny p. 45

Carolina sea robin See *northern sea robin:* p. 313

carp p. 68

carpel \\'kär-pəl\\ A modified leaf of a flower that alone or with others forms a pistil.

carpenter ant p. 15

carpet beetle pp. 36, 37

carrot p. 69

cartilage \\'kärt-əl-ij\\ The white elastic tissue that connects bones. Cartilage is also the tissue that makes up the skeletons of embryos and young animals. It later becomes bones.

cashew p. 69

Cassini's division p. 70

cast \\'kast\\ A fossil in which a mineral has filled in a hole or mold made by a decaying plant or animal. A cast is also a copy of a fossil or other object, made by man from a mold.

castor-oil plant p. 70

cat p. 71

Catalina goby p. 186

catalpa p. 71

catamount See *cougar:* p. 107

cataract p. 72

catbird p. 72

catbrier See *greenbrier:* p. 197

cat claw acacia pp. 1, 2

caterpillar The larva of a butterfly or moth.

catfish p. 73

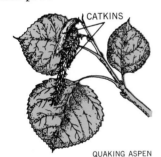

CATKINS

QUAKING ASPEN

catkin \\'kat-kən\\ A scaly, bract-covered structure on certain trees, such as the chestnut and willow.

catnip p. 73

cattail p. 73

cattle p. 74

cattleya p. 74

cauliflower See *cabbage:* p. 62

caverns \\'kav-ərnz\\ Caves. Caverns are usually large underground areas that are quite long.

cavy See *capybara:* p. 67; and *guinea pig:* p. 200

cayenne See *pepper:* p. 341

cecropia moth pp. 298, 299

cedar p. 75

cedar waxwing p. 476

celery p. 75

celestial equator \\sə-'les(h)-chəl i-'kwāt-ər\\ An imaginary circle on the celestial sphere. The celestial equator is in the same plane as the earth's equator and is halfway between the celestial poles.

celestial horizon \\sə-'les(h)-chəl hə-'rizⁿn\\ The imaginary circle on the celestial sphere that is halfway between the point directly above the observer and the point opposite that below the observer.

celestial meridian \\sə-'les(h)-chəl mə-'rid-ē-ən\\ The imaginary circle within the celestial sphere that passes through the celestial poles and the point directly above the observer.

celestial poles p. 76

celestial sphere \\sə-'les(h)-chəl 'sfir\\ An imaginary sphere going out from the earth for an unlimited distance. Objects in space seem to be located on its surface. It is divided by imaginary lines so that objects in space can be located at particular points on it.

cell In living tissue, the smallest unit of structure and function. A cell has a nucleus and cytoplasm. A cell is also a walled hole in the nonliving tissues of plants. A cell is sometimes called a protoplast.

cell division \\də-'vizh-ən\\ The way in which single-celled plants and animals reproduce. Cell division is also the process in which new cells divide to form 2 cells in animals and plants that have many cells.

cell membrane \\'mem-,brān\\ The thin, living layer that surrounds the materials of a cell.

cell sap A liquid that fills the vacuoles in plant cells. It is made up of water that has materials dissolved or suspended in it.

cellulose \\'sel-yə-,lōs\\ A carbohydrate that is the main part of the cell walls of plants.

cell wall An envelope of non-living material that surrounds some cells of plants. Plant cells usually have cellulose walls.

Cenozoic Era \\,sē-nə-'zō-ik 'ir-ə\\ See Geologic Time Chart, p. 493.

centipede p. 76

central mudminnow p. 301

central nervous system \\'sen-trəl 'nər-vəs 'sis-təm\\ In vertebrates, the part of the nervous system that receives sensory impulses and sends out motor impulses.

century plant See *agave:* p. 2

cephalothorax \\,sef-ə-lō-'thōr-,aks\\ The area of the combined head and thorax in spiders and certain crustaceans.

cepheid variable \\'sē-fē-əd 'ver-ē-ə-bəl\\ A star that grows dim and bright regularly and with the same amount of time between changes.

cerebellum \\,ser-ə-'bel-əm\\ In man, the part of the brain that is the center of coordination for movements of the muscles.

cerebrum \\sə-'rē-brəm\\ The largest part of the brain in man. It has 2 equal parts, called hemispheres.

chacma baboon p. 25

chalcedony p. 77

chalcopyrite p. 77

chalk p. 77

chambered nautilus p. 309

chameleon p. 78

chamois p. 78

channel catfish p. 73

channeled whelk p. 480

characteristics \,kar-ik-tə-'ris-tiks\ In animals and plants, traits that are passed on by inheritance and that can be modified by the environment. For example, behavior, size, shape or hair color are characteristics by which a single person or a group can be recognized.

cheetah p. 79

chemical weathering \'kem-i-kəl 'weth-ər-ing\ The breaking down of rock material by chemical processes. Chemical weathering results in a change in the makeup and the character of the original rock material.

chemosphere \'kem-ō-,sfir\ A layer of the atmosphere. It is usually thought of as beginning in the upper stratosphere, about 25 miles up, and extending into the ionosphere (50 to 275 miles up). The chemosphere is sometimes called the ozone layer because it contains ozone.

chemosynthesis \,kem-ō-'sin(t)-thə-səs\ In plants, the making of organic compounds by using the energy given off during chemical reactions.

chemotropism \ke-'mä-trə-,piz-əm\ The reaction of an organism or any of its parts in turning toward or away from a chemical substance.

cherrystone clam p. 89

cherry tree p. 79

chestnut p. 80

chestnut cowrie shell p. 108

chewing mouth parts The specialized movable jaws and lip-like parts of such insects as grasshoppers, roaches and termites. Insects with chewing mouth parts bite off and chew plant materials and other substances on which they feed.

chick The young of domestic chickens and some other birds.

chickadee p. 80

chicken p. 81

chicken hawk pp. 208, 209

chickweed p. 81

chicory p. 81

chili pepper p. 341

chimney rock p. 82

chimney swift p. 432

chimpanzee p. 82

chinch bug pp. 54, 55

chinchilla p. 83

Chinese mantis p. 274

chinook \shə-'nuk\ A southwest wind in the Sierra Nevada and Rocky Mountain regions. A chinook moves quickly down the eastern side of the mountains toward a low pressure area.

Chinooks are most common in winter and spring when the wind melts snow and causes warm temperatures in the valleys to the east.

chipmunk p. 83

chitin \'kīt-ən\ A hard, waterproof substance that forms the exoskeleton of such arthropods as the lobster.

chiton p. 84

Chlorella See *algae:* pp. 6–7

chlorite p. 84

chlorophyll \'klōr-ə-,fil\ The green-colored material in most plants. Chlorophyll is necessary to photosynthesis.

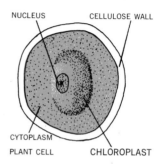

NUCLEUS   CELLULOSE WALL

CYTOPLASM

PLANT CELL   CHLOROPLAST

chloroplast \'klōr-ə-,plast\ A small body, or plastid, that contains chlorophyll. Chloroplasts occur in the cytoplasm of many plant cells.

chocolate See *cacao:* p. 62

cholesterol \kə-'les-tə-,rȯl\ A heavy, white or colorless form of alcohol. Cholesterol occurs mostly in animal tissues.

chordate \'kȯrd-ət\ Any vertebrate or marine animal that has an internal skeleton. At some stage in their early development, chordates have an elastic rod of cells that is later replaced by a backbone. They also have gill slits or pouches at some time.

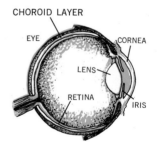

CHOROID LAYER

EYE

CORNEA

LENS

RETINA

IRIS

choroid layer \'kōr-,ȯid 'lā-ər\ The dark inside layer of the eyeball of vertebrates. It contains blood vessels and color cells.

Christmas fern pp. 148, 149

chromatin \'krō-mə-tən\ The grain-like materials in the nucleus of a cell. Chromatin forms the most noticeable part of the nuclear network and the chromosomes.

chromite p. 84

chromosome \'krō-mə-ˌsōm\ In plants and animals, any of the microscopic, thread-like bodies that control heredity. Chromosomes develop from chromatin in a cell nucleus before the cell divides. They occur in a certain number, form and size for each species of plant and animal.

chromosphere p. 85

chrysalis \'kris-ə-ləs\ An undeveloped butterfly, or pupa, in a protective covering.

chrysanthemum p. 85

chuckwalla p. 86

chukar partridge p. 334

cicada p. 86

cigar tree See *catalpa:* p. 71

cilia \'sil-ē-ə\ Tiny hair-like structures that grow from the outside surface of a 1-celled organism. The organism swims from place to place by moving its cilia back and forth in a kind of beating motion.

ciliate p. 87

cinder cone p. 87

cinnabar p. 87

cinnamon fern pp. 148, 149

circulatory system \'sər-kyə-lə-ˌtor-ē 'sis-təm\ In many animals, a closed network of tubes or vessels through which blood and the materials in it move to all parts of the body. A circulatory system also carries lymph.

circumpolar \ˌsər-kəm-'pō-lər\ At, near or around the celestial poles or the poles of the earth.

cirque p. 88

cirrocumulus clouds pp. 90, 91

cirrostratus clouds pp. 90, 91

cirrus clouds pp. 90, 91

cisco See *lake herring:* p. 245

citrus tree p. 88

civet cat See *ringtail cat:* p. 380

clam p. 89

clamworm See *nereis:* p. 311

class One of the divisions of a plant or animal phylum that is further divided into orders.

claw The nail on an animal's toe. In some arthropods such as crabs, a claw is the pincer-like ending on the legs.

cleavage \'klē-vij\ A characteristic that certain minerals and rocks have that makes them tend to split along definite planes spaced closely together.

click beetle pp. 36, 37

cliff A very steep slope, usually of rock.

climate \'klī-mət\ The weather conditions of a given area. The climate of an area is described in terms of temperature, pressure, winds, rain and evaporation for a long period of time.

climax \'klī-ˌmaks\ **community** A well-balanced community where living things can use the materials and energy found there.

cloud pp. 90–91

clover p. 92

club moss p. 92

cluster \'kləs-tər\ In plants, a grouping of individual parts that have the same structure and that grow together, such as bananas, grapes and the flowers of certain plants.

coachwhip snake pp. 410, 411

coal p. 93

coal sack p. 93

coastal plain pp. 351, 352

coastal rhododendron p. 379

coast range \'rānj\ A mountain range that is nearly parallel to the edge of a continent.

coatimundi p. 93

coat-of-mail shell See *chiton:* p. 84

coccus See *bacteria:* p. 25

cochlea \'käk-lē-ə\ In birds and most mammals except the egg-laying mammals, the spiral tube in the inner ear that contains a fluid, a membrane and the auditory nerve endings.

cockatoo p. 94

cockle button See *burdock:* p. 57

cockleshell p. 94

cockroach p. 95

cockscomb p. 95

cocoa tree See *cacao:* p. 62

coconut palm p. 330

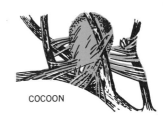

COCOON

cocoon The outer covering spun by the larvae of some insects before they enter the resting, or pupal stage. A cocoon is also the egg case of spiders and earthworms.

cod p. 96

coelacanth p. 96

coelenterate \si-'lent-ə-ˌrāt\ An animal having a body made up of chiefly 2 layers of tissue, a mouth-like opening that takes in food and gets rid of waste materials, a simple nervous system and protective structures such as tentacles and stinging cells around the mouth. Corals, hydras, jellyfish and sea anemones are coelenterates.

coffee tree p. 97

col p. 97

cold air mass \'mas\ A large body of air that is colder than the surface over which it is moving. A cold air mass begins as arctic or polar air. In the northern hemisphere, a cold air mass moves to the southeast and east.

cold-blooded Describing such animals as fish, amphibians and reptiles, whose body temperatures vary with the temperatures of their surroundings or habitat.

cold front The boundary line between a cold air mass and a warm air mass. The cold air mass is moving toward the warm air mass and pushing it under. A cold front may also be the line on the earth's surface where a cold air mass meets a warm air mass.

coleus p. 97

collared lemming p. 251

collared lizard p. 259

collared peccary pp. 338, 339

colon \'kō-lən\ In many higher animals, the main part of the large intestine.

colony \'käl-ə-nē\ A group of animals such as insects or seals, living together as a community. A colony is also a group of microorganisms that have grown from a single cell or a group of cells.

Colorado potato beetle pp. 36, 37

colt A young animal of the horse family, such as the zebra, ass or horse.

columbine p. 98

coma p. 98

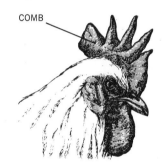

COMB

comb The fleshy growth or crest on the heads of domestic birds and some other birds such as grouse.

comet p. 99

commensalism \kə-'men(t)-sə-,liz-əm\ A relationship between 2 animals, such as a barnacle attached to a whale, where 1 animal benefits and the other neither suffers nor benefits.

commercial tobacco p. 446

common annual nasturtium p. 309

common annual ragweed p. 371

common barberry p. 29

common barn owl pp. 326, 327

common bean p. 33

common blue violet p. 464

common boat shell p. 402

common book louse p. 49

common burdock p. 57

common bushtit pp. 58, 59

common chameleon p. 78

common chickweed p. 81

common cockleshell pp. 94, 95

common crow p. 115

common cuttlefish p. 119

common dandelion p. 121

common dayflower p. 122

common domestic rat pp. 374, 375

common earthworm p. 136

common East African waterbuck p. 473

common edible morel p. 296

common eel pp. 137, 138

common eider p. 139

common fig tree p. 150

common foxglove p. 165

common gar p. 172

common garden hyacinth p. 222

common garden onion p. 320

common garden petunia p. 344

common garden snapdragon p. 412

common greenbrier p. 198

common haircap moss p. 297

common heliotrope p. 212

common hippopotamus p. 215

common horse sponge p. 418

common horsetail p. 221

common house centipede p. 76

common house mouse p. 301

common iguana p. 225

common Indian mongoose p. 291

common kiwi pp. 240, 241

common lilac p. 255

common loon p. 262

common mackerel p. 265

common mesquite p. 283

common milkweed p. 285

common morning glory p. 296

common nighthawk p. 312

common oat p. 316

common octopus p. 318

common opossum p. 321

common orange day lily p. 122

common papaw p. 331

common paramecium p. 333

common peafowl p. 336

common persimmon p. 342

common pickerelweed p. 346

common pitcher plant p. 351

common plantain p. 353

common plum tree p. 355

common poinsettia p. 356

common pompano p. 357

common roundworm See *ascaris:* p. 20

common scorpion p. 393

common screech owl p. 327

common silverfish p. 404

common skate p. 405

common skunk p. 406

common snipe p. 412

common South American tapir pp. 435, 436

common spiderwort p. 416

common starfish p. 422

common starling pp. 422, 423

common sunflower p. 428

common termite p. 439

common tern pp. 439, 440

common thresher shark pp. 400, 401

common thyme p. 442

common walkingstick p. 468

common water lily p. 474

common wheat p. 480

common wild lupine p. 264

common wild strawberry p. 425

common yarrow p. 488

common zebra p. 491

communal \kə-'myün-ᵊl\ Describing an association of certain animals that live and work together, such as ants.

complete metamorphosis \,met-ə-'mōr-fə-səs\ A kind of change in which a developing organism goes through 4 stages. The stages are the egg, larva, pupa and adult.

complex mountain p. 300

composite cone p. 99

compound eye In insects and crustaceans, an eye made up of several lenses or facets that contain separate nerve endings.

compound leaf A leaf whose blade is divided into 2 or more distinct parts called leaflets.

conch p. 99

concretion p. 100

condensation \,kän-,den-'sā-shən\ The process that changes a gas or vapor into a liquid, or solid.

condor p. 100

cone p. 101

coneflower See *yellow daisy:* p. 488

cones In vertebrates, the cone-shaped end organs of the visual cells in the retina of the eye. Cones are necessary to color vision.

cone shell See *cone:* p. 101

coney See *hyrax:* p. 223

conglomerate p. 101

CONIFER

SPRUCE TREE

conifer \'kän-ə-fər\ Any plant whose seeds are not produced in seed cases, but that bears cones. Conifers usually have needle-shaped leaves. Pines, spruces and firs are conifers.

connective tissue \kə-'nek-tiv 'tish-(,)ü\ Any fiber-like tissue that holds together and supports body structures in animals.

conservation \,kän(t)-sər-'vā-shən\ The protection, care and wise use of land, forests, water, animal life, minerals and fuels.

CONSTELLATION

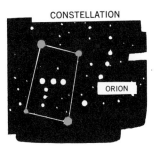

ORION

constellation \,kän(t)-stə-'lā-shən\ A number of stars that seem to form a group, named after an animal, a character from myths or an object. To astronomers, constellations are definite areas of the celestial sphere that are marked off by imaginary boundary lines.

constrictor \kən-'strik-tər\ A muscle that contracts or that makes an opening of the body smaller. A constrictor is also a snake that kills its prey by crushing it in its coils.

continent \'känt-ᵊn-ant\ Any 1 of the 7 major land masses on earth: North America, South America, Europe, Asia, Africa, Australia and Antarctica.

continental air mass \,känt-ᵊn-'ent-ᵊl 'ar 'mas\ A large, fairly dry body of air that has formed over a land area.

continental \,känt-ᵊn-'ent-ᵊl\ **drift** A theory having to do with the development of continents. The theory states that large continents broke up into smaller masses of land and slowly drifted apart. The continents became separated by seas.

continental shelf p. 101

continental slope p. 102

contractile vacuole \kən-'trak-tᵊl 'vak-yə-wōl\ A liquid-filled opening in 1-celled animals. It has to do with the giving off of water from the cell and with the control of osmotic pressure.

Cooper's hawk pp. 208, 209

coot p. 102

cootie See *louse:* p. 262

copepod p. 102

Copernican system \kō-'pər-ni-kən 'sis-təm\ The theory of Nicolaus Copernicus, stated in the sixteenth century, that the earth is a planet that rotates on its axis and revolves around the sun.

copper p. 103

copperhead pp. 410, 411

copper rockfish p. 383

coquina See *limestone:* p. 256

coral p. 103

coral snake pp. 410, 411

cordillera p. 103

core \'kōr\ The center of the earth. The earth's core is believed to be in 2 parts, a solid sphere surrounded by a liquid sphere. A core is also a rod-shaped sample of rock obtained with

Coriolis effect

special hollow drills. Such samples help man gain knowledge of the rocks below the surface of the earth. A core is also the inner part of fruits, that contains the seeds, as in apples and pears.

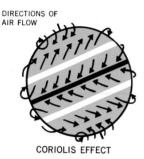

DIRECTIONS OF AIR FLOW

CORIOLIS EFFECT

Coriolis effect \\,kȯr-ē-'ō-ləs ə-'fekt\\ The turning aside of a moving mass from a north or south path, caused by the rotation of the earth. The Coriolis effect is most noticeable in winds, rockets, artillery shells and flowing water.

corm \\'kȯrm\\ A large, solid bulb that has scaly leaves and buds. The crocus and gladiolus grow from corms.

cormorant p. 104

corn p. 104

cornea \\'kȯr-nē-ə\\ The clear, tough, transparent part of the eyeball coating. It covers the iris and the pupil and lets light into the eye. The cornea is made up of layers or fibers that are connected to the rest of the eyeball covering.

cornflower See *bachelor's button:* p. 25

corn smut See *rust and smut:* p. 385

corona p. 105

corpuscle \\'kȯr-,pəs-əl\\ A particle of protoplasm, such as a red blood cell or a white blood cell or a blood platelet, that has a special function in the blood.

correlation \\,kȯr-ə-'lā-shən\\ The determination of the same geologic age in parts of a rock formation that are a great distance apart, or in different rock formations of the same age. A correlation is also the use of fossils or other evidence to show age relationships of rocks or events.

corundum p. 105

cos lettuce p. 253

cosmic dust p. 105

cosmic \\'käz-mik\\ **rays** Radiation from outer space that bombards the earth and its atmosphere. Primary cosmic rays enter the atmosphere and bump into atoms of oxygen and nitrogen. In this way, the primary rays give their energy to secondary rays that penetrate lower levels of the atmosphere.

cosmology \\käz-'mäl-ə-jē\\ The study of the universe.

cotton p. 106

cotton boll weevil p. 477

cottonmouth pp. 410, 411

cotton rat pp. 374, 375

cottonwood p. 106

cotyledon \\,kät-əl-'ēd-ən\\ A small leaf-like structure inside a plant seed of a young plant.

cougar p. 107

counterglow p. 107

covey \\'kəv-ē\\ A small group of game birds, such as quails or partridges, usually made up of 1 brood with or without the parents.

cowbird p. 107

cow killer See *velvet ant:* p. 461

cowrie p. 108

cowslip p. 108

coyote p. 109

coypu See *nutria:* p. 315

coypu rat See *nutria:* p. 315

crab p. 109

crab, horseshoe See *horseshoe crab:* p. 220

Crab nebula p. 310

cranberry p. 110

crane p. 110

crane fly pp. 160, 161

cranium \\'krā-nē-əm\\ The part of the skull that covers the brain.

crape myrtle p. 111

crappie p. 111

crater p. 111

crawdad See *crayfish:* p. 112

crawfish See *crayfish:* p. 112

crayfish p. 112

crazyweed See *locoweed:* p. 260

creosote bush p. 112

crescent \\'kres-ənt\\ Describing the appearance of the moon between new moon and first quarter, or between last quarter and new moon. The planets Venus and Mercury also have a crescent stage.

crescent moon See *moon:* p. 294

cress p. 112

Cretaceous Period \\kri-'tā-shəs 'pir-ē-əd\\ See Geologic Time Chart, p. 493.

crevasse p. 113

cricket p. 113

cricket frog pp. 166, 167

croaker p. 113

crocodile p. 114

crocus p. 114

Cro-Magnon man pp. 270, 271

crop In zoology, the first of the 3 stomachs of a bird. It stores and prepares the food for digestion in the other 2 stomachs. The crop is largest in birds that eat grains, but is missing in birds that eat insects and fruit. A crop is also a digestive organ in insects and other animals. A crop is also food that is grown and harvested.

crossbill p. 115

cross-pollination \\,krȯs-päl-ə-'nā-shən\\ The moving of pollen from a stamen of a flower to the pistil of another flower of the same kind, or species, by natural ways or by man.

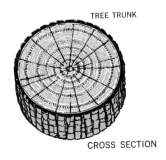

TREE TRUNK

CROSS SECTION

cross section \\'sek-shən\\ A crosswise slice of a material at right angles to an axis or plane.

crow p. 115

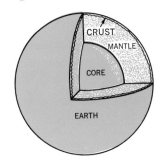

CRUST

MANTLE

CORE

EARTH

crust The outer layer or shell of the earth. It is up to 80 miles thick and is made up of rock and soil on top, with granite and basalt underneath.

crustacean p. 115

crystal p. 116

crystalline \\'kris-tə-lən\\ Describing a solid substance that has the properties of a crystal. Crystalline also describes particles that are usually hard or glossy.

cub The young of various mammals such as bears, foxes, lions and tigers.

cuckoo p. 116

cuckoo-button See *burdock:* p. 57

cucumber p. 117

cud \\'kəd\\ The food that is molded into pellets in the second compartment of the stomach of such ruminant mammals as cattle. The cud is then returned to the animal's mouth for more chewing.

cultivated geranium p. 177

cultivated gooseberry p. 189

cultivated hop vine pp. 216, 217

cultivated iris p. 228

cultivated tea rose p. 383

culture \\'kəl-chər\\ The growth of micro-organisms in a prepared substance that contains food for them.

cultured pearl p. 337

cumulonimbus clouds pp. 90, 91

cumulus clouds pp. 90, 91

cuprite p. 117

curlew p. 117

day lily

current \\'kər-ənt\\ A flow of water or air in a definite direction.

current marks p. 118

cuticle \\'kyüt-i-kəl\\ A skin, membrane or other hard covering of a cell or organ. A cuticle is also a thin, waxy, waterproof layer covering the outer surfaces of some plant leaves.

cutlip minnow pp. 287, 288

cutoff p. 118

cutting A twig, branch or leaf that is cut from a parent plant and put in soil, sand or water. In time, new roots, stems and leaves will grow from the cutting.

cuttlefish p. 119

cycle \\'sī-kəl\\ A series of stages in the life of a plant or animal. A cycle is also any series of events that always happen in the same order.

cyclone \\'sī-,klōn\\ An area of low atmospheric pressure in which winds move toward the center in a spiral pattern. In the northern hemisphere, the winds in a cyclone move in a counterclockwise direction. In the southern hemisphere, the winds in a cyclone move in a clockwise direction.

cynthia moth pp. 298, 299

cypress p. 119

cytoplasm \\'sīt-ə-,plaz-əm\\ The materials that surround the nucleus in a cell.

d

daddy longlegs See *crane fly:* p. 161; and *harvestman:* p. 207

daffodil See *narcissus:* p. 308

dahlia p. 120

damselfly p. 120

dark nebula See *nebula:* p. 309

darning needle See *damselfly:* p. 120; and *dragonfly:* p. 131

dandelion p. 120

daphnia p. 121

Darwinism \\'där-wə-,niz-əm\\ Charles Darwin's theory of evolution, which states that all species of plants and animals develop from earlier forms by a process called natural selection. In natural selection, each generation produces young whose characteristics differ slightly from those of the parents. Individuals that have characteristics best suited to their environment survive and reproduce. After many generations, a new species may be produced through this process.

day A unit of time determined by 1 rotation of the earth. A day is also the time from dawn to dark.

dayflower p. 121

day lily p. 122

521

deathwatch See *book louse:* p. 49

decay \di-'kā\ The breakdown of dead organisms by certain microorganisms.

deciduous \di-'sij-ə-wəs\ Describing plants that lose their leaves every year.

declination \,dek-lə-'nā-shən\ The angular measure of a star's distance from the celestial equator. Declination is figured on a great circle that passes through the celestial pole and the star. Declination is also the angle between a compass needle pointing toward magnetic north and a line indicating true north.

deep Any area of the sea that is more than 18,000 feet below the surface.

deer p. 122

deer fly pp. 160, 161

defense mechanism \'mek-ə-,niz-əm\ The means by which an organism defends itself against other organisms.

degeneration \di-,jen-ə-'rā-shən\ The gradual or slow change of an organism to a lower form of development. Degeneration is also the return of an organ to a simpler or useless state during the course of evolution.

degradation \,deg-rə-'dā-shən\ A wearing down or lowering of land surfaces through weathering, erosion and the effect of gravity on large and small masses of rock.

dehydration \,dē-,hī-'drā-shən\ A lessening of the amount of fluid or liquid in living tissues.

Deimos See *Mars:* p. 277

delphinium p. 123

delta p. 123

den The burrow, cave or other home of a wild animal. A den is also a cave where a female bear takes care of her cubs.

density current \'den(t)-sə-tē 'kər-ənt\ A current in fluids, such as water or air, that is caused by differences of density within the fluid.

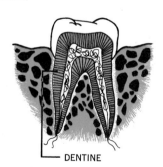

DENTINE

dentine \'den-,tēn\ The hard, dense tissue of the teeth that surrounds the pulp cavity. Dentine is covered with enamel. Dentine is also a substance in the tooth-like scales of sharks and related fish; also spelled dentin.

deoxyribonucleic \dē-,äk-sē-'rī-bō-n(y)ü-,klē-ik\ **acid** (DNA) A chemical substance carried by the proteins in the nucleus of living cells. It is important in the passing on of hereditary characteristics.

deposit Any earth material dropped by the action of wind, water or moving ice.

deposition \,dep-ə-'zish-ən\ The dropping of earth material from such natural carriers as floods, streams, seas, winds and glaciers.

depression \di-'presh-ən\ A low place on the surface of the earth. A depression is usually surrounded on all sides by higher ground. A depression is also an area of low atmospheric pressure in relation to the surrounding areas.

descendant \di-'sen-dənt\ Any offspring, no matter how many generations there are between it and a given ancestor.

desert A large, barren area with few living organisms. A desert may be hot and dry, as the Gobi Desert in Asia, or cold, as Antarctica. A desert is usually an area with very little rainfall.

detritus p. 124

develop \di-'vel-əp\ To grow through stages.

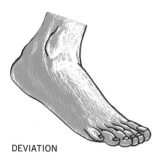

DEVIATION

deviation \,dē-vē-'ā-shən\ A variation that is not normal in the usual growth of an animal body part.

devilfish See *octopus:* p. 318

devil ray See *manta:* p. 273

devil's purses See *skate:* p. 405

Devonian Period \di-'vō-nē-ən 'pir-ē-əd\ See Geologic Time Chart, p. 493.

dew Small drops of water from the air that form on grass, leaves and other surfaces that are cooler than the surrounding air.

dewlap \'d(y)ü-,lap\ A loose fold of skin that hangs down under the throats of some animals.

dew point The temperature at which the atmosphere becomes saturated with water vapor.

diamond p. 124

diamondback rattlesnake pp. 410, 411

diamondback turtle pp. 456, 457

diaphragm \'dī-ə-,fram\ The muscular tissue that separates the abdominal cavity from the chest cavity. A diaphragm is also any thin membrane that separates parts of the body cavity in animals.

diatom p. 125

diatomaceous \,dī-ət-ə-'mā-shəs\ **earth** A light-colored, earthy material that is full of holes. It is made up of diatom shells of nearly pure silica.

dichotomous \dī-'kät-ə-məs\ Divided into 2 parts, pairs or branches.

dicotyledon \,dī-,kät-əl-'ēd-ən\ A plant that produces 2 cotyledons, such as most shrubs and trees that lose their leaves every year.

differentiation \,dif-ə-,ren-chē-'ā-shən\ The gradual changing of body parts, through evolution, to perform different or special functions.

diffuse nebula See *nebula:* p. 309

digestion \dī-'jes(h)-chən\ The changing of food into simpler chemical compounds that can be absorbed by the tissues. Digestion consists of both mechanical and chemical action.

digestive enzymes \dī-'jes-tiv 'en-,zīmz\ Chemical substances produced by the cells of an organism. Digestive enzymes help break down molecules of food during digestion.

digestive system \dī-'jes-tiv 'sis-təm\ All the parts of a many-celled organism that are involved in the process of digestion.

digitalis See *foxglove:* p. 165

dike \'dīk\ A bank or wall, usually built to protect lowlands from floods. A dike is also a formation of molten rock that hardened in a fissure. See *vein:* p. 461.

dilation \dī-'lā-shən\ The enlarging of a part of the body, such as an organ or duct, to bigger than its normal size.

dill p. 125

dimetrodon p. 126

dinoflagellate p. 126

dip The angle or slope of a layer of rock or other flat surface as measured from the horizontal.

diploid \'dip-,lȯid\ Having double the basic, or smallest, number of chromosomes.

dipping ducks pp. 132, 133

disconformity \,dis-kən-'fȯr-mət-ē\ An area that separates 2 parallel layers of layered rock. A disconformity is caused by the erosion of 1 layer that is then covered with another layer of rock.

discontinuity \(,)dis-,känt-ᵊn-'(y)ü-ət-ē\ A sudden or quick change in structure. A discontinuity is also the area between 2 air masses of different temperatures and pressures.

disintegration \(,)dis-,int-ə-'grā-shən\ The breakdown of a substance into smaller parts.

disk \'disk\ In vertebrates, a thin layer of fibrous cartilage located between each 2 vertebrae or bone sections of the spinal column. A disk is also one of the cup-like ends on the tendrils of climbing vines that cling to walls and trees.

dispersal \dis-'per-səl\ The moving of plants or animals to a new area. Dispersal is also the process of reaching a new area.

ditch moss See *elodea:* p. 141

diurnal \dī-'ərn-ᵊl\ Describing plants or animals that are active only during the daytime. Diurnal also describes the movement of celestial objects in relation to the earth during a day, or 24-hour period.

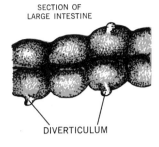

SECTION OF LARGE INTESTINE

DIVERTICULUM

diverticulum \,dī-vər-'tik-yə-ləm\ A sac or pouch leading from a hollow body part.

divide A spine-like elevation or high place, such as a mountain range, that separates 2 drainage systems or basins.

diving petrel p. 343

dobsonfly p. 126

dodo p. 127

dog p. 127

dog fennel p. 128

dog flea p. 156

dogwood p. 128

doldrums \'dōl-drəmz\ An area near the equator, especially over the oceans, where there are light, varying winds, calms or periods of no wind, and occasional storms or squalls. The doldrums also are called the doldrum belt or the equatorial belt.

dolomite p. 129

dolomitic limestone See *dolomite:* p. 129

dolphin p. 129

dome p. 129

domestic \də-'mes-tik\ Describing mammals and birds that have been tamed by man, or that in some way have become used to living near man. Rats and cockroaches are domestic pests.

domestic cat p. 71

domestic cattle p. 74

domestic goat p. 185

domestic llama pp. 259, 260

domestic pig See *swine:* p. 432

domestic pigeon See *dove* p. 131

domestic rabbit p. 370

domestic sheep p. 402

dominant \'däm-(ə-)nənt\ Describing a plant or animal, or a group of plants and animals, having the most influence in a particular environment.

dominant trait \'däm-(ə-)nənt 'trāt\ In genetics, 1 of a pair of opposite characters that is stronger than the other when factors for both are present in the cells.

donkey p. 130

dormant \'dȯr-mənt\ Resting, not active, as a seed or animal in hibernation.

dorsal \'dȯr-səl\ Describing the back or the area near the back of an animal. Dorsal also describes the upper surface of plants that do not have clearly separate roots, stems or leaves, such as algae.

double-crested cormorant p. 104

Douglas fir p. 130

dove p. 131

dragonfly p. 131

drainage \'drā-nij\ The flowing off of surface water into rivers and streams.

drift A collection of materials such as boulders, gravel, sand and clay that has been carried by glaciers and deposited by the melting ice or the water from it.

dromedary See camel: p. 65

drone fly pp. 160, 161

drought \'draủt\ A long period of time without rainfall.

drowned valley See estuary: p. 143; and valley: p. 459

duck pp. 132–133

duck-billed platypus p. 134

duck hawk pp. 208, 209

duct \'dəkt\ A tube or canal that carries away secretions and excretions, especially from glands.

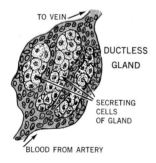

TO VEIN

DUCTLESS GLAND

SECRETING CELLS OF GLAND

BLOOD FROM ARTERY

ductless gland \'dək(t)-ləs 'gland\ A gland that produces hormones that are released directly into the bloodstream instead of through a duct.

dugong p. 134

dune \'d(y)ün\ A mound, hill or ridge of sand formed by the wind. Dunes usually form on deserts or along sea- or lakeshores.

duodenum \,d(y)ü-ə-'dē-nəm\ The upper or first part of the small intestine.

duplication \,d(y)ü-pli-'kā-shən\ The separation of a leaf or an organ of a flower into 2 or more parts by division during development. Duplication is also the doubling of the chromosomes into equal parts during mitosis.

dust-cloud hypothesis \hī-'päth-ə-səs\ A theory that the solar system was formed from whirling cosmic dust. The pressure of starlight forced the molecules together to form a rotating sun.

The planets and their moons condensed from matter thrown off by the sun.

Dutchman's-breeches See bleeding heart: p. 44

Dutchman's pipe See pipevine: p. 349

dwarf bean p. 33

dwarf marigold p. 275

dwarf poinciana p. 356

e

eagle p. 135

eardrum In many animals, the membrane that separates the outer ear from the middle ear. The eardrum carries vibrations to other structures in the ear. An eardrum is also a thin membrane that covers the hearing organ on the legs of certain insects.

ear shell See abalone: p. 1

earth Soil or loose material, other than rock, on land surfaces. Also, the planet Earth. See pp. 135, 498, 499, 502.

earth light Sunlight reflected to the moon from the daylight area of the earth. Earth light is sometimes called earthshine.

earthquake A tremor or shaking of the earth's crust. Earthquakes are caused by underground volcanic activity or by the shifting of rock beneath the surface.

earthquake belt Either of 2 areas, in the Pacific or in the Mediterranean, where earthquakes usually occur because the earth's crust is weak in those places.

earth science The study of the earth, its materials and the forces that act on them, and the earth's relationships to other bodies in space.

earthworm p. 136; see also worm: p. 486

eastern bluebird p. 46

eastern bobwhite p. 49

eastern chipmunk p. 83

eastern cottonwood pp. 106, 107

eastern goshawk p. 136

eastern hemlock p. 213

eastern kingbird p. 238

eastern mockingbird p. 289

eastern mole p. 290

eastern narrowmouth toad pp. 444, 445

eastern spadefoot toad pp. 444, 445

eastern starfish p. 422

eastern tent caterpillar pp. 438, 439

eastern white pine p. 348

echidna p. 136

eclipse p. 137

ecology \i-'käl-ə-jē\ The study of the relationships among living things and between them and their environment.

ectoderm \'ek-tə-,dərm\ The outer cell layer of an animal embryo. The nervous system, the skin, the teeth and other outer features develop from the ectoderm. The ectoderm is also the outer layer of cells, or membrane, of the body of some many-celled lower animals.

eddy \'ed-ē\ A whirlpool of water or air.

eel p. 137

eelgrass p. 138

efferent \'ef-ə-rənt\ **nerves** Nerves that carry impulses away from nerve centers to muscles and glands.

eft See *newt:* p. 312

egg A reproductive cell produced by the female.

CRAWFISH

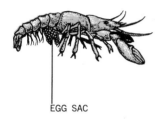

EGG SAC

egg sac \'sak\ A case that contains and protects the eggs of certain insects, spiders, crustaceans and mollusks.

egret p. 138

eider p. 139

electric eel p. 139

element \'el-ə-mənt\ A chemical substance that cannot be broken down into a simpler substance by ordinary chemical methods.

elephant p. 140

elliptical galaxy p. 170

elm p. 140

elodea p. 141

elver See *eel:* p. 137

embryo \'em-brē-,ō\ A young organism in the earliest stages of development. An embryo is also a partially developed plant in a seed.

FISH DEVELOPMENT

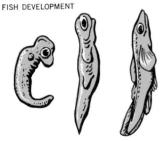

EMBRYOLOGY

embryology \,em-brē-'äl-ə-jē\ The branch of biology that has to do with the stages in the formation and development of the embryo in plants and animals.

emerald See *beryl:* p. 38

emergence \i-'mər-jən(t)s\ A process by which a sea or lake bottom becomes dry land. The water level becomes lower or the land is lifted up.

emery See *corundum:* p. 105

emperor penguin pp. 339, 340

emu p. 141

Encke's comet p. 99

end moraine p. 141; see also *moraine:* p. 295

endocrine gland \'en-də-krən 'gland\ Any of the ductless glands that produce and discharge one or more hormones into the blood and lymph systems.

endoderm \'en-də-,dərm\ The inner germ layer of an embryo. The linings of certain internal organs are formed from the endoderm. An endoderm is also the inner layer of cells or tissue in the bodies of several many-celled, lower animals.

endoskeleton \,en-(,)dō-'skel-ət-ᵊn\ The inner framework of bones and cartilage in most vertebrates.

English ivy See *ivy:* p. 229

English sparrow p. 142

English yew p. 490

Eniwetok Atoll p. 23

entomology \,ent-ə-'mäl-ə-jē\ The branch of zoology that deals with the study of insects.

envelope \'en-və-,lōp\ Any covering, enclosing membrane or shell. An envelope is also any enclosing leaves.

environment \in-'vī-rən-mənt\ The conditions or surroundings outside an individual plant or animal.

enzyme \'en-,zīm\ An organic substance in a living cell. Enzymes are made up of protein, or protein combined with other substances. Enzymes control chemical reactions in living matter.

Eocene Epoch \'ē-ə-,sēn 'ep-ək\ See Geologic Time Chart, p. 493.

eolith \'ē-ə-,lith\ A rough piece of flint that is believed to have been a tool or weapon of early Stone Age men.

eon \'ē-ən\ One of the longest geological periods. It is made up of at least 2 eras.

ephedra p. 142

ephedrine See *ephedra:* p. 142

epicenter \'ep-ə-,sen-tər\ The area that is directly over the focus of an earthquake. Earthquake movement is always most violent at the epicenter.

epidermis \,ep-ə-'dər-məs\ The outer layer of skin. It contains no blood vessels. Epidermis covers the true skin of higher vertebrate animals. Epidermis is also the outermost cell layer of roots, stems and leaves.

epoch \'ep-ək\ A division of geologic time, within a period.

equator \i-'kwāt-ər\ An imaginary line around the earth halfway between the North and South poles. It divides the earth into equal hemispheres, northern and southern. The equator is located at 0 degrees latitude.

equinox \\'ē-kwə-ˌnäks\\ Either of the 2 times of the year, about March 21 and September 23, when the sun appears directly overhead to an observer on the earth's equator. During the equinox, the days and nights are of equal length everywhere on earth.

era \\'ir-ə\\ Any of the 4 main divisions of geologic time. Each era includes 1 or more periods.

erosion \\i-'rō-zhən\\ The wearing away of rocks and other substances on the earth's surface by water, wind, waves and glaciers.

escarpment p. 143

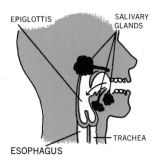

esophagus \\i-'säf-ə-gəs\\ In many animals, the muscular tube that connects the mouth with the stomach.

estivation \\ˌes-tə-'vā-shən\\ A state of certain animals that is something like sleep. Estivation takes place during the hot, dry summer months. Some toads and frogs estivate during the dry season, somewhat as bears hibernate in winter.

estuary p. 143

eucalyptus See *blue gum:* p. 47

euglena p. 143

European beech p. 35

European blackbird p. 42

European corn borer p. 144

European hedgehog p. 211

European medicinal leech pp. 250, 251

European nightingale p. 313

European nightjar See *goatsucker:* p. 186

European robin p. 381

European rock dove p. 131

European wild boar p. 144

evening primrose p. 145

evening star A name often given to Venus, or any other planet that sets after the sun.

evergreen \\'ev-ər-ˌgrēn\\ A tree or other plant that does not lose its leaves every year.

evolution \\ˌev-ə-'lü-shən\\ The long process of the development of a species from its earliest stages of life on earth.

excretion \\ek-'skrē-shən\\ The rejection of waste materials by an organism. Carbon dioxide is excreted from plant and animal cells.

Protein waste is removed from the blood by the kidneys and then excreted from the body.

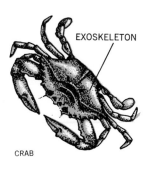

exoskeleton \\ˌek-(ˌ)sō-'skel-ət-ᵊn\\ The outside skeleton, or hard protective outer covering of such animals as crustaceans and insects.

exosphere \\'ek-sō-ˌsfir\\ The outer part of the earth's atmosphere. It begins beyond the ionosphere, at an altitude of 200 miles or more.

exotic \\ig-'zät-ik\\ Describing a cultivated plant not native to the land where it is grown.

expanding universe \\ik-'spand-ing 'yü-nə-ˌvərs\\ A theory stating that all the galaxies in the universe are constantly moving away from one another at a great speed. The theory is based on observations that show that all galaxies are moving away from the earth.

extinct \\ik-'sting(k)t\\ Describing a species or larger group that is no longer living.

eye In human beings and other animals, the complex organ of sight. An eye changes light into nerve impulses. An eye is also the fairly calm area at the center of a hurricane.

eyespot \\'ī-ˌspät\\ A primitive organ of sight that is sensitive to light. Some invertebrates and some 1-celled plants have eyespots.

f

face One of the flat surfaces of a crystal. A face is also any open or broken rock surface.

factor \\'fak-tər\\ A gene.

fairy shrimp p. 145

falcon p. 146

fall cankerworm p. 66

falling star See *meteor:* p. 284

falls The flow of water over a steep slope or over and upright separation in a stream bed.

family In the classification of plants and animals, a grouping or ranking that is above a genus and below an order.

fang \\'fang\\ One of the long, curved, hollow teeth in the front part of the jaw of a poisonous snake. The poison is released through the fangs. A fang is also 1 of the 4 long, pointed teeth that meat-eating animals use to grasp and tear their prey.

fat A greasy solid or liquid in the tissues of animals and certain plants. Some examples of fat are beef suet, lard, olive oil and peanut oil.

fatigue \fə-'tēg\ A temporary lessening of the ability of an organism or of its parts to function well. Fatigue occurs after a period of long or hard exercise or activity.

fault p. 146

fauna \'fon-ə\ The animals found in a certain area or a certain time. Fauna is also a listing and description of all the animals of an area.

fawn \'fon\ A young deer that usually still has its baby spots and drinks its mother's milk.

feather A light, horny outgrowth of skin that is the outer covering of birds. A feather has a main shaft with a hollow quill at the end of it. The quill is inside the skin. Smaller shafts, called vanes, stick out on both sides of the main shaft. Small fibers, called barbs, grow out from the vanes. Each barb has hooked structures called barbules, which interlock to form a strong surface.

feather duster worm See *worm:* p. 486

feldspar p. 147

female Describing the sex or the characteristics of the sex that bears young. Female also describes a pistillate plant.

fern pp. 148–149

ferret p. 150

fertilization \,fərt-ᵊl-ə-'zā-shən\ The joining of the egg cell of a female plant or animal with the sperm cell of a male plant or animal.

fetus \'fēt-əs\ An unborn animal that has the characteristics of the species to which it belongs. Fetus usually means the later stages of the unborn young of vertebrates.

fibrous \'fī-brəs\ Thread-like, stringy.

fiddler crab p. 109

field cricket p. 113

field sparrow p. 415

fig tree p. 150

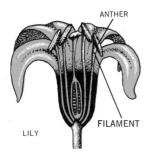

ANTHER

FILAMENT

LILY

filament \'fil-ə-mənt\ In flowers, the stalk of the stamen. A filament is also a row of thin cells found in certain algae.

filaria p. 151

fin \'fin\ A wing-like organ on the bodies of fish and certain other animals that live in water. Fins are used in swimming, turning and balancing the body.

fin-backed lizard See *dimetrodon:* p. 126

finback whale pp. 478, 479

finch p. 151

fir p. 152

firefly p. 152

fire opal p. 320

firn p. 153

first quarter moon See *moon:* p. 294

fish p. 153

fisher p. 153

fish hawk pp. 208, 209

fission \'fish-ən\ An asexual method of reproduction, in which a single cell divides into 2 or more cells of about the same size. Fission is also the splitting of the nucleus of an atom into 2 or more parts of about the same size. Large amounts of energy are released during nuclear fission.

fissure p. 154

5-lined skink p. 405

fixed star A star whose position in relation to the stars around it does not change over a long period of time.

flagellate p. 154

flagellum \flə-'jel-əm\ A long whip-like lengthening of bacteria, protozoa and certain cells. Such organisms move around by means of the whip-like motion of flagella.

flamingo p. 155

flash flood A sudden rush of water down a canyon or a valley after a heavy rain over higher ground nearby.

flatworm p. 155; see also *worm:* p. 486

flax p. 156

flea p. 156

fleece \'flēs\ The wool coat of a lamb, sheep, alpaca or similar animal.

fleshy roots Large, pulpy roots that are a source of food for the plants that grow from them.

flicker p. 157

flint p. 157

floating ribs In man, the 2 lowest pairs of ribs. They are attached to the vertebrae in the back but not to the breastbone or the cartilage of other ribs.

flock A large group of wild birds or mammals living together by choice. A flock is also a number of domestic animals taken care of as a group, as sheep, goats or chickens.

floe p. 158

flood plain p. 352

flora \'flōr-ə\ The plant life of a certain area or time. Flora is also a listing and description of all the plants of an area.

Florida water rat pp. 374, 375

flounder p. 158

flour corn p. 104

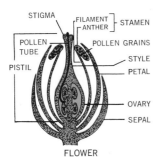

FLOWER

flower The part of certain plants that contains or is made up of the reproductive organs.

flowering dogwood p. 128

fluke p. 159; see also *flatworm*: p. 155

fluorescent See *fluorite*: p. 159

fluorite p. 159

fluted \\'flüt-əd\\ Describing a surface that bears parallel grooves and ridges, as the surface of a scallop shell.

fly pp. 160–161

flycatcher p. 162

flying fish p. 162

flying squirrel p. 421

foal \\'fōl\\ A young horse or animal of the horse family, usually less than 1 year old.

focus \\'fō-kəs\\ The center or source of an earthquake.

fog A concentration of water droplets suspended in the air and dense enough to reduce visibility. Fog usually occurs where warm, moist air is cooled to the dew point as it moves over a cold area.

fold Rock layers that have been bent into a wavelike pattern. Folds are caused by large, shifting movements of the earth's crust.

foliage \\'fō-l(ē)ij\\ All of the leaves growing on a plant or tree.

follicle \\'fäl-i-kəl\\ A small sac or gland, usually deep but narrow-mouthed. A follicle usually produces a substance, such as a hair that grows from a follicle in the skin.

food chain The natural pattern by which small animals are eaten by larger animals, which are in turn eaten by still larger animals. Another kind of food chain, sometimes called the food-and-energy chain, includes the green plants which use energy from the sun to make food for animals. When the animals die, their bodies return minerals to the soil and provide food for more green plants.

food web A number of different food chains existing together in a natural community where many different plants and animals depend on each other for food. A food web is sometimes called a food cycle.

"fool's gold" See *pyrite*: p. 367

forage \\'fòr-ij\\ Grass or other plant food that animals find for themselves.

foraminifer p. 162

forest A large area of land that is covered with a dense, natural growth of shrubs and trees.

forest buffalo p. 53

forestry \\'fòr-ə-strē\\ The science of tree care and forest management.

forget-me-not p. 163

formation \\fòr-'mā-shən\\ A mass of rock, all of the same kind and of the same age.

forsythia p. 164

fossil p. 164

4-toed echidna pp. 136, 137

Fowler's toad pp. 444, 445

fox p. 165

foxglove p. 165

foxtail grass pp. 194, 195

fracture \\'frak-chər\\ The irregular way a mineral breaks apart. The color or texture of the freshly broken surface is often helpful in identifying the mineral.

fraternal \\frə-'tərn-əl\\ **twins** Two humans that have developed from 2 eggs fertilized in the same manner at the same time. They may be of the same sex, or brother and sister. They resemble each other only as ordinary brothers and sisters do.

free-living In biology, plants or animals that can move about from 1 place to another.

French marigold p. 275

frigate bird See *man-o'-war bird*: p. 273

frigid \\'frij-əd\\ **zone** Either of the 2 polar zones where the climate is very cold. One frigid zone is within the Arctic Circle, while the other is within the Antarctic Circle.

fringed gentian p. 175

frog pp. 166–167

froghopper See *spittlebug*: p. 417

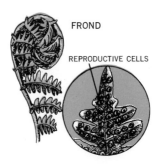

FROND

REPRODUCTIVE CELLS

frond \\'fränd\\ The leaf of a fern, made up of many small leaflets attached to a slender rib.

front In meteorology, the boundary between 2 different air masses.

frost Ice crystals that appear where water vapor has condensed on a surface that has a temperature of 32° F. or less.

frost action \\'ak-shən\\ In geology, the freezing and thawing of water that seeps into cracks in rocks. Since water expands as it freezes, frost action causes the rocks to break apart.

fruit The part of a plant that develops from the

ovary of the flower, and that contains the plant's seed. Some but not all fruits are edible.

fruit fly pp. 160, 161

FRY

fry Young animals, usually fish just hatched and not yet feeding themselves.

fuchsia p. 168

fucus See *algae:* pp. 6–7

Fuller's teasel p. 438

full moon See *moon:* p. 294

fumarole p. 168

fungus pp. 168, 169

fusion \\'fyü-zhən\\ In biology, the joining together of the nuclei of 2 or more cells, as when fertilization takes place.

g

gabbro p. 169

galactic \\gə-'lak-tik\\ Having to do with a galaxy.

galaxy p. 170

gale \\'gāl\\ A wind with a velocity of 32 to 63 miles per hour.

galena p. 170

gall \\'gȯl\\ A lump or swelling on a plant, usually caused by a parasitic insect.

gallbladder \\'gȯl-,blad-ər\\ In most vertebrates, a small sac that is attached to the liver, and that collects liver bile.

gallinule p. 170

game birds Birds that are legally hunted by sportsmen.

game fish Fish that are legally caught by sport fishermen.

gamete \\gə-'mēt\\ A reproductive cell that must join with another before a new organism can develop. Egg and sperm cells are gametes.

gametophyte \\gə-'mēt-ə-,fīt\\ In plants such as ferns and mosses, the part of the life cycle that produces gametes. The alternate generation, called a sporophyte, produces spores.

ganglion \\'gang-glē-ən\\ A group of nerve cells that form a center from which nerve impulses are passed on.

gannet p. 171

gar p. 172

garden beet p. 35

garden bleeding heart p. 44

garden carrot p. 69

garden cockscomb pp. 95, 96

garden cornflower See *bachelor's button:* p. 25

gardenia p. 172

garden parsley p. 334

garden pea p. 335

garden plum tree p. 355

garden tomato p. 447

garden zinnia p. 492

garnet p. 173

garter snake pp. 410, 411

gastrolith p. 173

gastropod p. 174

gazelle p. 174

gecko p. 175

gem \\'jem\\ A jewel. A gem is a precious or semiprecious stone valued for its beauty.

gemsbok See *oryx:* p. 323

gene \\'jēn\\ That part of a cell, usually the chromosome, that carries 1 inherited trait. Each gene is thought to be a molecule of DNA (deoxyribonucleic acid).

generation \\,jen-ər-'ā-shən\\ In biology, the process of reproducing. A generation is also a group of animals or plants having a common parent or parents.

genetics \\jə-'net-iks\\ The study of heredity, or how organisms vary and how inherited characteristics are passed on from the parent to the offspring.

gentian p. 175

genus \\'jē-nəs\\ A classification of plants or animals that is generally based on similar structure. It is a subdivision of the larger group called a family. The genus is subdivided into individual kinds or species.

geocentric \\,jē-ō-'sen-trik\\ Having the center of the earth as a point of reference, or having the earth as a center.

geode p. 176

geography The study of the climate and surface features of the earth, and how these matters relate to plant and animal life.

geologic column p. 176

geology \\jē-'äl-ə-jē\\ The study of the history and composition of the earth, particularly the composition of the earth's crust.

geomorphology \\,jē-ə-(,)mȯr-'fäl-ə-jē\\ The study of land masses and relief features, and how they were formed.

geophysics \\,jē-ə-'fiz-iks\\ The study of the earth that is primarily concerned with energy, motion and change. Geophysics includes study of climates, volcanoes, earthquakes, ocean currents, and the electrical and magnetic fields of the earth.

geosyncline p. 176

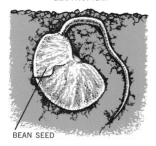

GEOTROPISM

BEAN SEED

geotropism \jē-'ä-trə-,piz-əm\ The response of growing plants to gravity. Because of gravity, the roots grow down while the stem grows up.

geranium p. 177

germ A microscopic organism, usually one of the disease-causing bacteria. A germ is also any small combination of cells, such as a fertilized egg, a seed or a bud, that is developing into something larger.

germinate \'jər-mə-,nāt\ To begin growing from a seed or spore.

germ layer \'lā-ər\ Any of the 3 layers of cells formed as a fertilized egg begins to develop into a new animal.

gestation \je-'stā-shən\ The period of time during which a young mammal develops inside the mother's body.

geyser p. 177

giant anteater p. 16

giant arborvitae See *cedar:* p. 75

giant cactus p. 63

giant cane See *bamboo:* p. 28

giant panda p. 178

giant pangolin p. 331

giant petrel p. 343

giant puffball p. 365

giant sequoia p. 398

giant tortoise p. 178

giant water bug pp. 54, 55

gibbon p. 179

gibbous moon See *moon:* p. 294

Gila monster p. 179

gill \'gil\ **cover** The flap of skin that covers and protects the gills of most fish.

GILL

GILL COVER

gills \'gilz\ The respiratory organs of fish and other animals that live in water. Blood circu-

lating through the gills absorbs oxygen from the water and carbon dioxide is released.

gill \'gil\ **slits** Narrow openings through which water passes to or from the gills of a fish.

ginger p. 180

ginkgo p. 180

giraffe p. 181

gizzard A part of the digestive system of seed-eating birds, earthworms and some other animals that have no teeth. A gizzard has strong, muscular walls and a tough lining. A gizzard crushes and grinds up food before it passes into the stomach.

glacial \'glā-shəl\ **drift** Rocks and soil moved by a glacier and deposited where the glacier melted.

glacial grooves p. 181

glacial striae p. 181

glaciation \,glā-s(h)ē-'ā-shən\ The changing of the earth's surface by glacial action.

glacier p. 182

gladiolus p. 182

gland \'gland\ A body organ that produces something, as a sweat gland, which produces perspiration.

globular cluster See *star cluster:* p. 422

glory-of-the-sea cone p. 101

glowworm p. 183

glucose \'glü-,kōs\ A simple sugar produced by plants during photosynthesis. Glucose occurs in fruit and honey, and in the body fluids of animals.

gnatcatcher p. 183

gneiss p. 184

gnu p. 184

goat p. 185

goatsbeard p. 185

goatsucker p. 186

goby p. 186

gold-and-blue macaw p. 265

golden agouti p. 3

golden beryl p. 38

golden-crowned kinglet p. 239

goldeneye See *duck:* pp. 132, 133

goldeneye lacewing p. 243

golden hamster pp. 205, 206

golden lion marmoset p. 276

golden ragwort See *groundsel:* p. 198

goldenrod p. 187

golden shiner pp. 402, 403

goldfinch p. 187

goldfish p. 188

gonad \'gō,nad\ In animals, a gland that produces gametes.

goose p. 188

gooseberry p. 189

gopher p. 189

gorge p. 190

gorilla p. 190

gourd p. 191

grackle p. 191

gradation \grā-'dā-shən\ In earth science, the erosion of hills or plateaus into nearly level plains.

grade The slope of an area, particularly the slant of a streambed where the water is neither eroding nor depositing sediments.

gradient \'grād-ē-ənt\ The slope of a line or surface, as measured from a horizontal line. A gradient is also the amount of change or rate of change of temperature or air pressure measured at regular intervals.

grafting \'graft-ing\ Attaching part of 1 plant onto part of another plant so that the parts unite and continue to grow.

grain The seeds of cereal plants such as wheat, rice and corn. In earth science, grains are small crystals or particles of rock that are either loose or bound together in a rock mass.

grama grass pp. 194, 195

granite p. 192

Grant's gazelle p. 174

granules \'gran-,yülz\ Areas on the surface of the sun that give a mottled appearance and are probably due to erupting gas. In biology, granules are small particles in cells that probably contain stored food.

grape p. 192

grape fern pp. 148, 149

grapefruit See *citrus tree:* p. 88

grape hyacinth p. 193

graphite p. 193

grass pp. 194–195

grasshopper p. 196

grass wrack See *eelgrass:* p. 138

gravel Loose fragments of rock, usually deposited by water and usually mixed with smaller particles of clay and sand.

gravitation \,grav-ə-tā-shən\ The attraction of all particles and masses in the universe by all other particles and masses.

gravity \'grav-ə-tē\ The force that attracts all bodies toward the center of the earth.

GRAVITY FAULT

gravity \'grav-ə-tē\ **fault** A break in the earth's surface. In a gravity fault, 1 large land mass sinks down below the level of another mass, along the break.

gray fox p. 165

gray seal p. 395

gray squirrel p. 421

gray whale p. 478, 479

gray wolf p. 483

great anteater p. 16

great auk p. 24

great barracuda p. 196

great bird of paradise pp. 40, 41

great black cockatoo p. 94

great blue heron pp. 213, 214

great-crested flycatcher p. 162

greater flamingo p. 155

greater Indian hill mynah pp. 307, 308

greater kudu p. 242

greater scaup See *duck:* pp. 132–133

greater yellowlegs pp. 196, 197

great gray kangaroo pp. 235, 236

great horned owl pp. 326, 327

great plains toad pp. 444, 445

grebe p. 197

Greek valerian See *Jacob's ladder:* p. 231

green algae p. 6

green anemone See *sea anemone:* p. 393

green anole p. 15

green bean p. 33

greenbottle fly pp. 160, 161

greenbrier, p. 197

green brittle star See *serpent star:* p. 399

green darner dragonfly p. 131

green lacewing p. 243

green monkey pp. 292, 293

green peach aphid p. 18

green pepper p. 341

green toad pp. 444, 445

grosbeak p. 198

grizzly bear p. 33

ground gecko p. 175

groundhog See *marmot:* p. 277; see also *woodchuck:* p. 485

ground moraine See *moraine:* p. 295

ground pine See *club moss:* p. 92

groundsel p. 198

ground squirrel p. 421

ground swell Broad, rolling waves on the surface of the sea, caused by a distant but long-lasting storm.

ground water Water that collects just below the surface of the earth. The top level of ground water is the water table.

grouper p. 199

grouse p. 199

growth rings Concentric circles of larger and smaller cells, visible on cross-sections of cut tree trunks and twigs, that mark years of growth. Growth rings are also rings on the outer edges of some fish scales.

grub \'grəb\ The worm-like larval stage in the development of some beetles.

guano See *cormorant:* p. 104

guava p. 200

guinea pig p. 200

gulf A large body of water that is surrounded by

land on 3 sides but open to the sea on the fourth side.

gulf fritillary butterfly pp. 60, 61

gull p. 201

gully p. 201

gum A sticky substance that oozes from certain trees and plants, and that hardens as it dries. Resins, amber and rubber are all gums.

guppy p. 202

guyot See *seamount:* p. 396

gymnosperm \'jim-nə-,spərm\ A plant whose seeds are not enclosed in seedcases. Pines and other cone-bearing trees are gymnosperms.

gypsum p. 202

gyrfalcon See *falcon:* p. 146

h

habitat \'hab-ə-,tat\ The natural living place of a plant or animal.

haddock p. 203

hagfish p. 203

hail Pellets of ice that form as frozen raindrops in cumulonimbus clouds.

hairy mopalia See *chiton:* p. 84

hairy-nosed wombat p. 484

hake p. 204

halibut p. 204; see also *flounder:* p. 158

halite p. 205

Halley's comet p. 99

halo p. 205

hammerhead shark pp. 400, 401

hamster p. 205

hanging valley p. 459

haploid \'hap-,lȯid\ Describing a cell that has the smallest number of chromosomes in a normal body cell. Gametes are haploid cells. Most body cells are diploid.

harbor porpoise p. 361

hard coal Anthracite coal.

hardness \'härd-nəs\ The resistance of a solid material to scratching or cutting.

hardshell clam p. 89

hardwood \'härd-,wud\ **trees** Trees that have broad leaves that fall from the branches in autumn, and that bear seeds in cases, as nuts and fruit.

hardy \'härd-ē\ Describing plants that live through the winter outdoors, without special protection. Hardy also describes plants or animals that can withstand unfavorable conditions such as poor soil or a severe climate.

hardy catalpa p. 71

hare p. 206

harebell See *bellflower:* p. 38

harlequin bug pp. 54, 55

harrier See *hawk:* pp. 208–209

hartebeest p. 206

harvest fly p. 207

harvestman p. 207

harvest moon See *moon:* p. 294

hawk pp. 208–209

hawk moth p. 299

hawthorn p. 210

hazel p. 210

headfish See *ocean sunfish:* p. 317

head lettuce p. 253

headwaters \'hed-,wȯt-ərz\ The small streams that form the beginning, or source, of a river.

heal-all p. 210

heart In animals, the body organ that acts as a pump to circulate blood. The heart is a hollow, muscular organ that pumps blood by relaxing and contracting.

heartwood \'härt-,wud\ The older, non-living wood in the center of a tree trunk or branch. Heartwood is usually harder and darker in color than the living sapwood that surrounds it.

heather p. 211

hedge apple See *osage orange:* p. 323

hedgehog p. 211

Heidelberg man pp. 270, 271

heliocentric \,hē-lē-ō-'sen-trik\ Having the center of the sun as a point of reference, or having the sun as a center.

heliotrope p. 212

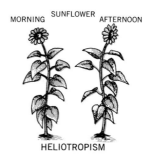

MORNING SUNFLOWER AFTERNOON

HELIOTROPISM

heliotropism \,hē-lē-'ä-trə-piz-əm\ The way a plant responds to sunlight, as a sunflower head turns to follow the sun across the sky.

hellgrammite See *dobsonfly:* p. 126

hematite p. 212

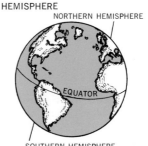

HEMISPHERE

NORTHERN HEMISPHERE

EQUATOR

SOUTHERN HEMISPHERE

hemisphere \'hem-ə-,sfir\ Either of 2 halves of

the earth (the northern or southern hemispheres), above or below the equator. In the brain, a hemisphere is either of the 2 halves or sides of the cerebrum or cerebellum.

hemlock tree p. 212

hemoglobin \'hē-mə-,glō-bən\ The substance in red blood corpuscles that carries oxygen and carbon dioxide.

hemp p. 213

hepatica p. 213

herb \'(h)erb\ A flowering plant with a soft rather than woody stem. Normally, plants that are herbs fall to the ground during the winter, while shrubs and trees stand erect.

herbarium \,(h)er-'bar-ē-əm\ A collection of dried and pressed flowers. A herbarium is also a building in which such a collection is kept.

herbivorous \,(h)er-'biv-ə-rəs\ Describing animals that feed only on plants.

herd A group of mammals that live, feed and move about together.

heredity \hə-'red-ə-tē\ In plants and animals, the passing on of genes through reproduction. Heredity causes the offspring to resemble 1 or both parents.

hermaphroditic \(,)hər-,maf-rə-'dit-ik\ Describing an animal, such as an earthworm or snail, that has both male and female reproductive organs.

hermit thrush p. 441

heron p. 213

herpetology \,hər-pə-'täl-ə-jē\ The study of reptiles, or of reptiles and amphibians.

herring p. 214

herring gull p. 201

hibernate \'hī-bər-,nāt\ To remain inactive during the winter months, as some mammals, reptiles and amphibians do.

hibiscus p. 214

hickory tree p. 215

high In meteorology, a region of high atmospheric pressure.

high-bush blueberry p. 45

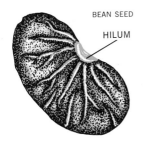

BEAN SEED

HILUM

hilum \'hī-ləm\ On a seed, the scar caused by the separation of the seed from its stalk.

hippopotamus p. 215

Hirudinea See *annelid:* p. 14

hoarfrost p. 216

hoary marmot p. 277

holly p. 216

hollyhock p. 216

homeostasis \,hō-mē-ō-'stā-səs\ In the bodies of animals, the way organs and systems work together to keep certain conditions the same, such as body temperature.

homogeneous \,hō-mə-'jē-nē-əs\ Describing forms of organisms, or parts of organisms, that are like each other because they are descended from a common ancestor.

homologous \hō-'mäl-ə-gəs\ Describing things that are like each other in structure and origin but not necessarily in function. The foreleg of a horse is homologous to the arm of a man.

honey bear See *kinkajou:* p. 239

honeybee p. 34

honey locust p. 261

honey mesquite p. 283

honeysuckle p. 216

hoof A horny structure that encloses the toes of many animals such as horses and sheep.

hookworm p. 217

hop p. 217

horizon \hə-'rīz-ᵊn\ The line or circle that appears to be the boundary between the earth and the sky.

hormone \'hor-,mōn\ In animals, a chemical substance manufactured by the endocrine glands and carried by the body fluids. The hormones have certain effects on other body organs. Hormones are also chemical substances in plants.

horn A hard, pointed growth, made of skin, on the heads of some hoofed mammals such as cattle and deer, sometimes used as a weapon.

hornblende p. 218; see also *amphibole:* p. 12

horned lark p. 248

hornet p. 218

horntail p. 219

horse p. 219

horse chestnut p. 220

horsefly pp. 160, 161

horse latitudes \'lat-ə-,t(y)üdz\ Either of 2 belts of high atmospheric pressure that extend around the world. The horse latitudes lie between the trade winds and the prevailing westerlies. One belt is about 30 degrees north of the equator, while the other is about 30 degrees south of the equator.

horseshoe crab p. 220

horsetail p. 221

horticulture \'hort-ə-,kəl-chər\ A branch of agriculture that deals with the growing of flowers, fruits and vegetables.

host A plant or animal that is a source of food for another plant or animal that lives in or on it as a parasite.

house finch p. 151

housefly pp. 160, 161

house mosquito p. 297

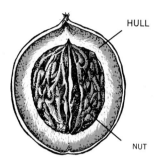

HULL

NUT

hull The husk or shell that is the outer covering of a seed or fruit.

human itch mite p. 289

humidity \hyü-'mid-ə-tē\ The amount of water vapor in the air.

hummingbird p. 222

hummingbird moth pp. 298, 299

humpback whale p. 478, 479

humus \'hyü-məs\ Decaying plant and animal matter. Usually, humus helps to make up the dark-colored parts of soil.

Hungarian partridge p. 334

hunter's moon See *moon:* p. 294

hurricane A severe windstorm or tropical cyclone 50 to 1,000 miles in diameter. Hurricanes usually originate in the West Indies. Hurricane winds have a velocity of more than 75 miles per hour.

hyacinth p. 222

hybrid \'hī-brəd\ The offspring of parents of different varieties. The offspring may resemble either parent or neither.

hybridization \,hī-brəd-ə-'zā-shən\ The producing of new forms of life by cross-breeding older, somewhat different forms. Hybridization is the opposite of inbreeding.

hydra p. 223

hydrangea p. 223

hydrogen \'hī-drə-jən\ A colorless, odorless chemical element that is part of water, all plants and animals and in all acids. Hydrogen by itself is a gas at ordinary temperatures and pressures.

hydrosphere \'hī-drə-,sfir\ The part of the earth that contains or is covered by water. The hydrosphere is also the envelope of water vapor that surrounds the earth.

hydrotropism \hī-'drä-trə-,piz-əm\ The response of a living plant to water, as when roots grow toward moisture.

hypha \'hī-fə\ A thread-like filament that makes up the plant body of a fungus.

hypocotyl \'hī-pə-,kät-əl\ A part of a plant embryo found inside a seed. The hypocotyl develops into the stem below the cotyledons.

hypothesis \hī-'päth-ə-səs\ A theory or explanation that is believed to be true, so long as known facts seem to support the theory and no known facts disprove it.

hyrax p. 223

i

ibex p. 224

ibis p. 224

ice age Any one of several periods of prehistoric time when glaciers covered much of the continents. Also, the Pleistocene Epoch, which was the most recent ice age.

iceberg A large mass or block of ice floating in the ocean.

icecap See *glacier:* p. 182

Iceland spar See *calcite:* p. 63

ice sheet A glacier or ice cap covering a land area.

ichthyology \,ik-thē-'äl-ə-jē\ The study of fish.

ichthyosaur p. 225

igneous rock p. 382

iguana p. 225

immunity \im-'yü-nə-tē\ The ability to resist a disease-causing organism, or some other natural hazard.

impala p. 226

inbreeding \'in-,brēd-ing\ The natural or controlled breeding of similar or closely related individuals. Inbreeding is the opposite of hybridization or cross-breeding.

incense cedar p. 226

incisor \in-'sī-zər\ A tooth adapted to cutting. In most mammals, incisors are the single-rooted teeth in the center of both upper and lower jaws.

inclination \,in-klə-'nā-shən\ Any slope or slant. In space science, inclination is the angle between the intersection of the plane of an orbit and the plane of the earth's orbit.

incomplete metamorphosis \,in-kəm-'plēt ,met-ə-'mȯr-fə-səs\ A pattern of insect development in which there is no resting or pupal stage. The insect passes directly from the larval stage, which usually lives in water, to the adult stage.

incubation \,in-kyə-'bā-shən\ The act of keeping fertilized eggs warm so that the embryos inside them can develop and hatch.

Indian buffalo p. 53

Indian cress See *nasturtium:* p. 309

Indian elephant p. 140

Indian paintbrush p. 227

Indian rhinoceros p. 379

Indian turnip See *jack-in-the-pulpit:* p. 230

indicolite See *tourmaline:* p. 448

indigo bunting p. 56

infection \in-'fek-shən\ The invasion of a plant

or animal by a disease-causing organism such as bacteria.

infertile \(')in-'fert-əl\ Unable to reproduce.

INGESTION

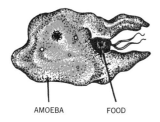

AMOEBA   FOOD

ingestion \in-'jes(h)-chən\ The taking in of food or some other substance.

inherited characteristics \in-'her-ət-əd ,kar(-i)k-tə-'ris-tiks\ Physical traits such as blue eyes or curly hair that are passed on from parent to offspring through genes.

inner \'in-ər\ **ear** In some animals, the part of the ear that includes the bony labyrinth, the cochlea and the semicircular canals. The inner ear has to do with the sense of balance as well as hearing.

insect p. 227

instinct \'in-,sting(k)t\ In an animal, any particular way of behaving that is predictable and largely inherited.

insulin \'in(t)-s(ə-)lən\ A hormone that regulates carbohydrate metabolism in the bodies of some animals.

intergalactic \,int-ər-gə'lak-tik\ Having to do with the vast spaces between and beyond the galaxies of the universe.

intermediate \,int-ər-'mēd-ē-ət\ **host** A plant or animal in which parasites live only while in a larval or immature stage of development. The parasite moves on to another host before becoming an adult.

interphase \'int-ər-,fāz\ The stage of the nucleus of a cell between mitotic cell divisions. The interphase is also called the resting stage.

interplanetary \,int-ər-'plan-ə-,ter-ē\ Having to do with the space between the planets in the solar system.

interrupted fern pp. 148, 149

interstellar \,int-ər-'stel-ər\ Having to do with the space between the stars of the Milky Way or of some other galaxy.

intestines \in-'tes-tənz\ In many animals, the long, tube-like part of the digestive tract to which food passes from the stomach. Digestion and absorption take place in the animal's intestines.

intrusive \in-'trü-siv\ Describing igneous rock that hardened under the earth's crust rather than on the surface of the earth.

invertebrate \(')in-'vərt-ə-brət\ Any animal that does not have a backbone. Protozoa, shellfish and insects are all invertebrates.

involuntary muscles \(')in-'väl-ən-,ter-ē 'məs-əlz\ Muscles that are not primarily controlled by the brain. Organs such as the heart and stomach are activated by involuntary muscles. Most invertebrates have only involuntary muscles.

io moth pp. 298, 299

ionosphere \ī-'än-ə-,sfir\ The layer of the earth's atmosphere that begins about 50 miles above the surface and extends to about 275 miles or more.

iridescent \,ir-ə-'des-ənt\ Describing changing, shimmering colors that result from the diffraction of light. Soap bubbles, certain birds and insects are iridescent.

iris p. 228

irregular galaxy p. 170

isinglass See *mica*: p. 284; and *muscovite*: p. 304

ISLAND

island A land area, smaller than a continent, that is surrounded by water.

isthmus p. 228

ivory The tooth-like material that makes up the tusks of elephants, walruses and some other mammals.

ivy p. 229

j

jackal p. 229
jack-in-the-pulpit p. 230
jackrabbit p. 230
Jacob's ladder p. 231
jaguar p. 231
Japanese barberry p. 29
Japanese beetle pp. 36, 37
Japanese ivy See *Boston ivy:* p. 50
Japanese yew p. 490
Java man pp. 270, 271
jay p. 232
jellyfish p. 232
jerboa p. 233

jet \'jet\ **stream** A swift-moving wind occurring at altitudes of 20,000 to 40,000 feet. The jet stream moves from west to east.

jimsonweed p. 233

Johnson grass pp. 194, 195

joint \\'joint\\ In the bodies of animals, a place where 2 or more bones are connected. In plants, a joint is the place where leaves or branches grow out from a stem.

jonquil See *narcissus:* p. 308

Joshua tree See *yucca:* p. 490

jugular \\'jəg-yə-lər\\ In some animals, any of several veins in the neck that carry blood from the head to the heart.

junco p. 234

June beetle pp. 36, 37

jungle Uncultivated land, usually tropical, with a dense growth of trees, vines and other plant life.

juniper p. 234

Jupiter pp. 234, 502

Jurassic Period \\jù-'ras-ik 'pir-ē-əd\\ See Geologic Time Chart, p. 493.

k

kame p. 235

kangaroo p. 235

kangaroo rat pp. 374, 375

kaolin p. 236

kaolinite See *kaolin:* p. 236

karst topography p. 236

katydid p. 237

kelp See *algae:* pp. 6–7

kelp blenny p. 45

Kentucky blue grass p. 195

kernel \\'kərn-əl\\ A plant seed, such as a grain of corn or wheat, that is protected by a hard covering or husk.

kettle p. 237

KEY

KEY WEST

key A low island of sand or coral near a coast. A key is usually part of a chain of islands.

kidney \\'kid-nē\\ In many animals, either of 2 bean-shaped glandular organs that filter waste products from the blood.

kidney bean p. 33

killer whale p. 478, 479

kingbird p. 238

kingdom Either of the 2 large groups, the plant and animal kingdoms, into which all living things are classed.

kingfisher p. 238

kinglet p. 239

king rail p. 372

kinkajou p. 239

kit A young fox, or the young of some other small fur-bearing animal.

kite p. 240

kiwi p. 240

klipspringer p. 241

koala p. 241

koodoo See *kudu:* p. 242

kudu p. 242

kumquat tree p. 242

l

labyrinth fish See *betta:* p. 39

laccolith p. 243

lacewing p. 243

lady's slipper p. 244

lagoon p. 244

lake p. 244

lake herring p. 245

lake sturgeon p. 425

lamantin manatee p. 272

lamprey p. 245

land breeze A movement of air from land areas toward a large lake or the sea. Warmer air over the water is rising, and cooler air from over the land is replacing it. A land breeze usually occurs at night and in the early morning because at those times the land is cooler than the water.

landslide p. 246

land snail p. 409

lantern fish p. 246

lapis lazuli p. 247

large intestine \\in-'tes-tən\\ In many animals, the last part of the digestive tract. It is made up of the caecum, the colon and the rectum.

largemouth black bass p. 247

lark p. 248

larva \\'lär-və\\ An early stage in the development of certain animals, after the embryo. Larvae change form before they become adults. The tadpole is the larva of a frog or toad. A caterpillar is the larva of a butterfly or moth.

larynx \\'lar-ing(k)s\\ The organ of voice in most mammals. It is located between the windpipe and the base of the tongue. The larynx contains the vocal cords.

latent \\'lāt-ᵊnt\\ Having to do with something that is present but is not active.

lateral \\'lat-ə-rəl\\ Having to do with the side, located on the side or branching from the middle toward the side.

lateral moraine See *moraine:* p. 295

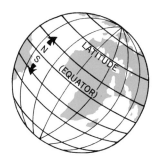

latitude \\'lat-ə-‚t(y)üd\\ A measurement, in degrees, of distance north or south of the earth's equator.

laughing hyena See *spotted hyena:* p. 419

laurel p. 248

lava p. 248

lavender p. 249

Laysan albatross p. 4

leaf In plants, an outgrowth from a stem. A leaf is usually a flat, green blade. It makes sugar by photosynthesis.

leafhopper p. 249

leaf lettuce p. 253

least weasel p. 477

leatherwood p. 250

leech p. 250; see also *annelid:* p. 14

leeward \\'lē-wərd\\ Describing a side or direction opposite the direction from which the wind blows.

legume \\'leg-‚yüm\\ A plant, such as the pea or bean, that grows pods containing a number of seeds in a row.

lemming p. 251

lemon See *citrus tree:* p. 88

lemon lily See *day lily:* p. 122

lemur p. 251

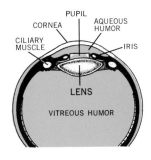

lens \\'lenz\\ In vertebrates, the part of the eye that focuses light rays on the retina. The lens is located just behind the iris.

lenticel \\'lent-ə-‚səl\\ In a plant stem, an opening that lets a gas pass inward and outward.

lentil p. 252

leopard p. 252

leopard cat See *ocelot:* p. 317

leopard frog pp. 166, 167

leopard lily p. 256

lesser kudu p. 242

lesser panda p. 253

lesser scaup See *duck:* pp. 132–133

lettuce p. 253

leukocyte \\'lü-kə-‚sīt\\ A white blood cell or corpuscle. Leukocytes destroy many organisms that cause disease. Also sometimes spelled leucocyte.

levee \\'lev-ē\\ A bank or wall built along a river to prevent flooding.

libration of the moon p. 254

lichen p. 254

licorice p. 255

life A state of matter with certain characteristics of function and structure. These are metabolism, growth, reproduction, sensitivity to stimulation, development of different cells or tissues and individual recognizable forms.

life cycle \\'sī-kəl\\ The series of changes in form and function that a plant or animal passes through during 1 complete generation.

ligament \\'lig-ə-mənt\\ Strong, tough strands of tissue that hold bones together at movable joints, or that hold certain internal organs in place.

lightning A discharge of static electricity between a cloud and the surface of the earth.

lightning bug See *firefly:* p. 152

light-year The distance that light travels in one year, or about 6 trillion miles.

lignite p. 255; see also *coal:* p. 93

lilac p. 255

lily p. 255

lily of the valley p. 256

lime See *citrus tree:* p. 88

limestone p. 256

ling See *heather:* p. 211

linnet p. 257

linseed oil See *flax:* p. 156

lion p. 257

lionfish p. 258

litter \\'lit-ər\\ Two or more young born at the same time to any of the smaller mammals that usually produce several young.

little brown bat p. 32

littleneck clam p. 89

liver A gland-like organ that produces fluids, such as bile, that are used in digestion. In vertebrates, the liver destroys worn-out red corpuscles and stores vitamin A and a form of carbohydrate.

liver fluke p. 159

liverwort p. 258; see also *hepatica:* p. 213

lizard p. 259

llama p. 259

loam \\'lōm\\ Soil made up mainly of sand and clay with different amounts of silt and organic matter.

lobe \\'lōb\\ A well-defined part of an organ such as a brain or liver. A lobe is also the rounded lower part of the outer ear. A lobe is also a rounded division of a leaf. A lobe is also a flap on the toes of such birds as coots and grebes.

lobster p. 260

locomotion \\,lō-kə-'mō-shən\\ The movement of an organism from one place to another.

locoweed p. 260

locust p. 261

lode \\'lōd\\ A mineral deposit formed in closely-spaced veins or fissures in rock. See *vein:* p. 461.

loess p. 261

loggerhead shrike p. 404

loggerhead turtle pp. 456, 457

long-billed curlew p. 118

long-eared owl pp. 326, 327

long-horned beetle pp. 36, 37

long-horned grasshopper p. 196

longitude \\'län-jə-,t(y)üd\\ The measurement, in degrees, of the distance east or west of the prime meridian, which passes through Greenwich, England.

longnose gar p. 172

long waves pp. 475, 476

loon p. 262

loris p. 262

louse p. 262

low An area where the atmospheric pressure is less than that of the areas around it. The atmospheric pressure in a low is usually less than normal atmospheric pressure (14.7 pounds per square inch at sea level).

lumbar \\'ləm-bər\\ Having to do with the lower part of the back.

luminosity \\,lü-mə-'näs-ə-tē\\ The brightness of a star as compared to the brightness of the sun.

lumpfish p. 263

lumpsucker See *lumpfish:* p. 263

luna moth pp. 298, 299

lunar \\'lü-nər\\ Having to do with the moon.

lunar eclipse p. 137

lung In man and higher vertebrates, either of 2 thin, elastic, sac-like organs that is a part of the respiratory system. Lungs absorb oxygen from the air and give off carbon dioxide from the body.

lungfish p. 263

lupine p. 264

lupulin See *hop:* p. 217

luster \\'ləs-tər\\ The way a mineral surface reflects light. Luster is one of many ways that minerals are identified. The luster of a mineral may be glassy, metallic, dull, silky, pearly, brilliant or greasy.

lymph \\'lim(p)f\\ A colorless fluid that bathes animal tissues. Lymph passes into lymphatic channels and ducts and is discharged into the blood by way of the thoracic duct. Lymph is made up of a liquid that is like blood plasma and contains many white blood cells.

lynx p. 264

lyreman See *harvest fly:* p. 207

m

macaw p. 265

mace See *nutmeg tree:* p. 315

mackerel p. 265

Magellanic clouds p. 265

maggot \\'mag-ət\\ Any soft-bodied insect larva that feeds on living organisms or on decaying matter. A maggot is usually the larva of the housefly. See *fly:* p. 161.

magma \\'mag-mə\\ A mass of melted rock minerals and dissolved gases under the surface of the earth. Lava is magma that flows from volcanoes.

magnetic poles p. 266

magnetite p. 266

magnificent frigate bird See *man-o'-war bird* p. 273

magnitude \\'mag-nə-,t(y)üd\\ A number used to indicate and compare the brightness of stars, planets or other celestial bodies.

magnolia p. 267

magpie p. 267

mahogany tree p. 268

maidenhair fern pp. 148, 149

maidenhair tree See *ginkgo:* p. 180

malachite p. 268; see also *azurite:* p. 24

malaria See *sporozoan:* p. 419

male Describing the sex that produces sperm that unites with the egg of a female to produce a new animal. Male also describes the characteristics of that sex. Male also describes a staminate plant or its organs.

mallard See *duck:* pp. 132–133

malleable \\'mal-ē-ə-bəl\\ Describing a substance such as gold that can be reshaped by pressure or hammering.

mallow See *hibiscus*: p. 214

mammal p. 269

mammoth p. 269

man pp. 270–271

manatee p. 272

mandible \\'man-də-bəl\\ A jaw, especially the lower jaw, of a mammal. A mandible is also either part of the beak of a bird. A mandible is also a biting part of the mouth of arthropods.

mandrill p. 272

mane Long, coarse hair that grows on the necks of some mammals, such as horses and male lions.

mango tree p. 272

man-o'-war bird p. 273

manta p. 273

mantis p. 274

mantle \\'mant-ᵊl\\ Either or both lobes in the body wall of a mollusk or similar animal. The lobes contain glands that give off a fluid that forms shells. A mantle is also the soft, outer wall of a tunicate or barnacle. A mantle is also the back and folded wings of a bird. The earth's mantle is the part of the earth between the crust and the core. It is about 1,800 miles thick.

maple p. 274

map turtle pp. 456, 457

marble p. 275

Marchantia See *liverwort*: p. 258

marigold p. 275

marihuana See *hemp*: p. 213

marine \\mə-'rēn\\ Having to do with the oceans, or living in an ocean or other body of saltwater.

marlin p. 276

marmoset p. 276

marmot p. 277

marrow \\'mar-ō\\ The soft, fatty tissue in the cavities of many bones.

Mars pp. 277, 502

marsh p. 278

marsh hawk pp. 208, 209

marsh marigold See *cowslip*: p. 108

marsupial \\mär-'sü-pē-əl\\ A mammal, such as a kangaroo, having an abdominal pouch for carrying its young.

marten See *American sable*: p. 10

martin p. 278

mastodon p. 278

maternal \\mə-'tərn-ᵊl\\ Of, like or characteristic of a mother.

matrix \\'mā-triks\\ Fine-grained minerals or particles of rock that fill in the spaces between larger particles, crystals or fossils. Matrix is also the material between the cells of a tissue. A matrix is also a place of origin and growth, such as the dermis of finger- and toenails.

mature \\mə-'t(y)ur\\ Ripe or adult. Mature also refers to the completion of the development of germ cells.

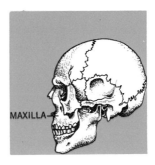

maxilla \\mak-'sil-ə\\ In man or many other mammals, the upper jaw. The maxilla is also a secondary mouth part of most arthropods.

mayflower p. 279; see also *hepatica*: p. 213

mayfly p. 279

Mayweed See *dog fennel*: p. 128

meadow buttercup p. 59

meadowlark p. 280

meadow mouse See *vole*: p. 467

meadow mushroom p. 305

meadow spittlebug pp. 417, 418

meadow vole p. 467

mealies See *sorghum*: p. 414

meander p. 280

mechanical weathering \\mi-'kan-i-kəl 'weth-ər-ing\\ The natural process that breaks rocks down into smaller and smaller fragments by expansion and contraction caused by changes in temperature, frost action, or by the action of water, ice or wind.

medulla \\mə-'dəl-ə\\ The innermost part of an organ, as contrasted with the cortex or outer part of the organ.

medusa \\mi-'d(y)ü-sə\\ A stage in the life cycle of the jellyfish.

meiosis \\mī-'ō-səs\\ Divisions of the nucleus of germ cells. Meiosis results in the formation of gametes in animals, and spores in higher plants.

melon p. 281

membrane \\'mem-,brān\\ A thin sheet of tissue that covers an organ or that lines such body cavities as the thorax and the abdomen.

Mendel's \\'men-dəlz\\ **laws** The three basic

principles of inheritance: the law of unit characters, the law of dominance and the law of segregation. The law of unit characters states that inherited characteristics are determined and passed on by individual factors that are paired. The law of dominance states that when two contrasting factors occur in an organism, one is stronger and keeps the other from showing. The law of segregation states that factors are separated and recombined by chance during sexual reproduction.

Mercury pp. 281, 502

meridian \mə-'rid-ē-ən\ An imaginary line that passes from the North Pole to the South Pole through any given place on the surface of the earth. A meridian is also one of the standard lines of longitude.

Merychippus p. 282

mesa p. 282; see also *butte:* p. 59

mesentery \'mes-ᵊn-ter-ē\ A fold in the tissue that lines the abdominal cavity of vertebrates.

Mesohippus p. 282

mesothorax \,mez-ə-'thōr-,aks\ In an insect, the middle section of the thorax. The mesothorax has the second pair of legs and the first pair of wings attached to it.

Mesozoic Era \,mez-ə-'zō-ik 'ir-ə\ See Geologic Time Chart, p. 493.

mesquite p. 283

metabolism \mə-'tab-ə-,liz-əm\ All the processes that are concerned with the activity, nourishment and growth of an organism.

metal p. 283

metamorphic rock p. 382

metamorphosis \,met-ə-'mȯr-fə-səs\ A series of growth changes in the development of an animal as it matures after birth or hatching.

metaphase \'met-ə-,fāz\ The stage in mitosis when the chromosomes are in the center of the cell just before they separate and move to opposite ends of the cell.

metathorax \,met-ə-'thōr-,aks\ In an insect, the end or last section of the thorax. Attached to the metathorax are the third or jumping pair of legs and the second pair of wings.

metazoa \,met-ə-'zō-ə\ An animal group that includes all many-celled types. It is usually considered to include coelenterates and higher animals.

meteor p. 284

meteorite \'mēt-ē-ə-,rīt\ A meteor, or a part of a meteor, that has fallen onto the earth's surface.

meteorology \,mēt-ē-ə-'räl-ə-jē\ The science that has to do with the atmosphere and weather.

mica p. 284

microbe \'mī-,krōb\ A microscopic plant or animal that is usually thought of in connection with disease or fermentation. A microbe is sometimes called a germ.

microbiology \,mī-krō-(,)bī-'äl-ə-jē\ The science of the nature, life and actions of microorganisms.

microcline See *feldspar:* p. 147

microorganism \,mī-krō-'ȯr-gə-,niz-əm\ Any living body so small that a microscope is needed to see it.

microscopic \,mī-krə-'skäp-ik\ Describing something that is too small to be seen clearly without a microscope.

middle ear In higher vertebrates, the cavity that includes the eardrum, the hammer, the anvil, the stirrup and the opening of the Eustachian tube.

midnight mollie See *black mollie:* p. 43

midnight sun The sun when it can be seen for 24 hours a day during part of arctic and antarctic summers.

mid-ocean ridge p. 285

midrib \'mid-,rib\ The single large vein in the center of a leaf. It runs from the petiole to the tip of the leaf.

midwife toad pp. 444, 445

migration \mī-'grā-shən\ The act of moving at regular periods of time from one geographical area to another.

MILDEW (MAGNIFIED)

mildew \'mil-,dü\ A fungus that produces an unpleasant, musty odor and then patches of grayish, fuzzy growth and finally decay. Mildew sometimes grows on objects made from plant or animal materials.

milk snake pp. 410, 411

milk teeth In mammals, the first set of teeth. They are later replaced by more permanent teeth.

milkweed p. 285

milkweed bug pp. 54, 55

Milky Way The galaxy to which the earth's solar system belongs. From earth, the Milky Way looks like a glowing band across the sky. It is sometimes called the Galaxy. See *galaxy:* p. 170.

millipede p. 286

mimicry \'mim-i-krē\ The form or color of an animal or plant that makes it look like some other plant or animal or like some object in its surroundings.

mimosa tree p. 286

mineral p. 286

mink p. 287

minnow p. 287

mint p. 288

Miocene Epoch \\'mī-ə-ˌsēn 'ep-ək\\ See Geologic Time Chart, p. 493.

mirage \\mə-'räzh\\ An image, on the eye, of a distant object. A mirage is caused by the total reflection of light from the meeting of warm and cool air masses. A mirage is usually upside down when compared with the object.

Mississippian Period \\ˌmis-(ə-)'sip-ē-ən 'pir-ē-əd\\ See Geologic Time Chart, p. 493.

mistletoe p. 288

mite p. 289

mitosis \\mī-'tō-səs\\ The division of a cell nucleus that occurs before the whole cell divides. The process includes the appearance of double chromosomes that separate and move to opposite sides of the cell. This separation results in 2 cells. Each of the 2 cells normally has an identical set of chromosomes.

moccasin flower See *lady's slipper:* p. 244

mockingbird p. 289

modern man pp. 270, 271

molar \\'mō-lər\\ In mammals, a double grinding tooth with a broad surface. The molars are behinds the incisors and canines.

mold \\'mōld\\ A small, furry-looking fungus that grows on wood, paper, leather and different food substances. See *slime mold:* p. 407, and *penicillium:* p. 341. A mold is also a natural or artificial impression of a plant part, shell or other organism.

mole p. 290

mollusk p. 290

Molly Miller See *blenny:* p. 44

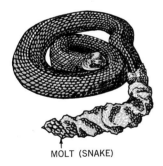

MOLT (SNAKE)

molt \\'mōlt\\ In many animals, birds, insects and reptiles, to shed feathers, hair, horns or an outer layer of skin. Molting is followed by a new growth of what was shed.

molybdenite p. 291

molybdenum See *molybdenite:* p. 291

monadnock p. 291

monarch butterfly pp. 60, 61

Mongolian pony p. 358

mongoose p. 291

monkey pp. 292–293

monocotyledon \\ˌmän-ə-ˌkät-ᵊl-'ēd-ᵊn\\ Any plant that has only 1 cotyledon in its seeds. Wheat, barley, corn, rye, bamboo, palms, lilies and orchids are monocotyledons.

monocular vision \\mä-'näk-yə-lər 'vizh-ən\\ Vision in which an image is seen separately by each eye, or by 1 eye. Monocular vision occurs when an animal's eyes are located on the sides of its head. An animal with monocular vision sees objects without depth or flat, as seen in a photograph.

monolith \\'män-ᵊl-ˌith\\ A large rock formation made up of just 1 kind of rock. It is usually a column-shaped, coarse-grained, igneous rock.

monsoon \\män-'sün\\ A wind system, mostly in the tropics, in which the wind blows from the sea to the land for about 6 months, and from the land to the sea for the next 6 months. A monsoon is also the season of the southwest monsoon during which there is heavy rainfall.

month The period of time that corresponds to about the period from new moon to new moon, or a little more than 29½ days.

moon pp. 294, 502

moonstone p. 294

moose p. 295

moraine p. 295

moray p. 295

morel p. 296

Mormon tea See *ephedra:* p. 142

morning glory p. 296

MORNING STAR   VENUS

morning star A planet, especially Mercury or Venus, that is seen in the east just before or at sunrise.

morphology \\mȯr-'fäl-ə-jē\\ A branch of biology dealing with the structure and form of plants and animals, their systems, organs, tissues and cells. Morphology is also the scientific study of the forms and structures of land.

mosquito p. 297

moss p. 297

moth pp. 298–299

Mother Carey's chickens See *petrel:* p. 343

motor nerve A nerve that carries impulses from a nerve center, such as the brain or the spinal cord, to a muscle.

mountain p. 300

mountain bluebird p. 46

mountain laurel p. 300

mountain lion See *cougar:* p. 107

mouse p. 300

mucus \\'myü-kəs\\ In many animals, a fluid given off by the glands that cover the inside linings of the digestive and respiratory tracts. Mucus is also a slimy fluid that moistens some of the outer surfaces of earthworms, fish and amphibians.

mud Fine-grained soil that contains much water and possibly some minerals.

mudcrack p. 301

MUDFLOW

mudflow \\'məd-flō\\ A kind of landslide or avalanche in which mud and debris move down a slope.

mudminnow p. 301

mud puppy p. 302

mud pusser See *black mollie:* p. 43

mud siren p. 405

mud turtle pp. 456, 457

mulberry p. 302

mule p. 303

mule deer p. 123

mullet p. 303

multicellular \\,məl-ti-'sel-yə-lər\\ Describing plants and animals made up of many cells.

murex p. 304

muscle \\'mus-əl\\ A tissue or organ in many animals that contracts to produce movement of the body or of parts of the body.

muscovite p. 304; see also *mica:* p. 284

mushroom p. 304

muskellunge p. 305

muskie See *muskellunge:* p. 305

musk-ox p. 305

muskrat p. 306

mussel p. 306

mussel worm See *nereis:* p. 311

mustard p. 307

mutant \\'myüt-ᵊnt\\ An individual plant or animal that shows some new characteristic that can be inherited. A mutant is sometimes called a sport.

mutation \\myü-'tā-shən\\ In an individual plant or animal, a change or characteristic that can be inherited. Such a characteristic is different from any characteristics of the parents. A mutation is probably caused by chemical or physical changes in the genes or chromosomes.

mute swan p. 430

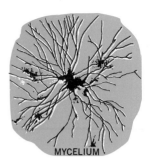

MYCELIUM

mycelium \\mī-'sē-lē-əm\\ The meshwork of fine filaments that makes up the plant body of most fungi.

myna See *mynah bird:* p. 307

mynah bird p. 307

myrtle p. 308

n

nadir \\'nā-,dir\\ In astronomy, the point in the celestial sphere that is directly below the observer. It is opposite the zenith, or point directly above the observer.

naked-nosed wombat p. 484

naked sole p. 414

narcissus p. 308

narrow-mouthed toad pp. 444, 445

nasal cavity \\'nā-zəl 'kav-ət-ē\\ In higher vertebrates, the part of the breathing passage that opens to the outside through the nostrils.

nasturtium p. 309

native \\'nāt-iv\\ Describing plants and animals that originated in a certain area. Native also describes characteristics that one is born with. Native also describes an element or mineral that is found uncombined with other elements, such as native gold. Native also describes rocks or minerals that are generally found in a certain area.

natural \\'nach-(ə-)rəl\\ **gas** A mixture of hydrocarbons, mainly methane, that occurs naturally in rock cavities as a gas, or dissolved in water, or with deposits of petroleum. Natural gas burns and is used as a fuel.

natural immunity \\'nach-(ə-)rəl im-'yü-nət-ē\\ The inborn ability of an organism to resist a certain disease.

natural resources \\'nach-(ə-)rəl 'rē-,sōrs-əz\\ The plant and animal life, minerals, water, oil and the land that is supplied by nature in any given area.

natural selection \\'nach-(ə-)rəl sə-'lek-shən\\

The theory of Charles Darwin that attempts to explain the causes of the changes in plants and animals. The theory states that individual plants and animals having characteristics best suited to a particular environment live to become the parents of the next generation. Those that are less well suited to the same environment do not live long enough to produce young. By this natural process of reproducing the characteristics most useful to survive, new species eventually arise that have characteristics different from those of their ancestors.

nautilus p. 309

navel \\'nā-vəl\\ The scar or depression in the middle of the abdomen of mammals that marks the place where the umbilical cord was attached before birth.

Neanderthal man pp. 270, 271

neap tide \\'nēp tīd\\ A tide that occurs during the first- and third-quarter moons. During neap tide, the high tide is lower and the low tide is higher than usual. This is because the gravitational pull of the moon and of the sun are at right angles to each other.

nebula p. 309

neck The part of the body of an animal that connects the head with the body or trunk. A neck is also a narrow section of a part, such as that in an organ or bone. A neck is also solid lava or other igneous rock that fills the opening in an extinct volcano and that has been exposed by erosion. A neck is also a narrow strip of land that connects 2 ridges or that connects a peninsula with the mainland.

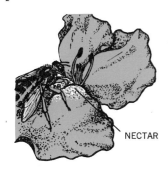

NECTAR

nectar \\'nek-tər\\ A sugary fluid given off by plants. Nectar is produced by glands that are usually located at the base of the pistils.

needlefish p. 310

neon goby p. 186

neon tetra p. 440

Neptune pp. 310, 502

nereis p. 311

nerve In many animals, any of the cord-like fibers outside the central nervous system that impulses travel along between the various parts of the body and the central nervous system. A nerve is made up of nerve fibers, blood and lymph vessels and connective tissue, or sheaths.

nerve cells Cells that make up nerve tissue. Each cell has a central body with a nucleus and cytoplasm. Fine thread-like fibers stick out from each cell. Nerve cells are also neurons.

nervous system \\'sis-təm\\ In vertebrates, the system made up of the brain, the spinal cord and the network of nerves and nerve fibers that carry impulses all through the body. The nervous system coordinates the activities of the other systems of the body.

nettle p. 311

neuron \\'nü-,rän\\ A nerve cell.

névé See *firn:* p. 153

new moon See *moon:* p. 294

newt p. 312

New World porcupine p. 359

nictitating membrane \\'nik-tə-,tāt-ing 'mem-,brān\\ A thin, movable membrane, or third eyelid, found in the eye of reptiles, birds, and certain mammals.

nighthawk p. 312

nightingale p. 312

nightjar See *goatsucker:* p. 186

nightshade p. 313

nimbostratus clouds pp. 90, 91

nimbus clouds pp. 90, 91

9-banded armadillo p. 20

9-spotted ladybird beetle pp. 36, 37

nitrogen \\'nī-trə-jən\\ An element that is a gas and that makes up about 78 percent of the earth's atmosphere. It has no color, odor or taste. It does not react with other substances at ordinary temperatures and pressures.

nitrogen cycle \\'nī-trə-jən sī-kəl\\ A continuous series of events in which nitrogen in the air is changed into nitrogen compounds by bacteria and by lightning. These compounds are used by plants to make amino acids. They are used by both plants and animals to make proteins. When a plant or animal dies, the proteins change to amino acids and ammonia by the process of decay. Then, the ammonia combines with oxygen to form nitrates and nitrites. The nitrates become available to the plants again, or, along with the nitrites, they are changed into nitrogen which is released into the air. This completes the cycle.

nitrogen fixation \\'ni-trə-jən fik-'sā-shən\\ Any of several chemical processes by which nitrogen from the air combines with another element or elements to form compounds.

nitrogen-fixing bacteria \\'ni-trə-jən 'fiks-ing bak-'tir-ē-ə\\ Bacteria that live in nodes on the roots of growing plants such as peas, beans or alfalfa. The bacteria use nitrogen from the air to make amino acids and proteins that are used by green plants.

nocturnal \\näk-'tərn-əl\\ Describing an animal that is most active during the night.

node \\'nōd\\ A mass of 1 kind of tissue within another kind of tissue. A node is also a small lump or swelling that is either normal or caused by infection. A node is also a joint between two parts of a plant stem. A node is also the part of the stem to which the plant leaf is attached.

normal fault p. 146

North American coral snake pp. 410, 411

North American ovenbird p. 325

North American oyster p. 328

North American wild turkey p. 454

North Atlantic gannet p. 171

northern anchovy p. 13

northern gannet p. 171

northern lights See *aurora:* p. 24

northern pike pp. 346, 347

northern porgy p. 360

northern puffer p. 365

northern sea robin p. 313

northern sea cucumber p. 394

northern sea horse p. 395

northern shrike p. 403

North Pole The most northern point on the earth's surface. It is 1 of 2 points through which pass the imaginary line that forms the earth's axis. The North Pole is sometimes called the geographic north pole to distinguish it from the magnetic north pole.

North Star Polaris, a fairly bright star located almost directly above the North Pole. The North Star marks the position of the north celestial pole.

Norway rat p. 374

Nostoc See *algae:* pp. 6–7

nostril The openings of the nose.

nova p. 314

nuclear membrane \'nü-,klē-ər 'mem-,brān\ A living double membrane that is made up of proteins and fatty substances. The nuclear membrane surrounds the nucleus of a cell and seems to control the passage of materials between the nucleus and the cytoplasm.

nucleic acid \nü-'klē-ik 'as-əd\ A complex compound that is found in all living cells. Nucleic acid is made up of carbon, hydrogen, oxygen, nitrogen and phosphorus. Along with proteins, it is thought to control the growth of the cell.

nucleolus \nü-'klē-ə-ləs\ A rounded body in the nuclei of cells that does not undergo cell division. The nucleolus is believed to take part in the control of the making of protein in cells.

nucleus \'nü-klē-əs\ A rounded body in the cytoplasm of most plant and animal cells. A nucleus is made up of chromosomes and 1 or more nucleoli suspended in protein gel, all surrounded by a membrane. A nucleus controls the metabolism, growth and division of its cell. A nucleus is also a dense, bright core, as of a comet or galaxy.

nurse shark pp. 400, 401

nut A dry fruit that does not open along definite seams when it is mature. A nut contains a single seed that is enclosed in a hard shell.

nuthatch p. 314

nutmeg tree p. 315

nutria p. 315

nymph \'nim(p)f\ An immature stage in the life cycle of an insect that undergoes gradual metamorphosis.

O

oak tree p. 316

oat p. 316

obsidian p. 316

occluded \ə-'klüd-əd\ **front** The weather condition in which a cold front catches up with a warm front, and the edge of one front moves up over the edge of the other.

ocean The large, continuous body of water that covers almost ¾ of the earth's surface. An ocean is also any 1 of the 5 regions into which this body is divided: Atlantic, Pacific, Indian, Arctic and Antarctic.

ocean currents \'kər-əntz\ The movement of warm water from areas around the equator to areas around the poles, and of cold water from the poles to areas around the equator. Ocean currents are produced and affected by the rotation of the earth, the difference in temperatures and the direction of the prevailing winds. See p. 501.

ocean perch See *rosefish:* p. 384

ocean sunfish p. 317

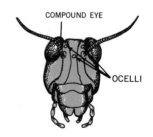

COMPOUND EYE

OCELLI

ocelli \ō-'sel-,ī\ In insects, the simple eyes which occur in twos and threes between the compound eyes.

ocelot p. 317

octopus p. 318

Oedogonium See *algae:* pp. 6–7

offshore bar See *barrier beach:* p. 30

Ohio buckeye p. 53

okapi p. 318

old-fashioned garden peony p. 341

Old World porcupine p. 360

oleander p. 318

olfactory \äl-'fak-t(ə-)rē\ Having to do with the organs of smell or with the sense of smell.

Oligocene Epoch \'äl-i-gō-,sēn 'ep-ək\ See Geologic Time Chart, p. 493.

Oligochaeta See *annelid:* p. 14

olive tree p. 319

olivine p. 319

omnivore \'äm-ni-,vōr\ An organism that eats living or dead animal and plant substances.

onion p. 319

onyx p. 320

oolitic limestone p. 256

ooze \'üz\ An ocean-bed deposit of shells, skeletons and fragments of animals. Ooze has a mud-like texture.

opal p. 320

opaque \ō-'pāk\ Having to do with a substance that does not let light pass through it.

open cluster See *star cluster:* p. 422

opium See *poppy:* p. 359

opium poppy p. 359

opossum p. 321

opposite \'äp-ə-zət\ Referring to leaves that grow in pairs, across from each other, on 2 sides of a stem or twig.

opposition \,äp-ə-'zish-ən\ The condition of a celestial body when it is on the side of the earth away from the sun so that a straight line from the celestial body would pass through the earth and the sun. Opposition is also the condition of any 2 celestial bodies located opposite each other on the celestial sphere, with a difference in longitude of 180 degrees.

orange See *citrus tree:* p. 88

orangutan p. 321

orbit \'ȯr-bət\ The circular or elliptical path in which a satellite, star, planet, meteor or comet revolves around another body.

orchid p. 322

order In the scientific classification of plants and animals, a group of organisms related to each other. Several orders may be placed together in a larger group called a class, or an order may be broken down into smaller groups called families.

Ord kangaroo rat pp. 374, 375

Ordovician Period \,ȯrd-ə-'vish-ən 'pir-ē-əd\ See Geologic Time Chart, p. 493.

ore \'ōr\ Any rock or natural minerals in rock that are found in the earth's crust and from which useful metals may be taken.

organ A group of cells or tissues that forms a functional part of a plant or animal.

organic \ȯr-'gan-ik\ Describing organisms that are alive or that were once alive.

organism \'ȯr-gə-,niz-əm\ An individual living plant or animal.

Oregon junco p. 234

oribi p. 322

Oriental jackal p. 229

origin \'ȯr-ə-jən\ The ancestry of an organism or group of organisms.

oriole p. 322

ornamental gourd p. 191

ornate chorus frog pp. 166, 167

ornithology \,ȯr-nə-'thäl-ə-jē\ The science of bird groups, forms, habits and development.

orthoclase See *feldspar:* p. 147

oryx p. 323

osage orange p. 323

Oscillatoria See *algae:* pp. 6–7

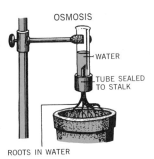

OSMOSIS

WATER

TUBE SEALED TO STALK

ROOTS IN WATER

osmosis \ä-'smō-səs\ The process of a liquid passing through a living membrane. The liquid passes from the side that has the densest material to the side that has the least dense material.

osmunda See *fern:* pp. 148–149

osprey See *hawk:* pp. 208–209

ostrich p. 324

otter p. 324

outcrop p. 325

outlier \'aut-,lī(-ə)r\ A rock mass that erosion has cut away from the material that formerly connected it to the rest of a mountain or cliff.

oval kumquat tree p. 242

ovary \'ōv-(ə-)rē\ A female organ of reproduction. In animals it produces egg cells. In plants it produces spores that develop into female gametophytes, which produce egg cells.

ovenbird p. 325

oviparous \ō-'vip-(ə-)rəs\ Describing the pattern of reproduction in which eggs are given off from the female and young hatch from eggs.

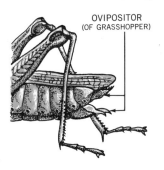

OVIPOSITOR (OF GRASSHOPPER)

ovipositor \'ō-və-,päz-ət-ər\ The egg-laying organ of an insect.

ovule \\'ō-vyül\\ In seed plants, the rounded sac-like part in which the ovary forms. After fertilization, the ovule develops into a seed.

ovum \\'ō-vəm\\ An egg cell.

owl pp. 326–327

oxbow lake p. 245

oxidation \\,äk-sə-'dā-shən\\ The process of combining with oxygen or with more oxygen.

oxygen \\'äk-si-jən\\ A gas that has no color nor odor at ordinary temperatures. It is the most plentiful element by weight in the known parts of the earth. Oxygen combines chemically with most other elements to form oxides.

oxygen-carbon dioxide cycle \\'äk-si-jən 'kär-bən dī-'äk-,sīd 'sī-kəl\\ The continuous replacement of the atmosphere by plants and animals. Plants and animals take in oxygen and give off carbon dioxide during breathing. Plants use carbon dioxide and give off oxygen during photosynthesis.

oyster p. 328; see also *clam*: p. 89

oyster drill p. 328

oystershell scale insect p. 391

ozone \\'ō-,zōn\\ A form of oxygen that has an odor. It reacts more easily with other elements than regular oxygen. Ozone is formed at high altitudes by ultraviolet light from the sun, that strikes regular oxygen in the atmosphere of the earth.

ozone layer \\'ō-,zōn 'lā-ər\\ A layer of the atmosphere. The layer contains ozone and absorbs ultraviolet light from the sun. The ozone layer begins in the upper stratosphere and extends into the ionosphere. The ozone layer is sometimes called the chemosphere.

p

Pacific anchovy p. 13

Pacific halibut p. 204

Pacific salmon p. 387

Pacific viperfish p. 329

paddlefish p. 329

pahoehoe See *lava*: p. 248

painted bunting p. 56

painted cup See *Indian paintbrush*: p. 227

painted lady butterfly pp. 60, 61

painted turtle pp. 456, 457

palate \\'pal-ət\\ In many mammals, the roof of the mouth. The palate is made up of a hard bony framework in front, and muscular fiber surrounded by a movable fold of mucous membrane in back.

Paleocene Epoch \\'pā-lē-ə-sēn 'ep-ək\\ See Geologic Time Chart, p. 493.

paleontology \\,pā-lē-(,)än-'täl-ə-jē\\ The scientific study of life in past geologic time. Paleontology is based on plant and animal fossils.

Paleozoic Era \\,pā-lē-ə-'zō-ik 'ir-ə\\ See Geologic Time Chart, p. 493.

palm p. 329

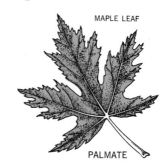

MAPLE LEAF

PALMATE

palmate \\'pal-,māt\\ Describing structures that branch out from a center, as the veins of a leaf or the leaflets of a compound leaf.

palm cockatoo p. 94

palmetto palm See *cabbage palmetto*: p. 62

paloverde p. 330

pancreas \\'pang-krē-əs\\ In man, a large digestive gland located behind the stomach and parallel to the duodenum. The pancreas gives off pancreatic juice which goes into the duodenum. It also contains the islands of Langerhans, glands that produce the hormone insulin.

panda See *giant panda*: p. 178; and *lesser panda*: p. 253

pangolin p. 330

pansy See *violet*: p. 464

panther See *cougar*: p. 107

papaw p. 331

papaya p. 331

paper mulberry p. 332

paper-white narcissus p. 308

papilla \\pə-'pil-ə\\ Tissue that connects with and carries food to the root of a tooth, hair or feather. A papilla is also one of the many tiny bumps on the upper surface of the inner layer of skin.

paprika See *pepper*: p. 341

parakeet p. 332

parallel venation \\'par-ə-,lel vā-'nā-shən\\ In a leaf, veins running side by side from the leafstalk to the tip of the blade. Parallel venation occurs in the leaves of grasses and lilies.

paramecium p. 333

parasite \\'par-ə-,sīt\\ An organism that lives in or on a host organism. A parasite takes its food from and is usually destructive to the host.

parietal \\pə-'rī-ət-əl\\ Having to do with, or next to, the walls of a cavity or part.

parrot p. 333

parsley p. 334

parsnip p. 334

parthenogenesis \\,pär-thə-nō-'jen-ə-səs\\ The development of an embryo without the fertilization of the egg. Parthenogenesis occurs among some invertebrates, such as aphids.

partridge p. 334; see also *bobwhite*: p. 49

passenger pigeon p. 335

pathogenic \'path-ə-'jen-ik\ Having to do with disease. Pathogenic often refers to organisms that cause disease.

pathology \pə-'thäl-ə-jē\ The study of diseases, especially the changes in behavior and form of body tissues and organs that may cause, or be caused by, a disease.

paw Usually, the clawed foot of a 4-footed animal, such as a lion, tiger, dog, cat or wolf.

pawpaw See *papaw*: p. 331

pea p. 335

peach tree p. 336

peacock See *peafowl*: p. 336

peafowl p. 336

peahen See *peafowl*: p. 336

peanut p. 337

pearl p. 337

pearly layer \'pər-lē lā-ər\ The smooth inner layer in the shells of such bivalves as clams and oysters.

pearly nautilus p. 309

pearly razor fish p. 377

pear tree p. 338

peat p. 338; see also *coal*: p. 93

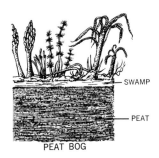

PEAT BOG

peat bog \'pēt bäg\ A swamp-like area that contains peat, a partly decayed, dark brown plant matter.

pecan See *hickory tree*: p. 215

peccary p. 338

pectoral \'pek-t(ə-)rəl\ Having to do with a part of an animal that is in, or on, the chest area. Pectoral also refers to either or both of the fins of a fish that are located behind the gills.

Peking man pp. 270, 271

pelican p. 339

pelvis \'pel-vəs\ The basin-like structure in the lower part of the skeleton of many vertebrates. The hind limbs are attached to the pelvis.

pelycosaur See *dimetrodon*: p. 126

penguin p. 339

penicillin See *penicillium*: p. 340

penicillium p. 340

peninsula \pə-'nin-sə-lə\ A large piece of land that sticks out into the water from the mainland. A peninsula is almost surrounded by

water and is connected by a narrow strip of land to the mainland.

Pennsylvanian Period \,pen-səl-'vā-nyən 'pir-ē-əd\ See Geologic Time Chart, p. 493.

Pensacola red snapper p. 412

penumbra p. 340

peony p. 341

pepper p. 341

peppercorn See *pepper*: p. 341

peppermint p. 341

perch p. 342

peregrine falcon See *hawk*: pp. 208–209

perennial \pə-'ren-ē-əl\ A plant that lives from year to year.

perfect flower A flower that contains both stamens and pistil, although some other parts may be missing.

peridot See *olivine*: p. 319

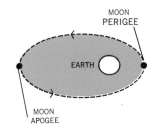

perigee \'per-ə-jē\ The point nearest the earth in the orbit of the moon or of a satellite.

perihelion \,per-ə-'hēl-yən\ The point nearest the sun in the orbit of a planet or comet.

period \'pir-ē-əd\ A division of geological time. A period is longer than an epoch and shorter than an era. Periods are known by the formation of certain rock layers or fossils in a certain order. A period is also the time it takes a planet, satellite, star or other celestial body to revolve around another celestial body.

periodical cicada pp. 86, 87

peristalsis \,per-ə-'stòl-səs\ In many animals, the wave-like contractions of the muscles in the walls of different organs of the body. Peristalsis occurs in the esophagus during swallowing.

peritoneum \,per-ət-°n-'ē-əm\ In mammals, a thin membrane that lines the abdominal cavity. The peritoneum covers the soft organs of the body. It is made up of cells that produce a colorless watery fluid.

permablack See *black mollie*: p. 43

permeable \'per-mē-ə-bəl\ Describing any substance through which liquids can pass.

Permian Period \'pər-mē-ən 'pir-ē-əd\ See Geologic Time Chart, p. 493.

persimmon tree p. 342

petal \'pet-°l\ One unit of the inner floral part of a flower. A petal is usually shaped like a leaf and is often colored.

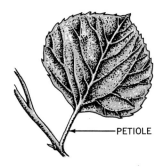

PETIOLE

MOTHS
PHOTOTROPISM

petiole \\'pet-ē-,ōl\\ The stalk of a leaf.

petrel p. 343

petrified wood p. 343

petroleum \\pə-'trō-lē-əm\\ An oily liquid, often called crude oil, that occurs in the upper part of the earth's crust. It is the material from which gasoline, oil, kerosene, paraffin and asphalt are made.

petunia p. 344

phagocyte \\'fag-ə-,sīt\\ Any body cell that gets its food by surrounding it. A phagocyte can move through tissue. In vertebrates, a phagocyte is a blood cell that feeds on bacteria.

pharynx \\'far-ing(k)s\\ In animals, a sac-like part of the digestive tract.

phase \\'fāz\\ Any of the changing and repeating stages of the amount of light reflected by the moon or planets. A phase is also any of the 5 stages of mitosis in the development of a plant or animal cell. A phase is also any of several skin or body-cover color variations, especially among amphibians.

pheasant p. 344

phenomenon \\fi-'näm-ə-,nän\\ A fact or event that may be described and explained on a scientific basis. A phenomenon is also an unusual or rare fact or event.

phloem \\'flō-em\\ In seed plants and ferns, food-carrying, tube-like tissue and other tissues that carry food both up and down.

phlogopite mica p. 284

phlox p. 344

Phobos See *Mars:* p. 277

phoebe p. 345

phosphorite p. 345

photosphere \\'fōt-ə-,sfir\\ The visible layer of gases that surrounds the sun or other stars. The photosphere of the sun is a few hundred miles thick and has a temperature of about 5,500°C. See *sun:* p. 427.

photosynthesis \\,fōt-ə-'sin-thə-səs\\ The process by which sugar is made in the cells of green plants. Carbon dioxide combines with water when there is light present, and with chlorophyll, necessary for the process. Through photosynthesis, plants make their own food.

phototaxis \\,fōt-ə-'tak-səs\\ In a free, simple organism, a movement that is stimulated by light, heat or a chemical change.

phototropism \\fō-'tä-trə-,piz-əm\\ In plants, animals or one of their parts, a movement stimulated by light.

phylum \\'fī-ləm\\ A division of animal and plant classification that includes one or more classes.

physiology \\,fiz-ē-'äl-ə-jē\\ The science that deals with the function of cells, tissues, organs and systems in living organisms.

pickerel frog pp. 166, 167

pickerelweed p. 346

pied-billed grebe p. 197

piercing and sucking mouth parts \\'pir-sing ənd 'sək-ing maùth pärts\\ The wide, sharp-pointed beaks with which certain insects feed on the blood of man and the larger animals.

pig See *swine:* p. 432

pigeon See *dove:* p. 131

pigeon hawk pp. 208, 209

pigeon horntail p. 219

pigmy shrew p. 403

pika p. 346

pike p. 346

pillbug See *sowbug and pillbug:* p. 414

pillow lava p. 249

pilot fish p. 347

pilot whale pp. 478, 479

pimento tree p. 347

pineal \\'pin-ē-əl\\ **body** A cone-shaped gland located in the mid-brain of all vertebrates. It has no known function or purpose.

pineapple p. 348

pine tree p. 348

pink and white lady's slipper p. 244

pink jellyfish p. 232

pink salmon p. 387

PINNATE

BLACK WALNUT LEAF

pinnate \\'pin-,āt\\ Similar to a feather, as similar

small leaves arranged on each side of a common stem.

pintail See *duck:* pp. 132–133

pinworm p. 348

pipevine p. 349

pipit p. 349

piranha p. 350

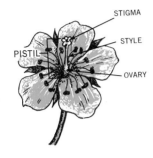

pistil \'pist-əl\ The female reproductive organs in a flower. The pistil usually includes the ovary, style and stigma.

pistillate \'pis-tə-,lāt\ Referring to flowers having pistils but no stamens, or no stamens that function.

pit The hard shell, in the center of certain fruits, that contains a single seed. A pit is also a fine pore in a vascular cell, especially in the wood of cone-bearing trees.

pitchblende p. 350

pitcher plant p. 351

pit viper p. 351; see also *snake:* pp. 410–411

placenta \plə-'sent-ə\ In most mammals, a disk-shaped organ that is full of blood vessels and capillaries. It spreads over the inner surface of the uterus during the development of an embryo. In plants, a placenta is a part of the ovary wall.

plain p. 351

plains pocket gopher p. 189

planarian p. 352; see also *flatworm:* p. 155

planet p. 352

planetary nebula See *nebula:* p. 309

plane tree See *sycamore:* p. 433

plankton p. 353; see also *dinoflagellate:* p. 126

plantain p. 353

plant classification \,klas-ə-fə-'kā-shən\ The division of the plant kingdom into related groups and subgroups. See pp. 496–497.

plant louse See *aphid:* p. 17

plants Living organisms that do not have nerves and sense organs. Plants usually have firm cell walls that contain cellulose. Plants make carbohydrates using minerals from the soil and energy from the sun. All green plants and some that are not green contain chlorophyll. Reproduction is carried on by seeds or spores, and by sprouting or spreading roots. Plants provide food for all other forms of life, either directly or indirectly.

plant succession \sək-'sesh-ən\ In a biological community, any series of changes in plants. Plant succession may result from the introduction of new forms of life, or from changes in climate or in the surface of the land.

plasma membrane \'plaz-mə 'mem-brān\ The outer membrane or exposed outer edge of the cytoplasm of a cell. The plasma membrane controls the flow of materials into and out of a cell.

plasmodium See *sporozoan:* p. 419

plasmolysis \plaz-'mäl-ə-səs\ The collapse or shrinking of protoplasm in a cell due to the loss of water by reverse osmosis.

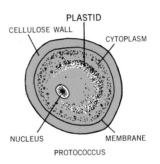

plastids \'plas-tədz\ Bodies in the cytoplasm of most plants and 1-celled organisms. Plastids are associated with the forming or storing, or both, of food. When plastids are colored, they are called chromoplasts.

plateau p. 354

platelets \'plāt-ləts\ In the blood of vertebrates, the smallest of the solid particles. Platelets have irregular shapes and no color. They are important in blood clotting. Platelets are also called thrombocytes.

platy p. 354

playa lake p. 245

Pleistocene Epoch \'plī-stə,sēn 'ep-ək\ See Geologic Time Chart, p. 493.

pleura \'plùr-ə\ In man and other mammals, a thin membrane that covers each lung. The pleura folds back to form a lining for the inside of the thoracic cavity. The pleura gives off a mucous that allows free motion of the lungs in breathing. In arthropods, the pleura is a heavy membrane that lines each side of a segment, as in crayfish, shrimp and spiders.

Pliocene Epoch \'plī-ə-,sēn 'ep-ək\ See Geologic Time Chart, p. 493.

plover p. 354

plumage \'plü-mij\ All the feathers of a bird.

plum tree p. 355

Pluto pp. 355, 502

pocket gopher See *gopher:* p. 189

pocket rat pp. 374, 375

poinciana p. 356

poinsettia p. 356

poison hemlock p. 356

poison ivy p. 357

poison oak See *poison ivy:* p. 357

poison sumac pp. 426, 427

polar air mass \'pō-lər 'ar 'mas\ A body of air that forms or gets its characteristics in polar regions. A polar air mass moves toward lower latitudes.

polar \'pō-lər\ front A surface or boundary between a polar air mass and a tropical air mass.

pole The point on any sphere where its axis of rotation meets the surface.

pole bean p. 33

polecat See *skunk:* p. 406

polecat weed See *skunk cabbage:* p. 406

polemonium See *Jacob's ladder:* p. 231

pollen \'päl-ən\ In plants, grains that produce the male sex cells. Pollen is formed in the anthers of flowers or in the male cones of evergreens.

pollination \,päl-ə-'nā-shən\ The fertilization of a flowering plant by transfer of pollen from anther to pistil by wind, water, gravity, insects, birds or other animals, or by people who breed plants.

Polychaeta See *annelid:* p. 14

polygamous \pə-'lig-ə-məs\ Bearing a flower that is either male or female as well as one that has both male and female reproductive organs. Both of these flowers are on the same plant. Polygamous also describes animals that have more than one mate at a time.

polyp \'päl-əp\ A coelenterate animal, such as a hydra, that has a hollow, tube-like body and a mouth that is surrounded by tentacles.

polyphemus moth pp. 298, 299

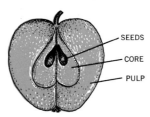

POME (APPLE)

pome \'pōm\ A pulpy fruit, such as an apple or pear, in the apple family. The seeds of a pome are in a core and are surrounded by a fleshy pulp called the receptacle.

pompano p. 357

pony p. 358

poorwill p. 358

poplar p. 358

poppy p. 359

population \,päp-yə-'lā-shən\ The living organisms that live in a given area or region.

porcupine p. 359

porcupine fish p. 360

HAIR SHAFT   PORE

pore \'pōr\ A small opening in skin or in membranes. Pores function in the processes of secretion, excretion, the loss of water by evaporation from plants, or absorption.

porgy p. 360

porous \'pōr-əs\ Full of pores or tiny holes, and able to absorb moisture.

porpoise p. 360

Portuguese man-of-war p. 361

posterior \pä-'stir-ē-ər\ Describing a part that is located behind another part, toward the rear or toward the back surface.

potato p. 361

potato leafhopper p. 249

pothole p. 362

prairie \'prer-ē\ A large area of grassland on a plain. A prairie never has large forests. In South America, a prairie is called a pampa. In Africa it is called a veldt. In Eurasia it is called a steppe.

prairie dog p. 362

praying mantis p. 274

Pre-Cambrian Eras \prē-'kam-brē-ən 'ir-əs\ See Geologic Time Chart, p. 493.

precious coral p. 103

precipitation \pri-,sip-ə-'tā-shən\ Form of rain, hail, sleet, snow, dew or frost.

predator \'pred-ət-ər\ Any animal that catches and eats other animals.

prehensile \prē-'hen-səl\ Describing a body part, such as a hand, foot, tail or upper lip, that is used for grasping or holding.

premolars \prē-'mō-lərs\ In certain mammals, large teeth in front of the molars. Premolars are used to tear, grind and crush such foods as plants and rough grasses. In man, premolars are the bicuspid teeth.

pressure \'presh-ər\ Any force applied by something to something else. In a plant, pressure is the force put forth in pushing the water absorbed in the root hairs upward. Pressure is also the force that helps hold young stems and flowers up straight. Pressure supplies the energy used by buds and flowers to swell and unfold.

pretty-faced wallaby p. 469

prevailing \pri-'vā-ling\ winds In any certain place, the winds that blow from one direction more often than from other directions.

primate p. 363

prime meridian \\'prīm mə-'rid-ē-ən\\ An imaginary line that runs north and south on the earth's surface and that passes through the Royal Observatory at Greenwich, England. The prime meridian stands for 0 degrees longitude. It divides the regions of east and west longitude.

primitive \\'prim-ət-iv\\ Describing the earliest recognizable form of a tissue or organ of an animal or plant. Primitive also describes an organ or part that is just starting to develop. Primitive also describes animals or plants having little or no change through evolution, as species closely related in structure to their ancestors.

primordial \\prī-'mȯrd-ē-əl\\ Describing the earliest recognizable form of a tissue or organ of an animal or plant. Primordial also describes substances that existed at the beginning of the universe, such as gases and dust.

primrose p. 363

principle \\'prin-sə-pəl\\ A general truth that is based on observed facts.

proboscis monkey pp. 292, 293

profile \\'prō-,fīl\\ A vertical section that shows the layers that make up soil. A profile is also a drawing that shows an outline of an earth surface and the vertical arrangement of materials under the surface.

promethea moth pp. 298, 299

propagation \\,präp-ə-'gā-shən\\ An increase in the number of plants by natural or artificial separation of the growing parts from the parent plant. These parts root and develop as individual plants.

prophase \\'prō-,fāz\\ The stage in mitosis when distinct chromosomes appear, a spindle is formed and the nuclear membrane dissolves.

protective coloration \\prə-'tek-tiv ,kəl-ə-'rā-shən\\ Color patterns or markings on an organism that blend in with the color patterns of its environment. Protective coloration seems to hide and protect the organism from its enemies.

protein \\'prō-,tēn\\ Substances necessary to all living cells. They are made up of carbon, hydrogen, nitrogen, oxygen and other elements.

protoplasm \\'prōt-ə-,plaz-əm\\ The complex matter that makes up living things.

protoplast \\'prōt-ə-,plast\\ The protoplasm of a single plant cell.

protozoan p. 364

pruning \\'prün-ing\\ Cutting off dead or extra branches, twigs or roots.

Przhevalski's horse See pony: p. 358

ptarmigan p. 364

puddingstone See conglomerate: p. 101

puffball p. 365

puffer p. 365

puffin p. 365

pulmonary \\'pu̇l-mə-,ner-ē\\ Having to do with the lungs.

pulpwood \\'pəlp-,wu̇d\\ Wood, mostly from cone-bearing trees, from which pulp for paper making is made.

puma See cougar: p. 107

pumice p. 366

pumpkin p. 366

pumpkinseed See sunfish: p. 428

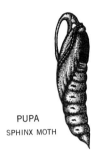

PUPA
SPHINX MOTH

pupa \\'pyü-pə\\ The form of an insect undergoing the third of four stages of metamorphosis. The pupa is often within a cocoon or other protective covering.

pupil In vertebrates and a few other animals, the rounded opening that is surrounded by the iris of the eye.

purple gallinule p. 171

purple grackle p. 191

purple martin p. 278

purple sea urchin p. 397

purple trillium pp. 450, 451

pussy willow p. 367

pygmy antelope See oribi: p. 322

pyrite p. 367

python pp. 410, 411

q

quahog See clam: p. 89

quail p. 368; see also bobwhite: p. 49

Quaker bonnet See lupine: p. 264

quaking aspen p. 368

quarry \\'kwȯr-ē\\ An open pit from which stone, such as granite, slate or limestone, is removed for commercial use.

quartz p. 368

quartzite p. 369

queen The reproductive female in a colony of social insects, such as bees, ants or termites.

queen angelfish pp. 13, 14

Queen Anne's lace See carrot: p. 69

queen conch pp. 99, 100

queen's crape myrtle p. 111

quicksand A mass of sand that contains enough water to be half liquid. It is usually deep and gummy.

quill \\'kwil\\ One of the large feathers in the wing or tail of a bird. A quill is also the hollow base of the shaft of a bird feather.

quince tree p. 369

r

rabbit p. 370

raccoon p. 370

race A group of similar organisms, not different enough from other organisms to be classified as a separate species.

radial \\'rād-ē-əl\\ Having to do with parts arranged like rays, such as the rays, or arms, of marine animals such as starfish. Radial also refers to the small flowers, arranged around a central point, that make up the flower heads of such plants as sunflowers, daisies and asters.

radial symmetry \\'rād-ē-əl 'sim-ə-trē\\ The form of an animal body in the general shape of a cylinder or bowl. Similar parts of such a body are arranged around a central axis, as in jellyfish and corals.

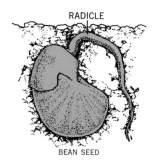

RADICLE

BEAN SEED

radicle \\'rad-i-kəl\\ The early root, or root and hypocotyl, of a seedling or plant embryo.

radio astronomy \\ə-'strän-ə-mē\\ The study of celestial bodies by the radio waves they give off. Radio astronomy is different from optical astronomy, in which light waves are studied.

radiolarian p. 371

radiolarian ooze See *radiolarian:* p. 371

radish p. 371

radius \\'rād-ē-əs\\ In man, 1 of the 2 bones in the arm, located on the same side as the thumb. In vertebrates higher than fishes, the radius is the similar part of the forelimb.

ragweed p. 371

rail p. 372

rainbow p. 372

rainbow shell See *abalone:* p. 1

rainbow trout p. 452

rain forest Any wooded area in which the yearly rainfall is at least 100 inches. Such an area has a large variety of tall trees. Little light passes through the trees to the forest floor. In tropical areas, a rain forest is called a jungle.

rain shadow p. 373

raspberry p. 373

rat pp. 374–375

rat flea p. 156

rattlesnake pp. 410, 411

rattlesnake fern pp. 148, 149

raven p. 376

ray Any of the whitish lines that appear to radiate from the craters of the moon. A ray is also any of the flower stalks of a cluster of flowers. A ray is also any one of the petals around the flower head of plants such as sunflowers, daisies and asters. A ray is also any of the bony parts that support the fins of a fish. A ray is also a radiating branch, as the arm of a starfish. A ray is also a kind of fish; see *ray:* p. 376.

razor fish p. 376

receptacle \\ri-'sep-ti-kəl\\ In a flower, the top of the stem, to which the parts of the flower are attached.

recessive trait \\ri-'ses-iv 'trāt\\ A hereditary characteristic that does not appear in descendants when it is combined with a dominant or stronger characteristic.

rectum \\'rek-təm\\ The end part of the food tube in an animal.

red abalone p. 1

red alder p. 5

red algae p. 6

red ash p. 21

red-backed woodland salamander p. 386

redbird See *cardinal:* p. 67

red-breasted nuthatch p. 315

red-breasted sapsucker p. 390

redbud tree p. 377

red cedar See *juniper:* p. 234

red clover p. 92

red corpuscle \\'kór-,pəs-əl\\ In vertebrates, a disk-shaped blood cell that is thinner in the center than around the edge. It contains hemoglobin that carries oxygen from the lungs or gills to the tissues.

red crossbill p. 115

red eft See *newt:* p. 312

red-eyed vireo p. 465

redfish See *rosefish:* p. 384

red gum See *sweet gum:* p. 431

red-headed woodpecker p. 485

red hibiscus p. 215

red mulberry p. 302

red mullet p. 303

red ocher See *hematite:* p. 212

red pepper p. 341

red raspberry p. 373

red-shafted flicker p. 157

red-shouldered hawk pp. 208, 209

red snapper p. 412

red-spotted newt p. 312

red-spotted purple butterfly pp. 60, 61

red-tailed hawk pp. 208, 209
redtop See *grass*: p. 195
red trillium pp. 450, 451
red-winged blackbird p. 42
redwood p. 377

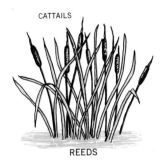

CATTAILS

REEDS

reed \\'rēd\\ Any of the various tall, hollow-stemmed grasses.

reef p. 378

regeneration \\ri-,jen-ə-'rā-shən\\ The natural replacement of body parts or of tissue that has been lost or destroyed by injury or normal wear. In certain simple animals, such as worms and sponges, regeneration of the entire body can occur. In man, only tissues such as hair, nails and skin are regenerated.

regurgitation \\rē-,gər-jə-'tā-shən\\ A process that is the opposite of swallowing. In ruminant mammals, food is regurgitated for further chewing.

reindeer See *caribou*: p. 68

reindeer moss See *lichen*: p. 254

relative humidity \\'rel-ət-iv hyü-'mid-ət-ē\\ The percentage of water vapor in the air compared to the largest amount of water vapor that the air could hold at that temperature.

relief \\ri-'lēf\\ The differences in the elevation or height above sea level of land surfaces. Relief is also the difference between the highest and lowest land surfaces in an area.

renal \\'rēn-əl\\ Having to do with kidneys or with their parts or functions.

reproduction \\,rē-prə-'dək-shən\\ The processes by which organisms produce offspring.

reptile p. 378

LONGLEAF PINE

RESIN

resin \\'rez-ᵊn\\ A secretion, such as pine resin,

from certain trees. Resin is used in making turpentine, glues and varnishes.

respiration \\,res-pə-'rā-shən\\ A process that occurs in all living cells. In respiration, energy is released from food by an oxidation reaction that is controlled by an enzyme. Respiration is also the process by which cells receive oxygen and give off carbon dioxide.

reticulated giraffe p. 181

retina \\'ret-ᵊn-ə\\ In vertebrates, an inner layer of tissue that lines the back part of the eyeball. The retina contains rods and cones.

reverse fault p. 147

revolution \\,rev-ə-'lü-shən\\ The act of a celestial body moving in its orbit. A revolution is also the time it takes a celestial body to make 1 orbit.

rex begonia p. 38

rhesus monkey pp. 292, 293

rhinoceros p. 378

rhizoid \\'rī-zȯid\\ One of the root-like growths on mosses, fern gametophytes, liverworts and fungi. A rhizoid absorbs food and it holds the plant to the material on which it grows.

rhizome \\'rī-,zōm\\ A horizontal stem with lumps, buds and branches. A rhizome often looks like a root and usually grows underground, as in grasses and lilies. A rhizome is sometimes called rootstock.

rhododendron p. 379

ribonucleic \\'rī-bō-n(y)ü-,klē-ik\\ acid (RNA) A complex chemical substance in all living cells. It is thought to serve as a pattern for the making of proteins and enzymes within the cell. Ribonucleic acid is also thought to make up the active part of a virus.

rice p. 379

rice rat pp. 374, 375

right whale p. 478, 479

rill p. 380

ringed plover pp. 354, 355

ring-necked pheasant p. 344

ringtail cat p. 380

ring-tailed lemur pp. 251, 252

rip current \\'kər-ənt\\ A strong current that flows out from the shore. A rip current returns the water brought to land by waves.

river p. 380

river ducks pp. 132, 133

river hog See *bushpig*: p. 58

river otter p. 325

roadrunner p. 381; see also *cuckoo*: p. 117

robin p. 381

roches moutonnées p. 382

rock p. 382

rock barnacle p. 30

rock crystal p. 382

rocket larkspur See *delphinium*: p. 123

rockfish p. 383; see also *grouper*: p. 199

rock lobster See *spiny lobster*: p. 417

rock pipit pp. 349, 350

rock ptarmigan p. 364

rockslide \\'räk-,slīd\\ A downward, usually fast movement of rock fragments over a sloped surface.

Rocky Mountain columbine p. 98

Rocky Mountain goat See *antelope:* p. 16

rodent \\'rōd-ənt\\ Any gnawing mammal, such as a squirrel, rat, mouse, gopher, porcupine or beaver.

rods \\'rädz\\ Rod-shaped nerve endings in the retina of the eye of vertebrates. Rods are sensitive to different amounts of light.

romaine lettuce p. 253

root A plant organ that usually grows in the ground. A root absorbs water and dissolved mineral salts from the soil. It also holds the plant in place. A root is also that part of an organ or structure that is buried in the tissue beneath it. A root is also that part of a nerve between the cells of its beginning or end and a ganglion.

rose p. 383

roseate spoonbill p. 418

rose beetle pp. 36, 37

rosefish p. 384

rose hip See *rose:* p. 383

rosemary p. 384

rose of Sharon See *hibiscus:* p. 214

rotation \\rō-'tā-shən\\ The turning of a celestial body on its axis.

rough-legged hawk pp. 208, 209

round-headed apple tree borer p. 50

roundworm See *worm:* p. 486

royal chinchilla p. 83

royal fern pp. 148, 149

rubellite See *tourmaline:* p. 448

ruby p. 384; see also *corundum:* p. 105

ruby spinel p. 417

ruby-throated hummingbird p. 222

ruffed grouse p. 200

rufous-sided towhee p. 448

rumen \\'rü-mən\\ The first, or largest, stomach of a ruminant mammal.

ruminant \\'rü-mə-nənt\\ A plant-eating mammal, such as cattle, deer, antelopes and camels, whose stomach has several compartments. A ruminant swallows its food whole. The food is then returned to the mouth for chewing while the animal rests. After the food is chewed and reswallowed, it is further digested as it passes through the other parts of the stomach.

rupture \\'rəp-chər\\ A break in rock, caused by folding or faulting.

runner A thin, horizontal plant stem, as in a strawberry plant, that takes root at its end and starts a new plant. A runner is sometimes called a stolon.

rush Long, thin, grass-like plants that are closely related to lilies. Rushes have leafless, unbranched, usually hollow stems. They bear tiny, greenish, lily-like flowers.

rust and smut p. 385

rusty blackbird p. 42

rutabaga See *turnip:* p. 455

rye p. 385

S

sable p. 386

sage p. 386

saguaro cactus p. 63

salamander p. 386

saline \\'sā-,lēn\\ Containing salt or salts.

saliva \\sə-'lī-və\\ A clear, somewhat sticky substance that is secreted by the salivary glands. Saliva moistens and softens food before the food is swallowed. In man, saliva contains mucus and enzymes.

salmon p. 387

salt See *halite:* p. 205

salt dome \\dōm\\ A round-topped deposit of rock salt that sometimes occurs between layers of sedimentary rocks.

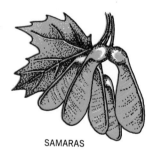

SAMARAS

samara \\'sam-ə-rə\\ The dry, winged fruit of the maple, ash or elm tree. A samara contains a single seed.

sand Mineral or rock particles 1/400 to 1/64 inch in size. Sand is often made up of quartz grains. Sand grains are particles of rock that has been broken down by the force of water or air. Sand is used in the manufacture of glass, mortar and concrete.

sandbar p. 387

sand dollar p. 387

sand dune p. 388

sandpiper p. 388

sandstone p. 388

sap Plant fluid made up mainly of mineral salts, gases and organic substances dissolved in water. Sap moves and is contained mainly in the phloem and xylem tissues.

sapphire p. 389; see also *corundum:* p. 105

saprophyte \\'sap-rə-,fīt\\ A plant that gets its food from dead organic matter. Typical saprophytes are mold that lives on bread, bacteria that sour milk or orchids that take their food from humus.

sapsucker p. 389

sapwood \\'sap-,wu̇d\\ The outer layer of wood that surrounds the heartwood of a stem. Sapwood is usually living. It is younger, lighter and softer than heartwood.

sarcastic blenny p. 45

sardine p. 390

Sargasso \\sär-'gas-ō\\ Sea A huge floating mass of seaweed in the North Atlantic Ocean. Small fish, mollusks, crabs, jellyfish, sea worms and various other many-colored deep-sea creatures live there.

sassafras p. 390

satellite \\'sat-əl-,īt\\ A celestial body, such as the earth's moon, that orbits around a larger body. A satellite is also any man-made object put into orbit around the earth, moon or other celestial body.

satinspar See *gypsum:* p. 202

saturated \\'sach-ə-,rāt-əd\\ Describing air that contains all the moisture it can hold at a given temperature.

saturation \\,sach-ə-'rā-shən\\ point The temperature at which dew is formed. The saturation point is also the largest number of organisms that can live and flourish in a given region.

Saturn pp. 390, 502

sawfish p. 391

saw-whet owl pp. 326, 327

scale Any of a certain kind of body cover. Scales are the flexible plates of fish, the sections of hardened skin on snakes, birds and some mammals, the broad hairs on butterfly wings. Scale is also the secretion that covers certain scale insects.

scale insect p. 391

scallop p. 392

scaly anteater See *pangolin:* p. 330

scarlet tanager p. 435

scaup See *duck:* pp. 132–133

scavenger \\'skav-ən-jər\\ An animal that feeds on dead animals, or that feeds on decaying plant materials.

schist p. 392

scoria p. 392

scorpion p. 393

scorpion fish p. 393; see also *lionfish:* p. 258

scoter See *duck:* pp. 132–133

screech owl p. 326

scup See *porgy:* p. 360

sea The great mass of salt water that covers a large part of the earth. A sea is also an ocean, such as the Pacific or Atlantic. A sea is also a body of salt water that is smaller than an ocean, such as the North Sea. A sea is also a large body of inland salt water.

sea anemone p. 393

sea blubber See *jellyfish:* p. 232

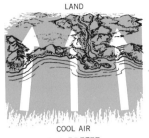

LAND
COOL AIR
SEA BREEZE

sea breeze A gentle-to-moderate wind that blows from water to land after the land has been heated by the sun. Rising air currents from the heated land lower the air pressure over the land so that wind blows toward the land.

sea cow See *manatee:* p. 272

sea crayfish See *spiny lobster:* p. 417

sea cucumber p. 394

sea ear See *abalone:* p. 1

sea fan p. 394

sea horse p. 395

seal p. 395

sea lamprey pp. 245, 246

sea level The average level of the ocean surface for all stages of the tide. The elevations of land masses are measured from sea level.

sea lion p. 395

seamount p. 396

sea otter p. 396

sea raven p. 397

seaside plantain p. 353

seasons The 4 periods of time in a year, spring, summer, autumn and winter. The seasons are caused by the position of the earth in its orbit around the sun, the rotation of the earth on its axis, and the tilting of the earth toward and away from the sun.

sea squab See *puffer:* p. 365

sea urchin p. 397

sebaceous glands \\si-'ba-shəs 'glandz\\ Sac-like glands that usually open into the small sacs around hair roots. Sebaceous glands secrete an oily fluid.

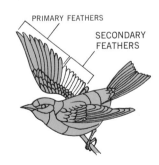

PRIMARY FEATHERS
SECONDARY FEATHERS

secondary \\'sek-ən-,der-ē\\ feathers The quill feathers that grow from the second, or inner, section of the wings in birds.

secretion \si-'krē-shən\ Any substance given off by certain cells in an animal or plant body.

sediment \'sed-ə-mənt\ Solid material such as rocks, gravel, sand and mud, carried along or deposited by water, wind or ice.

sedimentary \,sed-ə-'ment-ə-rē\ Having to do with rock formed from materials that are carried by wind or water, and often formed under water.

sedimentary rock p. 382

seed The ripened ovule of a flowering or cone-bearing plant. A seed is made up of the embryo, 1 or more seed coats and stored food.

seedling \'sēd-ling\ A small plant grown from seed. A seedling is also any young tree less than 3 feet tall.

seed plant Any plant that has flowers or cones, true roots, stems and leaves. Seed plants are also called spermatophytes.

segment \'seg-mənt\ A natural division in the body of an organism, such as 1 of the divisions in an earthworm or in the jointed parts of an arthropod.

seismology \sīz-'mäl-ə-jē\ The science that deals with the interior of the earth by measuring the speed with which earthquakes or artificial vibrations travel through it.

selenite p. 398; see also *gypsum:* p. 202

self-heal See *heal-all:* p. 210

self-pollination \'self-,päl-ə-'nā-shən\ The transfer of pollen from the stamen of a flower to its stigma, or to the stigma of another flower on the same plant.

semipalmated plover pp. 354, 355

sensation \sen-'sā-shən\ The emotion experienced when a sense organ, such as an eye, ear or skin, is acted upon by some kind of stimulus.

sense organ An organ sensitive to a certain kind of stimulation, as the ear to sound waves.

sensory \'sens-(ə-)rē\ **nerves** Nerves that carry impulses from various parts of the vertebrate body to the spinal cord and to the brain.

SEPALS

sepal \'sēp-əl\ One of the outermost leaf-like parts of a flower. Sepals are usually green.

sepia See *cuttlefish:* p. 119

sequoia p. 398

serpentine p. 398

serpent star p. 399

serum \'sir-əm\ Usually, the clear fluid that remains when blood clots.

17-year locust See *cicada:* p. 86

sex-linked character \'sek-,sling(k)t 'kar-ik-tər\ A hereditary characteristic that only appears when X chromosomes are present in cells.

sexual reproduction \'seksh-(ə-)wəl ,rē-prə-'dək-shən\ The production of a new individual through the union of sperm with an egg.

shale p. 399

shark pp. 400–401

sharp-shinned hawk pp. 208, 209

sheath \'shēth\ A plant part that covers another part.

sheep p. 402

sheet lava p. 249

shell p. 402

Shetland pony p. 358

shield \'shēld\ **volcano** A gently sloping volcanic cone formed by the overlapping of lava.

shiner p. 402

shooting star See *meteor:* p. 284

short-eared owl p. 326, 327

short-horned grasshopper p. 196

short waves p. 476

shoveler See *duck:* pp. 132–133

showy lady's slipper p. 244

shrew p. 403

shrike p. 403

shrimp p. 404

shrub \'shrəb\ A plant that has a woody stem that does not die to the ground in winter. A shrub differs from a tree in having several stems from the same root, or a single crooked stem.

Siamese fighting fish See *betta:* p. 39

sidereal \sī-'dir-ē-əl\ Having to do with the stars.

sidewinder pp. 410, 411

silica \'sil-i-kə\ The compound silicon dioxide. Opal, quartz and sand are impure forms of silica.

silk tree See *mimosa tree:* p. 286

silt \'silt\ Particles of earth materials that are smaller than sand grains and larger than clay particles.

Silurian Period \sī-'lur-ē-ən 'pir-ē-əd\ See Geologic Time Chart, p. 493.

silverfish p. 404

silver hake p. 204

sinkhole \'singk-,hōl\ A hole or depression in the ground that was made by the water that dissolved such rocks as limestone and gypsum.

siphon \'sī-fən\ A tube-like organ on bivalve mollusks. The siphon takes water to the gills or discharges water from the gill chamber.

siren p. 404

skate p. 405

skeletal muscle \'skel-ət-ᵊl 'məs-əl\ A voluntary muscle, connected to the bones, that moves some part of the vertebrate body.

skeleton \\'skel-ət-ᵊn\\ The rigid framework of an animal's body. A skeleton is usually jointed to allow movement.

skin In humans, the 2 main layers of the outer covering of the body. The outside layer is called the epidermis. Beneath this is the dermis.

skink p. 405

skipjack See *tuna:* p. 454

skull The part of the skeleton that makes up the bony part of the head of vertebrate animals.

skunk p. 406

skunk cabbage p. 406

slate p. 407

sleet \\'slēt\\ Rain that has been frozen or partly frozen into particles of ice.

slender dwarf siren p. 405

slender loris p. 262

slime mold p. 407

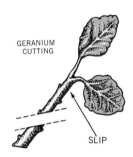

GERANIUM CUTTING

SLIP

slip A branch, twig or leaf cut from the parent plant and placed in soil, sand or water to grow. A slip is often called a cutting.

sloth p. 407

slow lemur See *loris:* p. 262

slug See *snail:* p. 409

small intestine \\in-'tes-tən\\ The coiled, tube-like part of the digestive tract in the abdomen. The small intestine connects the stomach to the large intestine.

smallmouth black bass p. 408

smalltooth sawfish p. 391

smelt p. 408

smog A combination of smoke and fog.

smooth dogfish p. 409

smooth hammerhead shark pp. 400, 401

smooth muscles \\'məs-əlz\\ Involuntary muscles. Smooth muscles have unmarked cells and occur in such places as the walls of a digestive organ.

smooth sumac p. 427

smut See *rust and smut:* p. 385

snail p. 409; see also *gastropod:* p. 174

snake pp. 410–411

snapdragon p. 412

snapper p. 412

snapping turtle pp. 456, 457

snipe p. 412

snow p. 413

snowball See *puffer* p. 365

snowy owl pp. 326, 327

soapstone See *talc:* p. 434

social \\'sō-shəl\\ **animal** An animal, such as an ant, that lives with a group of animals of the same species for most or all of its life cycle. A social animal performs a role that is a part of the total activities carried out by the group.

socket \\'säk-ət\\ In an animal body, a hollow or cavity such as the eye socket, which contains another part of the body.

soft coal Bituminous coal.

soil p. 413

solar eclipse p. 137

solar energy \\'sō-lər 'en-ər-jē\\ The radiant energy of the sun.

solar flare p. 413

solar system \\'sō-lər 'sis-təm\\ The sun, the 9 planets and their satellites, the asteroids and the meteors and comets.

sole p. 414

solstice \\'säl-stəs\\ Either of 2 times a year when the sun appears to reach its greatest distance from the celestial equator. In the northern hemisphere, these times are the first day of summer and the first day of winter.

solution \\sə-'lü-shən\\ A mixture of liquids, of solids or of gases.

sorghum p. 414

sound A narrow strip or passage of water that connects 2 large bodies of water. A sound is also a strip of water between an island and the mainland.

soupfin shark pp. 400, 401

sour cherry tree p. 79

sour gum See *black gum:* p. 43

South African bushpig p. 58

South African hartebeest pp. 206, 207

South American lungfish pp. 263, 264

southern lights See *aurora:* p. 24

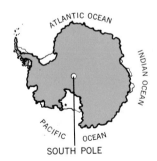

ATLANTIC OCEAN

INDIAN OCEAN

PACIFIC OCEAN

SOUTH POLE

South Pole The most southern point on the earth's surface. It is 1 of 2 points through which pass the imaginary line that forms the earth's axis. The South Pole is also called the geographical south pole to distinguish it from the south magnetic pole.

sowbug and pillbug p. 414

spadefoot toad pp. 444, 445

Spanish bayonet See *yucca:* p. 490

sparrow p. 415

sparrow hawk pp. 208, 209

spawn \\'spȯn\\ A mass of eggs deposited by egg-laying water animals.

spearmint p. 415

specialization \\,spesh-(ə-)lə-'zā-shən\\ The adaptation of a part of an organism to a certain function.

species \\'spē-shēz\\ A group of plants or animals so alike in structure and hereditary traits that their various forms will reproduce for several generations. Species is the classification unit below genus.

spectral tarsier p. 437

sperm \\'spərm\\ The male reproductive cell. In sexual reproduction, the sperm joins with an egg to form a developing individual.

spermatophytes \\spər-'mat-ə-,fīts\\ Plants that produce pollen tubes and seeds and that have true roots, stems and leaves. Spermatophytes are sometimes called seed plants.

sperm whale p. 478, 479

spice tree See *California laurel:* p. 64

spicule \\'spik-yül\\ One of the needle-like forms of calcium carbonate or silicon that make up the skeleton of some sponges.

spider p. 416

spider monkey pp. 292, 293

spiderwort p. 416

spike In plants, a long but narrow flower cluster, pointed at the tip.

spinach p. 416

spinal \\'spīn-əl\\ column In vertebrates, the part of the skeleton that is flexible. The spinal column is made up of vertebrae that are connected by fiber disks and ligaments.

spinal \\'spīn-əl\\ cord In vertebrates, a thick, rope-like structure inside the spinal column. The spinal cord is the main conductor of nerve impulses to and from the brain. It is also a center for many independent reflex actions.

spine \\'spīn\\ The spinal column of vertebrates. A spine is also a sharp pointed part on a plant, such as the thorn on a rose stem.

spinel p. 417

spinneret \\,spin-ə-'ret\\ In spiders and many caterpillars, a tube-like organ that discharges silk.

spiny anteater See *echidna:* p. 136.

spiny lobster p. 417

spiracle \\'spī-ri-kəl\\ An outside opening, or pore, of the breathing system of an insect.

spiral galaxy p. 170

spirillum See *bacteria:* p. 25

Spirogyra See *algae:* pp. 6–7

spittlebug p. 417

spleen \\'splēn\\ In most vertebrates, a large glandular organ that is a part of the lymphatic system.

sponge p. 418

spoonbill p. 418

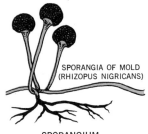

SPORANGIA OF MOLD (RHIZOPUS NIGRICANS)

SPORANGIUM

sporangium \\spə-'ran-jē-əm\\ A walled chamber or case in which asexual spores are formed in algae, fungi, mosses, ferns and certain protozoa.

spore \\'spōr\\ A reproductive body that develops into a separate organism without being fertilized. In plants, a spore is usually produced by a division of the nucleus of germ cells. In protozoa and bacteria, a spore may be formed by division, by enclosure of the protoplasm in a tough covering or it may be formed by both division and enclosure.

sporophyte \\'spōr-ə-,fīt\\ A spermatophyte, moss or fern that has developed from a fertilized egg. In a sporophyte, spores are produced.

sporozoan p. 419

spotted hyena p. 419

spotted moray pp. 295, 296

spotted sandpiper p. 388

spotted turtle pp. 456, 457

spring A season during which leaf and flower buds open, fertilization takes place and new wood grows under the bark of trees. A spring is also a deposit of water underground in porous rock or soil. The water flows from the ground through a natural opening.

spring cankerworm p. 66

spring crocus p. 114

spring peeper See *frog:* pp. 166–167

spring tide \\'tīd\\ The tide that rises highest above and falls lowest below average sea level. Spring tide occurs twice a month, near the times of new and full moon.

spruce p. 419

squall \\'skwȯl\\ line A long line of cumulus and cumulonimbus clouds that forms in front of a fast-moving cold front. A squall line is often the source of violent thunderstorms and sometimes of tornadoes.

squash p. 420

squash bug pp. 54, 55

squid p. 420

squirrel p. 421

squirrel corn See *bleeding heart:* p. 44

staghorn sumac p. 427

stalactite \\stə-'lak-,tīt\\ An icicle-shaped deposit of calcium carbonate crystals that hangs from the roof of a cave or cavern. A stalactite forms when water containing minerals seeps through a cave roof. The water evaporates and the minerals build up a deposit.

stalagmite \stə-'lag-ˌmīt\ A deposit of calcium carbonate crystals that sticks up from the floor of a cave or cavern. A stalagmite forms when water containing minerals seeps through a cave roof. The water evaporates and the minerals build up a deposit.

stamen \'stā-mən\ A flower organ made up of a stalk, or filament, and an anther in which pollen develops.

staminate \'stā-mə-nət\ **flower** A flower that bears stamens but no pistils.

star pp. 421, 502

starch \'stärch\ Any of a group of carbohydrate compounds found mainly in seeds, tubers and other plant parts.

star cluster p. 422

starfish p. 422

starling p. 422

star-of-Bethlehem p. 423

star sapphire p. 389

stationary \'stā-shə-ˌner-ē\ **front** The boundary between 2 masses of air that stay in 1 place for a period of time.

steady-state universe \'sted-ē 'stāt 'yü-nə-ˌvərs\ A theory stating that in the universe, the processes that change matter into energy in stars are balanced by the processes that change energy into matter in other areas of space.

stegosaur p. 423

stem A plant part that supports the plant and that contains sap-carrying tubes.

sterile \'ster-əl\ Describing any object made free of microorganisms by heat or antiseptic methods. Sterile also describes any plant or animal that is unable to reproduce.

stickleback p. 424

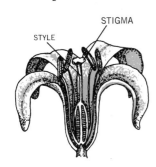

STIGMA
STYLE

stigma \'stig-mə\ In a flower, the surface at the tip of the style of the pistil. A stigma is usually covered with a sticky fluid or hairs. The stigma receives pollen from the stamen.

stilt p. 424

stimulus \'stim-yə-ləs\ Any condition or influence, either outside or inside an organism, that brings about a reaction.

stingaree See *ray:* p. 376

stinging nettle p. 311

stingray See *ray:* p. 376

stinkbug pp. 54, 55

STOLON

STRAWBERRY PLANT

stolon \'stō-lən\ A branch of a plant stem that runs horizontally at or below ground level. A stolon is also called a runner.

stomach \'stəm-ək\ The pouch-like digestive organ in man and in many other animals.

stomata \stō-'mat-ə\ The pores in leaves through which carbon dioxide is absorbed and mixed with water.

storm petrel p. 343

strait \'strāt\ A narrow stretch of sea or a waterway that connects 2 larger bodies of water.

stratified \'strat-ə-ˌfīd\ Describing horizontal layers or beds of rocks, soils or clouds.

stratified rock p. 424

stratocumulus clouds pp. 90, 91

stratosphere \'strat-ə-ˌsfir\ A layer of the earth's atmosphere. Its height averages from 6 to 50 miles above the surface. The heights are less at the poles and greater at the equator.

stratum \'strāt-əm\ A bed or layer of sedimentary rock. The rock layers above and below a stratum are usually different in thickness and makeup.

strawberry p. 425

stream See *river:* p. 380

striated muscles \'strī-ˌāt-əd 'məs-əlz\ Muscles with fibers divided or marked by tiny, crosswise bands.

string bean p. 33

striped blenny p. 45

striped blister beetle pp. 36, 37

striped mullet p. 303

striped skunk p. 406

striped tuna p. 454

sturgeon p. 425

style \'stīl\ The usually slender part of the pistil of most flowers. The style grows from the top of the ovary.

submarine canyon \'səb-mə-ˌrēn 'kan-yən\ A steep-sided and deep valley on the ocean floor.

subsoil See *soil:* p. 413

substratum \'səb-ˌstrāt-əm\ A bed or layer of earth or rock that is directly under another layer.

subterranean \ˌsəb-tə-'rā-nē-ən\ Describing something beneath the surface of the earth.

succession \sək-'sesh-ən\ Any process of change in a biological community.

sucking louse p. 263

sucking mouth parts The tube- and siphon-like beaks of some insects, such as leafhoppers, moths and aphids. Such insects suck juices from the leaves and stems of plants or nectar from flowers.

sugar beet p. 35

sugarcane p. 426

sugar maple p. 274

sulfur p. 426

sumac p. 426

summer squash p. 420

summer tanager p. 435

sun pp. 427, 502

sundew p. 427

sun drop See *evening primrose:* p. 145

sunfish p. 428

sunflower p. 428

sun jellyfish p. 232

sunspot p. 429

superior \sü-'pir-ē-ər\ Describing a structure or organ of the body that is located above some other part. Superior also describes the orbits of the planets or the planets further away from the sun than the earth.

supernova p. 429

surf scoter See *duck:* p. 132

Surinam toad pp. 444, 445

survival of the fittest \sər-'vī-vəl əv thə 'fit-əst\ A part of Charles Darwin's theory of evolution. Only the better-adapted individuals of one generation live long enough to become the parents of the next generation.

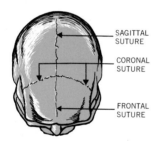

SUTURE

suture \'sü-chər\ The line in the fruit or seed of a legume along which it bursts open to discharge seeds. A suture is also the line of joining of 2 bones, as that of a skull.

swallow p. 429

swallowtail butterfly p. 60

swallow-tailed kite p. 240

swamp An area of land that is saturated with water, usually because of poor natural drainage. A swamp is sometimes called a bog.

swamp cabbage See *skunk cabbage:* p. 406

swan p. 430

sweat glands \'glandz\ The tube-shaped organs in the skin that empty their secretions onto the surface of the body. In man, sweat glands help cool the body by secreting a watery fluid that evaporates from the surface of the skin.

sweet basil p. 430

sweet bay See *laurel:* p. 248

sweet cherry tree p. 79

sweet gum p. 431

sweet potato p. 431

sweet sorghum p. 414

swift p. 432

swim bladder \'blad-ər\ In most fish, a long sac that is filled with air. The swim bladder allows the fish to remain at a particular depth. A swim bladder is also called an air bladder.

swine p. 432

Swiss chard See *beet:* p. 35

swordfish p. 432

swordtail platy p. 354

sycamore p. 433

symbiosis \sim-bē-'ō-səs\ The partnership between 2 different organisms where both organisms benefit, as between lichens and algae or between legumes and certain bacteria.

sympathetic nervous system \sim-pə-'thet-ik 'nər-vəs 'sis-təm\ In vertebrates, a division of the automatic nervous system. The sympathetic nervous system opposes and balances the involuntary actions of such organs as the heart, salivary glands, small intestine, stomach and eyes.

syncline p. 433; see also *anticline:* p. 17

synodic \sə-'näd-ik\ **month** The time between 2 new moons, an average of 29 days, 12 hours, 44 minutes and 2.8 seconds. A synodic month is also called a lunar month.

Syrian hyrax p. 223

system \'sis-təm\ A group of organs that have a related purpose, as in the circulatory system.

t

tactile \'tak-təl\ Having to do with the sense of touch or the organs of touch.

tadpole The larva of a toad or frog. See *frog:* p. 166. A tadpole has external gills that later become internal, a large, vertically flattened tail and no mouth. A tadpole undergoes many body changes. The tail is absorbed into the body, a mouth with horny jaws develops, and lungs and legs are gradually grown.

talc p. 434

talon \'tal-ən\ The sharp, strong claw of a flesh-eating bird, such as a hawk.

talus p. 434; see also *detritus:* p. 124

tanager p. 434

tangerine See *citrus tree:* p. 88

tapeworm p. 435; see also *flatworm:* p. 155
tapir p. 435

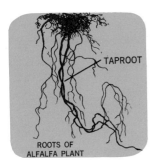

taproot \\'tap-,rüt\\ The main root of a plant. A taproot develops from the primary root and grows downward.
tarantula p. 436
tarn p. 436
tarsier p. 437
taste buds In man and other vertebrates, the receptors for the sense of taste. The taste buds are usually located in bundles on the upper surface and sides of the tongue. They seem to respond only to substances, in solutions, that are sour, sweet, bitter or salty.
taxonomy \\tak-'sän-ə-mē\\ The science of plant and animal classification.
tea p. 437
teak p. 438
teal See *duck:* pp. 132–133
tear gland \\'gland\\ In higher vertebrates, a gland behind the upper eyelid at the outer corner of the eye. A tear gland produces a watery liquid that washes the surface of the eye.
tea rose p. 383
teasel p. 438
telophase \\'tel-ə-,fāz\\ The final stage of mitotic cell division. During telophase, the cytoplasm divides and nuclei form in the two cells that result.
temperate zone Either of 2 areas of the earth in the middle latitudes, north and south. The north temperate zone is the area between the Tropic of Cancer and the Arctic Circle. The south temperate zone is the area between the Tropic of Capricorn and the Antarctic Circle.
tendon \\'ten-dən\\ In vertebrates, a cord of strong, flexible, connective tissue in which the fibers of a muscle end. A tendon connects the muscle to a bone or other structure.
tendril \\'ten-drəl\\ Usually, a modified stem, as in grapes or gourds, that wraps itself around an available support. A tendril may be a modified leaf, as in sweet peas or vetches.
tent caterpillar p. 438
terminal moraine See *end moraine:* p. 141; and *moraine:* p. 295
termite p. 439

tern p. 439
tetra p. 440
Texas bluebonnet See *lupine:* p. 264
theory \\'thē-ə-rē\\ An explanation of relationships among observed scientific facts, events or phenomena.
third quarter moon See *moon:* p. 294
thistle p. 440
thorax \\'thōr-,aks\\ In vertebrates, the part of the body between the head and abdomen. In insects, the thorax is the body part that usually has three pairs of legs and often two pairs of wings.
thousand-legged worm See *millipede:* p. 286
thrasher p. 441
3-spined stickleback p. 424
3-toed echidna p. 137
thresher shark pp. 400, 401
thrush p. 441
thrust fault p. 147
thunder The sound that results when lightning heats the air along its path. The air expands suddenly and produces a sound wave.
thunder lizard See *brontosaur:* p. 52
thyme p. 441

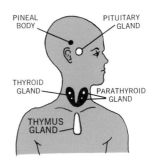

thymus gland \\'thī-məs 'gland\\ In most vertebrate young, a ductless, gland-like body in the chest cavity near the base of the neck. Its function is not understood.
thyroid gland \\'thīr-,oid 'gland\\ In many vertebrates, an endocrine gland in the neck. The thyroid gland is made up of 2 connected lobes, 1 on each side of the trachea. This gland controls and regulates much of the metabolism of the body.
tick p. 442
tidal theory \\'tīd-əl 'thē-ə-rē\\ A theory of the origin of the solar system. The theory states that as a star approached the sun, a tidal wave of gaseous material occurred on the sun's surface. Part of this material was pulled away from the sun and later condensed to form the planets and their natural satellites.
tidal \\'tīd-əl\\ wave The rise and fall of the ocean surface due to the gravitational pull of the sun and moon.
tide \\'tīd\\ The rise and fall of the surface of the sea. Tides occur twice every 24 hours and 52

minutes. They are caused by the gravitational pull of the sun and the moon.

tiger p. 442

tiger cat See *ocelot:* p. 317

tigerfish See *lionfish:* p. 258

tiger shark pp. 400, 401

tiger swallowtail butterfly pp. 60, 61

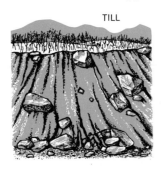

TILL

till A glacial deposit that contains rocks and earth materials. Till is sometimes called boulder clay.

timberline p. 443

timber wolf p. 483

time zones The 24 imaginary divisions on the earth, each about 15 degrees wide and centered on a meridian. Each division has a standard time that is based on the solar time of its meridian.

timothy grass pp. 194, 195

tissue \'tish-ü\ A group of cells that are alike and that perform special as well as similar functions.

titmouse p. 443

toad pp. 444–445

tobacco p. 446

tokay p. 446

tomato p. 447

tonsils \'tän-səlz\ In man, the 2 small masses of tissue at the sides of the throat. Tonsils are believed to produce white corpuscles that destroy bacteria in the mouth and pharynx.

tooth shell p. 402

topaz p. 447

topography \tə-'päg-rə-fē\ The study and description of the physical features of the earth's surface. Topography is also the physical features themselves, such as rivers and mountains.

topsoil See *soil:* p. 413

tornado \tȯr-'nād-ō\ A small but violent storm that has a funnel-shaped cloud in which the wind may whirl at speeds up to several hundred miles per hour. Tornadoes occur over land under certain combinations of low atmospheric pressure, high temperature and high humidity.

torrid \'tȯr-əd\ **zone** The area around the equator and bounded by the Tropics of Cancer and Capricorn. The torrid zone is the largest of the earth's climatic zones.

tortoise \'tȯrt-əs\ The name given to some turtles that live on dry land.

touch-me-not See *balsam:* p. 27

tourmaline p. 448

towhee p. 448

toxin \'täk-sən\ Any poison produced and secreted by an animal or plant. When a toxin is secreted by a parasite and causes disease, the host may produce antibodies, called antitoxins, to counteract the toxin.

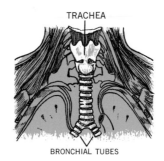

TRACHEA

BRONCHIAL TUBES

trachea \'trā-kē-ə\ In vertebrates, a tube or passage that begins at the larynx and goes to the bronchi. The trachea is the air passage to and from the lungs. The trachea is sometimes called the windpipe.

trade winds Frequent winds from a given direction in the regions of latitudes 30 to 35 degrees north and south of the equator. Trade winds blow toward the low-pressure region of the equator.

trailing arbutus See *mayflower:* p. 279

trait \'trāt\ Usually, a physical characteristic that is inherited.

translucent \trans-'lüs-ᵊnt\ Describing a substance that lets light rays pass partly through it, but that spreads the rays out. Things seen through a translucent substance are not clear.

transparent \trans-'par-ənt\ Describing a substance that lets light rays pass through it. Things can be seen clearly through a transparent substance.

transpiration \,trans-pə-'rā-shən\ The loss of water by evaporation from leaves and other plant parts exposed to the air.

transverse \'trans-,vərs\ Describing a part or structure at right angles to the long or main part of the body or an organ.

trap See *basalt:* p. 30

traprock See *basalt:* p. 30

travertine p. 448

tree frog pp. 166, 167

tree iguana p. 225

tremor \'trem-ər\ A small earthquake.

trench p. 449

triceratops p. 449

trichina p. 450

trillium p. 450

trilobite p. 451

tropical fish p. 451

tropical \'träp-i-kəl\ year The time needed for 1 revolution of the earth around the sun from the time of year when the sun appears directly overhead at noon to an observer on the equator. The length of a tropical year is 365 days, 5 hours, 48 minutes and 46 seconds.

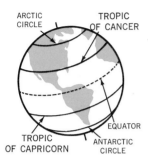

Tropic of Cancer \'träp-ik ev 'kan-sər\ An imaginary line parallel to the earth's equator at a latitude of 23½ degrees north. To an observer on the Tropic of Cancer, the sun would seem to pass directly overhead on June 22, the summer solstice.

Tropic of Capricorn \'träp-ik ev 'kap-ri-kȯrn\ An imaginary line parallel to the earth's equator at a latitude of 23½ degrees south. To an observer on the Tropic of Capricorn, the sun would seem to pass directly overhead on December 22, the winter solstice.

tropics \'träp-iks\ The area of the earth's surface between the Tropics of Cancer and Capricorn. The tropics include all points over which the sun is directly overhead at some time during the year. The tropics is also called the torrid zone.

tropism \'trō-,piz-əm\ The movement of an organism or of part of an organism toward or away from outside stimuli such as light, water, gravity or heat.

tropopause \'trō-pə-,pȯz\ The layer of the atmosphere between the troposphere and the bottom of the stratosphere. The tropopause averages about 7 miles up. Its altitude changes with latitude and season.

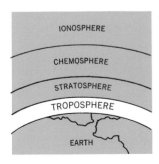

troposphere \'trō-pə-,sfir\ The lower layer of the earth's atmosphere. The troposphere varies in thickness from 30,000 to 60,000 feet.

trough p. 451

trout p. 452

true forget-me-not p. 163

true salmon p. 387

trypanosome p. 452

tsunami p. 453

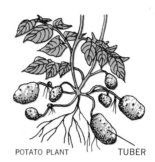

POTATO PLANT   TUBER

tuber \'tü-bər\ A short, fleshy, underground stem, as a potato. A tuber functions in food storage and asexual reproduction.

tufa See *limestone:* p. 256

tufted titmouse p. 443

tulip tree p. 453

tuna p. 454

tundra \'tən-drə\ Any swampy plain at high altitudes in the Arctic and sub-Arctic areas of North America, Europe and Asia. A tundra has a large area of black muck or swampland soil covering permanently frozen subsoil.

tupelo See *black gum:* p. 43

turbid \'tər-bəd\ Describing water or some other liquid that is cloudy or not clear.

turbulence \'tər-byə-lən(t)s\ A condition of irregular air or water movements. Turbulence is caused by unequal up and down movement of currents, by air or water flowing over an uneven surface or by winds or currents of different directions or speeds flowing past one another.

turkey p. 454

turkeyfish See *lionfish:* p. 258

turkey vulture p. 467

turnip p. 455

turquoise p. 455

turtle pp. 456–457

twins Two individuals born at a single birth. Identical twins result from 1 complete division of a fertilized egg. Fraternal twins result from 2 fertilized eggs.

2-toed sloth p. 408

tympanum \'tim-pə-nəm\ The thin, vibrating tissue of a hearing organ. A tympanum is sometimes called an eardrum.

typhoon \tī-'fün\ A severe windstorm, hurricane or tropical cyclone that usually originates in the Far East region of the Pacific Ocean.

tyrannosaur p. 458

u

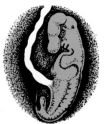

UMBILICAL CORD

DEVELOPING PIG EMBRYO

umbilical \ˌəm-'bil-i-kəl\ **cord** In mammals, a tube that connects the unborn young to the placenta. An umbilical cord contains blood vessels.

umbra \'əm-brə\ The dark, central part of the shadow of a planet or a satellite. No sunlight reaches the umbra. An umbra is also the central, darker region of a sunspot.

umbrella magnolia p. 267

underwing moth pp. 298, 299

ungulate \'əng-gyə-lət\ Having hoofs or shaped like a hoof.

unicellular \ˌyü-ni-'sel-yə-lər\ Describing an organism made up of 1 cell.

UNIVALVE

SNAIL

univalve \'yü-ni-ˌvalv\ Describing an organism with a 1-piece shell, as a snail.

universe \'yü-nə-ˌvərs\ The entire celestial arrangement that has been seen or about which theories have been stated. All matter exists in the universe and all events occur in it.

unsaturated \ˌən-'sach-ə-ˌrāt-əd\ Describing air that contains less water vapor than it can normally hold at a given temperature.

unstratified \ən-'strat-ə-ˌfīd\ Describing rock structures or deposits of loose material that are not formed in beds or layers.

upland cotton p. 106

upland plover p. 458

Uranus pp. 459, 502

urea \yu-'rē-ə\ In mammals and some lower animals, the main nitrogen-containing compound in urine. Urea is the final waste product from the decomposition of protein compounds in the body. Urea is believed to form in the liver from amino acids and the ammonia compounds.

ureter \yu-'rēt-ər\ In mammals, a tube that carries urine from the kidney to the urinary bladder. In other vertebrate animals, the ureter is a tube from the kidney to the outside of the body.

urethra \yu-'rē-thrə\ In mammals, the canal that leads from the urinary bladder to the outside of the body.

urinary bladder \'yur-ə-ˌner-ē 'blad-ər\ A sac made up of membranes that is located in the front part of the pelvic cavity in mammals. The urinary bladder is a temporary storage place for urine.

urine \'yur-ən\ In vertebrates, the waste material given off by the kidneys. Urine is mostly a water solution of urea.

U-shaped valley p. 459

uterus \'yüt-ə-rəs\ In female mammals, the thick-walled, hollow, muscular organ in which the young develop before birth. The uterus contracts during birth and pushes the young through the birth passage.

v

vaccine \vak-'sēn\ A suspension of killed or weakened microorganisms, or of the poisons they produce or of both. Vaccine is injected to prevent or treat an infectious disease.

vacuole \'vak-yə-ˌwōl\ A usually spherical opening in the cytoplasm of plant and animal cells. A vacuole is surrounded by a membrane and is filled with liquid or solid matter, or with both. Vacuoles function in digestion, getting rid of wastes, and storing food.

valley p. 459

valley glacier p. 182

valve \'valv\ A gate-like structure, such as a fold of membrane tissue, in an organ or vessel. A valve prevents the fluid that leaves the organ or passage from flowing back.

Van Allen belts p. 460

vanilla p. 460

variation \ˌver-ē-'ā-shən\ The difference in a certain characteristic among the offspring of a certain species, or between offspring and their parents. Variation is also the angle between magnetic north and true north.

variety \və-'rī-ət-ē\ A kind, much like others of the same kind, but different in color or in some other way. Ruby and sapphire are varieties of the mineral corundum. In plants and animals, a variety is a classification smaller than species. Varieties are often developed by breeders to meet special needs.

vascular system \\'vas-kyə-lər 'sis-təm\\ Any arrangement of vessels that allows flow or circulation of liquids, as xylem and phloem tissues in ferns and seed plants, and blood vessels and lymph vessels in vertebrate animals.

vein \\'vān\\ In vertebrates, any of the blood vessels that return blood from the lungs or body tissues to the heart. A vein is also a bundle of xylem and phloem tissues in a leaf. A vein is also a mineral deposit in a rock or rock formation; see *vein:* p. 461.

velvet ant p. 461

venation \\vā-'nā-shən\\ The arrangement of veins in a leaf. The veins may be side by side from the base to the tip, as in grass. They may be in a network pattern, as in the blade of a maple leaf. Venation is also the pattern of veins in an insect's wings.

ventifact p. 461

ventral \\'ven-trəl\\ Describing the underside or lower surface of an organism or structure.

ventricle \\'ven-tri-kəl\\ Either of the 2 lower chambers of the heart.

Venus pp. 462, 502

Venus's-flytrap p. 462

verbena p. 463

vermiculite p. 463

vertebra \\'vərt-ə-brə\\ Any of the bones that make up the spinal column of vertebrate animals. Vertebrae are usually separated by elastic disks of cartilage. Each vertebra contains an opening through which the spinal cord passes.

vertebrate \\'vərt-ə-brət\\ Any organism, such as a fish, amphibian, reptile, bird or mammal, that has a spinal column made up of vertebrae.

vestigial \\ve-'stij-(ē-)əl\\ Referring to an organ or part of an organism that serves no useful purpose. A vestigial organ or part represents an earlier stage of the part or a needed organ in a related organism.

viable \\'vī-ə-bəl\\ Describing an organism that is alive and able to continue to live in a normal way.

vicuna p. 464

VILLI

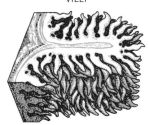

WALL OF SMALL INTESTINE

villi \\'vi-ˌlī\\ Small, finger-like projections on the

inside lining of the small intestine. Villi are absorption surfaces for digested food in the small intestine.

violet p. 464

violet-tip butterfly pp. 60, 61

vireo p. 465

Virginia bluebell p. 465

Virginia deer p. 123

virulent \\'vir-(y)ə-lənt\\ Describing microorganisms that are strong causes of disease. Such organisms are usually bacteria or viruses that quickly break down the natural defenses of a host organism.

virus \\'vī-rəs\\ A tiny organism that is like a parasite because it is active in living cells and able to produce only within living cells. Viruses are smaller and simpler than 1-celled algae, protozoa and bacteria. Viruses usually can cause disease.

viscera \\'vis-(ə-)rə\\ All the organs contained in the chest and abdomen of a body.

vitamin \\'vīt-ə-mən\\ Any of certain substances in foods required for good health.

vitreous \\'vi-trē-əs\\ Describing minerals that have a glassy luster, such as quartz and calcite.

vitreous humor \\'vi-trē-əs 'hyü-mər\\ A clear, jelly-like substance that fills the cavity in the eyeball between the lens and the retina.

viviparous \\vī-'vip-(ə-)rəs\\ Describing the reproduction pattern in which the young are born alive instead of hatching from incubated eggs.

vocal \\'vō-kəl\\ **cords** Either of 2 pairs of folds in the larynx. Vocal cords are made up of white bands of fiber. The lower pair produces sounds when the fibers are vibrated by air passing between the folds.

volcanic cone p. 465

volcanic neck p. 466

volcano p. 466

vole p. 467

voluntary muscles \\'väl-ən-ˌter-ē 'məs-əlz\\ Muscles that are consciously controlled, as arm or leg muscles.

Volvox See *algae:* pp. 6–7

V-shaped valley p. 459

vug \\'vəg\\ A hole or cavity in rock. If mineral-bearing water seeps into a vug, the vug may become filled or lined with crystals.

vulture p. 467

wahoo p. 468

walking fern pp. 148, 149

walking leaves See *walkingstick:* p. 468

walkingstick p. 468

wallaby p. 468

walleye p. 469
walleyed pike See *walleye:* p. 469
walnut tree p. 470
walrus p. 470
wandering albatross p. 4
waning moon See *moon:* p. 294
wapiti p. 471
warbler p. 471
warm air mass \\'mas\\ A large body of air that is warmer than the surface over which it passes, or that is warmer than nearby air masses.
warm-blooded Describing any animal whose body temperature stays about the same. The body temperatures of warm-blooded animals are often higher than the average temperatures of the environments in which they live.

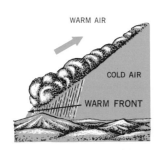

WARM AIR
COLD AIR
WARM FRONT

warm front The gently sloping boundary layer between a moving warm air mass and an air mass of lower temperature.
warping \\'wȯrp-ing\\ The bending of a large area of the earth's crust, usually hundreds of square miles. Warping is caused by strong gradual underground pressures. Warping may raise up or lower large areas over long periods of time.
Warsaw grouper p. 199
warthog p. 472
wasp p. 472
water A fluid that is odorless and tasteless when pure and at temperatures between 0° C. and 100° C. Water is made up of hydrogen and oxygen. Many other substances will dissolve in it. The freezing point of water is 0° C. and its boiling point is 100° C.
waterbuck p. 473
water buffalo p. 53
watercress See *cress:* pp. 112, 113
water cycle \\'si-kəl\\ The constant process in which water evaporates from the surface of oceans, lakes, ground plants and animals. The water rises in the atmosphere, condenses and falls back to earth as rain or other forms of precipitation.
water flea See *copepod:* p. 102, and *daphnia:* p. 121
water gap p. 473
water lily p. 473
watermelon p. 474

water pig See *capybara:* p. 67
water pipit pp. 349, 350
waterspout p. 474
water strider p. 475

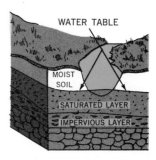

WATER TABLE
MOIST SOIL
SATURATED LAYER
IMPERVIOUS LAYER

water table The level beneath the ground surface below which water fills all spaces. Although a water table may change, it is usually parallel to the ground surface.
water vapor \\'vā-pər\\ Water in a gaseous state. Water vapor is an important part of the atmosphere. The amount of water vapor in the atmosphere varies with temperature, since warm air can hold more water vapor than cooler air.
waterweed See *elodea:* p. 141
waves p. 475

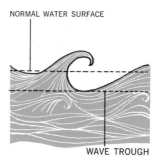

NORMAL WATER SURFACE
WAVE TROUGH

wave trough \\'trȯf\\ In a water wave, the point that is farthest below the normal surface of the water.
waxing moon See *moon:* p. 294
waxwing p. 476
weasel p. 477
weathering \\'weth-ər-ing\\ The decay and coming apart of rocks and minerals by mechanical and chemical processes.
weeping golden bell See *forsythia:* p. 164
weeping willow p. 482
weevil p. 477
western bluebird p. 46
western catalpa p. 71
western kingbird p. 238
western red cedar p. 75
western tanager p. 435
western toad pp. 444, 445
whale pp. 478–479
whale shark pp. 400, 401

wheat p. 480
wheat rust See *rust and smut:* p. 385
whelk p. 480
whippoorwill p. 481
white ant See *termite:* p. 439
white birch pp. 39, 40
white-breasted nuthatch p. 315
white clover p. 92

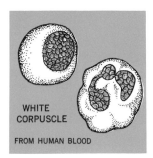

WHITE
CORPUSCLE

FROM HUMAN BLOOD

white corpuscle \'kȯr-,pəs-əl\ Any one of a number of colorless blood cells of various sizes, shapes, structures and purposes. White corpuscles are formed mainly in the red bone marrow and in lymphatic tissue. A white corpuscle is often called a leukocyte.

white crappie p. 111
white curlew See *ibis:* p. 224
white-handed gibbon p. 179
white ibis p. 224
white-lined sphinx moth pp. 298, 299
white-lipped land snail p. 409
white marlin p. 276
white mulberry p. 302
white pepper p. 341
white perch p. 481
white rat p. 374
white shark pp. 400, 401
white-tailed deer p. 123
white-tailed jackrabbit p. 230
white-tailed prairie dog p. 362
whooping crane p. 110
wild blackberry pp. 41, 42
wildebeest See *gnu:* p. 184
wild honeysuckle pp. 216, 217
wild New England aster p. 22
wild rice p. 481
wild sweet William See *phlox:* p. 344
Williamson's sapsucker p. 390
willow p. 482
wind Any noticeable, natural and usually horizontal movement of air. Wind is caused by the unequal heating of air masses, which results in high- and low-pressure areas. Wind speed and direction are influenced by differences in pressure and the rotation of the earth. Winds blow from high pressure areas to low pressure areas.
wind erosion \i-'rō-zhən\ The removal, carrying and depositing of rock and soil particles by the wind.

winter fern See *poison hemlock:* p. 356
winter flounder p. 158
winter squash p. 420
wireworm See *beetle:* p. 36
witch hazel p. 482
wolf p. 483
wolverine p. 483
wombat p. 484
woodchuck p. 485; see also *marmot:* p. 277
wood duck pp. 132, 133
wood frog pp. 166, 167
woodland caribou p. 68
woodpecker p. 485
wood rat pp. 374, 375
woolly bear p. 486
woolly locoweed p. 260
woolly mammoth p. 269
woolly monkey pp. 292, 293
worm p. 486
wren p. 487

X

X chromosome \'krō-mə-,sōm\ The chromosome that determines the sex of an organism. The X chromosome promotes the development of female characteristics. Each female cell contains 2 X chromosomes, while each male cell has 1 X and 1 Y chromosome.

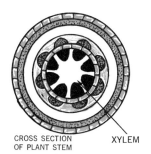

CROSS SECTION
OF PLANT STEM   XYLEM

xylem \'zī-ləm\ Plant tissue that carries water from roots to leaves. Xylem forms wood and is made up of several kinds of cells.

y

yak p. 487
yarrow p. 488
yazoo stream See *river:* p. 380
Y chromosome \'krō-mə-,sōm\ The partner of the X chromosome in the cell nuclei of most

male organisms. The Y chromosome helps decide the sex of an individual.

year The time it takes the earth to make 1 revolution around the sun. A year is a unit for measuring time. A tropical year is 365 days, 5 hours, 48 minutes and 46 seconds long.

yeast p. 488

yellow-bellied sapsucker pp. 389, 390

yellow-billed magpie p. 267

yellow bullhead p. 56

yellow cockleshell pp. 94, 95

yellow daisy p. 488

yellow-headed blackbird p. 42

yellow jacket p. 489

yellow paloverde p. 330

yellow perch p. 342

yellow poplar See *tulip tree:* p. 453

yellow-shafted flicker p. 157

yellowtail p. 489

yew p. 490

yolk A fatty, protein substance that is found in granules in the cytoplasm of eggs. Yolk is food for a developing embryo.

yucca p. 490

Z

zebra p. 491

zebra swallowtail butterfly pp. 60, 61

zebu p. 491

zenith \'zē-nəth\ On the celestial sphere, the point directly above an observer.

Zinjanthropus man pp. 270, 271

zinnia p. 491

zircon p. 492

zodiac \'zōd-ē-,ak\ The imaginary, narrow belt of 12 constellations through which the sun seems to pass during 1 year. The 12 signs of the zodiac are Aries, Taurus, Gemini, Cancer, Leo, Virgo, Libra, Scorpio, Sagittarius, Capricorn, Aquarius and Pisces.

zodiacal light p. 492

zoeae See *crab:* p. 109

zoologist \zō-'äl-ə-jəst\ A scientists who studies animal life.

zoology \zō-'äl-ə-jē\ A branch of biology that has to do with the life, structure, development and classification of animals.

ZOOPHYTE

— SEA ANEMONE

zoophyte \'zō-ə-,fīt\ An invertebrate animal that looks like a plant, such as a coral or a sponge.

zucchini See *squash:* p. 420

zygote \'zī-,gōt\ A fertilized egg or cell. A zygote results from the joining of 2 gametes, or sex cells.